THE LIFE OF GOETHE

George Henry Lewes

THE LIFE
OF GOETHE

Introduction by
VICTOR LANGE

With many contemporary illustrations

FREDERICK UNGAR PUBLISHING CO.
NEW YORK

Printed in the United States of America

Library of Congress Catalog Card No. 65–21308

INTRODUCTION

1.

George Henry Lewes' *Life of Goethe* is an altogether remarkable book. When it was published in 1855 it was the
first comprehensive study in any language of that German
writer whose fascinating and productive life, and whose
immense influence at home and abroad, had given to German literature a degree of self-confidence and reputation
that it had never had before. It is true that two or three
German biographies had summed up, before Lewes, a mass
of information and gossip, repetitious and trivial though
it often was. But there was no study that had attempted
to assess the whole of an incomparably rich and diversified
life. This Lewes proposed to offer.

In the 1840's and 1850's, Goethe's work, as impressive
in its scope as in its variety, had in some measure lost its
stirring immediacy, its experimental and imaginative appeal: the ideals of the romantic generation had long ago
superseded the more classicist convictions which Goethe
and Schiller had evolved in their plays, their poetry and
their criticism. Goethe's scientific pursuits, to which he
himself attached at times greater importance than to his
literary accomplishments, were not widely or not seriously
respected. As a public figure he had all too often shown
himself in disagreement with prevailing opinion: his political sympathies had not been with the French Revolution
but rather, as he saw it, with the forces of order and European integration that he recognized in Napoleon. To the
German nationalists he had, before 1813, appeared un-
patriotic, and the subsequent generation of aggressive

liberals regarded him as the embodiment of the conservative and authoritarian past.

In the small town of Weimar with its provincial but cultivated court society to which Goethe had contributed so much during his life, the memory of the great man had, of course, long after his death remained vivid and exemplary. Many of those who had known and worked with the urban but often crotchety old master were still alive, and became the object of worshipful curiosity among the countless visitors to the town.

In 1854 a young English journalist, George Henry Lewes, a friend of Carlyle and of Herbert Spencer and an extraordinarily effective writer on philosophical and sociological issues, arrived in Weimar to gather material for a biography of Goethe that he had planned for several years and which it now seemed to him peculiarly appropriate to complete. Although he was married and the devoted father of three children, he had recently decided to leave his family and, divorce being at that time out of the question, to live with a young woman who enjoyed a solid reputation as essayist and editor and who was much later to emerge as the author of *Adam Bede* and of *Middlemarch*.

Lewes had met George Eliot a few years earlier in London. To many their friendship seemed puzzling enough: he was then thirty-six, a brilliant but, as some felt at the time, "a rather vulgar little man," who had turned from medicine to playwriting and journalism, contributing incisive literary and theatrical reviews to several prominent magazines. His domestic life was the subject of much scandalized irritation: he and his wife lived, together with three other couples and two unmarried sisters, in a large house in Bayswater, demonstratively and shockingly dedicated to the communal ideals of Fourier, Shelley and Godwin. His vivacity and wit must have been irresistible and disarming: one of his acquaintances thought that the "brightness and versatility of Lewes, and the wonderful expressiveness of his eyes, made one forget the unlovely rest." It is true that he was fond of discoursing on "the most delicate matters of physiology," that he was at the time "an airy loose-tongued merry-hearted being with more sail than ballast," and that he showed his versatility "by convulsing the men over the port with unrespectable French stories and charming the women in the drawing room a little later with nursery anecdotes."

But there was another, more serious and impressive side to him which was grudgingly admitted by Carlyle and praised by Herbert Spencer. He had written two undistinguished novels and a number of first-rate political, philosophical and scientific papers of indubitable originality and had made a "prodigious sensation" as a controversial lecturer on the history of speculative philosophy. In his *Biographical History of Philosophy* (1845-46) he had shown considerable technical and historical competence as well as a most respectable skill of popularization: it was written to show the "vanity of all metaphysics." As a man not only of striking intellectual mobility but of decided philosophical convictions he cannot have failed to impress George Eliot. The two shared, in any case, an interest in contemporary materialistic thought, which, for Lewes, was most convincingly represented by Comte's *Positive Philosophy;* George Eliot, in turn, had begun her literary career by translating in 1846 D. F. Strauss' *Life of Jesus*, a militant attack on the credibility of the Gospels, and was now persuaded by Lewes to translate Feuerbach's anthropological and psychological criticism of religion, *The Essence of Christianity.*

Lewes had been educated in France and had spent two years studying post-Hegelian philosophy in Germany: he knew many of the conspicuous European men of letters personally. For Goethe he had early developed a lively interest: he admired above all the independence, as he thought, of Goethe's social and personal life and the skeptical and experimental character of Goethe's humanism. It was undoubtedly difficult for a more transcendental-minded devotee of Goethe such as Margaret Fuller, whom Lewes met at the Carlyles', to sympathize with these motives: Lewes is, she writes, "a witty, French, flippant sort of man [who is] now writing a life of Goethe, a task for which he must be as unfit as irreligion and sparkling shallowness can make him." She was not alone in under-rating the qualities of mind and judgment that were only a few years later to produce one of the finest biographies in English literature.

2.

Lewes and George Eliot arrived in Weimar in August, 1854, and found it at first "more like a huge village, or market town than the precincts of a court," an unlikely setting for the most important literary figure that Germany had produced. "It was inconceivable that the stately Jupiter *en redingote,* so familiar to us all through Rauch's statuette, could have habitually walked along these rude streets and among these slouching mortals." Their dislike of German provincial ways was justified by what they saw of the inhabitants: "they seemed to us to have more than the usual heaviness of Germanity; even their stare was slow, like that of herbiverous quadrupeds." They were received with the respect that was customarily shown to English visitors and were soon captivated by the charms of the surrounding countryside and touched by the constant reminders of Goethe's life. In an entertaining essay George Eliot later described these "Three Months in Weimar." They often walked for hours ("we carried provisions with us, and Keats' poems") and visited Schiller's and Goethe's houses (at that time still privately owned), looked at the collections and manuscripts that were displayed, and were given special permission by Goethe's daughter-in-law to see his private rooms. "Among such memories one breathes deeply and tears rush to one's eyes." They went on excursions to Jena and Ilmenau, and watched Liszt conducting Wagner operas. They worked hard and with a purpose. The list of books they read together during these three months is formidable: it includes nearly all of Goethe's literary works but beyond it, Schiller, Lessing and Heine, much French literature and philosophy, Shakespeare—in Schlegel's German translation as well as in English—and dozens of works on history, contemporary philosophy and criticism.

When they left in November for Berlin, "to seek fresh streets and new faces," Lewes' book had progressed satisfactorily. They shared again in the literary, musical and intellectual life of a city that struck them as bleak but quite remarkably energetic and cosmopolitan. Varnhagen von Ense, one of the most ardent Goethe propagandists, welcomed them warmly; he permitted Lewes to use his library, which "supplied all the deficiencies of the public one, where to ask for books was generally like 'sinking buckets into empty wells'." In March, 1855, they left Berlin, and by the spring of the next year Lewes had finished the manuscript of his *Life of Goethe*. It appeared in November, 1855, dedicated to Carlyle, "who first taught England to appreciate Goethe," and was immediately a success: at least a thousand copies were bought at once, "a wonderfully good sale in less than three months for a thirty-shilling book." By 1900, eighteen English editions had been published.

The biography of Goethe remained Lewes' only sustained piece of literary research; he soon turned (or returned) to more specifically scientific interests. In a succession of important books he provided popular but lucid, serious and in many respects original discussions of various aspects of contemporary science: his *Seaside*

Studies (1858) is a pioneering work in marine biology; in his *Physiology of Common Life* (1859), in *Studies in Animal Life* (1862) and in numerous other publications he developed a theory of the homogeneity of all nervous structures that was to be of considerable influence upon Wundt and Pavlov. In his most ambitious work, *The Problems of Life and Mind* (1874-77), he attempted a system of scientific psychology in which, beyond empirical research into the organic functions of the nervous system, an understanding of the social and historical conditions of behavior was to provide a total view of the phenomena of mind.

3.

Lewes' contributions to the history of science were considerable, and the breadth of his philosophical culture and his untiring advocacy of a nonspeculative sort of humanism make him a remarkable if not, perhaps, fully recognized figure in the intellectual life of nineteenth-century England. But the achievement that has alone assured him a place of indisputable greatness in English literature is his *Life of Goethe*.

What gives to this book its remarkable and to this day undiminished excellence is, of course, in the first place the ease and clarity of his style: Lewes was by all accounts the best London journalist of his time. But he was more than a skillful writer. His mind was sharp, discriminating and well trained in philosophical matters, he recognized intellectual and imaginative strength, and he knew, above all, how to arouse the interest of a cultivated audience. These qualities of a first-rate mind Lewes now brought to bear upon a man of letters in whose work a coherent attitude toward life, a peculiarly modern sensibility, had been given most impressive shape. The person behind the work, the concrete embodiment of conviction in a canon of superb imaginative writing, was for Lewes the chief object of curiosity and admiration. His study of Goethe, this is to say, is a biography rather than a piece of what we would more narrowly consider literary criticism. His discussion of Goethe's writings are at once enlivened and limited by this deliberate purpose, and we must be prepared to accept many of his particular literary judgments or misjudgments not as flaws of an obtuse critic but as logical corollaries of his assessment of Goethe the human being.

Goethe's discursive works, his novels, his essays, his plays were thus for Lewes more telling or more directly revealing documents than his poetry: he considered literature to be essentially the persuasive and stirring evidence of a remarkable mind, and to make the whole scope of that mind intelligible, its private and public aspects, its abundance, its exemplary character as well as its human failings—this was Lewes' central intention. He wrote from a point of view that was conditioned by his historical and national predispositions: Goethe was for him the pragmatic realist in a world beclouded by what the Englishman with admirable good sense felt to be the petty social and spiritual conventions of German life. He would not conceal his dislike of what he considered the sham profundity, the mysticism and the pomposity of the Germans. German style, whether in manners or in writing, seemed to him often clumsy and pretentious, and where he thought to detect it in Goethe or his work, he was not embarrassed to say so.

If his judgment was refreshingly independent, he was nevertheless at pains to provide for his audience a persuasive, detailed and leisurely view of Goethe the man, and of the times that produced him. His accounts of Frankfurt in the eighteenth century, of the social and intellectual climate in which Goethe's work developed, of the political background, of those incomparable decades between the French Revolution and the defeat of Napoleon—all these are carefully and intelligently related. We may now and again differ from Lewes' estimate of the men and women, great or casual, who played a role in Goethe's long life. His dislike for Lenz, for instance, is palpable, and Charlotte von Stein does not seem to us—as she did to Lewes—merely a selfish coquette; we think of Goethe's relationship to her as a more profound experience that affected, for better or worse, much of his later work. But Lewes' judgment of men and circumstances remains in all important respects clearsighted and reasonable.

Goethe's scientific work, in particular, seemed to Lewes of greater interest than was at the time commonly conceded: it had undoubtedly drawn him to the poet in the first place and now enabled him to write judiciously and in detail of the character of Goethe's scientific pursuits and the importance of his discoveries. Here, too, Lewes anticipated more recent critics who agree that, while Goethe's experiments and theories may as such not have been decisive in the history of science, they must be recognized as determining factors in his development as a modern, naturalistic and, in Lewes' vocabulary, antimetaphysical poet.

4.

What a modern biographer of Goethe would modify is the perspective of Goethe's life as a whole. For Lewes it was the young genius and the man of resolute imaginative maturity that offered the most impressive model of personal and spiritual achievement. His own affinities were decidedly with the Goethe before the turn of the century. "It is Goethe's misfortune with posterity that he is mostly present to our minds as the calm old man, seldom as the glorious youth." The aging Goethe who was still familiar to so many living witnesses struck him as a pale reminder of earlier greatness; he had, in any case, been adequately and all too deferentially represented in the published memoirs of several of Goethe's associates. Lewes and George Eliot had interviewed as many of these as were still alive: they had talked at length to Kräuter, Goethe's last secretary and, especially, visited Eckermann, whose *Conversations with Goethe* had done more than any other book to establish in the minds of the Germans the statuesque image of the venerable sage. "We were fortunate enough to be in time to see poor Eckermann before his *total* death. His mind was already half gone, but the fine brow and eyes harmonized entirely with the interest we had previously felt in him. We saw him in a small lodging, surrounded by singing birds, and tended by his son."

Eckermann's Goethe in his skeptical aloofness, his detachment from the present, his magisterial preoccupation with himself as an historical figure was for Lewes hardly in need of understanding or interpretation: in fifty pages he deals all too summarily with the incomparably productive last twenty years of Goethe's life. If he insists again and again on the inaccuracies and shortcomings of Goethe's autobiography, *Poetry and Truth*, it is because, having been written as late as 1814, it struck him as a dubious effort to force the years of effervescent youth into a pattern of abstraction; the tone of urbane reflection, the thought, falsified the character of the early years. The works after Schiller's death, *Elective Affinities*, the *Divan* poems, *Wilhelm Meister's Travels* and, above all, the second part of *Faust* baffled and irritated him; they were, he was convinced, much inferior to the output of the first half of Goethe's life. His understanding of the shape and function of literature was inevitably personal: he was not in sympathy with the rarefied or, as he would disapprovingly say, the "allegorical" mode of the very works of the late Goethe that we would today regard as his greatest. With one blunt sentence—"Nothing worthy of special notice occurs in the last two acts" — he merely obscures the superb crescendo of *Faust II*, one of the poetic triumphs of German literature; and *Wilhelm Meister's Travels*, for us an intriguing piece of fiction in a modern key, Lewes intensely disliked: "it is unintelligible, it is tiresome, it is fragmentary; it is dull, and it is often ill-written."

But these personal opinions, forcefully and unequivocally put, though never foolish and always fairly reasoned, are part of the very quality of Lewes' mind, of the vivacity and independence of his judgment, and it is this quality that has assured his work its continuing appeal. To this day *The Life of Goethe* has, in any language, remained one of the wisest and richest accounts of the greatest German writer.

VICTOR LANGE

PREFACE TO THE SECOND EDITION
(PARTLY REWRITTEN) 1864

THERE was, perhaps, some temerity in attempting a *Life of Goethe* at a time when no German author had undertaken the task; but the reception which my work has met with, even after the appearance of the biographies by Viehoff and Schäfer, is a justification of the temerity. The sale of thirteen thousand copies in England and Germany, and the sympathy generously expressed, not unmingled, it is true, with adverse and even angry criticism, are assurances that my labours were not wholly misdirected, however far they may have fallen short of their aim. For the expressions of sympathy, public and private, I cannot but be grateful; and I have done my best to profit by criticism even when it was most hostile.

I wish to make special mention of the assistance tendered me by the late Mr. Franz Demmler. Although a stranger to me, this accomplished student of Goethe kindly volunteered, amid many and pressing avocations, to re-read my book with the express purpose of annotating it; and he sent me several sheets of notes and objections, all displaying the vigour of his mind and the variety of his reading. Some of these I was glad to use; and even those which I could not agree with or adopt, were always carefully considered. On certain points our opinions were diametrically opposed; but it was always an advantage to me to read criticisms so frank and acute.

The present edition is altered in form and in substance.
It has been rewritten in parts, with a view not only of introducing all the new material which several important publications have furnished, but also of correcting and reconstructing
it so as to make it more worthy of public favour. As there is
little probability of any subsequent publication bringing to
light fresh material of importance, I hope that this reconstruction of my book will be final.

With respect to the use I have made of the materials at
hand, especially of Goethe's *Autobiography*, I can but repeat
what was said in the Preface to the First Edition : the *Dichtung und Wahrheit* not only wants the egotistic garrulity and
detail which give such confessions their value, but presents
great difficulties to a biographer. The main reason of this is
the abiding inaccuracy of *tone*, which, far more misleading
than the many inaccuracies of *fact*, gives to the whole youthful period, as narrated by him, an aspect so directly contrary
to what is given by contemporary evidence, especially his own
letters, that an attempt to reconcile the contradiction is futile.
If any one doubts this, and persists in his doubts after
reading the first volume of this work, let him take up
Goethe's Letters to the Countess von Stolberg, or the recently
published letters to Kestner and Charlotte, and compare their
tone with the tone of the *Autobiography*, wherein the old
man depicts the youth as the old man saw him, not as the
youth felt and lived. The picture of youthful follies and
youthful passions comes softened through the distant avenues
of years. The turbulence of a youth of genius is not indeed
quite forgotten, but it is hinted with stately reserve. Jupiter
serenely throned upon Olympus forgets that he was once a
rebel with the Titans.

When we come to know the real facts, we see that the

Autobiography does not so much misstate as understate; we, who can 'read between the lines', perceive that it errs more from want of sharpness of relief and precision of detail than from positive misrepresentation. Controlled by contemporary evidence, it furnishes one great source for the story of the early years; and I greatly regret there is not more contemporary evidence to furnish more details.

For the later period, besides the mass of printed testimony in shape of Letters, Memoirs, Reminiscences, etc., I have endeavoured to get at the truth by consulting those who lived under the same roof with him, those who lived in friendly intercourse with him, and those who have made his life and works a special study. I have sought to acquire and to reproduce a definite image of the living man, and not simply of the man as he appeared in all the reticences of print. For this purpose I have controlled and completed the testimonies of print by means of papers which have never seen the light, and papers which in all probability never will see the light—by means of personal corroboration, and the many slight details which are gathered from far and wide when one is alive to every scrap of authentic information and can see its significance; and thus comparing testimony with testimony, completing what was learned yesterday by something learned to-day, not unfrequently helped to one passage by details furnished from half a dozen quarters, I have formed the conclusions which appear in this work. In this difficult, and sometimes delicate task, I hope it will be apparent that I have been guided by the desire to get at the truth, having no cause to serve, no partisanship to mislead me, no personal connexion to trammel my judgment. It will be seen that I neither deny, nor attempt to slur over, points which may tell against my hero. The man is too great and

too good to forfeit our love, because on some points he may
incur blame.

Considerable space has been allotted to analyses and criticisms of Goethe's works; just as in the life of a great
Captain, much space is necessarily occupied by his campaigns.
By these analyses I have tried to be of service to the student
of German literature, as well as to those who do not read
German ; and throughout it will be seen that pains have not
been spared to make the reader feel at home in this foreign
land.

The scientific writings have been treated with what pro-
portionately may seem great length ; and this, partly because
science filled a large portion of Goethe's life ; partly, because,
even in Germany, there was nothing like a full exposition of
his aims and achievements in this direction.

G. H. L.

CONTENTS

BOOK III: 1771 TO 1775

BOOK IV: 1775 TO 1779

Contents

ILLUSTRATIONS

Illustrations

xxv

Facing Page

Illustrations   xxv

Facing Page

Christiane Vulpius
Drawing by Goethe[1]   320

Christiane sleeping
Drawing by Goethe   322

Goethe's home in Weimar[4]   382
    The yellow room[3]
    Small dining room[3]
    The staircase[3]
    Juno room[3]
    The big collection room[3]
    Urbino room[3]
    Goethe's workroom[3]

Friedrich von Schiller
Drawing by Reisz after sculpture by Dannecker   388

Wilhelm von Humboldt
Chalk drawing[3]   394

Alexander von Humboldt   396

Friedrich von Müller   428

Schiller's home in Weimar   440

Bettina Brentano   500

Friedrich Wilhelm Riemer
Chalk drawing by Schmeller[3]   504

Minna Herzlieb
Oil painting by Seidler[3]   510

Life mask of Goethe[1]   516

Johann Heinrich Meyer   522

Ottilie von Goethe[3]
Drawing by Müller   530

Karl Friedrich Zelter
Oil painting by Begas[3]   532

Johann Peter Eckermann   538

[1] Bruckmann—Art Reference Bureau
[2] Freies Deutsches Hochstiff Frankfurter Goethe-Museum
[3] Nationale Forschungs- und Gedenkstätten der klassischen deutschen
  Literatur in Weimar
[4] Marburg—Art Reference Bureau

LIFE AND WORKS OF GOETHE

BOOK THE FIRST

1749 to 1765

CHAPTER I

PARENTAGE

QUINTUS CURTIUS tells us that, in certain seasons, Bactria
was darkened by whirlwinds of dust, which completely covered
and concealed the roads. Left thus without their usual landmarks,
the wanderers awaited the rising of the stars :

> To light them on their dim and perilous way.

May we not say the same of Literature? From time to time its
pathways are so obscured beneath the rubbish of the age, that
many a footsore pilgrim seeks in vain the hidden route. In such
times let us imitate the Bactrians : let us cease to look upon the
confusions of the day, and turning our gaze upon the great
Immortals who have gone before, seek guidance from their light.
In all ages the biographies of great men have been fruitful in
lessons. In all ages they have been powerful stimulants to a noble
ambition. In all ages they have been regarded as armouries
wherein are gathered the weapons with which great battles have
been won.

There may be some among my readers who will dispute Goethe's
claim to greatness. They will admit that he was a great poet, but
deny that he was a great man. In denying it, they will set forth
the qualities which constitute their ideal of greatness, and finding him deficient in some of these qualities, will dispute his claim.
But in awarding him that title, I do not mean to imply that he was
an ideal man ; I do not present him as the exemplar of all
greatness. No man can be such an exemplar. Humanity reveals
itself in fragments. One man is the exponent of one kind of
excellence, another of another. Achilles wins the victory, and

Homer immortalizes it : we bestow the laurel crown on both.   In virtue of a genius such as modern times have only seen equalled once or twice, Goethe deserves the epithet of great ; unless we believe a great genius can belong to a small nature.   Nor is it in virtue of genius alone that he deserves the title.   Merck said of him that what he lived was more beautiful than what he wrote ; and his Life, amid all its weaknesses and all its errors, presents a picture of a certain grandeur of soul, which cannot be contemplated unmoved.   I shall make no attempt to conceal his faults.   Let them be dealt with as harshly as severest justice may dictate, they will not eclipse the central light which shines throughout his life. But although I neither wish to excuse nor to conceal faults which he assuredly had, we must always bear in mind that the faults of a celebrated man are apt to carry an undue emphasis ; they are thrown into stronger relief by the very splendour of his fame.   Had Goethe never written *Faust* no one would have heard that he was an inconstant lover, or a tepid politician.   His glory immortalizes his shame.

Let us begin as near the beginning as may be desirable, by glancing at his ancestry.   That he had inherited his organization and tendencies from his forefathers, and could call nothing in himself original, he has told us in these verses :

> Vom Vater hab' ich die Statur,
>   Des Lebens ernstes Führen ;
> Von Mütterchen die Frohnatur,
>   Die Lust zu fabuliren.
> Urahnherr war der Schönsten hold,
>   Das spukt so hin und wieder ;
> Urahnfrau liebte Schmuck und Gold,
>   Das zuckt wohl durch die Glieder.
> Sind nun die Elemente nicht,
>   Aus dem Complex zu trennen,
> Was ist denn an dem ganzen Wicht
>   Original zu nennen ? *

* From my father I inherit my frame, and the steady guidance of life ; from dear little mother my happy disposition, and love of story-telling. My ancestor was a 'ladies' man', and that habit haunts me now and then ; my ancestress loved finery and show, which also runs in the blood.   If, then, the elements are not to be separated from the whole, what can one call original in the descendant ?

This is a very inadequate translation ; but, believing that to leave German untranslated is unfair to those whose want of leisure or inclination has prevented their acquiring the language, I shall throughout translate every word cited.   At the same time it is unfair to the poet, and to the writer quoting the poet, to be forced to give translations which are after all felt *not* to represent the force and spirit of the original. I will do my best to give *approximative* translations, which the reader will be good enough to accept as such, rather than be left in the dark.

The first glimpse we get of his ancestry carries us back to about the middle of the seventeenth century. In the Grafschaft of Mansfeld, in Thuringia, the little town of Artern numbered among its scanty inhabitants a farrier, by name Hans Christian Goethe. His son, Frederick, being probably of a more meditative turn, selected a more meditative employment than that of shoeing horses : he became a tailor. Having passed an apprenticeship (not precisely that of *Wilhelm Meister*), he commenced his Wanderings, in the course of which he reached Frankfurt. Here he soon found employment, and being, as we learn, 'a ladies' man', he soon also found a wife. The master tailor, Sebastian Lutz, gave him his daughter, on his admission to the citizenship of Frankfurt and to the guild of tailors. This was in 1687. Several children were born, and vanished ; in 1700 his wife, too, vanished, to be replaced, five years afterwards, by Frau Cornelia Schellhorn, the daughter of another tailor, Georg Walter ; she was then a widow, blooming with six-and-thirty summers, and possessing the solid attractions of a good property, namely, the hotel *Zum Weidenhof*, where her new husband laid down the scissors and donned the landlord's apron. He had two sons by her, and died in 1730, aged seventy-three.

Of these two sons, the younger, Johann Caspar, was the father of our poet. Thus we see that Goethe, like Schiller, sprang from the people. He makes no mention of the lucky tailor, nor of the Thuringian farrier, in his autobiography. This silence may be variously interpreted. At first, I imagined it was aristocratic prudery on the part of *von* Goethe, minister and nobleman ; but it is never well to put ungenerous constructions, when others, equally plausible and more honourable, are ready ; let us rather follow the advice of Arthur Helps, to 'employ our *imagination* in the service of charity'. We can easily imagine that Goethe was silent about the tailor, because, in truth, having never known him, there was none of that affectionate remembrance which encircles the objects of early life, to make this grandfather figure in the autobiography beside the grandfather Textor, who *was* known and loved. Probably, also, the tailor was seldom talked of in the parental circle. There is a peculiar and indelible ridicule attached to the idea of a tailor in Germany, which often prevents people of much humbler pretensions than Goethe, from whispering their connexion with such a trade. Goethe does mention this grandfather in the Second Book of his *Autobiography*, and tells us how he was teased by the taunts of boys respecting his humble parentage ; these taunts even wen so far as to imply that he might possibly have had several grand-fathers; and he began to speculate on the possibility of some latent aristocracy in his descent. This made him examine with some curiosity the portraits of noblemen to try and detect a likeness.

Johann Caspar Goethe received a good education, travelled into Italy, became an imperial councillor in Frankfurt, and married, in 1748, Katharina Elizabeth, daughter of Johann Wolfgang Textor, the chief magistrate (*Schultheiss*)*.

The genealogical tables of kings and conquerors are thought of interest, and why should not the genealogy of our poet be equally interesting to us? In the belief that it will be so, I here subjoin it.

Goethe's father was a cold, stern, formal, somewhat pedantic, but truth-loving upright-minded man. He hungered for knowledge; and, although in general of a laconic turn, freely imparted all he learned. In his domestic circle his word was law. Not only imperious, but in some respects capricious, he was nevertheless greatly respected, if little loved, by wife, children, and friends. He is characterized by Krause as *ein geradliniger Frankfurter Reichsbürger*—'a formal Frankfurt citizen', whose habits were as measured as his gait†. From him the poet inherited the well-built frame, the erect carriage, and the measured movement which in old age became stiffness, and was construed as diplomacy or haughtiness; from him also came that orderliness and stoicism which have so much distressed those who cannot conceive genius otherwise than as vagabond in its habits. The craving for know-ledge, the delight in communicating it, the almost pedantic attention to details, which are noticeable in the poet, are all traceable in the father.

The mother was more like what we conceive as the proper parent for a poet. She is one of the pleasantest figures in German literature, and one standing out with greater vividness than almost

---

* The family of Textor and Weber exists to this day, and under both names, in the Hohenlohe territory. Karl Julius Weber, the humorous author of *Democritus* and of the *Briefe eines in Deutschland reisenden Deutschen* was a member of it. In the description of the *Jubilæum* of the Nürnberg University of Altorf, in 1723, mention is made of one Joannes Guolfgangus Textor as a bygone ornament of the faculty of law; and Mr. Demmler, to whom I am indebted for these particulars, suggests the probability of this being the same John Wolfgang, who died as Oberbürgermeister in Frankfurt, 1701.

† Perhaps *geradliniger* might be translated as 'an old square-toes', having reference to the antiquated cut of the old man's clothes. The fathers of the present generation dubbed the stiff coat of their grandfathers, with its square skirts and collars, by the name of *magister matheseos*, the name by which the Pythagorean proposition is known in Germany.

Johann Kaspar Goethe, the poet's father

GENEALOGICAL TABLE OF THE GOETHE FAMILY

FRIEDRICH GEORG GOETHE

Born Sept. 7, 1657, at Artern, in the county of Mansfeld, where his father was a farrier; from 1687 a citizen and tailor in Frankfort-on-the-Maine; married first, ANNA ELISABETH LUTZ, a tailor's daughter (died 1700); secondly, May 4, 1705, MRS. CORNELIA SCHELLHORN (born Sept. 27, 1668; buried March 28, 1754); died as keeper of the inn *zum Weidenhof* at Frankfort; buried Feb. 13, 1730

JOHANN MICHAEL GOETHE, died 1733

JOHANN CASPAR GOETHE, born July 31, 1710; died 27 May, 1782, as Imperial Counsellor in Frankfort; married Aug. 20, 1748, KATHARINA ELIZABETH TEXTOR (born Feb. 19, 1731; died Sept. 13, 1808)

JOHANN WOLFGANG VON GOETHE born Aug. 28, 1749; died March 22, 1832; from July 13, 1788, lived with CHRISTIANE VULPIUS (died June 6, 1816); married her, Oct. 19, 1806

CORNELIE FRIEDRICA CHRISTIANE born Dec. 7, 1750; died June 8, 1777, at Emmendingen; married Nov. 1, 1773, JOH. GE. SCHLOSSER (born 1739; died 1799, at Frankfort)

HERMANN JACOB born Nov. 26, 1752; died Jan. 11, 1759

KATHARINA ELIZABETH born Sept. 8, 1754; died Jan. 19, 1756

JOHANNA MARIA born March 28, 1756; died Aug. 9, 1759

GEORG ADOLF born June 14, 1760; died Feb. 16, 1761

JULIUS AUGUST WALTHER von GOETHE, born Dec. 25, 1789, in Weimar; died as Privy Counsellor, Oct. 28, 1830, at Rome; married April, 1817, OTTILIE von POGWISCH

MARIE ANNA LUISE SCHLOSSER born Oct. 28, 1774; died Sept. 28, 1811; married 1795, NICOLOVIUS, at Eutin (died 1839)

ELISABETH KATHARINA JULIE SCHLOSSER, born May 10, 1777; died July 5, at Emmendingen

---

WALTHER WOLFGANG v. GOETHE born Feb. 1818

WOLFGANG MAX. v. GOETHE, born Sept. 18, 1820

ALMA v. GOETHE, born Oct. 1827

GENEALOGICAL TABLE OF THE TEXTOR FAMILY

GEORG WEBER
Citizen of Weickersheim, a small town in the Jaxt district, near Mergentheim

WOLFGANG WEBER
Counsellor at Hohenlohe, and Director of the Chancery at Neuenstein; according to the custom of the time, translated his family name WEBER into Latin, and called himself TEXTOR

JOHANN WOLFGANG TEXTOR
Born at Neuenstein; until 1690, Vice Court Judge and President-Vicar at the Electoral Court of Justice at Heidelberg; afterwards Consul and First Syndic at Frankfort; died there Dec. 27, 1701

CHRISTOPH HEINRICH TEXTOR, Counsellor of Justice and Advocate at the Elector Palatine; died 1716

JOHANN NICOLAUS TEXTOR, Colonel and City Commandant; married 1737, a widow von BARCKHAUSEN, born von KLETTENBERG

JOHANN WOLFGANG TEXTOR, born Dec. 12, 1693; died Feb. 6, 1771, as Imperial Counsellor and Magistrate at Frankfort; married ANNA MARGARETHA LINDHEIMER, daughter of DR. CORNELIUS LINDHEIMER, Procurator of the Imperial Chamber of Justice at Wetzlar (born July 31, 1711; died April 15, 1783

KATHARINA ELISABETH born Feb. 19, 1731; died Sept. 13, 1808; married Aug. 20 1748, the father of the Poet, Counsellor GOETHE

JOHANNA MARIA, born 1734; married Nov. 11, 1751, the druggist MELBER, in Frankfort

ANNA MARIA, born 1738; married Nov. 2, 1756, the clergyman M. STARK, in Frankfort

JOHANN JOST, born 1739; died Sept. 19, 1792, as Sheriff in Frankfort

ANNA CHRISTINA, born Oct. 24, 1743

any other. Her simple, hearty, joyous, and affectionate nature
endeared her to all. She was the delight of children, the favourite
of poets and princes. To the last retaining her enthusiasm and
simplicity, mingled with great shrewdness and knowledge of
character, *Frau Aja*, as they christened her, was at once grave
and hearty, dignified and simple. She had read most of the best
German and Italian authors, had picked up considerable desultory
information, and had that 'mother wit' which so often in women
and poets seems to render culture superfluous, their rapid intuitions
anticipating the tardy conclusions of experience. Her letters are
full of spirit : not always strictly grammatical ; not irreproachable
in orthography ; but vigorous and vivacious. After a lengthened
interview with her, an enthusiast* exclaimed, 'Now do I understand how Goethe has become the man he is !' Wieland, Merck,
Bürger, Madame de Stael, Karl August, and other great people
sought her acquaintance. The Duchess Amalia corresponded with
her as with an intimate friend ; and her letters were welcomed
eagerly at the Weimar Court. She was married at seventeen to a
man for whom she had no love, and was only eighteen when the
poet was born†. This, instead of making her prematurely old,
seems to have perpetuated her girlhood. 'I and my Wolfgang',
she said, 'have always held fast to each other, because we were
both young together'. To him she transmitted her love of story-
telling, her animal spirits, her love of everything which bore the
stamp of distinctive individuality, and her love of seeing happy
faces around her. 'Order and quiet', she says in one of her
charming letters to Freiherr von Stein, 'are my principal characteristics. Hence I despatch at once whatever I have to do, the most
disagreeable always first, and I gulp down the devil without
looking at him. When all has returned to its proper state, then I
defy any one to surpass me in good humour'. Her heartiness and
tolerance are the causes, she thinks, why every one likes her. 'I
am fond of people, and *that* every one feels directly—young and
old. I pass without pretension through the world, and that gratifies
men. I never *bemoralize* any one—*always seek out the good that
is in them, and leave what is bad to him who made mankind, and
knows how to round off the angles.* In this way I make myself
happy and comfortable'. Who does not recognize the son in those

---

* *Ephemeriden der Literatur*, quoted in *Nicolovius über Goethe*.
† Lovers of parallels may be reminded that Napoleon's mother was only eighteen
when the hero of Austerlitz was born.

accents? The kindliest of men inherited his loving happy nature from the heartiest of women.

He also inherited from her his dislike of unnecessary agitation and emotion; that deliberate avoidance of all things capable of disturbing his peace of mind, which has been construed as coldness. Her sunny nature shrank from storms. She stipulated with her servants that they were not to trouble her with afflicting news, except upon some positive necessity for the communication. In 1805, when her son was dangerously ill at Weimar, no one ventured to speak to her on the subject. Not until he had completely recovered did she voluntarily enter on it. 'I knew it all', she remarked, 'but said nothing. Now we can talk about him without my feeling a stab every time his name is mentioned'.

In this voluntary insulation from disastrous intelligence, there is something so antagonistic to the notorious craving for excitement felt by the Teutonic races, something so unlike the morbid love of intellectual drams—the fierce alcohol of emotion with which we intoxicate ourselves, that it is no wonder if Goethe has on this account been accused of insensibility. Yet, in truth, a very superficial knowledge of his nature suffices to show that it was not from coldness he avoided indulgence in the 'luxury of woe'. It was excess of sensibility, not want of sympathy. His delicate nature shrank from the wear and tear of excitement. That which to coarser natures would have been a stimulus, was to him a disturbance. It is doubtless the instinct of an emotional nature to seek such stimulants; but his reason was strong enough to keep this instinct under control. Falk relates that when Goethe heard he had looked upon Wieland in death, 'and thereby procured myself a miserable evening, and worse night, he vehemently reproved me for it. Why, said he, should I suffer the delightful impression of the features of my friend to be obliterated by the sight of a disfigured mask? I carefully avoided seeing Schiller, Herder, or the Duchess Amalia, in the coffin. I, for my part, desire to retain in my memory a picture of my departed friends more full of soul than the mere mask can furnish me'.

This subjection of the instinct of curiosity to the dictates of reason is not coldness. There is danger indeed of carrying it too far, and of *coddling* the mind; but into this extreme neither Goethe nor his mother can be said to have fallen. At any rate, let the reader pronounce what judgment he thinks fit, it is right that he should at the outset distinctly understand it to be a character-

Katharina Elisabeth Goethe, the poet's mother

istic of the man. The self-mastery it implies forms the keystone of his character. In him the *emotive* was subjected to the *intellectual.* He was 'king over himself'. He, as he tells us, found men eager enough to lord it over others, while indifferent whether they could rule themselves

> Das wollen alle Herren seyn,
> Und keiner ist Herr von sich!

He made in his study to subdue into harmonious unity the rebellious impulses which incessantly threatened the supremacy of reason. Here, on the threshold of his career, let attention be called to this cardinal characteristic : his footsteps were not guided by a light tremulous in every gust, liable to fall to the ground amid the hurrying agitation of vulgar instincts, but a torch grasped by an iron will, and lifted high above the currents of those lower gusts, shedding a continuous steady gleam across the troubled path. I do not say he never stumbled. At times the clamorous agitation of rebellious passions misled him as it misleads others, for he was very human, often erring ; but viewing his life as it disposes itself into the broad masses necessary for a characteristic appreciation, I say that in him, more than in almost any other man of his time, naked vigour of resolution, moving in alliance with steady clearness of intellect, produced a self-mastery of the very highest kind*.

This he owed partly to his father and partly to his mother. It was from the latter he derived those characteristics which determined the movement and orbit of his artistic nature : her joyous, healthy temperament, humour, fancy, and suceptibility, were, in him, creative, owing to the marvellous insight which gathered up the scattered and vanishing elements of experience into new and living combinations.

CHAPTER II

THE PRECOCIOUS CHILD

JOHANN WOLFGANG GOETHE was born on the 28th August, 1749, as the clock sounded the hour of noon, in the busy town of Frankfurt-on-the-Maine. The busy town, as may be supposed, was quite heedless of what was then passing in the

---

* 'All I have had to do I have done in kingly fashion', he said : 'I let tongues wag as they pleased. What I saw to be the right thing that I did '.

corner of that low, heavy-beamed room in the *Grosse Hirsch Graben*, where an infant, black, and almost lifeless, was watched with agonizing anxiety—an anxiety dissolving into tears of joy, as the aged grandmother exclaimed to the pale mother : ' *Räthin, er lebt!* he lives !' But if the town was heedless, not so were the stars, as astrologers will certify ; the stars knew who was gasping for life beside his trembling mother, and in solemn convocation they prefigured his future greatness. Goethe, with a grave smile, notes this conjunction of the stars.

Whatever the stars may have betokened, this August 1749 was a momentous month to Germany, if only because it gave birth to the man whose influence on his nation has been greater than that of any man since Luther, not even excepting Lessing. A momentous month in very momentous times. It was the middle of the eighteenth century : a period when the movement which had culminated in Luther was passing from religion to politics, and freedom of thought was translating itself into liberty of action. From theology the movement had communicated itself to philosophy, morals, and politics. The agitation was still mainly in the higher classes, but it was gradually descending to the lower. A period of deep unrest : big with events which would expand the conceptions of all men, and bewilder some of the wisest.

It is not the biographer's province to write a history of an epoch while telling the story of a life ; but some historical indication is necessary, in order that the time and place should be vividly before the reader's mind ; and perhaps the readiest way to call up such a picture in a paragraph will be to mention some of the ' notables ' of that period, and at what points in their career they had arrived. In that very month of August Madame du Chatelet, the learned translator of Newton, the loving but pedantic *Uranie* of Voltaire, died in childbed, leaving him without a companion and without a counsellor to prevent his going to the court of Frederick the Great. In that year Rousseau was seen in the brilliant circle of Madame d'Epinay, disputing with the Encyclopædists, declaiming eloquently on the sacredness of maternity, and going home to cast his newborn infant into the basket of the Foundling Hospital. In that year Samuel Johnson was toiling manfully over his English dictionary ; Gibbon was at Westminster, trying with unsuccessful diligence to master the Greek and Latin rudiments ; Goldsmith was delighting the Tony Lumpkins of his district, and the 'wandering bear-leaders of genteeler sort', with his talents, and enjoying

The house in which Goethe was born (from a model)

that 'careless idleness of fireside and easy chair', and that 'tavern excitement of the game of cards, to which he looked back so wistfully from his first hard London struggles'. In that year Buffon, whose *scientific* greatness Goethe was one of the first to perceive, produced the first volume of his *Histoire Naturelle*. Haller was at Göttingen performing those experiments on sensibility and irritability which were to immortalize him. John Hunter, who had recently left Scotland, joined Cheselden at the Chelsea Hospital. Mirabeau and Alfieri were tyrants in their nurseries ; and Marat was an innocent boy of five years old, toddling about in the Val de Travers, unmolested as yet by the wickedness of 'les aristocrats'.

If these names have helped to call up the period, we must seek in Goethe's own pages for a picture of the place. He has painted the city of Frankfurt as one who loved it. No city in Germany was better fitted for the birthplace of this cosmopolitan poet. It was rich in speaking memorials of the past, remnants of old German life, lingering echoes of the voices which sounded through the middle ages : such as a town within a town, the fortress within a fortress, the walled cloisters, the various symbolical ceremonies still preserved from feudal times, and the Jews' quarter, so picturesque, so filthy, and so strikingly significant. But if Frankfurt was thus representative of the past, it was equally representative of the present. The travellers brought there by the Rhine-stream, and by the great northern roads, made it a representative of Europe, and an emporium of Commerce. It was thus a centre for that distinctively modern idea—Industrialism—which began, and must complete, the destruction of Feudalism. This two-fold character Frankfurt retains to the present day : the storks, perched upon its ancient gables, look down upon the varied bustle of Fairs held by modern Commerce in the ancient streets.

The feeling for antiquity, and especially for old German life, which his native city would thus picturesquely cultivate, was rivalled by a feeling for Italy and its splendours which was cultivated under the paternal roof. His father had lived in Italy, and had retained an inextinguishable delight in all its beauties. His walls were hung with architectural drawings and views of Rome ; and the poet was thus familiar from infancy with the Piazza del Popolo, St. Peter's, the Coliseum, and other centres of grand associations. Typical of his own nature and strivings is this conjunction of the Classic and the German—the one lying nearest to him, in homely intimacy, the other lying outside, as a mere *scene* he was to contemplate. Goethe by nature was more Greek than German, but he never freed himself from German influence.

Thus much on time and place, the two cardinal conditions of life. Before quitting such generalities for the details of biography, it may be well to call attention to one hitherto unnoticed, viz., the moderate elevation of his social status. Placed midway between the two perilous extremes of affluence and want, his whole career received a modifying impulse from this position. He never knew adversity. This alone must necessarily have deprived him of one powerful chord which vibrates through literature. Adversity, the sternest of teachers, had nothing to teach him. He never knew the gaunt companionship of Want, whispering terrible suggestions. He never knew the necessity to conquer for himself breathing-room in the world ; and thus all the feelings of bitterness, opposition, and defiance, which accompany and perplex the struggle of life, were to him almost unknown ; and he was taught nothing of the aggressive and practical energy which these feelings develop in impetuous natures. How much of his serenity, how much of his dislike to politics, may be traced to this origin ?

That he was the loveliest baby ever seen, exciting admiration wherever nurse or mother carried him, and exhibiting, in swaddling clothes, the most wonderful intelligence, we need no biographer to tell us. Is it not said of every baby? But that he was in truth a wonderful child we have undeniable evidence, and of a kind less questionable than the statement of mothers and relatives. At three years old he could seldom be brought to play with little children, and only on the condition of their being pretty. One day, in a neighbour's house, he suddenly began to cry and exclaim, 'That black child must go away ! I can't bear him !' And he howled till he was carried home, where he was slowly pacified ; the whole cause of his grief being the ugliness of the child.

A quick, merry little girl grew up by the boy's side. Four other children also came, but soon vanished. Cornelia was the only companion who survived, and for her his affection dated from her cradle. He brought his toys to her, wanted to feed her and attend on her, and was very jealous of all who approached her. 'When she was taken from the cradle, over which he watched, his anger was scarcely to be quieted. He was altogether much more

Cornelia, Goethe's sister

easily moved to anger than to tears'. To the last his love for Cornelia was passionate.

In old German towns, Frankfurt among them, the ground-floor consists of a great hall where the vehicles are housed. This floor opens in folding trap-doors, for the passage of wine-casks into the cellars below. In one corner of the hall there is a sort of lattice, opening by an iron or wooden grating upon the street. This is called the *Geräms*. Here the crockery in daily use was kept; here the servants peeled their potatoes, and cut their carrots and turnips, preparatory to cooking; here also the housewife would sit with her sewing, or her knitting, giving an eye to what passed in the street (when anything did pass there) and an ear to a little neighbourly gossip. Such a place was of course a favourite with the children.

One fine afternoon, when the house was quiet, Master Wolfgang, with his cup in his hand and nothing to do, finds himself in this *Geräms*, looking out into the silent street; and telegraphing to the young Ochsensteins, who dwelt opposite. By way of doing something he begins to fling the crockery into the street, delighted at the smashing music which it makes, and stimulated by the approbation of the brothers Ochsenstein, who chuckle at him from over the way. The plates and dishes are flying in this way, when his mother returns: she sees the mischief with a housewifely horror, melting into girlish sympathy, as she hears how heartily the little fellow laughs at his escapade, and how the neighbours laugh at him.

This genial, indulgent mother employed her faculty for story-telling to his and her own delight. 'Air, fire, earth, and water I represented under the forms of princesses; and to all natural phenomena I gave a meaning, in which I almost believed more fervently than my little hearers. As we thought of paths which led from star to star, and that we should one day inhabit the stars, and thought of the great spirits we should meet there, I was as eager for the hours of story-telling as the children themselves; I was quite curious about the future course of my own improvization, and any invitation which interrupted these evenings was disagreeable. There I sat, and there Wolfgang held me with his large black eyes; and when the fate of one of his favourites was not according to his fancy, I saw the angry veins swell on his temples, I saw him repress his tears. He often burst in with "But, mother, the princess won't marry the nasty tailor, even if he does kill the

giant ". And when I made a pause for the night, promising to
continue it on the morrow, I was certain that he would in the
meanwhile think it out for himself, and so he often stimulated my
imagination. When I turned the story according to his plan, and
told him that he had found out the dénouement, then was he all
fire and flame, and one could see his little heart beating underneath his dress ! His grandmother, who made a great pet of him,
was the confidant of all his ideas as to how the story would turn
out, and as she repeated these to me, and I turned the story
according to these hints, there was a little diplomatic secrecy
between us, which we never disclosed. I had the pleasure of
continuing my story to the delight and astonishment of my
hearers, and Wolfgang saw with glowing eyes the fulfilment of
his own conceptions, and listened with enthusiastic applause '.
What a charming glimpse of mother and son !

The grandmother here spoken of lived in the same house, and
when lessons were finished, away the children hurried to her room,
to play. The dear old lady, proud as a grandmother, ' spoiled '
them of course, and gave them many an eatable, which they would
get only in her room. But of all her gifts nothing was comparable
to the puppet-show with which she surprised them on the Christmas
eve of 1753, and which Goethe says ' created a new world in the
house '. The reader of *Wilhelm Meister* will remember with what
solemn importance the significance of such a puppet-show is treated,
and may guess how it would exercise the boy's imagination.

There was also the grandfather Textor, whose house the children
gladly visited, and whose grave personality produced an impression
on the boy, all the deeper because a certain mysterious awe surrounded the monosyllabic dream-interpreting old gentleman. His
portrait presents him in a *perruque à huit étages*, with the heavy
golden chain round his neck, suspending a medal given him by the
Empress Maria Theresa ; but Goethe remembered him more vividly
in his dressing-gown and slippers, moving amid the flowers of his
garden, weeding, training, watering ; or seated at the dinner table
where on Sundays he received his guests.

The mother's admirable method of cultivating the inventive activity of the boy, finds its pendant in the father's method of cultivating
his receptive faculties. He speaks with less approbation than it
deserved of his father's idea of education ; probably because late in
life he felt keenly his deficiencies in systematic training. But the
principle upon which the father proceeded was an excellent one,

namely, that of exercising the intellect rather than the memory.
An anecdote was dictated, generally something from every-day life
or perhaps a trait from the life of Frederick the Great ; on this the
boy wrote dialogues and moral reflections in Latin and German.
Some of these have been preserved and published ; a glance at
them shows what a mastery over Latin was achieved in his eighth
year.   We can never be *quite* certain that the hand of the master
is not mingled with that of the child ; but the very method of
independence which the master throughout pursued is contrary to
a supposition of his improving the exercises, although the style is
certainly above what even advanced pupils usually achieve.   Dr.
Wisemann of Frankfurt, to whom we are indebted for these exercises and compositions, written during Goethe's sixth, seventh, and
eighth years, thinks there can be no doubt of their being the un-
assisted productions of the boy.   In one of the dialogues there is
a pun which proves that the dialogue was written in Latin first,
and then translated into German.   It is this : the child is making
wax figures, his father asks him why he does not relinquish such
trivialities.   The word used is *nuces*, which, meaning trivialities in
a metaphorical sense, is by the boy wilfully interpreted in its
ordinary sense, as *nuts*—'*cera nunc ludo non nucibus*'—I play with
wax, not with nuts.   The German word *nüsse* means nuts simply,
and has no metaphorical meaning.

Here is one of his moral reflections.   ' Horatius and Cicero were
indeed Heathens, yet more sensible than many Christians ; for the
one says silver is baser than gold, gold than virtue ; and the other
says nothing is so beautiful as virtue.   Moreover, many Heathens
have surpassed Christians in virtue.   Who was truer in friendship
than Damon ?, more generous than Alexander ?, more just than
Aristides ?, more abstinent than Diogenes ?, more patient than
Socrates ?, more humane than Vespasian ?, more industrious than
Apelles and Demosthenes ?'   Platitudes these, doubtless ; but
they are platitudes which serve many as the ripe maxims of
maturity.   They give us a notion of the boy being somewhat ' old-
fashioned ', and they show great progress in culture.   His progress
in Greek was remarkable, as may be seen from his published
exercises.   Italian he learned by listening to his father teaching
Cornelia.   He pretended to be occupied with his own lesson, and
caught up all that was said.   French, too, he learned, as the exercises testify ; and thus before he is eight, we find him writing
German, French, Italian, Latin, and Greek.

He was, in fact, a precocious child. This will probably startle many readers, especially if they have adopted the current notion that precocity is a sign of disease, and that marvellous children are necessarily evanescent fruits which never ripen, early blossoms which wither early. *Observatum fere est celerius occidere festinatam maturitatem*, says Quintilian, in the mournful passage which records the loss of his darling son ; and many a proud parent has seen his hopes frustrated by early death, or by natural mediocrity following the brilliant promise. It may help to do away with some confusion on this subject, if we bear in mind that men distinguish themselves by *receptive* capacity and by *productive* capacity ; they learn, and they invent. In men of the highest class these two qualities are united. Shakespeare and Goethe are not less remarkable for the variety of their knowledge, than for the activity of their invention. But as we call the child clever who learns his lessons rapidly, and the child clever who shows wit, sagacity, and invention, this ambiguity of phrase has led to surprise when the child who was 'so clever' at school, turns out a mediocre man ; or, conversely, when the child who was a dunce at school, turns out a man of genius.

Goethe's precocity was nothing abnormal. It was the activity of a mind at once greatly receptive and greatly productive. Through life he manifested the same eager desire for knowledge, not in the least alarmed by that bugbear of 'knowledge stifling originality', which alarms some men of questionable genius and unquestionable ignorance. He knew that if abundant fuel stifles miserable fires, it makes the great fire blaze.

> Ein Quidam sagt : 'Ich bin von keiner Schule ;
> Kein Meister lebt mit dem ich buhle ;
> Auch bin ich weit davon entfernt
> Dass ich von Todten was gelernt'.
> Das heisst, wenn ich ihn recht verstand :
> 'Ich bin ein Narr auf eigne Hand !' *

In the summer of 1754 the old house was entirely rebuilt, Wolfgang officiating at the ceremony of laying the foundation, dressed

---

* An exquisite epigram, which may be rendered thus :
> An author boasting said : 'I follow none ;
> I owe my wisdom to myself alone ;
> To neither ancient nor to modern sage
> Am I indebted for a single page'.—
> To place this boasting in its proper light :
> This author is—a Fool in his own Right !

as a little bricklayer. The quick, observant boy found much in
this rebuilding of the paternal house to interest him ; he chatted
with the workmen, learning their domestic circumstances, and
learning something of the builder's art, which in after years so
often occupied him. This event, moreover, led to his being sent
to a friend during the restoration of the upper part of the house—
for the family inhabited the house during its reconstruction, which
was made storey by storey from the ground upwards—and the
event also led to his being sent to school.

Viehoff thinks that Germany would have had quite another
Goethe had the child been kept at a public school till he went to
the university ; and quotes Gervinus to the effect that Goethe's
home education prevented his ever thoroughly appreciating
history, and the struggles of the masses. Not accepting the
doctrine that Character is formed by Circumstances, I cannot
accept the notion of school life affecting the poet to this extent.
We have only to reflect how many men are educated at public
schools *without* their imbibing a love of history and sympathy
with the masses, to see that Goethe's peculiarities must have had
some other source than home education. That source lay in his
character. Moreover, it is extremely questionable whether Goethe
could have learned to sympathize with the masses in a school of
one of the German imperial towns, where there could be no
'masses', but only close corporations, ruled and ruling according
to narrow and somewhat sordid ideas. From intercourse with the
sons of Frankfurt citizens, no patriotism, certainly no republicanism,
was to be learned. Nor was the public teaching, especially the
historical teaching, likely to counteract this influence, or to inspire
the youth with great national sympathies. Those ideas had not
penetrated schools and universities. History, as taught by Schiller
and Heeren, was undreamed of. 'When I entered at Tübingen
in 1826', writes Mr. Demmler to me, 'the university of Paulus,
Schelling, Hegel, and, in days of yore, of Melanchthon, Reuchlin,
and Kepler, traditions were still surviving of the lectures of Rosler,
professor of history. In one of them, as I was told by a fellow of
the college who had heard it, the old cynical sceptic said, "As
regards the Maid of Orleans, I conclude she was a cow girl, and
was, moreover, on a very friendly footing with the young officers".
Another time he said, "Homer was a blind schoolmaster and
wandering minstrel, and I cannot comprehend the fuss that is
made about his poems"'. If this was the man who instructed

Schelling and Hegel (1790–94), we may form some estimate of what Goethe would have heard forty years earlier.

One thing, however, he did learn at school, and that was disgust at schools. He, carefully trained at home, morally as well as physically, had to mingle with schoolboys who were what most schoolboys are,—dirty, rebellious, cruel, low in their tastes and habits. The contrast was very painful to him, and he was glad when the completion of his father's house once more enabled him to receive instruction at home.

One school anecdote he relates which well illustrates his power of self-command. Fighting during school time was severely punished. One day the teacher did not arrive at the appointed time. The boys played together till the hour was nearly over, and then three of them, left alone with Wolfang, resolved to drive him away. They cut up a broom, and reappeared with the switches. 'I saw their design, but I at once resolved not to resist them till the clock struck. They began pitilessly lashing my legs. I did not stir, although the pain made the minutes terribly long. My wrath deepened with my endurance, and on the first stroke of the hour I grasped one of my assailants by the hair and hurled him to the ground, pressing my knee on his back ; I drew the head of the second, who attacked me behind, under my arm and nearly throttled him ; with a dexterous twist I threw the third flat on the ground. They bit, scratched, and kicked. But my soul was swelling with one feeling of revenge, and I knocked their heads together without mercy. A shout of murder brought the household round us. But the scattered switches and my bleeding legs bore witness to my story '.

CHAPTER III

EARLY EXPERIENCES

IT is profoundly false to say that 'Character is formed by Circumstance', unless the phrase, with unphilosophic equivocation, include the whole complexity of circumstances, from Creation downwards. Character is to outward Circumstance what the Organism is to the outward world : living *in* it, but not specially determined *by* it. A wondrous variety of vegetable and animal organisms live and flourish under circumstances which furnish the *means* of living, but do not determine the *specific forms* of each organism. In the same way *various* characters live under *identical* circumstances, nourished by them, not formed by them. Each character assimilates, from surrounding circumstance, that which is by it assimilable, rejecting the rest ; just as from the earth and air the plant draws those elements which will serve it as food, rejecting the rest. Every biologist knows that Circumstance has a *modifying* influence ; but he also knows that those modifications are only possible within certain limits. Abundance of food and peculiar treatment will modify the ferocity of a wild beast ; but it will not make the lion a lamb. I have known a cat, living at a mill, from abundance of fish food take spontaneously to the water : but the cat was distinctively a cat, and not an otter, although she had lost her dread of water. Goethe truly says that if Raphael were to paint peasants at an inn he could not help making them look like Apostles, whereas Teniers would make his Apostles look like Dutch boors ; each artist working according to his own inborn genius.

Instead, therefore, of saying that man is the creature of Circumstance, it would be nearer the mark to say that man is the architect of Circumstance. It is Character which builds an existence out of Circumstance. Our strength is measured by our plastic power. From the same materials one man builds palaces, another hovels, one warehouses, another villas ; bricks and mortar are mortar and bricks, until the architect can make them something else. Thus it is that in the same circumstances, one man rears a stately edifice, while his brother, vacillating and incompetent, lives for ever amid ruins : the block of granite which was an obstacle on the pathway of the weak, becomes a stepping-stone on the pathway of the strong*.

If the reader agrees with this conception of the influence of circumstances, he will see that I was justified in laying some stress on Goethe's social position, though I controverted Viehoff and Gervinus on the point of school education. The continued absence of Want is one of those permanent and powerful conditions which necessarily modify a character. The well-fed lion loses his ferocity.

* ' The greatness or the smallness of a man is determined for him at his birth, as strictly as it is determined for a fruit, whether it is to be a currant or an apricot. Education, favourable circumstances, resolution, industry, may do much, in a certain sense they do *everything;* that is to say, they determine whether the poor apricot shall fall in the form of a green bead, blighted by the east wind, and be trodden under foot ; or whether it shall expand into tender pride and sweet brightness of golden velvet '.— RUSKIN, *Modern Painters*, iii, p. 44.

But the temporary and incidental effect of school education, and other circumstances of minor importance, can never be said to modify a character ; they only more or less accelerate its development.

Goethe furnishes us with a striking illustration of the degree in which outward circumstances affect character. He became early the favourite of several eminent painters, was constantly in their ateliers, playing with them, and making them explain their works to him. He was, moreover, a frequent visitor at picture sales and galleries, till at last his mind became so familiarized with the subjects treated by artists, that he could at once tell what historical or biblical subject was represented in every painting he saw. Indeed, his imagination was so stimulated by familiarity with these works, that in his tenth or eleventh year he wrote a description of twelve possible pictures on the history of Joseph, and some of his conceptions were thought worthy of being executed by artists of renown. It may be further added, in anticipation, that during the whole of his life he was thrown much with painters and pictures, and was for many years tormented with the desire of becoming an artist. If, therefore, Circumstance had the power of forming faculty, we ought to find him a painter. What is the fact? The fact is that he had *not* the faculty which makes a painter ; he had no faculty, properly speaking, for plastic art, and years of labour, aided by the instruction and counsel of the best masters, were powerless to give him even a respectable facility. All therefore that Circumstance did in this case was to give his other faculties the opportunity of exercising themselves in art ; it did not create the special faculty required. Circumstance can create no faculty : it is food, not nutrition ; opportunity, not character.

Other boys, besides Goethe, heard the Lisbon earthquake eagerly discussed ; but they had not their religious doubts awakened by it, as his were awakened in his sixth year. This catastrophe, which, in 1755, spread consternation over Europe, he has described as having greatly perturbed him. The narratives he heard of a magnificent capital suddenly smitten—churches, houses, towers, falling with a crash—the bursting land vomiting flames and smoke—and sixty thousand souls perishing in an instant—shook his faith in the beneficence of Providence. 'God, the creator and preserver of heaven and earth', he says, ' whom the first article of our creed declared to be so wise and benignant, had not displayed paternal care in thus consigning both the just and the unjust to the same destruction. In vain my young mind strove to resist these impressions. It was impossible; the more so as the wise and religious themselves could not agree upon the view to be taken of the event'.

At this very time Voltaire was agitating the same doubts :

> Direz-vous, en voyant cet amas de victimes :
> Dieu s'est vengé, leur mort est le prix de leur crimes?
> Quel crime, quelle faute ont commis ces enfans
> Sur le sein maternel écrasés et sanglans?
> Lisbonne qui n'est plus, eût-elle plus de vices
> Que Londres, que Paris, plongés dans les délices?
> Lisbonne est abîmée ; et l'on danse à Paris.

We are not, however, to suppose that the child rushed hastily to such a conclusion. He debated it in his own mind as he heard it debated around him. Bettina records that on his coming one day from church, where he had listened to a sermon on the subject, in which God's goodness was justified, his father asked him what impression the sermon had made. 'Why', said he, 'it may after all be a much simpler matter than the clergyman thinks ; God knows very well that an immortal soul can receive no injury from a mortal accident'.

Doubts once raised would of course recur, and the child began to settle into a serious disbelief in the benignity of Providence, learning to consider God as the wrathful Deity depicted by the Hebrews. This was strengthened by the foolish conduct of those around him, who, on the occasion of a terrible thunderstorm which shattered the windows, dragged him and his sister into a dark passage, 'where the whole household, distracted with fear, tried to conciliate the angry Deity by frightful groans and prayers'. Many children are thus made sceptics ; but in a deeply reflective mind such thoughts never long abide, at least not under the influences of modern culture, which teaches that Evil is essentially a narrow finite thing, thrown into obscurity on any comprehensive view of the Universe ; and that the amount of evil massed together from every quarter must be held as small compared with the broad beneficence of Nature.

The doubts which troubled Wolfgang gradually subsided. In his family circle he was the silent, reflective listener to constant theological debates. The various sects separating from the established church all seemed to be animated by the one desire of approaching the Deity, especially through Christ, more nearly than seemed possible through the ancient forms. It occurred to him that he, also, might make such an approach, and in a more direct way. Unable to ascribe a form to the Deity, he 'resolved to seek Him in His works, and in the good old Bible fashion, to build an altar to Him'. For this purpose he selected some types, such as ores and other natural productions, and arranged them in symbolical order on the elevations of a music stand ; on the apex was to be a flame typical of the soul's aspiration, and for this a pastille did duty. Sunrise was awaited with impatience. The glittering of the house tops gave signal ; he applied a burning-glass to the pastille, and thus was the worship consummated by a priest of seven years old, alone in his bedroom !*

Lest the trait just cited should make us forget that we are tracing the career of a child, it may be well to recall the anecdote related by Bettina, who had it from his mother; it will serve to set us right as to the childishness. One day his mother, seeing him from her window cross the street with his comrades, was amused with the gravity of his carriage, and asked laughingly, if he meant thereby to distinguish himself from his companions. The little fellow replied, 'I *begin* with this. Later on in life I shall distinguish myself in far other ways'.

On another occasion, he plagued her with questions as to whether the stars would perform all they had promised at his birth. 'Why', said she, 'must you have the assistance of the stars, when other people get on very well without?' 'I am not to be satisfied with what does for other people !' said the juvenile Jupiter.

He had just attained his seventh year when the Seven Years' War broke out. His grandfather espoused the cause of Austria, his father that of Frederick. This difference of opinion brought with it contentions, and finally separation between the families. The exploits of the Prussian army were enthusiastically cited on the one side and depreciated on the other. It was an all-absorbing topic, awakening passionate partisanship. Men looked with strange feelings on the struggle which the greatest captain of his age was maintaining against Russia, Austria, and France. The ruler of not more than five millions of men was fighting unaided against the rulers of more than a hundred millions ; and, in spite of his

---

* A similar anecdote is related of himself by that strange Romancist, once the idol of his day, and now almost entirely forgotten, Restif de la Bretonne.—See *Les Illuminés*, par GÉRARD DE NERVAL.

alleged violation of honour, it was difficult to hear without enthusiasm of his brilliant exploits. Courage and genius in desperate circumstances always awaken sympathy ; and men paused not to ask what justification there was for the seizure of Silesia, nor why the Saxon standards drooped heavily in the churches of Berlin. The roar of victorious cannon stunned the judgment ; the intrepid general was blindly worshipped. The Seven Years' War soon became a German epos. Archenholtz wrote its history (1791) ; and this work—noisy with guard-room bragging and folly, the rant of a *miles gloriosus* turned *philosophe*—was nevertheless received with enthusiasm, was translated into Latin, and read in school in company with Tacitus and Cæsar.

This Seven Years' War was a circumstance from which, as it is thought, Goethe ought to have received some epic inspiration. He received from it precisely that which was food to his character. He caught the grand enthusiasm, but, as he says, it was the *personality* of the hero, rather than the greatness of his cause, which made him rejoice in every victory, copy the songs of triumph, and the lampoons directed against Austria. He learnt now the effects of party spirit. At the table of his grandfather he had to hear galling sarcasms and vehement declamations showered on his hero. He heard Frederick ' shamefully slandered '. ' And as in my sixth year, after the Lisbon earthquake, I doubted the beneficence of Providence, so now, on account of Frederick, I began to doubt the justice of the world '.

Over the doorway of the house in which he was born was a lyre and a star, announcing, as every interpreter will certify, that a poet was to make that house illustrious. The poetic faculty early manifested itself. We have seen him inventing conclusions for his mother's stories ; and as he grew older he began to invent stories for the amusement of his playfellows, after he had filled his mind with images

> Lone sitting on the shores of old Romance.

He had read the *Orbis Pictus*, Ovid's *Metamorphoses*, Homer's *Iliad* in prose, *Virgil* in the original, *Telemachus*, *Robinson Crusoe*, *Anson's Voyages*, with such books as *Fortunatus*, *The Wandering Jew*, *The Four Sons of Aymon*, etc. He also read and learned by heart most of the poets of that day : Gellert, Haller, who had really some gleams of poetry ; and Canitz, Hagedorn, Drollinger, —writers then much beloved, now slumbering upon dusty shelves, unvisited, except by an occasional historian, and by spiders of an inquiring mind.

Not only did he tell stories, he wrote them also, as we gather from a touching little anecdote preserved by Bettina. The small-pox had carried off his little brother Jacob. To the surprise of his mother, Wolfgang shed no tears, believing Jacob to be with God in heaven. ‘Did you not love your little brother, then’, asked his mother, ‘that you do not grieve for his loss?’ He ran to his room, and from under the bed drew a quantity of papers on which he had written stories and lessons. ‘All these I had written that I might teach them to him’, said the child. He was then nine years old.

Shortly before the death of his brother he was startled by the sound of the warder’s trumpet from the chief tower, announcing the approach of troops. This was in January 1759. It seemed as if the warder never *would* cease blowing his sounding horn. On came the troops in continuous masses, and the rolling tumult of their drums called all the women to the windows, and all the boys in admiring crowds into the streets. The troops were French. They seized the guard-house, and in a little while the city was a camp. To make matters worse, these troops were at war with Frederick, whom Wolfgang and his father worshipped. They were soon billeted through the town, and things relapsed into their usual routine, varied by a military occupation. In the Goethe-house an important person was quartered,—Count de Thorane, the king’s lieutenant, a man of taste and munificence, who assembled round him artists and celebrities, and won the affectionate admiration of Wolfgang, though he failed to overcome the hatred of the old councillor.

This occupation of Frankfurt brought with it many advantages to Goethe. It relaxed the severity of paternal book education, and began another kind of tuition—that of life and manners. The perpetual marching through the streets, the brilliant parades, the music, the ‘pomp, pride, and circumstance’ were not without their influence. Moreover, he now gained conversational familiarity with French*, and acquaintance with the theatre. The French nation always carries its ‘civilization’ with it, namely, a café and a theatre. In Frankfurt both were immediately opened, and Goethe was presented with a ‘free admission’ to the theatre, a privilege he used daily, not always understanding, but always enjoying what

---

* He says that he had never learned French before; but this is erroneous, as his exercises prove.

he saw. In tragedy the measured rhythm, slow utterance, and abstract language enabled him to understand the scenes, better than he understood comedy, wherein the language, besides moving, amid the details of private life, was also more rapidly spoken. But at the theatre, boys are not critical, and do not need to understand a play in order to enjoy it*. A *Racine*, found upon his father's shelves, was eagerly studied, and the speeches were declaimed with more or less appreciation of their meaning.

The theatre, and acquaintance with a chattering little braggart, named Derones, gave him such familiarity with the language, that in a month he surprised his parents with his facility. This Derones was acquainted with the actors, and introduced him 'behind the scenes'. At ten years of age to go 'behind the scenes' means a great deal. We shall see hereafter how early he was introduced behind the scenes of life. For the present let it be noted that he was a frequenter of the green-room, and admitted into the dressing-room, where the actors and actresses dressed and undressed with philosophic disregard to appearances ; and this, from repeated visits, he also learned to regard as quite natural.

A grotesque scene took place between these two boys. Derones excelled, as he affirmed, in 'affairs of honour'. He had been engaged in several, and had always managed to disarm his antagonist, and then nobly forgive him. One day he pretended that Wolfgang had insulted him : satisfaction was peremptorily demanded, and a duel was the result. Imagine Wolfgang, aged twelve, arrayed in shoes and silver buckles, fine woollen stockings, dark serge breeches, green coat with gold facings, a waistcoat of gold cloth, cut out of his father's wedding waistcoat, his hair curled and powdered, his hat under his arm, and little sword, with silk sword-knot. This little manikin stands opposite his antagonist with theatrical formality ; swords clash, thrusts come quick upon each other, the combat grows hot, when the point of Derones' rapier lodges in the bow of Wolfgang's sword-knot ; hereupon the French boy, with great magnanimity, declares that he is satisfied !

* Well do I remember, as a child of the same age, my intense delight at the French theatre, although certainly no three consecutive phrases could have been understood by me. Nay, so great was this delight, that although we regarded the French custom, of opening theatres on Sunday, with the profoundest sense of its 'wickedness', the attraction became irresistible : and one Sunday night, at Nantes, my brother and I stole into the theatre with pricking consciences. To this day I see the actors gesticulating, and hear the audience cry *bis! bis!* redemanding a *couplet* (in which we joined with a stout British *encore!*) ; and to this day I remember how we laughed at what we certainly understood only in passing glimpses. Goethe's ignorance of the language was, I am sure, no obstacle to his enjoyment.

The two embrace, and retire to a café to refresh themselves with a glass of almond milk*.

Theatrical ambition, which stirs us all, soon prompted Wolfgang. As a child he had imitated Terence ; he was now to make a more elaborate effort in the style of Piron. When the play was completed he submitted it to Derones, who, pointing out several grammatical blunders, promised to examine it more critically, and talked of giving it *his* support with the manager. Wolfgang saw, in his mind's eye, the name of his play already placarded at the corners of the street ! Unhappily Derones in his critical capacity was merciless. He picked the play to pieces, and stunned the the poor author with the critical jargon of that day ; proclaimed the absolute integrity of the Three Unities, abused the English, laughed at the Germans, and maintained the sovereignty of French taste in so confident a style, that his listener was without a reply. If silenced, however, he was not convinced. It set him thinking on those critical canons. He studied the treatise on the Unities by Corneille, and the prefaces of Racine. The result of these studies was profound contempt for that system ; and it is, perhaps, to Derones that we owe something of the daring defiance of all 'rule', which startled Germany in *Goetz von Berlichingen*.

CHAPTER IV

VARIOUS STUDIES

AT length, June 1761, the French quitted Frankfurt ; and studies were seriously resumed. Mathematics, music, and drawing were commenced under paternal superintendence. For mathematics Wolfgang had no aptitude ; for music little ; he learned to play on the harpsichord, and subsequently on the violoncello, but he never attained any proficiency. Drawing continued through life a pleasant exercise.

Left now to the calm of uninterrupted studies, he made gigantic strides. Even the hours of recreation were filled with some useful occupation. He added English to his polyglot store ; and to keep up his several languages, he invented a Romance, wherein six or seven brothers and sisters scattered over the world corresponded

* To remove incredulity, it may be well to remind the reader that to this day German youths fight out their quarrels with swords—not fists.

with each other. The eldest describes in good German all the
incidents of his travels ; his sister answers in womanly style with
short sharp sentences, and nothing but full stops, much as *Siegwart*
was afterwards written. Another brother studies theology, and
therefore writes in Latin, with postcripts in Greek. A third and
a fourth, clerks at Hamburg and Marseilles, take English and
French ; Italian is given to a musician ; while the youngest, who
remains at home, writes in Jew-German. This romance led him
to a more accurate study of geography. Having placed his
characters in various parts of the globe, he was not satisfied till he
had a distinct idea of these localities, so that the objects and
events should be consonant with probability. While trying to
master the strange dialect—Jew-German—he was led to the study
of Hebrew. As the original language of the Old Testament this
seemed to him an indispensable acquisition. His father consented
to give him a Hebrew master ; and although he attained no
scholarship in that difficult language, yet the reading, translating,
and committing to memory of various parts of the Bible, brought
out the meaning more vividly before him ; as every one will
understand who compares the lasting effect produced by the
laborious school reading of Sallust and Livy, with the facile
reading of Robertson and Hume. The Bible made a profound
impression upon him. To a boy of his constitutional reflectiveness,
the severe study of this book could not fail to exercise a deep and
permeating influence ; nor, at the same time, in one so accustomed
to think for himself, could it fail to awaken certain doubts. 'The
contradiction', he says, 'between the actual or possible, and
tradition, forcibly arrested me. I often posed my tutors with the
sun standing still on Gideon, and the moon in the valley of Ajalon ;
not to mention other incongruities and impossibilities. All my
doubts were now awakened, as in order to master the Hebrew I
studied the literal version by Schmidt, printed under the text'.

One result of these Hebrew studies was a biblical poem on
Joseph and his Brethren ; which he dictated to a poor half idiot
who lived in his father's house, and who had a mania for copying
or writing under dictation. Goethe soon found the process of
dictation of great service ; and through life it continued to be his
favourite mode of composition. All his best thoughts and expressions, he says, came to him while walking ; he could do nothing
seated.

To these multifarious studies in Literature must be added

multifarious studies of Life.   The old Frankfurt city with its busy crowds, its fairs, its mixed population, and its many sources of excitement, offered great temptations, and great pasture to so desultory a genius.   This is perhaps a case wherein Circumstance may be seen influencing the direction of Character.   A boy of less impressionable nature, of less many-sided curiosity, would have lived in such a city undisturbed ; some eyes would see little of the variety, some minds would be unsolicited by the exciting objects.   But Goethe's desultory, because impulsive, nature found continual excitement in fresh objects ; and he was thus led to study many things, to grasp at many forms of life, instead of concentrating himself upon a few.   A large continuity of thought and effort was perhaps radically uncongenial to such a temperament ; yet one cannot help speculating whether under other circumstances he might not have achieved it.   Had he been reared in a quiet little old German town, where he would have daily seen the same faces in the silent streets, and come in contact with the same characters, his culture might have been less various, but it might perhaps have been deeper.   Had he been reared in the country, with only the changing seasons and the sweet serenities of Nature to occupy his attention when released from study, he would certainly have been a different poet.   The long summer afternoons spent in lonely rambles, the deepening twilight filled with shadowy visions, the slow uniformity of his external life necessarily throwing him more and more upon the subtler diversities of inward experience, would inevitably have influenced his genius in quite different directions, would have animated his works with a very different spirit.   Yet who shall say that to him this would have been all gain?   Who shall say that it would not have been a loss?   For such an organization as his the life he led was perhaps the very best.   He was desultory, and the varieties of objects which solicited his attention, while they helped to encourage that tendency, also helped to nourish his mind with images and experience, such as afterwards became the richest material for his art.   His mind was concrete, and in this many-coloured life at Frankfurt it found abundant material.

At any rate it is idle to speculate on what would have been ; we must concern ourselves with what was.   The boy saw much of life, in the lower as in the upper classes.   He passed from the society of the Count de Thorane, and of the artists whom the Count assembled round him (from whom the boy learned some-

François de Théas, Count de Thorane (the King's Lieutenant)

thing of the technical details of painting), to the society of the Jews in the strange, old, filthy, but deeply interesting *Judengasse;* or to that of various artizans, in whose shops his curiosity found perpetual food. The Jews were doubly interesting to him : as social pariahs, over whom there hovered a mingled mystery of terror and contempt ; and as descendants of the Chosen People, who preserved the language, the opinions, and many of the customs of the old biblical race. He was impressed by their adherence to old customs ; by their steadfastness and courageous activity ; by their strange features and accents ; by their bright cleverness and good nature. The pretty Jewish maidens, also, smiled agreeably upon him. He began to mingle with them ; managed to get permission to attend some of their ceremonies ; and attended their schools. As to artizans, he was all his life curious about their handicrafts, and fond of being admitted into their family circles. Scott himself was not fonder of talking to one ; nor did Scott make better use of such manifold experience. Frederika's sister told her visitor that Goethe knew several handicrafts, and had even learned basket-making from a lame man in Sesenheim. Here in Frankfurt the boy was welcome in many a shop. The jeweller, Lautensack, gladly admitted him to witness the mysteries of his art, while he made the bouquet of jewels for the Kaiser, or a diamond snuff-box which Rath Goethe had ordered as a present for his wife ; the boy eagerly questioning him respecting precious stones, and the engravings which the jeweller possessed. Nothnagel, the painter, had established an ʼoil-cloth manufactory ; and the boy not only learned all the processes, but lent a helping hand.

Besides these forms of life, there were others whose influence must not be overlooked ; one of these bring before us the Fräulein von Klettenburg, of whom we first get a glimpse in connection with his Confirmation, which took place at this period, 1763. The readers of *Wilhelm Meister* are familiar with this gentle and exquisite character, where she is represented in the ' Confessions of a Beautiful Soul ' *. In the ' Confessions ' we see that the ' piety ' and retirement are represented less as the consequences of evangelical illumination, than of moral serenity and purity shrinking from contact with a world of which it has been her fate

---

* Or as we in England, following Carlyle, have been misled into calling it, the ʻConfessions of a Fair Saint'. The *schöne Seele—une belle âme*, was one of the favourite epithets of the last century. Goethe applies it to Klopstock, who was neither ' saint nor fair '.

to see the coarsest features. The real Fräulein von Klettenburg it is perhaps now impossible to separate from the ideal so beautifully painted by Goethe. On him her influence was avowedly very great, both at this period and subsequently. It was not so much the effect of religious discussion, as the experience it gave him of a deeply religious nature. She was neither bigot nor prude. Her faith was an inner light which shed mild radiance around her †. Moved by her influence, he wrote a series of *Religious Odes*, after the fashion of that day, and greatly pleased his father by presenting them copied neatly into a quarto volume. His father begged that every year he would present him with such a volume.

A very different sort of female influence has now to be touched on. His heart began to flutter with the emotions of love. He was not quite fifteen, when Gretchen, the sister of one of his disreputable companions, first set his youthful pulses throbbing to the movements of the divine passion. The story is told in a rambling way in the Autobiography, and may here be very briefly dismissed. He had often turned his poetical talents to *practical* purposes, namely, writing wedding and funeral verses, the produce of which went in joyous feastings. In these he was almost daily thrown with Gretchen ; but she, though kind, treated him as a child, and never permitted the slightest familiarity. A merry life they led, in picnics and pleasure bouts ; and the coronation of the Kaiser Joseph II. was the occasion of increased festivity. One night, after the fatigues of a sight-seeing day, the hours rolled unheeded over these thoughtless, merry heads, and the stroke of midnight startled them. To his dismay, Wolfgang found he had forgotten the door-key with which hitherto he had been able to evade paternal knowledge of his late hours. Gretchen proposed that they should all remain together, and pass the night in conversation. This was agreed on. But, as in all such cases, the effort was vain. Fatigue weighed down their eyelids ; conversation became feebler and feebler ; two strangers already slumbered in corners of the room ; one friend sat in a corner with his betrothed, her head reposing on his shoulder ; another crossing his arms upon the table, rested his head upon them—and snored. The noisy room had become silent. Gretchen and her lover sat by the window talking in undertones. Fatigue at length conquered her also, and drooping her head upon his shoulder she too slept. With tender

† In Varnhagen von Ense's *Vermischte Schriften* (vol. iii, p. 33), the reader will find a few significant details respecting this remarkable person, and some of her poems.

pride he supported that delicious burden, till like the rest he gave
way, and slept.

It was broad day when he awoke. Gretchen was standing
before a mirror arranging her cap. She smiled on him more
amiably than ever she had smiled before ; and pressed his hand
tenderly as he departed. But now, while he seemed drawing
nearer to her, the dénouement was at hand. Some of the joyous
companions had been guilty of nefarious practices, such as
forgeries of documents. His friend and Gretchen were involved
in the accusation, though falsely. Wolfgang had to undergo a
severe investigation, which, as he was perfectly innocent, did not
much afflict him ; but an affliction came out of the investigation,
for Gretchen in her deposition concerning him, said, ' I will not
deny that I have often seen him, and seen him with pleasure, but
I treated him as a child, and my affection for him was merely that
of a sister'. His exasperation may be imagined. A boy aspiring
to the dignity of manhood knows few things more galling than to
be treated as a boy by the girl whom he has honoured with his
homage. He suffered greatly at this destruction of his romance :
nightly was his pillow wet with tears ; food became repugnant
to him ; life had no more an object.

But pride came to his aid ; pride and that volatility of youth,
which compensates for extra sensitiveness by extra facility for
forgetting. He threw himself into study, especially of philosophy,
under guidance of a tutor, a sort of *Wagner* to the young *Faust*.
This tutor, who preferred dusty quartos to all the landscapes in the
world, used to banter him upon being a true German, such as
Tacitus describes, avid of the emotions excited by solitude and
scenery. Laughter weaned him not from the enjoyment. He
was enjoying his first sorrow : the luxury of melancholy, the
romance of a forlorn existence, drove him into solitude. Like
Bellerophon he fed upon his own heart, away from the haunts of
men. He made frequent walking excursions. Those mountains
which from earliest childhood had stood so distant, ' haunting
him like a passion ', were now his favourite resorts. He
visited Homburg, Kronburg, Königstein, Wiesbaden, Schwalbach,
Biberich. These filled his mind with lovely images.

Severer studies were not neglected. To please his father he
was diligent in application to jurisprudence ; to please himself he
was still more diligent in literature : *Morhof's Polyhistor, Gessner's
Isagoge*, and *Bayle's Dictionary*, filled him with the ambition to

become an University Professor. Herein, as, indeed, throughout his career, we see the strange impressibility of his nature, which, like the fabled chameleon, takes its colour from every tree it lies under.

The melancholy fit did not last long. A circle of lively friends, among them Horn, of whom we shall hear more anon, drew him into gaiety again. Their opinion of his talents appears to have been enormous; their love for him, and interest in all he did, was of the kind which followed him through life. No matter what his mood—in the wildest student-period, in the startling genius-period, and in the diplomatic-period — whatever offence his manner created, was soon forgotten in the irresistible fascination of his nature. The secret of that fascination was his own overflowing lovingness, and his genuine interest in every individuality, however opposite to his own.

With these imperfect glances at his early career we close this book, on his departure from home for the university of Leipsic. Before finally quitting this period, we may take a survey of the *characteristics* it exhibits, as some guide in our future inquiries.

CHAPTER V

THE CHILD IS FATHER TO THE MAN

AS in the soft round lineaments of childhood we trace the features which after years will develop into more decided forms, so in the moral lineaments of the Child may be traced the characteristics of the Man. But an apparent solution of continuity takes place in the transition period; so that the Youth is in many respects unlike what he has been in childhood, and what he will be in maturity. In youth, when the passions begin to stir, the character is made to swerve from the orbit previously traced. Passion, more than Character, rules the hour. Thus we often see the prudent child turn out an extravagant youth; but he crystallizes once more into prudence, as he hardens with age.

This was certainly the case with Goethe, who, if he had died young, like Shelley or Keats, would have left a name among the most *genial*, not to say extravagant, of poets; but who, living to the age of eighty-two, had fifty years of crystallization to acquire a definite figure which perplexes critics. In his childhood, scanty as the details are which enable us to reconstruct it, we see the main features of the man. Let us glance rapidly at them.

And first of his *manysidedness.* Seldom has a boy exhibited such variety of faculty. The multiplied activity of his life is prefigured in the varied tendencies of his childhood. We see him as an orderly, somewhat formal, inquisitive, reasoning, deliberative child, a precocious learner, an omnivorous reader, and a vigorous logician who thinks for himself—so independent, that at six years of age he doubts the beneficence of the Creator ; at seven, doubts the competence and justice of the world's judgment. He is inventive, poetical ; proud, loving, volatile, with a mind open to all influences, swayed by every gust, and yet, while thus swayed as to the direction of his activity, master over that activity. The most diverse characters, the most antagonistic opinions interest him. He is very studious : no bookworm more so ; alternately busy with languages, mythology, antiquities, law, philosophy, poetry, and religion ; yet he joins in all festive scenes, gets familiar with life in various forms, and stays out late o' nights. He is also troubled by melancholy, dreamy moods, forcing him ever and anon into solitude.

Among the dominant characteristics, however, are seriousness, formality, rationality. He is by no means a naughty boy. He gives his parents no tremulous anxiety as to what will become of him. He seems very much master of himself. It is this which in later years perplexed his judges, who could not reconcile this appearance of self-mastery, this absence of enthusiasm, with their conceptions of a poet. Assuredly he had enthusiasm, if ever man had it : at least, if enthusiasm (being 'full of the God') means being filled with a divine idea, and by its light working steadily. He had little of the other kind of enthusiasm—that insurrection of the feelings carrying away upon their triumphant shoulders the Reason which has no longer power to guide them ; for his intellect did not derive its main momentum from his feelings. And hence it is that whereas the quality which first strikes us in most poets is *sensibility*, with its caprices, infirmities, and generous errors ; the first quality which strikes us in Goethe—the Child and Man, but *not* the Youth—is *intellect*, with its clearness and calmness. He has also a provoking immunity from error. I say *provoking*, for we all gladly overlook the errors of enthusiasm ; some, because these errors appeal to our compassion ; and some, because these errors establish a community of impulse between the sinner and ourselves, forming, as it were, broken edges which show us where to look for support—scars which tell of wounds we have escaped. Whereas, we are pitiless to the cold prudence which shames our weakness and asks no alms from our charity. Why do we all preach Prudence, and secretly dislike it? Perhaps, because we dimly feel that life without its generous errors might want its lasting enjoyments; and thus the very mistakes which arise from an imprudent, unreflecting career, are absolved by that instinct which suggests other aims for existence beyond prudential aims. This is one reason why the erring lives of Genius command such deathless sympathy.

Having indicated so much, I may now ask those who are distressed by the calm, self-sustaining superiority of Goethe in old age, whether, on deeper reflection, they cannot reconcile it with their conceptions of the poet's nature? We admire Rationality, but we sympathize with Sensibility. Our dislike of the one arises from its supposed incompatibility with the other. But if a man unites the mastery of Will and Intellect to the profoundest sensibility of Emotion, shall we not say of him that he has in living synthesis vindicated both what we preach and what we love? That Goethe united these will be abundantly shown in this Biography. In the chapters about to follow we shall see him wild, restless, aimless, erring, and extravagant enough to satisfy the most ardent admirer of the vagabond nature of genius: the Child and the Man will at times be scarcely traceable in the Youth.

One trait must not be passed over, namely, his *impatient susceptibility*, which, while it prevented his ever thoroughly mastering the technic of any one subject, lay at the bottom of his multiplied activity in directions so opposed to each other. He was excessively impressible, caught the impulse from every surrounding influence, and was thus never constant to one thing, because his susceptibility was connected with an impatience which soon made him weary. There are men who learn many languages, and never thoroughly master the grammar of one. Of these was Goethe. Easily excited to throw his energy in a new direction, he had not the patience which begins at the beginning, and rises gradually, slowly into assured mastery. Like an eagle he swooped down upon his prey; he could not watch for it, with cat-like patience. It is to this impatience we must attribute the fact of so many works being left fragments, so many composed by snatches during long intervals.

Prometheus, Mahomet, Die Natürliche Tochter, Elpenor, Achilleis, Nausikäa, remain fragments. *Faust, Egmont, Tasso, Iphigenia, Meister,* were many years in hand. Whatever could be done in a few days—while the impulse lasted—was done ; longer works were spread over a series of years.

BOOK THE SECOND

1765 to 1771

CHAPTER I

THE LEIPSIC STUDENT

I N the month of October 1765, Goethe, aged sixteen, arrived in Leipsic, to commence his collegiate life, and to lay, as he hoped, the solid foundation of a future professorship. He took lodgings in the Feuerkugel, between the Old and New Markets, and was by the rector of the University inscribed on the 19th a student 'in the Bavarian nation'. At that period, and until quite recently, the University was classed according to four 'Nations', viz., the *Mísnian*, the *Saxon*, the *Bavarian*, and the *Polish*. When the inscription was official, the 'nations' were vhat in Oxford and Paris are called 'tongues'; when not official, hey were students' clubs, such as they exist to this day. Goethe, as a Frankfurter, was placed in the Bavarian*.

If the reader has any vivid recollection of the Leipsic chapters in the *Autobiography*, let me beg him to dismiss them with all haste from his mind; that very work records the inability of recalling the enchanting days of youth 'with the dimmed powers of an aged mind'; and it is evident that the calm narrative of his Excellency J. W. von Goethe very inaccurately represents the actual condition of the raw, wild student, just escaped from the paternal roof, with money which seems unlimited in his purse, with the world before him which his genius is to open. His own letters, and the letters of his friends, enable us 'to read between the lines' of the *Autobiography*, and to read there a very different account.

He first presented himself to Hofrath Böhme, a genuine German professor, shut within the narrow circle of his speciality. To him, Literature and the Fine Arts were trivialities; and when

---

* Otto Jahn, in the *Briefe an Leipziger Freunde*, p. 9.

the confiding youth confessed his secret ambition of studying *belles lettres*, in lieu of the jurisprudence commanded by his father, he met with every discouragement. Yet it was not difficult to persuade this impressible student that to rival Otto and Heineccius was the true ambition of a vigorous mind. He set to work in earnest, at first, as students usually do on arriving at seats of learning. His attendance at the lectures on philosophy, history of law, and jurisprudence, was assiduous enough to have pleased even his father. But this flush of eagerness quickly subsided. Logic was invincibly repugnant to him. He hungered for realities, and could not be satisfied with definitions. To see operations of his mind which, from childhood upwards, had been conducted with perfect ease and unconsciousness, suddenly pulled to pieces, in order that he might gain the superfluous knowledge of what they were, and what they were called, was to him tiresome and frivolous. ' I fancied I knew as much about God and the world as the professor himself, and logic seemed in many places to come to a dead standstill'. We are here on the threshold of that experience which has been immortalized in the scene between Mephistopheles and the Student. Jurisprudence soon became almost equally tiresome. He already knew as much law as the professor thought proper to communicate ; and what with the tedium of the lectures, and the counter-attraction of delicious fritters, which used to come 'hot from the pan precisely at the hour of lecture', no wonder that volatile Sixteen soon abated attendance.

Volatile he was, wild, and somewhat rough, both in appearance and in speech. He had brought with him a wild, uneasy spirit struggling towards the light. He had also brought with him the rough manners of Frankfurt, the strong Frankfurt dialect and colloquialisms, rendered still more unfit for the Leipsic salon by a mixture of proverbs and biblical allusions. Nay, even his costume was in unpleasant contrast with that of the society in which he moved. He had an ample wardrobe, but unhappily it was doubly out of fashion : it had been manufactured at home by one of his father's servants, and thus was not only in the Frankfurt style, but grotesquely made in that style. To complete his discomfiture, he saw a favourite low comedian throw an audience into fits of laughter by appearing on the stage dressed precisely in that costume, which he had hitherto worn as the latest novelty ! All who can remember the early humiliations of being far behind

their companions in matters of costume, will sympathize with
this youth.   From one of his letters written shortly after his
arrival, we may catch a glimpse of him.   'To-day I have heard
two lectures : Böhme on law, and Ernesti on Cicero's *Orator*.
That'll do, eh ?   Next week we have collegium philosophicum et
mathematicum.   I haven't seen Gottsched yet.   He is married
again.   She is nineteen and he sixty-five.   She is four feet high,
and he seven feet.   She is as thin as a herring, and he as broad
as a feathersack.   I make a great figure here !   But as yet I
am no dandy.   I never shall become one.   I need some skill to
be industrious.   In society, concerts, theatre, feastings, promenades,
the time flies.   Ha !   it goes gloriously.   But also expensively.
The devil knows how my purse feels it.   Hold ! rescue ! stop !
There go two louis d'or.   Help ! there goes another.   Heavens !
another couple are gone.   Pence are here as farthings are with
you.   Nevertheless one can live cheaply here.   So I hope to get
off with two hundred thalers—what do I say ? with three hundred.
N.B. Not including what has already gone to the devil'.

Dissatisfied with College, he sought instruction elsewhere.   At
the table where he dined daily, kept by Hofrath Ludwig the rector,
he met several medical students.   He heard little talked of but
medicine and botany, and the names of Haller, Linnæus, and
Buffon were incessantly cited with respect.   His ready quickness
to interest himself in all that interested those around him, threw
him at once into these studies, which hereafter he was to pursue
with passionate ardour, but which at present he only lightly
touched.   Another source of instruction awaited him, one which
through life he ever gratefully acknowledged, namely, the society
of women.   Willst du genau erfahren was sich ziemt,
            So frage nur bei edlen Frauen an ! *

So he speaks in *Tasso;* and here, in Leipsic, he was glad to learn
from Frau Böhme not only some of the requisites for society, but
also some principles of poetic criticism.   This delicate, accomplished
woman was able to draw him into society, to teach him l'ombre
and picquet, to correct some of his awkwardnesses, and lastly to
make him own that the poets he admired were a deplorable set,
and that his own imitations of them deserved no better fate than
the flames.   He had got rid of his absurd wardrobe at one fell
swoop, without a murmur at the expense.   He now had also to

---

* Wouldst clearly learn what the Becoming is, inquire of noble-minded women !

cast away the poetic wardrobe brought from home with so much pride. He saw that it was poetic frippery—saw that his own poems were lifeless ; accordingly, a holocaust was made of all his writings, prose and verse, and the kitchen fire wafted them into space.

But society became vapid to him at last. He was not at his ease. Cards never amused him, and poetical discussion became painful. ' I have not written a long while', he writes to his friend Riese. ' Forgive me. Ask not after the cause ! It was not occupation, at all events. You live contented in Marburg ; I live so here. Solitary, solitary, quite solitary. Dear Riese, this solitude has awakened a certain sadness in my soul :

> It is my only pleasure,
> Away from all the world,
> To lie beside the streamlet,
> And think of those I love.

But contented as I am, I still feel the want of old companions. I sigh for my friends and my maiden, and when I feel that my sighs are vain,

> Then fills my heart with sorrow,
> My eye is dim ;
> The stream which softly passed me,
> Roars now in storm.
> No bird sings in the bushes,
> The zephyr which refreshed me
> Now storms from the north,
> And whirls off the blossoms.
> With tremor I fly from the spot,—
> I fly, and seek in deserted streets
> Sad solitude.

Yet how happy I am, quite happy ! Horn has drawn me from low spirits by his arrival. He wonders why I am so changed.

> He seeks to find the explanation,
> Smiling thinks o'er it, looks me in the face ;
> But how can he find out my cause of grief?
> I know it not myself.

But I must tell you something of myself :

> Quite other wishes rise within me now,
> Dear friend, from those you have been wont to hear.
> You know how seriously I wooed the Muse ;
> With what a hate I scorned those whom the Law

And not the Muses beckoned.   And you know
How fondly I (alas ! most falsely) hoped
The Muses loved me,—gave me gift of song !
My Lyre sounded many a lofty song,
But not the Muses, not Apollo sent them.
True, it is my pride made me believe
The Gods descended to me, and no Master
Produced more perfect works than mine !
No sooner came I here, than from my eyes
Fell off the scales, as I first learned to prize
Fame, and the mighty efforts fame required.
Then seemed to me my own ambitious flight
But as the agitation of a worm,
Who in the dust beholds the eagle soar,
And strives to reach him ; strains every nerve,
Yet only agitates the dust he lies in.
Sudden the wind doth rise, and whirls the dust
In clouds, the worm is also raisèd with it :
Then the poor worm believes he has the wings
Of eagles, raising him too in the air !
But in another moment lulls the wind,
The cloud of dust drops gently on the ground,
And with the dust the worm, who crawls once more !

Don't be angry with my galimathias.   Good-bye.   Horn will finish
this letter'.

Not only is this letter curious in its revelations of his state of
mind, but the verses into which it spontaneously flows, and
which I have translated with more jealous fidelity to the meaning
than to poetical reproduction, show how among his friends he was
even then regarded as a future poet.   The confession uttered in the
final verses clearly owes its origin to Frau Böhme's criticisms ;
but it is not every young poet who can be so easily discouraged.
Even *his* discouragement could not last long.   Schlosser, afterwards his brother-in-law, came to Leipsic, and by his preaching
and example once more roused the productive activity which
showed itself in German, French, English, and Italian verses.

Schlosser, who was ten years his senior, not only awakened
emulation by his own superior knowlege and facility, but further
aided him by introducing him to a set of literary friends, with
whom poetic discussions formed the staple of conversation.   This
circle met at the house of one Schönkopf, a *Weinhändler* and
Hauswirth, living in the Brühl, No. 79*.   To translate these

* The house still stands there, but has been almost entirely remodelled.

words into English equivalents would only mislead the reader. Schönkopf kept neither an hotel, nor a public house, but what in Germany is a substitute for both. He sold wine, and kept a *table d'hôte;* occasionally also let bedrooms to travellers. His wife, a lively, cultivated woman, belonging to a good family in Frankfurt, drew Frankfurt visitors to the house; and with her Goethe soon became on terms of intimacy, which would seem surprising to the English reader who only heard of her as an innkeeper's wife. He became one of the family, and fell in love with the daughter. I must further beg the reader to understand that in Germany, to this day, there is a wide difference between the dining customs and our own. The English student, clerk, or bachelor, who dines at an eating-house, chop-house, or hotel, goes there simply to get his dinner, and perhaps look at *The Times.* Of the other diners he knows nothing, cares little. It is rare that a word is interchanged between him and his neighbour. Quite otherwise in Germany. There the same society is generally to be found at the same table. The *table d'hôte* is composed of a circle of *habitués*, varied by occasional visitors, who in time become, perhaps, members of the circle. Even with strangers conversation is freely interchanged; and in a little while friendships are formed over these dinner tables, according as natural tastes and likings assimilate, which, extending beyond the mere hour of dinner, are carried into the current of life. Germans do not rise so hastily from the table as we; for time with them is not so precious; life is not so crowded; time can be found for a quiet after-dinner talk. The cigars and coffee, which appear before the cloth is removed, keep the company together; and in that state of suffused comfort which quiet digestion creates, they hear without anger the opinions of antagonists. In such a society we must imagine Goethe in the Schönkopf establishment, among students and men of letters, all eager in advancing their own opinions, and combating the false taste which was not their own.

To complete this picture, and to separate it still more from our English customs, you must imagine host and hostess dining at the table, while their charming daughter, who had cooked or helped to cook the dinner, brought them the wine. This daughter was the Anna Katharina, by intimates called Käthchen, and by Goethe, in the *Autobiography*, designated as Annchen and Annette. Her portrait, still extant, is very pleasing. She was then nineteen, lively, and loving; how could she be insensible to the love of this glorious youth, in all the fervour of genius, and with all the attractions of beauty? They saw each other daily, not only at dinner but in the evenings, when he accompanied the piano of her brother by a feeble performance on the flute. They also got up private theatricals, in which Goethe and Käthchen played the lovers. *Minna von Barnhelm*, then a novelty, was among the pieces performed. That these performances were of a strictly amateur order may be gathered from the fact that in one of them the part of a nightingale, which is important, was represented by a handkerchief, rolled up into such ornithological resemblance as art could reach.

Two letters, quite recently discovered, have fallen into my hands; they give us a curious glimpse of him at this time, such as one may look for in vain in his own account of himself, or in the accounts of any other writer. They are from his friend Horn, whose arrival he mentioned in the letter previously quoted, and who was one of his daily companions in Frankfurt. The first is dated 12th of August, 1766, and is addressed to one Moors, a Frankfurt companion.

'To speak of our Goethe! He is still the same proud, fantastic personage as when I came hither. If you only saw him, you would either be mad with anger or you would burst with laughter. I cannot at all understand how a man can so quickly transform himself. His manners and his whole bearing, at present, are as different as possible from his former behaviour. Over and above his pride, he is a dandy; and all his clothes, handsome as they are, are in so odd a taste that they make him conspicuous among all the students. But this is indifferent to him; one may remonstrate with him for his folly as much as one likes

> Man mag Amphion seyn und Feld und Wald bezwingen,
> Nur keinen Goethe nicht kann man zur Klugheit bringen*.

All his thought and effort is only to please himself and his lady-love. In every circle he makes himself more ridiculous than agreeable. Merely because the lady admires it, he has put on tricks and gestures that one cannot possibly refrain from laughing at. He has adopted a walk which is quite insufferable. If you only saw it!   Il marche à pas comptés,
> Comme un Recteur suivi des quatre Facultés.

---

* One may be Amphion and coerce the trees and rocks, but not bring Goethe to his senses.

Anna Katharina Schönkopf

His society is every day more intolerable to me, and he, too, tries
to avoid me whenever he can.   I am too plain a man for him to
walk across the street with me.   What would the "king of Holland"
say if he saw him in this guise?   Do write again to him soon and
tell him your opinion ; else he and his lady-love will remain as
silly as ever.   Heaven only preserve me, as long as I am here,
from any sweetheart, for the women here are the very devil.
Goethe is not the first who has made a fool of himself to please
his Dulcinea.   I only wish you could see her just for once : she is
the most absurd creature in the world.   Her *mine coquette avec
un air hautain* is all with which she has bewitched Goethe.   Dear
friend ! how glad should I be if Goethe were still what he was in
Frankfurt!   Good friends as we were formerly, we can now scarcely
endure each other for a quarter of an hour.   Yet with time I still
hope to convert him, though it is a hard matter to make a coxcomb
wise.   But I will venture everything for the sake of it.

> Ach ! früchtete dies mien Bemühn !
> Ach ! könnt' ich meinen Zweck erreichen !
> Ich wollt' nicht Luther, nicht Calvin,
> Noch einem der Bekehrer weichen*.

I cannot write to him again what I have here told you.   I shall be
delighted if you will do so.   I care neither for his anger nor for
that of his lady-love.   For, after all, he is not easily offended with
me ; even when we have quarrelled he sends for me next day.   So
much of him ; more another time.

Live and forget not thy   HORN '.

Moors followed Horn's advice, and expressed to Goethe, apparently in very plain terms, his astonishment and dissatisfaction at
the disadvantageous change.   In October of the same year, he
received from Horn the following explanation :

' But, dear Moors ! how glad you will be to learn that we have
lost no friend in our Goethe, as we falsely supposed.   He had so
travestied himself as to deceive not only me but a great many
others, and we should never have discovered the real truth of the
matter, if your letter had not threatened him with the loss of a
friend.   I must tell you the whole story as he himself told it to me,
for he has commissioned me to do so in order to save him the

---

* Ah, if my attempt succeed, I should not envy Luther, Calvin, nor any other Con-
verter.

trouble. He is in love, it is true—he has confessed it to me, and will confess it to you ; but his love, though its circumstances are sad, is not culpable, as I formerly supposed. He loves. But not that young lady whom I suspected him of loving. He loves a girl beneath him in rank, but a girl whom—I think I do not say too much—you would yourself love if you saw her. I am no lover, so I shall write entirely without passion. Imagine to yourself a woman, well grown, though not very tall ; a round, agreeable, though not extraordinarily beautiful face ; open, gentle, engaging manners ; a very pretty understanding, without having had any great education. He loves her very tenderly, with the perfect, honest intentions of a virtuous man, though he knows that she can never be his. Whether she loves him in return I know not. You know, dear Moors, that is a point about which one cannot well ask ; but this much I can say to you, that they seem to be born for each other. Now observe his cunning ! That no one may suspect him of such an attachment, he undertakes to persuade the world of precisely the opposite, and hitherto he has been extraordinarily successful. He makes a great parade, and seems to be paying court to a certain young lady of whom I have told you before. He can see his beloved and converse with her at certain times without giving occasion for the slightest suspicion, and I often accompany him to her. If Goethe were not my friend I should fall in love with her myself. Meanwhile he is supposed to be in love with the Fräulein —— (but what do you care about her name ?) and people are fond of teasing him about her. Perhaps she herself believes that he loves her, but the good lady deceives herself. Since that time he has admitted me to closer confidence, has made me acquainted with the affairs, and shown me that his expenditure is not so great as might be supposed. He is more of a philosopher and moralist than ever ; and innocent as his love is, he nevertheless disapproves it. We often dispute about this, but let him take what side he will, he is sure to win ; for you know what weight he can give to only apparent reasons. I pity him and his good heart, which really must be in a very melancholy condition, since he loves the most virtuous and perfect of girls without hope. But if we suppose that she loves him in return, how miserable must he be on that very account ! I need not explain that to you, who so well know the human heart. He has told me that he will write you one or two things about it himself. There is no necessity for me to

recommend silence to you on this subject; for you yourself see
how necessary it is. . . . '

Imagine this somewhat fantastic youth assured that his passion
is returned, and then imagine him indulging in the boyish
caprice of tormenting his beloved. There is nothing more cruel
than youth; and youthful lovers, once assured of victory, are
singularly prone to indulge in the most frivolous pretexts for
ingeniously tormenting. 'Man loves to conquer, likes not to feel
secure', Goethe says, in the piece wherein he dramatized this
early experience:

> Erringen will der Mensch; er will nicht sicher seyn.

Had Käthchen conquetted with him, keeping him in the exquisite
pain of suspense, she would have been happier: but as he said
in his little poem, *Der Wahre Genuss*, 'she is perfect, and her only
fault is that she loves me':

> Sie ist volkommen, und sie fehlet
> Darin allein dass sie mich liebt.

He teased her with trifles and idle suspicions; was jealous without
cause, convinced without reason; plagued her with fantastic
quarrels, till at last her endurance was exhausted, and her love
was washed away in tears. No sooner was he aware of this than
he repented, and tried to recover the jewel which like a prodigal
he had cast away. In vain. He was in despair, and tried in
dissipation to forget his grief. A better issue was poetry. Several
of his lyrics bore the burden of this experience; and one entire
play, or pastoral, is devoted to a poetical representation of these
lovers' quarrels: this is *Die Laune des Verliebten*, which is very
curious as the earliest extant work of the great poet, and as the
earliest specimen of his tendency to turn experience into song.
In the opera of *Erwin und Elmire* he subsequently treated a
similar subject, in a very different manner. The first effort is the
more curious of the two. The style of composition is an imitation
of those pastoral dramas, which, originated by Tasso and Guarini
in the soft and almost luscious *Aminta* and *Pastor Fido*, had by
the French been made popular all over Europe.

Two happy and two unhappy lovers are somewhat artificially
contrasted; the two latter representing Käthchen and the poet.
Action there is none; the piece is made up of talk about love,
some felicitous verses of the true stamp and ring, and an occasional

glimpse of insight into the complexities of passion. Eridon, the jealous lover, torments his mistress in a style at once capricious and natural ; with admirable truth she deplores his jealousy and excuses it :

> Zwar oft betrübt er mich, doch rührt ihn auch mein Schmerz.
> Wirft er mir etwas vor, fängt er mich an zu plagen,
> So darf ich nur ein Wort, ein gutes Wort nur sagen,
> Gleich ist er umgekehrt, die wilde Zanksucht flieht,
> Er weint sogar mit mir, wenn er mich weinen sieht*.

It is admirably said that the very absence of any cause for grief prompts him to create a grief :

> *Da er kein Elend hat, will er sich Elend machen.*

Amine is also touched with a delicate pencil. Her lovingness, forgivingness, and endurance are from the life. Here is a couplet breathing the very tenderness of love :

> Der Liebe leichtes Band machst du zum schweren Joch.
> Du quälst mich als Tyrann ; und ich? *ich lieb dich noch !*†

One more line and I have done : Eglé is persuading Eridon that Amine's love of dancing is no trespass on her love for him ; since, after having enjoyed her dance, her first thought is to seek him :

> *Und durch das Suchen selbst wirst du ihr immer lieber‡.*

In such touches as these lurks the future poet ; still more so in the very choice of the subject. Here, as ever, he does not cheat himself with pouring feigned sorrows into feigning verse : he embalms his own experience. He does not trouble himself with drawing characters and events from the shelves of the library : his soul is the fountain of his inspiration. His own life was uniformly the text from which he preached. He sang what he had felt, and because he had felt it ; not because others had sung before him. He was the echo of no man's joys and sorrows, he was the lyrist of his own. This is the reason why his poems have an endless charm : they are as indestructible as passion itself. They reach our hearts because they issue from his. Every bullet

---

* 'Tis true he vexes me, and yet my sorrow pains him.
  Yet let him but reproach—begin to tease me,
  Then need I but a word, a single kind word utter,
  Away flies all his anger in a moment,
  And he will weep with me, because he sees me weep.
† The fairy link of Love thou mak'st a galling yoke.
  Thou treat'st me as a slave ; and I? I love thee still !
‡ And in the very search her heart grows fonder of thee.

hits the mark, according to the huntsman's superstition, if it have first been dipped in the marksman's blood.

He has told us emphatically, that *all his works are but fragments of the grand confession of his life.* Of him we may say what Horace so well says of Lucilius, that he trusted his secrets to books as to faithful friends :

> Ille velut fidis arcana sodalibus olim
> Credebat libris ; neque, si male cesserat, unquam
> Decurrens alio, neque si bene : *quo fit, ut omnis*
> *Votiva pateat veluti descripta tabella*
> *Vita senis* *.

How clearly he saw the nullity of every other procedure is shown in various passages of his letters and conversations. Riemer has preserved one worth selecting : 'There will soon be a poetry without poetry, a real ποίησις, where the subject matter is ἐν ποιήσει, in the *making:* a manufactured poetry'†. He dates from Leipsic the origin of his own practice, which he says was a tendency he never could deviate from all his life : 'namely, the tendency to transform into an image, a poem, everything which delighted or troubled me, or otherwise occupied me, and to come to some distinct understanding with myself upon it, to set my inward being at rest'. The reason he gives for this tendency is very questionable. He attributes it to the isolation in which he lived with respect to matters of taste forcing him to look within for poetical subjects. But had not the tendency of his genius lain in that direction, no such circumstances could have directed it.

Young, curious, and excitable as he was, nothing is more natural than that he should somewhat shock the respectabilities by his pranks and extravagancies. His constant companion was Behrisch, one of the most interesting figures among these Leipsic friends. With strongly marked features and a certain dry causticity of manner, always well dressed, and always preserving a most staid demeanour, Behrisch was about thirty years of age, and had an ineradicable love of fun and mystification. He could treat trifles with an air of immense importance. He would invent narratives about the perversity and absurdity of others, in order

---

* *Sermon.*, lib. II, I.

† *Briefe von und an Goethe.* Herausgeg. von RIEMER. 1846. What follows is untranslateable, from the play on words : 'Die Dichter heissen dann so, wie schon Moritz spasste, *a spissando, densando,* vom Dichtmachen, weil sie Alles zusammendrängen, und kommen mir vor wie eine Art Wurstmacher, die in den Darm des Hexameters oder Trimeters ihre Wort- und Sylbenfülle stopfen'.

to convulse his hearers with the unction of his philippics against such absurdity. He was fond of dissipation, into which he carried an air of supreme gravity. He rather affected the French style of *politesse*, and spoke the language well; and, above all, he had some shrewd good sense, as a buttress for all his follies. Behrisch introduced him to some damsels who 'were better than their reputation', and took him into scenes more useful to the future poet than advantageous to the repute of the young student. He also laughed him out of all respect for gods, goddesses, and other mythological inanities which still pressed their heavy dullness on his verse; would not let him commit the imprudence of rushing into print, but calmed the author's longing, by beautifully copying his verses into a volume, adorning them with vignettes. Behrisch was, so to speak, the precursor of Merck; his influence not so great, but somewhat of the same kind. The friends were displeased to see young Goethe falling thus away from good society into such a disreputable course; but just as Lessing before him had neglected the elegant Leipsic world for actors and authors of more wit than money, and preferred Mylius, with his shoes down at heel, to all that the best dressed society could offer; so did young Goethe neglect salon and lecture-hall for the many-coloured scene of life in less elegant circles. Enlightened by the result, we foresee that the poet will receive little injury from these sources; he is gaining experience, and experience even of the worst sides of human nature will be sublimated into noble uses, as carrion by the wise farmer is turned into excellent manure. In this great drama of life every Theatre has its Green-room; and unless the poet know how it is behind the scenes he will never understand how actors speak and move.

Goethe had often been 'behind the scenes', looking at the skeleton which stands in almost every house. His adventure with Gretchen, and its consequences, early opened his eyes to the strange gulfs which lie under the crust of society. 'Religion, morals, law, rank, habits', he says, 'rule over the *surface* of social life. Streets of magnificent houses are kept clean; every one outwardly conducts himself with propriety; but the disorder within is often only the more desolate; and a polished exterior covers many a wall which totters, and falls with a crash during the night, all the more terrible because it falls during a calm. How many families had I not more or less distinctly known in which bankruptcy, divorce, seduction, murder, and robbery had wrought

destruction ! Young as I was, I had often, in such cases, lent my
succour ; for as my frankness awakened confidence, and my dis-
cretion was known, and as my activity did not shun any sacrifice
—indeed, rather preferred the most perilous occasions—I had
frequently to mediate, console, and try to avert the storm ; in the
course of which I could not help learning many sad and humiliat-
ing facts '.

It was natural that such sad experience should at first lead him
to view the whole social fabric with contempt.   To relieve himself
he—being then greatly captivated with Molière's works,—sketched
the plans of several dramas, but their plots were so uniformly
unpleasant, and the catastrophes so tragic, that he did not work
out these plans. 'The Fellow Sinners' (*Die Mitschuldigen*) is the
sole piece which was completed, and it now occupies a place among
his writings.   Few, in England at least, ever read it ; yet it is worth
a rapid glance, and is especially remarkable as the work of a youth
not yet eighteen.   It is lively, and strong with effective situations and two happily sketched characters,—Söller, the scampish
husband, and his father-in-law, the inquisitive landlord.   The plot is
briefly this : Söller's wife—before she became his wife—loved a
certain Alcest ; and her husband's conduct is not such as to make
her forget her former lover, who, at the opening of the play, is
residing in her father's hotel.   Alcest prevails upon her to grant
him an interview in his own room, while her husband, Söller, is at
the masquerade.   Unluckily, Söller has determined to rob Alcest
that very night.   He enters the room by stealth—opens the escri-
toire—takes the money—is alarmed by a noise—hides himself in
an alcove, and then sees his father-in-law, the landlord, enter the
room !   The old man, unable to resist a burning curiosity to know
the contents of a letter which Alcest has received that day, has
come to read it in secret.   But he in turn is alarmed by the appearance of his daughter, and, letting the candle fall, he escapes.
Söller is now the exasperated witness of an interview between
Alcest and his wife : a situation which, like the whole of the play,
is a mixture of the ludicrous and the painful—very dramatic and
very unpleasant.

On the following day the robbery is discovered.   Sophie thinks
the robber is her father ; he returns her the compliment—nay,
more, stimulated by his eager curiosity, he consents to inform
Alcest of his suspicion in return for the permission to read the
contents of the mysterious letter.   A father sacrificing his daughter

to gratify a paltry curiosity is too gross; it is the only trait of juvenility in the piece—a piece otherwise prematurely old. Enraged at such an accusation, Sophie retorts the charge upon her father, and some unamiable altercations result. The piece winds up by the self-betrayal of Söller, who, intimating to Alcest that he was present during a certain nocturnal interview, shields himself from punishment. The moral is—' Forget and forgive among fellow-sinners '.

CHAPTER II

MENTAL CHARACTERISTICS

THE two dramatic works noticed towards the close of the last chapter may be said to begin the real poetic career of their author, because in them he drew from his actual experience. They will furnish us with a text for some remarks on his peculiar characteristics, the distinct recognition of which will facilitate the comprehension of his life and writings. We make a digression, but the reader will find that in thus swerving from the direct path of narrative, we are only tacking to fill our sails with wind.

Frederick Schlegel (and after him Coleridge) aptly indicated a distinction, when he said that every man was born either a Platonist or an Aristotelian. This distinction is often expressed in the terms *subjective* and *objective* intellects. Perhaps we shall best define these by calling the objective intellect one which is eminently *impersonal*, and the subjective intellect one which is eminently *personal ;* the former disengaging itself as much as possible from its own prepossessions, striving to see and represent objects as they exist ; the other viewing all objects in the light of its own feelings and preconceptions. It is needless to add that no mind can be exclusively objective, nor exclusively subjective ; but every mind has a more or less dominant tendency in one of these directions. We see the contrast in Philosophy, as in Art. The realist argues from Nature upwards, argues inductively, starting from reality, and never long losing sight of it ; even in the adventurous flights of hypothesis and speculation, being desirous that his hypothesis shall correspond with realities. The idealist argues from an Idea downwards, argues deductively, starting from some conception, and seeking in realities only visible illustrations of a deeper existence. The achievements of modern Science, and the masterpieces of Art, prove that the grandest generalizations and the most elevated types can only be reached by the former method ; and that what is called the 'ideal school', so far from having the superiority which it claims, is only more lofty in its *pretensions;* the realist, with more modest pretensions, achieves loftier results.   The Objective and Subjective, or, as they are also called, the Real and Ideal, are thus contrasted as the termini of two opposite lines of thought.   In Philosophy, in Morals, and in Art, we see a constant antagonism between these two principles.   Thus in Morals the Platonists are those who seek the highest morality *out* of human nature, instead of in the healthy development of all human tendencies, and their due co-ordination ; they hope, in the *suppression* of integral faculties, to attain some superhuman standard.   They call that Ideal which no Reality can reach, but for which we should strive.   They superpose *ab extra*, instead of trying to develop *ab intra*.   They draw from their own minds, or from the dogmas handed to them by tradition, an arbitrary mould, into which they attempt to fuse the organic activity of Nature.

If this school had not in its favour the imperious instinct of progress, and aspirations after a better, it would not hold its ground.   But it satisfies that craving, and thus deludes many minds into acquiescence.   The poetic and enthusiastic disposition most readily acquiesces : preferring to overlook what man *is*, in its delight of contemplating what the poet makes him.   To such a mind all conceptions of man must have a halo round them,— half mist, half sunshine ; the hero must be a Demigod, in whom no *valet de chambre* can find a failing : the villain must be a Demon, for whom no charity can find an excuse.

Not to extend this to a dissertation, let me at once say that Goethe belonged to the *objective* class.   'Everywhere in Goethe', said Franz Horn, 'you are on firm land or island ; nowhere the infinite sea'.   A better characterization was never written in one sentence.   In every page of his works may be read a strong feeling for the real, the concrete, the living ; and a repugnance as strong for the vague, the abstract, or the supersensuous.   His constant striving was to study Nature, so as to see her *directly*, and not through the mists of fancy, or through the distortions of prejudice,—to look at men, and *into* them,—to apprehend things as they were.   In his conception of the universe he could not separate God *from* it, placing Him above it, beyond it, as the philosophers did who represented God whirling the universe round His finger, 'seeing it go'. Such a conception revolted him. He animated the universe with God ; he animated fact with divine life ; he saw in Reality the incarnation of the Ideal ; he saw in Morality the high and harmonious action of all human tendencies ; he saw in Art the highest representation of Life. If we look through his works with critical attention, we shall observe the *concrete* tendency determining—first, his choice of subjects ; secondly, his handling of character ; and, thirdly, his style. Intimately connected with this concreteness is that other characteristic of his genius, which determined his *creative impulses only in alliance with emotions he himself had experienced.* His imagination was not, like that of many others, incessantly at work in the combination and recombination of images, which could be accepted for their own sake, apart from the warrant of preliminary confrontation with fact. It demanded the confrontation ; it moved with ease only on the secure ground of Reality. In like manner we see that in science there are men whose active imaginations carry them into hypothesis and speculation, all the more easily because they do not bring hypothesis to the stern test of fact. The mere delight in combining ideas suffices them ; provided the deductions are *logical*, they seem almost indifferent to their *truth*. There are poets of this order ; indeed most poets are of this order. Goethe was of a quite opposite tendency. In him, as in the man of science, an imperious desire for reality controlled the errant facility of imagination. 'The first and last thing demanded of Genius', he says, 'is love of truth'.

Hence we see why he was led to portray men and women instead of demigods and angels : no Posas and Theklas, but Egmonts and Clärchens. Hence also his portraitures carry their moral *with* them, *in* them, but have no moral superposed—no accompanying verdict as from some outstanding judge. Further, —and this is a point to be insisted on,—his style, both in poetry and prose, is subject to the same law. It is vivid with pictures, but it has scarcely any imagery. Most poets describe objects by metaphors or comparisons ; Goethe seldom tells you what an object is *like*, he tells you what it *is*. Shakespeare is very unlike Goethe in this respect. The prodigal luxuriance of his imagery often entangles, in its overgrowth, the movement of his verse. It is true, he also is eminently concrete : he sees the real object vividly, and he makes us see it vividly ; but he scarcely ever paints it save in the colours of metaphor and simile. Shakespeare's imagery bubbles up like a perpetual spring : to say that it repeatedly *overflows*, is only to say that his mind was lured by its own sirens away from the direct path. He did not master his Pegasus at all times, but let the wild careering creature take its winged way. Goethe, on the contrary, always masters his : perhaps because his steed had less of restive life in its veins. Not only does he master it, and ride with calm assured grace : he seems so bent on reaching the goal, that he scarcely thinks of anything else. To quit metaphor, he may be said to use with the utmost sparingness all the aids of imagery, and to create images of the objects, rather than images of what the objects are like.

Shakespeare, like Goethe, was a decided realist. He, too, was content to let his pictures of life carry their own moral with them. He uttered no moral verdict ; he was no Chorus preaching on the text of what he pictured. Hence we cannot gather from his works what were his opinions. But there is this difference between him and Goethe, that his intense sympathy with the energetic passions and fierce volitions of our race made him delight in heroic characters, in men of robust frames and impassioned lives. Goethe, with an infusion of the best blood of Schiller, would have been a Shakespeare ; but, such as Nature made him he was—not Shakespeare.

Turning from these abstract considerations to the two earliest works which form our text, we observe how the youth is determined in the choice of his subject by the realistic tendency. Instead of ranging through the enchanted gardens of Armida—instead of throwing himself back into the distant Past, thus escaping from the trammels of a modern subject, which the confrontation of reality always makes more difficult, this boy fashions into verse his own experience, his own observation. He looks into his own heart,—he peers into the byways of civilization, walking with curious observation through squalid streets and dark fearful alleys. Singular, moreover, is the absence of any fierce indignation, any cry of pain at the sight of so much corruption underlying the surface of society. In youth the loss of illusions is generally followed by a cynical misanthropy, or a vehement protest. But Goethe is neither cynical nor indignant. He seems to accept the fact as a thing to be admitted, and quietly striven against, with a view to its amelioration. He seems to think with the younger

Pliny, that indulgence is a part of justice, and would cite with approval the favourite maxim of the austere yet humane Thraseas, *qui vitia odit homines odit*,—he who hates vices hates mankind*. For in the *Mitschuldigen* he presents us with a set of people whose consolation is to exclaim ' Rogues all !'—and in after years he wrote of this piece, that it was dictated, though unconsciously, by 'far-sighted tolerance in the appreciation of moral actions, as expressed in the eminently Christian sentence, *Let him who is without sin among you cast the first stone*'.

CHAPTER III

ART STUDIES

FRAU BÖHME died.   In her he lost a monitress and friend, who had kept some check on his waywardness, and drawn him into society.   The Professor had long since cooled towards him, after giving up all hopes of making him another Heineccius.   It was pitiful.   A youth with such remarkable dispositions, who would *not* be assiduous in attendance at lecture, and whose amusement during lecture was to sketch caricatures of various law dignitaries in his note book : another ornament to jurisprudence irrecoverably lost !   Indeed, the collegiate aspect of this Leipsic residence is not one promising to professors ; but we—instructed by the result—know how much better he was employed, than if he had filled a hundred volumes of note books by diligent attendance at lecture.   He studied much, in a desultory manner ; he studied Molière and Corneille ; he began to translate *Le Menteur*.   The theatre was a perpetual attaction ; and even the uneasy, unsatisfied condition of his affections, was instructing him in directions whither no professor could lead him.   But greater than all was the influence of Shakspeare, whom he first learned a little of through Dodd's *Beauties of Shakspeare*, a work not much prized in England, where the plays form part of our traditional education, but which must have been a revelation to the Germans, something analogous to what Charles Lamb's *Specimens of the Old English Drama* was to us.   The marvellous strength and beauty of language, the bold and natural imagery of these *Beauties*, startled the young

---

* PLINY, *Epist.*, lib. VIII, 22.   After the text was written, SCHöLL published Goethe's note-book kept at Strasburg, wherein may be read this very aphorism transcribed.   It was just the sort of passage to captivate him.

poets of that day, like the discovery of huge fossil remains of some antediluvian fauna ; and to gratify the curiosity thus awakened, he says there came Wieland's prose translation of several plays, which he studied with enthusiasm*.

There are no materials to fill up the gaps of his narrative here, so that I am forced to leave much indistinct. For instance, he has told us that Käthchen and he were no longer lovers ; but we find him writing to her in a friendly and even lover-like tone from Frankfurt, and we know that friendly intercourse still subsisted between them. Of this, however, not a word occurs in the *Autobiography*. Nor are we accurately informed how he made the aquaintance of the Breitkopf family. Breitkopf was a bookseller in Leipsic, in whose house Literature and Music were highly prized. Bernhard, the eldest son, was an excellent performer, and composed music to Goethe's songs, which were published in 1769, under this title : *Neue Lieder in Melodieen gesetzt von Bernhart Theodor Breitkopf.* The poet is not named. This *Liederbuch* contains twenty songs, the majority of which were subsequently reprinted in the poet's works. They are love songs, and contain a love-philosophy more like what is to be found in Catullus, Horace, and Wieland, than what one would expect from a boy, did we not remember how the braggadocio of youth delights in expressing *roué* sentiments, as if to give itself airs of profound experience. This youth sings with gusto of inconstancy:

> Da fühl ich die Freuden der wechselden Lust.

He gaily declares that if one mistress leaves you another will love you, and the second is sweeter to kiss than the first :

> Es küsst sich so süsse der Busen der Zweiten,
> Als kaum sich der Busen der Ersten geküsst.

Another acquaintance, and one more directly influential, was that of Oeser, the director of the Drawing Academy. He had been the friend and teacher of Winckelmann, and his name stood high among connoisseurs. Goethe, who at home had learned a little drawing, joined Oeser's class, where, among other fellow-students, was the Hardenberg who afterwards made such a noise in the Prussian political world. He joined the class, and did his best to acquire by labour the skill which only talent can acquire. That he made little progress in drawing, we learn from his

---

* It is possible that Wieland's translation only then fell into Goethe s hands, but the publication was commenced before his arrival in Leipsic, namely, in 1761.

subsequent confession, no less than from his failure ; but tuition
had this effect at least—it taught him to use his eyes.   In a future
chapter * I shall have occasion to enter more fully on this subject.
Enough if for the present a sentence or two from his letters tell
us the enthusiasm Oeser inspired.   'What do I not owe to you',
he writes to him, 'for having pointed out to me the way of the
True and the Beautiful !' and concludes by saying, 'the undersigned
is your work !'   Writing to a friend of Oeser's, he says that Oeser
stands beside Shakspeare and Wieland in the influence exercised
over him.   'His instruction will influence my whole life.   He it
was who taught me that the Ideal of Beauty is Simplicity and
Repose, and thence it follows that no youth can be a master'.

Instruction in the theory of Art he gained from Oeser, from
Winckelmann, and from *Laocoon*, the incomparable little book
which Lessing at this period carelessly flung upon the world.   Its
effect upon Goethe can only be appreciated by those who early in
life have met with this work, and risen from it with minds widened,
strengthened, and inspired †.   It opened a pathway amid confusion,
throwing light upon many of the obscurest problems which torment the artist.   It awakened in Goethe an intense yearning to
see the works of ancient masters ; and these beckoned from
Dresden.   To Dresden he went.   But here, in spite of Oeser,
Winckelmann, and Lessing, in spite of grand phrases about Art,
the invincible tendency of his nature asserted itself, and instead of
falling into raptures with the great Italian pictures, he confesses
that he took their merits upon trust, and was really charmed by
none but the landscape and Dutch painters, whose subjects
appealed directly to his experience.   He did not feel the greatness
of Italian Art ; and what he did not feel he would not feign.

It is worth noticing that this trip to Dresden was taken in absolute secrecy.   As, many years later, he stole away to Italy without
letting his friends even suspect his project, so now he left Leipsic
for Dresden without a word of intimation.   Probably the same
motive actuated him in both instances.   He went to see, to enjoy,
to learn, and did not want to be disturbed by personal influence—
by other people's opinions.

On his return he was active enough with drawing.   He made

* See Book V, ch. v.

† Macaulay told me that the reading of this little book formed an epoch in his mental
history, and that he learned more from it than he had ever learned elsewhere.   [*Laocoon*,
translated, with Introduction and Notes by Sir Robert Phillimore, Bart., is now obtain-
able in Routledge's New Universal Library, 1*s*. net.]

Adam Friedrich Oeser

the acquaintance of an engraver named Stock*, and with his usual propensity to try his hand at whatever his frends were doing, he forthwith began to learn engraving. In the *Morgenblatt* for 1828 there is a detailed account of two of his engravings, both representing landscapes with small cascades shut in by rocks and grottoes ; at the foot of each are these words : *peint par A. Theile, gravé par Goethe.* One plate is dedicated *à Monsieur Goethe, Conseillier actuel de S. M. Impériale, par son fils très obéissant.* In the room which they show to strangers in his house in Frankfurt, there is also a specimen of his engraving—very amateurish ; but Madame von Goethe showed me one in her possession which really has merit.

Melancholy, wayward, and capricious, he allowed Lessing to pass through Leipsic without making any attempt to see the man he so much admired : a caprice he afterwards repented, for the opportunity never recurred. Something of his hypochondria was due to mental, but more to physical causes. Dissipation, bad diet (especially the beer and coffee), and absurd endeavours to carry out Rousseau's preaching about returning to a state of nature, had seriously affected his health. The crisis came at last. One summer night (1768) he was seized with violent hæmorrhage. He had only strength enough to call to his aid the fellow-student who slept in the next room. Medical assistance promptly came. He was saved ; but his convalescence was embittered by the discovery of a tumour on his neck, which lasted some time. His recovery was slow, but it seemed as if it relieved him from all the peccant humours which had made him hypochondriacal, leaving behind an inward lightness and joyousness to which he had long been a stranger. One thing greatly touched him—the sympathy expressed for him by several eminent men ; a sympathy he felt to be quite undeserved, for there was not one among them whom he had not vexed or affronted by his caprices, extravagances, morbid opposition, and stubborn persistence.

One of these friends, Langer, not only made an exchange of books with him, giving a set of Classic authors for a set of German, but also, in devout yet not dogmatic conversation, led his young friend to regard the Bible in another light than that of a merely human composition. 'I loved the Bible and valued it, for it was almost the only book to which I owed my moral culture. Its

---

* This Stock had two amiable daughters, one of whom married (1785) Körner, the correspondent of Schiller, and father of the poet.

events, dogmas, and symbols were deeply impressed on my mind'. He therefore felt little sympathy with the Deists who were at this time agitating Europe ; and although his tendency was strongly against the Mystics, he was afraid lest the poetical spirit should be swept away along with the prophetical.. In one word, he was in a state of religious doubt—'destitute of faith, yet terrified at scepticism'.

This unrest and this bodily weakness he carried with him, September 1768, from Leipsic to Frankfurt, whither we will follow him.

CHAPTER IV

RETURN HOME

HE returned home a boy in years, in experience a man. Broken in health, unhappy in mind, with no strong impulses in any one direction, uncertain of himself and of his aims, he felt, as he approached his native city, much like a repentant prodigal, who has no vision of the fatted calf awaiting him. His father, unable to perceive the real progress he had made, was very much alive to the slender prospect of his becoming a distinguished jurist. The fathers of poets are seldom gratified with the progress in education visible to them ; and the reason is that they do not know their sons to be poets, nor understand that the poet's orbit is not the same as their own. They tread the common highway on which the mile-stones accurately mark distances ; and seeing that their sons have trudged but little way according to this measurement, their minds are filled with misgivings. Of that silent progress, which consists less in travelling on the broad highway, than in development of the limbs which will make a sturdy traveller, parents cannot judge.

Mother and sister, however, touched by the worn face, and, woman-like, more interested in the man than what he had achieved, received him with an affection which compensated for his father's coldness. There is quite a pathetic glimpse given of this domestic interior in the *Autobiography*, where he alludes to his father's impatience at his illness, and anxiety for his speedy recovery. And we gladly escape from this picture to the letters written from Frankfurt to his old love, Käthchen Schönkopf*. It

* Printed in *Goethe's Briefe an seine Leipziger Freunde.* Herausgegeben von OTTO JAHN.

appears that he left Leipsic without saying adieu. He thus refers to it :

'Apropos, you will forgive me that I did not take leave of you. I was in the neighbourhood, I was even below at the door ; *I saw the lamp burning and went to the steps, but I had not the courage to mount.* For the last time—how should I have come down again ?

'Thus I now do what I ought to have done then : I thank you for all the love and frendship which you have constantly shown me, and which I shall never forget. I need not beg you to remember me,—a thousand occasions will arise which must remind you of a man who for two years and a half was part of your family, who indeed often gave you cause for displeasure, but still was always a good lad, and whom it is to be hoped you will often miss ; at least, I often miss you'.

The tumour on his neck became alarming : the more so as the surgeons, uncertain about its nature, were wavering in their treatment. Frequent cauterization, and constant confinement to his room, were the worst parts of the cure. He read, drew, and etched to wile away the time ; and by the end of the year was pronounced recovered. This letter to Käthchen announces the recovery.

'My best, anxious friend,

'You will doubtless have heard from Horn, on the new year, the news of my recovery ; and I hasten to confirm it. Yes, dear friend, it is over, and in future you must take it quietly, even if you hear —he is laid up again ! You know that my constitution often makes a slip, and in a week gets on its legs again ; this time it was bad, and seemed yet worse than it was, and was attended with terrible pains. Misfortune is also a good. I have learned much in illness which I could have learned nowhere else in life. It is over, and I am quite brisk again, though for three whole weeks I have not left my room, and scarcely any one has visited me but my doctor, who, thank God ! is an amiable man ! An odd thing it is in us men : when I was in lively society I was out of spirits, now I am forsaken by all the world I am cheerful ; for even throughout my illness my cheerfulness has comforted my family, who were not in a condition to comfort themselves, to say nothing of me. The new year's song which you have also received, I composed during an attack of great foolery, and had it printed for the sake of amusement. Besides this, I draw a great deal, write tales, and am contented with myself. God give me, this new year, what is good for me ; may He do the same for all of us, and if we pray for nothing more than this, we may certainly hope that He will give it us.   If I can only get along till April, I shall easily reconcile myself to my condition.   Then I hope things will be better ; in particular my health may make progress daily, because it is now known precisely what is the matter with me.   My lungs are as sound as possible, but there is something wrong at the stomach.   And, in confidence, I have had hopes given me of a pleasant, enjoyable mode of life, so that my mind is quite cheerful and at rest.   As soon as I am better again I shall go away into foreign countries, and it must depend only on you and another person how soon I shall see Leipsic again ; in the meantime I think of going to France to see what French life is, and learn the French language. So you can imagine what a charming man I shall be when I return to you.   It often occurs to me, that it would be a laughable affair, if, in spite of all my projects, I were to die before Easter.   In that case I would order a gravestone for myself in Leipsic churchyard, that at least every year on St. John's day you might visit the figure of St. John and my grave.   What do you think ? '

To celebrate his recovery, Rath Moritz gave a great party, at which all the Frankfurt friends assembled.   In a little while, however, another illness came to lay the poet low ; and, worse than all, there came the news from Leipsic that Käthchen was engaged to a Dr. Kanne, whom Goethe had introduced to her.   This for ever decided his restlessness about her.   Here is a letter from him.

' My dear, my beloved friend,

' A dream last night has reminded me that I owe you an answer.   Not that I had entirely forgotten it,—not that I never think of you : no, my dear friend, every day says something to me of you and of my faults.   But it is strange, and it is an experience which perhaps you also know, the remembrance of the absent, though not extinguished by time, is veiled.   The distractions of our life, acquaintance with new objects, in short, every change in our circumstances, do to our hearts what smoke and dirt do to a picture,—they make the delicate touches quite undiscernible, and in such a way that one does not know how it comes to pass.   A thousand things remind me of you ; I see your image a thousand times, but as faintly, and often with as little emotion, as if I thought of some one quite strange to me ; it often occurs to me that I owe you an answer, without my feeling the slightest impulse to write to you. Now, when I read your kind letter, which is already some months old, and see your friendship and your solicitude for one so unworthy, I am shocked at myself, and for the first time feel what a change has taken place in my heart, that I can be without joy at that which formerly would have lifted me up to heaven. Forgive me this! Can one blame an unfortunate man because he is unable to rejoice? My wretchedness has made me dead to the good which still remains to me. My body is restored, but my mind is still uncured. I am in dull, inactive repose; that is not happiness. And in this quietude my imagination is so stagnant, that I can no longer picture to myself what was once dearest to me. It is only in a dream that my heart often appears to me as it is,—only a dream is capable of recalling to me the sweet images, of so recalling them as to reanimate my feelings; I have already told you that you are indebted to a dream for this letter. I saw you, I was with you; how it was, is too strange for me to relate to you. In one word, you were married. Is that true? I took up your kind letter, and it agrees with the time; if it is true, O may that be the beginning of your happiness!

'When I think of this disinterestedly, how does it rejoice me to know that you, my best friend, you, before every other who envied you and fancied herself better than you, are in the arms of a worthy husband; to know that you are happy, and freed from every annoyance to which a single state, and especially your single state, was exposed! I thank my dream that it has vividly depicted your happiness to me, and the happiness of your husband, and his reward for having made you happy. Obtain me his friendship in virtue of your being my friend, for you must have all things in common, even including friends. If I may believe my dream we shall see each other again, but I hope not so very quickly, and for my part I shall try to defer its fulfilment. If, indeed, a man can undertake anything in opposition to destiny. Formerly I wrote to you somewhat enigmatically about what was to become of me. Now I may say more plainly that I am about to change my place of residence, and move farther from you. Nothing will any more remind me of Leipsic, except, perhaps, a restless dream; no friend who comes from thence; no letter. And yet I perceive that this will be no help to me. Patience, time, and distance will do that which nothing else can do; they will annihilate every unpleasant impression, and give us back our

friendship, with contentment, with life, so after a series of years
we may see each other again with altogether different eyes, but
with the same heart.   Within a quarter of a year you shall have
another letter from me, which will tell you of my destination and
the time of my departure, and which can once more say to superfluity what I have already said a thousand times.   I entreat you
not to answer me any more; if you have anything more to say to
me, let me know it through a friend.   That is a melancholy
entreaty, my best! you, the only one of all her sex, whom I
cannot call friend, for that is an insignificant title compared with
what I feel.   I wish not to see your writing again, just as I wish
not to hear your voice; it is painful enough for me that my
dreams are so busy.   You shall have one more letter; that
promise I will sacredly keep, and so pay a part of my debts; the
rest you must forgive me.'

To round off this story, the following extract may be given from
the last letter which has been preserved of those he wrote to her.
It is dated Frankfurt, January 1770.

'That I live peacefully is all that I can say to you of myself,
and vigorously, and healthily, and industriously, for I have no
woman in my head.   Horn and I are still good friends, but, so
it happens in the world, he has his thoughts and ways, and I have
my thoughts and ways, and so a week passes and we scarcely see
each other once.   But, everything considered, I am at last tired of
Frankfurt, and at the end of March I shall leave it.   I must not
yet go to you, I perceive; for if I came at Easter you could not
be married.   And Käthchen Schönkopf I will not see again, if I
am not to see her otherwise than so.   At the end of March,
therefore, I go to Strasburg; if you care to know that, as· I believe
you do.   Will you write to me to Strasburg also?   You will play
me no trick.   For, Käthchen Schönkopf, now I know perfectly
that a letter from you is as dear to me as from any hand in the
world.   You were always a sweet girl and will be a sweet woman.
And I, I shall remain Goethe.   You know what that means.   If I
name my name, I name my whole self, and you know that so
long as I have known you I have lived only as part of you'.

So fall away the young blossoms of love which have not the
force to ripen into fruit.   'The most loveable heart', he writes to
Käthchen, with a certain bit of humour, 'is that which loves the
most readily; but that which easily loves also easily forgets'.
It was his case; he could not be happy without some one to love;

but his mobile nature soon dried the tears wrung from him by her loss.

Turning once more to his domestic condition, we find him in cold, unpleasant relations with his father, who had almost excited the hatred of his other child, Cornelia, by the stern, pedantic, pedagogic way in which he treated her. The old man continued to busy himself with writing his travels in Italy, and with instructing his daughter. She, who was of a restless, excitable, almost morbid disposition, secretly rebelled against his tyranny, and made her brother the confidant of all her griefs. The poor mother had a terrible time of it, trying to pacify the children, and to stand between them and their father.

Very noticeable is one detail recorded by him. He had fallen ill again ; this time with a stomach disorder, which no therapeutic treatment in the power of Frankfurt medicine seemed to mitigate. The family physician was one of those duped dupers who still clung to the great promises of Alchemy. It was whispered that he had in his possession a marvellous panacea, which was only to be employed in times of greatest need, and of which, indeed, no one dared openly speak. Frau Aja, trembling for her son, besought him to employ this mysterious salt. He consented. The patient recovered, and belief in the physician's skill became more complete. Not only was the poet thus restored once more to health, he was also thereby led to the study of Alchemy, and, as he narrates, employed himself in researches after the 'virgin earth'. In the little study of that house in the *Hirsch-graben*, he collected his glasses and retorts, and following the directions of authorities, sought, for a time, to penetrate the mystery which then seemed so penetrable. It is characteristic of his ardent curiosity and volatility that he should have now devoted the long hours of study to works such as Welling's *Opus Mago-cabbalisticum et Theosophicum*, and the unintelligible mystifications and diatribes of Paracelsus. He also tried Van Helmont (an interesting though fantastic writer), Basil Valentine, and other Alchemists. These, however, must quickly have been laid aside. They were replaced by the *Compendium* and the *Aphorisms* of Boerhaave, who at that period filled Europe with the sound of his name*. Goethe's studies of these writings were valuable as preparations for *Faust ;*

---

* So little can contemporary verdicts settle an author's position, that Boerhaave, whose *Institutions* were thought worthy of a Commentary in seven quartos by the great Haller, and whose *Aphorisms* were expanded into five quartos by the illustrious Van Swieten, is now nothing but a name.

and were not without influence on his subsequent career in science.

Renewed intercourse with Fräulein von Klettenberg, together with much theological and philosophical reading, brought Religion into prominence in his thoughts. He has given a sketch of the sort of Neoplatonic Christianity into which his thoughts moulded themselves ; but as this sketch was written so very many years after the period to which it relates, one cannot well accept its authenticity. For biographic purposes it is enough to indicate that, besides these Alchemic studies, Religion rose also into serious importance. Poetry seemed quite to have deserted him, although he still occasionally touched up his two plays. In a letter he humorously exposes the worthlessness of the *Bardenpoesie*, then in fashion among versifiers, who tried to be patriotic and Tyrtæan by huddling together golden helmets, flashing swords, the tramp of horses, and when the verse went lame for want of a syllable, supplying an *Oh!* or *Ha!* 'Make me feel', he says, 'what I have not yet felt,—make me think what I have not yet thought, then I will praise you. But shrieks and noise will never supply the place of pathos'.

Paoli, the Corsican patriot, passed through Frankfurt at this time, and Goethe saw him in the house of Bethmann, the rich merchant ; but, with this exception, Frankfurt presented nothing remarkable to him, and he was impatient to escape from it. His health was sufficiently restored for his father to hope that now Jurisprudence could be studied with some success ; and Strasburg was the university selected for that purpose.

CHAPTER V

STRASBURG

HE reached Strasburg on the 2nd April, 1770. He was now turned twenty, and a more magnificent youth never, perhaps, entered the Strasburg gates. Long before celebrity had fixed all eyes upon him he was likened to an Apollo ; and once, when he entered a dining-room, people laid down their knives and forks to stare at the beautiful youth. Pictures and busts, even when most resembling, give but a feeble indication of that which was most striking in his appearance ; they give the form of features, but

Strasbourg Cathedral

not the play of features ; nor are they very accurate as to the form. His features were large and liberally cut, as in the fine sweeping lines of Greek art.   The brow was lofty and massive, and from beneath it shone large lustrous brown eyes of marvellous beauty, their pupils being of almost unexampled size.   The slightly aquiline nose was large, and well cut.   The mouth was full, with a short, arched upper lip, very sensitive and expressive.   The chin and jaw boldly proportioned ; and the head rested on a handsome and muscular neck.

In stature he was rather above the middle size ; but although not really tall, he had the aspect of a tall man, and is usually so described, because his presence was very imposing*.   His frame was strong, muscular, yet sensitive.   Dante says this contrast is in the nature of things, for

> Quanta la cosa è più perfetta,
> Più senta 'l bene, e così la doglienza.

Excelling in all active sports, he was almost a barometer in sensitiveness to atmospheric influences.

Such, externally, was the youth who descended at the hotel *zum Geist*, in Strasburg, this 2nd April, and who, ridding himself of the dust and *ennui* of a long imprisonment in the diligence, sallied forth to gaze at the famous Cathedral, which made a wonderful impression on him as he came up to it through the narrow streets.   The Strasburg Cathedral not inaptly serves as the symbol of his early German tendencies ; and its glorious tower is always connected, in my mind, with the brief but ardent endeavours of his Hellenic nature to throw itself into the old German world.   German his spirit was not, but we shall see him, under the shadow of this tower, for a moment inspired with true German enthusiasm.

His lodgings secured—No. 80, on the south side of the Fish-market—he delivered his letters of introduction, and arranged to dine at a *table d'hôte* kept by two maiden ladies, named Lauth, in the Krämergasse, No. 13.   The guests here were about ten in number, mostly medical.   Their president was Dr. Salzmann, a clean old bachelor of eight and forty, scrupulous in his stockings, immaculate as to his shoes and buckles, with hat under his arm, and scarcely ever on his head—a neat, dapper old gentleman,

---

* Rauch, the sculptor, who made the well-known statuette of Goethe, explained this to me as owing to his large bust and erect carriage,

well instructed, and greatly liked by the poet, to whom he gave excellent advice, and for whom he found a valuable *repetent**.   In spite of the services of this excellent repetent, jurisprudence wearied him considerably, according to his account ; at first, however, he seems to have taken to it with some pleasure, as we learn by a letter, in which he tells Fräulein von Klettenberg a different story : ' Jurisprudence begins to please me very much. Thus it is with all things as with Merseburg beer : the first time we shudder at it, and having drunk it for a week, we cannot do without it '.   The study of jurisprudence, at any rate, did not absorb him.   Schöll has published a notebook kept during this period, which reveals an astonishing activity in desultory research†. When we remember that the society at his *table d'hôte* was principally of medical students, we are prepared to find him eagerly throwing himself into the study of anatomy and chemistry. He attended Lobstein's lectures on anatomy, Ehrmann's clinical lectures, with those of his son on midwifery, and Spielman's on chemistry.   Electricity occupied him, Franklin's great discovery having brought that subject into prominence.   No less than nine works on electricity are set down in the notebook to be studied. We also see from this notebook that chromatic subjects begin to attract him—the future antagonist of Newton was preluding in the science.   Alchemy still fascinated him ; and he wrote to Fräulein von Klettenberg, assuring her that these mystical studies were his secret mistresses.   With such a direction of his thoughts, and the influence of this pure, pious woman still operating upon him, we can imagine the disgust which followed his study of the *Système de la Nature*, then making so great a noise in the world. This dead and dull exposition of an atheism as superficial as it was dull, must have been everyway revolting to him : irritating to his piety, and unsatisfying to his reason.   Voltaire's wit and Rousseau's sarcasms he could copy into his notebook, especially when they pointed in the direction of tolerance ; but he who could read Bayle, Voltaire, and Rousseau with delight, turned from the *Système de la Nature* with scorn ; especially at a time when we find him taking the sacrament, and trying to keep up an acquaint-

---

* The medical student will best understand what a repetent is, if the word be translated a *grinder;* the university student, if the word be translated a *coach*. The repetent prepares students by an examination, and also by repeating and explaining in private what the professor has taught in the lecture hall.

† *Briefe und Aufsätze von Goethe.* Herausgegeben von ADOLF SCHÖLL. In this, as in his other valuable work, Schöll is not content simply to reprint papers entrusted to him, but enriches them by his own careful, accurate editing.

ance with the pious families to which Fräulein von Klettenberg had introduced him. I say *trying*, because even his goodwill could not long withstand their dulness and narrowness ; he was forced to give them up, and confessed so much to his friend.

Shortly after his arrival in Strasburg, namely in May 1770, an event occurred which agitated the town, and gave him an opportunity of seeing, for the first time, Raphael's cartoons. Marie Antoinette, the dauphiness of France elect, was to pass through on her way to Paris. On a small island on the Rhine a building was erected for her reception ; and this was adorned with tapestries worked after the cartoons. These tapestries roused his enthusiasm ; but he was shocked to find that they were placed in the side chambers, while the chief salon was hung with tapestries worked after pictures by modern French artists. That Raphael should thus be thrown into a subordinate position was less exasperating to him than the *subjects* chosen from the modern artists. 'These pictures were the history of Jason, Medea, and Creusa—consequently, a story of a most wretched marriage. To the left of the throne was seen the bride struggling against a horrible death, surrounded by persons full of sympathetic grief ; to the right stood the father, horror-struck at the murdered babes at his feet ; whilst the fury, in her dragon car, drove through the air'.

All the ideas which he had learned from Oeser were outraged by this selection. He did not quarrel so much with the arrangement which placed Christ and the Apostles in side chambers, since he had thereby been enabled to enjoy the sight of them. 'But a blunder like that of the grand saloon put me altogether out of my self-possession, and with loud and vehement cries I called to my comrades to witness the insult against feeling and taste. "What !" I exclaimed, regardless of bystanders, "can they so thoughtlessly place before the eyes of a young queen, on her first setting foot in her dominions, the representation of the most horrible marriage perhaps that ever was consummated ! Is there among the architects and decorators no one man who understands that pictures *represent something*—that they work upon the mind and feelings—that they produce impressions and excite forebodings ? It is as if they had sent a ghastly spectre to meet this lovely, and as we hear most joyous, lady at the very frontiers !"' To him, indeed, pictures meant something ; they were realities to him, because he had the true artistic nature. But to the French architects, as to the Strasburg officials, pictures were pictures—ornaments betokening more or less luxury and taste, flattering the eye, but never touching the soul.

Goethe was right; and omen-lovers afterwards read in that picture the dark foreshadowing of her destiny. But no one then could have foreseen that her future career would be less triumphant than her journey from Vienna to Paris. That smiling, happy, lovely princess of fifteen, whose grace and beauty extort expressions of admiration from every beholder, as she wends her way along roads lined with the jubilant peasantry leaving their fields to gaze upon her, through streets strewn with nosegays, through triumphal arches, and rows of maidens garlanded, awaiting her arrival to offer her spring-flowers as symbols—can her joy be for a moment dashed by a pictured sorrow? Can omens have a dark significance to her?

'I still vividly remember', says Goethe, 'the beauteous and lofty mien, as charming as it was dignified, of the young princess. Plainly visible in her carriage, she seemed to be jesting with her female attendants respecting the throng which poured forth to meet her train'. Scarcely had the news of her happy arrival in the capital reached them, than it was followed by the intelligence of the accident which had disturbed the festivities of her marriage. Goethe's thoughts naturally recurred to the ominous pictures: a nature less superstitious would not have been entirely unmoved by such a coincidence.

'The excitement over, the Strasburgers fell into their accustomed tranquillity. The mighty stream of courtly magnificence had now flowed by, and left me no other longing than that for the tapestries of Raphael, which I could have contemplated and worshipped every hour. Luckily my earnest desires succeeded in interesting several persons of consequence, so that the tapestries were not taken down till the very last moment'.

The reëstablished quiet left him time for studies again. In a letter of this date, he intimates that he is 'so improved in knowledge of Greek as almost to read Homer without a translation. I am a week older; *that* you know says a great deal with me, not because I do much, but many things'. Among these many things, we must note his ardent search through mystical metaphysical writings for the material on which his insatiable appetite could feed. Strange revelations in this direction are afforded by his Notebook. On one page there is a passage from Thomas à Kempis, followed

by a list of mystical works to be read ; on another page, sarcastic
sentences from Rousseau and Voltaire ; on a third a reference to
Tauler. The book contains an analysis of the *Phædon* of Moses
Mendelssohn, contrasted with that of Plato ; and a defence of
Giordano Bruno against the criticism of Bayle.

Apropos of Bruno, one may remark the early tendency of
Goethe's mind towards Nature-worship. Tacitus, indeed, noticed
the tendency as national*. The scene in Frankfurt, where the
boy-priest erected his Pantheistic altar, will help to explain the
interest he must have felt in the glimpse Bayle gave him of the
great Pantheist of the sixteenth century—the brilliant and luckless
Bruno, who after teaching the heresy of Copernicus at Rome and
Oxford, after combating Aristotle and gaining the friendship of
Sir Philip Sidney, was publicly burnt on the 17th February, 1600,
in the presence of the Roman crowd : expiating thus the crime of
teaching that the earth moved, when the Church declared it to be
stable. A twofold interest attached itself to the name of Bruno.
He was a martyr of Philosophy, and his works were rare ; every
one abused him, few had read him. He was almost as much hated
as Spinoza, and scarcely any one knew the writings they reviled.
The rarity of Bruno's works made them objects of bibliopolic
luxury ; some were among the black swans of literature. The
Spaccio had been sold for thirty pounds in England, and three
hundred florins in Holland. Hamann, whom Herder and Goethe
ardently admired, searched Italy and Germany for the *De la Causa*
and *Del Infinito* in vain. Forbidden fruit is tempting ; but when
the fruit is rare, as well as forbidden, the attraction is irresistible†.
Pantheism, which captivates poetical minds, has a poetical grandeur
in the form given to it by Bruno which would have allured Goethe
had his tendencies not already lain in that direction. To preach
that doctrine Bruno became a homeless wanderer, and his wanderings ended in martyrdom. Nothing could shake his faith ; as he
loftily says, ' con questa filosofia l'anima mi s'aggrandisce e mi si
magnifica l'intelletto '.

Goethe's notes on Bayle's criticism may be given here, as illustrating his metaphysical opinions and his mastery of French

---

* *German.*, IX, *sub fine*. What Tacitus there represents as a more exalted creed
than anthropomorphism, was really a lower form of religious conception—the Fetichism,
which in primitive races precedes Polytheism.

† Since then the works have been made accessible through the cheap and excellent
edition collected by A. WAGNER : *Opere di Giordano Bruno Nolano*. 2 vols. Leipsic :
1830. But I do not observe that, now they are accessible, many persons interest themselves enough in Bruno to read them ; yet they are worth studying.

composition. We can be certain of the authenticity of the French : in spite of inaccuracies and inelegancies, it is fluent and expressive, and gives one the idea of greater conversational command of the language than he reports of himself.

'Je ne suis pas du sentiment de M. Bayle à l'égard de Jor. Brunus, et je ne trouve ni d'impiété ni d'absurdité dans les passages qu'il cite, quoique d'ailleurs je ne prétende pas d'excuser cet homme paradoxe. "L'uno, l'infinito, lo ente e quello ch' è in tutto, e per tutto anzi è l'*istezzo* ubique. E che *cosse* la infinita dimenzione per non essere magnitudine coincide coll' individuo, come la infinita moltitudine, per non esser numero coincide coll' unita". *Giord. Brun. Epist. Ded. del Tratt. de la Causa Principio et Uno**.

'Ce passage mériteroit une explication et une recherche plus philosophiques que le disc. de M. Bayle. Il est plus facile de prononcer un passage obscur et contraire à nos notions que de le déchiffrer, et que de suivre les idées d'un grand homme. Il est de même du passage où il plaisante sur une idée de Brunus, que je n'applaudis pas entièrement, si peu que les précédentes, mais que je crois du moins profondes et peut-être fécondes pour un observateur judicieux. Notez, je vous prie, de B. une absurdité : il dit que ce n'est point l'être qui fait qu'il y a beaucoup de choses, mais que cette multitude consiste dans ce qui paroit sur la superfice de la substance'.

In the same Notebook there is a remarkable comment on a chapter in Fabricius (*Bibliog. Antiq.*) which Goethe has written in Latin, and which may be thus rendered : 'To discüss God apart from Nature is both difficult and perilous ; it is as if we separated the soul from the body. We know the soul only through the medium of the body, and God only through Nature. Hence the absurdity, as it appears to me, of accusing those of absurdity who philosophically have united God with the world. For everything which exists necessarily pertains to the essence of God, because God is the one Being whose existence includes all things. Nor does the Holy Scripture contradict this, although we differently interpret its dogmas each according to his views. All antiquity thought in the same way ; an unanimity which to me has great significance. To me the judgment of so many men speaks highly

---

* 'The One, the Infinite, the Being, and that which is in all things is everywhere the same. Thus infinite extension not being magnitude coincides with the individual, as infinite multitude because it is not number coincides with unity'. The words in italics are given as in Goethe—carelessly copied for *l'istesso* and *cosi*. See BRUNO, *Opere*, I, p. 211, ed. Wagner.

for the rationality of the doctrine of emanation ; though I am of
no sect, and grieve much that Spinoza should have coupled this
pure doctrine with his detestable errors'*. This reference to
Spinoza, whom he subsequently reverenced as one of his best
teachers, is easily explicable when we reflect that he then knew no
more of Spinoza than could be gathered from Bayle.

Time was not all consumed by these studies, multifarious as
they were. Lively Strasburg had its amusements, and Goethe
joined his friend Salzmann in many a pleasant party. The various
pleasure grounds and public gardens were always crowded with
promenaders, and there the mixture of the old national costume
with modern fashions gave charming variety to the scene, and
made the pretty women still more attractive.

He found himself in the presence of two sharply defined nation-
alities. Alsatia, and especially Strasburg, although belonging to
France, still preserved its old German character. Eight hundred
years of national life were not to be set aside at once, when it
pleased the powers, at the peace of Westphalia, to say that Alsatia
should be French. Until the middle of the eighteenth century the
old German speech, costume, and manners were so dominant that
a Frankfurter, or a Mainzer, found himself at once at home
there. But just before the outbreak of the French Revolution the
gradual influx of officials brought about a sort of fashion in French
costume. Milliners, friseurs, and dancing masters had done their
best, or their worst, to 'polish' society. But the surface was rough,
and did not take kindly to this polishing. Side by side with the
French *employé*, there was the old German professor, who obstinately declined to acquire more of the foreigners' language than
sufficed for daily needs and household matters ; for the rest he
kept sturdily Teutonic. Even in costume the imitation was mainly
confined to the upper classes †. Goethe describes the maidens
of the bourgeoisie still wearing their hair in one long plait,

---

* I subjoin the original, as the reader may not be displeased to see a specimen of
Goethe's Latin composition : Separatim de Deo, et natura rerum disserere difficile et
pericolosum est, eodem modo quam si de corpore et anima sejunctim cogitamus.
Animam nonnisi mediante corpore, Deum nonnisi perspecta natura cognoscimus ; hinc
absurdum mihi videtur, eos absurditatis accusare, qui ratiocinatione maxime philo-
sophica Deum cum mundo conjunxere. Quæ enim sunt omnia ad essentiam Dei
pertinere necesse est, cum Deus sit unicum existens et omnia comprehendat. Nec
Sacer Codex nostræ sententiæ refragatur, cujus tamen dicta ab unoquoque in sententiam
suam torqueri patientur ferimus. Omnis antiquitatis ejusdem fuit sententiæ, cui con-
sensui quam multum tribuo. Testimonio enim mihi est virorum tantorum sententia
rectæ rationi quam convenientissimum fuisse systema emanativum, licet nulli subscribere
velim sectæ, valdeque doleam Spinozismum, teterrimis erroribus ex eodem fonte man-
antibus, doctrinæ huic purissimæ iniquissimum fratrem natum esse.

† STOEBER: *Der Aktuar Salzmann:* 1855, p. 7.

falling behind, and their petticoats of picturesque but perilous brevity.

Salzmann introduced him to several families, and thus more than by all his advice helped to soften down the exuberant expression of animal spirits which very often sinned against quiet conventionalities ; for by inducing him to frequent society, it forced him to learn that demeanour which society imperatively demands. In *Wilhelm Meister* great stress is laid upon the culture necessary to fit a man of genius for society ; and one of the great motives advanced for the pursuance of a theatrical career is the facility it affords a man of gaining address.

An excitable, impetuous youth, ambitious of shining in society, yet painfully conscious of the unsuitableness of his previous training for the attainment of that quietness deemed so necessary, would require to attend to every trifle which might affect his deportment. Thus, although he had magnificent hair, he allowed the hairdresser to tie it up in a bag, and affix a false queue. This obliged him to remain propped up powdered, from an early hour of the morning, and also to keep from overheating himself and from violent gestures, lest he should betray the false ornament. ' This restraint contributed much towards making me for a time more gentle and polite in my bearing ; and I got accustomed to shoes and stockings, and to carrying my hat under my arm ; I did not, however, neglect wearing fine understockings as a protection against the Rhine gnats '. To these qualifications as a cavalier, he added those of an excellent swordsman and rider. With his fellow-students he had abundant exercise in the use of the rapier ; and prompted, I presume, by his restless desire to do all that his friends did, he began to learn the violoncello !

His circle of friends widened ; and even that of his fellow-boarders in the Krämergasse increased. Among the latter, two deserve special mention—Jung Stilling and Franz Lerse. Stilling has preserved an account of their first meeting*. About twenty were assembled at dinner, when a young man entered the room in high spirits, whose large clear eyes, splendid brow, and beautifully proportioned figure, irresistibly drew the attention of Troost and Stilling. The former remarked, ' That must be an extraordinary man ! ' Stilling assented ; but feared lest they might be somewhat annoyed by him, he looked such a wild rollicking fellow. Meanwhile they learned that this student, whose unconstrained freedom

* STILLING'S *Wanderschaft*, p. 158.

Johann Heinrich Jung Stilling

and *àplomb* made them draw under their shells, was named Herr Goethe. Dinner proceeded. Goethe, who sat opposite Stilling, had completely the lead in conversation, without once seeking it. At length one of the company began quizzing the wig of poor Stilling ; and the fun was relished by all except Troost, Salzmann, and one who, indignantly reproving them for making game of so inoffensive a person, silenced the ridicule immediately ; this was none other than the large-eyed student whose appearance had excited Stilling's uneasiness. The friendship thus begun, was continued by the sympathy and tender affectionateness Goethe always displayed towards the simple, earnest, and unfriended thinker, whose deep religious convictions, and trusting child-like nature, singularly interested him. Goethe was never tired of listening to the story of his life. Instinctively he sought on all sides to penetrate the mysteries of humanity, and, by probing every man's experience, to make it his own. Here was a poor charcoal-burner, who from tailoring had passed to keeping a school; that failing, he had resumed his needle ; and having joined a religious sect, had, in silent communion with his own soul, gained for himself a sort of culture which raised him above the ordinary height of men :—what was there in his life or opinions to captivate the riotous, sceptical, prosperous student ? There was *earnestness*—there was *genuineness*. Goethe was eminently qualified to become the friend of one who held opposite convictions to his own, for his tolerance was large and genuine, and he respected every real conviction. Sympathizing with Stilling, listening to him, and dexterously avoiding any interference with his religious faith, he was not only enabled to be his friend, but also to learn quietly and surely the inner nature of such men.

Franz Lerse attracted him by different qualities : upright manliness, scrupulous orderliness, dry humour, and a talent for reconciling antagonists. As a memorial of their friendship his name is given to the gallant fellow in *Götz von Berlichingen*, who knows how to subordinate himself with dignity.

Salzmann had some years before founded a sort of club, or, as Stilling calls it, *Gesellschaft der schönen Wissenschaften*, the object of which was to join a book society with a debating club. In 1763-4 this club had among its members no less a person than O. F. Müller, the renowned helminthologist ; and now in 1770-1 it numbered, among others, Goethe, Lerse, Jung Stilling, Lenz, Weyland, and, as a guest, was honoured by the presence of Herder, who was then writing his work on the *Origin of Language.*

Generally speaking, Goethe is so liberal in information about his friends and contemporaries, and so sparing of precise indications of his own condition, that we are left in the dark respecting much that would be welcome knowledge. There is one thing mentioned by him which is very significant : although his health was sufficiently established for ordinary purposes, he still suffered from great irritability. Loud sounds were disagreeable to him ; diseased objects aroused loathing and horror. And he was especially troubled with giddiness, which came over him whenever he looked down from a height. All these infirmities he resolved to conquer, and that somewhat violently. In the evening when they beat the tattoo, he went close to the drums, though the powerful rolling and beating of so many seemed enough to make his heart burst in his bosom. Alone he ascended the highest pinnacle of the cathedral, and sat in what is called the neck, under the crown, for a quarter of an hour before venturing to step out again into the open air. Standing on a platform, scarcely an ell square, he saw before him a boundless prospect, the church and the supports of his standing place being concealed by the ornaments. He felt exactly as if carried up in a balloon. These painful sensations he repeated until they became quite indifferent ; he subsequently derived great advantage from this conquest, in mountainous excursions and geological studies. Anatomy was also of double value, at it taught him to tolerate the most repulsive sights while satisfying his thirst for knowledge. He succeeded so well, that no hideous sight could disturb his self-possession. He also sought to steel himself against the terrors of imagination. The awful and shuddering impressions of darkness in churchyards, solitary places, churches and chapels by night, he contrived to render indifferent— so much so, that when a desire came over him to recall in such scenes the pleasing shudder of youth, he could scarcely succeed even by the strangest and most terrific images.

Two love poems, written during this year—*Stirbt der Fuchs so gilt der Balg*, and *Blinde Kuh*—put us on the scent of flirtations. He is silent respecting Dorilis and Theresa in his *Autobiography;* and in ordinary cases a biographer would accept that silence, without drawing any conclusion from the poems. No one hereafter will think of identifying the Claribels, Isabels, and Madelines, with young ladies whom our poets met in society, and who led captive their inconstant hearts. With Goethe it is otherwise. All his poems grow out of occasions : they are flowers of which circumstance is the earth. Utterances of real feelings to real beings, they are unlike all coquettings with imaginary beauties. His poems are evidences*. Unhappily, the bare *fact* in this instance is all we can discover.

One flirtation, however, was not so easily effaced. From childhood his strange didactic father had instructed him and his sister in dancing, a task which seems rather ludicrous as we picture to ourselves the cold, formal, rigorous old Frankfurter. He was perfectly unconscious of any incongruity. With the utmost gravity he drilled them into a minuet, playing to them on a flageolet. Goethe's dancing had been for some time neglected, and when he stood up to a minuet once at Leipsic, he got through it so awkwardly as to draw upon himself the suspicion of having done so to prevent being invited again.

A handsome youth unable to dance was an anomaly in Strasburg. Not a Sunday evening passed without the pleasure gardens being crowded with gay dancers ; galas frequently enlivened the week ; and the merry Alsatians, then as now, seldom met but they commenced spinning round in the waltz. Into these gardens, amidst these waltzers, Goethe constantly went—yet could not waltz. He resolved at length to learn. A friend recommended him to a dancing-master of repute, who soon pronounced himself gratified with the progress made.

This master, a dry, precise, but amiable Frenchman, had two daughters, who assisted him at his lessons, acting both as partners and correctors. Two pretty girls, both under twenty, charming with French vivacity and coquetry, could not fail to interest the young poet ; nor could the graceful, handsome youth fail to create an impression on two girls whose lives were somewhat lonesome. Symptoms of this interest very soon showed themselves. The misfortune was that the state of their feelings made what dramatists call 'a situation'. Goethe's heart inclined towards Emilia, who loved another ; while that of Lucinda, the elder sister, was bestowed upon him. Emilia was afraid to trust herself too much with him ; but Lucinda was always at hand, ready to waltz with him, to protract his lesson, or to show him little attentions. There

---

* I find Viehoff insisting on a similar clue : he supposes Dorilis and Theresa (probably one and the same person) to be real persons, and that Goethe knew them through Salzmann. Mr. Demmler argues with some force that Dorilis can be none other than Frederika,—of whom more anon.

were not many pupils ; so that he often remained after his lesson
to chat away the time, or to read aloud to them a romance :
dangerous moments !

He saw how things stood, yet puzzled himself about the reserve
of the younger sister. The cause of it came out at last. One
evening, after the dance was over, Lucinda detained him in the
dancing-room, telling him that her sister was in the sitting-room
with a fortune-teller, who was disclosing the condition of a lover
to whom the girl's heart was given. 'Mine', said Lucinda, 'is
free, and I must get used to its being slighted'.

He tried to parry this thrust by divers little compliments ; and,
indiscreetly enough, advised her to try her own fate with the
fortune-teller, offering to do the same himself. Lucinda did not
like that tampering with fate, declaring that the disclosures of the
oracle were too true to be made a matter of sport. Probably this
piqued him into a little more earnestness than he had shown, for
ultimately he persuaded her to go into the sitting-room with him.
They found Emilia much pleased with the information that she had
received from the pythoness, who was highly flattered at the new
devotee to her shrine. A handsome reward was promised her if
she should disclose the truth. With the customary ceremonial she
began to tell the fortune of the elder sister. She hesitated. 'Oh,
I see', said Emilia, 'that you have something unpleasant to tell'.
Lucinda turned pale, but said, 'Speak out ; it will not cost me my
life'. The fortune-teller heaved a deep sigh, and proceeded with
her disclosures. Lucinda, she said, was in love ; but her love was
not returned ; another person standing in the way. And she went
on with more in the same style. It is not difficult to imagine that
the sybil should readily enough interpret the litttle drama which
was then acting by the youth and two girls before her eyes.
Lucinda showed evidence of distress ; and the old woman endeavoured to give a better turn to the affair by throwing out hopes
of letters and money. 'Letters', said Lucinda, 'I do not expect ;
and money I do not want. If I love as you say, I have a right to
be loved in return'. The fortune-teller shuffled the cards again ;
but that only made matters worse ; the girl now appeared in the
oracular vision in great trouble, her lover at a greater distance. A
third shuffle of the cards was still worse ; Lucinda burst into a
passionate flood of tears, and rushed from the room. 'Follow
her', said Emilia, 'and comfort her'. But he hesitated, not seeing
what comfort he could well give, as he could not assure her of

some return for her affection. 'Let us go together', he replied.
Emilia doubted whether her presence would do good; but she
consented. Lucinda had locked herself in; and paying the old
woman for her work, Goethe left the house.

He had scarcely courage to revisit the sisters; but on the
third day Emilia sent for him, and he received his lesson as usual.
Lucinda, however, was absent; and when he asked for her,
Emilia told him that she was in bed, declaring that she should die.
She had thrown out great reproaches against him for his ungrate-
ful behaviour. 'And yet I do not know', said he, 'that I am
guilty of having expressed any sort of affection for her. I know
somebody who can bear me witness of that'. Emilia smiled. 'I
comprehend', she said; 'but if we are not careful we shall all find
ourselves in a disastrous position. Forgive me if I say that you
must not go on with your lessons. My father says that he is
ashamed to take your money any longer, unless you mean to
pursue the art of dancing; since you know already what is
needed by a young man in the world'. 'Do you tell me to avoid
the house, Emilia?' he asked. 'Yes', she said; 'but not on my
own account. When you had gone the other day, I had the cards
cut for you; and the same answer was given thrice. You were
surrounded by friends, and all sorts of good fortune; but the
ladies kept aloof from you; my poor sister stood furthest of all.
One other constantly came near to you; but never close; for a
third person, a man, always came between. I will confess that I
thought I was myself this second lady; and now you will understand my advice. I have promised myself to another, and until
now I loved him more than any one. Yet your presence might
become more dangerous to me than it has been; and then what a
position would be yours between two sisters, one of whom you
would have made miserable by your affection, and the other by
your coldness'. She held out her hand and bade him farewell;
she then led him to the door; and in token that it was to be their
last meeting, she threw herself upon his bosom and kissed him
tenderly. Just as he had put his arms round her, a side door flew
open, and her sister, in a light but decorous dressing gown, rushed
in, crying, 'You shall not be the only one to take leave of him!'
Emilia released him. Lucinda took him in her arms, pressed her
black locks against his cheeks; remained thus for some time, and
then drawing back looked him earnestly in the face. He took her
hand, and tried to muster some kind expressions to soothe her;

but she turned away, walked passionately up and down the room, and then threw herself in great agitation into a corner of the sofa. Emilia went up to her, but was violently repulsed ; and a scene ensued, which had in it, says the principal performer, nothing really theatrical, although it could only be represented on the stage by an actor of sensibility. Lucinda poured forth reproaches against her sister. 'This', said she, 'is not the first heart beating for me that you have wheedled away. Was it not so with the one now betrothed to you, while I looked on and bore it ? I, only, know the tears it cost me ; and now you would rob me of this one. How many would you manage to keep at once ? I am frank and easy-tempered, and all think they understand me at once, and may slight me. You are secret and quiet, and make people wonder at what may be concealed behind : there is nothing there but a cold, selfish heart, sacrificing everything to itself'. Emilia seated herself by her sister, and remained silent, while Lucinda, growing more excited, began to betray matters not quite proper for him to hear. Emilia made a sign to him to withdraw. But Lucinda caught the sound, sprang towards him, and then remained lost in thought. 'I know that I have lost you', she said : 'I claim you no more ;—but neither shall you have him'. So saying, she grasped him wildly by the head, with her hands thrust among his hair, pressed her face to his, and kissed him repeatedly on the mouth. 'Now fear my curse ! Woe upon woe, for ever and ever, to her who for the first time after me kisses these lips ! Dare to sport with him now ! Heaven hears my curse ! And you begone, begone while you may !'

He hurried from the house never to return. Is not this narrative like a scene in a novel? The excited little Frenchwoman—the bewildered poet—the old fortune-teller, and the dry old dancing-master, faintly sketched, in the background, are the sort of figures a novelist would delight in.

CHAPTER VI

HERDER AND FREDERIKA

ONE thing very noticeable in this Strasburg period is the thoroughly *German* culture it gave him. In those days culture was mostly classical and French. Classical studies had never exercised much influence over him ; and, indeed, throughout his

Johann Gottfried Herder

career, he approached antiquity more through Art than through the Greek and Roman writers. To the French, on the other hand, he owed a great deal, both of direction and material. A revival of the old German nationality was, however, actively agitated at this epoch. Klopstock, Lessing, Herder, Shakespeare, and Ossian were the rivals opposed to France. A feeling of national pride gave its momentum to this change in taste. Gothic art began to be considered the true art of modern times.

At the *table d'hôte* our friends, all German, not only banished the French language, but made a point of being in every way unlike the French. French literature was ridiculed as affected, insincere, unnatural. The truth, homely strength, and simplicity of the German character were set against this literature of courtiers. Goethe had been dabbling in mediæval studies, had been awe-struck by the cathedral, had been inspired by Shakespeare, and had seen Lessing's iconoclastic wit scattering the pretensions of French poetry. Moreover, he had read the biography of *Götz von Berlichingen*, and the picture of that Titan in an age of anarchy had so impressed itself upon him, that the conception of a dramatic reproduction of it had grown up in his mind. *Faust* also lay there as a germ. The legend of that wonder-worker especially attracted him, now that he was in the condition into which youths so readily fall after a brief and unsatisfactory attempt to penetrate the mysteries of science. ' Like him, too, I had swept the circle of science, and had early learned its vanity ; like him I had trodden various paths, always returning unsatisfied'. The studies of alchemy, medicine, jurisprudence, philosophy, and theology, which had so long engaged him, must have made him feel quite a personal interest in the old Faust legend.

In such a mood the acquaintance with Herder was of great importance. Herder was five years his senior, and had already created a name for himself. He came to Strasburg with an eye-disease, which obliged him to remain there the whole winter, during the cure. Goethe, charmed with this new vigorous intellect, attended on him during the operation, and sat with him morning and evening during his convalescence, listening to the wisdom which fell from those lips, as a pupil listens to a much-loved master. Great was the contrast between the two men, yet the difference did not separate them. Herder was decided, clear, pedagogic ; knowing his own aims, and fond of communicating his ideas. Goethe was sceptical and inquiring. Herder rude, sarcastic, and bitter ;

Goethe amiable and infinitely tolerant. The bitterness which
repelled so many friends from Herder could not repel Goethe :
it was a peculiarity of his to be at all times able to learn from
antagonistic natures ; meeting them on the common ground of
sympathy, he avoided those subjects on which inevitably they must
clash. It is somewhat curious that although Herder took a great
liking to his young friend, and was grateful for his kind attentions,
he seems to have had little suspicion of his genius. The only fragment we have of that period, which gives us a hint of his opinion,
is in a letter to his bride, dated February 1772 : 'Goethe is really a
good fellow, only somewhat light and sparrow-like*, for which I
incessantly reproach him. He was almost the only one who visited
me during my illness in Strasburg whom I saw with pleasure ; and
I believe I influenced him in more ways than one to his advantage'.
His own conceit may have stood between Goethe and himself ; or
he may have been too conscious of his young friend's defects to
think much of his genius. 'Herder, Herder', Goethe writes to him
from Strasburg, 'be to me what you are. If I am destined to be
your planet, so will I be, and willingly and truly, a friendly moon
to your earth. But you must feel that I would rather be Mercury,
the last, the smallest of the seven, to revolve with you about the
sun, than the first of the five which turn round Saturn't. In one
of the many inaccuracies of his *Autobiography*, he says, that he
withheld from Herder his intention of writing *Götz;* but there is
a passage in Herder's work on German Art, addressed to Goethe,
which very plainly alluded to this intention‡. Such oversights are
inevitable in retracing the minor details of the past.

There was indeed contrast enough between the two, in age, character, intellect, and knowledge, to have prevented any very close
sympathy. Herder loved the abstract and ideal in men and things,
and was for ever criticizing and complaining of the individual,
because it did not realize his ideal standard. What Gervinus says
of Herder's relation to Lessing, namely, that he loved him when
he considered him as a whole, but could never cease plaguing him
about details, holds good also of his relation to Goethe through

---

* *Nur etwas leicht und Spatzenmässig:* I translate the phrase, leaving the reader
to interpret it, for twenty Germans have given twenty different meanings to the word
'sparrow-like', some referring to the chattering of sparrows, others to the boldness of
sparrows, others to the curiosity of sparrows, and others to the libertine character of
sparrows. Whether Herder meant gay, volatile, forward, careless, or amorous, I cannot
decide.
† *Aus Herder's Nachlass,* I, p. 28.
‡ HERDER : *Von deutschen Art und Kunst,* p. 112.

life. Goethe had little of that love of mankind in the abstract
which to Herder, and so many others, seems the substitute for
individual love,—which animates philanthropists who are sincere
in their philanthropy, even when they are bad husbands, bad
fathers, bad brothers, and bad friends. He had, instead of this,
the most overflowing love for individual men. His concrete and
affectionate nature was more attracted to men than to abstractions.
It is because many do not recognize this that they declaim against
him for his 'indifference' to political matters, to history, and to
many of the great questions which affect Humanity.

Herder's influence on Goethe was manifold, but mainly in the
direction of poetry. He taught him to look at the Bible as a
magnificent illustration of the truth that Poetry is the product of a
national spirit, not the privilege of a cultivated few. From the
poetry of the Hebrew People he led him to other illustrations of
national song ; and here Homer and Ossian were placed highest.
It was at this time that Ossian made the tour of Europe, and
everywhere met believers. Goethe was so delighted with the wild
northern singer, that he translated the song of *Selma*, and afterwards incorporated it in *Werther*. Besides Shakespeare and
Ossian, he also learned, through Herder, to appreciate the *Vicar
of Wakefield;* and the exquisite picture there painted, he was now
to see living in the parsonage of Frederika's father.

Upon the broad and lofty gallery of the Strasburg Cathedral he
and his companions often met to salute the setting sun with
brimming goblets of Rhine wine. The calm wide landscape
stretched itself for miles before them, and they pointed out
the several spots which memory endeared to each. One spot,
above all others, has interest for us—Sesenheim, the home of
Frederika. Of all the women who enjoyed the distinction of
Goethe's love, none seem to me so fascinating as Frederika.
Her idyllic presence is familiar to every lover of German literature, through the charming episode of the *Autobiography*, over
which the poet lingered with peculiar delight. The secretary is
now living to whom this episode was dictated, and he remembers
vividly how much affected Goethe seemed to be as these scenes
revisited memory ; walking up and down the room, with his hands
behind him, he often stopped in his walk, and paused in the dictation ; then after a long silence, followed by a deep sigh, he
continued the narrative in a lower tone.

Weyland, a fellow-boarder, had often spoken of a clergyman

who with his wife and two amiable daughters, lived near Drusenheim, a village about sixteen miles from Strasburg.   Early in
October 1770, Weyland proposed to his friend to accompany him
on a visit to the worthy pastor.   It was agreed between them that
Weyland should introduce him under the guise of a shabby theological student.   His love of incognito often prompted him to
such disguises.   In the present instance he borrowed some old
clothes, and combed his hair in such a way that when Weyland
saw him he burst out into a fit of laughter.   They set forth in high
glee.   At Drusenheim they stopped, Weyland to make himself
spruce, Goethe to rehearse his part.   Riding across the meadows
to Sesenheim, they left their horses at the inn, and walked leisurely
towards the parsonage,—an old and somewhat dilapidated farm-
house, but very picturesque, and very still.   They found pastor
Brion at home, and were welcomed by him in a friendly manner.
The rest of the family were in the fields.   Weyland went after
them, leaving Goethe to discuss parish interests with the pastor,
who soon grew confidential.   Presently the wife appeared ; and she
was followed by the eldest daughter bouncing into the room, inquiring after Frederika, and hurrying away again to seek her.

   Refreshments were brought, and old acquaintances were talked
over with Weyland,—Goethe listening.   Then the daughter returned, uneasy at not having found Frederika.   This little domestic
fuss about Frederika prepared the poet for her appearance.   At
length she came in.   Both girls wore the national costume, with
its short, white, full skirt and furbelow, not concealing the neatest
of ankles, a tight bodice and black taffeta apron.   Frederika's
straw hat hung on her arm ; and the beautiful braids of her fair
hair drooped on a delicate white neck.   Merry blue eyes, and a
piquant little *nez retroussé*, completed her attractions.   In gazing
on this bright young creature, then only sixteen, Goethe felt
ashamed of his disguise.   It hurt his amour-propre to appear thus
before her like a bookish student, shorn of all personal advantages.
Meanwhile conversation rattled on between Weyland and his
family.   Endless was the list of uncles, aunts, nieces, cousins,
gossips, and guests they had something to say about, leaving him
completely excluded from the conversation.   Frederika seeing this,
seated herself by him, and with charming frankness began to talk
to him.   Music was lying on the harpischord ; she asked him if
he played, and on his modestly qualified affirmative begged him
'to favour them'.   Her father, however, suggested that *she* ought

Friederike Brion

to begin, by a song. She sat down to the harpsichord, which was
somewhat out of tune, and, in a provincial style, performed several
pieces, such as then were thought enchanting. After this she
began to sing. The song was tender and melancholy, but she was
apparently not in the mood, for acknowledging her failure she rose
and said, ' If I sing badly it is not the fault of my harpsichord nor
of my teacher : let us go into the open air, and then you shall hear
my Alsatian and Swiss songs '. Into the air they went, and soon
her merry voice carolled forth :

> ' I come from a forest as dark as the night,
> And believe me, I love thee, my only delight.
> Ei ja, ei ja, ei, ei, ei, ei, ja, ja, ja ! ' *

He was already a captive.

His tendency to see pictures and poetry in the actual scenes of
life, here made him see realized the Wakefield family. If pastor
Brion did not accurately represent Mr. Primrose, yet he might
stand for him ; the elder daughter for Olivia, the younger for
Sophia ; and when at supper a youth came into the room, Goethe
involuntarily exclaimed ' What, Moses too ! ' A very merry supper
they had ; so merry that Weyland, fearing lest wine and Frederika
should make his friend betray himself, proposed a walk in the
moonlight. Weyland offered his arm to Salome, the elder
daughter (always named *Olivia* in the *Autobiography*), Frederika
took Goethe's arm. Youth and moonlight—need one say more ?
Already he began to scrutinize her tone in speaking of cousins
and neighbours, jealous lest it should betray an affection. But
her blithe spirit was as yet untroubled, and he listened in delicious
silence to her unembarrassed loquacity.

On retiring for the night the friends had much to talk over.
Weyland assured him the incognito had not been betrayed ; on
the contrary, the family had inquired after the young Goethe, of
whose joviality and eccentricities they had often heard. And now
came the tremulous question : was Frederika engaged ? No.
That was a relief ! Had she ever been in love ? No. Still
better ! Thus chatting, they sat till deep in the night, as friends
chat on such occasions, with hearts too full and brains too heated
for repose. At dawn Goethe was awake, impatient to see Frederika
with the dew of morning on her cheek. While dressing he looked

---

* The entire song is to be found in the *Sesenheimer Liederbuch* and in Viehoff :
Goethe Erläutert, vol. i, p. 110.

at his costume in disgust, and tried in vain to remedy it. His hair could be managed ; but when his arms were thrust into his threadbare coat, the sleeves of which were ludicrously short, he looked pitiable ; Weyland, peeping at him from under the coverlet, giggled. In his despair he resolved to ride back to Strasburg, and return in his own costume. On the way another plan suggested itself. He exchanged clothes with the son of the landlord at the Drusenheim Inn, a youth of his own size ; corked his eyebrows, imitated the son's gait and speech, and returned to the parsonage the bearer of a cake. This second disguise also succeeded, so long as he kept at a distance ; but Frederika running up to him and saying, ' George, what do you here ?' he was forced to reveal himself. ' Not George, but one who asks forgiveness '. ' You shocking creature ! ' she exclaimed, ' how you frightened me !' The jest was soon explained and forgiven, not only by Frederika, but by the family, who laughed heartily at it.

Gaily passed the day ; the two hourly falling deeper and deeper in love. Passion does not chronicle by time : moments are hours, hours years, when two hearts are rushing into one. It matters little, therefore, that the *Autobiography* speaks of only two days passed in this happy circle, whereas a letter of his says distinctly he was there ' some days—*einige Tage*' (*less* than three cannot be understood by *einige*). He was there long enough to fall in love, and to captivate the whole family by his gaiety, obligingness, and poetic gifts. He had given them a taste of his quality as a romancist, by telling the story of *The New Melusina* (subsequently published in the *Wanderjahre*). He had also interested himself in the pastor's plans for the rebuilding of the parsonage, and proposed to take away the sketches with him to Strasburg.

The pain of separation was lightened by the promise of speedy reunion. He returned to Strasburg with new life in his heart. He had not long before written to a friend that for the first time he knew what it was to be happy without his heart being engaged. Pleasant people and manifold studies left him no time for *feeling*. ' Enough, my present life is like a sledge journey, splendid and sounding, but with just as little for the heart as it has much for eyes and ears '. Another tone runs through his letters now, to judge from the only one which has been recovered*. It is addressed to Frederika, dated the 15th October.

* SCHÖLL, *Briefe und Aufsätze*, p. 51. The letters in Pfeiffer's book are manifest forgeries.

'Dear new friend,

'I dare to call you so; for if I can trust the language of eyes, then did mine in the first glance read the hope of this new friendship in yours—and for our hearts I will answer. You, good and gentle as I know you, will you not show some favour to one who loves you so?

'Dear, dear friend,

'That I have something to say to you there can be no question; but it is quite another matter whether I exactly know wherefore I now write, and *what* I may write. Thus much I am conscious of by a certain inward unrest: that I would gladly be by your side, and a scrap of paper is as true a consolation and as winged a steed for me here in noisy Strasburg, as it can be to you in your quiet, if you truly feel the separation from your friend.

'The circumstances of our journey home you can easily imagine, if you marked my pain at parting, and how I longed to remain behind. Weyland's thoughts went forwards, mine backwards; so you can understand how our conversation was neither interesting nor copious.

'At the end of the Wanzenau we thought to shorten our route, and found ourselves in the midst of a morass. Night came on; and we only needed the storm which threatened to overtake us, to have had every reason for being fully convinced of the love and constancy of our princesses*.

'Meanwhile, the scroll which I held constantly in my hand— fearful of losing it—was a talisman, which charmed away all the perils of the journey. And now?—Oh I dare not utter it—either you can guess it, or you will not believe it!

'At last we arrived, and our first thought, which had been our joy on the road, was the project soon to see you again.

'How delicious a sensation is the hope of seeing again those we love! And we, when our coddled heart is a little sorrowful, at once bring it medicine and say: Dear little heart, be quiet, you will not long be away from her you love; be quiet, dear little heart! Meanwhile we give it a chimera to play with, and then is it good and still as a child to whom the mother gives a doll instead of the apple which it must not eat.

'Enough, we are *not* here, and so you see you are wrong. You would not believe that the noisy gaiety of Strasburg would be

---

* An allusion doubtless intelligible to the person addressed, but I can make nothing of it.

disagreeable to me after the sweet country pleasures enjoyed with you. Never, Mamsell, did Strasburg seem so empty to me as now. I hope, indeed, it will be better when the remembrance of those charming hours is a little dimmed—when I no longer feel so vividly how good, how amiable my friend is. Yet ought I to forget that, or to wish it? No; I will rather retain a little sorrow and write to you frequently.

'And now many, many thanks and many sincere remembrances to your dear parents. To your dear sister many hundred . . . what I would so willingly give you again!'

A few days after his return, Herder underwent the operation previously alluded to. Goethe was constantly with him; but as he carefully concealed all his mystical studies, fearing to have them ridiculed, so one may suppose he concealed also the new passion which deliciously tormented him. In silence he occupied himself with Frederika, and carefully sketched plans for the new parsonage. He sent her books, and received from her a letter, which of course seemed priceless.

In November he was again at Sesenheim. Night had already set in when he arrived; his impatience would not suffer him to wait till morning, the more so as the landlord assured him the young ladies had only just gone home, where 'they expected some one'. He felt jealous of this expected friend; and he hastened to the parsonage. Great was his surprise to find them *not* surprised; greater still to hear Frederika whisper 'Did I not say so? Here he is!' Her loving heart had prophesied his coming, and had named the very day.

The next day was Sunday, and many guests were expected. Early in the morning Frederika proposed a walk with him, leaving her mother and sister to look after domestic preparations. Who shall describe that walk, wherein the youthful pair abandoned themselves without concealment to all the delightful nothings of commencing love? They talked over the expected pleasures of the day, and arranged how to be always together. She taught him several games; he taught her others; and underneath these innocent arrangements, Love serenely smiled. The church bell called them from their walk. To church they went, and listened—not very attentively—to the worthy pastor. Another kind of devotion made their hearts devout. He meditated on her charming qualities, and as his glance rested on her ruddy lips, he recalled the last time woman's lips had been pressed to his own; recalled the curse which the excited French girl had uttered, a curse which hitherto had acted like a spell.

This superstition not a little troubled him in games of forfeits, where kisses always form a large proportion ; and his presence of mind was often tried in the attempts to evade them ; the more so as many of the guests, suspecting the tender relation between him and Frederika, sportively took every occasion to make them kiss. She, with natural instinct, aided him in his evasions. The time came, however, when, carried away by the excitement of the dance and games, he felt the burning pressure of her lips crush the superstition in a

> Kiss, a long, long kiss
> Of youth and beauty gathered into one.

He returned to Strasburg, if not a formally betrothed, yet an accepted lover. As such the family and friends seem to have regarded him. Probably no betrothal took place, on account of his youth, and the necessity of obtaining his father's consent. His muse, lately silent, now found voice again, and several of the poems Frederika inspired are to be read in his published works*.

He had been sent to Strasburg to gain a doctor's degree. His Dissertation had been commenced just before this Sesenheim episode. But Shakespeare, Ossian, *Faust*, *Götz*, and, above all, Frederika, scattered his plans, and he followed the advice of friends to choose, instead of a Dissertation, a number of Theses, upon which to hold a disputation. His father would not hear of such a thing, but demanded a regular Dissertation. He chose, therefore, this theme, '*That it is the duty of every law-maker to establish a certain religious worship binding upon clergy and laity*'. A theme he supported by historical and philosophical arguments. The Dissertation was written in Latin, and sent to his father, who received it with pleasure. But the dean of the faculty would not receive it—either because its contents were paradoxical, or because it was not sufficiently erudite. In lieu thereof he was permitted to choose Theses for disputation. The Disputation was held on the 6th of August 1771, his opponent being Franz Lerse, who pressed him hard. A jovial *schmaus*, a real students' banquet, crowned this promotion of Dr. Goethe †.

---

* The whole have been reprinted in the *Sesenheimer Liederbuch;* and in VIEHOFF's *Goethe Erläutert.*

† There is some obscurity on this point. From a letter to Salzmann, it seems he only got a licentiate degree at this time. The doctorate he certainly had ; but *when* his diploma was prepared is not known.

He could find no time for visits to Sesenheim during this active preparation for his doctorate ; but he was not entirely separated from Frederika : her mother had come with both daughters to Strasburg, on a visit to a rich relative.   He had been for some time acquainted with this family, and had many opportunities of meeting his beloved.   The girls, who came in their Alsatian costume, found their cousins and friends dressed like French-women ; a contrast which greatly vexed Olivia, who felt 'like a maidservant' among these fashionable friends.   Her restless manners evidently made Goethe somewhat ashamed of her.   Frederika, on the other hand, though equally out of her element in this society, was more self-possessed, and perfectly contented so long as he was by her side.   There is in the *Autobiography* a significant phrase : this visit of the family is called a 'peculiar test of his love'.   And test it was, as every one must see who considers the relations in which the lovers stood.   He was the son of an important Frankfurt citizen, and held almost the position of a noble-man in relation to the poor pastor's daughter.   Indeed, the social disparity was so great, that many explain his not marrying Fred-erika on the ground of such a match being impossible,—'his father', it is said, 'would not have listened to such a thing for a moment'.   Love in nowise troubles itself about station, never asks 'what will the world say ?' but there is quite a different solicitude felt by Love when approaching Marriage.   In the first eagerness of passion, a prince may blindly pursue a peasant ; but when his love is gratified by return, when reflection reasserts its duties, then the prince will consider what in other minds will be the estimation of his mistress.   Men are very sensitive to the opinions of others on their mistresses and wives ; and Goethe's love must indeed have been put to the test, at seeing Frederika and her sister thus in glaring contrast with the society in which he moved.   In the groves of Sesenheim she was a wood-nymph ; but in Strasburg salons the wood-nymph seemed a peasant.   Who is there that has not experienced a similar destruction of illusion, in seeing an ad-mired person lose almost all charm in the change of environment?

Frederika laid her sweet commands on him one evening, and bade him entertain the company by reading *Hamlet* aloud.   He did so, to the great enjoyment of all, especially Frederika, 'who from time to time sighed deeply, and a passing colour tinged her cheeks'.   Was she thinking of poor Ophelia—placing herself in that forlorn position ?

> For Hamlet and the trifling of his favour,
> Hold it a fashion and a toy in blood !

She may have had some presentiment of her fate. The applause,
however, which her lover gained was proudly accepted by her,
'and in her graceful manner she did not deny herself the little
pride of having shone through him'.

It is quite certain that his passion gave him vague uneasiness.
'How happy is he', he writes, 'whose heart is light and free !
Courage urges us to confront difficulties and dangers, and only by
great labour are great joys obtained. That, perhaps, is the worst
I have to allege against love. They say it gives courage : never !
The heart that loves is weak. When it beats wildly in the bosom,
and tears fill our eyes, and we sit in an inconceivable rapture as
they flow—then, oh ! then, we are so weak, that flower-chains
bind us, not because they have the strength of any magic, but
because we tremble lest we break them'.

The mention of *Hamlet* leads us naturally into the society
where he sought oblivion, when Frederika quitted Strasburg.
Her departure, he confesses, was a *relief* to him. She herself
felt on leaving that the end of their romance was approaching.
He plunged into gaiety to drown tormenting thoughts. 'If you
could but see me', he wrote to Salzmann, after describing a dance
which had made him forget his fever : ' my whole being was sunk
in dancing. And yet could I but say : I am happy ; that would
be better than all. "Who is't can say I am at the worse?" says
Edgar (in *Lear*). That is some comfort, dear friend. My heart
is like a weathercock when a storm is rising, and the gusts are
changeable'. Some days later he wrote : 'All is not clear in my
soul. I am too curiously awake not to feel that I grasp at shadows.
And yet . . . To-morrow at seven my horse is saddled, and then
adieu !'

Besides striving to drown in gaiety these tormenting thoughts,
he also strove to divert them into channels of nobler activity ;
stimulated thereto by the Shakespearean fanaticism of his new
friend Lenz.

Reinhold Lenz, irrevocably forgotten as a poet, whom a vain
effort on the part of Gruppe has tried to bring once more into
public favour*, is not without interest to the student of German
literature during the *Sturm und Drang* period. He came to

---

* GRUPPE : *Reinhold Lenz Leben und Werke:* 1861.

Strasburg in 1770, accompanying two young noblemen as their tutor, and mingling with them in the best society of the place ; and, by means of Salzmann, was introduced to the Club. Although he had commenced by translating Pope's *Essay on Criticism*, he was, in the strictest sense of the word, one of the Shakespeare bigots, who held to the severest orthodoxy in Shakespeare as a first article of their creed, and who not only maintained the Shakespeare clowns to be incomparable, but strove to imitate them in their language. Many an entravagant jest, and many an earnest discussion served to vary the hours. It is not easy for us to imagine the effect which the revelation of such a mind as Shakespeare's must have produced on the young Germans. His colossal strength, profundity of thought, originality and audacity of language, his beauty, pathos, sublimity, wit, and wild overflowing humour, and his accuracy of observation as well as depth of insight into the mysteries of passion and character, were qualities which no false criticism, and, above all, no national taste, prevented Germans from appreciating. It was very different in France. There an established form of art, with which national pride was identified, and an established set of critical rules, upon which Taste securely rested, necessarily made Shakespeare appear like a Cyclops of Genius—a monster, though of superhuman proportions. Frenchmen could not help being shocked at many things in Shakespeare ; yet even those who were most outraged, were also most amazed at the pearls to be found upon the dunghill. In Germany the pearls alone were seen. French taste had been pitilessly ridiculed by Lessing. The French Tragedy had been contrasted with Shakespeare, and pronounced unworthy of comparison. To the Germans, therefore, Shakespeare was a standard borne by all who combated against France, and his greatness was recognized with something of wilful preference. The state of German literature also rendered his influence the more prodigious. Had Shakespeare been first revealed to *us* when Mr. Hayley was the great laureate of the age, we should have felt something of the eagerness with which the young and ardent minds of Germany received this greatest poet of all ages.

I am fortunately enabled, thanks to Otto Jahn, to give here a very interesting illustration of the enthusiasm with which these young men studied Shakespeare ; and among the new materials this Biography contains, perhaps nothing will be so welcome in

Reinhold Lenz

England. It is an oration prepared by Goethe for one of the
meetings of the Shakespeare-circle before mentioned. To hear the
youth of one-and-twenty thus eloquent on his great idol, lets us
intimately into the secret of his mental condition.

ORATION ON SHAKESPEARE.

'In my opinion, the noblest of our sentiments is the hope of
continuing to live, even when destiny seems to have carried us
back into the common lot of non-existence. This life, gentlemen,
is much too short for our souls ; the proof is, that every man, the
lowest as well as the highest, the most incapable as well as the
most meritorious, will be tired of anything sooner than of life, and
that no one reaches the goal towards which he set out ; for however long a man may be prosperous in his career, still at last, and
often when in sight of the hoped-for object, he falls into a grave,
which God knows who dug for him, and is reckoned as nothing.
Reckoned as nothing? I? who am everything to myself, since I
know things only through myself ! So cries every one who is
truly conscious of himself ; and makes great strides through this
life—a preparation for the unending course above. Each, it is
true, according to his measure. If one sets out with the sturdiest
walking pace, the other wears seven-leagued boots and outstrips
him ; two steps of the latter are equal to a day's journey of the
former. Be it as it may with him of the seven-leagued boots, this
diligent traveller remains our friend and our companion, while we
are amazed at the gigantic steps of the other and admire them,
follow his footsteps and measure them with our own.

'Let us up and be going, gentlemen ! To watch a solitary
march like this enlarges and animates our souls more than to stare
at the thousand footsteps of a royal procession. To-day we
honour the memory of the greatest traveller on this journey of life,
and thereby we are doing an honour to ourselves. When we know
how to appreciate a merit we have the germ of it within ourselves.
Do not expect that I should say much or methodically ; mental
calmness is no garment for a festival ; and as yet I have thought
little upon Shakespeare ; to have glimpses, and, in exalted passages,
to feel, is the utmost I have been able to obtain. The first page of
his that I read made me his for life : and when I had finished a
single play, I stood like one born blind, on whom a miraculous
hand bestows sight in a moment. I saw, I felt, in the most vivid
manner, that my existence was infinitely expanded, everything was

now unknown to me, and the unwonted light pained my eyes. By little and little I learned to see, and, thanks to my receptive genius, I continue vividly to feel what I have won. I did not hesitate for a moment about renouncing the classical drama. The unity of place seemed to me irksome as a prison, the unities of action and of time burthensome fetters to our imagination ; I sprang into the open air, and felt for the first time that I had hands and feet. And now that I see how much injury the men of rule did me in their dungeon, and how many free souls still crouch there, my heart would burst if I did not declare war against them, and did not seek daily to batter down their towers.

'The Greek drama, which the French took as their model, was both in its inward and outward character such, that it would be easier for a marquis to imitate Alcibiades than for Corneille to follow Sophocles. At first an *intermezzo* of divine worship, then a mode of political celebration, the tragedy presented to the people great isolated actions of their fathers with the pure simplicity of perfection ; it stirred thorough and great emotions in souls because it was itself thorough and great. And in what souls? Greek souls ! I cannot explain to myself what that expresses, but I feel it, and appeal for the sake of brevity to Homer and Sophocles, and Theocritus ; they have taught me to feel it.

'Now hereupon I immediately ask : Frenchman, what wilt thou do with the Greek armour ? it is too strong and too heavy for thee.

'Hence, also, French tragedies are parodies of themselves. How regularly everything goes forward, and how they are as like each other as shoes, and tiresome withal, especially in the fourth act,—all this, gentlemen, you know from experience, and I say nothing about it.

'Who it was that first thought of bringing great political actions on the stage I know not ; this is a subject which affords an opportunity to the amateur for a critical treatise. I doubt whether the honour of the invention belongs to Shakespeare ; it is enough that he brought this species of drama to the pitch which still remains the highest, for few eyes can reach it and thus it is scarcely to be hoped that any one will see beyond it or ascend above it. Shakpeare, my friend ! if thou wert yet amongst us, I could live nowhere but with thee ; how gladly would I play the subordinate character of a Pylades, if thou wert Orestes ; yes, rather than be a venerated highpriest in the temple of Delphos.

'I will break off, gentlemen, and write more to-morrow, for I am in a strain which, perhaps, is not so edifying to you as it is heartfelt by me.

'Shakespeare's dramas are a beautiful casket of rarities, in which the history of the world passes before our eyes on the invisible thread of time. His plots, to speak according to the ordinary style, are no plots, for his plays all turn upon the hidden point (which no philosopher has yet seen and defined), in which the peculiarity of our *ego*, the pretended freedom of our will, clashes with the necessary course of the *whole*. But our corrupt taste so beclouds our eyes, that we almost need a new creation to extricate us from this darkness.

'All French writers, and Germans infected with French taste, even Wieland, have in this matter, as in several others, done themselves little credit. Voltaire, who from the first made a profession of vilifying everything majestic, has here also shown himself a genuine Thersites. If I were Ulysses, his back should writhe under my sceptre. Most of these critics object especially to Shakespeare's characters. And I cry, nature, nature! nothing so natural as Shakespeare's men.

'There I have them all by the neck. Give me air that I may speak! He rivalled Prometheus, and formed his men feature by feature, only of *colossal size;* therein lies the reason that we do not recognize our brethren ; and then he animated them with the breath of *his* mind ; *he* speaks in all of them, and we perceive their relationship.

'And how shall our age form a judgment as to what is natural? Whence can we be supposed to know nature, we who, from youth upwards, feel everything within us, and see everything in others, laced up and decorated? I am often ashamed before Shakespeare, for it often happens that at the first glance I think to myself I should have done that differently ; but soon I perceive that I am a poor sinner, that nature prophesies through Shakespeare, and that my men are soap-bubbles blown from romantic fancies.

'And now to conclude,—though I have not yet begun. What noble philosophers have said of the world, applies also to Shakespeare ;—namely, that what we call evil is only the other side, and belongs as necessarily to its existence and to the Whole, as the torrid zone must burn and Lapland freeze, in order that there may be a temperate region. He leads us through the whole world, but we, enervated, inexperienced men, cry at every strange grasshopper that meets us : He will devour us.

' Up, gentlemen ! sound the alarm to all noble souls who are in the elysium of so-called good taste, where drowsy in tedious twilight they are half alive, half not alive, with passions in their hearts and no marrow in their bones ; and because they are not tired enough to sleep, and yet are too idle to be active, loiter and yawn away their shadowy life between myrtle and laurel bushes '.

In these accents we hear the voice of the youth who wrote *Götz with the Iron Hand.* If the reader turn to the *Autobiography* and see there what is said of Shakespeare, he will be able to appreciate what I meant in saying that the *tone* of the *Autobiography* is unlike the reality. The tone of this speech is that of the famous *Sturm und Drang* (storm and stress) period, which in after life became so very objectionable to him. How differently Schiller was affected by Shakespeare may be read in the following confession : ' When at an early age I first grew acquainted with this poet, I was indignant at his coldness—indignant with the insensibility which allowed him to jest and sport amidst the highest pathos. Led by my knowledge of more modern poets to seek the poet in his works ; to meet and sympathize with his heart ; to reflect with him over his object ; it was insufferable to me that this poet gave me nothing of himself. Many years had he my reverence—certainly my earnest study, before I could comprehend his individuality. I was not yet fit to comprehend nature at first hand '.

The enthusiasm for Shakespeare naturally incited Goethe to dramatic composition, and, besides *Götz* and *Faust* before mentioned, we find in his Notebook the commencement of a drama on *Julius Cæsar.*

Three forms rise up from out the many influences of Strasburg into distinct and memorable importance : Frederika ; Herder ; the Cathedral. An exquisite woman, a noble thinker, and a splendid monument, were his guides into the regions of Passion, Poetry, and Art. The influence of the Cathedral was great enough to make him write the little tractate on German architecture *D. M. Erwini à Steinbach;* the enthusiasm of which was so incomprehensible to him in after years, that he was with difficulty persuaded to reprint the tractate among his works. Do we not see here—as in so many other traits—how different the youth is from the child and man ?

How thoroughly he had entered into the spirit of Gothic architecture is indicated by the following anecdote. In company with some friends he was admiring the Strasburg Cathedral, when one remarked, 'What a pity it was not finished, and that there should be only one steeple'. Upon this he answered, 'It is a matter of equal regret to me to see this solitary steeple unfinished ; the four spiral staircases leave off too abruptly at the top ; they ought to have been surmounted by four light pinnacles, with a higher one rising in the centre instead of the clumsy mass'. Some one, turning round to him, asked him who told him *that ?* 'The tower itself', he answered ; 'I have studied it so long, so attentively, and with so much love, that at last it has confessed to me its open secret'. Whereupon his questioner informed him that the tower had spoken truly, and offered to show him the original sketches, which still existed among the archives.

Inasmuch as in England many professed admirers of architecture appear imperfectly acquainted with the revival of the taste for Gothic art, it may not be superfluous to call attention to the fact that Goethe was among the very first to recognize the peculiar beauty of that style, at a period when classical, or pseudo-classical, taste was everywhere dominant. It appears that he was in friendly correspondence with Sulpiz Boisserée, the artist who made the restored design of Cologne Cathedral ; from whom he doubtless learned much. And we see by the *Wahlverwandtschaften* that he had a portfolio of designs illustrative of the principle of the pointed style. This was in 1809, when scarcely any one thought of the Gothic ; long before Victor Hugo had written his *Notre Dame de Paris ;* long before Pugin and Ruskin had thrown their impassioned energy into this revival ; at a time when the church in Langham Place was thought beautiful, and the Temple Church was considered an eyesore.

And now he was to leave Strasburg,—to leave Frederika. Much as her presence had troubled him of late, in her absence he only thought of her fascinations. He had not ceased to love her, although he already felt she never would be his. He went to say adieu. 'Those were painful days, of which I remember nothing. When I held out my hand to her from my horse, the tears were in her eyes, and I felt sad at heart. As I rode along the footpath to Drusenheim a strange phantasy took hold of me. I saw in my mind's eye my own figure riding towards me, attired in a dress I had never worn—pike grey with gold lace. I shook off this phantasy, but eight years afterwards I found myself on the very road, going to visit Frederika, and that too in the very dress which

I had seen myself in, in this phantasm, although my wearing it was quite accidental'. The reader will probably be somewhat sceptical respecting the dress, and will suppose that this prophetic detail was afterwards transferred to the vision by the imagination of later years*.

And so farewell, Frederika, bright and exquisite vision of a poet's youth ! We love you, pity you, and think how differently *we* should have treated you ! We make pilgrimages to Sesenheim as to Vaucluse, and write legibly our names in the Visitors' Album, to testify so much. And we read, not without emotion, narratives such as that of the worthy philologist Näke, who in 1822 made the first pilgrimage†, thinking, as he went, of this enchanting Frederika (and somewhat also of a private Frederika of his own), examined every rood of the ground, dined meditatively at the inn (with a passing reflection that the bill was larger than he anticipated), took coffee with the pastor's successor ; and, with a sentiment touching in a philologist, bore away a sprig of the jessamine which in days gone by had been tended by the white hands of Frederika, and placed it in his pocket-book as an imperishable souvenir.

---

* The correspondence with the Frau von Stein contains a letter written by him a day or two after this visit, but, singularly enough, *no* mention of this coincidence.
† *Die Wahlfahrt nach Sesenheim.*

Sulpiz Boisserée

BOOK THE THIRD

1771 to 1775

CHAPTER I

DR. GOETHE'S RETURN

ON the 25th or 28th of August 1771, he quitted Strasburg. His way led through Mannheim ; and there he was first thrilled by the beauty of ancient masterpieces, some of which he saw in plaster cast. Whatever might be his predilection for Gothic Art, he could not view these casts without feeling himself in presence of an Art in its way also divine ; and his previous study of Lessing lent a peculiar interest to the Laocoon group, now before his eyes.

Passing on to Mainz, he fell in with a young wandering harpist, and invited the ragged minstrel to Frankfurt, promising him a public in the Fair and a lodging in his father's house. It was lucky that he thought of acquainting his mother with this invitation. Alarmed at its imprudence, she secured a lodging in the town, and so the boy wanted neither shelter nor patronage.

Rath Goethe was not a little proud of the young Doctor. He was also not a little disturbed by the young Doctor's manners ; and often shook his ancient respectable head at the opinions which exploded like bombshells in the midst of conventions. Doctoral gravity was but slightly attended to by this young hero of the *Sturm und Drang*. The revolutionary movement known by the title of the *Storm and Stress* was then about to astonish Germany, and to startle all conventions, by works such as Gerstenberg's *Ugolino*, Goethe's *Götz von Berlichingen*, and Klinger's *Sturm und Drang* (from whence the name). The wisdom and extravagance of that age united in one stream : the masterly criticisms of Lessing,—the enthusiasm for Shakespeare,—the mania for Ossian and the northern mythology,—the revival of ballad literature,—and imitations of Rousseau, all worked in one rebellious current against established authority. There was one universal shout for

Nature. With the young, Nature seemed to be a compound of volcanoes and moonlight ; her force explosion, her beauty sentiment. To be insurgent and sentimental, explosive and lachrymose, were the true signs of genius. Everything established was humdrum. Genius, abhorrent of humdrum, would neither spell correctly, nor write correctly, nor demean itself correctly. It would be *German*—lawless, rude, and natural. Lawless it was, and rude it was, but not natural, according to the nature of any reputable type.

It is not easy, in the pages of the *Autobiography*, to detect in Goethe an early leader of the *Sturm und Drang ;* but it is easy enough to detect this in other sources. Here is a glimpse, in a letter from Mayer of Lindau (one of the Strasburg set) to Salzmann, worth chapters of the *Autobiography* on such a point. ' *O Corydon, Corydon quæ te dementia cepit!* According to the chain in which our ideas are linked together, *Corydon* and *dementia* put me in mind of the extravagant Goethe. He is still at Frankfurt, is he not ?'

That such a youth, whose wildness made friends nickname him the 'bear' and the ' wolf', could have been wholly pleasing to his steady, formal father, is not to be expected. Yet the worthy sire was not a little proud of his son's attainments. The verses, essays, notes, and drawings which had accumulated during the residence in Strasburg were very gratifying to him. He began to arrange them with scrupulous neatness, hoping to see them shortly published. But the poet had a virtue, perhaps of all virtues the rarest in youthful writers,—a reluctance to appear in print. Seeing, as we daily see, the feverish alacrity with which men accede to that extremely imaginary request, 'request of friends', and dauntlessly rush into print,—seeing the obstinacy with which they cling to all they have written, and insist on what they have written being printed—Goethe's reluctance demands an explanation. And, if I may interpret according to my own experience, the explanation is, that his delight in composition was rather the pure delight of intellectual activity, than a delight in the result : delight, not in the *work*, but in the *working*. Thus, no sooner had he finished a poem than his interest in it began to fade ; and he passed on to another. Thus it was that he left so many works fragments, his interest having been exhausted before the whole was completed.

He had a small circle of literary friends to whom he communicated his productions, and this was publication enough for him.

We shall see him hereafter, in Weimar, writing solely for a circle of friends, and troubling himself scarcely at all about a public. It was necessary for him to occupy himself with some work which should absorb him, as *Götz* did at this time, for only in work could he forget the pain, almost remorse, which followed his renunciation of Frederika. If at Strasburg he had felt that an end was approaching to this sweet romance, at Frankfurt, among family connections, and with new prospects widening before him, he felt it still more. He wrote to her. Unhappily that letter is not preserved. It would have made clear much that is now conjectural. 'Frederika's answer', he says, 'to the letter in which I had bidden her adieu, tore my heart. I now, for the first time, became aware of her bereavement, and saw no possibility of alleviating it. She was ever in my thoughts ; I felt that she was wanting to me ; and, worst of all, I could not forgive myself ! Gretchen had been taken from me ; Annchen had left me ; but now, for the first time, I was guilty ; I had wounded, to its very depths, one of the most beautiful and tender of hearts. And that period of gloomy repentance, bereft of the love which had so invigorated me, was agonizing, insupportable. But man will live ; and hence I took a sincere interest in others, seeking to disentangle their embarrassments, and to unite those about to part, that they might not feel what I felt. Hence I got the name of the "Confidant", and also, on account of my wanderings, I was named the "Wanderer". Under the broad open sky, on the heights or in the valleys, in the fields and through the woods, my mind regained some of its calmness. I almost lived on the road, wandering between the mountains and the plains. Often I went, alone or in company, right through my native city as though I were a stranger in it, dining at one of the great inns in the High Street, and after dinner pursuing my way. I turned more than ever to the open world and to Nature ; there alone I found comfort. During my walks I sang to myself strange hymns and dithyrambs. One of these, the *Wanderer's Sturmlied*, still remains. I remember singing it aloud in an impassioned style amid a terrific storm. The burden of this rhapsody is that man of genius must walk resolutely through the storms of life, relying solely on himself', a burden which seems to give expression to what he then felt respecting his relation to Frederika.

Although we have no exact knowledge of the circumstances, from the height of which to judge his conduct, the question must be put, Why did he not marry Frederika? It is a question often raised, and as often sophistically answered. By one party he is angrily condemned; disingenuously absolved by another. But he himself acknowledged his fault. He himself never put forth any excuse. He does not hint at disparity of station, he does not say, there were objections from his parents. He makes *no* excuse, but confesses the wrong, and blames himself without sophistication. Yet the excuses he would not suggest, partisans have been eager to suggest for him. Some have sought far and wide in the gutters of scandal for materials of defence. One gets up a story about Frederika being seduced by a Catholic priest; whence it is argued that Goethe could not be expected to marry one so frail; whence also it follows, by way of counterblast, that it was *his* desertion which caused her fall*. The basis of fact on which this lie is reared (there is usually some basis, even for the wildest lies), is that Frederika brought up the orphan child of her sister Salome.

Let me endeavour, without sophistication, to state the real case, at least as far as the imperfect evidence admits of a judgment. It seems always to have been forgotten by the many writers who have discussed this topic, that our judgment is misled by the artistic charm which he has thrown over the narrative: we fail to separate the Fact from the Fiction; we read the poem he has made up from his early experience, and read it as if the poem were an unvarnished record of that experience. He has painted Frederika so charmingly; he has told the story of their simple youthful love with so much grace, and quiet emotion; he has made us believe so entirely in the Idyl, that our sympathies are rudely disturbed when we find the Idyl is not to end in a marriage.

But if we consider the case calmly, divesting it, as much as possible, of the illusive suggestions of romance, we may, perhaps, come to the conclusion, that it was, after all, only a 'love-affair' between a boy and a girl, a temporary fascination, such as often stirs the affections of youth, without deepening into serious thought of marriage. Doubtless the reader can from his or her own history rapidly recall such an experience; certainly the experience of their friends will supply such cases. If we read the story in this light all is clear. The boy and girl are fascinated by each other; they look into each other's eyes, and are happy; they walk together, talk together, and, when separated, think of each

---

* Strangely enough, although Goethe read the MS. in which Näke repeats this story, he takes no notice of it.

other. But they never think of marriage; or think of it vaguely as a remote contingency. Young love's dream is enough for them. They are pained at parting; perhaps all the more so, because they dimly feel that the awakening is at hand. But there is a sort of tacit understanding that marriage is not the issue to be looked for. Had any one hinted to either Goethe or Frederika that their passion was but a 'youthful stirring of the blood', and not an eternal union of souls, they would assuredly have resented it with emphatic denial. Yet so it was. Goethe soon consoled himself; and there is positive evidence that Frederika, shortly afterwards, allowed herself to be consoled by Lenz.

Such, after mature deliberation, I believe to have been the real story. When in old age Goethe, reviewing the pleasant dreams of youth, and weaving them into an artistic narrative, avowedly half fiction, came to that episode with Frederika, he thought of it as we all think of our early loves, with a mingled tenderness and pain; his imagination was kindled, and he turned his experience into a poem. But the fact thus idealized was a very ordinary fact; the story thus poetized was a very common story, and could be told by ninety out of every hundred students, who do *not* marry the idol of the last university term. That Goethe, with his affectionate sensitive nature, was for a time in love with Frederika, is possible. It is certain that whatever the agitation of his feelings, they were not *deeply* moved; she had laid no firm hold of his soul; there were none of those ties between them which grow stronger with advancing time.

No sooner had he made this decisively clear to himself, than he wrote to Frederika to tell her so. No woman can be given up without feeling pain, and probably Frederika's affections were far more deeply engaged than his were; nevertheless, in spite of the pain she doubtless felt, and pathetically expressed in her letter to him, we find her presently engaged in another 'love-affair', with the poet Lenz, which, though it ended in a breach, certainly went so far as the exchange of vows; and, accordingly to Lenz, the growth of the passion was rapid. 'It was with us both', he writes to his friend, 'as with Cæsar: *veni, vidi, vici*. Through unconscious causes grew our confidence—and now it is sworn, and indissoluble'. When, in after years, Goethe visited Frederika, she—having long given up Lenz,—whose madness must have made her rejoice in her escape—told him of Lenz having pretended to be in love with her, but omitted to say anything about her own reciprocity ; and she omitted this from motives which every woman will appreciate. But however obscure the story may be, it seems certain that at least for a short time she ·believed in and returned Lenz's passion*.

After this exposition of what I conceive to be the real case, it will be easy to answer the outcry of the sentimentalists against Goethe's 'faithlessness' and his 'cruel treatment of Frederika', without recurring to the excuses sometimes put forth, that to have been faithful to her he must have been faithless to his genius ; and that it was better one woman's heart should be broken (which it was *not*) than that the poet's experience should be narrowed within the small circle of domestic life. It is a mistake to speak of faithlessness at all. We may regret that he did not feel the serious affection which would have claimed her as a wife ; we may upbraid him for the thoughtlessness with which he encouraged the sentimental relation ; but he was perfectly right to draw back from an engagement which he felt his love was not strong enough properly to fulfil. It seems to me that he acted a more moral part in relinquishing her, than if he had swamped this lesser in a greater wrong, and escaped one breach of faith by a still greater breach of faith—a reluctant, because unloving, marriage. The thoughtlessness of youth, and the headlong impetus of passion, frequently throw people into rash engagements ; and in these cases the *formal* morality of the world, more careful of externals than of truth, declares it to be nobler for such rash engagements to be kept, even when the rashness is felt by the engaged, than that a man's honour should be stained by a withdrawal. The letter thus takes precedence of the spirit. To satisfy this prejudice a life is sacrificed. A miserable marriage rescues the honour ; and no one throws the burden of that misery upon the prejudice. I am not forgetting the necessity of being stringent against the common thoughtlessness of youth in forming such relations ; but I say that this thoughtlessness once having occurred, reprobate it as we may, the pain which a separation may bring had better be endured, than evaded by an unholy marriage, which cannot come to good.

Frederika herself must have felt so too, for never did a word of blame escape her ; and we shall see how affectionately she welcomed him, when they met after the lapse of years. This, however, does not absolve him from the blame of having thoughtlessly incurred the responsibility of her affection. That blame he

* For full details see GRUPPE : *Reinhold Lenz, Leben und Werke*, 1861, pp. 11, *sq.*

must bear. The reader will apportion it according as he estimates the excuses of temperament, and the common thoughtlessness of us all in such matters.

Although I think Goethe's conduct in this matter perfectly upright, and justifiable from a far more serious point of view than that of being faithful to his genius, I am not at all disposed to acquiesce in the assumption that marriage with Frederika would have crippled his genius by narrowing his sympathies. The cause of his relinquishing her was the want of a sufficiently powerful love ; and that also is his justification. Had he loved her enough to share a life with her, his experience of woman might have been less extensive, but it would assuredly have gained an element it wanted. It would have been deepened. He had experienced, and he could paint (no one better), the exquisite devotion of woman to man ; but he had scarcely ever felt the peculiar tenderness of man for woman, when that tenderness takes the form of vigilant protecting fondness. He knew little, and that not until late in life, of the subtle interweaving of habit with affection, which makes life saturated with love, and love itself become dignified through the serious aims of life. He knew little of the exquisite *companionship* of two souls striving in emulous spirit of longing rivalry to become better, to become wiser, teaching each other to soar. He knew little of this ; and the kiss he feared to press upon the loving lips of Frederika—the life of sympathy he refused to share with her—are wanting to the greatness of his works.

In such a mood as that which followed the rupture with Frederika, it is not wonderful if Frankfurt and the practice of law were odious to him. Nothing but hard work could do him good : and he worked hard. From the Herder Correspondence it appears that he read Greek writers with some eagerness, his letters being studded with citations from Plato, Homer, and Pindar. *Die griechen sind mein einzig Studium*, he says. We find him also working at *Götz von Berlichingen*. Gothic Art, a kindred subject, occupies him, and from thence, by an easy transition, he passes to the Bible to study it anew. The results of this study are seen in two little tractates published in 1773, one called *Brief des Pastor's zu * * * an den neuen Pastor zu * * **; the other, *Zwei wichtige bisher unerörtete biblische Fragen, zum erstenmal gründlich beantwortet von einem Landgeistlichen in Schwaben.* The influence of Fräulein von Klettenberg is traceable in the religious sentiment of these works; while his own affectionate nature speaks in the tolerance preached. Of the two biblical questions, one goes to prove that it was not the ten commandments which stood on the tables of Moses, but ten laws of the Israelitish-Jehovah covenant. The second is an answer, by no means clear, to the question: 'What is it to speak with tongues?' which he explains as a 'speech of the Spirit, more than pantomime and yet inarticulate'.

Among the friends to whom he communicated his plans and ideas, two must be named: Schlosser, whom we have seen at Leipsic, and Merck, whose influence was very beneficial. The portrait sketched of this remarkable man in the *Autobiography* gives a very incorrect idea to those who cannot control what is there said by other direct evidence; especially calculated to mislead is the nickname 'Mephistopheles Merck', for whatever tendency to sarcasm Merck may have indulged in, it is quite clear that his admiration was generous and warm, his influence over Goethe being uniformly one of friendly incitement, or of friendly warning.

Johann Heinrich Merck was born in Darmstadt, 1741. The son of an apothecary, he raised himself to the companionship of princes. He was at this time *Kriegsrath* in Darmstadt, and in correspondence with most of the notabilities of the day; among them Herder, who had the highest opinion of his abilities, and the most jealous anxiety to retain his friendship, fearing lest the new friendship with Goethe should step between them; as, indeed, eventually it did. Merck, whose significance in the history of German literature is considerable, and whose correspondence shows him to have critically influenced men greatly his superiors in production, was one of the most zealous propagators of English literature. He began by translating Hutcheson *On Beauty*, Addison's *Cato*, and Shaw's *Travels in the Levant*. The Shakespeare neophytes found him prepared to share their enthusiasm; and when, in 1772, he persuaded Schlosser to undertake the editing of the *Frankfurter Gelehrten Anzeigen*, and to make it the Moniteur of the *Sturm und Drang* party, his own contributions were numerous and valuable*. His official duties do not seem to have pressed very heavily upon him, for he made frequent excursions, and seems to have stayed some time at Frankfurt. The friendship between him and Goethe was warm. He saw more deeply than Herder into this singular genius, and on many critical

---

* See for further information the work of STAHR: *Johann Heinrich Merck. Ein Denkmal.*

occasions we find him always manifesting a clear insight, and a real regard.

The *Frankfurter Gelehrten Anzeigen* was a point of reunion, bringing Goethe into relation with many persons of ability. It also afforded him an opportunity of exercising himself in criticism. Thirty-five of the articles he wrote for this journal have been collected into his works, where the curious student will seek them. In these studies the time flew swiftly. He had recommenced horse and sword exercise, and Klopstock having made skating illustrious, it soon became an amusement of which he was never tired; all day long and deep into the night he was to be seen wheeling along; and as the full moon rose above the clouds over the wide nocturnal fields of ice, and the night wind rushed at his face, and the echo of his movements came with ghostly sound upon his ear, he seemed to be in Ossian's world. Indoors there were studies and music. 'Will you ask my violoncello master', he writes to Salzmann, 'if he still has the sonatas for two basses, which I played with him, and if so, send them to me as quickly as convenient? I practise this art somewhat more earnestly than before. As to my other occupations, you will have gathered from my drama (*Götz*), that the purposes of my soul are becoming more earnest'.

It has before been hinted that *Sturm und Drang*, as it manifested itself in the mind and bearing of the young doctor, was but very moderately agreeable to the old Rath Goethe; and whatever sympathy we may feel with the poet, yet, as we are all parents, or hope to be, let us not permit our sympathy to become injustice; let us admit that the old Rath had considerable cause for parental uneasiness, and let us follow the son to Wetzlar without flinging any hard words at his father.

CHAPTER II

'GÖTZ VON BERLICHINGEN'

ALTHOUGH *Götz* was not published until the summer of 1773, it was written in the winter of 1771, or, to speak more accurately, the first of the three versions into which the work was shaped, was written at this time. We must bear in mind that there are three versions: the first is entitled the *Geschichte Gott-*

friedens von Berlichingen mit der eisernen Hand, dramatisirt*, which was not published until very many years afterwards. The second is entitled *Götz von Berlichingen, Schauspiel*†, and is the form in which the work was *originally* published. The third is an adaptation of this second piece, with a view to stage representation, which adaptation was made with Schiller during the efforts to create a national stage at Weimar‡.

The first form is the one I most admire, and the one which, biographically, has most interest. While he is on his way to Wetzlar we will open his portfolio, and take out this manuscript for closer scrutiny, instead of waiting till he publishes the second version. From a letter to Salzmann we learn that it was written in November 1771. 'My whole genius is given to an undertaking which makes me forget Shakespeare, Homer, everything ; I am dramatizing the history of the noblest of Germans, to rescue the memory of a brave man ; and the labour it costs me kills time here, which is at present so necessary for me'. He gives the following account of its composition, in the *Autobiography :* 'An unceasing interest in Shakespeare's works had so expanded my mind, that the narrow compass of the stage and the short time allotted to a representation, seemed to me insufficient for the development of an important idea. The life of *Götz von Berlichingen*, written by himself, suggested the historic mode of treatment ; and my imagination took so wide a sweep, that my dramatic construction also went beyond all theatrical limits in seeking more and more to approach life. I had, as I proceeded, talked the matter over with my sister, who was interested heart and soul in such subjects ; and I so often renewed this conversation, without taking any steps towards beginning the work, that at last she impatiently and urgently entreated me not to be always talking, but, once for all, to set down upon paper that which must be so distinct before my mind. Moved by this impulse, I began one morning to write, without having made any previous sketch or plan. I wrote the first scenes, and in the evening they were read aloud to Cornelia. She greatly applauded them, but doubted whether I should go on so ; nay, she even expressed a decided unbelief in my perseverance. This only incited me the more ; I wrote on the next day, and also on the third. Hope increased with the daily communications, and step by step everything gained more life as I mastered the con-

---

* *Werke*, vol. xxxiv, of the edition of 1840.   † *Werke*, vol. ix.
‡ *Werke*, vol. xxxv.

ception. Thus I kept on, without interruption, looking neither backwards nor forwards, neither to the right nor to the left; and in about six weeks I had the pleasure of seeing the manuscript stitched'.

Gottfried von Berlichingen, surnamed of the Iron Hand, was a distinguished predatory Burgrave of the sixteenth century*; one of the last remains of a turbulent, lawless race of feudal barons, whose personal prowess often lent the lustre of romance to acts of brigandage. Gottfried with the Iron Hand was a worthy type of the class. His loyalty was as unshakable as his courage. Whatever his revered emperor thought fit to do, he thought right to be done. Below the emperor he acknowledged no lord. With his fellow barons he waged continual war. Against the Bishop of Bamberg, especially, he was frequently in arms; no sooner was a peace arranged with him, than the Bishop of Mainz was attacked. War was his element. With something of Robin Hood chivalry, he was found on the side of the weak and persecuted; unless when the Kaiser called for his arm, or unless when tempted by a little private pillage on his own account. To his strong arm the persecuted looked for protection. A tailor earns two hundred florins by shooting at a mark; the sum is withheld; he goes to Götz with a piteous tale; instantly the Iron Hand clutches the recalcitrant debtors travelling that way, and makes them pay the two hundred florins.

It was a tempting subject for a poet of the eighteenth century, this bold, chivalrous robber, struggling single-handed against the advancing power of civilization, this lawless chieftain making a hopeless stand against the Law, and striving to perpetuate the feudal spirit. Peculiarly interesting to the poet was the consecration of *individual* greatness in Götz. Here was a man great not by privilege, but by Nature; his superiority given him by no tradition, by no court favour, but by favour only of his own strong arm and indomitable spirit. And was not the struggle of the whole eighteenth century a struggle for the recognition of individual worth, of Rights against Privileges, of Liberty against Tradition? Such also was the struggle of the sixteenth century. The Reformation was to Religion what the Revolution was to Politics: a stand against the tyranny of Tradition—a battle for the rights of *individual* liberty of thought and action, against the absolute prescriptions of privileged classes.

---

* Scott by an oversight makes him flourish in the fifteenth century. He was born in 1482, and thus reached man's estate with the opening of the sixteenth century.

In the *Chronicle of Götz von Berlichingen* his deeds are recorded by himself with unaffected dignity. There Goethe found materials, such as Shakespeare found in Holingshed and Saxo-Grammaticus ; and used them in the same free spirit. He has dramatized the *chronicle*—made it live and move before us ; but he has dramatized a chronicle, not written a drama. This distinction is drawn for a reason which will presently appear.

Viehoff has pointed out the use which has been made of the chronicle, and the various elements which have been added from the poet's own invention. The English reader cannot be expected to feel the same interest in such details as the German reader does ; it is enough therefore to refer the curious to the passage *, and only cite the characters invented by Goethe ; these are Adelheid, the voluptuous, fascinating demon ; Elizabeth, the noble wife, in whom Goethe's mother saw herself; Maria, a reminiscence of Frederika ; Georg, Franz Lerse, Weislingen, and the Gypsies. The death of Götz is also new. The tower mentioned by Goethe is still extant at Heilbronn, under the name of Götzen's Thurm. The rest, including the garden, is the creation of the poet. Götz was confined for only one night in that tower. His death, which according to the play must have happened in 1525, did not occur till 1562, when the burly old knight, upwards of eighty, died at his castle of Horberg, at peace with all men, and in perfect freedom. His tomb may be seen at the monastery of Schönthal †.

Götz was a dramatic chronicle, not a drama. It should never have been called a drama, but left in its original shape with its original title. This would have prevented much confusion ; especially with reference to Shakespeare, and his form of dramatic composition. While no one can mistake the *influence* of Shakespeare in this work, there is great laxity of language in calling it Shakespearean ; a laxity common enough, but not admissible. Critics are judges who rely on precedents with the rigour of judges on the bench. They pronounce according to precedent. That indeed is their office. No sooner has an original work made its appearance, than one of these two courses is invariably pursued : it is rejected by the critics because it does not range itself under any acknowledged class, and thus is branded because

---

* *Goethe's Leben*, vol. II, pp. 77, 79.

† Count Joseph Berlichingen, the present representative of the family, has recently published a *Life of Götz*, but it has not reached me.

it is not an imitation ; or it is quietly classified under some acknowledged head. The latter was the case with *Götz von
Berlichingen*. Because it set the unities at defiance, and placed
the people beside the nobles on the scene ; because instead of
declaiming, as in French tragedy, the persons spoke dramatically
to the purpose ; because, in short, it did *not* range under the
acknowledged type of French tragedy, it was supposed to range
under the Shakespearean type—the only accepted antagonist to
the French.

Is it like *Othello ?* Is it like *Macbeth ?* Is it like *Richard III,
Henry IV, King John; Julius Cæsar*, or any one unquestioned
play by Shakespeare? Unless the words 'Shakespearean style' are
meaningless people must mean that *Götz* resembles Shakespeare's
plays in the structure and organization of plot, in the delineation
of character, and in the tone of dialogue ; yet a cursory review of
the play will convince any one that in all these respects it is
singularly *unlike* Shakespeare's plays.

In *construction* it differs from Shakespeare, first, as intended to
represent an *epoch* rather than a *story;* secondly, as taking the
licences of narrative art, instead of keeping the stage always in
view, and submitting to the stern necessities of theatrical representation ; thirdly, as wanting in that central unity round which all
the persons and events are grouped, so as to form a work of art.
It is a succession of scenes ; a story of episodes.

In the presentation of character the work is no less un-Shake-
spearean. Our national bigotry, indeed, assumes that every
masterly portraiture of character is Shakespearean ; an assumption
which can hardly maintain itself in the presence of Sophocles,
Racine, and Goethe. Each poet has a manner of his own, and
Shakespeare's manner is assuredly not visible in *Götz von Berlichingen*. The characters move before us with singular distinctness
in their external characteristics, but they do not, as in Shakespeare,
involuntarily betray the inmost secret of their being. We know
them by their language and their acts ; we do not know their
thoughts, their self-sophistications, their involved and perplexed
motives, partially obscured even to themselves, and seen by us in
the cross lights which break athwart their passionate utterances.
To take a decisive example : Weislingen is at once ambitious and
irresolute, well-meaning and weak *. The voice of friendship

---

* In his vacillation, Goethe meant to stigmatize his own weakness with regard to
Frederika, as he tells us in the *Wahrheit und Dichtung*.

awakens remorse in him, and forces him to accept the proffered hand of Götz. He swears never again to enter the bishop's palace. But, easily seduced by noble thoughts, he is afterwards seduced as easily by vanity: tempted he falls, turns once more against his noble friend, and dies betrayed and poisoned by the wife to whom he has sacrificed all—dies unpitied by others, despicable to himself. This vacillation is truthful, but not truth-fully represented. We who only see the conduct cannot explain it. We stand before an enigma, as in real life; not before a character such as Art enables us to see, and see through. It is not the business of Art to present enigmas; and Shakespeare, in his strongest, happiest moods, contrives to let us see into the wavering depths of the *souls*, while we follow the *actions* of his characters. Contrast Weislingen with such vacillating characters as Richard II, King John, or Hamlet. The difference is not of degree, but of kind.

Nor is the language Shakespearean. It is powerful, picturesque, clear, dramatic; but it is not pregnant with thought, obscured in utterance, and heavy with that superfœtation of ideas, which is a characteristic and often a fault in Shakespeare. It has not his redundancy, and prodigal imagery. Indeed it is very singular, and as the production of a boy especially so, in the absence of all rhetorical amplification, and of all delight in imagery for its own sake.

It was the first-born of the Romantic School, or rather of the tendency from which that school issued; and its influence has been wide-spread. It gave the impulse and direction to Scott's historical genius, which has altered our conceptions of the past, and given new life to history. It made the Feudal Ages a subject of eager and almost universal interest. It decided the fate of French tragedy in German literature. But its influence on dramatic art has been, I think more injurious than beneficial, and mainly because the distinction between a dramatized chronicle and a drama has been lost sight of.

This injurious influence is traceable in the excessive importance it has given to local colour, and the intermingling of the historic with the dramatic element. Any one at all acquainted with the productions of the Romantic School in Germany or France will understand this. Goethe's object not being to write a drama, but to dramatize a picture of the times, local colour was of primary importance; and because he made it so attractive, others have imitated him in departments where it is needless. Nay, critics are so persuaded of its importance, that they strain every phrase to show us that Shakespeare was also a great painter of times ; forgetting that local colouring is an appeal to a critical and learned audience, not an appeal to the heart and imagination. It is history, not drama. Macbeth, in a bag-wig, with a small sword at his side, made audiences tremble at the appalling ruin of a mind entangled in a crime. The corrected costume would not make that tragedy more appalling, had we not now grown so critical that we demand historical 'accuracy', where, in the true dramatic age, they only demanded passion. The merest glance at our own dramatic literature will suffice to show the preponderating (and misplaced) influence of History, in the treatment, no less than in the subjects chosen.

Götz, as a picture of the times, is an animated and successful work ; but the eighteenth century is on more than one occasion rudely thrust into the sixteenth ; and on this ground Hegel denies its claim to the highest originality. 'An original work appears as the creation of *one* mind, which, admitting of no external influence, fuses the whole work in one mould, as the events therein exhibited were fused. If it contains scenes and motives which do not naturally evolve themselves from the original materials, but are brought together from far and wide, then the internal unity becomes necessarily destroyed, and these scenes betray the author's subjectivity. For example, Goethe's *Götz* has been greatly lauded for originality, nor can we deny that he has therein boldly trampled under foot all the rules and theories which were then accepted : but the execution is notwithstanding not thoroughly original. One may detect in it the poverty of youth. Several traits, and even scenes, instead of being evolved from the real subject, are taken from the current topics of the day. The scene, for example, between Götz and Brother Martin, which is an allusion to Luther, contains notions gathered from the controversies of Goethe's own day, when—especially in Germany—people were pitying the monks because they drank no wine, and because they had passed the vows of chastity and obedience. Martin, on the other hand, is enthusiastic in his admiration of Götz, and his knightly career : "When you return back laden with spoils, and say, such a one I struck from his horse ere he could discharge his piece ; such another I overthrew, horse and man ; and then, returning to your castle, you find your wife." . . . Here Martin wipes his eye and pledges the wife of Götz. Not so—not with such thoughts did Luther begin, but with quite another religious conviction !'

'In a similar style', Hegel continues, 'Basedow's pedagogy is introduced. Children, it was said, learn much that is foolish and unintelligible to them; and the real method was to make them learn objects, not names. Karl thus speaks to his father just as he would have spoken in Goethe's time from parrot-memory: "Jaxt-hausen is a village and castle upon the Jaxt, which has been the property and heritage for two hundred years of the Lords of Berlichingen". "Do you know the Lord of Berlichingen?" asks Götz; the child stares at him, and from pure erudition, knows not his own father. Götz declares that *he* knew every pass, pathway, and ford about the place, before he knew the name of village, castle, or river '*.

Considered with reference to the age in which it was produced, *Götz von Berlichingen* is a marvellous work: a work of daring power, of vigour, of originality; a work to form an epoch in the annals of letters. Those who now read it as the work of the great Goethe may be somewhat disappointed; but at the time of its appearance no such 'magnificent monster' had startled the pedantries and proprieties of the schools ;—'a piece', said the critic in the *Teutsche Mercur* of the day, 'wherein the three unities are shamefully outraged, and which is neither a tragedy nor a comedy, and is, notwithstanding, the most beautiful, the most captivating monstrosity'.

The breathless rapidity of movement renders a first reading too hurried for proper enjoyment; but on recurring to the briefly indicated scenes, we are amazed at their fullness of life. How marvellous, for example, is that opening scene of the fifth act (removed from the second version), where Adelheid is in the gipsies' tent! Amid the falling snow shines the lurid gleam of the gipsy fire, around which move dusky figures; and this magnificent creature stands shuddering as she finds herself in the company of an old crone who tells her fortune, while a wild-eyed boy gazes ardently on her and alarms her with his terrible admiration; the whole scene *lives*, yet the touches which call it into life are briefer than in any other work I can remember.

* HEGEL's *Vorlesungen über die Æsthetik*, I, p. 382,

CHAPTER III

WETZLAR

IN the spring of 1772 he arrived at Wetzlar with *Götz* in his
portfolio, and in his head many wild, unruly thoughts. A
passage in the *Autobiography* amusingly illustrates his conception
of the task he had undertaken in choosing to inform the world of
his early history. Remember that at Wetzlar he fell in love with
Charlotte, and lived through the experience which was fused into
Werther, and you will smile as you hear him say: 'What occurred
to me at Wetzlar is of no great importance, but it may receive a
higher interest if the reader will allow me to give a cursory glance
at the history of the Imperial Chamber, in order to present to his
mind the unfavourable moment at which I arrived'. This it is to
write autobiography when one has outlived almost the memories
of youth, and lost sympathy with many of its agitations. At the
time he was in Wetzlar he would have looked strangely on any
one who ventured to tell him that the history of the Imperial
Chamber was worth a smile from Charlotte; but at the time of
writing his meagre account of Wetzlar, he had, perhaps, some
difficulty in remembering what Charlotte's smiles were like. The
biographer has a difficult task to make any coherent story out of
this episode*.

In Wetzlar there were two buildings interesting above all others
to us—the Imperial Court of Justice, and *Das teutsche Haus*.
The Imperial Court was a Court of Appeal for the whole empire,
a sort of German Chancery. Imagine a *German* Chancery! In
no country does Chancery move with railway speed, and in
Germany even the railways are slow. Such a chaotic accumulation
of business as this Wetzlar *Kammer-Gericht* presented, was
perhaps never seen before. Twenty thousand cases lay undecided
on Goethe's arrival, and there were but seventeen lawyers to
dispose of them. About sixty was the utmost they could get
through in a year, and every year brought more than double that

---

* Fortunately, during the very months in which I was rewriting this work, there
appeared an invaluable record in the shape of the correspondence between Goethe and
Kestner, so often alluded to by literary historians, but so imperfectly known. (*Goethe
und Werther. Briefe Goethe's, meistens aus seiner Jugendzeit.* Herausgegeben von
A. Kestner: 1854.) This book, which is very much in need of an editor, is one of the
richest sources to which access has been had for a right understanding of Goethe's
youth; and it completes the series of corroborative evidence by which to control the
Autobiography.

number to swell the heap. Some cases had lingered through a century and a half, and still remained far from a decision. This was not a place to impress the sincere and eminently practical mind of Goethe with a high idea of Jurisprudence.

Das teutsche Haus was one of the remnants of the ancient institution of the *Teutsche Ritter*, or Teutonic Order of Knighthood, celebrated in German mediæval history. The student is familiar with the black armour and white mantles of these warrior-priests, who fought with the zeal of missionaries and the terrible valour of knights, conquering for themselves a large territory, and still greater influence. But it fared with them as with the knights of other Orders. Their strength lay in their zeal ; their zeal abated with success. Years brought them increasing wealth, but the spiritual wealth and glory of their cause departed. They became what all corporations inevitably become ; and at the time now written of they were reduced to a level with the knights of Malta. The Order still possessed property in various parts of Germany, and in certain towns there was a sort of steward's house, where rents were collected and the business of the Order trans-acted ; this was uniformly styled *das teutsche Haus*. There was such a one in Wetzlar ; and the *Amtmann*, or steward, who had superintendence over it, was a certain Herr Buff, on whom the reader is requested to fix his eye, not for any attractiveness of Herr Buff, intrinsically considered, but for the sake of his eldest daughter, Charlotte. She is the heroine of this Wetzlar episode.

Nor was this house the only echo of the ancient Ritterthum in Wetzlar. Goethe, on his arrival, found there another, and more consciously burlesque parody, in the shape of a Round Table and its Knights, bearing such names as St. Amand the Opiniative, Eustace the Prudent, Lubormirsky the Combative, and so forth. It was founded by August Friedrich von Goué, secretary to the Brunswick Embassy, of whom we shall hear more : a wild and whimsical fellow, not without a streak of genius, who drank him-self to death. He bore the title of Ritter Coucy, and christened Goethe ' *Götz von Berlichingen der Redliche*—Götz the Honest '. In an imitation of *Werther* which Goué wrote*, a scene introduces this Round Table at one of its banquets at the Tavern ; a knight sings a French song, whereupon Götz exclaims, ' Thou, a German Ritter, and singest foreign songs ! ' Another knight asks Götz, ' How far have you advanced with the monument which you are to

* *Masuren, oder der junge Werther. Ein Trauerspiel aus dem Illyrischen.* 1775.

erect to your ancestor?' Götz replies, 'It goes quietly forward.
Methinks it will be a slap in the face to pedants and the public∗'.

Of this Round Table and its buffooneries, Goethe has merely
told us that he entered heartily into the fun at first, but soon
wearying of it, relapsed into his melancholy fits. 'I have made
many acquaintances', says Werther, 'but have found no society. I
know not what there is about me so attractive that people seek my
company with so much ardour. They hang about me, though I
cannot walk two steps in their path'. A description of him,
written by Kestner at this period, is very interesting, as it gives us
faithfully the impression he produced on his acquaintances before
celebrity had thrown its halo round his head, and dazzled the
perceptions of his admirers :

'In the spring there came here a certain Goethe, by trade† a
Doctor Juris, twenty-three years old, only son of a very rich
father ; in order—this was his father's intention—that he might
get some experience in *praxi*, but according to his own intention,
that he might study Homer, Pindar, etc., and whatever else his
genius, his manner of thinking, and his heart might suggest to
him.

'At the very first the *beaux esprits* here announced him to the
public as a colleague, and as a collaborator in the new Frankfurt
Gelehrte Zeitung, parenthetically also as a philosopher, and gave
themselves trouble to become intimate with him. As I do not
belong to this class of people, or rather am not so much in general
society, I did not know Goethe until later, and quite by accident.
One of the most distinguished of our *beaux esprits,* the Secretary
of Legation Gotter, persuaded me one day to go with him to the
village of Garbenheim—a common walk. There I found him on
the grass, under a tree, lying on his back, while he talked to some
persons standing round him—an epicurean philosopher (von Goué,
a great genius), a stoic philosopher (von Kielmansegge), and a
hybrid between the two (Dr. König)—and thoroughly enjoyed
himself. He was afterwards glad that I had made his acquaintance
under such circumstances. Many things were talked of—some of
them very interesting. This time, however, I formed no other
judgment concerning him than that he was no ordinary man. You
know that I do not judge hastily. I found at once that he had

---

∗ *Ein Stück das Meister und Gesellen auf's Maul schlägt.* Cited by APPELL :
Werther und seine Zeit, p. 38.
† *Seiner Handthierung nach.* The word is old German, and now fallen out of use,
although the verb *handthieren* is still occasionally used.

genius, and a lively imagination ; but this was not enough to make me estimate him highly.

'Before I proceed further, I must attempt a description of him, as I have since learned to know him better. He has a great deal of talent, is a true genius and a man of character ; possesses an extraordinarily vivid imagination, and hence generally expresses himself in images and similes. He often says, himself, that he always speaks figuratively, and can never express himself literally ; but that when he is older he hopes to think and say the thought itself as it really is. He is ardent in all his affections, and yet has often great power over himself. His manner of thinking is noble : he is so free from prejudices that he acts as it seems good to him, without troubling himself whether it will please others, whether it is the fashion, whether conventionalism allows it. All constraint is odious to him.

'He is fond of children, and can occupy himself with them very much. He is *bizarre*, and there are several things in his manners and outward bearing which might make him disagreeable. But with children, women, and many others, he is nevertheless a favourite. He has a great respect for the female sex. In *principiis* he is not yet fixed, and is still striving after a sure system. To say something of this, he has a high opinion of Rousseau, but is not a blind worshipper of him. He is not what is called orthodox. Still this is not out of pride or caprice, or for the sake of making himself a *rôle*. On certain important subjects he opens himself to few, and does not willingly disturb the contentment of others in their own ideas. It is true he hates scepticism, strives after truth and after conviction on certain main points, and even believes that he is already convinced as to the weightiest ; but as far as I have observed, he is not yet so. He does not go to church or to the sacrament, and prays seldom. For, says he, I am not hypocrite enough for that. Sometimes he seems in repose with regard to certain subjects, sometimes just the contrary. He venerates the Christian religion, but not in the form in which it is presented by our theologians. He believes in a future life, in a better state of existence. He strives after truth, yet values the feeling of truth more than the demonstration. He has already done much, and has many acquirements, much reading ; but he has thought and reasoned still more. He has occupied himself chiefly with the *belles lettres* and the fine arts, or rather with all sorts of knowledge, except that which wins bread '.

On the margin of this rough draft, Kestner adds : 'I wished to describe him, but it would be too long a business, for there is much to be said about him. In one word, *he is a very remarkable man*'.

Further on : 'I should never have done, if I attempted to describe him fully'.

The Gotter referred to at the opening of this letter was a young man of considerable culture, with whom Goethe became intimate over renewed discussions on art and criticism. 'The opinions of the ancients', he says, 'on these important topics I had studied by fits and starts for some years. Aristotle, Cicero, Quinctilian, Longinus—none were neglected, but they did not help me, for they presupposed an experience which I needed. They introduced me to a world infinitely rich in works of art ; they unfolded the merits of great poets and orators, and convinced me that *a vast abundance of objects must lie before us ere we can think upon them*—that we must accomplish something, nay fail in something, before we can learn our own capacities and those of others. My knowledge of much that was good in ancient literature was merely that of a schoolboy, and by no means vivid. The most splendid orators, it was apparent, had *formed themselves in life*, and we could never speak of them as artists without at the same time mentioning their personal peculiarities. With the poets this was perhaps less the case : but everywhere nature and art came in contact only through life. And thus the result of all my investigations was my old resolution to study Nature, and to allow her to guide me in loving imitation'.

Properly to appreciate this passage we must recall the almost universal tendency of the Germans to construct poems in conformity with definite rules, making the poet but a development of the critic. Lessing nobly avowed that he owed all his success to his critical sagacity ; Schiller, it is notorious, hampered his genius by fixing on his Pegasus the leaden wings of Kant's philosophy ; and Klopstock himself erred in too much criticism. Goethe was the last man to disdain the rich experience of centuries, the last man to imagine that ignorance was an advantageous basis for a poet to stand upon, but he was too thoroughly an artist not to perceive the insufficiency of abstract theories in the production of a work of art which should be the expression of real experience.

In conjunction with Gotter he translated Goldsmith's *Deserted Village*, though he speaks slightingly of his share in it. Through

Gotter's representations he was also persuaded to publish some little poems in Boie's *Annual*. 'I thus* came into contact with those', he says, 'who, united by youth and talent, afterwards effected so much in various ways. Bürger, Voss, Hölty, the two Counts Stolberg, and several others grouped round Klopstock; and in this poetical circle, which extended itself more and more, there was developed a tendency which I know not exactly how to name. One might call it that need of independence which always arises in times of peace—that is to say precisely when, properly speaking, one is not dependent. In war we bear restraints of force as well as we can; we are physically, but not morally wounded; the restraint disgraces no one; it is no shame to serve the time; we grow accustomed to suffering both from foes and friends; we have wishes rather than definite views. On the contrary, in times of peace our love of freedom becomes more and more prominent, and the greater our freedom, the more we wish for it; we will tolerate nothing above us; we will not be restrained; no one shall be restrained! This tender, sometimes morbid feeling, assumes in noble souls the form of justice: such a spirit then manifested itself everywhere; and because but few were oppressed, it was wished to free these from occasional oppression. And thus arose a certain moral contest between individuals and the government, which, however laudable its origin, led to unhappy results. Voltaire, reverenced for his conduct in the affair of Calais, had excited great attention; and in Germany Lavater's proceedings against the *Landvogt* (sheriff of the province) had perhaps been even more striking. The time was approaching when dramatists and novelists sought their villains among ministers and official persons; hence arose a world, half real, half imaginary, of action and reaction, in which the most violent accusations and instigations were made by writers of periodical journals, under the garb of justice, who produced the more powerful effect because they made the public imagine that it was itself the tribunal—*a foolish notion, as no public has an executive power;* and in Germany, dismembered as it was, public opinion neither benefited nor injured any one'.

It was a period of deep unrest in Europe: the travail of the French Revolution. In Germany the spirit of the Revolution issued

---

* Düntzer in his *Studien* has thrown doubts on this connexion with the Göttingen school having originated in Wetzlar. But the point is of no importance, and Goethe's own version is left undisturbed in the text.

from the study and the lecture hall ; it was a literary and philosophic insurrection, with Lessing, Klopstock, Kant, Herder, and
Goethe for leaders.   Authority was everywhere attacked, because
everywhere it had shown itself feeble, or tyrannous.   The majestic
peruke of Louis XIV was lifted by an audacious hand, which thus
revealed the baldness so long concealed.   No one *now* believed in
that Grand Monarque ; least of all Goethe, who had *Götz von
Berlichingen* in his portfolio, and to whom Homer and Shakespeare
were idols.   'Send me no more books', writes Werther, ' I will no
longer be led, incited, spurred by them.   There is storm enough
in this breast.   I want a cradle-melody, and that I have in all its
fullness in Homer.   How often do I lull with it my raging blood to
rest !'   The Kestner correspondence proves, what before was
known, that *Werther* is full of biography, and that Goethe was
then troubled with fits of depression following upon days of the
wildest animal spirits.   He was fond of solitude ; and the lonely
hours passed in reading, or making sketches of the landscape in
his rough imperfect style.

   'A marvellous serenity has descended on my spirit', writes
Werther, 'to be compared only to the sweet mornings of spring
which so charm my heart.   I am alone, and here life seems
delicious in this spot formed for natures like mine.   I am so happy,
so filled with the calm feeling of existence, that my art suffers.   I
cannot sketch, yet never was I a greater painter than at this
moment !   When the dear valley clothes itself in vapour, and the
sun shines on the top of my impenetrable forest and only a few
gleams steal into its sanctuary, while I lie stretched in the tall
grass by the cascade, curiously examine the many grasses and
weeds, and contemplate the little world of insects with their
innumerable forms and colours, and feel within me the presence of
the Almighty who formed us after his own image, the breath of the
All-loving who sustains us in endless bliss,—my friend, when my
eyes are fixed on all these objects, and the world images itself in
my soul like the form of a beloved, then I yearn and say : Ah !
couldst thou but express that which lives within thee, that it should
be the mirror of thy soul, as thy soul is the mirror of the Infinite
God !'

   The image of Frederika pursued him.   It could only be banished
by the presence of another.   'When I was a boy', he prettily says
in a letter to Salzmann, 'I planted a cherry-tree, and watched its
growth with delight.   Spring frost killed the blossoms, and I had

to wait another year before the cherries were ripe—then the birds ate them ; another year the caterpillars—then a greedy neighbour —then the blight.   Nevertheless, when I have a garden again, I shall again plant a cherry-tree !'   He did so :

> And from Beauty passed to Beauty,
> Constant to a constant change*.

The image which was to supplant that of Frederika was none other than that of the Charlotte Buff, before mentioned.   Two years before his arrival, her mother had died.   The care of the house and children devolved upon her ; she was only sixteen, yet good sense, housewifely aptitude, and patient courage, carried her successfully through this task.   She had for two years been betrothed to Kestner, secretary to the Hanoverian legation, then aged four-and-twenty : a quiet, orderly, formal, rational, cultivated man, possessing great magnanimity, as the correspondence proves, and a dignity which is in nowise represented in the Albert of *Werther*, from whom we must be careful to distinguish him, in spite of the obvious identity of position.   How Goethe came to know Kestner has already been seen ; how he came to know Lotte may now be told†.   The reader with *Werther* in hand may compare the narrative there given with this extract from Kestner's letter to a friend.   ' It happened that Goethe was at a ball in the country where my maiden and I also were.   I could only come late, and was forced to ride after them.   My maiden, therefore, drove there in other society.   In the carriage was Dr. Goethe, who here first saw Lottchen.   He has great knowledge, and has made Nature in her physical and moral aspects his principal study, and has sought the true beauty of both.   No woman here had pleased him.   Lottchen at once fixed his attention.   She is young, and although not regularly beautiful, has a very attractive face.   Her glance is as bright as a spring morning, and especially it was so that day, for she loves dancing.   She was gay, and in quite a simple dress.   He noticed her feeling for the beauty of Nature, and her unforced wit,—rather humour than wit.   He did not know she was betrothed.   I came a few hours later ; and it is not our custom in public to testify anything beyond friendship to each other.   He was excessively gay (this he often is, though at

* Monckton Milnes.
† Lotte and Lottchen, it is perhaps not altogether superfluous to add, are the favourite diminutives of Charlotte.

Charlotte Buff

other times melancholy) ; Lottchen quite fascinated him, the more
so because she took no trouble about it, but gave herself wholly to
the pleasure of the moment.   The next day, of course, Goethe
called to inquire after her.   He had seen her as a lively girl, fond
of dancing and pleasure ; he now saw her under another and a
better aspect,—in her domestic quality '.

To judge from her portrait, Lotte must, in her way, have been a
charming creature : not intellectually cultivated, not poetical,—
above all, not the sentimental girl described by *Werther ;* but a
serene, calm, joyous, open-hearted German maiden, an excellent
housewife, and a priceless manager.   Goethe at once fell in love
with her.   An extract from Kestner's account will tell us more.
After describing his engagement to Lotte, he adds,—' She is not
strictly a brilliant beauty, according to the common opinion ; to
me she is one : she is, notwithstanding, the fascinating maiden
who might have hosts of admirers, old and young, grave and gay,
clever and stupid, etc.   But she knows how to convince them
quickly that their only safety must be sought in flight or in friendship.   One of these, as the most remarkable, I will mention,
because he retains an influence over us.   A youth in years
(twenty-three), but in knowledge, and in the development of his
mental powers and character, already a man, an extraordinary
genius, and a man of character, was here,—as his family believed,
for the sake of studying the law, but in fact to track the footsteps
of Nature and Truth, and to study Homer and Pindar.   He had
no need to study for the sake of a maintenance.   Quite by chance,
after he had been here some time, he became acquainted with
Lottchen, and saw in her his ideal : he saw her in her joyous
aspect, but was soon aware that this was not her best side ; he
learned to know her also in her domestic position, and, in a word,
became her adorer.   It could not long remain unknown to him
that she could give him nothing but friendship ; and her conduct
towards him was admirable.   Our coincidence of taste, and a
closer acquaintance with each other, formed between him and me
the closest bond of friendship.   Meanwhile, although he was
forced to renounce all hope in relation to Lottchen, and *did*
renounce it, yet he could not, with all his philosophy and natural
pride, so far master himself as completely to repress his inclination.   And he has qualities which might make him dangerous
to a woman, especially to one of susceptibility and taste.   But
Lottchen knew how to treat him so as not to encourage vain hope,

and yet make him admire her manner towards him.   His peace of
mind suffered : there were many remarkable scenes, in which
Lottchen's behaviour heightened my regard for her ; and he also
became more precious to me as a friend ; but I was often inwardly
astonished that love can make such strange creatures even of the
strongest and otherwise the most self-sustained men.   I pitied
him, and had many inward struggles ; for, on the one hand, I
thought that I might not be in a position to make Lottchen so
happy as he would make her ; but, on the other hand, I could not
endure the thought of losing her.   The latter feeling conquered,
and in Lottchen I have never once been able to perceive a shadow
of the same conflict'.

Another extract will place this conflict in its true light :—' I am
under no further engagement to Lottchen than that under which
an honourable man stands when he gives a young woman the
preference above all others, makes known that he desires the like
feeling from her, and when she gives it, receives from her not only
this, but a complete acquiescence.   This I consider quite enough
to bind an honourable man, especially when such a relation lasts
several years.   But in my case there is this in addition, that
Lottchen and I have expressly declared ourselves, and still do so
with pleasure, without any oaths and asseverations '.   This absence
of any *legal* tie between them must have made Kestner's position
far more trying.   It gives a higher idea both of his generous for-
bearance and of the fascination exercised by Goethe : for what a
position ! and how much nobility on all sides was necessary to
prevent petty jealousies ending in a violent rupture !   Certain it is
that the greatest intimacy and the most affectionate feelings were
kept up *without* disturbance.   Confident in the honour of his friend
and the truth of his mistress, Kestner never spoiled the relation
by a hint of jealousy.   Goethe was constantly in Lotte's house,
where his arrival was a jubilee to the children, who seized hold of
him, as children always take loving possession of those who are
indulgent to them, and forced him to tell them stories.   It is a
pleasant sight to see Goethe with children ; he always shows
such hearty fondness for them ; and these brothers and sisters
of Lotte were doubly endeared to him because they belonged
to her.

One other figure in this Wetzlar set arrests our attention : it is
that of a handsome blonde youth, with soft blue eyes and a settled
melancholy expression.   His name is Jerusalem, and he is the son

of the venerable Abbot of Riddagshausen*. He is here attached as secretary to the Brunswick Legation, a colleague, therefore, of von Goué. He is deeply read in English literature, and has had the honour of Lessing's friendship; a friendship subsequently expressed in the following terms, when Lessing, acting as his editor, wrote the preface to his Philosophical Essays: 'When he came to Wolfenbüttel he gave me his friendship. I did not enjoy it long, but I cannot easily name one who in so short a space of time excited in me more affection. It is true I only learned to know one side of his nature, but it was the side which explains all the rest. It was the desire for clear knowledge; the talent to follow truth to its last consequences; the spirit of cold observation; but an ardent spirit not to be intimidated by truth. . . . How sensitive, how warm, how active this young inquirer was, how true a man among men, is better known to more intimate friends'. The Essays which these words introduce are five in number; the titles are given below†.

The melancholy of his disposition led him to think much of suicide, which he defended on speculative grounds. And this melancholy, and these meditations, were deepened by an unhappy passion for the wife of one of his friends. The issue of that passion we shall have to narrate in a future chapter. For the present it is enough to indicate the presence of this youth among the circle of Goethe's acquaintances. They saw but little of each other, owing to the retiring sensitiveness of Jerusalem; probably the same cause had kept them asunder years before in Leipsic, where they were fellow-students; but their acquaintance furnished Goethe with material which he was afterwards to use in his novel.

Jerusalem's unhappy passion and Goethe's unhappy passion, one would think, must have been a bond of union between them; but in truth Goethe's passion can scarcely have been called 'unhappy' —it was rather a delicious uneasiness. Love, in the profound, absorbing sense, it was not. It was an *imaginative passion,* in which the poet was more implicated than the man. Lotte excited his imagination; her beauty, her serene gaiety, her affectionate manners, charmed him; the romance of his position heightened the charm, by giving an *unconscious security* to his feelings. I am

* No Catholic, as this title might seem to imply, but a Protestant; his Abbey, secularized two centuries before, yielded him only a title and revenues.
† I. *Dass die Sprache dem ersten Menschen durch Wunder nicht mitgetheilt sein kann.* II. *Ueber die Natur und den Ursprung der allgemeinen und abstrakten Begriffe.* III. *Ueber die Freiheit.* IV. *Ueber die Mendelssohnsche Theorie vom sinnlichen Vergnügen.* V. *Ueber die vermischten Empfindungen.*

persuaded that if Lotte had been free, he would have fled from her as he fled from Frederika. In saying this, however, I do not mean that the impossibility of obtaining her gave him any comfort. He was restless, impatient, and, in a certain sense, unhappy. He believed himself to be desperately in love with her, when in truth he was only in love with the indulgence of the emotions she excited; a paradox which will be no mystery to those acquainted with the poetic temperament.

Thus passed the summer. In August he made a little excursion to Giessen, to see Professor Höpfner, one of the active writers in the *Frankfurter Gelehrten Anzeigen*. Characteristically he calls on the professor incognito, presenting himself as a shy, awkward student; which, as Höpfner only knows him through correspondence, is facile enough. The comic scene ends by his jumping into the professor's arms, exclaiming, 'I am Goethe!' In Giessen, he found Merck. He persuaded him to return to Wetzlar, to be introduced to Lotte. Merck came; but so far from undervaluing her, as the very inaccurate account in the *Autobiography* would have us understand, Merck wrote to a friend: 'J'ai trouvé aussi l'amie de Goethe, cette fille dont il parle avec tant d'enthousiasme dans toutes ses lettres. Elle mérite réellement tout ce qu'il pourra dire du bien sur son compte'*. He exasperated Goethe by preferring the 'Juno form' of one of her friends, and pointing her out as the more worthy of attention, because she was disengaged. That Goethe should have been offended, was in the order of things; but in the retrospective glance which he gave to this period in his old age, he ought to have detected the really friendly spirit animating Merck; he ought not to have likened him to Mephistopheles; the more so as Merck's representations were really effectual, and hastened the dénouement. Every day made Goethe's position less tenable. At last he consented to tear himself away, and accompany Merck in a trip down the Rhine. It was time. Whatever factitious element there may have been in his romance, the situation was full of danger; indulgence in such emotions would have created at last a real and desperate passion; there was safety but in flight.

Merck left Wetzlar, having arranged that Goethe should join him at Coblentz. The following extracts from Kestner's *Diary* will remind the reader of Goethe's departure from Leipsic without saying adieu to Käthchen. His dislike of 'scenes' made him

* *Briefe aus dem Freundeskreise von Goethe, Herder, Merck*, p. 59.

shrink from those emotions of leave-taking usually so eagerly sought by lovers.

'*Sept.* 10*th*, 1772. To-day Dr. Goethe dined with me in the garden ; I did not know that it was the last time. In the evening Dr. Goethe came to the *teutsche Haus*. He, Lottchen, and I, had a remarkable conversation about the future state ; about going away and returning, etc., which was not begun by him, but by Lottchen. We agreed that the one who died first, should, if he could, give information to the living, about the conditions of the other life. Goethe was quite cast down, for he knew that the next morning he was to go'.

'*Sept.* 11*th*, 1772. This morning at seven o'clock Goethe set off without taking leave. He sent me a note with some books. He had long said that about this time he would make a journey to Coblentz, where the pay-master of the forces, Merck, awaited him, and that he would say no good-byes, but set off suddenly. So I had expected it. But that I was, notwithstanding, unprepared for it, I have felt—felt deep in my soul. In the morning I came home. "Herr Dr. Goethe sent this at ten o'clock." I saw the books and the note, and thought what this said to me— "He is gone!"—and was quite dejected. Soon after Hans* came to ask me if he were really gone? The *Geheime Räthin* Langen had sent to say by a maid-servant: "It was very ill-mannered of Dr. Goethe to set off in this way, without taking leave". Lottchen sent word in reply: "Why had she not taught her nephew better?" Lottchen, in order to be certain, sent a box which she had of Goethe's, to his house. He was no longer there. In the middle of the day the *Geheime Räthin* Langen sent word again: "She would, however, let Dr. Goethe's mother know how he had conducted himself". Every one of the children in the *teutsche Haus* was saying: "*Doctor Goethe is gone!*" In the middle of the day I talked with Herr von Born, who had accompanied him, on horseback, as far as Brunnfells. Goethe had told him of our evening's conversation. Goethe had set out in very low spirits. In the afternoon I took Goethe's note to Lottchen. She was sorry about his departure ; the tears came into her eyes while reading. Yet it was a satisfaction to her that he was gone, since she could not give him the affection he desired. We spoke only of him ; indeed, I could think of nothing else, and defended the manner of his leaving, which was blamed by a silly person ;

---

* One of Lotte's brothers.

I did it with much warmth. Afterwards I wrote him word what had happened since his departure'.

How graphically do these simple touches set the whole situation before us : the sorrow of the two lovers at the departure of their friend, and the consternation of the children on hearing that Dr. Goethe is gone! One needs such a picture to reassure us that the episode, with all its strange romance, and with all its danger, was not really a fit of morbid sentimentalism. Indeed, had Goethe been the sentimental Werther he has represented, he would never have had the strength of will to tear himself from such a position. He would have blown his brains out, as Werther did. On the other hand, note what a worthy figure is this of Kestner, compared with the cold Albert of the novel. A less generous nature would have rejoiced in the absence of a rival, and forgotten, in its joy, the loss of a friend. But Kestner, who knew that his friend was his rival,—and such a rival, that doubts crossed him whether this magnificent youth were not really more capable of rendering Lotte happy than he himself was,—grieved for the absence of his friend !

Here is Goethe's letter, referred to in the passage just quoted from the *Diary :*

'He is gone, Kestner ; when you get this note, he is gone ! Give Lottchen the enclosed. I was quite composed, but your conversation has torn me to pieces. At this moment I can say nothing to you but farewell. If I had remained a moment longer with you I could not have restrained myself. Now I am alone, and to-morrow I go. O my poor head !'

This was the enclosure, addressed to Lotte :

'I certainly hope to come again, but God knows when ! Lotte, what did my heart feel while you were talking, knowing, as I did, that it was the last time I should see you? Not the last time, and yet to-morrow I go away. He is gone ! What spirit led you to that conversation? When I was expected to say all I felt, alas ! what I cared about was here below, was your hand, which I kissed for the last time. The room, which I shall not enter again, and the dear father who saw me to the door for the last time. I am now alone, and may weep ; I leave you happy, and shall remain in your heart. And shall see you again ; *but not to-morrow is never!* Tell my boys, He is gone. I can say no more'.

CHAPTER IV

PREPARATIONS FOR 'WERTHER'

HAVING sent his luggage to the house of Frau von Laroche, where he was to meet Merck, he made the journey down the Lahn, on foot. A delicious sadness subdued his thoughts as he wandered dreamily along the river banks; and the lovely scenes which met his eye solicited his pencil, awakening once more the ineffectual desire (which from time to time haunted him) of becoming a painter. He had really no faculty in this direction, yet the desire often suppressed now rose up in such a serious shape, that he resolved to settle for ever whether he should devote himself to the art or not. The test was curious. The river glided beneath, now flashing in the sunlight, now partially concealed by willows. Taking a knife from his pocket he flung it with his left hand into the river, having previously resolved that if he saw it fall he was to become an artist; but if the sinking knife were concealed by the willows he was to abandon the idea. No ancient oracle was ever more ambiguous than the answer now given him. The willows concealed the sinking knife, but the water splashed up like a fountain, and was distinctly visible. So indefinite an answer left him in doubt*.

He wandered pleasantly on the banks till he reached Ems, and then journeyed down the river in a boat. The old Rhine opened upon him; and he mentions with peculiar delight the magnificent situation of Oberlahnstein, and, above all, the majesty of the castle of Ehrenbreitstein. On arriving at the house of Geheimrath von La Roche, where he had been announced by Merck, he was most kindly received by this excellent family. His literary tendencies bound him to the mother; his joyousness and strong sense, to the father; his youth and poetry, to the daughters. The Frau von Laroche, Wieland's earliest love, had written a novel in the Richardson style, *Die Geschichte des Fräuleins von Stern-heim*; and Schäfer remarks that she probably gathered Merck,

---

* This mode of interrogating fate recalls that strange passage in ROUSSEAU'S *Confessions* (Livre VI), where he throws a stone at a tree: if he hits, it is a sign of salvation; if he misses, of damnation! Fortunately he hits: 'Ce qui, véritablement, n'étais pas difficile, car j'avais eu le soin de le choisir fort gros et fort près; depuis lors je n'ai plus douté de mon salut'. Had Goethe read this passage? The *Confessions* appeared in 1768, that is, four years before this journey down the Lahn. Yet from a passage in one of his letters to the Frau von Stein, it seems as if he then, 1782, first read the *Confessions*.

Goethe, and others into her house with a view to favourable criticisms of this novel. If this were her design, she succeeded with Goethe, who reviewed her book in the *Frankfurter Gelehrten Anzeigen.* Whether this compliance was extorted by herself, or by the charms of her daughter Maximiliane, history saith not ; certain it is that the dark eyes of the daughter made an impression on the heart of the young reviewer. She is the Mlle B. introduced in *Werther ;* but she is even still more interesting to us as the future mother of Bettina. They seem to have looked into each other's eyes, flirted and sentimentalized, as if no Lotte had been left in Wetzlar. Nor will this surprise those who have considered the mobile nature of our poet. He is miserable at moments, but the fullness of abounding life, the strength of victorious will, and the sensibility to new impressions, keep his overactive nature from the despondency which killed Werther. He is not always drooping because Charlotte is another's. He is open to every new impression, serious or gay. Thus, among other indications, we find him throwing off in *Pater Brey* and *Satyros,* sarcasm and humour which are curious as products of the Werther period, although of no absolute worth ; and we follow him up the Rhine, in company with Merck and his family, leisurely enjoying Rheinfels, St. Goar, Bacharach, Bingen, Elfeld, and Biberich,—

> The blending of all beauties ; streams and dells,
> Fruit, foliage, crag, wood, cornfield, mountain, vine,
> And chiefless castles, breathing stern farewells
> From gray but leafy walls where Ruin greenly dwells–

sketching as if life were a leisure summer day.

He returned to Frankfurt, and busied himself with law, literature, and painting. Wandering Italians, then rare, brought casts of antique statues to Frankfurt ; and with delighted eagerness he purchased a complete set, thus to revive as much as possible the grand impression he received at Mannheim. Among his art-studies must be noted the attention bestowed on the Dutch painters. He began to copy some still-life pictures ; one of these he mentions with pride, and what, think you, this one was?—a copy of a tortoiseshell knife-handle inlaid with silver ! He has *Götz von Berlichingen* in his portfolio, and delights in copying a knife-handle !

To law he devoted himself with greater assiduity than ever. His father, delighted at going through the papers with him, was peculiarly gratified at this honourable diligence, and in his delight was willing to overlook the other occupations of 'this singular creature', as he rightly named him. Goethe's literary plans were numerous, and the *Frankfurt Journal* gave him constant opportunities for expressing himself on poetry, theology, and even politics. Very significant is the following passage from one of these articles, in reply to the complaint that the Germans had no Fatherland, no Patriotism : ' When we have a place in the world where we can repose with our property, a field to nourish us, and a house to cover us, have we not there our Fatherland ? and have not thousands upon thousands in every city got this ? and do they not live happy in their limited sphere ? Wherefore, then, this vain striving for a sentiment we neither have nor can have, a sentiment which only in certain nations, and in certain periods, is the result of many concurrent circumstances ? Roman patriotism ! God defend us from it, as from a giant ! we could not find the stool upon which to sit, nor the bed on which to lie in such patriotism !' He was also rewriting *Götz von Berlichingen*. He found, on rereading the manuscript, that, besides the unities of time and place, he had sinned against the higher unity of composition. He says,—

' In abandoning myself to my imagination, I had not deviated much in the beginning, and the first acts were pretty much as had been intended. In the following acts, however, and especially towards the end, I was unconsciously led away by a singular passion. In making Aldelheid so lovable, I had fallen in love with her myself,—my pen was unconsciously devoted to her alone,—the interest in her fate gained the preponderance ; and as, moreover, Götz, towards the end, has little to do, and afterwards only returns to an unhappy participation in the Peasant War, nothing was more natural than that a charming woman should supplant him in the mind of the author, who, casting off the fetters of art, thought to open a new field. I was soon sensible of this defect, or rather this culpable superfluity, since my poetical nature always impelled me to unity. Instead of the biography of Götz and German antiquities, I now confined my attention to my own work, to give it more and more historical and national substance, and to cancel that which was fabulous or passionate. In this I indeed sacrificed much, as the inclination of the man had to yield to the conviction of the artist. Thus, for instance I had placed Aldelheid in a terrific nocturnal gipsy scene, where she produced a great effect by her beautiful presence. A nearer examination banished her ; and the love affair between Franz and his gracious lady, which was very circumstantially carried on in the fourth and fifth acts, was much condensed, and only the chief points indicated.

'Without altering the manuscript, which I still possess in its original shape, I determined to rewrite the whole, and did this with such activity, that in a few weeks I produced an entirely new version. It had never been my intention to have the second poem printed, as I looked upon this likewise as no more than a preparatory exercise, the foundation of a new work, to be accomplished with greater industry and deliberation.

'When I suggested my plans to Merck, he laughed at me, and asked what was the meaning of this perpetual writing and rewriting? The work, he said, by this means, only becomes different, and seldom better ; you must see what effect one thing produces, and then try something new. "Be in time at the hedge, if you would dry your linen", he exclaimed, in the words of the proverb : hesitation and delay only make uncertain men. On the other hand, I pointed out how unpleasant it would be to offer a bookseller a work on which I had bestowed so much affection, and perhaps have it refused ; for how would they judge of so young, nameless, and audacious an author? As my dread of the press gradually vanished, I wished to see printed my comedy *Die Mitschuldigen*, upon which I set some value, but I found no publisher inclined to undertake it.

'Here the mercantile taste of my friend was at once excited. He proposed that we should publish at our own expense this singular and striking work, from which we should derive large profit. Like many others, he used often to reckon up the bookseller's profit, which with many works was certainly great, especially if what was lost by other writings and commercial affairs was left out of the calculation. We settled that I should procure the paper, and that he should answer for the printing. To work we went, and I was pleased to see my wild dramatic sketch in clean proof sheets ; it looked really better than I myself expected. We completed the work, and it was sent off in several parcels. It was not long before the attention it excited became universal. But as, with our limited means, the copies could not be forwarded, a pirated edition suddenly made its appearance. As, moreover, there could be no immediate return, especially in ready money, for the copies sent out, and as my treasury was not very flourishing at the time when much attention and applause was bestowed upon me, I was extremely perplexed how to pay for the paper by means of which I had made the world acquainted with my talent. On the other hand, Merck, who knew better how to help himself, was certain that all would soon come right again ; but I never perceived that to be the case.'

There is some inaccuracy in the foregoing, which a comparison of the first and second versions of the work will rectify. The changes he effected were very slight, and mainly consist in the striking out of the two scenes in which Adelheid plays so conspicuous a part.

A greater inaccuracy, amounting to injustice, is contained in the passage about Herder, as we now learn from the *Posthumous Papers* of the latter, from which it is clear that he *did* greatly admire *Götz*, and wrote warmly of it to his betrothed, saying, 'you will have some heavenly hours of delight when you read it, for there is in it uncommon German strength, depth, and truth, although here and there it is rather schemed than artistically wrought (*nur gedacht*)'. Probably in writing to Goethe he was more critical, and as usual with him, somewhat pedagogic ; but it is also probable that he was loud in praise, since the poet replies, 'Your letter was a consolation. I already rank the work much lower than you do. Your sentence that Shakespeare has quite spoiled me, I admit to the full. The work must be fused anew, freed from its dross, and with newer, better metal cast again. Then it shall appear before you'. He seems to have been nettled (not unnaturally) at the sentence, 'all is rather schemed than artistically wrought', which, he says, is true of *Emilia Galotti*, and prevents his altogether liking it, although a masterpiece. Judging from a tolerably extensive acquaintance with authors in relation to criticism, I should think it highly probable that the longer Goethe pondered on Herder's letter the fainter became his pleasure in the praise, and the stronger his irritation at the blame. I have known a feeling of positive gratitude for a criticism, slowly change into an uneasy and almost indignant impression of injustice having been done. That Goethe did not, on reflection, so entirely concur with the objections he was at first ready to admit, appears from the fact that he did not recast his work.

When *Götz* appeared the effect on the public was instantaneous, startling. Its bold expression of the spirit of Freedom, its defiance of French criticism, and the originality no less than the power of the writing, carried it triumphant over Germany. It was pronounced a masterpiece in all the *salons* and in all the beer-houses of that uneasy time. Imitations followed with amazing rapidity; the stage was noisy with the clang of chivalry, and the bookshelves creaked beneath the weight of resuscitated Feudal Times.

An amusing example of 'the trade' is mentioned by Goethe. A bookseller paid him a visit, and with the air of a man well satisfied with his proposal, offered to give an *order* for a dozen plays in the style of *Götz*, for which a handsome *honorarium* should be paid. His offer was the more generous, because such was the state of literature at this period, that, in spite of the success *Götz* achieved, it brought no money to its author—pirated editions circulating everywhere, and robbing him of his reward. Moreover, what the bookseller proposed was what the public expected. When once a writer has achieved success in any direction, he must continue in that direction, or peril his reputation. An opinion has been formed of him; he has been *classed;* and the public will not have its classification disturbed. Nevertheless, if he repeat himself, this unreasoning public declaims against his 'poverty'. No man ever repeated himself less than Goethe. He did not model a statue, and then amuse himself with taking casts of it in different materials. He lived, thought, and suffered; and because he had lived, thought, and suffered, he wrote. When he had once expressed his experience in a work, he never recurred to it. The true artist, like the snake, casts his skin, but never resumes it. He works according to the impulse from within, not according to the demand from without. And Goethe was a genuine artist, never exhausting a lucky discovery, never working an impoverished vein. Every poem came fresh from life, coined from the mint of his experience.

Götz is the greatest product of the *Sturm und Drang* movement. As we before hinted, this period is not simply one of vague wild hopes and retrospections of old German life, it is also one of unhealthy sentimentalism. Goethe, the great representative poet of his day—the secretary of his age—gives us masterpieces which characterize both these tendencies. Beside the insurgent *Götz* stands the dreamy *Werther*. And yet, accurately as these two works represent two active tendencies of that time, they are both far removed above the perishing extravagances of that time; they are both *ideal* expressions of the age, and as free from the disease which corrupted it as Goethe himself was free from the weakness of his contemporaries. Wilkes used to say that he had never been a Wilkite. Goethe was never a Werther. To appreciate the distance which separated him and his works from his sentimental contemporaries and their works, we must study the characters of such men as Jacobi, Klinger, Wagner, and Lenz, or we must read such works as *Woldemar*. It will then be plain why Goethe turned with aversion from such works, his own included, when a few years had cleared his insight, and settled his aims. Then also will be seen the difference between genius which idealizes the spirit of the age, and talent which panders to it*.

It was, indeed, a strange epoch ; the unrest was the unrest of disease, and its extravagances were morbid symptoms. In the letters, memoirs, and novels, which still remain to testify to the follies of the age, may be read a self-questioning and sentimental introspection, enough to create in healthy minds a distaste both for sentiment and self-questioning. A factitious air is carried even by the most respectable sentiments ; and many *not* respectable array themselves in rose-pink. Nature is seldom spoken of but in hysterical enthusiasm. Tears and caresses are prodigally scattered, and upon the slightest provocations. In Coburg an *Order of Mercy and Expiation* is instituted by sensitive noodles. Leuchsenring, whom Goethe satirized in *Pater Brey* as a professional sentimentalist, gets up a secret society, and calls it the *Order of Sentiment*, to which tender souls think it a privilege to belong. Friendship is fantastically deified ; brotherly love draws trembling souls together, not on the solid grounds of affection and mutual service, but on entirely imaginary grounds of 'spiritual communion'; whence arose, as Jean Paul wittily says, 'an universal love for all men and beasts—except reviewers'. It was a sceptical epoch, in which everything established came into question. Marriage, of course, came badly off among a set of men who made the first commandment of genius to consist in loving your neighbour *and* your neighbour's wife.

These were symptoms of disease ; the social organization was out of order ; a crisis, evidently imminent, was heralded by extravagances in literature, as elsewhere. The cause of the disease was want of faith. In religion, in philosophy, in politics,

---

* As Karl Grün epigrammatically says of Goethe and his contemporaries, ' he was at once patient and physician, they were patients and nothing else '.

in morals, this eighteenth century was ostentatious of its disquiet and disbelief. The old faith, which for so long had made European life an organic unity, and which in its tottering weakness had received a mortal blow from Luther, was no longer universal, living, active, dominant ; its place of universal directing power was vacant ; a new faith had not arisen. The French Revolution was another crisis of that organic disturbance which had previously shown itself in another order of ideas,—in the Reformation. Beside this awful crisis, other minor crises are noticeable. Everywhere the same Protestant spirit breaks through traditions in morals, in literature, and in education. Whatever is established, whatever rests on tradition, is questioned. The classics are no longer believed in ; men begin to maintain the doctrine of progress, and proclaim the superiority of the moderns. Art is pronounced to be in its nature progressive. Education is no longer permitted to pursue its broad traditional path ; the methods which were excellent for the past, no longer suffice for the present; everywhere new methods rise up to ameliorate the old. The divine right of institutions ceases to gain credence. The individual claimed and proclaimed his freedom : freedom of thought and freedom of act. Freedom is the watchword of the eighteenth century.

Enough has been said to indicate the temper of those times, and to show why *Werther* was the expression of that temper. Turning to the novel itself, we find it so bound up with the life of its author, that the history of his life at this epoch is the record of the materials from which it was created ; we must, therefore, retrace our steps again to the point where Goethe left Wetzlar, and, by the aid of his letters to Kestner, follow the development of this strange romance.

Götz was published in the summer of 1773. It was in the autumn of 1772 that Goethe left Wetzlar, and returned home. His letters to Kestner and Charlotte are full of passionate avowals and tender reminiscences. The capricious orthography and grammar to be noticed in them belong to a period when it was thought unworthy of a genius to conform to details so fastidious as correct spelling and good grammar ; but the affectionate nature which warms these letters, the abundant love the writer felt and inspired, these belong to him, and not to his age. If a proof were wanted of Goethe's loving disposition, we might refer to these letters, especially those addressed to the young brother of Charlotte. The reader of this Biography, however, will need no such proof, and we may therefore confine ourselves to the relation of Goethe to the Kestners. 'God bless you, dear Kestner', runs one of the early letters, 'and tell Lotte that I often believe I can forget her ; but then I have a relapse, and it is worse with me than ever'. He longs once more to be sitting at her feet, letting the children clamber over him. He writes in a strain of melancholy, which is as much poetry as sorrow : when a thought of suicide arises, it is only one among the many thoughts which hurry through the mind. There is a very significant passage in the *Autobiography*, which aptly describes his real state of mind : 'I had a large collection of weapons, and among them a very handsome dagger. This I place by my bedside every night, and before extinguishing my candle I made various attempts to pierce the sharp point a couple of inches into my breast ; but not being able to do it I laughed myself out of the notion, threw aside all hypochondriacal fancies, and resolved to live'. He played with suicidal thoughts, because he was restless, and suicide was a fashionable speculation of the day ; but whoever supposes these thoughts of suicide were serious, has greatly misunderstood him. He had them not, even at this period ; and when he wrote *Werther* he had long thrown off even the faint temptation of poetic longings for death. In October 1772 the report reaches him that his Wetzlar friend, Goué, has shot himself : 'Write to me at once about Goué', he says to Kestner ; '*I honour such an act, and pity mankind*, and let all the Philisters make their tobacco-smoke comments on it and say : There, you see ! Nevertheless, I hope never to make my friends unhappy by such an act myself'. He was too full of life to do more than coquette with the idea of death. Here is a confession : 'I went to Homburg, and there gained new love of life, seeing how much pleasure the appearance of a miserable thing like me can give such excellent people'. On the 7th of November he suddenly appeared in Wetzlar with Schlosser, and stayed there till the 10th, in a feverish, but delicious enthusiasm. He writes to Kestner on reaching home : 'It was assuredly high time for me to go. Yesterday evening I had thoroughly criminal thoughts as on the sofa. . . . And when I think how above all my hopes your greeting of me was, I am very calm. I confess I came with some anxiety. I came with a pure, warm, full heart, dear Kestner, and it is a hell-pain when one is not received in the same spirit as one brings. But so—God give you a whole life such as those two days were to me !'

The report of Goué's suicide, before alluded to, turned out to be false ; but the suicide of Jerusalem was a melancholy fact.   Goethe immediately writes to Kestner :

'Unhappy Jerusalem !   The news was shocking, and unexpected ; it was horrible to have this news as an accompaniment to the pleasantest gift of love.   The unfortunate man !   But the devil, that is, the infamous men who enjoy nothing but the chaff of vanity, and have the lust of idolatry in their hearts, and preach idolatry, and cramp healthy nature, and overstrain and ruin the faculties, are guilty of this misery, of our misery.   If the cursed parson is not guilty, God forgive me that I wish he may break his neck like Eli.   The poor young man !   When I came back from a walk, and he met me in the moonlight, I said to myself, he is in love.   Lotte must still remember that I laughed about it.   God knows, loneliness undermined his heart, and for seven years* his form has been familiar to me.   I have talked little with him. When I came away, I brought with me a book of his ; I will keep that and the remembrance of him as long as I live'.

Among the many inaccuracies of the *Autobiography*, there is one of consequence on the subject of *Werther*, namely, the assertion that it was the news of Jerusalem's suicide which suddenly set him to work.   The news reached him in October 1772, and in November Kestner sent him the narrative of Jerusalem's last days.   Not until the middle and end of 1773 did he write *Werther*.   In fact, the state of his mind at this period is by no means such as the *Autobiography* describes.   Read this letter written in December : 'That is wonderful !   I was about to ask if Lenchen† had arrived, and you write to tell me she is.   If I were only there I would nullify your discourse, and astonish all the tailors ; I think I should be fonder of her than of Lotte. From the portrait she must be an amiable girl, much better than Lotte, if not precisely the . . . *And I am free and thirsting for love.*   I must try and come ; yet that would not help me.   Here am I once more in Frankfurt, and carry plans and fancies about with me, which I should not do if I had but a maiden'.   In January he seems to have found a maiden, for he writes : 'Tell Lotte there is a certain maiden here whom I love heartily, and whom I would choose before all others if I had any thought of marriage, and she also was born on the 11th January‡.   It would

* This 'seven years' refers to the first sight of Jerusalem at Leipsic.
† A sister of Charlotte's.   ‡ Lotte's birthday.

be pretty: such a pair! Who knows what God's will is?' I agree with Viehoff against Düntzer, that this alludes to Anna Antoinette Gerock, a relation of Schlosser's, who is known to have loved him passionately, and to have furnished some traits for Mignon. Clear it is that he is not very melancholy. 'Yesterday I skated from sunrise to sunset. And I have other sources of joy which I can't relate. Be comforted that I am almost as happy as people who love, like you two, that I am as full of hope, and that I have lately *felt* some poems. My sister greets you, my maiden also greats you, my gods greet you'. Thus we see, that, although Lotte's picture hangs by his bedside, although her image hovers constantly before him, and the *Teutsche Haus* is the centre of many yearning thoughts, he is not pining despondently for Charlotte. He has rewritten *Götz*, and allowed Merck to carry it to the printer's. He is living in a very merry circle, one figure in which is Antoinette Gerock, as we gather from a letter written in February 1773, a month after that in which he refers to his 'maiden'. Here is the passage: 'At Easter I will send you a quite adventurous novelty*. My maiden greets Lotte. In character she has much of Lenchen, and my sister says resembles her portrait. If we were but as much in love as you two—meanwhile I will call her my "dear little wife", for recently she fell to me in a lottery as my wife'. She was then only fifteen, and their relation to each other will be described in chap. VI.

And now the day approaches when Lotte is to be married and leave Wetzlar. He writes to her brother Hans, begging him, when Lotte departs, to write at least once a week, that the connexion with the *Teutsche Haus* may not be broken, although its jewel is carried away. He writes to Kestner to be allowed to get the wedding ring. 'I am wholly yours, but from henceforth care not to see you nor Lotte. Her portrait too shall away from my bedroom the day of her marriage, and shall not be restored till I hear she is a mother; and from that moment a new epoch begins, in which I shall not love her but her children, a little indeed on her account, but that's nothing to do with it; and if you ask me to be godfather, my spirit shall rest upon the boy, and he shall make a fool of himself for a maiden like his mother'. Enclosed was this note to Lotte; 'May my memory with this ring for ever remain with you in your happiness. Dear Lotte, some time hence we shall see each other again, you with this ring on your finger,

* *Götz*.

and I as always thine. I know no name or bye-name to sign this with. You know me'. When the marriage takes place he writes to Kestner. 'God bless you; you have surprised me. I had meant to make a holy sephulchre on Good Friday, and bury Lotte's portrait. But it hangs still by my bed, and shall remain there till I die. Be happy. Greet for me your angel, and Lenchen; she shall be the second Lotte, and it shall be as well with her. I wander in the desert where no water is, my hair is my shade, and my blood my spring'. The bridesmaid brings him the bridal bouquet, a flower of which he sticks in his hat, as he walks to Darmstadt, in a melancholy mood; but to show that his passion for Charlotte was after all only a poetic passion, here is a passage in the letter he sent to Kestner immediately after the marriage: 'O Kestner, when have I envied you Lotte in the human sense? for not to envy you her in the spiritual sense I must be an angel without lungs and liver. Nevertheless I must disclose a secret to you. That you may know and behold. When I attached myself to Lotte, and you know that I was attached to her from my heart, Born talked to me about it, *as people are wont to talk*. "If I were K. I should not like it. How can it end? You quite cut him out!" and the like. Then I said to him in these very words, in his room, it was in the morning: "The fact is, I am fool enough to think the girl something remarkable; if she deceived me, and turned out to be as girls usually are, and used K. as capital in order to make the most of her charms, the first moment which discovered that to me, the first moment which brought her nearer to me, would be the last of our acquaintance", and this I protested and swore. And between ourselves, without boasting, I understand the maiden somewhat, and you know how I have felt for her and for everything she has seen and touched, and wherever she has been, and shall continue to feel to the end of the world. And now see how far I am envious, and must be so. For either I am a fool, which it is difficult to believe, or she is the subtlest deceiver, or then—Lotte, the very Lotte of whom we are speaking'. A few days afterwards he writes: 'My poor existence is petrified to barren rock. This summer I lose all. Merck goes. My sister too. And I am alone'.

The marriage of Cornelia, his much-loved sister, was to him a very serious matter, and her loss was not easily supplied. It came, too, at a time when other losses pained him. Lotte was married, Merck was away, and a dear friend had just died.

Nevertheless, he seems to have been active in plans. Among them was most probably that of a drama on *Mahomet*, which he erroneously places at a later period, after the journeys with Lavater and Basedow, but which Schäfer, very properly, restores to the year 1773, as Boie's *Annual* for 1774 contains the *Mahomet's song*. Goethe has narrated in full the conception of this piece, which is very grand ; he tells us the idea arose within him of illustrating the sad fact, noticeable in the biographies of genius, that every man who attempts to realize a great idea comes in contact with the lower world, and must place himself on its level in order to influence it, and thus compromises his higher aims, and finally forfeits them. He chose Mahomet as the illustration, never having regarded him as an impostor. He had carefully studied the Koran and Mahomet's life, in preparation. 'The piece', he says, 'opened with a hymn sung by Mahomet alone under the open sky. He first adores the innumerable stars as so many gods ; but as the star god (Jupiter) rises, he offers to him, as the king of the stars, exclusive adoration. Soon after, the moon ascends the horizon, and claims the eye and heart of the worshipper, who, refreshed and strengthened by the dawning sun, is afterwards stimulated to new praises. But these changes, however delightful, are still unsatisfactory, and the mind feels that it must rise still higher, and mounts therefore to God, the One Eternal, Infinite, to whom all these splendid but finite creatures owe their existence. I composed this hymn with great delight ; it is now lost, but might easily be restored as a cantata, and is adapted for music by the variety of its expression. It would, however, be necessary to imagine it sung according to the original plan, by the leader of a caravan with his family and tribe ; and thus the alternation of the voices and the strength of the chorus would be secured.

'Mahomet converted, imparts these feelings and sentiments to his friends ; his wife and Ali become unconditional disciples. In the second act, he attempts to propagate this faith in the tribe ; Ali still more zealously. Assent and opposition display themselves according to the variety of character. The contest begins, the strife becomes violent, and Mahomet flies. In the third act, he defeats his enemies, make his religion the public one, and purifies the Kaaba from idols ; but this being impracticable by force, he is obliged to resort to cunning. *What in his character is earthly increases and develops itself; the divine retires and is obscured.* In the fourth act, Mahomet pursues his conquests, his doctrine becomes a *means* rather than an *end*, all kinds of practices are employed, nor are horrors wanting. A woman, whose husband has been condemned by Mahomet, poisons him. In the fifth act he feels that he is poisoned. His great calmness, the return to himself and to his better nature, make him worthy of admiration. He purifies his doctrine, establishes his kingdom, and dies.

'This sketch long occupied my mind; for, according to my custom, I was obliged to let the conception perfect itself before I commenced the execution. All that genius, through character and intellect, can exercise over mankind, was therein to be represented and what it gains and loses in the process. Several of the songs to be introduced in the drama were rapidly composed; the only one remaining of them, however, is the *Mahomet's Gesang*. This was to be sung by Ali, in honour of his master, at the apex of his success, just before the change resulting from the poison'. Of all his unrealized schemes, this causes me the greatest regret. In grandeur, depth, and in the opportunities for subtle psychological unravelment of the mysteries of our nature, it was a scheme peculiarly suited to his genius. How many *Clavigos* and *Stellas* would one not have given for such a poem?

Maximiliane Laroche had recently married Brentano, a Frankfurt merchant, a widower, many years her senior, with five children. Goethe became intimate at their house; and, as Merck writes, 'il joue avec les enfants et accompagne le clavecin de madame avec la basse. M. Brentano, quoique assez jaloux pour un Italien, l'aime et veut absolument qu'il fréquente la maison'. The husband wanted his presence, often as an umpire in the disputes with his wife; and the wife, also, chose him umpire in her disputes with her husband; nay, Merck hints, 'il a la petite Madame Brentano à consoler sur l'odeur de l'huile, du fromage, et des manières de son mari'. So passed autumn and winter, in a tender relation, such as in those days was thought blameless enough, but such as modern writers cannot believe to have been so blameless. For my part I cannot disbelieve his own word on this matter, when he says, 'My former relation to the young wife, which was, properly speaking, only that of a brother to a sister, was resumed after marriage. Being of her own age, I was the only one in whom she heard an echo of those voices to which she had been accustomed in her youth. We lived in childish confidence; and, *although there was nothing passionate in our intercourse*, it was painful, because she was unable to reconcile herself to her new

condition'. If not passionate, the relation was certainly sentimental and dangerous. Hear how he writes to Frau Jacobi:
'It goes well with me, dear lady, and thanks for your double, triple
letter. The last three weeks there has been nothing but excitement,
and now we are as contented and happy as possible. I say *we*, for
since the 15th of January not a branch of my existence has been
solitary. And Fate, which I have so often vituperated, is now
courteously entitled beautiful, wise Fate, for since my sister left me,
this is the first gift that can be called an equivalent. The Max is
still the same angel whose simple and darling qualities draw all
hearts towards her, and the feeling I have for her—wherein her
husband would find cause for jealousy—now makes the joy of my
existence. Brentano is a worthy fellow, with a frank, strong
character, and not without sense. The children are lively and
good'. An anecdote, related by his mother to Bettina, gives us
an amusing picture of him parading before Max. The morning
was bright and frosty. 'Wolfgang burst into the room where his
mother was seated with some friends: "Mother, you have never
seen me skate, and the weather is so beautiful to-day". I put on
my crimson fur cloak, which had a long train, and was closed in
front by golden clasps, and we drove out. There skated my son,
like an arrow among the groups. The wind had reddened his
cheeks, and blown the powder out of his brown hair. When he
saw my crimson cloak he came towards our carriage and smiled
coaxingly at me. "Well", said I, "what do you want?" "Come,
mother, you can't be cold in the carriage, give me your cloak".
"You won't put it on, will you?" "Certainly". I took it off, he put
it on, threw the train over his arm, and away he went over the ice
like a son of the gods. Oh, Bettina, if you could have seen him!
Anything so beautiful is not to be seen now! I clapped my hands
for joy. Never shall I forget him, as he darted out from under
one arch of the bridge and in again under the other, the wind
carrying the train behind him as he flew! Your mother, Bettina,
was on the ice, and all this was to please her'.

No thought of suicide in *that* breast!

Quite in keeping with this anecdote is the spirit of the satirical
farce *Götter, Helden, und Wieland*, which is alluded to in this
passage of a letter to Kestner, May 1774, and must therefore have
been written some time before: 'My rough joke against Wieland
makes more noise than I thought. He behaves very well in the
matter, as I hear, so that I am in the wrong'. The origin of this

farce was a strong feeling in the circle of Goethe's friends, that Wieland had modernized, misrepresented, and traduced the Grecian gods and heroes. One Sunday afternoon 'the rage for dramatizing everything' seized him, and with a bottle of Burgundy by his side he wrote off the piece just as it stands. The friends were in raptures with it. He sent it to Lenz, then at Strasburg, who insisted on its at once being printed. After some demurring, consent was given, and at Strasburg the work saw the light. In reading it, the public, unacquainted with the circumstances and the mood to which it owed its origin, unacquainted also with the fact of its never having been designed for publication, felt somewhat scandalized at its fierceness of sarcasm. But in truth there was no malice in it. Flushed with the insolence and pride of wit, he attacked a poet whom, on the whole, he greatly loved; and Wieland took no offence at it, but reviewed it in the *Teutsche Mercur*, recommending it to all lovers of pasquinade, *persiflage*, and sarcastic wit. This reminds one of Socrates standing up in the theatre, when he was lampooned by Aristophanes, that the spectators might behold the original of the sophist they were hooting on the stage. *Götter, Helden, und Wieland* is really amusing, and under the mask of its buffoonery contains some sound and acute criticism*. The peculiarity of it, however, consists in its attacking Wieland for treating heroes unheroically, at a time when, from various parts of Germany, loud voices were raised against Wieland, as an immoral, an unchristian, nay, even an atheistical writer. Lavater called upon Christians to pray for this sinner; theologians forbade their followers to read his works; pulpits were loud against him. In 1773 the whole Klopstock school rose against him† in moral indignation, and burned his works on Klopstock's birthday. Very different was Goethe's ire. He saw that the gods and heroes were represented in perruques and satin breeches, that their cheeks were rouged, their thews and sinews shrunk to those of a petit maître; and against such a conception of the old Pagan life he raised his voice.

'I cannot blame you', he writes to Kestner, 'for living in the world and making acquaintances amongst men of rank and influence. Intercourse with the great is always advantageous to him who knows properly how to use it. I honour gunpowder, if

---

* It called forth a retort, *Thiere, Menschen, und Goethe;* which has not fallen in my way. Critics speak of it as personal, but worthless.

† *Gervinus*, IV, p. 285.

only for its power of bringing me a bird down out of the air. . . .
So in God's name continue, and don't trouble yourself about the
opinions of others, shut your heart to antagonists as to flatterers.
. . . O Kestner, I am in excellent spirits, and if I have not you
by my side, yet all the dear ones are ever before me. The circle
of noble natures is the highest happiness I have yet achieved.
And now, my dear *Götz*, I trust in his strong nature, he will
endure. He is a human offspring with many sins, and nevertheless one of the best. Many will object to his clothing and
rough angles ; yet I have so much applause that it astonishes me.
I don't think I shall soon write anything which will again find its
public. Meanwhile I work on, in the hope that something striking
in the whirl of things may be laid hold of'.

On Christmas Day 1773, in answer to Kestner's wish that he
should come to Hanover and play a part there, he writes this
noticeable sentence. 'My father would not object to my entering
foreign service, and no hope or desire of an office detains me
here—but, dear Kestner, *the talents and powers which I have, I
need too much for my own aims; I am accustomed to act according
to my instinct, and therewith can no prince be served'*. In less
than two years he was to accept service under a prince ; but we
shall see that he did so with full consciousness of what was
required, and of what he could afford to give.

The mention of that prince leads me to make an important
correction in the date of the first acquaintance with him, erroneously placed in the December of 1774 by Goethe. It is useless
to inquire how Goethe's memory could so have deceived him
as to bring this important event in conjunction with his first
acquaintance with Lili ; the dates of the Knebel correspondence
are beyond question. On the 11th February Knebel paid him a
visit, and informed him that the two princes, Karl August and
Constantine, were desirous of seeing him. He went, and was
received with flattering kindness, especially by Karl August, who
had just read *Götz*. He dined with his royal hosts in a quiet way,
and left them, having received and produced an agreeable impression. They were going to Mainz, whither he promised to
follow them. His father, like a sturdy old burgher who held aloof
from princes, shook his sceptical head at the idea of this visit. To
Mainz, however, the poet went a day or two afterwards, and spent
several days with the young princes, as their guest. This was his
first contact with men of high rank.

In the following May he hears with joy that Lotte is a mother, and that her boy is to be called Wolfgang, after him ; and on the 16th of June he writes to Lotte : 'I will soon send you a friend who has much resemblance to me, and hope you will receive him well; he is named Werther, and is and was—but that he must himself explain'.

Whoever has followed the history thus far, moving on the secure ground of contemporary document, will see how vague and inaccurate is the account of the composition of *Werther* given by its author in his restrospective narrative. It was not originated by growing despair at the lost of Charlotte. It was not originated by tormenting thoughts of self-destruction. It was not to free himself from suicide that he wrote this story of suicide. All these several threads were woven into its woof ; but the rigour of dates forces us to the conviction that *Werther*, although taken from his experience, was not written while that experience was being undergone. Indeed, the true philosophy of art would, *à priori*, lead us to the conviction that, although he cleared his 'bosom of the perilous stuff' by moulding this perilous stuff into a work of art, he must have essentially outlived the storm before he painted it,—conquered his passion, and subdued the rebellious thoughts, before he made them plastic to his purpose. The poet cannot see to write when his eyes are full of tears ; cannot sing when his breast is swollen with sighs, and sobs choke utterance. He must rise superior to his grief before he can sublimate his grief in song. The artist is a master, not a slave ; he *wields* his passion, he is not hurried along by it ; he possesses, and is not possessed. Art enshrines the great sadness of the world, but is itself not sad. The storm of passion weeps itself away, and the heavy clouds roll off in quiet masses, to make room for the sun, which, in shining through, touches them to beauty with its rays. While pain is in its newness, it is pain, and nothing else ; it is not Art, but Feeling. Goethe could not write *Werther* before he had outlived Wertherism. It may have been, as he says, a 'general confession', and a confession which brought him certain relief; but we do not confess until we have repented, and we do not repent until we have outlived the error.

Werther was written rapidly. 'I completely isolated myself', he says ; 'nay, prohibited the visits of my friends, and put aside everything that did not immediately belong to the subject. Under such circumstances, and under so many preparations in secret, I wrote it in four weeks without any scneme of the whole, or treatment of any part being previously put on paper'. It is of this seclusion Merck writes: 'Le grand succès que son drame a eu lui tourne un peu la tête. Il se détache de tous ses amis, et n'existe que dans les compositions qu'il prépare pour le public'.

It is a matter of some interest to ascertain the exact truth respecting the date of the composition of *Werther*. As before stated, his own account is manifestly inaccurate; and the only thing which renders it difficult to assign the dates with tolerable precision is his statement that it was written in four weeks, without any scheme of the whole or treatment of any part having been previously put on paper. If we consent to believe that his memory in this case deceived him, the correspondence of the period furnishes hints from which we may conclude that in 1772, on the arrival of the news about Jerusalem's suicide, he made a general sketch, either in his mind or on paper; and that during the following year he worked at it from time to time. In June 1773 he writes to Kestner: 'And thus I dream and ramble through life, writing plays and *novels*, and the like'. In July he writes: 'I am working my own situation into art for the consolation of gods and men. I know what Lotte will say when she sees it, and I know what I shall answer her'. The word in the original is *Schauspiel* —play, drama; Viehoff suggests that he does not mean drama, but a work which will bring his situation *zur Schau*—before the public eye. In September of the same year he writes: 'You are always by me when I write. At present I am working at a novel, but it gets on slowly'. In November Frau Jacobi writes to him, acknowledging the receipt of a novel, in manuscript, no doubt, which delights her. In February 1774 Merck writes of him: 'Je prévois qu'un roman, qui paraîtra de lui à pâques, sera aussi bien reçu que son drame'. As we have nowhere a hint of any other novel besides *Werther* at this epoch, it is difficult to resist the evidence of these dates; and we must therefore conclude that the assertion in the *Autobiography* is wholly inexact.

In September 1774 he wrote to Lotte, sending her a copy of *Werther:* 'Lotte, how dear this little book is to me thou wilt feel in reading it, and this copy is as dear to me as if it were the only one in the world. Thou must have it, Lotte; I have kissed it a hundred times; have kept it locked up that no one might touch it. O Lotte! And I beg thee let no one except Meyers see it yet; it will be published at the Leipsic fair. I wish each to read it alone, thou alone,—Kestner alone,—and each to write me a little word about it. Lotte, adieu Lotte!'

Let us now take a glance at this work, which startled Europe, and which for a long while was all that Europe knew of Goethe*.

CHAPTER V

'WERTHER'

AUJOURDHUI l'homme désire immensément, mais il veut faiblement: In these words Guizot has written an epigraph for *Werther;* a book composed out of a double history, the history of its author's experience and the history of one of his friends.

The story of Jerusalem, whom he met in the Wetzlar circle, furnished Goethe with the machinery by which to introduce his own experience. He took many of the details from Kestner's long letter, sent shortly after the catastrophe : the letter may therefore be here abridged, as an introduction to the novel. Jerusalem, melancholy by temperament, was unhappy during the whole of his Wetzlar residence. He had been denied admittance into the high diplomatic society to which his position gave him claims ; he had been in unpleasant relations with his ambassador, whose secretary he was ; and he had fallen in love with the wife of his friend. Thus oppressed, he shunned company, was fond of long moonlight walks, and once lost himself in the wood, wandering about the whole night. But he was solitary even in his grief, told none of his friends the causes of his melancholy, and solaced himself with novels—the wretched novels of that day. To these he added all the tragedies he could get hold of ; English writers, especially the gloomy writers ; and various philosophical works. He wrote also essays, one on suicide, a subject which greatly occupied him. Mendelssohn's *Phædon* was his favourite work†. When the rumour reached Wetzlar of Goué's suicide he said that Goué was not a fit man for such a deed, but defended the act. A few days before his own unhappy end he was talking with

---

* SCOTT in prefacing his translation of *Götz* says : 'It was written by the *elegant* author of the *Sorrows of Werther*'.

† Goethe, it will be remembered, in Strasburg made an analysis of this work, contrasting it with Plato's.

Schleimitz about suicide, and said, 'It would be a bad look-out, however, if the shot were not to take effect!' The rest of the narrative must be told in Kestner's own words, the simple circumstantial style best fitting such a history.

'Last Tuesday he comes with a discontented look to Kielmansegge, who was ill. The latter asks how he is? "Better than I like to be". He also that day talked a good deal about love, which he had never done before ; and then about the *Frankfurter Zeitung*, which had for some time pleased him more than usual. In the afternoon (Tuesday) he goes to Secretary H.'s. Until eight o'clock in the evening they play tarock together. Annchen Brandt was also there ; Jerusalem accompanied her home. As they walk, Jerusalem often strikes his forehead, gloomily and repeatedly says : "If one were but dead—if one were but in heaven!" Annchen joked him about it ; he bargains for a place by her side in heaven, and at parting he says : "It is agreed, then, that I shall have a place by you in heaven".

'On Wednesday, as there were great doings at the Crown Prince, and everybody invited everybody, he went there to dinner, though he generally dined at home, and he brought Secretary H. with him. He did not behave there otherwise than usual ; if anything, he was more cheerful. After dinner, Secretary H. takes him home with him to see his wife. They take coffee ; Jerusalem says to Mrs. H. : "Dear Mrs. H., this is the last coffee I shall drink with you". She thinks it a joke, and answers in that tone. The same afternoon (Wednesday) Jerusalem was alone at H.'s : what took place there is unknown ; perhaps herein lies the cause of what followed. In the evening, just as it was dark, Jerusalem comes to Garbenheim, into tne usual inn, asks whether any one is in the room above? On the answer, No, he goes up, soon comes down again, goes out into the yard, towards the left, comes back after a little while, goes into the garden ; it becomes quite dark, he remains there a long time, the hostess makes her remarks upon this, he comes out of the garden, goes past her with hasty steps, all without saying a word, into the yard, hurrying straight away from it.

'In the meantime, or still later, something passed between H. and his wife, concerning which H. confides to a female friend that they quarrelled a little about Jerusalem ; and his wife at last desired that he would forbid him the house, whereupon he did so the following day, in a note.

'[It is said* that Secretary H. has given secret information that on the Wednesday before Jerusalem's death, when he was with H. and his wife taking coffee, the husband was obliged to go to the ambassador. When he returns, he observes an extraordinary seriousness in his wife, and a silence in Jerusalem, which appear strange to him, especially as he finds them so much changed after his return. Jerusalem goes away. Secretary H. makes his observations on the above-mentioned circumstances : he contracts suspicion that something injurious to him may have happened in his absence ; for he is very suspicious and jealous. Nevertheless he puts on a composed and cheerful air, and determines to put his wife to the test. He says : Jerusalem has often invited him to dinner ; what does she think of their asking Jerusalem for once to dine with them ? She, the wife, answers : No ; and she must entirely break off intercourse with Jerusalem ; he begins to behave in such a way that she must altogether avoid his society. And she held herself bound to tell him, her husband, what had passed in his absence. Jerusalem had thrown himself at her feet, and had wanted to make a formal declaration of love to her. She was naturally indignant at this, and had uttered many reproaches to him, etc. She now desired that her husband would forbid him, Jerusalem, the house, for she could and would neither see nor hear anything more of him.

'Hereupon, it is said, H. the next morning wrote the note to Jerusalem, etc.]

'In the night of Wednesday-Thursday he got up at two o'clock, awakened the servant, said he could not sleep, he was not well, has a fire lighted, tea made, yet is afterwards, to all appearance, very well.

'Thursday morning, Secretary H. sends Jerusalem a note. The maid will not wait for an answer, and goes away. Jerusalem has just been shaved. At eleven o'clock Jerusalem sends a note to Secretary H., who does not take it from the servant, and says he requires no answer, he cannot enter into any correspondence, and besides they saw each other every day at the office. When the servant brings back the note unopened, Jerusalem throws it on the table and says : Very good. (Perhaps to make the servant believe that it related to some indifferent matter.)

'In the middle of the day he dines at home, but takes little—

---

* The passage in brackets occurs in a subsequent letter ; it is inserted here to give the story continuity.

some soup. At one o'clock he sends a note to me, and at the same time one to his ambassador, in which he begs the latter to send him his money for this (or the following) month. The servant comes to me. I am not at home, nor is my servant. Jerusalem in the meantime is gone out, comes home about a quarter-past three, the servant gives him the note again. Jerusalem asks him why he did not leave it at my house with some maid-servant? He replies, because it was open and unsealed. Jerusalem: That was of no consequence, every one might read it; he must take it again. The servant thinks himself hereby warranted to read it also, reads it, and then sends it by a boy who waits in the house. I, in the meantime, had come home; it might be half-past three when I received the following note: "Might I beg of you to lend me your pistols for a journey which I am about to take?—J."* As I knew nothing of all this that I have told you, or of his principles, having never had any particular intercourse with him, I had not the least hesitation in sending him the pistols.

'The servant had read in the note that his master intended to make a journey, and indeed the latter had himself told him so, also had ordered everything for the journey the next morning at six o'clock, even the *friseur*, without his (the servant's) knowing whither, or with whom, or in what way. But as Jerusalem always kept his engagements secret from him, this did not arouse his suspicion. Nevertheless he thought to himself: " Is master perhaps going secretly to Brunswick, leaving me here alone?" etc. He had to take the pistols to a gunmaker's to get them loaded.

'The whole afternoon Jerusalem was busy alone; rummaged among his papers, wrote, walked, as the people below in the house heard, rapidly up and down the room. He also went out several times and paid his small debts; he had taken a pair of ruffles, he said to the servant; they did not satisfy him, he must return them to the tradesman; if he did not like to take them again, there was the money for them, which in fact the tradesman preferred.

'About seven o'clock the Italian master came to him. He found him restless and out of humour. He complained that he had his hypochondriasis again strongly, and about various things; said also, that the best he could do would be to take himself out of the world. The Italian urged upon him very seriously that such passions

* '*Dürfe ich Ew. Wohlgeb. wohl zu einer vorhabenden Reise um ihre Pistolen gehorsamst ersuchen?*' The German epistolary forms of civility are not translatable.

must be repressed by philosophy, etc. Jerusalem : That is not so easily done ; he would rather be alone to-day, he might leave him, etc. The Italian : He must go into society, amuse himself, etc. Jerusalem : Well, he was going out again. The Italian, seeing the pistols on the table, is anxious about the result, goes away at eight o'clock and to Kielmansegge, to whom he talks of nothing but Jerusalem, his restlessness and discontent, without, however, mentioning his anxiety, because he believed that he might be laughed at for it.

'The servant went to Jerusalem to take off his boots. But he said, he was going out again ; as he really did, before the Silberthor on the Starke Weide and elsewhere in the streets, where, with his hat pressed over his eyes, he rushed by several persons, with rapid steps, without seeing any one. He was also seen about this time standing a long time by the river, in a position as if he meant to throw himself in (so they say).

'Before nine o'clock he comes home, says to the servant that there must be more fuel put in the stove, because he shall not go to bed yet, also tells him to get everything ready for six o'clock in the morning, and has a pint of wine brought to him. The servant, that he may be ready very early, because his master was always very punctual, goes to bed in his clothes.

'As soon as Jerusalem was alone, he seems to have prepared everything for the dreadful deed. He tore up his correspondence and threw it under the table, as I have myself seen. He wrote two letters, one to his relations, the other to H. ; it is thought also that he wrote one to the ambassador Höffler, which the latter perhaps suppresses. They lay on the writing table. The first, which the medical man saw the next morning, contained in substance only what follows, as Dr. Held, who read it, related to me :

'" Dear father, dear mother, dear sisters and brother-in-law, forgive your unhappy son and brother ; God, God bless you ! "

'In the second, he entreated H. for forgiveness that he had disturbed the peace and happiness of his married life, and created dissension between this dear couple, etc. At first his inclination for H.'s wife had been only virtuous, etc. It is said to have been three sheets long, and to have ended thus :—" One o'clock. In the other life we shall see each other again ". (In all probability he shot himself immediately on finishing this letter.)'

The sensation produced in Wetzlar by this suicide was immense.

People who had scarcely seen Jerusalem were unable to quiet their agitation ; many could not sleep ; the women especially felt the deepest interest in the fate of this unhappy youth ; and *Werther* found a public ready for it.

With these materials in hand, let us take up the novel to see how Goethe employs them. Werther is a man who, not having yet learned self-mastery, imagines that his immense desires are proofs of immense superiority : one of those of whom it has been wittily said that they fancy themselves great painters because they paint with a big brush. He laughs at all rules, whether they be rules of Art, or rules which Convention builds like walls around our daily life. He hates order—in speech, in writing, in costume, in office. In a word, he hates all control. Gervinus remarks that he turns from men to children because they do not pain him, and from them to Nature because she does not contradict him ; from truth to poetry, and in poetry from the clear world of Homer to the formless world of Ossian. Very characteristic of the epoch is the boundless enthusiasm inspired by Ossian, whose rhetorical trash the Germans hailed as the finest expression of *Nature's* poetry. Old Samuel Johnson's stern, clear sense saw into the very heart of this subject when he said, 'Sir, a man might write such stuff for ever if he would but *abandon* his mind to it'. It is abandonment of the mind, throwing the reins on the horse's neck, which makes such writing possible ; and it was precisely this abandonment to impulse, this disregard of the grave remonstrances of reason and good sense, which distinguished the Werther epoch.

Werther is not Goethe. Werther perishes because he is wretched, and is wretched because he is so weak. Goethe was 'king over himself'. He saw the danger, and evaded it ; tore himself away from the woman he loved, instead of continuing in a dangerous position. Yet although Werther is not Goethe, there is one part of Goethe living in Werther. This is visible in the incidents and language as well as in the character. It is the part we see reappearing under the various masks of Weislingen, Clavigo, Faust, Fernando, Edward, Meister, and Tasso, which no critic will call the same lay figure variously draped, but which every critic must see belong to one and the same genus : men of strong desires and weak volitions, wavering impressionable natures unable to attain self-mastery. Goethe was one of those who are wavering because impressionable, but whose wavering is not weakness ; they oscillate, but they return into the direct path which their wills have prescribed. He was tender as well as impressionable. He could not be stern, but he could be resolute. He had only therefore, in imagination, to keep in abeyance the native force of resolution which gave him mastery, and in that abeyance a weak wavering character stood before him, the original of which was himself.

When a man delineates himself, he always shrinks from a complete confession. Our moral nature has its modesty. Strong as the impulse may be to drag into light that which lies hidden in the recesses of the soul, pleased as we may be to create images of ourselves, we involuntarily keep back something, and refuse to identify ourselves with the creation. There are few things more irritating than the pretension of another to completely understand us. Hence authors never thoroughly portray themselves. Byron, utterly without self-command, is fond of heroes proud and self-sustaining. Goethe, the strongest of men, makes heroes the footballs of circumstance. But he also draws from his other half the calm, self-sustaining characters. Thus we have the antithesis of Götz and Weislingen—Albert and Werther—Carlos and Clavigo —Jarno and Meister—Antonio and Tasso—the Captain and Edward ; and, deepened in colouring, Mephistopheles and Faust.

Werther is not much read nowadays, especially in England, where it labours under the double disadvantage of a bad name and an execrable translation. Yet it is well worth reading in the original, where it will be found very unlike the notion of it current among us. I remember many years ago reading it in the execrable English version with astonishment and contempt ; this contempt remained, until accidentally falling in with a Spanish translation, the exquisite beauty of the pictures changed my feeling into admiration, and Goethe's own wonderful prose afterwards fixed that admiration for ever. It is a masterpiece of style ; we may look through German literature in vain for such clear sunny pictures, fullness of life, and delicately managed simplicity. Its style is one continuous strain of music, which, restrained within the limits of prose, fulfils all the conditions of poetry ; dulcet as the sound of falling waters, and as full of sweet melancholy as an autumnal eve.

Nothing can be simpler than the structure of this book, wherein, as M. Marmier well remarks*, every detail is so arranged as to

* *Etudes sur Goethe*, p. 11.

lay bare the sufferings of a diseased spirit. Werther arrives at his chosen retreat, believing himself cured, and anticipating perfect happiness. He is painter and poet. The fresh spring mornings, the sweet cool evenings, soothe and strengthen him. He selects a place under the limes to read and dream away the hours. There he brings his pencil and his Homer. Everything interests him—the old woman who brings his coffee, the children who play around him, the story of a poor family. In this serene convalescence he meets with Charlotte, and a new passion agitates his soul. His simple uniform existence becomes changed. He endeavours by bodily activity to charm away his desires. The days no longer resemble each other : now ecstatic with hope, now crushed with despair. Winter comes : cold, sad, gloomy. He must away. He departs, and mingles with the world, but the world disgusts him. The monotony and emptiness of official life are intolerable to his pretensions ; the parchment pride of the noblesse is insulting to his sense of superiority. He returns to the peaceful scene of his former contentment, and finds indeed Charlotte, the children, his favourite woods and walks, but not the calmness which he seeks. The hopelessness of his position overwhelms him. Disgusted with the world—unsatisfied in his cravings—he dies by his own hand.

Rosenkrantz—in the true spirit of that criticism which seeks everywhere for meanings more recondite than the author dreamt of—thinks that Goethe exhibits great art in making Werther a diplomatist, because a diplomatist is a man of *shams* (*Scheinthuer*) ; but the truth is, Goethe made him precisely what he found him. His art is truth. He is so great an artist that the simplest realities have to him significance. Charlotte cutting bread and butter for the children—the scene of the ball—the children clinging around Werther for sugar, and pictures of that kind, betray so little inventive power, that they have excited the ridicule of some English critics, to whom poetry is a thing of pomp, not the beautiful vesture of reality. The beauty and art of Werther are not in the incidents (a Dumas would shrug despairing shoulders over such invention), but in the representation. What *is* Art but Representation ?*

The effect of *Werther* was prodigious. 'That nameless unrest',

* ' *L'art n'est qu'une forme*', says George Sand, with a truth few critics have penetrated ; let me add Goethe's own opinion—surely of weight in such matters : ' None will comprehend the simple truth that the highest, the only operation of art is representation'. (*Gestaltung.*)

says Carlyle, 'the blind struggle of a soul in bondage, that high, sad, longing discontent which was agitating every bosom, had driven Goethe almost to despair. All felt it; he alone could give it voice. And here lies the secret of his popularity; in his deep, susceptive heart he felt a thousand times more keenly what every one was feeling; with the creative gift which belonged to him as a poet, he bodied it forth into visible shape, gave it a local habitation and a name; and so made himself the spokesman of his generation. *Werther* is but the cry of that dim, rooted pain under which all thoughtful men of a certain age were languishing: it paints the misery, it passionately utters the complaint; and heart and voice all over Europe loudly and at once respond to it. True it prescribes no remedy; for that was a far different, far harder enterprise, to which other years and a higher culture were required; but even this utterance of pain, even this little, for the present is grasped at, and with eager sympathy appropriated in every bosom. If Byron's life weariness, his moody melancholy, and mad, stormful indignation, borne on the tones of a wild and quite artless melody could pierce so deep into many a British heart, now that the whole matter is no longer new—is indeed old and trite—we may judge with what vehement acceptance this *Werther* must have been welcomed, coming, as it did, like a voice from the unknown regions: the first thrilling peal of that impassioned dirge which, in country after country, men's ears have listened to till they were deaf to all else. For *Werther*, infusing itself into the core and whole spirit of literature, gave birth to a race of sentimentalists who have raged and wailed in every part of the world, till the better light dawned on them, or, at worst, exhausted Nature laid herself to sleep, and it was discovered that lamenting was unproductive labour. These funereal choristers, in Germany, a loud, haggard, tumultuous, as well as tearful class, were named the *Kraftmänner*, or Powermen; but have long since, like sick children, cried themselves to rest*'

Perhaps there never was a fiction which so startled and enraptured the world. Men of all kinds and classes were moved by it. It was the companion of Napoleon, when in Egypt; it penetrated into China. To convey in a sentence its wondrous popularity, we may state that in Germany it became a people's book, hawked about the streets, printed on miserable paper, like an

* *Miscellanies*, vol. 1, p. 272.

ancient ballad; and in the Chinese empire, Charlotte and Werther were modelled in porcelain*.

Objectors of course there were. Lessing, for example, who neither suffered from the disease of the epoch, nor tolerated any approach to sentimentality, thought so fiery a production ought to have a cold epilogue to counteract it. ' Do you believe', he wrote, 'that any Roman or Grecian youth would *thus* and *therefore* have committed suicide? Certainly not. They knew how to guard themselves from the extravagances of love, and in the days of Socrates such an ἐξ ἔρωτος κατοχὴ whom τι τολμᾶν παρὰ φύσιν impelled, would scarcely be pardoned even by a girl. Such little-great questionable originals only suit our Christian culture, which knows so well how to transform a corporeal necessity into a spiritual perfection. So, worthy Goethe, let us have a concluding chapter ; and the more cynical the better †'. This is a misstatement of the whole question. It is not the extravagance of love which causes Werther's suicide : it is his own diseased moral nature which makes life insupportable, and which makes unhappy love the spark that fires the train. Moveover, one reads with surprise this reference to Greek and Roman life, coming from so admirable a scholar as Lessing. He forgot that Sophocles, in the *Antigone*,

---

* While in Italy, he received a letter from a young Frenchman, who said : ' Oui, Monsieur, je vous dois la meilleure action de ma vie, par conséquent, la racine de plusieurs autres, et pour moi votre livre est bon. Si j'avais le bonheur d'habiter le même pays que vous, j'irais vous embrasser, et vous dire mon secret ; mais malheureusement j'en habite un où personne ne croirait au motif qui vient de me déterminer à cette démarche. Soyez satisfait, Monsieur, d'avoir pu à trois cents lieues de votre demeure ramener la cœur d'un jeune homme à l'honnêteté et à la vertu, toute une famille va être tranquille, et mon cœur jouit d'une bonne action '.

Let me not forget the visit of his English admirer, who accosted him on the stairs with ' You must be the author of *Werther!*' adding that he could not wait a moment longer, all he wanted to say was this, ' I will not repeat what you must have heard from thousands, for indeed your work has not affected me so much as it has others; but when I think what it required to write such a book, I am lost in astonishment '. Having eased his mind of this weight, he wished Goethe a hearty farewell, and ran downstairs.

A similar story is told by Schiller in a letter to Körner. ' A shrivelled figure entered my room, and asked me if I was not Councillor Schiller. I replied 'in the affirmative. "I heard that you were here, and could not restrain myself from seeing the author of *Don Carlos*". "*Gehorsamer Diener!* your most obedient servant", said I ; "whom have I the honour of addressing?" " I have not the happiness of being known to you. My name is Vulpius ". " I am indebted to you for your politeness; unluckily I have an engagement ". " Oh, sir, I beg you won't mention it. I am quite satisfied with having seen you "'.—*Briefwechsel*, i, p. 105.

At the risk of swelling this note to unreasonable dimensions, I must quote a passage from *Pliny's Letters*, which records a similar anecdote : ' Nunquamne legisti Gaditanum quemdam Titi Livii nomine gloriaque commotum ad visendum eum ab ultimo terrarum orbe venisse, statimque ut viderat abiisse '.—*Lib.* ii, *Ep.* iii.

† LESSING : *Werke*, x, 225, Letter to Eschenberg.

It is surmised that Lessing's objections to *Werther* were sharpened by his dislike at recognizing his young friend, Jerusalem, thus brought into a fiction. A letter from Weisse to Garve, quoted by APPELL, *Werther und seine Zeit*, p. 50, confirms this.

makes an unhappy lover commit suicide because his mistress is lost to him.   He forgot, also, that the Stoics introduced the 'fashion' of suicide into Rome ; and in Alexandria the Epicureans established a 'society for the suppression of life'—the συναποθανούμενοι —where, having exhausted every pleasure, the members assembled at a feast, the wine-cup went freely round, and in the midst of this orgie they quietly put an end to their contemptible existences :—a new variation of the conversazione, at which, instead of music and æsthetic tea, the guests were invited to supper and suicide.

The Berlin Aristarchus—Nicolai—an upright, but narrow-minded man, and a great enemy of all *Schwärmerei*, wrote by way of criticism a parody called the *Joys of Young Werther*, in which sentimentalism is ridiculed :—Werther shoots himself with chicken's blood only, and marries Charlotte 'and lives happy all the rest of his life'.

Goethe's answer to this was 'a burlesque poem called *Nicolai at Werther's grave*, which, however, cannot be communicated'.   This poem has been recovered and printed by Boas*.   It is exceedingly coarse, and not very humorous.   The admirers of Werther, of course, are greatly incensed against Nicolai ; but they forget that Nicolai never denied the talent of the work, he only echoed Lessing's objection to its tendency.   His criticism, moreover, was but a feather in the scale against the praise which poured in from all sides.

While the public was reading the tragic story of *Werther* through fast-flowing tears, a painful sense of indignation rose in the breasts of Kestner and Charlotte at seeing themselves thus dragged into publicity, their story falsified.   The narrative was in many respects too close to reality not to be very offensive in its *deviations* from reality.   The figures were unmistakable ; and yet they were not the real figures.   The eager public soon found out who were the principal personages, and that a real history was at the bottom of the romance ; but as the whole truth could not be known, the Kestners found themselves in a very false light.   They were hurt by this indiscretion of their friend ; more hurt perhaps than they chose to confess ; and we may read, in the following fragment of the sketch of the letter sent by Kestner on receipt of the book, the accents of an offended friend whose pride restrains the full expression of his anger :

'Your *Werther* might have given me great pleasure, since it

* *Nachträge zu Goethe's Werke:* Lief. 1, p. 12.

could have reminded me of many interesting scenes and incidents. But as it is, it has in certain respects given me little edification. You know I like to speak my mind.

'It is true, you have woven something new into each person, or have fused several persons into one. So far good. But if in this interweaving and fusing you had taken counsel of your heart, you would not have so prostituted the real persons whose features you borrow. You wished to draw from nature, that your picture might be truthful ; and yet you have combined so much that is contradictory, that you have missed the very mark at which you aimed. The distinguished author will revolt against this judgment, but I appeal to reality and truth itself when I pronounce that the artist has failed. The real Lotte would, in many instances, be grieved if she were like the Lotte you have there painted. I know well that it is said to be a character compounded of two, but the Mrs. H. whom you have partly inwoven was also incapable of what you attribute to your heroine. But this expenditure of fiction was not at all necessary to your end, to nature and truth, for it was without any such behaviour on the part of a woman—a behaviour which must ever be dishonourable even to a more than ordinary woman —that Jerusalem shot himself.

'The real Lotte, whose friend you nevertheless wish to be, is in your picture, which contains too much of her not to suggest her strongly : is, I say—but no, I will not say it, it pains me already too much only to think it. And Lotte's husband—you called him your friend, and God knows that he was so—is with her.

'The miserable creature of an Albert ! In spite of its being an alleged fancy picture and not a portrait, it also has such traits of an original (only external traits, it is true, thank God, only external), that it is easy to guess the real person. And if you wanted to have him act so, need you have made him such a blockhead ? that forthwith you might step forward and say, See what a fine fellow I am !'

Kestner here touches on a point of morality in literature worth consideration. While emphatically declaring that the artist must take his materials from reality, must employ his own experience, and draw the characters he has really known, we must as emphatically declare that he is bound to represent his experience in forms sufficiently different from the reality to prevent the public reading actual histories beneath his invention, and recognizing the persons he has employed as lay figures, whenever those persons are assigned parts which they would reject. There is, of course, great difficulty in keeping to truth while avoiding the betrayal of actual occurrences ; but it is a difficulty which is commanded by morality.

Goethe was evidently astounded at the effect his book had produced on his friends : ' I must at once write to you, my dear and angry friends, and free my heart. The thing is done ; the book is out ; forgive me if you can. I will hear nothing till the event has proved how exaggerated your anxiety is, and till you have more truly felt, in the book itself, the innocent mingling of fiction and truth. Thou hast, dear Kestner, exhausted everything, cut away all the ground of my excuse, and left me nothing to say ; yet I know not, my heart has still more to say, although I cannot express it. I am silent, but the sweet presentiment I must still retain, and I hope eternal Fate has that in store for me which will bind us yet closer one to the other. Yes, dear ones, I who am so bound to you by love, must still remain debtor to you and your children for the uncomfortable hours which my—name it as you will—has given you. . . . And now, my dear ones, when anger rises within you, think, oh think only that your old Goethe, ever and ever, and now more than ever, is your own '.

Their anger fell. They saw that he had committed an indiscretion, but had done no more. They wrote forgiveness, as we gather from this letter Goethe sent on the 21st of November :

' Here I have thy letter, Kestner ! On a strange desk, in a painter's studio, for yesterday I began to paint in oil, I have thy letter, and must give thee my thanks ! Thanks, dear friend ! Thou art ever the same good soul ! O that I could spring on thy neck, throw myself at Lotte's feet, one, one minute, and all, all that should be done away with, explained, which I could not make clear with quires of paper ! O ye unbelieving ones ! I could exclaim. Ye of little faith ! Could you feel the thousandth part of what *Werther* is to a thousand hearts, you would not reckon the sacrifice you have made towards it ! Here is a letter, read it, and send me word quickly what thou thinkest of it, what impression it makes on thee. Thou sendest me Hennings' letter ; he does not condemn me ; he excuses me. Dear brother Kestner ! if you will wait, you shall be contented. I would not, to save my own life, call back *Werther*, and believe me, believe in me, thy anxieties, thy *gravamina* will vanish like phantoms of the night if thou hast patience ; and then, between this and a year, I

promise you in the most affectionate, peculiar, fervent manner, to
disperse, as if it were a mere north-wind fog and mist, whatever
may remain of suspicion, misinterpretation, etc., in the gossiping
public, though it is a herd of swine. *Werther* must—must be !
You do not feel *him*, you only feel *me* and *yourselves;* and that
which you call *stuck on*, and in spite of you, and others, is *interwoven.* If I live, it is thee I have to thank for it ; thus thou art
not Albert. And thus—

  'Give Lotte a warm greeting for me, and say to her : "To know
that your name is uttered by a thousand hallowed lips with reverence, is surely an equivalent for anxieties which would scarcely,
apart from anything else, vex a person long in common life, where
one is at the mercy of every tattler".

  'If you are generous and do not worry me, I will send you
letters, cries, sighs after *Werther*, and if you have faith, believe
that all will be well, and gossip is nothing, and weigh well your
philosopher's letter, which I have kissed.

  'O then !—hast not felt how the man embraces thee, consoles
thee, and in thy—-in Lotte's worth, finds consolation enough under
the wretchedness which has terrified you even in the fiction? Lotte,
farewell,—Kestner, love me, and do not worry me'.

  The pride of the author in his darling breaks out in this letter,
now his friends have forgiven him. We must admit that Kestner
had reason to be annoyed ; the more so as his friends, identifying
him with the story, wrote sympathetically about it. He had to
reply to Hennings on the subject, and in telling him the true
story, begged him to correct the false reports. He says : 'In
the first part of *Werther*, Werther is Goethe himself. In Lotte
and Albert he has borrowed traits from us, my wife and myself.
Many of the scenes are quite true, and yet partly altered ; others
are, at least in our history, unreal. For the sake of the second
part, and in order to prepare for the death of Werther, he has
introduced various things into the first part which do not at all
belong to us. For example, Lotte has never either with Goethe
or with any one else stood in the intimate relation which is there
described ; in this we have certainly great reason to be offended
with him, for several accessory circumstances are too true and
too well known for people not to point to us. He regrets it now,
but of what use is that to us? It is true he has a great regard
for my wife ; but he ought to have depicted her more faithfully in
this point, that she was too wise and delicate ever to let him go

so far as is represented in the first part. She behaved to him in such a way as to make her far dearer to me than before, if this had been possible. Moreover, our engagement was never made public, though not, it is true, kept a secret : still she was too bashful ever to confess it to any one. And there was no engagement between us but that of hearts. It was not till shortly before my departure (when Goethe had already been a year away from Wetzlar at Frankfurt, and the disguised Werther had been dead half a year) that we were married. After the lapse of a year, since our residence here, we have become father and mother. The dear boy lives still, and gives us, thank God, much joy. For the rest, there is in Werther much of Goethe's character and manner of thinking. Lotte's portrait is completely that of my wife. Albert might have been made a little more ardent. The second part of *Werther* has nothing whatever to do with us. . . . When Goethe had printed his book, he sent us an early copy, and thought we should fall into raptures with what he had done. But we at once saw what would be the effect, and your letter confirms our fears. I wrote very angrily to him. He then for the first time saw what he had done ; but the book was printed, and he hoped our fears were idle '. In another letter to the same, Kestner says : ' You have no idea what a man he is. But when his great fire has somewhat burnt itself out, then we shall all have the greatest joy in him '.

We have thus brought to a close the history of *Werther*, its composition and effect : a history so important in the biography of its author, that we might have been excused for having devoted so much space to it, even if the letters, which have furnished the evidence, did not throw so strong a light upon a period very inadequately represented in the *Wahrheit und Dichtung*.

On the 28th August 1849, the hundredth anniversary of the great poet's birth, when all Germany joined in a jubilee, a small marble monument was erected in the well-known *Wertherplatz* without the Wetzlar gates, where Goethe was wont to sit and muse ; three lime trees are planted round it, bearing this inscription :

RUHEPLATZ DES DICHTERS

GOETHE

ZU SEINEM ANDENKEN FRISCH BEPFLANZT
BEI DER JUBELFEIER AM 28 AUG. 1849.

CHAPTER VI

THE LITERARY LION

GOETHE was now at the perilous juncture in an author's career, when having just achieved a splendid success, he is in danger either of again snatching at laurels in presumptuous haste, or of suffering himself to repose upon the laurels he has won, talking of greatness, instead of learning to be great. Both perils he avoided. He neither traded on his renown, nor conceived that his education was complete. Wisely refraining from completing fresh important works, he kept up the practice of his art by trifles, and the education of his genius by serious studies.

Among these trifles are *Clavigo*, the *Jahrmarktsfest zu Plundersweilen*, and the *Prolog zu Bahrdt's Neuesten Offenbarungen*. For the composition of *Clavigo* we must retrace our steps a little, and once more see him in the Frankfurt circle during the summer of 1774, that is, before the *publication* of *Werther*, which was delayed till October. In his sister's pleasant circle we have already noticed Antoinette Gerock, who was fascinating enough to fix his attentions. They were accustomed to meet once a week, in picnics and pleasure parties ; at one of these it was agreed to institute a marriage lottery. He thus speaks of it : 'Every week lots were drawn to determine the couples who should be symbolically wedded ; for it was supposed that every one knew well enough how lovers should conduct themselves, but few had any proper conceptions of the requisite demeanour between man and wife. General rules were laid down to the effect that these wedded couples should preserve a polite indifference, not sitting near each other, nor speaking to each other too often, much less indulging in anything like caresses. At the same time, side by side with this polite indifference, this well-bred calm, anything like discord or suspicion was to be sedulously avoided ; and whoever succeeded in gaining the affections of his wife without using the importunities of a lover, was supposed to have achieved their ideal. Much sportive confusion and agreeable pleasantry of course arose from this scheme '. Strangely enough, to him it fell thrice to have the same girl appointed by hazard to fill the place of his wife. When fate had brought them together for the third time, it was resolved unanimously that they should be no longer separated, that heaven had spoken, and that hereafter they were to consider themselves as man and wife, and not to draw lots as the others did. At these reunions something new was generally read aloud by one of the party. One evening Goethe brought with him as a novelty the *Mémoire* of Beaumarchais. During the conversation which ensued, Goethe's partner said to him : ' If I were thy liege lady, and not thy wife, I would command thee to change this memoir into a play, to which it seems well suited'. He answered : 'That thou mayst see, my love, that liege lady and wife are one, I here undertake that this day week I will read a play on this very matter'. So bold a promise excited astonishment, but he resolved on fulfilling it. 'What, in such cases', he says, 'is termed invention, was with me spontaneous. While escorting my titulary wife home I was silent ; and on her inquiring the cause, I told her that I was thinking out the play, and had already got into the middle of it— intending to show her how gladly I would do anything to please her. Upon which she pressed my hand, and I snatched a kiss. "Thou must not step out of thy character", she exclaimed : "they say it is not proper for married folks to be loving". "Let them say what they please", I replied, "we will have it our own way"'.

He confesses that before reading the memoir aloud, the subject had appeared to him eminently dramatic ; though without such a stimulus as he had received, this piece, like so many others, would have remained among the number of *possible* creations. The only novelty in it was his mode of treating the villains. He was weary of these characters so frequently represented, who, from revenge, or from hate, or from trivial motives, ruin a noble nature ; and he wished in Carlos to show the working of clear good sense, against passion and inclination. Justified by the precedent of Shakespeare, he translated, word for word, such portions of the memoir as were dramatic ; borrowing the dénouement from an English ballad*. He was ready before the week expired, and read the piece to a delighted audience.

A few words on this memoir may be useful. Beaumarchais had two sisters living in Madrid, one married to an architect, the other, Marie, engaged to Clavijo, a young author without fortune. No sooner had Clavijo obtained the office he had long solicited, than he refused to fulfil his promise. Beaumarchais hurried to Madrid ; his object was twofold : to save the reputation of his

---

* So he says ; but his memory deceived him. The ballad was an old German ballad, *Das Lied vom Herren und der Magd.* See HERDER's *Nachlass*, I, 159.

sister, and to put a little speculation of his own on foot. He sought Clavijo, and by his sangfroid and courage extorted from him a written avowal of his contemptible conduct. No sooner is this settled, than Clavijo, alarmed at the consequences, solicits a reconciliation with Marie, offering to marry her. Beaumarchais consents, but just as the marriage is about to take place he learns that Clavijo is secretly conspiring against him, accusing him of having extorted the marriage by force, in consequence of which he has procured an order from the government to expel Beaumarchais from Madrid. Irritated at such villainy, Beaumarchais goes to the ministers, reaches the king, and avenges himself by getting Clavijo dismissed from his post. This is, in brief, the substance of the *Mémoire* which appeared in February 1774. The adventure occurred in 1764, so that Clavijo, who subsequently became a distinguished writer, might have seen himself not only held up to odium in the sparkling pages of Beaumarchais, but represented on the stage of every German theatre. He died in 1806, vice-president of the Natural History Society in Madrid, having previously translated Buffon, and edited the *Mercurio historico y politico de Madrid*. We must suppose that Goethe knew nothing of the existence of Clavijo, when he wrote the drama.

With Beaumarchais in our hands it is curious to read *Clavigo*, which is as close a reproduction as the dramatic form admits ; and is an evidence that Goethe did wisely in not at once proceeding to complete *Faust* (fragments of which were written) or *Cæsar*. He would infallibly have repeated himself. He has repeated himself in *Clavigo :* the external circumstances are changed, but the experience is the same. Clavigo is another Weislingen, and was meant to be so : ' I have written a tragedy ', Goethe writes to Schönborn, ' *Clavigo*, a modern anecdote, dramatized with the greatest simplicity and heartfelt truth. My hero is an irresolute, half-great, half-little man, the pendant to Weislingen, or rather Weislingen himself as the chief person '. He has well portrayed the weak, ambitious nature of one who hopes to rise still higher in the world, but feels his career obstructed by a passion which made him happy in the obscure days of penniless youth. The popular author and court favourite aspires to some woman of rank ; an aspiration in which he is encouraged by his friend Carlos, who mockingly strips off the garlands with which the poet's imagination had decked his mistress.

Marie is a weak, sensitive creature, without much individuality, and is perhaps the poorest sketch Goethe has given of a woman. There is, however, one little touch that shows the poet; it is a sentence which escapes Marie, when Clavigo returns repentant to her feet, appealing to her affection: she throws herself on his neck, exclaiming, 'Ah, sister, whence knows he that I love him so—*woher weiss er dass ihn so liebe!*'

Marie is overjoyed at Clavigo's return, but her joy is brief. The demon of ambition, aided by the cold sarcasms of Carlos (in whom we see the germ of Mephistopheles), once more troubles Clavigo, and turns him from a marriage so ill suited to his hopes. Carlos bitterly, but truly, says to him, 'There is nothing in the world so pitiable as an undecided man, who wavers between two feelings, hoping to reconcile them'.—He suggests that Beaumarchis should be assassinated. 'He who orders the assassination of the brother, pantomimically intimates that he will have nothing to do with the sister', adds Carlos, quite in the Mephistophelic tone. They determine on a contemptible plan. Beaumarchais is to be imprisoned for having insulted and threatened Clavigo under his own roof. The order for arrest arrives, and Marie dies broken-hearted at the treachery of her lover.

Up to this point—short at least of the death of Marie—Beau-marchais' *Mémoire* has been faithfully followed; a fifth act is added, with a dénouement to fit it for the stage.

Powerful as this scene is in theatrical effect, one cannot but admit that æsthetically it is poor and almost commonplace. The clumsiness by which the meeting is contrived has been noticed by Rosenkranz *. Clavigo is seeking Carlos; he orders the servant who lights the way *not* to pass through the street where the Beaumarchais family resides, yet the servant actually leads him there because it is the shorter route. The whole tone of this fifth act is not in harmony with what precedes. The act is *grafted on*—it does not *grow out of*—the subject.

As a stage play the interest is great: the situations are effective; the dramatic collision perfect; the plot is clearly and rapidly evolved; the language vigorous, passionate, and pointed. But it must not be tried by any high standard. Merck, anxious about his friend's reputation, would not consent to judge the play according to the theatre standard, but exclaimed, 'Such trash as this you must not write again; others can do that!' Goethe

* *Goethe und seine Werke*, p. 185.

Friedrich Gottlieb Klopstock

says, that in this Merck was wrong, and for the first time did him an injury. 'We should not in all things transcend the notions which men have already formed ; it is right that much should be done in accordance with the common way of thinking. Had I written a dozen such pieces (and it would have been easy to do so with a little stimulus), three or four of them would perhaps have kept their place upon the stage'.

This can scarcely be accepted as conclusive reasoning. Merck might have replied, 'Perhaps so; but you have genius fit for higher things than stage plays'. Nevertheless, as before hinted, I think Goethe was right in his course, although the reasons he alleges are unsatisfactory. *Clavigo*, like the other trifles he composed at this period, must be regarded as the sketches with which an artist fills his portfolio, not the works which are to brighten galleries. The impulse to create was imperious ; if trifles were demanded, he created trifles. His immense activity was forced to expend itself on minor works, because he dimly felt himself unripe for greater works.

He was beginning to feel himself a man of consequence ; the notable men of the day eagerly sought his acquaintance. Among these men we must note Klopstock, Lavater, Basedow, Jacobi, and the Stolbergs. Correspondence led to personal intercourse. Klopstock arrived in Frankfurt in this October 1774, just before *Werther* appeared. Goethe saw him, read the fragments of *Faust* to him, and discussed skating with him. But the great religious poet was too far removed from the strivings of his young rival to conceive that attachment for him which he felt for men like the Stolbergs, or to inspire Goethe with any keen sympathy.

In June, Lavater also came to Frankfurt. This was a few months before Klopstock's visit. He had commenced a correspondence with Goethe on the occasion of the *Briefe des Pastors*. Those were great days of correspondence. Letters were written to be read in circles, and were shown about like the last new poem. Lavater pestered his friends for their portraits, and for ideal portraits (according to their conception) of our Saviour, all of which were destined for the work on *Physiognomy* on which he was then engaged. The artist who took Goethe's portrait sent Lavater the portrait of Bahrdt instead, to see what he would make of it ; the physiognomist was not taken in ; he stoutly denied the possibility of such a resemblance. Yet when he saw the actual

Goethe he was not satisfied. He gazed in astonishment, exclaiming, ' *Bist's ?* Art thou he ? ' ' *Ich bin's.* I am he ', was the answer ; and the two embraced each other. Still the physiognomist was dissatisfied. ' I answered him with my native and acquired realism, that as God had willed to make me what I was, he, Lavater, must even so accept me '.

The first surprise over, they began to converse on the weightiest topics. Their sympathy was much greater than appears in Goethe's narrative, written many years after the characters of both had developed themselves : Goethe's into what we shall subsequently see ; Lavater's into that superstitious dogmatism and priestly sophistication which exasperated and alienated many of his friends.

Lavater forms a curious figure in the history of those days : a compound of the intolerant priest and the factitious sentimentalist. He had fine talents, and a streak of genius, but he was ruined by vanity. In his autobiographic sketch* he has represented himself indicating as a child the part he was to play as a man. Like many other children, he formed for himself a peculiar and intimate re-lation with God, which made him look upon his playfellows with scorn and pity, because they did not share his ' need and use of God '. He prayed for wonders, and the wonders came. God corrected his school exercises. God concealed his many faults, and brought to light his virtuous deeds. In fact, Lavater was said to have been ' from the beginning the friend of Lies, who stooped to the basest flatteries to gain influence '. To this flattering, cring-ing softness he united the spirit of priestly domination. His first works made a great sensation. In 1769 he translated Bonnet's *Palingénésie*, adding notes in a strain of religious sentimentalism then very acceptable. At a time when the critics were rehabili-tating Homer and the early singers, it was natural that the religious world should attempt a restoration of the early Apostolic spirit. At a time when belief in poetic inspiration was a first article of the creed, belief in prophetic inspiration found eager followers. I have already touched on the sentimental extravagance of the time. The lovely Countess Branconi writes to him : ' O toi chéri pour la vie, l'âme de mon âme ! Ton mouchoir, tes cheveux, sont pour moi ce que mes jarretières sont pour toi ! ' etc., which is surpassed by what he allowed to be addressed to him by another admirer : ' Oh that I could lie on thy breast in Sabbath holy

* See GESSNER'S *Biographie Lavaters.*

Johann Kaspar Lavater

evening stillness—oh thou angel!' This kind of rhodomontade went all round. They wept, and were wept on.

At the time of his arrival in Frankfurt, Lavater was in the first flush of renown. Goethe was peculiarly attracted to him, not only by the singularity of his character, but by a certain community of religious *sentiment*. Community of creed there was not, and could not be. What Goethe *felt* we may gather from his attachment to Fräulein von Klettenberg ; what he *thought* may be seen in such letters as this to Pfenninger, a friend of Lavater's : ' Believe me, dear brother, the time will come when we shall understand each other. You talk to me as a sceptic, who wishes to *understand*—to have all *demonstrated*—who has had no experience. The contrary of all this is the fact. Am I not more resigned in matters of Understanding and Demonstration than you are ? I am, perhaps, a fool to express myself in your language to please you. I ought, by a purely experimental pyschology, to place my inmost being before you to show that I am a man, and hence can only feel as other men feel, and that all which appears contradiction between us is only dispute about words, arising from my inability to feel things under other combinations than those actually felt by me, and hence, in expressing their relation to me, I name them differently, which has been the eternal source of controversy, and will for ever remain so. And yet you always want to oppress me with *evidences*. Wherefore ? Do I need evidence of my own existence ? Evidence that I feel ? I only treasure, love, and demand evidences which convince me that thousands (or even one) have felt before me that which strengthens and invigorates me. And thus to me the word of man becomes like unto the word of God. With my whole soul, I throw myself upon the neck of my brother : Moses, Prophet, Evangelist, Apostle, Spinoza, or Machiavelli ! To each, however, I would say : Dear friend, it is with you as it is with me. Certain details you apprehend clearly and powerfully, but the whole can no more be conceived by you than by me '.

He names Spinoza in this very remarkable passage ; and the whole letter seems like a reproduction of the passage in the *Ethics*, where that great thinker, anticipating modern psychology, shows ' that each person judges of things according to the disposition of his brain, or rather accepts the affections of his imaginations as real things. It is no wonder therefore (as we may note in passing) that so many controversies have arisen among men, and that these controversies have at last given birth to scepticism. For although human bodies are alike in many things, there are more in which they differ, and thus what to one appears good, to another appears evil ; what to one appears order, to another appears confusion ; what to one is pleasant, to another is unpleasant* '.

It is unnecessary to interrupt the narrative here by more closely scrutinizing his studies of Spinoza ; enough, if the foregoing citation has made present to our minds the probable parentage of Goethe's opinions. The contrast between Lavater's Christianity and the Christianity of Fräulein von Klettenberg interested him, and gave him matter for thought. He agreed somewhat with both, but he agreed perfectly with neither. The difference between Faith and Knowledge he thus reconciled : ' In Faith everything depends on the fact of believing ; *what* we believe is quite secondary. Faith is a profound sense of security, springing from confidence in the All-powerful, Inscrutable Being. The strength of this confidence is the main point. But *what* we think of this Being depends on other faculties, or even on other circumstances, and is altogether indifferent. Faith is a holy vessel, into which every man may pour his feelings, his understanding, and his imagination, as entirely as he can. Knowledge is the antipode of Faith. Therein the point is not *whether* we know, but *what* we know, *how much* we know, and *how well* we know it. Hence men may dispute about knowledge, because it can be widened, corrected ; but not about Faith '.

So strong was the attraction of Lavater's society that Goethe accompanied him to Ems. The journey was charming ; beautiful summer weather, and Lavater's cheerful gaiety formed pleasant accompaniments to their religious discussions. On returning to Frankfurt, another and very different celebrity was there to distract his attention—Basedow, the education reformer. No greater contrast to Lavater could have been picked out of the celebrities of that day. Lavater was handsome, clean, cheerful, flattering, insinuating, devout ; Basedow ugly, dirty among the dirty, sarcastic, domineering, and aggressively heterodox. One

---

* ' Que omnia satis ostendunt, unumquemque *pro dispositione cerebri de rebus judicasse*, vel potius imaginationis affectiones pro rebus accepisse. Quare non mirum est (ut hoc etiam obiter notemus) quod inter homines tot, quot experimur, controversiæ ortæ sint ex quibus tandem Scepticismus. Nam quamvis humana corpora in multis conveniunt, in plurimis tamen discrepant, et ideo id quod uni bonum alteri malum videtur ; quod uni ordinatum, alteri confusum ; quod uni gratum, alteri ingratum est '.
—*Ethices : Pars* I, *Append.*

tried to restore Apostolic Christianity ; the other could not restrain the most insolent sarcasms on the Bible, the Trinity, and every form of Christian creed. One set up as a Prophet, the other as a Pedagogue.

Basedow (born 1723) was also early in indicating his future part. At school the wild and dirty boy manifested rebellious energy against all system and all method ; studied in a desultory, omnivorous manner, as if to fit himself for everything ; ran away from home, and became a lackey in a nobleman's house ; caught up Rousseau's doctrine about a state of nature, which he applied to Education ; wrote endless works, or rather incessant repetitions of one work ; shouted with such lusty lungs that men could not but hear him ; appealed to the nation for support in his philanthropic schemes ; collected 'a rent' from philanthropists and dupes ; attacked established institutions, and parenthetically all Christian tenets ; and proved himself a man of restless energy, and of vast and comprehensive ignorance. He made considerable noise in the world ; and in private lived somewhat the life of a restless hog who has taken to philanthropy and freethinking.

Much as such a character was opposed to his own, Goethe, eager and inquiring, felt an attraction towards it, as towards a character to study. Like many other studies, this had its drawbacks. He was forced to endure the incessant smoking and incessant sarcasms of the dirty educationist. The stench he endured with firmness ; the anti-Christian tirades he answered with paradoxes wilder than any he opposed. ' Such a splendid opportunity of exercising, if not of elevating, my mind ', he says, ' was not to be thrown away ; so prevailing on my father and friends to undertake my law business, I once more set off for the Rhine in Basedow's company '. Basedow filled the carriage with smoke, and killed the time with discussions. On the way they fell in with Lavater, and the three visited several chateaux, especially those of noble ladies, everywhere anxious to receive the literary Lions. Goethe, we may parenthetically note, is in error when he says that he was on this voyage greatly pestered by the women wanting to know all about the truth of *Werther ;* the fact being that *Werther* did not appear until the following October ; for although the exigencies of my narrative have caused a certain anticipation in chronology, this journey with Lavater and Basedow, here made to follow the publication of *Werther*, came *before* it in Goethe's life. If we are not to believe that the women crowded round him with questions about Lotte, we can readily believe that children crowded round him, begging him to tell them stories.

Wild and 'genius-like' was his demeanour. 'Basedow and I', he says, 'seemed to be ambitious of proving who could behave the most outrageously'. Very characteristic is the glimpse we catch of him quitting the ball-room, after a heating dance, and rushing up to Basedow's room. The Philanthropist did not go to bed. He threw himself in his clothes upon the bed, and there, in a room full of tobacco smoke and bad air, dictated to his scribe. When fatigue overcame him, he slept awhile, his scribe remaining there, pen in hand, awaiting the awakening of the Philanthropist, who, on opening his eyes, at once resumed the flow of his dictation. Into such a room sprang the dance-heated youth, began a fierce discussion on some problem previously mooted between them, hurried off again to look into the eyes of some charming partner, and before the door closed, heard Basedow recommence dictating.

This union of philosophy with amusement, of restless theorizing with animal spirits, indicates the tone of his mind. 'I am contented', he said to Lavater, 'I am happy. That I feel; and yet the whole centre of my joy is an overflowing yearning towards something which I have not, something which my soul perceives dimly'. He could reach that 'something' neither through the pious preaching of Lavater, nor through the aggressive preaching of Basedow. Very graphic and ludicrous is the picture he gives of his sitting like a citizen of the world between a prophet on the right and a prophet on the left hand—

> Prophete rechts, Prophete links,
> Das Welt-Kind in der Mitten—

quietly eating a chicken while Lavater explains to a country parson the mystery of the Revelation, and Basedow astonishes a dancing-master with a scornful exposure of the inutility of baptism *.

Nor could he find this 'something' in Jacobi, with whom he now came into sentimental intimacy. He could to some extent sympathize with Jacobi's sentimental cravings, and philosophic, religious aspirations, for he was bitten with the Wertherism of the epoch. He could gaze with him in uneasy ecstasy upon the moonlight quivering on the silent Rhine, and pour forth the songs which were murmuring within his breast. He could form a friendship, believing it to rest upon an eternal basis of perfect sympathy ;

* See the poem *Diné zu Coblentz.*

Friedrich Heinrich Jacobi

but the inward goad which drove him onwards and onwards was not to be eradicated until fresh experience had brought about fresh metamorphoses in his development. It is the Youth we have before us here, the Youth in his struggles and many-wandering aims, not the man grown into clearness.

Jacobi thought that in Goethe he had at length found the man his heart needed, whose influence could sustain and direct him. 'The more I consider it', he wrote to Wieland, 'the more intensely do I feel how impossible it is for one who has not seen and heard Goethe to write a word about this extraordinary creation of God's. One needs be with him but an hour to see that it is utterly absurd to expect him to think and act otherwise than as he does. I do not mean that there is no possibility of an improvement in him ; but nothing else is possible with his nature, which develops itself as the flower does, as the seed ripens, as the tree grows into the air and crowns itself'.

Goethe's wonderful *personality* seems almost everywhere to produce a similar impression. Heinse, the author of *Ardinghello,* writes of him at this period to Gleim : 'Goethe was with us, a beautiful youth of five-and-twenty, who is all genius and strength from head to foot, his heart full of feeling, his soul full of fire and eagle-winged ; I know no man in the whole History of Literature who at such an age can be compared to him in fullness and completeness of genius '. Those, and they are the mass, who think of him as the calm and stately minister, the old Jupiter throned in Weimar, will feel some difficulty perhaps in recognizing the young Apollo of this period. But it must be remembered that not only was he young, impetuous, bursting into life, and trying his eagle wings with wanton confidence of strength ; he was, moreover, a Rhinelander, with the gay blood of that race stimulated by the light and generous wine of the Rhine—not a Northern muddled with beer. When I cöntrast young Goethe with a Herder, for example, it is always as if a flask of Rhenish glittered beside a seidel of Bavarian beer.

Such answer to his aspirations as the youth could at this period receive, he found in Spinoza. In his father's library there was a little book written against Spinoza, one of the many foolish refutations which that grand old Hebrew's misunderstood system called forth. 'It made little impression on me, for I hated controversies, and always wanted to know *what* a thinker thought, and not what another conceived he *ought to have thought*'. It made him, however, once more read the article Spinoza, in Bayle's *Dictionary*, which he found pitiable—as indeed it is. If a philosophy is to be judged by its fruits, the philosophy which guided so great and so virtuous a life as that of Spinoza, could not, Goethe thought, deserve the howls of execration which followed Spinozism. He procured the *Opera Posthuma* and studied them ; with what fruit let the following confession indicate. He is speaking of his new friendship with Jacobi : ' The thoughts which Jacobi imparted to me flowed immediately from his heart. How deeply was I moved when in unlimited confidence he revealed to me the deepest wants and aspirations of his soul. From so amazing a combination of mental wants, passion, and ideas, I could only gather presentiment of what might, perhaps, hereafter grow clearer to me. Fortunately, my mind had already been prepared, if not thoroughly cultivated in this direction, having in some degree appropriated the results and style of thought of an extraordinary man, and though my study had been incomplete and hasty, I was yet already conscious of important influences derived from this source. This man, who had wrought so powerfully on me, and who was destined to affect so deeply my entire mode of thinking, was Spinoza. After looking around the world in vain for the means of developing my strange nature, I met with the *Ethics* of that philosopher. Of what I read *in* the work, and of what I read *into* it, I can give no account, but I found in it a sedative for my passions, and it seemed to unveil a clear, broad view over the material and moral world. But what especially riveted me to him was the boundless disinterestedness which shone forth in every sentence. That wonderful sentiment, " *He who truly loves God must not require God to love him in return*", together with all the preliminary propositions on which it rests, and all the consequences deduced from it, filled my mind*. To be disinterested in everything, but most of all in love and friendship, was my highest desire, my maxim, my practice, so that that saucy speech of *Philine's*, " If I love thee, what is that to thee ? " was spoken right out of my heart. Moreover, it must not be forgotten here that the closest unions rest on contrasts. The all-equalizing calmness of Spinoza was in striking contrast with my all-disturbing activity ; his mathematical method was the direct opposite of my poetic style of thought and feeling, and that very precision which was thought ill adapted to moral subjects made me

---

* The proposition to which Goethe refers is doubtless the xix of Book v : '*Qui Deum amat, conari non potest, ut Deus ipsum contra amet.*'

his enthusiastic disciple, his most decided worshipper. Mind and heart, understanding and sense, sought each other with eager affinity, binding together the most different natures. But now all within was fermenting and seething in action and reaction. Fritz Jacobi, the first whom I suffered to look into the chaos, and whose nature was also toiling in its own unfathomable depths, heartily responded to my confidence, and endeavoured to convert me to his own opinions. He, too, felt an unspeakable spiritual want ; he, too, would not have it appeased by *outward* aid, but aimed at development and illumination from *within*. I could not comprehend what he communicated to me of the state of his mind ; the less, indeed, as I could form no adequate conception of my own. Still, being far in advance of me in philosophical thought, and even in the study of Spinoza, he was able to guide and enlighten my efforts'.

Although he studied Spinoza much and reverently, he never studied him systematically. The mathematical form into which that thinker casts his granite blocks of thought, was an almost insuperable hindrance to systematic study on the part of one so impatient, so desultory, and so unmathematical as Goethe. But a study may be very fruitful which is by no means systematic ; a phrase may fructify, when falling on a proper soil. It has doubtless happened to the reader in his youth to meet with some entirely novel and profoundly suggestive idea, casually cited from an ancient author ; if so, he will remember the over-mastering influence it exercised, the longing it awakened for a nearer acquaintance with that author. The casual citation of a passage from Spinoza made my youth restless, and to this day I remember the aspect of the page where it appeared, and the revolution in thought which it effected. A few ideas determined the direction of Goethe's mind. Although he did not study the system of Spinoza with any view of adopting it as a system, he studied it to draw therefrom food which his own mind could assimilate and work into new forms. Spinoza was to him what Kant was to Schiller ; but, with characteristic difference, Schiller studied systematically, and tried systematically to reproduce what he had studied.

Side by side with Spinozism, we have to note his struggles to gain clearness respecting Christianity. The influence of Fräulein von Klettenberg attracted him to the Moravians, who seemed to realize early Christianity ; with his usual impressionability he studied their history and their doctrines, and gave them some hopes that he would become a convert ; but his enthusiasm cooled down when he discovered the wide chasm that separated him from them. 'That which separated me from this brotherhood', he says, 'as well as from many other worthy Christians, was the very point which has more than once torn the Church with dissent. One party maintained that by the Fall, human nature had been so corrupted to its inmost core, that not a trace of good could be found in it ; and that, therefore, man must renounce all trust in his own powers, and look only to the effect of grace. The opposite party, admitting the hereditary imperfections of man, ascribed to nature a certain internal germ of good which, animated by divine grace, was capable of growing up into a joyous tree of spiritual happiness. This latter conviction penetrated to the depths of my soul all the time that I was, with tongue and pen, maintaining the opposite doctrine. But I had so dawdled along without thinking (*ich dämmerte so hin*) that I had never clearly stated the dilemma to myself'.

In spite of all his differences, however, with this sect or that sect, nothing, as he says, could rob him of his love for the Holy Scriptures and for the Founder of Christianity. He therefore wrought out for his own private use a Christianity of his own ; and as everything which took possession of his soul always assumed a poetic form, he now conceived the idea of treating epically the history of the *Wandering Jew.* 'The legend ran that in Jerusalem there was a shoemaker named Ahazuerus. The shoemaker whom I had known in Dresden supplied me with the main features of his character ; and I animated them with the spirit and humour of an artisan of the school of Hans Sachs, ennobling him by a great love for Christ. In his open workshop he talked with the passers-by, and jested with them after the Socratic fashion ; so that the people took pleasure in lingering at his booth. Even the Pharisees and Sadducees spoke to him ; and our Saviour himself, and his disciples, often stopped before his door. The shoemaker, whose thoughts were altogether worldly, I nevertheless depicted as feeling a special affection for our Lord, which chiefly showed itself in a desire to convert this great man, whose mind he did not comprehend, to his own way of thinking. He therefore gravely incited Christ to abandon contemplation, to cease wandering through the country with such idlers, and drawing the people away from their work into the desert; because an assembled multitude, he said, was always excitable, and no good could come out of such a life. Our Lord endeavoured by parables to instruct him in his higher views, but they were all thrown away on the rough shoemaker. As Christ grew into greater importance, and became a public character, the well-meaning workman pronounced his opinion still more sharply and angrily, declaring that nothing but disorder and tumult could result from such proceedings, and that Christ would at length be compelled to place himself at the head of a party, which certainly was not his design. And now when these consequences had ensued, Christ having been seized and condemned, Ahazuerus gives full vent to his indignation, as Judas, who in appearance had betrayed our Lord, enters the workshop in despair, with loud lamentations, telling of the frustration of his plan. He had been, no less than the shrewdest of the other disciples, thoroughly persuaded that Christ would declare himself Regent and Chief of the people, and thought by this violence to compel him, whose hesitation had been hitherto invincible, to hasten the declaration*. In this persuasion he had roused the priesthood to an act from which they had hitherto shrunk. The disciples, on their side, were not unarmed; and probably all would have gone well, had not our Lord given himself up, and left them in the most helpless condition. Ahazuerus, by no means propitiated by this narrative, embitters the state of the wretched ex-apostle, who has no resource left but to hang himself. As our Saviour is led past the workshop of the shoemaker, on his road to execution, the well-known scene of the legend occurs. The sufferer faints under the burden of the cross, which Symon of Cyrene undertakes to carry. At this moment Ahazuerus steps forward; and, in the style of those harsh common-sense people who, seeing a man miserable through his own fault, feel no compassion, but rather, in their ill-timed justice, make the matter worse by reproaches, repeats all his former warnings, which he now turns into vehement accusations, springing, as it were, from his very love for the sufferer. Our Saviour answers not, but at that instant Veronica covers his face with a napkin, and there, as she removes it and raises it aloft, Ahazuerus sees depicted the features of our Lord, not in their present agony, but radiant with celestial life. As-

* This new light thrown upon that strange history, though adverse from all tradition, is in strict accordance with our knowledge of human nature. It has been adopted by Archbishop Whately, to whom, indeed, it is generally attributed; and has furnished the subject of a miracle-play to R. H. Horne. See his *Judas Iscariot*.

tounded at the sight, he turns away his eyes, and hears the words, " Over the earth shalt thou wander till thou shalt once more see me in this form ".   Overwhelmed by the sentence, he is some time before he recovers himself ; *he then finds that every one has gone to the place of execution, and that the streets of Jerusalem are empty.* Unrest and yearnings drive him forth, and his wanderings begin '.

This legendary conception he never executed.   It lived within him for a long while, and during his travels in Italy he again thought of taking it up ; but, like so many other plans, it remained a mere scheme, from the want of some external stimulus urging him to give it a shape.

Another subject also worthy of elaborate treatment is thus mentioned by him : ' The common burthen of humanity which we have all to bear falls most heavily on those whose intellectual powers expand early.   We may grow up under the protection of parents, we may lean for a while upon our brothers and friends, be amused by acquaintances, rendered happy by those we love, but in the end man is always driven back upon himself ; and it seems as if the Divinity had so placed himself in relation to man as not always to respond to his reverence, trust, and love, at least not in the terrible moment of need.   Early and often enough had I learned that the call to us is " Physician, heal thyself " ; and how frequently had I been compelled to exclaim in my pain, " I tread the wine-press alone ! "   So now, looking round for support to my self-dependence, I felt that the surest basis on which to build was my own productive activity.   For many years I had never known it fail me.   What I had seen by day often shaped itself into magnificent dreams at night.   My time for writing was early in the morning ; but in the evening, or deep in the night, when wine and social intercourse had elevated my spirits, you might demand whatever you wanted : only let a subject with some character in it be proposed, and I was at once prepared and ready.   In reflecting on this natural gift, I saw that it belonged to me *as my own,* and could neither be fostered nor hindered by any external circumstances ; so I sought to make it the basis of my whole existence. This notion transformed itself into an image.   The old mythological figure of Prometheus occurred to me ; who, severed from the gods, peopled the world from his own workshop.   I clearly felt that nothing important could be produced without self-isolation.   My productions had been the children of solitude ; and since I had formed wider relations with the world there had

Goethe as a young man

been no want of power or of *pleasure of invention*, but the *execu-tion* halted, because I had neither in prose nor in verse, what could properly be called a style of my own, and thus with every new work had to begin at the beginning, and make experiments. As in this I had to exclude all aid from men, so, after the fashion of Prometheus, I separated myself from the gods also ; and this the more naturally as, with my mode of thinking, one tendency always swallowed up and repelled every other.

'The fable of Prometheus lived within me. The old Titan web I cut up according to my own stature, and began to write a play expressing the incongruous relation in which Prometheus stood with respect to Jupiter and the later gods, in consequence of his making men with his own hand, giving them life by the aid of Minerva, and thus founding a third dynasty. To this strange composition belongs the monologue which has become famous in German literature, because it called forth a declaration from Lessing against Jacobi on certain important matters of doctrine*'.

Of this *Prometheus* we possess but a fragment, but the fragment is of such excellence as to make us regret that it never was completed. It lies there among his works, like the torso of the Theseus, enough to prove the greatness of the artist, if not enough to satisfy the spectator. Grand in conception, simple in style, luminous with great thoughts, it would have been an exemplar of the adaptation of an antique symbol to modern meanings, not the idle imitation of a bygone creed.

Nothing can be more unlike Æschylus. The Greek Titan glories in his audacity :

Ἑκὼν ἑκὼν ἥμαρτον, οὐκ ἀρνήσομαι.

'Willingly, willingly I did it, never will I deny the deed!' but while glorying, he *complains :* the injustice of the tyrant wrings from him cries of pain, cries of physical and cries of moral agony. The whole tragedy is one wild outburst of sorrow. The first words he utters fling his clamorous sorrow on the air, call on the Divine Ether and the swift winged Winds, on the Sea Springs and the multitudinous laughter of the waves, on the Universal Mother, the Earth—and on the all-seeing Eye, the Sun, to witness what he, a

* He alludes to the discussion on Spinoza between Jacobi and Lessing, which gave rise to Jacobi's book, *Ueber die Lehre des Spinozas.* This feeble book made a great noise in its day.

god, must suffer. These are his opening words ; the closing words carry the same burden. He wails over the pangs that are and are to be :

Αἰ, αἰ τὸ παρὸν τὸ τ' ἐπερχόμενον
Πῆμα στενάχω.

This is antique. The Titan in Goethe utters *no* complaint. There is no bravado in his defiance ; the defiance is uncompromising and sublime. His contempt for Zeus is founded on his knowledge of the subordination of Zeus to a higher power—Destiny. ' Away', he exclaims, ' I serve no slave '.

Geh ! Ich diene nicht Vasallen !

In this he resembles the Titan drawn by Shelley, in the *Prometheus Unbound*, who, to Mercury's warning of the years of coming torture, calmly and grandly answers :

Perchance no thought can count them—yet they pass !

On this conviction rests his self-reliance. He knows the reign of tyranny must end, and he awaits that end.

In Æschylus also, the Titan knows that Zeus must fall ; he foresees his own release, and, foreseeing it, resolves to bear his fate as well as he can, 'for it is vain to struggle against fate' (v. 105). Nevertheless, the knowledge of an end, and the philosophy which preaches acquiescence, does not prevent him from *complaining*. And this is very Greek. Homer makes even Mars, when wounded, howl with pain ; and Sophocles has filled the *Philoctete* with cries of physical pain. The Greeks had none of our modern notions respecting the effeminacy of complaint.

It may be objected perhaps to the foregoing view of the Titan, that Æschylus has in the first scene made him imperturbably silent, disdaining to answer the taunts of Power and the pity of Vulcan, as they bind him to the rock. These draw from him no groan, no word, no gesture ; he has no defiance for the one nor friendly gratitude for the other. It is not until he is left alone that he appeals to Earth, Air, and Ocean. This silence, followed by this passion, produces a sublime effect. But the sublimity was *not* the poet's intention ; it is an accidental effect. The silence was simply a *stage necessity*, as I have elsewhere shown. Whether owing to some eurhythmic tendency in the construction of Greek plays, as

Gruppe*, and after him Bode†, have maintained; or, more probably from motives of economy with respect to the actors, as Geppert asserts‡; certain it is that in the plays of Æschylus more than *two speakers* were never together on the stage, with one trivial exception in the *Choëphoræ*, where Pylades says a few words. Hence scholars have been puzzled to account for the distribution of the *Prometheus* into parts. In the first scene the protagonist would take Power and the deuteragonist Vulcan. Prometheus therefore *must* be silent, for there is no one to speak for him. Here comes the difficulty: If Prometheus is necessarily silent during the prologue, how does he become eloquent immediately on being left alone? Welcker§ supposes that Prometheus was represented by a picture, and the protagonist at the close of the prologue got behind it, and spoke through it; an explanation accepted by Hermann‖, but shown by Schömann¶ to be full of difficulties. Let that point be settled as it may, the fact remains that the silence of Prometheus was forced by stage necessities, and was *not* meant as an indication of his self-reliance; the further proof of which is to be seen in his wailings and writhings throughout the play—notably in the scene with Mercury (v. 905), where Prometheus is scurrilously fluent.

Shelley never makes his Titan flinch. He stands there as the sublime of *endurance:*

> To suffer woes which Hope thinks infinite;
> To forgive wrongs darker than death or night;
> To defy power which seems omnipotent;
> To love and bear; to hope till Hope creates
> From its own wreck the thing it contemplates;
> Neither to change, nor falter, nor repent.

This is grand; but grander far the conception of Goethe, whose Titan knows that he is a god, and that if he be true to himself no power can trouble or destroy his heritage of life and activity:

> Das was ich habe können sie nicht rauben,
> Und was *sie* haben mögen sie beschützen;
> Hier Mein und Dein,
> Und so sind wir geschieden.

---

* *Ariadne: oder die tragische Kunst der Griechen*, p. 143.
† *Geschichte der Hellen, Dichtkunst*, III, p. 233.
‡ *Alt-Griechische Bühne*, p. 58. ‖ *Trilogie*, p. 30.
§ *Opusc.* II, p. 146. ¶ *Prometheus*, p. 85.

EPIMETHEUS.

Wie vieles ist denn Dein?

PROMETHEUS.

Der Kreis den meine Wirksamkeit erfüllt*.

This is a profound truth strikingly brought out. Godlike energy is seen only in creation ; what we can *do* we *are;* our strength is measured by our plastic power. Thus the contempt of Prometheus for the idleness, the uncreativeness of the gods is both deep and constant.

Curtain thy heavens, Zeus,
With clouds, with mist !
And, like a boy that crushes thistle-tops,
Loosen thy rage on oaks and mountain ridges.
Yet must thou leave
Me my earth standing ;
My hut, which myself built ;
My hearth, with its bright flame,
Which thou dost envy.
I know nought so pitiful
Under the sun as ye gods !
Scantily nourishing
With the forced offerings
Of tremulous prayer
Your divinity !
Children and beggars,
And fools hope-deluded,
Keep ye from starving !
Who gave me succour
From the fierce Titans?
Who rescued me
From slavery?
Thou ! thou, my soul, glowing
With holiest fire !
Yet didst thou, credulous,
Pour forth thy thanks to him
Who slumbers above !

---

* That which I have they cannot rob me of; that which they have, let them guard
Here mine, here thine ; and thus are we distinguished.

EPIMETHEUS.
What, then, is thine?

PROMETHEUS.
The circle my activity doth fill !

I reverence thee ?   Wherefore ?
Hast lightened the woes
Of the heavily laden ?
Hast *thou* dried the tears
Of the troubled in spirit ?
Who fashioned me man ?
   Was it not almighty Time—
   And Fate eternal,
   Thy lords and mine ?
Here I sit and shape
Man in my image :
A race like myself,
That will suffer and weep,
Will rejoice and enjoy,
And scorn thee,
As I !

Even in this rough plaster-cast of translation, does not the
grandeur and beauty of the original shine through ?

CHAPTER VII

LILI

'I MUST tell you something which makes me happy ; and that
is the visit of many excellent men of all grades, and from all
parts, who, among unimportant and intolerable visitors, call on me
often, and stay some time.   We first know that we exist, when we
recognize ourselves in others (*man weiss erst dass man ist, wenn
man sich in andern wiederfindet*)'.   It is thus he writes to the
Countess Augusta von Stolberg, with whom he had formed,
through correspondence, one of those romantic friendships which
celebrated men, some time in their lives, are generally led to form.
This correspondence is among the most characteristic evidences
we have of his mental condition, and should be read by every one
who wishes to correct the *tone* of the *Autobiography*.   Above all,
it is the repository of his fluctuating feelings respecting Lili, the
woman whom, according to his statement to Eckermann, he loved
more than any other.   'She was the first, and I can also add she
is the last, I truly loved ; for all the *inclinations* which have since
agitated my heart were superficial and trivial in comparison'*.

* *Gespräche*, III, p. 299.

There is no statement he has made respecting a matter of feeling, to which one may oppose a flatter contradiction. Indeed we find it difficult to believe he uttered such a sentence, unless we remember how carelessly in conversation such retrospective statements are made, and how, at his very advanced age, the memory of youthful feelings must have come back upon him with peculiar tenderness. Whatever caused him to make that statement, the statement is very questionable. I do not think that he loved Lili more than Frederika ; and we shall hereafter have positive evidence that his love for the Frau von Stein, and for his wife, was of a much deeper and more enduring nature. ' My love for Lili ', he said to Eckermann, ' had something so peculiar and delicate that even now it has influenced my style in the narrative of that painfully happy epoch. When you read the fourth volume of my *Autobiography*, you will see that my love was something quite different from love in novels '.

Well, the fourth volume is now open to every one, and he must have peculiar powers of divination who can read any profound passion in the narrative. A colder love-history was never written by a poet. There is no emotion warming the narrative ; there is little of a loving recollection, gathering all details into one continuous story ; it is, indeed, with great difficulty one unravels the story at all. He seems to seize every excuse to interrupt the narrative by general reflections, or by sketches of other people. He speaks of himself as ' the youth of whom we now write ! ' He speaks of her, and her circle, in the vaguest manner ; and the feelings which agitated him we must ' read between the lines '.

It is very true, however, that the love there depicted is unlike the love depicted in novels. In novels, whatever may be the amount of foolishness with which the writers adumbrate their ideal of the passion, this truth, at least, is everywhere set forth, that to love we must render up body and soul, heart and mind, all interests and all desires, all prudences and all ambitions, identifying our being with that of another, in union to become elevated. To love is for the soul to choose a companion, and travel with it along the perilous defiles and winding ways of life ; mutually sustaining, when the path is terrible with dangers, mutually exhorting, when it is rugged with obstructions, and mutually rejoicing, when rich broad plains and sunny slopes make the journey a delight, showing in the quiet distance the resting-place we all seek in this world.

Lili Schönemann

It was not such companionship he sought with Lili ; it was not such self-devotion which made him restlessly happy in her love. This child of sixteen, in all the merciless grace of maidenhood, proudly conscious of her power, ensnared his roving heart through the lures of passionate desire, but she never touched his soul ; as the story we have to tell will sufficiently prove.

Anna Elizabeth Schönemann, immortalized as Lili, was the daughter of a great banker in Frankfurt, who lived in the splendid style of merchant princes. She was sixteen when Goethe first fell in love with her. The age is significant. It was somewhat the age of Frederika, Lotte, Antoinette, and Maximiliane. An age when girlhood has charms of grace and person, of beauty and freshness, which even those will not deny who profoundly feel the superiority of a developed woman. There is poetry in this age ; but there is no depth, no fullness of character. Imagine the wide-sweeping mind of the author of *Götz*, *Faust*, *Prometheus*, *The Wandering Jew*, *Mahomet*, in companionship with the mind of a girl of sixteen !

Nor was Lili an exceptional character. Young, graceful, and charming, she was confessedly a coquette. Early in their acquaintance, in one of those pleasant hours of overflowing egotism wherein lovers take pride in the confession of faults (not without imitation also of nobler qualities), Lili told him the story of her life ; told him what a flirt she had been ; told him, moreover, that she had tried her spells on him, and was punished by being herself ensnared. Armida found herself spell-bound by Rinaldo ; but this Rinaldo followed her into the enchanted gardens more out of adventurous curiosity than love.

There was considerable difference in their stations ; and the elegant society of the banker's house was every way discordant to the wild youth, whose thoughts were of Nature and unconstrained freedom. The balls and concerts to which he followed her were little to his taste. ' If ', he writes to Augusta von Stolberg, ' If you can imagine a Goethe in a braided coat, from head to foot in the gallantest costume, amid the glare of chandeliers, fastened to the card table by a pair of bright eyes, surrounded by all sorts of people, driven in endless dissipation from concert to ball, and with frivolous interest making love to a pretty blonde, then will you have a picture of the present Carnival-Goethe '. In the following poem he expresses Lili's fascination and his uneasiness ; the translation aims at accuracy

of meaning rather than poetry, because the meaning is here the
motive for my citing the poem :

> Wherefore so resistlessly dost draw me
>   Into scenes so bright?
> Had I not enough to soothe and charm me
>   In the lonely night?
>
> Homely in my little room secluded,
>   While the moon's bright beams
> In a shimmering light fell softly on me,
>   As I lay in dreams.
>
> Dreaming thro' the golden hours of rapture
>   Soothed my heart to rest,
> As I felt thy image sweetly living
>   Deep within my breast.
>
> Can it be I sit at yonder table,
>   Gay with cards and lights,
> Forced to meet intolerable people,
>   Because 'tis *she* invites?
>
> Alas! the gentle bloom of spring no longer
>   Cheereth my poor heart,
> There is only spring, and love, and nature,
>   Angel, where thou art!

The real Goethe is thus drawn in contrast by himself in his
letter to Augusta. 'But there is another, who in grey beaver
coat, with boots, and a brown silk neckerchief, who, ever living
in himself, working and striving, now throwing the innocent
feelings of youth into little poems, now the strong spices of life
into dramas, sketching his friends in chalk, asking neither right
nor left what will be thought of his doings, because he always
rises through work a step higher, because he springs at no ideal,
but lets his nature develop itself fighting and playing'. Here
the true chord vibrates. Born for poetry, and not to pass his
life in ball-rooms dangling after a pretty blonde who coquetted
with him and with others, he feels that his passion is a folly.
Now when a man feels that—'Cupid may have tapped him on
the shoulder, but I warrant him heart whole'. Read this poem,
and read in it the struggle :

> Heart, my heart, what is this feeling,
>   That doth weigh on thee so sore?
> What new life art thou revealing,
>   That I know myself no more?

> Gone is all that once was dearest,
> Gone the care that once was nearest,
> Gone the labour, gone the bliss,
> Ah ! whence comes such change as this ?
> Art thou spell-bound by the beauty
>   Of a sweétly blooming face ;
> Beauteous shape, and look so truthful,
>   And an all-resistless grace ?
> When the bonds I strive to sever,
> Man myself to flee for ever,
> Vain are all my efforts, vain !
> And but lead me back again.

> With such magic-web she binds me,
>   To burst through I have no skill ;
> All-absorbing passion blinds me,
>   Paralyses my poor will.
> In her charmèd sphere delaying,
> I must live, her will obeying :
> Great, oh ! great to me the change !
> Love, oh ! free me ! let me range ! *

Lili coquetted, and her coquetry seems to have cooled his passion
for a while, though she knew how to rekindle it. She served him
as he served poor Käthchen, in Leipsic ; and as in Leipsic he
dramatized his experience under the form of *Die Laune des
Verliebten,* so here he dramatizes the new experience in an opera,
Erwin und Elmire, wherein the coquetry of a mistress brings a
lover to despair—a warning to Lili, which does not seem to have
been altogether without effect.

Not only had he to suffer from her thoughtlessness, but also
from the thoughtfulness of parents on both sides. It was not a
marriage acceptable to either house. The banker's daughter, it
was thought, should marry into some rich or noble family. A
poet, who belonged to a well-to-do yet comparatively unimportant
family, was not exactly the bridegroom most desired. On the
other hand, the proud, stiff old Rath did not greatly rejoice in the
prospect of having a fine lady for his daughter-in-law. Cornelia,
who knew her father, and knew his pedantic ways, wrote strongly
against the marriage. Merck, Crespel, Horn, and other friends,
were all decidedly opposed to so incompatible a match. But of

---

* No one can be more sensible than I am of the inadequacy of this translation, but
the English reader would rather have a poor translation than an original he could not
understand ; and the German reader has only to turn to the original if it does not linger
in his memory.

course the lovers were only thrown closer together by these attempts to separate them.

A certain Demoiselle Delf managed to overcome objections, and gain the consent of both families. ' How she commenced it, how she got over the difficulties I know not, but one evening she came to us bringing the consent. "Take each other's hands", she cried in a half-pathetic, half-imperious manner : I advanced to Lili and held out my hand : in it she placed hers, not indeed reluctantly, yet slowly. With a deep sigh we sank into each other's arms greatly agitated'. No formal betrothal seems to have taken place. Indeed, the consent which was obtained seems in nowise to have altered the feeling of friends and relatives. The nearer marriage seemed, the more impracticable it appeared. To Goethe, after the first flush of joy had subsided, the idea of marriage was in itself enough to make him uneasy, and to sharpen his sense of the *disparity* in station. The arrival of the two Counts Stolberg, and their proposal that he should accompany them in a tour through Switzerland, gave an excuse for freeing himself from Lili, ' as an experiment to try whether he could renounce her '.

Before accompanying him on his journey, it is necessary to cast a retrospective glance at some biographical details omitted while the story of Lili was narrated. The mornings were devoted to poetry, the middle of the day to jurisprudence. Poetry was the breathing-room of his heart. In it he sought to escape from the burden of intolerable doubts. ' If I did not write dramas I should be lost ', he tells Augusta von Stolberg. Among these dramas we must place *Stella*, for which, as we learn from a letter to Merck, the publisher offered twenty dollars,—that is to say, three pounds sterling. What an insight that gives into the state of Literature ; the author of two immensely popular works is offered three pounds for a drama in five acts ! Poor Schiller, subsequently, was glad to write histories and translate memoirs for fifteen or eighteen shillings a sheet of sixteen pages.

In *Stella* I can trace no biographical element, and perhaps the absence of this element makes the weakness of the drama. A poorer production was never owned by a great poet ; although there have not been wanting critics to see in this also the broad handling of a master. It is the old story of the Count von Gleichen and his two wives. Fernando has deserted his wife, and formed an attachment to Stella ; but the peculiarity of the situation is, that he quitted Cecilia, his wife, from no assignable

cause, without even having outlived his love for her.   He has
indeed every reason to respect and cherish her as the mother of
his child, and as a high-principled, virtuous woman ; but he flies
from her like a coward, flies to one more passionate, because she
gives him the transports of passion in exchange for his wife's calm
affection.   The two women meet, and discover their love for the
same man.

Here is a fine dramatic collision.   On the one side Fernando
sees Duty in the shape of a noble, suffering wife, and an engaging
daughter ; on the other, Passion in the shape of a fascinating
mistress.   But with this suggestive subject Goethe has done
little.   He shows us the contemptible weakness of the wavering
Fernando, but the subject he has not powerfully wrought out.   As
I cannot recommend any one to read this play, the two masterly
touches it contains may here be cited.   The following is delicately
observed :

We women believe in men ! *In the ardour of passion they deceive themselves, how then can we help being deceived by them ?*

This also is charming : Ferdinand returns to Stella after a long
absence, and in their endearments she says :

Stella.   How we love you ! We do not think of the grief you cause us !
Fernando (stroking her hair).   And has the grief made your hair grey ?
It is fortunate your hair is so golden . . . nay, none seems to have fallen
out ! (*Takes the comb from her hair, which falls on her shoulders.   He
then twines the hair round his arm, exclaiming:*) Rinaldo once more in
the ancient chains !

Artists complain of the dearth of subjects ; will no one try his
hand at that ?   Originally the *dénouement* of this ' Play for lovers '
(as it was called) solved the difficulty by a romantic piece of
bigamy.   Fernando is about to fly with Cecilia—about to return to
his duty, when his wife—compassionating the situation of Stella
if Fernando should leave her—resolves to sacrifice her conjugal
claims, and to *share* him with Stella !   The curtain falls as he
embraces them both, exclaiming, ' Mine ! mine ! '

This roused vehement opposition.   It was said to be a plea in
favour of bigamy.   The public dimly felt that instead of being a
proper solution of the problem, it was on the whole rather ridiculous.   Still more unsatisfactory, however, if deeply considered,
is the *dénouement* which was added when the play was produced
at Weimar, and which now takes the place of the original in his

collected works.   Therein Fernando, unable to quit Stella, and unable to quit his wife, weeps with both, and blows his brains out. This is an *evasion* of the difficulty, not a solution.

In 1798, a feeble translation of *Stella* was published in England, and suggested to Canning his admirable caricature, *The Rovers*, familiar to all readers of the *Antijacobin*.   Among the ludicrous passages of this parody is the famous vow of friendship :

> *Matilda.*   A sudden thought strikes me.   Let us swear an eternal friendship.
> *Cecilia.*   Let us agree to live together.

But this is really a very slight variation from the original :

> *Stella.*   Madame !   Da fährt mir ein Gedanke durch den Kopf—Wir wollen einander das seyn, was sie uns hätten werden sollen !   Wir wollen beisammen bleiben !—Ihre hand !—Von diesen Augenblick an, lass' ich Sie nicht !

Besides *Stella*, he seemed to have worked at *Faust*, and to have written the opera of *Claudine von Villa Bella*, several passages for Lavater's *Physiognomy*, and many smaller poems.

The Stolbergs, with whom the Swiss journey was made, were two ardent admirers of Klopstock, and two specimens of the defiant 'genius' class which scorned convention.   They hated imaginary tyrants ; outraged sober citizens by their reckless recurrence to a supposed state of nature ; and astonished sensible citizens by their exaggerated notions of friendship.   Merck was pitiless in his sarcasms and warnings.   He could not tolerate the idea of Goethe's travelling with these *Burschen*.   But Goethe had too much of kindred devilry in him, breaking out at moments, to object to the wildness of his companions ; though he began to suspect all was not right when, after violating every other *convenance*, they insisted on bathing in public.   Nature having nothing to say against naked youths in the bright sunshine, what business had old Humdrum to cover its eyes with modest hands, and pretend to be shocked ? However, so little prepossessed was Humdrum in favour of the Nude, that stones were showered upon these children of Nature ; a criticism which effectively modified their practice, if it failed to alter their views.

Drinking the health of Stolberg's mistress, and then dashing the glasses against the wall to prevent their being desecrated by other lips after so solemn a consecration (a process which looked less heroic when *item'd* in the bill next day), and otherwise demeaning themselves like true children of 'genius', they passed a wild and merry time. This journey need not longer detain us. Two visits alone deserve mention. One was to Karl August, who was then in Karlsruhe arranging his marriage with the Princess Luise, and who very pressingly invited the poet to Weimar. The other was to his sister Cornelia, who earnestly set before him all the objections to a marriage with Lili. 'I made no promises', he says, 'although forced to confess that she had convinced me. I left her with that strange feeling in my heart with which passion nourishes itself; for the boy Cupid clings obstinately to the garment of Hope even when she is preparing with long strides to depart'. The image of Lili haunted him amid the lovely scenes of Nature :

> Dearest Lili, if I did not love thee
>   How entrancing were a scene like this !
> Yet, my Lili, if I did not love thee,
>   What were any bliss?

It was her image which endeared him to his native land. His father, always desirous he should see Italy, was now doubly anxious he should go there, as the surest means of a separation from Lili. But 'Lombardy and Italy', says the poet, 'lay before me a strange land ; while the dear home of Germany lay behind, full of sweet domesticities, and where—let me confess it—*she* lived who so long had enchained me, in whom my existence was centred. A little golden heart, which in my happiest hours I had received from her, still hung round my neck. I drew it forth and covered it with kisses'.

On his return to Frankfurt he learned that Lili's friends had taken advantage of his absence, to try and bring about a separation, arguing, not without justice, that his absence was a proof of lukewarmness. But Lili remained firm ; and it was said that she had declared herself willing to go with him to America. A sentence from the *Autobiography* is worth quoting, as a specimen of that love 'so unlike the love to be found in novels', which he declared had given a peculiar tone to his narrative. It is in reference to this willingness of Lili to go to America : 'the very thing which should have animated my hopes depressed them. My fair paternal house, only a few hundred paces from hers, was after all more endurable and attractive than a remote, hazardous spot beyond the seas !' A sentence which recalls Gibbon's antithesis, on the resignation of his early love : 'I sighed as a lover, I obeyed as a son'.

He was restless and unhappy during these months, for he was not strong enough to give up Lili, nor sufficiently in love to marry her ; jealous of those who surrounded her, hurt by her coldness, he was every now and then led captive by her tenderness.   There were moments when bygone days seemed once more restored, and then instantly vanished again.   His poem of *Lili's Menagerie* expresses his surly disgust at the familiar faces which surround her.   The Bear of the menagerie is a portrait of himself.

Turning to Art for consolation, he began the tragedy of *Egmont*, which he completed many years afterwards in Italy.   It was a work which demanded more repose than could be found in his present condition, and I hasten to the *dénouement* of an episode, which, amid fluctuations of feeling, steadily advanced to an end that must have been foreseen.   The betrothal was cancelled.   He was once more free.   Free, but not happy.   His heart still yearned for her, rather because there lay in his nature a need of loving, than because she was the woman fitted to share his life.   He lingered about the house o' nights, wrapped in his mantle, satisfied if he could catch a glimpse of her shadow on the blind, as she moved about the room.   One night he heard her singing at the piano.   His pulses throbbed, as he distinguished his own song :

Wherefore so resistlessly dost draw me
Into scenes so bright ?—

the song he had written in the morning of their happiness !   Her voice ceased.   She rose, and walked up and down the room, little dreaming that her lover was beneath her window.

To give decision to his wavering feelings, there came, most opportunely, a visitor to Frankfurt.   This was in September.   Karl August, with his bride, on his way to Weimar, once more pressed him to spend a few weeks at his Court.   The rapid inclination which had sprung up between the Prince and the Poet—the desire to see something of the great world—the desire, moreover, to quit Frankfurt, all combined to make him eagerly accept the invitation.   His father, indeed, tried to dissuade him ; partly because he did not like the intercourse of plain citizens with princes ; partly because the recent experience of Voltaire with Frederick the Great seemed to point to an inevitable termination in disgrace, if not evaded by servility.   His consent was extorted at last, however, and Goethe quitted for ever the paternal roof.

BOOK THE FOURTH

1775 to 1779

CHAPTER I

WEIMAR IN THE EIGHTEENTH CENTURY

ON the 7th of November, 1775, Goethe, aged twenty-six,
    arrived at the little city on the banks of the Ilm, where his
long residence was to confer on an insignificant Duchy the immortal renown of a German Athens.

Small indeed is the space occupied on the map by the Duchy of
Saxe-Weimar; yet the historian of the German Courts declares,
and truly, that after Berlin there is no Court of which the nation is
so proud*.   Frederick the Great and Wolfgang Goethe have
raised these Courts into centres of undying interest.   Of Weimar
it is necessary we should form a distinct idea, if we would understand the outward life of the poet.

> Klein ist unter den Fürsten Germaniens freilich der meine,
> Kurz und schmal ist sein Land, mässig nur was er vermag.

'Small among German princes is mine, poor and narrow his kingdom, limited his power of doing good'.   Thus sings Goethe in
that poem, so honourable to both, wherein he acknowledges his
debt to Karl August.   The geographical importance of Weimar
was, and is, small; but we in England have proud reason to know
how great a place in the world can be filled by a nation whose
place is trivial on the map.   We know, moreover, that the Athens,
which it is the pride of Weimar to claim as a patronymic, was but
a dot upon the surface of Europe, a dot of earth, feeding some
twenty thousand freemen, who not only extended the empire of
their arms from Eubœa to the Thracian Bosphorus, but who left
their glories in Literature, Philosophy, and Art, as marvels and as
models for the civilized world.   It is interesting, therefore, to know

---

* VEHSE : *Geschichte der Deutschen Höfe seit der Reformation*, vol. XXVIII, p. 3.

how small this Duchy of Saxe-Weimar was, that we may appreciate the influence exercised by means so circumscribed. We must know how absurdly scant the income of its generous prince, who, as I am credibly informed, would occasionally supply the deficiencies of his purse by the princely unprinceliness of selling to the Jews a diamond ring, or ancestral snuff-box, that he might hand the proceeds to some struggling artist or poet. I mention this lest it should be supposed that a sarcastic spirit has dictated the enumeration of unimposing details, in the following attempt to reconstruct some image of Weimar and its Court.

Weimar is an ancient city on the Ilm, a small stream rising in the Thuringian forests, and losing itself in the Saal, at Jena ; this stream, on which the sole navigation seems to be that of ducks, meanders peacefully through pleasant valleys, except during the rainy season, when mountain-torrents swell its current, and overflow its banks. The Trent, between Trentham and Stafford—'the smug and silver Trent', as Shakespeare calls it— will give an idea of this stream. The town is charmingly placed in the Ilm valley, and stands some eight hundred feet above the level of the sea. 'Weimar', says the old topographer, Mathew Merian, 'is *Weinmar*, because it was the wine market for Jena and its environs. Others say it was because some one here in ancient days began to plant the vine, who was hence called *Weinmayer*. But of this each reader may believe just what he pleases*'.

On a first acquaintance, Weimar seems more like a village bordering a park, than a capital with a Court, having all courtly environments. It is so quiet, so simple ; and although ancient in its architecture, has none of the picturesqueness which delights the eye in most old German cities. The stone-coloured, light brown, and apple-green houses have high-peaked slanting roofs, but no quaint gables, no caprices of architectural fancy, none of the mingling of varied styles which elsewhere charms the traveller. One learns to love its quiet simple streets and pleasant paths, fit theatre for the simple actors moving across the scene ; but one must live there some time to discover its charm. The aspect it presented, when Goethe arrived, was of course very different from that presented now ; but by diligent inquiry we may get some rough image of the place restored. First be it noted that the city walls were still erect ; gates and portcullis still spoke of days of warfare. Within these walls were six or seven hundred houses,

* *Topographia Superioris Saxoniæ Thuringiæ*, etc., 1650, p. 188.

The Duke's castle in Weimar before it burned down in 1774

not more, most of them very ancient. Under these roofs were about seven thousand inhabitants—for the most part not handsome. The city gates were strictly guarded. No one could pass through them in cart or carriage without leaving his name in the sentinel's book; even Goethe, minister and favourite, could not escape this tiresome formality, as we gather from one of his letters to the Frau von Stein, directing her to go out alone, and meet him beyond the gates, lest their exit together should be known. During Sunday service a chain was thrown across the streets leading to the church, to bar out all passengers, a practice to this day partially retained : the chain is fastened, but the passengers step over it without ceremony. There was little safety at night in those silent streets; for if you were in no great danger from marauders, you were in constant danger of breaking a limb in some hole or other; the idea of lighting streets not having presented itself to the Thuringian mind. In the year 1685, the streets of London were first lighted with lamps; in 1775 Germany had not yet ventured on that experiment. If in 1854 Weimar is still innocent of gas, and perplexes its inhabitants with the dim obscurity of an occasional oil-lamp slung on a cord across the streets, we can understand that in 1775 it had not even advanced so far. And our supposition is exact*.

The palace, which now forms three sides of a quadrangle, and is truly palatial in appearance, was in ashes when Goethe arrived. The ducal pair inhabited the Fürstenhaus, which stands opposite. The park was not in existence. In its place there was the *Welsche Garten*, a garden arranged after the pattern of Versailles, with trees trimmed into set shapes, with square beds, canals, bridges, and a Babylonic spiral tower called *Die Schnecke*, in which the people assembled to hear music, and to enjoy punch and sweet cakes. To the left of this garden stood the nucleus of the present park, and a wooded mass stretching as far as Upper Weimar.

Saxe-Weimar has no trade, no manufactures, no animation of commercial, political, or even theological activity. This part of Saxony, be it remembered, was the home and shelter of Protestantism in its birth. Only a few miles from Weimar stands the Wartburg, where Luther, in the disguise of Squire George,

---

* In a decree made at Cassel, in 1775, this sentence is noticeable : ' In every house as soon as the alarum sounds at night, every inhabitant must hold out a lighted lantern, in order that the people may find their way in the streets '. Quoted by BIEDERMANN : *Deutschland im 18ten Jahrhundert*, I, p. 370.

lived in safety, translating the Bible, and hurling his inkstand at the head of Satan, like a rough-handed disputant as he was.   In the market-place of Weimar stand, to this day, two houses from the windows of which Tetzel advertised his indulgences, and Luther afterwards in fiery indignation fulminated against them. These records of religious struggle still remain, but are no longer suggestions for the continuance of the strife.   The fire is burnt out ; and perhaps in no city of Europe is theology so placid, so entirely at rest.   The Wartburg still rears its picturesque eminence over the lovely Thuringian valleys ; and Luther's room is visited by thousands of pilgrims ; but in this very palace of the Wartburg, besides the room where Luther struggled with Satan, the visitors are shown the Banqueting Hall of the Minnesingers, where poet challenged poet, and the *Sängerkrieg*, or Minstrels' Contest, was celebrated.   The contrast may be carried further.   It may be taken as a symbol of the intellectual condition of Saxe-Weimar that while the *relics* of Luther are simply preserved, the Minstrel Hall is now being restored in more than its pristine splendour. Lutheran theology is crumbling away, just as the famous *inkspot* has disappeared beneath the gradual scrapings of visitors' pen-knives ; but the minstrelsy of which the Germans are so proud daily receives fresh honour and adulation.   Nor is this adulation a mere revival.   Every year the Wartburg saw assembled the members of that numerous family (the Bachs) which, driven from Hungary in the early period of Reform, had settled in Saxony, and had given, besides the great John Sebastian Bach, many noble musicians to the world.   Too numerous to gain a livelihood in one city, the Bachs agreed to meet every year at the Wartburg. This custom, which was continued till the close of the eighteenth century, not only presented the singular spectacle of one family consisting of no less than a hundred and twenty musicians, but was also the occasion of musical entertainments such as were never heard before.   They began by religious hymns, sung in chorus ; they then took for their theme some popular song, comic or licentious, varying it by the improvisation of four, five, or six parts ; these improvisations were named *Quolibets*, and are considered by many writers to have been the origin of German opera.

The theologic fire has long burnt itself out in Thuringia.   In Weimar, where Luther preached, another preacher came, whom we know as Goethe.   In the old church there is one portrait of Luther, painted by his friend Lucas Kranach, greatly prized, as well it may be ; but for this one portrait of Luther, there are a hundred of Goethe. It is not Luther, but Goethe, they think of here ; poetry, not theology, is the glory of Weimar. And, corresponding with this, we find the dominant characteristic of the place to be no magnificent church, no picturesque ancient buildings, no visible image of the earlier ages, but the sweet serenity of a lovely park. The park fills the foreground of the picture, and always rises first in the memory. Any one who has spent happy hours wandering through its sunny walks and winding shades, watching its beauties changing through the fullness of summer, and the striking contrasts of autumn as it deepens into winter, will easily understand how Goethe could have been content to live in so small a city, which had, besides its nest of friends, so charming a park. It was indeed mainly his own creation ; and as it filled a large space in his life, it demands more than a passing allusion here.

Southwards from the palace it begins, with no obstacle of wall or iron gate, servant or sentinel, to *seem* to shut us out, so let us enter and look round. In the dew of morning, and in the silence of moonlight, we may wander undisturbed as if in our own grounds. The land stretches for miles away without barrier ; park and yellow cornlands forming one friendly expanse. If we pass into it from the palace gates, a winding path to the right conducts us into the Belvedere Allée : a magnificent avenue of chestnut trees, two miles long, stretching from the new street to the summer palace of Belvedere. This affords a shaded promenade along the park, in summer grateful for its coolness, in autumn looking like an avenue of golden trees. It terminates in the gardens of the Belvedere, which has its park also beautifully disposed. Here the Weimarians resort, to enjoy the fresh air after their fashion, namely, with accompaniments of bad beer, questionable coffee, and detestable tobacco.

If, instead of turning into the Belvedere Allée, we keep within the park, our walks are so numerous that choice becomes perplexing. Let us cross the *Stern Brücke*, a bridge leading from the palace. Turning to our right we pass along through noble trees, charmed by

> The sound of a hidden brook
> In the leafy month of June,
> Which to the quiet trees all night
> Singeth a quiet tune.

We reach the broad road leading to Upper Weimar. On this road, which skirts a meadow washed by the Ilm, we shall pass Goethe's *Gartenhaus* (Garden House, to be described hereafter), and then winding round the meadow, cross another bridge, and enter a shadowy path, picturesque with well-grouped trees—the solemn pine, the beech, whose dark-green patches of moss increase the brilliancy of its silver bark, the weeping birch with its airy elegance of form, the plane tree, the elm, the chestnut and the mountain ash, brilliant with berries hanging like clusters of coral against the deep blue of the sky. One steep side of this path is craggy with masses of moss-covered rock ; beneath the other flows the Ilm. A few paces from the bridge which leads us here, stands the *Borkenhaus* (Bark House), a hermit's hut, erected by Goethe for a fête of the duchess, and subsequently the favourite residence of the duke. It is only twenty feet long and fourteen deep, built entirely of wood, and plastered (so to speak) with the bark of trees. It rests against a rock amid the trees, and is surrounded by a wooden gallery, reached by rough wooden steps. Where is the prince who would live in such a hut nowadays? Where are the ministers who would attend council in such a hut? Yet here Karl August lived alone, glad to escape from the tedium of etiquette and the palling pleasures of a little Court. Here he debated affairs of state, not less momentous to him because they were trivial in European politics. Here he bathed in the Ilm running beneath. Here he could see the Garden House of his poet, and telegraph to him across the park. In this single room, which was at once dining-room, council-chamber, study, and bed-room, the manly duke lived alone for months.

From the *Borkenhaus* a small flight of stone steps conducts us to a mimic ruin, and thence a narrow winding path leads to a stone monument, interesting as a witness to the growth of a mythos. It is an antique column, four feet high, round which a serpent winds, in the act of devouring the offering cakes on the top. The inscription says, *Genio Loci*. But the Weimar *plebs*, disregarding antique symbols, and imperfectly acquainted with Virgil, has a legend to tell ; a legend sprung, no one knows whence, rapid and mysterious as the growth of fungi, like most legends, to satisfy the imperious craving for *explanations;* a legend which certifies how, formerly, a huge serpent dwelt in this spot, the terror of Weimar, until a cunning baker bethought him of placing poisoned cakes within the monster's reach ; and when the greedy ignorance of the serpent had relieved Weimar of the monster, a grateful people erected this monument to an energetic and inventive baker. *Et voilà, comme on écrit l'histoire.*

I will not fatigue the reader by dragging him all over this much-loved park, which must be enjoyed directly, not through description *; enough for present purposes if it be added that while the summer palace of Belvedere is connected with Weimar by the chestnut avenue, the summer palace and park of Tiefurt is also connected with Weimar by a richly wooded road, the Webicht. This Tiefurt is a tiny little place, quite a curiosity of diminutiveness. The park, through which runs a branch of the Ilm, is tiny but picturesque. The upper story of the palace is a labyrinth of tiny rooms, some of them so small that, standing with your back against one wall, you can touch the opposite wall with your hand. It was here the Duchess Amalia lived.

' I have lived here fifty years ', said Goethe to Eckermann, ' and where have I not been? but I was always glad to return to Weimar '. The stranger may wonder wherein lies the charm ; but a residence at Weimar soon reveals the secret. Among the charms are the environs. First there is Ettersburg, with its palace, woods, and park, some seven miles distant. Then there is Bercka with its charming valley, dear to all pedestrians, within half-a-dozen miles ; a little further is Jena and its enchanting valley, from whose heights we look down on the sombre city, rendered illustrious by so many sounding names. Jena was to science what Weimar was to poetry. Assembled there were men like Griesbach, Paulus, Baumgarten-Crusius, and Danz, to teach theology ; Schelling, Fichte, Hegel, Reinhold, and Fries, to teach philosophy ; Loder, Hufeland, Oken, Döbereiner, to teach science ; Luden, Schultz, and others, for history. The Schlegels and the Humboldts also lent their lustre to the place. Besides Jena, we must mention Ilmenau, Eisenach, the Thuringian forests, and the valley of the Saal : environs attractive enough for the most restless wanderer.

Having thus sketched the main features of the *place*, it will now be desirable to give some indication of the *times*, that we may understand the atmosphere in which Goethe lived. Difficult as the restoration of Weimar has been to me, and only possible through the aid of what still remains from the old time, the

---

* If a fuller description be desired, the reader will find one in the charming pages of Stahr's *Weimar und Jena*, to which I take this occasion of acknowledging a large debt.

difficulty has been tenfold with regard to the more changing aspects of society and opinion. Curiously enough the Germans, famous for writing on all subjects, have produced no work on the state of manners and the domestic conditions of this much-bewritten period. The books on Goethe are endless ; there is not one which tells us of the outward circumstances among which he moved. From far and wide I have gathered together some details which may aid in forming a picture.

Remember that we are in the middle of the eighteenth century. The French Revolution is as yet only gathering its forces together ; nearly twenty years must elapse before the storm breaks. The chasm between that time and our own is vast and deep. Every detail speaks of it. To begin with Science—everywhere the torch of civilization—it is enough to say that Chemistry did not then exist. Abundant materials indeed existed, but that which makes a Science, viz. the power of *prevision* based on *quantitative* knowledge, was still absent ; and Alchemy maintained its place among the conflicting hypotheses of the day. Goethe in Frankfurt was busy with researches after the 'virgin earth'. The philosopher's stone had many eager seekers. In 1787, Semler sent to the Academy of Berlin his discovery that gold grew in a certain atmospheric salt, when kept moist and warm. Klaproth, in the name of the Academy, examined this salt, and found indeed gold leaf in it—which had been put there by Semler's servant to encourage his master's credulity. This age, so incredulous in religion, was credulous in science. In spite of all the labours of the encyclopædists, in spite of all the philosophic and religious 'enlightenment', in spite of Voltaire and La Mettrie, it was possible for Count St. Germain and Cagliostro to delude thousands ; and Casanova found a dupe in the Marquise d'Urfé, who believed he could restore her youth, and make the moon impregnate her ! It was in 1774 that Mesmer astonished Vienna with his marvels of mystic magnetism. The secret societies of Freemasons and Illuminati, mystic in their ceremonies and chimerical in their hopes—now in quest of the philospher's stone, now in quest of the perfectibility of mankind—a mixture of religious, political, and mystical reveries, flourished in all parts of Germany, and in all circles.

With Science in so imperfect a condition, we are sure to find a corresponding poverty in material comfort and luxury. High-roads, for example, were only found in certain parts of Germany ;

Goethe in cavalier's garb

Prussia had no chaussée till 1787. Milestones were unknown, although finger-posts existed. Instead of facilitating the transit of travellers, it was thought good political economy to obstruct them, for the longer they remained the more money they spent in the country. A century earlier, stage coaches were known in England; but in Germany, public conveyances, very rude to this day in places where no railway exists, were few and miserable ; nothing but open carts with unstuffed seats. Diligences on springs were unknown before 1800 ; and what they were, even twenty years ago, many readers doubtless remember. Then as to speed. In 1754 there was 'the flying coach' running from Manchester to London, but taking four days and a half on the journey. In 1763 there was a coach between Edinburgh and London, once a month ; it passed twelve or fourteen days on the road ; though even in our own stage-coach days the distance was performed in forty-eight hours. And as England was a busy nation, always in a hurry, we may gather from these details some idea of the rapidity of German travel. Germans were not flurried by agitations as to loss of time : if you travelled post, it was said with pride that seldom more than an hour's waiting was necessary before the horses were got ready,—at least on frequented routes. Mail travelling was at the rate of five English miles in an hour and a quarter. Letters took nine days from Berlin to Frankfurt, which in 1854 required only twenty-four hours. So slow was the communication of news that, as we learn from the Stein correspondence, the death of Frederick the Great was only known in Carlsbad as a rumour a week afterward. 'By this time', writes Goethe, 'you must know in Weimar if it be true'. With these obstacles to locomotion, it was natural that men travelled but rarely, and mostly on horseback. What the inns were may be imagined from the infrequency of travellers, and the general state of domestic comfort.

The absence of comfort and luxury (luxury as distinguished from ornament) may be gathered from the Memoirs of the time, and from such works as Bertuch's *Mode Journal*. Such necessities as good locks, doors that shut, drawers opening easily, tolerable knives, carts on springs, or beds fit for a Christian of any other than the German persuasion, are still rarities in Thuringia ; but in those days, when sewers were undreamed of, and a post office was only a vision, much that we moderns consider as comfort was necessarily wanting. The furniture, even of palaces, was extremely simple. In the houses of wealthy bourgeois, chairs and tables were of common fir ; not until the close of the eighteenth century did mahogany make its appearance. Looking-glasses followed. The chairs were covered with a coarse green cloth ; the tables likewise ; and carpets are only now beginning to loom upon the national mind as a possible luxury. The windows were hung with woollen curtains, when the extravagance of curtains was ventured on. Easy-chairs were unknown ; the only arm-chair allowed was the so-called *Grandfather's chair*, which was reserved for the dignity of grey hairs, or the feebleness of age.

The *salon de reception*, or drawing-room, into which greatly honoured visitors were shown, had of course a kind of Sunday splendour, not dimmed by week-day familiarity. There hung the curtains ; the walls were adorned with family portraits or some work of native talent ; the tables alluring the eye with china, in guise of cups, vases, impossible shepherds, and very allegorical dogs. Into this room the honoured visitor was ushered ; and there, no matter what the hour, refreshment of some kind was handed. This custom—a compound product of hospitality and bad inns—lingered until lately in England, and perhaps is still not unknown in provincial towns.

On eating and drinking was spent the surplus now devoted to finery. No one then, except gentlemen of the first water, boasted of a gold snuff-box ; even a gold-headed cane was an unusual elegance. The dandy contented himself with a silver watch. The fine lady blazoned herself with a gold watch and heavy chain ; but it was an heirloom ! To see a modern dinner service glittering with silver, glass, and china, and to think that even the nobility in those days ate off pewter, is enough to make the lapse of time very vivid to us. A silver teapot and teatray were held as princely magnificence.

The manners were rough and simple. The journeymen ate at the same table with their masters, and joined in the coarse jokes which then passed for hilarity. Filial obedience was rigidly enforced ; the stick or strap not unfrequently aiding parental authority. Even the brothers exercised an almost paternal authority over their sisters. Indeed, the position of women was by no means such as our women can hear of with patience ; not only were they kept under the paternal, marital, and fraternal yoke, but society limited their actions by its prejudices still more than it does now. No woman of the better class of citizens could go out alone ; the servant-girl followed her to church, to a shop, or even to the promenade.

The coarseness of language may be imagined from our own literature of that period. The roughness of manners is shown by such a scene as that in *Wilhelm Meister*, where the *Schöne Seele* in her confessions (speaking of high, well-born society) narrates how, at an evening party, forfeits were introduced ; one of these forfeits is, that a gentleman shall say something gallant to every lady present ; he whispers in the ear of a lady, who boxes his ears, and boxes it with such violence that the powder from his hair flies into a lady's eyes ; when she is enabled to see again, it is to see that the husband of the lady has drawn his sword, and stabbed the offender, and that a duel, in the very presence of these women, is only prevented by one of the combatants being dragged from the room.

The foregoing survey would be incomplete without some notice of the *prices* of things ; the more so as we shall learn hereafter that the pension Karl August gave Schiller was 200 thalers—about £30 of our money ; that the salary of Seckendorff as *Kammerherr* was only 600 thalers, or about £100 ; and that the salary Goethe received, as Councillor of Legation, was only 1,200 thalers, about £200 per annum. It is necessary I should indicate something like the real relation of these sums to the expense of living. We find, in Schiller's correspondence with Körner, that he hires a riding-horse for sixpence a day (vol. I, p. 84), and gets a manuscript fairly copied at the rate of three halfpence a sheet of sixteen pages (vol. I, p. 92), with us the charge is twopence for every seventy-two words ; the whole of *Don Carlos* cost but three and sixpence for copying. He hires a furnished apartment, consisting of two rooms and a bedroom, for two pounds twelve and sixpence a quarter (Charlotte von Kalb writing to Jean Paul, November 1776, says his lodgings will only cost him ten dollars, or thirty shillings, a quarter) ; while his male servant, who in case of need can act as secretary, is to be had for eighteen shillings a quarter (vol. I, p. 111). Reckoning up his expenses he says, 'Washing, servants, the barber, and such things, all paid quarterly, and none exceeding six shillings : so that, speaking in round numbers, I shall hardly need more than four hundred and fifty dollars' (vol. II, p. 94)—that is, about £70 a year. Even when he is married, and sees a family growing round him, he says, 'With eight hundred dollars I can live here, in Jena, charmingly—*recht artig*' (vol. II, p. 153).

It is evident that in Weimar they led no very sumptuous life.

A small provincial town overshadowed by a Court, its modes of life were the expression of this contrast. The people, a slow, heavy, ungraceful, ignorant, but good-natured, happy, honest race, feeding on black bread and sausages ; rising higher, there were the cultivated classes of employés, artists, and professors ; and, higher still, the aristocracy. In the theatre, until 1825, the nobility alone were allowed admission to the boxes ; and when the Jena students crowded the pit, elbowing out the Weimar public, that public was forced to return home, or jostle with the students for seats in pit and gallery. Even when the theatre was rebuilt, and the bourgeoisie was permitted a place in the boxes, its place was on the left side of the house, the right being rigorously reserved for the *Vons.* This continued until 1848 ; since that year of revolutions the public has had the place it can pay for.

It is quite true, the Weimar Court but little corresponded with those conceptions of grandeur, magnificence, and historical or political importance, with which the name of Court is usually associated. But just as in gambling the feelings are agitated less by the greatness of the stake than by the variations of fortune, so in the social gambling of court intrigue, there is the same ambition and agitation, whether the green cloth be an empire or a duchy. Within its limits Saxe-Weimar displayed all that an imperial Court displays in larger proportions ; it had its ministers, its army, its chamberlains, pages, and sycophants. Court favour, and disgrace, elevated and depressed, as if they had been imperial smiles, or autocratic frowns. A standing army of six hundred men, with cavalry of fifty hussars, had its War Department, with war minister, secretary, and clerk*.

As the nobles formed the predominating element of Weimar, we see at once how, in spite of the influence of Karl August, and the remarkable men he assembled round him, no real public for Art could be found there. Some of the courtiers played more or less with Art, some had real feeling for it ; but the majority set decided faces against all the *beaux esprits.* When the Duchess Amalia travelled with Merck in 1778, Weimar was loud in anticipatory grumblings : ' She will doubtless bring back some *bel esprit* picked up *en route !* ' was the common cry. And really when we have learned, as we shall learn in a future chapter, the habits of

---

* Lest this should appear too ridiculous, I will add that one of the small German princes (the Graf von Limburg Styrum) kept a corps of hussars, which consisted of a colonel, six officers, and two privates !

these *beaux esprits*, and their way of making life 'genial', impartiality will force us to confess that this imperfect sympathy on the part of the *Vons* was not without its reason.

Not without profound significance is this fact that in Weimar the poet found a Circle, but no Public. To welcome his productions there were friends and admirers; there was no Nation. Germany had no public; nor has it to this day. It was, and is, a collection of cities, not a Nation. To appreciate by contrast the full significance of such a condition we must look at Greece and Rome. There the history of Art tells the same story as is everywhere told by the history of human effort. It tells us that to reach the height of perfection there must be the co-operation of the Nation with individual Genius. Thus it is necessary for the development of science that science should cease to be the speculation of a few, and become the minister of the many; from the constant pressure of unsatisfied *wants*, science receives its energetic stimulus; and its highest reward is the satisfaction of those wants. In Art the same law holds. The whole Athenian Nation co-operated with its artists; and this is one cause why Athenian Art rose into unsurpassed splendour. Art was not the occupation of a few, ministering to the luxury of a few; it was the luxury of all. Its triumphs were not hidden in galleries and museums; they blazed in the noonday sun; they were admired and criticized by the whole people; and, as Aristotle expressly says, every free citizen was from youth upwards a critic of Art. Sophocles wrote for all Athens, and by all Athens was applauded. The theatre was open to all free citizens. Phidias and Praxiteles, Scopas and Myron, wrought their marvels in brass and marble, as expressions of a national faith, and the delights of a national mind. Temples and market-places, public groves and public walks, were the galleries wherein these sculptors placed their works. The public treasury was liberal in its rewards; and the rivalry of private munificence was not displayed to secure works for private galleries, but to enrich the public possessions. In this spirit the citizens of Gnidos chose to continue the payment of an onerous tribute rather than suffer their statue of Venus to quit their city. And when some murmurs rose against the expense which Pericles was incurring in the building of the Parthenon, he silenced those murmurs by the threat of furnishing the money from his private purse, and then placing his name on the majestic work.

Stahr, who has eloquently. described the effects of such national co-operation in Art, compares the similar influence of publicity during the Middle Ages, when the great painters and sculptors placed their works in cathedrals,—open all day long, in council-houses and market-places, whither the people thronged,—with the fact that in our day Art finds refuge in the galleries of private persons, or in museums closed on Sundays and holidays*.

Nor is this all. The effect of Art upon the Nation is visible in the striking fact that in Greece and Rome the truly great men were crowned by the public, not neglected for any artist who pandered to the fashion and the tastes of the few, or who flattered the *first* impressions of the many. It was young Phidias whom the Athenians chose to carve the statue of Pallas Athene, and to build the Parthenon. Suppose Phidias had been an Englishman, would he have been selected by government to give the nation a statue of Wellington, or to build the Houses of Parliament? The names most reverenced by contemporaries in Greece, and in Italy, are the names which posterity has declared to be the highest. Necessarily so. The verdict of the public, when that public includes the whole intelligence of the nation, *must* be the correct verdict in Art.

CHAPTER II

THE NOTABILITIES OF WEIMAR

The Dowager Duchess Amalia. Mlle. Göchhausen. Wieland. Einsiedel. Corona Schröter. Bertuch. Musæus. Seckendorf. The Duchess Luise. Karl August. Gräfin Werther. Frau von Stein. Knebel. Herder.

HAVING endeavoured to reconstruct some image of Weimar and its people, we may now descend from generals to particulars, and sketch rapidly the principal figures which will move across that scene, during the first years of Goethe's residence.

The Dowager DUCHESS AMALIA is a very interesting figure. She had the Brunswick blood, with its capriciousness, love of pleasure, and frivolity ; but she had also a mind well cultivated, not poorly gifted, and ready in appreciating men of talent. Although a niece of Frederick the Great, she did not follow the princely fashion of the day, and turn her eyes away from German Literature, to fix them only upon France. She chose Wieland as

* See his *Torso*, pp. 147–51.

The Dowager Duchess Anna Amalia

the tutor of her son, and made him her own dear friend. Schiller, a rash judge of persons, and not very keen in his perception of woman's character, wrote to Körner, after his first interview with the Duchess : ' She has made no conquest of me. I cannot like her physiognomy. Her intellect is extremely limited, nothing interests her but what is based on the sensuous : hence the taste she has, or affects to have, for music, painting, and the rest. She is a composer herself, and has set Goethe's *Erwin und Elmire* to music. She speaks little ; but has, at any rate, the merit of throwing aside all the stiffness of ceremony'. Schiller's verdict cannot be accepted by any one who reflects, that, besides her appreciation of men of talent, who found delight in her society, she learned Greek from Wieland, read Aristophanes, and translated Propertius, was a musical composer, a tolerable judge of art, discussed politics with the Abbé Raynal and Greek and Italian literature with Villoison ; that, moreover, with all her multifarious reading and enjoyments, she contrived to superintend the education of her sons, and managed her kingdom with unusual success. This is not to be done by an ' extremely limited intellect'.

The ' sensuous basis ' alluded to by Schiller was certainly there. One sees it in her portraits. One sees it also in the glimpses of her joyous, pleasure-loving existence. Biographers and eulogists omit such details ; for in general the biographical mind moves only through periods of rhetoric, which may be applied with equal felicity to every prince or princess of whom it is the cue to speak. But it is by such details that the image of the Duchess can alone be made a *living* one. Here, for example, is a sketch of her, given by an anonymous traveller*. ' She is small in stature, good-looking, with a very *spirituelle* physiognomy ; she has the Brunswick nose, lovely hands and feet, a light yet princely gait, speaks well but rapidly, and has something amiable and fascinating in her nature. . . . This evening there was a Redoute, tickets one gulden (*two francs*) each. The Court arrived at eight. The Duchess was magnificent, *en domino*, and brilliant with jewels. She dances well, lightly and gracefully. The young princes, who were attired as *Zephyr* and *Amour*, also danced well. The masquerade was very full, lively, and varied. A faro table was laid out : the smallest stake being half a gulden. The Duchess staked dollars and half-louis, played generously and lost.

---

* Quoted from BERNOUILLI by VEHSE : *Geschichte der Deutschen Höfe*, vol. XXVIII, p. 60.

But as she was glad to dance, she did not play long. She danced with every mask who invited her, and stayed till nearly three o'clock, when almost every one had gone home'. The same writer also speaks of another Redoute. 'The Duchess appeared *en reine grecque*, a very beautiful costume, which suited her well. The ball was very brilliant ; some students from Jena were there. At the last ball of the season, the Duchess sent me one of her own Savoyard dresses, and I was *frisé* and dressed like a woman by the Countess von Görtz's maid. The young Count was likewise dressed as a woman, and we went to Court so, dined there, and drove thence to the ball, which lasted till six o'clock'.

This pleasure-loving Duchess, who knew so well how to manage her kingdom, cared little for the dignities of her state. According to Wieland, she lived sometimes in student fashion, especially at Belvedere, where student-songs, not always the most decorous, rang joyously through the moonlit gardens. Driving once with seven friends in a haycart from Tiefurt, and overtaken by a storm, she made no more ado, but drew over her light clothing Wieland's great coat, and in *that* costume drove on.

Her letters, especially those to Goethe's mother, several of which I have seen, have great heartiness, and the most complete absence of anything like formality. In one of them, I remember, she apologizes for not having written for some time, not from want of friendship, but lack of news : to show that she has been thinking of *Frau Aja*, she sends her a pair of garters worked by herself. '*Liebe Frau Aja!*' she writes on another occasion, 'my joy at the receipt of your letter is not easily described, nor will I attempt it, for true feelings are too sacred to be set down in black and white. You know, dear mother, what you are to me, and can believe how infinitely your remembrance of me has rejoiced me*'.

Beside the figure of the Duchess Amalia, we see that of the merry little humpbacked GÖCHHAUSEN, her maid of honour, by intimates named *Thusnelda*. One sees not why this sprightly little *démon de bonne compagnie* should have been named after the wife of Arminius. She was a great favourite with Amalia, with Karl August also, who was constantly engaged in 'wit combats' with her, not always of the mildest. She animated

---

* Here is another extract, which I leave in the original : 'Ach Mutter, Mutter!—sie errathen wohl meine Gedanken! was macht der alte Vater? er sollte ja nicht wohl seyn. Grüssen sie ihn von mir, und das tausendmal. Leben Sie wohl, beste Mutter; behalten Sie mir lieb und denken fleissig an ihre Freundin. *Amalia*'.

Grand Duke Karl August von Sachsen-Weimar

society with her devices, and kept up a voluminous correspondence with wits and notabilities in other cities. She was very fond of Goethe, and wrote constantly to his mother. But Karl August was her darling; perhaps because he plagued her so incessantly. As a sample of the lengths to which tricks were carried, consider the following anecdote, which I have from Frau von Goethe, who had it from her father-in-law, an accomplice in the deed. One night as *Thusnelda* came up the stairs leading to her bedroom, her candle was blown out. Not much heeding this, she went on, reached the gallery into which her bedroom opened, and walked on *feeling* for the door. There is no great difficulty in finding the door of your own room in the dark, yet Thusnelda groped, and groped, and groped in vain : no lock met her hand, a smooth blank wall allowed her hand to pass and repass over it with increasing confusion. Where was the door? Where was she? After groping some time, her perplexity growing into undefined alarm, she descended to the·Duchess's room ; but she found that closed ; the Duchess was asleep ; and her gentle knockings were not answered. Upstairs she went again, again to pass her hands along the wall, but still to find no door. The night was cold, and she was half-frozen with cold and fear before the mystery was explained : the Duke and Goethe had removed her door, and built up the wall in its place.

WIELAND had established his paper, the *Teutsche Merkur*, which was not without its influence. When he ceased to be the Prince's tutor, he remained the valued friend of the Duchess. He was in all the pleasure parties. So also was EINSIEDEL, who, at first Court page, became chamberlain to the Duchess Amalia in 1776. A jovial, careless epicurean ; everywhere known as *l'ami*, from his good nature and eccentricity ; filling the mouth of gossip with his extravagances ; poet and musician in a small way ; actor and inventor of amusements, his name meets us on every page of the Weimar chronicles.

Einsiedel makes us think of CORONA SCHRÖTER, the *Hofsängerin* (singer to the Court—we have no such word, because we have no such thing). Goethe had known this beautiful and accomplished creature while he was a student at Leipzig, and when, shortly after his arrival at Weimar, he made an expedition to Leipsic with the Duke, he saw her there again, and induced her to come to Weimar. She was the grace of their private theatricals, and the original personator of Iphigenia.

Als eine Blume zeigt sie sich der Welt,

says Goethe of her, in that passage wherein he has immortalized her and Mieding *. What a description!

She, like a flower, opens to the world.

Corona painted, sang, played, was learned in music, and declaimed with peculiar elegance,

The Muses lavished on her every art.

According to Karl August, she was 'marble-beautiful, but marble-cold'; Goethe says of her:

Und hoch erstaunt, seht Ihr in ihr vereint
Ein Ideal, das Künstlern nur erscheint†.

There is a notion current, originating with Riemer, but shown by Schöll to be very improbable, that Goethe had a *liaison* with Corona. I not only agree with Schöll's reasoning, but can corroborate it by the testimony of the Frau von Goethe, who assured me her father-in-law expressly and emphatically told her that he never had a passion for any actress. Varnhagen von Ense suspects that Corona was privately married to Einsiedel ; if not, her letters, still extant although inedited, prove that they were on the footing of lovers.

Another chamberlain, poet, and musician was SECKENDORF, who translated *Werther* into French, a year after Goethe's arrival (*Les Souffrances du Jeune Werther.* Par le B. S. d. S. Erlangen, 1776) ; and to these gay companions must be added BODE, the translator of Smollett ; BERTUCH, the treasurer and the translator of Cervantes ; and MUSÆUS, a passionate lover of gardening, who gave Weimar its pleasant *Erholung*, and who might be seen daily crossing the quiet streets with a cup of coffee in one hand, his garden tools in the other, trudging along to that loved retreat. At other times he might be seen plying the ex-drummer, Rüppler, with inspiring *schnapps* to unlock the casket of his memory, wherein were stored the legends and superstitions of the peasantry which Musæus afterwards dressed up in his own style in his celebrated *Volksmärchen.* There was much humour in Musæus ; he furnished his Weimar friends with many a pleasant quip and crank. Heinrich Schmidt tells the following. One day Musæus,

* See the poem *Mieding's Tod.*
† And gently awed, you feel in her combined
   What is Ideal in the artist's mind.

The Grand Duchess Luise

after a long illness, came to dine with the Schmidts. Every one was amazed at his healthy aspect. He received their reiterated compliments with perfect gravity, till his wife, unable longer to contain herself, confessed that before setting out he had rouged his cheeks ! *

These are the principal figures of Amalia's Court. We may now glance at the Court of the reigning Duke and Duchess— Karl August and Luise.

Of the DUCHESS LUISE no one ever speaks but in terms of veneration. She was one of those rare beings who, through circumstances the most trying, as well as through the ordinary details of life, manifest a *noble character*. The Queen of Prussia and the Duchess of Saxe-Weimar are two of the great figures in modern German history ; they both opposed the chief man of the age, Napoleon, and were both admired by him for that very opposition. Luise was of a cold temperament, somewhat rigid in her enforcement of etiquette (unlike the dowager), and wore to the last the old costume which had been the fashion in her youth ; apt in the early years of her marriage to be a little querulous with her husband, but showing throughout their lives a real and noble friendship for him.

And he was worthy of that friendship, much as his strange, and in many respects opposite nature, may have tried her. KARL AUGUST, whom Frederick the Great pronounced, at fourteen, to be the prince, of all he had seen, who gave the greatest promise, was in truth a very mixed, but very admirable, character. He can afford to be looked at more closely and familiarly than most princes. He was a man whose keen appreciation of genius not only drew the most notable men of the day to Weimar, but whose own intrinsically fine qualities *kept* them there. It is easy for a prince to assemble men of talent. It is not easy for a prince to make them remain beside him, in the full employment of their faculties, and in reasonable enjoyment of their position. Karl August was the prince who with the smallest means produced the greatest result in Germany. He was a man of restless activity. His eye was on every part of his dominions ; his endeavours to improve the condition of the people were constant. The recently published correspondence shows how active were his intellectual sympathies. In his tastes no man in Germany was so simple, except his dearest friend, Goethe, with whom, indeed, he had

* SCHMIDT : *Erinnerungen eines weimarischen Veteranen*, p. 21.

many cardinal points in common. I remember, on first seeing their busts together, being struck with a sort of faint family resemblance between them. Karl August might have been a younger brother, considerably 'animalized', but still belonging to the family. They had both, on the paternal side, Thuringian blood in their veins ; and in many respects Amalia and Frau Aja were akin. But while Karl August had the active, healthy, sensuous, pleasure-loving temperament of his friend, he wanted the *tact* which never allowed Goethe, except in his wildest period, to overstep limits ; he wanted the tenderness and chivalry which made the poet so uniformly acceptable to women. He was witty, but his *bon-mots* are mostly of that kind which, repeated after dinner, are not considered fit for drawing-room publication. Very characteristic is it of him, who had bestowed unusual pains in collecting a *Bibliotheca Erotica*, that when Schiller wrote the *Maid of Orleans* he fancied Schiller was going to give another version of *La Pucelle*, and abetted his mistress, the Frau von Heygendorf, in her refusal to play the part of the rehabilitated Maiden ! He was rough, soldierly, brusque, and imperious. He was at home when in garrison with Prussian soldiers, but out of his element when at foreign Courts, and not always at ease in his own. Goethe describes him longing for his pipe at the Court of Brunswick in 1774 : 'De son coté notre bon Duc s'ennuie terrible-ment, il cherche un interet, il n'y voudrait pas etre pour rien, la marche très bien mesurée de tout ce qu'on fait ici le gene, il faut qu'il renonce a sa chere pipe et une fee ne pourroit lui rendre un service plus agreable qu'en changeant ce palais dans une cabane de charbonnier '*.

In a letter (unprinted), he writes to Goethe, then at Jena, saying he longs to be with him to watch sunrise and sunset, for he can't see the sunset in Gotha, hidden as it is by the crowd of courtiers, who are so *comme il faut*, and know their 'fish duty' with such terrible accuracy, that every evening he feels inclined to give himself to the devil. His delight, when not with soldiers, was to be with dogs, or with his poet alone in their simple houses, discussing philosophy, and 'talking of lovely things that conquer death'. He mingled freely with the people. At Ilmenau he and Goethe put on the miners' dress, descended into the mines, and danced all night with peasant girls. Riding across country, over

---

* *Briefe an Frau von Stein*, III, p. 85. The French is Goethe's, as also the spelling and accentuation, or rather want of accentuation.

Corona Schröter

rock and stream, in manifest peril of his neck; teasing the maids of honour, sometimes carrying this so far as to offend his more princely wife; wandering alone with his dogs, or with some joyous companion; seeking excitement in wine, and in making love to pretty women, without much respect of station; offending by his roughness and wilfulness, though never *estranging* his friends— Karl August, often grieving his admirers, was, with all his errors, a genuine and admirable character. His intellect was active, his judgment, both of men and things, sound and keen. Once, when there was a discussion about appointing Fichte as professor at Jena, one of the opponents placed a work of Fichte's in the Duke's hands, as sufficient proof that *such* a teacher could not hold a chair. Karl August read the book—and appointed Fichte. He had great aims; he also had the despotic will which bends circumstances to its determined issues. 'He was always in progress', said Goethe to Eckermann; 'when anything failed, he dismissed it at once from his mind. I often bothered myself how to excuse this or that failure; but he ignored every shortcoming in the cheerfullest way, and always went forward to something new'.

Such was Karl August, as I conceive him from the letters of the period, and from the reports of those who knew him. Eight years younger than Goethe, he attached himself to him as to a brother. We shall see this attachment and its reciprocal influence in the following pages; clouds sometimes gather, quarrels and dissatisfaction are not absent (from what long friendship are they absent?); but fifty years of mutual service, and mutual love, proved the genuineness of both their characters.

Among the Weimar notables, FRAU VON STEIN must always have conspicuous eminence. In a future chapter we shall learn more of her. Enough for the present to say that she was *Hofdame* (Lady of Honour) to the Duchess Amalia, and for many years passionately loved by Goethe. Beside her we may mention the COUNTESS VON WERTHER, who was to Karl August what the Baroness von Stein was to Goethe. She, as is well known, is the original of the charming Countess in *Wilhelm Meister*, and her husband is still more eccentric than the eccentric Count. It is related of him that once when the Duke and some other illustrious guests were in his château, he collected several of his peasants, dressed them in his livery, and blacked their faces to make them pass as negroes!

To close this list we have MAJOR VON KNEBEL, the translator of Lucretius and Propertius, an honest, upright, satirical republican, the intimate friend of Karl August and Goethe, the 'philanthropic Timon', as Herder called him, severe against all shams and insincerities, but loving the human nature he declaimed against. As one looks upon his rough, genial, Socratic head, one seems to hear the accents of an independent thoroughly honest nature give weight to what he says.

I have omitted HERDER. He did not come to Weimar till after Goethe, and indeed was drawn thither by Goethe, whose admiration for him, begun at Strasburg, continued unabated. The strange bitterness and love of sarcasm in Herder's nature, which could not repel the young student, did not alter the affection of the man. In one of Goethe's unpublished letters to the Duchess Amalia, there is an urgent appeal on behalf of Herder, whose large family had to be supported on very straitened means; the Duke had promised to provide for one of the children, and Goethe writes to Amalia, begging her to do the same for another. No answer coming to this appeal, or at any rate no prompt notice being taken, he writes again more urgently, adding, that if she does not provide for the child, he (Goethe), out of his small income, will! And this was at a time when Herder was most bitter against Goethe. Well might Merck exclaim: 'No one can withstand the disinterestedness of this man!'

CHAPTER III

THE FIRST WILD WEEKS AT WEIMAR

THIS was the circle into which Goethe entered in all the splendour of youth, beauty, and fame: Youth, which, according to the fine conception of the Greeks, is 'the herald of Venus'; Beauty, which those Greeks adored as the splendour of Truth; and Fame, which has at all times been a halo dazzling to mortal eyes. Thus equipped for conquest, how can we wonder that he conquered? Even Amalia, angry with him for having ridiculed her darling Wieland, could not withstand the magic of his presence. Her love of genius left her no choice. She was fascinated by his wild ways, and by his splendid talents. One moment he startled her with a paradox, the next moment he

Karl Ludwig von Knebel

sprang from his seat, waltzing and whirling round the room with antics which made her scream with laughter. And Wieland?—he was conquered at once. He shall speak for himself, in a letter written after their first interview : 'How perfectly I felt, at the first glance, he was a man after my own heart ! How I loved the magnificent youth as I sat beside him at table ! All that I can say (after more than one crisis which I have endured) is this : since that morning my soul is as full of Goethe as a dewdrop of the morning sun. . . . I believe the godlike creature will remain longer with us than he intended ; and if Weimar *can* do anything, his presence will accomplish it'. This is very honourable to Wieland : Nestor gazes with unenvious delight upon the young Achilles. Heroic eyes are always proud to recognize heroic proportions.

After Wieland and the Duchess, the rest were easy to conquer. 'He rose like a star in the heavens', says Knebel. 'Everybody worshipped him, especially the women'. In the costume of his own Werther, which was instantly adopted by the Duke, he seemed the ideal of a poet. To moderns there are no very sentimental suggestions in a costume which was composed of blue coat and brass buttons, topboots, and leather breeches, the whole surmounted by powder and pigtail ; but in those days this costume was the suggestion of everything tender and romantic. Werther had consecrated it*. The Duke not only adopted it, but made all around him adopt it also, sometimes paying the tailor's bill himself. Wieland alone was excepted ; he was too old for such masqueradings.

Thoroughly to appreciate the effect of Goethe's influence with women, we must remember the state of feeling and opinion at the time. Those were the days of gallantry, the days of

Puffs, paints, and patches, powders, billets doux.

The laxity of German morals differed from the more audacious licentiousness of France : it had sentimentalism, in lieu of gaiety and luxuriousness, for its basis. The heart of a French marquise was lost over a supper-table sparkling with champagne and *bon-mots :* the heart of a German Gräfin yielded more readily to moonlight, melancholy, and a copy of verses. Wit and audacity were the batteries for a Frenchwoman ; the German was stormed

---

* It should be remembered, that in Germany, at that time, *boots* were only worn in very bad weather; and in the presence of women no one ever appeared except in shoes and silk stockings.

with sonnets and a threat of suicide. For the one, Lothario needed sprightliness and *bon ton;* for the other, turbulent disgust at all social arrangements, expressed in interjectional rhetoric, and a deportment outrageous to all conventions. It is needless to add that marriage was to a great extent what Sophie Arnould with terrible wit called it—'the sacrament of adultery'; and that on the subject of the sexes the whole tone of feeling was low. Poor, simple, earnest Schiller, whom no one will excuse of laxity, admired *Les Liaisons Dangereuses*, and saw no reason why women should not read it; although to our age the infamy of that book is so great as to stamp a brand upon the society which produced and applauded it. Yet even Schiller, who admired this book, was astounded at the condition of women at Weimar. 'There is hardly one of them', he writes to Körner, 'who has not had a *liaison*. They are all coquettes. . . . One may very easily fall into an "affair of the heart", though it will not *last* any time'. It was thought, apparently, that since Eros had wings, he must use them—and fly.

With this tone of society we can understand how, as Goethe in after-life confessed to Eckermann, the first years at Weimar were 'perplexed with love affairs'. A great admirer of women, and greatly admired by them, it was natural he should fall into their snares. Many charmers are named; among them, Fräulein von Kalb, Corona Schröter, and Kotzebue's sister, Amalia; but I am bound to say that, after the most diligent inquiry, I can find *no* reliable evidence for believing any one of those named to have been really loved by him. We must content ourselves with the fact of his having flirted considerably: making love to every bright pair of eyes which for a moment could make him believe what he said*.

For the first few months he gave himself up to the excitement of this new life. Among other things he introduced skating. Weimar had hitherto seen no gentleman on the ice; but now, Klopstock having made skating famous by his poetry, Goethe made it fashionable by his daring grace. The Duchess soon excelled in the art. Skating on the *Schwansee* became 'the rage'. Sometimes the banks were illuminated with lamps and torches, and music and fireworks animated the scene. The Duchess and ladies,

---

* 'Ich log und trog mich bei allen hübschen Gesichtern herum, und hatte den Vortheil immer ein Augenblick zu glauben was ich sagte', he says in a letter to the Frau von Stein, vol. 1, p. 5.

Christoph Martin Wieland

masked as during carnival, were driven in sledges over the noisy ice. 'We are somewhat mad here', Goethe writes to Merck, 'and play the devil's own game'. Wieland's favourite epithet for him was *wüthig*—outrageous ; and *wüthig* he was. Strange stories are told of him, now dashing across the ice, now loosening his long hair in Bertuch's room, and, with locks flowing over his shoulders, whirling round in mad Bacchante waltz ; and finally, standing in the Jena market-place with the Duke, by the hour together, smacking huge sledge whips for a wager. Imagine a Duke and a Poet thus engaged in a public market-place !

His constant companion, and in all devilries and dissipation his most jovial associate, was Karl August. All ceremony was laid aside between them. They dined together, often shared the same bedroom, and called each other by the brotherly *thou*. 'Goethe will never leave this place again', writes Wieland ; 'K. A. can no longer swim or wade without him. The Court, or rather his *liaison* with the Duke, wastes his time, which is really a great pity—and yet—with so magnificent and godlike a creature nothing is ever lost !' Weimar was startled in its more respectable circles by the conduct of these two, and their associates : conduct quite in keeping with the period named 'the *genial**'. In their orgies they drank wine out of skulls (as Byron and his friends did in their wild days), and in ordinary intercourse exhibited but a very mitigated respect for *meum* and *tuum*, borrowing handkerchiefs and waiscoats which were never returned. The favourite epithet of that day was 'infinite' : Genius drank infinitely, loved infinitely, and swallowed infinite sausages.

But the poet's nature soon wearies of such scenes. After some two months of dissipation, in masking, skating, hunting, drinking, and dicing, the want to be once more among simple people and lovely scenes drove him away from Weimar to Waldeck. Amid the crowded tumult of life he ever kept his soul sequestered ; and from the hot air of society he broke impatiently away to the serenity of solitude. While on this journey along the pine-clad mountains, there came over him a feeling of the past, in which the image of Lili painfully reappeared.

He was called back to Weimar by the Duke, impatient of his absence ; and, while debating in his own mind whether he should

---

* It is difficult to find an English word to express the German *genial*, which means pertaining to genius. The genial period was the period when every extravagance was excused on the plea of genius.

accept a place there, or return to Frankfurt, he began to take his seat, as a guest, in the Privy Council. He had tried the Court, and now he was about to try what virtue lay in government. ' I am here as if at home', so runs one of his letters, 'and the Duke daily becomes dearer to me'. Indeed his father's prognostications had failed. The connexion between his son and the Duke was of a totally different kind from that between Voltaire and Fritz. In secret, Voltaire despised the verses of his patron, as his patron in secret despised the weakness of Voltaire. A few unguarded expressions were enough to snap the link which bound them together ; but a lifetime only deepened the regard of Goethe and Karl August. Nor must it be supposed that their friendship was merely that of boon-companions. Both had high aims and strong wills. Prince Hal might recreate himself with Falstaff, Pistol, Bardolph, and the rest ; but while chucking Mrs. Quickly under the chin, he knew he was one day to be England's lord. Karl August and Goethe were not the men to lose themselves in the fleeting hours of dissipation ; serious, steady business was transacted almost the moment before some escapade. In their retreat at Ilmenau the poet writes :

> Mein Carl und ich vergessen hier
> Wie seltsam uns ein tiefes Schicksal leitet.
> Und ach ! ich fühl's, im stillen werden wir
> Zu neuen Scenen vorbereitet.

' My Karl and I here forget the strange mysterious Fate which guides us ; and I feel that in these quiet moments we are preparing for new scenes'. Yes, they learned 'in the happy present to forecast the future'.

The Duke knew what he was doing when he overstepped all precedent, and, in June 1776, elected Goethe to the post of Geheime Legations Rath, with a seat and voice in the Privy Council, and a salary of 1200 thalers. In writing to Goethe's father, the Duke intimated that there was absolute freedom of leaving the service at will, and that indeed the appointment was a mere formality, no measure of his affection. ' Goethe can have but one position—that of my friend. All others are beneath him'.

The post of Geheime Legations Rath at Weimar is not a very magnificent post ; and the salary of 1200 thalers (about £200) seems still less magnificent when we remember that at that period the King of Prussia gave the Barberini, an Italian dancer, exactly *ten* times the sum. But, such as it was, the appointment created great noise. Weimar was thunderstruck. The favour shown to Wieland had not passed without scandal; but alarming indeed was this elevation of a Frankfurt bourgeois. A poet, who had gone through none of the routine of business, whose life was anything but 'respectable', to be lifted suddenly over the plodding heads of legitimate aspirants! If *this* was to be, what reward could meritorious mediocrity expect? what advantage had slowly acquired routiniary knowledge?

So murmured scandalized officials and their friends. At last these murmurs expressed themselves distinctly in the shape of a protest. The Duke thought the act worthy of a deliberate justification, and with his own hand added these words to the protocol of the acts of his ministry :

'Enlightened persons congratutate me on possessing such a man. His genius and capacity are well known. To employ a man of such a stamp in any other functions than those in which he can render available the extraordinary gifts he possesses, is to abuse them. As to the observation that persons of merit may think themselves unjustly passed over: I observe, in the first place, that nobody to my knowledge, in my service, has a right to reckon on an equal degree of favour; and I add that I will never consent to be governed by mere length of service or rotation in my choice of a person whose functions place him in such immediate relation to myself, and are so important to the happiness of my people. In such a case I shall attend to nothing but the degree of confidence I can repose in the person of my choice. The public opinion which perhaps censures the admission of Dr. Goethe to my council without having passed through the previous steps of Amtmann, Professor, Kammerath, or Regierungsrath, produces no effect on my own judgment. The world forms its opinion on prejudices; but I watch and work—as every man must who wishes to do his duty—not to make a noise, not to attract the applause of the world, but to justify my conduct to God and my conscience'.

Assuredly we may echo M. Dumont's sentiment, that 'the prince, who, at nineteen, wrote those words, was no ordinary man'. He had not only the eye to see greatness, he had also the strong Will to guide his conduct according to his views, untrammelled by routine and formulas. 'Say what you will, it is only like can recognize like, and a prince of great capacity will always recognize and cherish greatness in his servants*'. People saw that the Duke was resolved. Murmurs were silenced; or only percolated the gossip of private circles, till other subjects buried them, as all gossip is buried.

* Goethe in *Eckermann*, III, p. 232.

The mode of life which the *genial* company led was not only the subject of gossip in Weimar, it grew and grew as scandals grow, *not* losing substance on the way, and reached the ears of distant friends.   Thus, only a month before the appointment, Klopstock wrote to Goethe a letter which scandal extorted from friendship.

' *Hamburg, 8th of May,* 1776.

' Here is a proof of my friendship, dearest Goethe ! It is somewhat difficult, I confess, to give it, but it must be given.   Do not fancy that I wish to preach to you about your doings ; or that I judge harshly of you because you have other views than mine.   But your views and mine quite set aside, what will be the inevitable consequence if your present doings continue ?   The Duke, if he continues to drink as he does, instead of strengthening, as he says, his constitution, will ruin it, and will not live long.   Young men of powerful constitutions—and that the Duke is not—have in this way early perished.   The Germans have hitherto, and with justice, complained that their princes would have nothing to do with authors.   They now gladly make an exception in favour of the Duke. But what a justification will not the other princes have, if you continue your present tone ?   If only that should happen which I feel will happen ! The Duchess will perhaps still subdue her pain, for she has a strong, manly intellect.   But that pain will become grief !   And can *that* be so suppressed ?   Louisa's grief, Goethe ! . . . I must add a word about Stolberg.   He goes to Weimar out of friendship for the Duke.   He must also live well with him.   But how ?   In *his* style ?   No ! unless he, too, becomes altered, he will go away.   And then what remains for him ?   Not in Copenhagen, not in Weimar.   I must write to Stolberg ; what shall I say to him ?   You may please yourself about showing this letter to the Duke.   I have no objection against it.   On the contrary ; for he is assuredly not yet arrived at that point when he will not listen to the honest word of a friend.   ' KLOPSTOCK '.

Goethe's answer, dated the 21st of May, a fortnight later, there-fore, runs thus :

' In future, spare us such letters, dear Klopstock !   They do no good, and only breed bad blood.   You must feel yourself that I have no answer to make.   Either I must, like a schoolboy, begin a *Pater peccavi*, or sophistically excuse, or as an honest fellow defend, and perhaps a mingling of all these might express the truth, but to what purpose ?   Therefore, not a word more between us on this subject.   Believe me I should not have a moment's rest if I replied to all such admonitions.   It pained the Duke a moment to think it was Klopstock.   He loves and honours you ; you know I do the same.   Good-bye.   Stolberg must come all the same.   We are no worse ; and with God's help will be better than what he has seen us '.

To this Klopstock indignantly replied—

'You have much misunderstood the proof of my friendship, which was great, precisely because of my reluctance to mix myself unasked in the affairs of others. And as you include *all* such letters and *all* such admonitions (your expressions are as strong as that) in the same class with the letter which contained this proof of my friendship, I hereby declare you unworthy of that friendship. Stolberg shall not come, if he listens to me, or rather if he listens to his own conscience'.

The breach thus made was never repaired. Stolberg did not come to Weimar ; and Klopstock wrote no more.

To return : whatever basis there may have been for the reports which Gossip magnified, certain it is that the Duke did not forget the cares of state in these wild orgies. Both he and his friend were very active and very serious. If Weimar, according to the historian of Germany*, stands as an illustrious exception among the German Courts, it was because Karl August, upheld by his friend, knew how to carry into earnest practice the axiom of Frederick the Great : 'A king is but the first of subjects'. Goethe's beneficent activity is seen less in such anecdotes as those often cited of his opening a subscription for Bürger to enable him to complete his translation of *Homer*, and of his relieving Jung Stilling from distress, than in the constant and *democratic* sympathy with which he directed the Duke's endeavours.

That he had not the grave deportment of a councillor is very evident. Imagine him as in this anecdote related by Gleim : ' Soon after Goethe had written *Werther* I came to Weimar, and wished to know him. I had brought with me the last *Musen Almanach*, a literary novelty, and read here and there a poem to the company in which I passed the evening. While I was reading, a young man, booted and spurred, in a short green shooting-jacket thrown open, came in and mingled with the audience. I had scarcely remarked his entrance. He sat down opposite to me and listened attentively. I scarcely knew what there was about him that particularly struck me, except a pair of brilliant black Italian eyes. But it was decreed that I should know more of him.

' During a short pause, in which some gentlemen and ladies were discussing the merits of the pieces I had read, lauding some and censuring others, the gallant young sportsman (for such I took him to be) arose from his chair, and bowing with a most

---

* MENZEL, CCXLI.

courteous and ingratiating air to me, offered to relieve me from time to time in reading, lest I should be tired. I could do no less than accept so polite an offer, and immediately handed him the book. But oh! Apollo and all ye Muses—not forgetting the Graces—what was I then to hear? At first, indeed, things went on smoothly enough :

> Die Zephyr'n lauschten,
> Die Bäche rauschten,
> Die Sonne
> Verbreitet ihr Licht mit Wonne—

the somewhat more solid, substantial fare of Voss, Stolberg, and Bürger was delivered in such a manner that no one had any reason to complain.

'All at once, however, it was as if some wild and wanton devil had taken possession of the young reader, and I thought I saw the Wild Huntsman bodily before me. He read poems that had no existence in the *Almanach;* broke out into all possible modes and dialects. Hexameters, iambics, doggerel verses one after another, or blended in strange confusion, came tumbling out in torrents. What wild and humorous fancies did he not combine that evening! Amidst them came such noble, magnificent thoughts, thrown in detached and flitting, that the authors to whom he ascribed them must have thanked God on their knees if they had fallen upon their desks.

'As soon as the joke was discovered, universal merriment spread through the room. He put everybody present out of countenance in one way or the other. Even my Mæcenasship, which I had always regarded it as a sort of duty to exercise towards young authors, poets, and artists, had its turn. Though he praised it highly on the one side, he did not forget to insinuate on the other that I claimed a sort of property in the individuals to whom I afforded support and countenance. In a little fable composed extempore in doggerel verses, he likened me wittily enough to a worthy and most enduring turkey hen, that sits on a great heap of eggs of her own and other people's, and hatches them with infinite patience ; but to whom it sometimes happens to have a chalk egg put under her instead of a real one : a trick at which she takes no offence.

'"That is either Goethe or the Devil!" cried I to Wieland, who sat opposite me. "Both", he replied'.

Silhouette of Goethe (between 1776 and 1780)

It is worth bearing in mind *what* the young Goethe was, that we may the better understand the reason of what he became. No sooner had he commenced his career as politician, than he began to tone down the extravagance of his demeanour; without foregoing any enjoyments, he tried to accord more with those in whom a staid demeanour was necessitated by their more flagging pulses of lethargic life. One month after his appointment Wieland writes of him : ' Goethe did in truth, during the first months of his visit here, scandalize most people (never me); but from the moment that he decided on becoming a man of business, he has conducted himself with blameless σωφροσύνη and all worldly prudence'. Elsewhere he says : ' Goethe, with all his real and apparent *sauvagerie*, has, in his little finger, more *conduite* and *savoir faire* than all the Court parasites, Boniface sneaks, and political cobweb-spinners have in their whole bodies and souls. So long as Karl August lives no power can remove him'.

As we familiarize ourselves with the details of this episode, there appears less and less plausibility in the often-iterated declamation against Goethe on the charge of his having 'sacrificed his genius to the Court'. It becomes indeed a singularly foolish display of rhetoric. Let us for a moment consider the charge. He had to choose a career. That of poet was then, as it is still, terribly delusive ; verse could create fame, but no money : *fama* and *fames* were then, as now, in terrible contiguity. No sooner is the necessity for a career admitted than much objection falls to the ground ; for those who reproach him with having wasted his time on Court festivities, and the duties of government which others could have done as well, must ask whether he would have *saved* that time had he followed the career of jurisprudence and jostled lawyers through the courts at Frankfurt ? or would they prefer seeing him reduced to the condition of poor Schiller, wasting so much of his precious life in literary 'hackwork', translating French books for a miserable pittance ? *Time*, in any case, would have been claimed ; in return for that given to Karl August he received, as he confesses in the poem addressed to the Duke, 'what the great seldom bestow—affection, leisure, confidence, garden and house. No one have I had to thank but him ; and much have I wanted, who, as a poet, ill-understood the arts of gain. If Europe praised me, what has Europe done for me ? Nothing. Even my works have been an expense to me'.

In 1801, writing to his mother on the complaints uttered against him by those who judged falsely of his condition, he says they only saw what he gave up, not what he gained—they could not comprehend how he grew daily richer, though he daily gave up so much.   He confesses that the narrow circle of a burgher life would have ill-accorded with his ardent and wide-sweeping spirit. Had he remained at Frankfurt, he would have been ignorant of the world.   But here the panorama of life was unrolled before him, and his experience was every way enlarged.   Did not Leonardo da Vinci spend much of his time charming the Court of Milan with his poetry and lute-playing? did he not also spend time in mechanical and hydrostatical labours for the State?   No reproach is lifted against his august name; no one cries out against *his* being false to his genius; no one rebukes him for having painted so little at one period.   The 'Last Supper' speaks for him.   Will not *Tasso, Iphigenia, Hermann und Dorothea, Faust, Meister*, and the long list of Goethe's words, speak for *him?*

I have dealt mainly on the dissipation of his *time*, because the notion that a Court life affected his genius by 'corrupting his mind' is preposterous.   No reader of this biography, it is to be hoped, will fail to see the true relations in which he stood to the Duke; how free they were from anything like servility, or suppression of genuine impulse.   Indeed, one of the complaints against him, according to the unexceptionable authority of Riemer, was that made by the subalterns, 'of his not being sufficiently attentive to Court etiquette'.   To say, as Niebuhr says, that the 'Court was a Delilah to which he sacrificed his locks', is profoundly to misunderstand his genius, profoundly to misread his life.   Had his genius been of that stormy kind which produces great Reformers and great Martyrs,—had it been his mission to agitate mankind by words which, reverberating to their inmost recesses, called them to lay down their lives in the service of an Idea,—had it been his tendency to meditate upon the far-off destinies of man, and sway men by the coercion of grand representative abstractions—then, indeed, we might say his place was aloof from the motley throng, and not in sailing down the swiftly flowing stream to sounds of mirth and music on the banks.   But he was not a Reformer, not a Martyr.   He was a Poet, whose religion was Beauty, whose worship was of Nature, whose aim was Culture. His mission was to paint Life, and for that it was requisite he should see it.   Happier circumstances might indeed have surrounded him, and given him a greater sphere.   It would have been very different, as he often felt, if there had been a Nation to appeal to, instead of a heterogenous mass of small peoples, willing enough to talk of Fatherland, but in nowise prepared to *become* a Nation. There are many other *ifs* in which much virtue could be found; but inasmuch as he could not create circumstances, we must follow his example, and be content with what the gods provided. I do not, I confess, see what other sphere was open to him in which his genius could have been more sacred; but I do see that he built out of circumstances a noble Temple in which the altar-flame burnt with a steady light. To hypothetical biographers be left the task of settling what Goethe *might have been;* enough for us to catch some glimpse of what he was.

'Poetry', says Carlyle, 'is the attempt which man makes to render his existence harmonious'. It is the flower into which a life expands; but it is not the life itself, with all daily needs, daily struggles, daily prosaisms. The true poet manfully accepts the conditions in which destiny has placed him, and therein tries to make his existence harmonious; the sham poet, like a weak workman, fretful over his tools, is loud in his assurances of what he *might* be, were it his lot to live in other circumstances. Goethe was led by the current of events to a little Court, where he was arrested by friendship, love, leisure, and opportunities of a freer, nobler life than Frankfurt Law Courts offered him. After much deliberation he chose his career: these pages will show how in it he contrived to be *true* to his genius.

It is scarcely worth while to notice trash about his servility and Court slavery. He was not required to be servile; and his nature was as proud as any prince's. 'They call me a prince's servant', he said to Eckermann, 'and a prince's slave; as if there were any meaning in such words! Whom do I serve? A tyrant—a despot? Do I serve one who lives for his own pleasures at the people's cost? Such princes and such times are, thank God! far enough from us. For more than half a century I have been connected in the closest relations with the Grand Duke, and for half a century have striven and toiled with him; but I should not be speaking truth were I to say that I could name a single day on which the Duke had not his thoughts busied with something to be devised and effected for the good of the country; something calculated to better the condition of each individual in it. As for himself, personally, what has his princely state given him but a burden and a task? Is his dwelling, or his dress, or his table more sumptuously provided than that of any private man in easy circumstances? Go into our maritime cities, and you will find the larder and cellar of every considerable merchant better filled than his. If, then, I am a prince's slave, it is at least my consolation that I am but the slave of one who is himself a slave of the general good'.

And to close this subject, read the following passage from Merck's letter to Nicolai—(the Merck who is said by Falk to have spoken so bitterly of the waste of Goethe's life at Weimar): 'I have lately paid Goethe a visit at the Wartburg, and we have lived together for ten days like children. I am delighted to have seen with my own eyes what his situation is. The Duke is the best of all, and has a character firm as iron : *I would do, for love of him, just what Goethe does.* . . . I tell you sincerely that the Duke is most worthy of respect, and one of the cleverest men that I have ever seen,—and consider that he is a prince, and only twenty years of age !' The long and friendly correspondence Merck kept up with the Duke is the best pledge that the foregoing estimate was sincere.

CHAPTER IV

THE FRAU VON STEIN

FROM out the many flirtations that amused him, there arises one which grew into predominant importance, swallowing up all the others, and leaping from lambent flame into eager and passionate fire. It was no transitory flash, but a fire which burnt for ten years ; and thereby is distinguished from all previous attachments. It is a silver thread woven among the many-coloured threads which formed the tapestry of his life. I will here detach it, to consider it by itself.

The Baroness von Stein, 'Hofdame', and wife of the Master of the Horse, was, both by family and position, a considerable person. To us she is interesting, as having sprung from a Scotch family, named Irving, and as being the sister-in-law to that Baron Imhoff who sold his first wife to Warren Hastings. She was the mother of seven children, and had reached that age which, in fascinating women, is of perilous fascination—the age of three-and-thirty.

Charlotte von Stein

We can understand something of her power if we look at her portrait, and imagine those delicate, coquettish features animated with the lures of sensibility, gaiety, and experience of the world. She sang well, played well, sketched well, talked well, appreciated poetry, and handled sentiment with the delicate tact of a woman of the world. Her pretty fingers had turned over many a serious book ; and she knew how to gather honey from weeds. With moral deficiencies, which this history will betray, she was to all acquaintances a perfectly *charming* woman ; and retained her charm even in old age, as many living witnesses testify. Some years after her first acquaintance with Goethe, Schiller thus writes of her to his friend Körner : 'She is really a genuine, interesting person, and I quite understand what has attached Goethe to her. Beautiful she can never have been ; but her countenance has a soft earnestness, and a quite peculiar openness. A healthy understanding, truth, and feeling, lie in her nature. She has more than a thousand letters from Goethe ; and from Italy he writes to her every week. They say the connexion is perfectly pure and blameless '.

It was at Pyrmont that Goethe first saw the Frau von Stein's portrait, and was three nights sleepless in consequence of Zimmermann's description of her. In sending her that flattering detail, Zimmermann added, 'he will assuredly come to Weimar to see you '. Under her portrait Goethe wrote, 'What a glorious poem it would be to see how the world mirrors itself in this soul ! She sees the world as it is, and yet withal sees it through the medium of love ; hence sweetness is the dominant expression '. In her reply to Zimmermann she begs to hear more about Goethe, and intimates her desire to see him. This calls forth a reply that she 'has no idea of the danger of his magical presence '. Such dangers pretty women gladly run into, especially when, like Charlotte von Stein, they are perfect mistresses of themselves.

With his heart still trembling from the agitations of victory over its desires, after he had torn himself away from Lili, he saw this charming woman. The earth continues warm long after the sun has glided below the horizon ; and the heart continues warm some time after the departure of its sun. Goethe was therefore prepared to fall desperately in love with one who 'viewed all things through the medium of love '. And there is considerable interest in noting the *kind* of idol now selected. Hitherto he has been captivated only by very young girls, whose youth, beauty, and girlishness, were the charms to his wandering fancy; but now he is fascinated by a *woman*, a woman of rank and elegance, a woman of culture and experience, a woman who, instead of abandoning herself to the charm of his affection, knew how, without descending from her pedestal, to keep the flame alive. The others loved him,—showed him their love,—and were forgotten. She contrived to keep him in the pleasant fever of hope; made herself necessary to him; made her love an aim, and kept him in the excitement of one

Who never is, but always to be blest.

Considering the state of society and opinion at that period, and considering moreover that, according to her son's narrative, her husband was scarcely seen in his own home more than once a week, and that no pretence of affection existed between them, we could understand how Goethe's notorious passion for her excited sympathy in Weimar. Not a word of blame escaped any one on this subject. They saw a lover whose mistress gave him just enough encouragement to keep him eager in pursuit, and who knew how to check him when that eagerness would press on too far. In his early letters to her there are sudden outbreaks and reserves; sometimes the affectionate *thou* escapes, and the next day, perhaps even in the next sentence, the prescribed *you* returns. The letters follow almost daily. So early as January 1776 this significant phrase escapes: 'Adieu, angel! I shall never become more prudent; and have to thank God for it. Adieu! and yet it grieves me that I love thee so—and precisely thee!'

Here is an answer, apparently, to something she has written (for unhappily we have none of *her* letters: she had taken the precaution to demand her letters back from him, and burnt them, carefully preserving his):

'Wherefore must I plague thee! dearest creature! Wherefore deceive myself and plague thee! We can be nothing to each other, and yet are too much to each other. Believe me thou art in all things one with me—but because I see things as they are it makes me mad! Good night, angel, and good morning. I will see thee no more . . . Only . . . Thou knowest all . . . My heart is . . . All I can say is mere folly. In future I shall see thee as men see the stars'. A few days after, he writes, 'Adieu, dear sister, since it must be so'.

I select the following as indicating the tone: '1*st May*. To-

day I shall not see you.   Your presence yesterday made so
wonderful an impression on me, that I know not as yet whether I
am well or ill from it.   Adieu, dearest lady'.   '1*st May. Evening.*
Thou art right to make me a saint, that is to say, to remove me
from thy heart.   Holy as thou art I cannot make *thee* a saint.   To-
morrow, therefore . . .   Well, I will not see thee.   Good night!'
On the 24th of May, a passionate letter reveals that she had written
or spoken to him in a decided tone about 'appearances' and 'the
world' :   'So the purest, most beautiful, truest relation, I ever had
to a woman, except to my sister, *that* also must be disturbed !
I was prepared for it ; but I suffered infinitely on account of the
past and the future, and of the poor child thus consecrated in
sorrow.   I will not see you ; your presence would make me sad.
If I am not to live with you, your love will help me no more than
the love of those absent, in which I am so rich.   *Presence*, in the
moment of need, discerns, alleviates, and strengthens.   The
absent comes with the hose when the fire is extinguished—
and all for the sake of the world !   The world which can be
nothing to me, will not let thee be anything to me.   You know
not what you do. . . .   The hand of one in solitude who hears not
the voice of love, presses hard where it rests.   Adieu, best of
women!'   '25*th May.*   You are always the same, always infinite
love and goodness.   Forgive me if I make you suffer.   I will
learn to bear my suffering alone'.   '2*nd June.*   Adieu.   Love
me as ever, I will come seldomer and write seldomer'.   '4*th June.*
Here, dear lady, is the tribute.   I will see if I can keep my resolution not to come.   You are not quite safe with me.   Yesterday
there were again some moments in which I truly felt how I love
you'.   '6*th June.*   So you could do me the unkindness of remaining away yesterday.   Truly what you do must be right in my
eyes !!   But it made me sad'.   '7*th June.*   You are a darling to
have told me all !   When one loves one should tell everything.
Dearest angel, and I have again three words which will set you at
rest, but only words from me to thee !   I shall come to-day'.

She was forced to quit Weimar for a while.   'Dearest lady', he
writes, 'I dare not think you are going away on Tuesday, and that
you will be away from me six months.   For what avails all else ?
It is *presence* alone which influences, consoles, and edifies ! even
thought it sometimes torments—torment is the sunshower of love'.

Here is a curious passage : 'Last night as I lay in bed half
asleep, Philip brought me a letter ; half stupefied, I read—that

Lili is betrothed!! I turn round and fall asleep. How I pray that fate may act so by me in the right moment. Dear angel, good night'. One more extract. 'Oh! you have a way of giving pain which is like that of destiny, which admits of no complaint, however it may grieve'.

In a little while the tone grows more subdued. Just as the tone of his behaviour in Weimar, after the first wild weeks, became softened to a lower key, so in these letters we see, after a while, fewer passionate outbreaks, fewer interjections, and no more *thou's*. But love warms them still. The letters are incessant, and show an incessant preoccupation. Certain sentimental readers will be shocked, perhaps, to find so many details about eating and drinking; but when they remember Charlotte cutting bread and butter, they may understand the author of *Werther* eloquently begging his beloved to send him a sausage.

The visitor may still read the inscription, at once homage and souvenir, by which Goethe connected the happy hours of love with the happy hours of active solitude passed in his Garden House in the park. Fitly is the place dedicated to the Frau von Stein. The whole spot speaks of her. Here are the flower-beds from which almost every morning flowers, with the dew still on them, accompanied letters, not less fresh and beautiful, to greet the beloved. Here are the beds from which came the asparagus he was so proud to send her. Here is the orchard in which grew the fruit he so often sent. Here is the room in which he dreamt of her; here the room in which he worked, while her image hovered round him. The house stands within twenty minutes' walk from the house where she lived, separated by clusters of noble trees.

If the reader turns back to the description of the park, he will ascertain the position of this *Gartenhaus*. Originally it belonged to Bertuch. One day, when the Duke was earnestly pressing Goethe to take up his residence in Weimar, the poet (who then lived in the Jägerhaus in the Belvedere Allée), undecided as to whether he should go or remain, let fall, among other excuses, the want of a quiet bit of land, where his taste for gardening could be indulged. 'Bertuch, for example, is very comfortable; if I had but such a piece of ground as that!' Hereupon the Duke, very characteristically, goes to Bertuch, and without periphrasis, says, 'I must have your garden'. Bertuch starts: 'But your highness——' 'But me no buts' replies the young Prince; 'I can't help you.

Goethe's garden house in Weimar

Goethe wants it, and unless we give it to him we shall never keep him here·; it is the only way to secure him '. This reason would probably not have been so cogent with Bertuch, had not the Duke excused the despotism of his act by giving in exchange more than the value of the garden. It was at first only lent to Goethe ; but in 1780 it was made a formal gift.

It is charmingly situated, and, although of modest pretensions, is one of the most enviable houses in Weimar. The Ilm runs through the meadows which front it. The town, although so near, is completely shut out from view by the thick-growing trees. The solitude is absolute, broken only by the occasional sound of the church clock, the music from the barracks, and the screaming of the peacocks spreading their superb beauty in the park. So fond was Goethe of this house, that winter and summer he lived there for seven years ; and when, in 1782, the Duke made him a present of the house in the *Frauenplan,* he could not prevail upon himself to sell the Gartenhaus, but continued to make it a favourite retreat. Often when he chose to be alone and undisturbed, he locked all the gates of the bridges which led from the town to his house, so that, as Wieland complained, no one could get at him except by aid of picklock and crowbar.

It was here, in this little garden, he studied the development of plants, and made many of those experiments and observations which have given him a high rank among the discoverers in Science. It was here the poet escaped from Court. It was here the lover was happy in his love. How modest this Garden House really is ; how far removed from anything like one's preconceptions of it ! It is true, that the position is one which many a rich townsman in England would be glad of, as the site for a handsome villa : a pretty orchard and garden on a gentle slope ; in front, a good carriage road, running beside a fine meadow, encircled by the stately trees of the park. But the house, a half-pay captain with us would consider a miserable cottage ; yet it sufficed for the Court favourite and minister. Here the Duke was constantly with him ; sitting up, till deep in the night, in earnest discussion ; often sleeping on the sofa instead of going home. Here both Duke and Duchess would come and dine with him, in the most simple, unpretending way ; the whole banquet in one instance consisting, as we learn from a casual phrase in the Stein correspondence, of ‘ a beer soup and a little cold meat *’.

* Compare also the *Briefwechsel zwischen Karl August und Goethe,* I, 27.

There is something very pleasant in noticing these traits of the simplicity which was then practised. The Duke's own hut— the *Borkenhaus*—has already been described (p. 196). The hut, for it was nothing else, in which Goethe lived in the Ilmenau mountains, and the more than bourgeois simplicity of the Garden House, make us aware of one thing among others, namely, that if he sacrificed his genius to a Court, it assuredly was not for loaves and fishes, not for luxury and material splendour of any kind. Indeed, such things had no temptation to a man of his simple tastes. 'Rich in money', he writes to his beloved, 'I shall never become ; but, therefore, all the richer in Confidence, Good Name, and Influence over the minds of men'.

It was his love of Nature which made him so indifferent to luxury. That love gave him simplicity and hardihood. In many things he was unlike his nation : notably in his voluntary exposure to two bright, wholesome things, which to his contemporaries were little less than bugbears—I mean fresh air and cold water. The nation which consented to live in the atmosphere of iron stoves, tobacco, and bad breath, and which deemed a pint of water all that man could desire for his ablutions, must have been greatly perplexed at seeing Goethe indulge in fresh air and cold water as enjoyingly as if they were vices.

Two anecdotes will bring this contrast into relief. So great was the German reluctance to even a necessary exposure to the inclemencies of open-air exercise, that historians inform us 'a great proportion, especially among the learned classes, employed a miserable substitute for exercise in the shape of a machine, by means of which they comfortably took their dose of movement without leaving their rooms*'. And Jacobs, in his *Personalien*, records a fact which, while explaining how the above-named absurdity could have gained ground, paints a sad picture of the life of German youth in those days. Describing his boyish days at Gotha, he says : 'Our winter pleasures were confined to a not very spacious courtyard, exchanged in summer for a little garden within the walls, which my father hired. *We took no walks. Only once a year, when the harvest was ripe, our parents took us out to spend an evening in the fields†*'. So little had Goethe of this prejudice against fresh air, that when he began the rebuilding of his Gartenhaus, instead of sleeping at an hotel or at the house

---

* BIEDERMANN: *Deutschland's Politische Materielle und Sociale Zustände*, i, p. 343.   † Quoted by Mrs. AUSTIN: *Germany from 1760 to 1814*, p. 85.

Goethe and Fritz von Stein

of a friend, he lived there through all the building period ; and we find him writing, 'At last I have a window once more, and can make a fire'. On the 3rd of May he writes, 'Good morning : here is asparagus. How were you yesterday ? Philip baked me a cake ; and thereupon, wrapped up in my blue cloak, I laid myself on a dry corner of the terrace and slept amid thunder, lightning, and rain, so gloriously that my bed was afterwards quite disagreeable'. On the 19th he writes, 'Thanks for the breakfast. I send you something in return. Last night I slept on the terrace, wrapped in my blue cloak, awoke three times, at 12, 2, and 4, and *each time there was a new splendour in the heavens'*. There are other traces of this tendency to bivouac, but these will suffice. He bathed, not only in the morning sunlight, but also in the Ilm, when the moonlight shimmered on it. Always in the free air seeking vigour—

> Tauche mich in die Sonne früh
> Bad' ab im Monde des Tages Müh'.

The Duke shared this love of bathing, which December's cold could not arrest. It was here Goethe learned to swim by the aid of 'corks' (which so often served him as an illustration), and no inclemency of the weather could keep him out of the water. The fascination of water luring into its treacherous depths is wonderfully expressed by him in that ballad, which every one knows, and almost every one tries to translate. I have tried my hand in this version :

THE FISHERMAN.

> The water rushed, the water swelled :
>   A fisherman sat by,
> And gazed upon his dancing float
>   With tranquil-dreaming eye.
> And as he sits, and as he looks,
>   The gurgling waves arise :
> A maid, all bright with water-drops,
>   Stands straight before his eyes.
>
> She sang to him, she spake to him :
>   ' My fish why dost thou snare
> With human wit and human guile
>   Into the killing air ?
> Couldst see how happy fishes live
>   Under the stream so clear,
> Thyself would plunge into the stream,
>   And live for ever there.

> 'Bathe not the lovely sun and moon
>   Within the cool deep sea,
> And with wave-breathing faces rise
>   In two-fold witchery?
> Lure not the misty heaven-deeps
>   So beautiful and blue?
> Lures not thine image, mirrored in
>   The fresh eternal dew?'
>
> The water rushed, the water swelled,
>   It clasped his feet, I wis;
> A thrill went through his yearning heart
>   As when two lovers kiss!
> She spake to him, she sang to him:
>   Resistless was her strain;
> Half drew him in, half lured him in;
>   He ne'er was seen again.

One night, while the moon was calmly shining on our poetical bather, a peasant, returning home, was in the act of climbing over the bars of the floating bridge; Goethe espied him, and moved by that spirit of devilry which so often startled Weimar, he gave utterance to wild sepulchral tones, raised himself half out of water, ducked under, and reappeared howling, to the horror of the aghast peasant, who, hearing such sounds issue from a figure with long floating hair, fled as if a legend of devils were at hand. To this day there remains an ineradicable belief in the existence of the water-sprite who howls among the waters of the Ilm.

CHAPTER V

PRIVATE THEATRICALS

' LET my present life', writes Goethe to Lavater, January 1777, 'continue as long as it will, at any rate I have heartily enjoyed a genuine experience of the variegated throng and press of the world—Sorrow, Hope, Love, Work, Wants, Adventure, Ennui, Impatience, Folly, Joy, the Expected and the Unknown, the Superficial and the Profound—just as the dice threw—with fêtes, dances, sledgings—adorned in silk and spangles—a marvellous *ménage!* And withal, dear brother, God be praised, in myself and in my real aims in life I am quite happy'.

'Goethe plays indeed a high game at Weimar', writes Merck,

'but lives at Court after his own fashion. The Duke is an excellent man, let them say what they will, and in Goethe's company will become still more so. What you hear is Court scandal and lies. It is true the intimacy between master and servant is very great, but what harm is there in that? *Were Goethe a nobleman it would be thought quite right.* He is the soul and direction of everything, and all are contented with him, because he serves many and injures no one. Who can withstand the disinterestedness of this man?'

He had begun to make his presence felt in the serious department of affairs ; not only in educating the Duke who had chosen him as his friend, but also in practical ameliorations. He had induced the Duke to call Herder to Weimar, as *Hof Prediger* (Court chaplain) and *General-superintendent;* whereat Weimar grumbled and gossiped, setting afloat stories of Herder having mounted the pulpit in boots and spurs. Not content with these efforts in a higher circle, Goethe sought to improve the condition of the people ; and among his plans we note one for the opening of the Ilmenau mines, which for many years had been left untouched.

Amusement went hand in hand with business. Among the varied amusements, one, which greatly occupied his time and fancy, deserves a more special notice, because it will give us a glimpse of the Court, and will also show us how the poet turned sport into profit. I allude to the private theatricals which were started shortly after his arrival. It should be premised that the theatre was still in ashes from the fire of 1774 *. Seyler had carried his troupe of players elsewhere ; and Weimar was without its stage. Just at this period private theatricals were even more 'the rage' than they are in England at present. In Berlin, Dresden, Frankfort, Augsburg, Nuremberg, and Fulda were celebrated amateur troupes. In Würtzburg, for a long while, a *noble* company put on sock and buskin ; in Eisenach, Prince and Court joined in the sport. Even the Universities, which in earlier times had, from religious scruples, denounced the drama, now forgot their antagonism, and in Vienna, Halle, Göttingen, and Jena, allowed the students to have private stages.

The Weimar theatre surpassed them all. It had its poets, its composers, its scene painters, its costumiers. Whoever showed

* On the state of the theatre before Goethe's arrival and subsequently, see PASQUÉ : *Goethe's Theaterleitung in Weimar,* 1863.

any talent for recitation, singing, or dancing, was pressed into
service, and had to work as hard as if his bread depended on it.
The almost daily rehearsals of drama, opera, or ballet, occupied
and delighted men and women glad to have something to do.
The troupe was distinguished : the Duchess Amalia, Karl August,
Prince Constantine, Bode, Knebel, Einsiedel, Musæus, Seckendorf,
Bertuch, and Goethe ; with Corona Schröter, Kotzebue's sister
Amalia, and Fräulein Göchhausen.   These formed a curious
strolling company, wandering from Weimar to all the palaces in
the neighbourhood—Ettersburg, Tiefurt, Belvedere, even to Jena,
Dornburg, and Ilmenau.   Often did Bertuch, as Falk tells us,
receive orders to have the sumpter wagon, or travelling kitchen,
ready for the early dawn, when the Court would start with its
wandering troupe.   If only a short expedition was intended, three
sumpter asses were sufficient.   If it was more distant, over hill and
dale, far into the distant country, then indeed the night before was
a busy one, and all the ducal pots and pans were in requisition.
Such boiling and stewing and roasting ! such slaughter of capons,
pigeons, and fowls !   The ponds of the Ilm were dragged for
fish ; the woods were robbed of their partridges ; the cellars were
lightened of their wines.   With early dawn rode forth the merry
party, full of anticipation, wild with animal spirits.   On they went
through solitudes, the grand old trees of which were wont only to
see the soaring hawk poised above their tops, or the wild-eyed deer
bounding past the hut of the charcoal-burner.   On they went :
youth, beauty, gladness, and hope, a goodly train, like that which
animated the forest of Ardennes, when 'under the shade of
melancholy boughs' the pensive Duke and his followers forgot
awhile their cares and 'painted pomps'.

Their stage was soon arranged.   At Ettersburg the traces are
still visible of this forest stage, where, when weather permitted,
the performances took place.   A wing of the chateau was also
made into a theatre.   But the open-air performances were most
relished.   To rehearsals and performances in Ettersburg the actors,
sometimes as many as twenty, were brought in the Duke's equip-
ages ; and in the evening, after a joyous supper often enlivened
with songs, they were conducted home by the Duke's body-
guard of Hussars bearing torches.   It was here they performed
Einsiedel's opera, *The Gypsies*, with wonderful illusion.   Several
scenes of *Götz von Berlichingen* were woven into it.   The
illuminated trees, the crowd of gypsies in the wood, the dances

and songs under the blue starlit heavens, while the sylvan bugle sounded from afar, made up a picture, the magic of which was never forgotten.   On the Ilm also, at Tiefurt, just where the river makes a beautiful bend round the shore, a regular theatre was constructed.   Trees, and other poetical objects, such as fishermen, nixies, water-spirits, moon, and stars,—all were introduced with effect.

The performances were of the same varied nature as the theatres.   Sometimes French comedies, sometimes serious works of art, often broad extravaganzas.   Occasionally they played charades, in which the plan was prearranged, but the dialogue left to the improvisation of the actors.   Once when an actor grew wordy and wandering, they rushed on the stage, carried him off by force, and informed the audience (as if it were part of the piece) that he was suddenly taken ill.   The records of that time have preserved for us the outline of a magical piece, got up in honour of Goethe's birthday—*Minerva's Birth, Life, and Deeds*. It was a magnificent magic-lantern piece, with music by Seckendorf.   The characters were not represented by puppets, but by gentlemen and ladies, in the so-called *Petit Colisée* at Tiefurt.   On the site of this new temple of the Muses stood formerly a solitary wood hut.   In the representation every appliance was sought after which external effect demanded.   It took place behind a large white curtain, *en silhouette*.   In the *Histoire universelle des Théâtres* there is only one example of a theatrical representation of this kind, namely, the drama which Chiron presented to his pupil, Achilles, and which had the same object and significance as the Tiefurt drama.   In antiquity such representations were called *umbræ palpitantes*, by moderns, *ombres chinoises*.   They were introduced at the Weimar Court about this time, by the Duke George of Saxe-Meiningen, and were very much in favour there.

The subject of this Tiefurt piece is remarkable : Jupiter (in the person of the painter Kraus, on whose shoulders was placed a colossal paste-board head), in order to frustrate the prophecy that on the *accouchement* of his wife Metis, he would be thrust from the throne, has devoured Metis.   Thereupon he suffers terrible pains in the head ; Ganymede, hovering behind him on a great eagle, offers him the cup of nectar : the pains of the Thunderer increase visibly, and Ganymede soars into the air to fetch Æsculapius and Vulcan.   Æsculapius seeks in vain to cure his master.   A Cyclops, who is summoned, bleeds him at the nose, without effect. Then comes the powerful Vulcan (represented by the young Duke Karl August), who, holding in one hand his hammer, in the other a great iron bar, and encircled by an apron, approaches his suffering father, and with one good stroke of the hammer splits his divine skull, out of which proceeds Minerva, the goddess of wisdom (represented by Corona Schröter), at first quite a small figure, but by means of appropriate machinery becoming larger and larger every moment, till at last the whole of her tall, slim form is revealed, enveloped in light gauze. She is received by Father Zeus in the most friendly manner; and rich gifts are presented to her by all the gods. She is furnished with a helmet, an ægis, and a lance; Ganymede places Jupiter's owl at her feet, and amidst music and choral singing the curtain falls.

In the third and last act, the poet departed from the materials of the myth. He made the new-born goddess read in the Book of Fate, and find there the 28*th of August** marked as one of the most fortunate days. She says that ' on that day three-and-thirty years ago a man was given to the world, who will be honoured as one of the best and wisest'. Then appears a winged genius in the clouds, bearing Goethe's name. Minerva crowns this name, and at the same time dedicates to it the divine gifts which have been immemorially the tokens of her favour; for example, the golden lyre of Apollo, and the flowery wreath of the Muses. The whip of Momus alone, on the thong of which stood the word 'Aves', is laid aside and rejected by the goddess; while the names Iphigenia and Faust appear in the clouds in fire transparencies. At the close, Momus advances unabashed, and brings the reprobated symbol of his Art as a present to Goethe.

Such was the opening and dedication of the new Weimar-Tiefurt Court Theatre. It is obvious that the piece was intended purely to celebrate the birthday of Goethe, the director of this social theatre; and gives us not a bad idea of the ingenuity and pains bestowed upon these amusements. The reader will not fail to notice that if Goethe prepared fêtes for the birthday of his Duchess, Weimar also prepared fêtes for the birthday of its poet.

Another favourite magic-lantern piece was *King Midas*, which is mentioned in Amalia's letters to Knebel in the year 1781. But the best known of the Tiefurt dramas is Goethe's operetta, *Die Fischerin*, performed in the summer of 1782. The charming text, beginning with the famous Erl-König, is preserved in Goethe's

* Goethe's birthday.

works.   The piece was represented in the Tiefurt Park, partly on
the bank of the Ilm near the bridge, partly on the Ilm itself, which
was illuminated with numerous torches and lamps.   Under lofty
alders against the river were placed scattered huts of fishermen ;
nets, boats, and fishing implements stood around.   On Dorten's
(Corona Schröter) hearth fire was burning.   At the moment in
which the fishermen, who had been called together, lighted their
strips of wood and torches, and spread themselves with their
brilliant lights in boats and on the banks of the river, to search for
the lost maiden, the light flashed suddenly up from the necks of
land which stretched forward into the Ilm, illuminating the nearest
objects, and showing their reflection in the water, while the more
distant groups of trees and hills lay in deep night.   The spectators
had assembled in great numbers, and as they crowded on the
wooden bridge, the better to catch the magical effect of the
illumination on the water, their weight crushed the bridge in, and
the eager gazers fell into the river.   No one, however, was injured.
The involuntary bathers were heartily laughed at, and the accident
was regarded as an amusing interlude.

I find further that when a travesty of the 'Birds' of Aristophanes was performed at Ettersburg, the actors were all dressed
in real feathers, their heads completely covered, though free to
move.   Their wings flapped, their eyes rolled, and ornithology
was absurdly parodied.   It is right to add, that besides these
extravagances and *ombres chinoises*, there were very serious
dramatic efforts : among them we find Goethe's second dramatic
attempt, *Die Mitschuldigen*, which was thus cast :—

Alceste .	.	.	Goethe.
Söller .	.	.	Bertuch.
Der Wirth	.	.	Musäus.
Sophie .	.	.	Corona Schröter.

Another play was the *Geschwister*, written in three evenings, it is
said, but without evidence, out of love for the sweet eyes of
Amalia Kotzebue, sister of the dramatist, then a youth.   Kotzebue
thus touches the point in his *Memoirs :* 'Goethe had at that time
just written his charming piece, *Die Geschwister*.   It was performed at a private theatre at Weimar, he himself playing William
and my sister Marianne—while to me, yes to me—was allotted the
important part of postilion !   My readers may imagine with what
exultation I trod the stage for the first time before the mighty

public itself'. Another piece was Cumberland's *West Indian*, in which the Duke played *Major O'Flaherty*, Eckhoff (the great actor) the Father, and Goethe *Belcour*, dressed in a white coat with silver lace, blue silk vest, and blue silk knee-breeches, in which they say he looked superb.

While mentioning these I must not pass over the *Iphigenia* (then in prose), which was thus cast :

Orestes	Goethe.
Pylades	Prince Constantine.
Thoas	Knebel.
Arkas	Seidler.
Iphigenia	Corona Schröter.

'Never shall I forget', exclaims Dr. Hufeland, 'the impression Goethe made as Orestes, in his Grecian costume ; one might have fancied him Apollo. Never before had there been seen such union of physical and intellectual beauty in one man!' His acting, as far as I can learn, had the ordinary defects of amateur acting : it was impetuous and yet stiff, exaggerated and yet cold : and his fine sonorous voice displayed itself without nice reference to shades of meaning. In comic parts, on the other hand, he seems to have been excellent ; the broader the fun, the more at home he felt ; and one can imagine the rollicking animal spirits with which he animated the Marktschreier in the *Plundersweilern;* one can picture him in the extravagance of the *Geflickte Braut**, giving vent to his sarcasm on the 'sentimental' tone of the age, ridiculing his own *Werther*, and merciless to *Waldemar*†.

I have thus brought together, irrespective of dates, the scattered indications of these theatrical amusements. How much enjoyment was produced by them! what social pleasure! and what endless episodes, to which memory recurred in after times, when they were seated round the dinner table! Nor were these amusements profitless. *Wilhelm Meister* was designed and partly written about this period ; and the reader, who knows Goethe's tendency to make all his works biographical, will not be surprised at the amount of theatrical experience which is mirrored in that work ; nor at the earnestness which is there made to lurk beneath amusement, so that what to the crowd seems no more than a flattery of their tastes, is to the man himself a process of the highest culture.

---

* Published, under a very mitigated form, as the *Triumph der Empfindsamkeit.* See the next chapter for further notice of this piece.

† Jacobi and Wieland were both seriously offended with his parodies of their writings ; but both soon became reconciled to him.

Boar-hunting in the light of early dawn, sitting in the middle of the day in grave diplomacy and active council, rehearsing during the afternoon, and enlivening the evening with grotesque serenades or torchlight sledgings—thus passed many of his days ; not to mention flirtations, balls, masquerades, concerts, and verse-writing. The muse was, however, somewhat silent, though *Hans Sachs' poetische Sendung*, *Lila*, some charming lyrics, and the dramas and operas written for the occasion, forbid the accusation of idleness. He was storing up materials. *Faust*, *Egmont*, *Tasso*, *Iphigenia*, and *Meister* were germinating.

The muse was silent, but was the soul inactive? As these strange and variegated scenes passed before his eyes, was he a *mere* actor, and not also a spectator? Let his works answer. To some indeed it has seemed as if in thus lowering great faculties to the composition of slight operas and festive pieces, Goethe was faithless to his mission, false to his own genius. This is but a repetition of Merck's exclamation against *Clavigo*, and may be answered as that was answered. Herder thought that the Chosen One should devote himself to great works. This is the objection of a man of letters who can conceive no other aim than the writing of books. But Goethe needed to *live* as well as to write. Life is multiplied and rendered infinite by Feeling and Knowledge. He sought both to feel and to know. The great works he has written—works high in conception, austerely grand in execution, the fruits of earnest toil and lonely self-seclusion—ought to shield him *now* from any charge of wasting his time on frivolities, though to Herder and Merck such a point of view was denied.

It was his real artistic nature, and genuine poetic mobility, that made him scatter with a prodigal hand the trifles which distressed his friends. Poetry was the melodious voice breathing from his entire manhood, not a profession, not an act of duty. It was an impulse : the sounding chords of his poetic nature vibrated to every touch, grave and stately, sweet and impassioned, delicate and humorous. He wrote not for Fame. He wrote not for Pence. He wrote poetry because he had *lived* it ; and sang as the bird sings on its bough. Open to every impression, touched to ravishment by beauty, he sang whatever at the moment filled him with delight—now trilling a careless snatch of melody, now a simple ballad, now a majestic hymn ascending from the depths of his soul on incense-bearing rhythms, and now a grave quiet chant, slow with its rich burden of meanings. Men in whom the productive activity is great cannot be restrained from throwing off trifles, as the plant throws off buds beside the expanded flowers. Michael Angelo carved the Moses, and painted the ceiling of the Sistine Chapel, but did he not also lend his master-hand to the cutting of graceful cameos?

CHAPTER VI

MANY-COLOURED THREADS

HITHERTO our narrative of this Weimar period has moved mainly among generalities, for only by such means could a picture of this episode be painted. Now, as we advance further, it is necessary to separate the threads of his career from those of others with which it was interwoven.

It has already been noted, that he began to tire of the follies and extravagances of the first months. In this year, 1777, he was quiet in his Garden House, occupied with drawing, poetry, botany, and the one constant occupation of his heart—love for the Frau von Stein. Love and ambition were the guides which led him through the labyrinth of the Court. Amid those motley scenes, amid those swiftly succeeding pleasures, Voices, sorrowing Voices of the Past, made themselves audible above the din, and recalled the vast hopes which once had given energy to his aims ; and these reverberations of an ambition once so cherished, arrested and rebuked him, like the deep murmurs of some solemn bass moving slowly through the showering caprices of a sportive melody. No soul can endure uninterrupted gaiety and excitement. Weary intervals will occur : the vulgar soul fills these intervals with the long lassitude of its ennui ; the noble soul with reproaches at the previous waste of irrevocable hours.

The quiet influence exercised by the Frau von Stein is visible in every page of his letters. As far as I can divine the state of things in the absence of her letters, I fancy she coquetted with him ; when he showed any disposition to throw off her yoke, when his manner seemed to imply less warmth, she lured him back with tenderness ; and vexed him with unexpected coldness when she had drawn him once more to her feet. 'You reproach me', he writes, 'with alternations in my love. It is not true ; but it is well that I do not every day feel how utterly I love you'. Again :

' I cannot conceive why the main ingredients of your feeling have lately been Doubt and want of Belief. But it is certainly true that one who did not hold firm his affection might have that affection doubted away, just as a man may be persuaded that he is pale and ill '. That she tormented him with these coquettish doubts is but too evident ; and yet when he is away from her she writes to tell him he is become dearer ! ' Yes, my treasure ! ' he replies, ' I believe you when you say your love increases for me during absence. When away, you love the idea you have formed of me ; but when present, that idea is often disturbed by my folly and madness. . . . I love you better when present than when absent : hence I conclude my love is truer than yours '. At times he seems himself to have doubted whether he really loved her, or only loved the delight of her presence.

With these doubts mingles another element, his ambition to do something which will make him worthy of her. In spite of his popularity, in spite of his genius, he has not subdued her heart, but only agitated it. He endeavours, by *devotion*, to succeed. Thus love and ambition play into each other's hands, and keep him in a seclusion which astonishes and pains several of those who could never have enough of his company.

In the June of this year his solitude was visited by one of the agitations he could least withstand—the death of his only sister Cornelia. *Sorrows and dreams*, is the significant entry of the following day in his journal.

It was about this time that he undertook the care of Peter Imbaumgarten, a Swiss peasant boy, the protégé of his friend Baron Lindau. The death of the Baron left Peter once more without protection. Goethe, whose heart was open to all, especially to children, gladly undertook to continue the Baron's care ; and as we have seen him sending home an Italian image-boy to his mother at Frankfurt, and *Wilhelm Meister* undertaking the care of *Mignon* and *Felix*, so does this ' cold ' Goethe add love to charity, and become a father to the fatherless.

The autumn tints were beginning to mingle their red and yellow with the dark and solemn firs of the Ilmenau mountains ; Goethe and the Duke could not long keep away from the loved spot, where poetical and practical schemes occupied the day, and many a wild prank startled the night. There they danced with peasant girls till early dawn ; one result of which was a swelled face, forcing Goethe to lay up.

On his return to Weimar he was distressed by the receipt of one of the many letters which *Werther* drew upon him. He had made sentimentality poetical ; it soon became a fashion. Many were the melancholy youths who poured forth their sorrows to him, demanding sympathy and consolation. Nothing could be more antipathetic to his clear and healthy nature. It made him ashamed of his *Werther*. It made him merciless to all Wertherism. To relieve himself of the annoyance, he commenced the satirical extravaganza of the *Triumph der Empfindsamkeit*. Very significant, however, of the unalterable kindliness of his disposition is the fact, that although these sentimentalities had to him only a painful or a ludicrous aspect, he did not suffer his repugnance to the malady to destroy his sympathy for the patient. There is a proof of this in the episode he narrates of his Harz journey, made in November and December of this year*, known to most readers through his poem, *Die Harzreise in Winter*. The object of that journey was twofold ; to visit the Ilmenau mines, and to visit an unhappy misanthrope whose Wertherism had distressed him. He set out with the Duke, who had arranged a hunting party to destroy 'a great thing of a boar' then ravaging the country round Eisenach ; but, although setting out with them, he left them, *en route*, for purposes of his own.

Through hail, frost, and mud, lonely, yet companioned by great thoughts, he rode along the mountainous solitudes, and reached at last the *Brocken*. A bright sun shone on its eternal snows as he mounted, and looked down upon the cloud-covered Germany beneath him. Here he felt the air of freedom swell his breast. The world with its conventions lay beneath him ; the Court with its distractions was afar ; and the poet stood amidst these snowy solitudes communing with that majestic spirit of beauty which animates Nature.   There,

> . . . high above the misty air
> And turbulence of murmuring cities vast†,

he was lost in reveries of his future life :

> Dem Geier gleich
> Der auf schweren Morgenwolken,
> Mit sanftem Fittig ruhend,
> Nach Beute schaut,
> Schwebe mein Lied.

* And *not* in 1776, as he says; that date is disproved by his letters to the Frau von Stein   † Wordsworth.

This image of the hawk poised above the heavy morning clouds looking for his prey, is (I adopt his own explanation) that of the poet on the snowy heights looking down on the winter landscape, and with his mind's eye seeking amidst the perplexities of social life for some object worthy of his muse.

Writing to his beloved, he speaks of the good effect this journeying amid simple people (to whom he is only known as Herr Weber, a landscape painter) has upon his imagination. It is like a cold bath, he says. And *à propos* of his disguise, he remarks how very *easy* it is to be a rogue, and what advantages it gives one over simple honest men to assume a character that is not your own.

But now let us turn to the *second* object of his journey. The letter of the misanthrope just alluded to was signed Plessing, and dated from Wernigerode. There was something remarkable in the excess of its morbidity, accompanied by indications of real talent. Goethe did not answer it, having already hampered himself in various ways by responding to such extraneous demands upon his sympathy ; another and more passionate letter came imploring an answer, which was still silently avoided. But now the idea of personally ascertaining what manner of man his correspondent was, made him swerve from his path ; and under his assumed name he called on Plessing.

On hearing that his visitor came from Gotha, Plessing eagerly inquired whether he had not visited Weimar, and whether he knew the celebrated men who lived there. With perfect simplicity Goethe replied that he did, and began talking of Kraus, Bertuch, Musäus, Jagemann, etc., when he was impatiently interrupted with 'But why don't you mention Goethe?' He answered that Goethe also had he seen ; upon this he was called upon to give a description of that great poet, which he did in a quiet way, sufficient to have betrayed his incognito to more sagacious eyes.

Plessing then with great agitation informed him that Goethe had not answered a most pressing and passionate letter in which he, Plessing, had described the state of his mind, and had implored direction and assistance. Goethe excused himself as he best could ; but Plessing insisted on reading him the letters, that he might judge whether they deserved such treatment.

He listened, and tried by temperate sympathetic counsel to wean Plessing from his morbid thoughts by fixing them on external objects, especially by some active employment. These were impatiently rejected, and he left him, feeling that the case was almost beyond help.

He was subsequently able to assist Plessing, who, on visiting him at Weimar, discovered his old acquaintance the landscape painter *. But the characteristic part of this anecdote—and that which makes me cite it here—is, the practical illustration it gives of his fundamental realism, which looked to nature and earnest activity as the sole cure for megrims, sentimentalisms, and self-torturings. Turn your mind to realities, and the self-made phantoms which darken your soul will disappear like night at the approach of dawn.

In the January of the following year (1778) Goethe was twice brought face to face with Death. The first was during a boar-hunt : his spear snapped in the onslaught, and he was in imminent peril, but fortunately escaped. On the following day, while he and the Duke were skating (perhaps talking over yesterday's escape), there came a crowd over the ice, bearing the corpse of the unhappy Fräulein von Lassberg, who, in the despair of un-requited love, had drowned herself in the Ilm, close by the very spot where Goethe was wont to take his evening walk. At all times this would have been a shock to him, but the shock was greatly intensified by the fact that in the pocket of the unfortunate girl was found a copy of *Werther!* † It is true we never re-proach an author in such cases. No reflecting man ever re-proached Plato with the suicide of Cleombrotus, or Schiller with the brigandage of highwaymen. Yet when fatal coincidences occur, the author, whom we absolve, cannot so lightly absolve himself. It is in vain to argue that the work does not, rightly considered, lead to suicide ; if it does so, *wrongly* considered, it is the proximate cause ; and the author cannot easily shake off that weight of blame. Goethe, standing upon logic, might have said : ' If Plato instigated the suicide of Cleombrotus, certainly he averted that of Olympiodorus ; if I have been one of the many causes which moved this girl towards that fatal act, I have also

---

* In 1788, Plessing was appointed professor of philosophy in the university of Duisburg, where Goethe visited him on his return home from the campaign in France, 1792. The reader may be interested to know that Plessing entirely outlived his morbid melancholy, and gained a respectable name in German letters. His principal works are *Osiris und Socrates*, 1783; *Historische und Philosophische Untersuchungen über die Denkart Theologie und Philosophie der ältesten Völker*, 1785; and *Memnonium, oder Versuche zur Enthüllung der Geheimnisse des Alterthums*, 1787. He died 1806.

† Riemer, who will never admit anything that may seem to tell against his idol, endeavours to throw a doubt on this fact, saying it was reported only out of malice. But he gives no reasons.

certainly been the cause of saving others, notably that young
Frenchman who wrote to thank me'. He might have argued
thus ; but Conscience is tenderer than Logic ; and if in firing at a
wild beast I kill a brother hunter, my conscience will not leave me
altogether in peace.

The body was borne to the house of the Frau von Stein,
which stood nearest the spot, and there he remained with it the
whole day, exerting himself to console the wretched parents.
He himself had need of some consolation. The incident affected
him deeply, and led him to speculate on all cognate subjects,
especially on melancholy. 'This inviting sadness', he beautifully
says, 'has a dangerous fascination, *like water itself, and we are
charmed by the reflex of the stars of heaven which shines through
both*'.

He was soon, however, '*forced* into theatrical levity' by the
various rehearsals necessary for the piece to be performed on the
birthday of the Duchess. This was the *Triumph der Empfindsamkeit.* The adventure with Plessing, and finally the tragedy of
the Fräulein von Lassberg had given increased force to his
antagonism against Wertherism and Sentimentality, which he now
lashed with unsparing ridicule. The hero of his extravaganza is a
Prince, whose soul is only fit for moonlight ecstasies and sentimental rhapsodies. He adores Nature ; not the rude, rough,
imperfect Nature whose gigantic energy would alarm the sentimental mind ; but the beautiful rose-pink Nature of books. He
likes Nature as one sees it at the Opera. Rocks are picturesque it
is true ; but they are often crowned with tiaras of snow, sparkling,
but apt to make one 'chilly' ; turbulent winds howl through their
clefts and crannies, alarming to delicate nerves. The Prince is
not fond of the winds. Sunrise and early morn are lovely—but
damp ; and the Prince is liable to rheumatism.

To obviate all such inconveniences he has had a mechanical
imitation of Nature executed for his use ; and this accompanies
him on his travels ; so that at a moment's notice, in secure
defiance of rheumatism, he can enjoy a moonlight scene, a sunny
landscape, or a sombre grove.

He is in love ; but his mistress is as factitious as his landscapes.
Woman is charming but capricious, fond but exacting ; and therefore the Prince has a doll dressed in the same style as the woman
he once loved. By the side of this doll he passes hours of
rapture ; for it he sighs ; for it he rhapsodizes.

The *real* woman appears—the original of that much-treasured image. Is he enraptured? Not in the least. His heart does not palpitate in her presence; he does not recognize her; but throws himself once more into the arms of his doll, and thus sensibility triumphs.

There are five acts of this 'exquisite fooling'. Originally it was much coarser, and more personal than we now see it. Böttiger says that there remains scarcely a shadow of its flashing humour and satiric caprice. The whip of Aristophanes was applied with powerful wrist to every fashionable folly, in dress, literature, or morals, and the spectators saw themselves as in a mirror of sarcasm. At the conclusion, the doll was ripped open, and out fell a multitude of books, such as were then the rage, upon which severe and ludicrous judgments were passed—and the severest upon *Werther*. The whole piece was interspersed with ballets, music, and comical changes of scene; so that what now appears a tiresome farce was then an irresistible extravaganza.

This extravaganza has the foolery of Aristophanes, and the physical fun of that riotous wit, whom Goethe was then studying. But when critics are in ecstasies with its wit and irony, I confess myself at a loss to conceive clearly what they mean. National wit, however, is perhaps scarcely amenable to criticism. What the German thinks exquisitely ludicrous, is to a Frenchman, or an Englishman, generally of mediocre mirthfulness. Wit requires delicate handling; the Germans generally touch it with gloved hands. Sarcasm is with them too often a sabre, not a rapier, hacking the victim where a thrust would suffice. It is a noticeable fact that amid all the riches of their Literature they have little that is comic of a high order. They have produced no Comedy. To them may be applied the couplet wherein the great original of Grotesque Seriousness set forth its verdict:

Κωμῳδοδιδασκαλίαν εἶναι χαλεπώτατον ἔργον ἀπάντων·
Πολλῶν γὰρ δὴ πειρασάντων αὐτήν ὀλίγοις χαρίσασθαι*.

which I will venture to turn thus:

Miss Comedy is a sad flirt,—you may guess
From the number who court her, the few she doth bless.

* ARISTOPHANES, *Equites*, v, 516.

CHAPTER VII

THE REAL PHILANTHROPIST

A STRANGE phantasmagoria is the life he leads at this epoch. His employments are manifold, yet his studies, his drawing, etching, and rehearsing are carried on as if they alone were the occupation of the day. His immense activity, and power of varied employment, scatter the energies which might be consecrated to some great work; but, in return, they give him the varied store of material of which he stood so much in need. At this time he is writing *Wilhelm Meister* and *Egmont; Iphigenia* is also taking shape in his mind. His office gives him much to do; and Gervinus, who must have known how great were the calls upon his time, should have paused ere he threw out the insinuation of 'diplomatic rudeness' when Goethe answered one of his brother-in-law's letters through his secretary. Surely with a brother-in-law one may take such latitude?*

This man, whose diplomatic coldness and aristocratic haughtiness have formed the theme of so many long tirades, was of all Germans the most sincerely democratic, until the Reign of Terror in France frightened him, as it did others, into more modified opinions. Not only was he always delighted to be with the people, and to share their homely ways, which were consonant with his own simple tastes, but we find him in the confidence of intimacy expressing his sympathy with the people in the heartiest terms. When among the miners he writes to his beloved, 'How strong my love has returned upon me for these lower classes! which one calls the lower, but which in God's eyes are assuredly the highest! Here you meet all the virtues combined: Contentedness, Moderation, Truth, Straightforwardness, Joy in the slightest good, Harmlessness, Patience—Patience—Constancy in——in . . . I will not lose myself in panegyric!' Again, he is writing *Iphigenia*, but the news of the misery and famine among the stocking-weavers of Apolda paralyses him. 'The drama will not advance a step: it is cursed; the King of Tauris must speak as if no stocking-weaver in Apolda felt the pangs of hunger!'

* Since the text was written, the correspondence with the Frau v. Stein has appeared; and from it we learn that in Switzerland he even dictated some letters to *her*! It could not have been 'diplomatic rudeness', inasmuch as he usually wrote to the Duke himself through his amanuensis.

In striking contrast stands the expression of his contempt for what was called the great world, as he watched it in his visits to the neighbouring Courts. If affection bound him to Karl August, whom he was forming, and to Luise, for whom he had a chivalrous regard, his eyes were not blind to the nullity of other princes and their followers. 'Good society have I seen', runs one of his epigrams, 'they call it the "good" whenever there is not in it the material for the smallest of poems'.

> Gute Gesellschaft hab' ich gesehen ; man nennt sie die gute
> Wenn sie zum kleinsten Gedicht keine Gelegenheit giebt.

Notably was this the case in his journey with the Duke to Berlin, May 1778. He only remained a few days there ; *saw* much, and not without contempt. ' I have got quite close to old Fritz, having seen his way of life, his gold, his silver, his statues, his apes, his parrots, and heard his own curs twaddle about the great man'. Potzdam and Berlin were noisy with preparations for war. The great King was absent; but Prince Henry received the poet in a friendly manner, and invited him and Karl August to dinner. At table there were several generals ; but Goethe, who kept his eyes open, sternly kept his mouth closed. He seems to have felt no little contempt for the Prussian Court, and its great men, who appeared very small men in his eyes. ' I have spoken no word in the Prussian dominions which might not be made public. Therefore I am called haughty and so forth'. Varnhagen intimates that the ill-will he excited by not visiting the literati, and by his reserve, was so great as to make him averse from hearing of his visit in after years*. What, indeed, as Varnhagen asks, had Goethe in common with Nicolai, Ramler, Engel, Zellner, and the rest? He did visit the poetess Karschin and the artist Chodowiecki ; but from the rest he kept aloof. Berlin was not a city in which he could feel himself at home ; and he doubtless was fully aware of the small account in which he was held by Frederick, whose admiration lay in quite other directions. What culture the King had was French, and his opinion of German literature had been explicitly pronounced in a work published this year, in which *Götz von Berlichingen* was cited as a sample of the reigning bad taste. The passage is too curious to be omitted. ' Vous y verrez représenter les abominables pièces de Shakespeare traduites en notre langue, et tout l'auditoire se pâmer d'aise en entendant ces

---

* *Vermischte Schriften*, III, p. 62.

farces ridicules, et dignes *des sauvages de Canada'*. That certainly
was afflicting to 'le bon goût'; but *that* was not the worst.
Shakespeare might be pardoned for *his* faults, 'car la naissance des
arts n'est jamais le point de leur maturité. Mais voilà encore un
Goetz de Berlichingen qui parait sur la scène, imitation détestable
de ces mauvaises pièces anglaises, et le parterre applaudit et
demande avec enthousiasme la répétition de *ces dégoûtantes
platitudes !'*

Thus the two German Emperors, Fritz and Wolfgang, held no
spiritual congress ; perhaps no good result *could* have been elicited
by their meeting. Yet they were, each in his own sphere, the two
most potent men then reigning. Fritz did not directly assist the
literature of his country, but his *indirect* influence has been
indicated by Griepenkerl †. He awoke the Germans from their
sleep by the rolling of drums ; those who least liked the clang of
arms or the 'divisions of a battlefield' were nevertheless awakened
to the fact that something important was going on in life, and they
rubbed their sleepy eyes, and tried to *see* a little into that. The
roll of drums has this merit, at all events, that it draws men from
their library table to the window, and so makes them look out
upon the moving, living world of action, wherein the erudite
may see a considerable sensation made even by men unable to
conjugate a Greek verb in ' $\mu\iota$ ' ‡.

On returning to Weimar, Goethe occupied himself with various
architecture studies, *à propos* of the rebuilding of the palace ; and
commenced those alterations in the park which resulted in the
beautiful distribution formerly described. But I pass over many
details of his activity, to narrate an episode which must win the
heart of every reader. In these pages it has been evident, I hope,
that no compromise with the truth has led me to gloss over faults,
or to conceal shortcomings. All that testimony warrants I have
reproduced : good and evil, as in the mingled yarn of life. Faults
and deficiences, even grievous errors, do not estrange a friend
from our hearts ; why should they lower a hero ? Why should the
biographer fear to trust the tolerance of human sympathy ? Why
labour to prove a hero faultless ? The reader is no *valet de*

---

* *De la Littérature Allemande*, p. 46. His opinion of the newly discovered
Niebelungen Lied was no less characteristically contemptuous ; he declared he would
not give such rubbish house-room.

† *Der Kunstgenius der Deutschen Literatur des letzten Jahrhunderts*, I, p. 52.

‡ Dr. George has become famous (or *did* become so—for, alas ! what is fame ?) by
his shrewd suspicion that Frederick with all his victories could not accomplish *that* feat
of intellectual vigour. Many men still measure greatness by verbs in $\mu\iota$.

chambre incapable of crediting greatness in a *robe de chambre*. Never should we forget the profound saying of Hegel in answer to the vulgar aphorism ('No man is a hero to his *valet de chambre*'); namely, 'This is not because the Hero is no Hero, but because the Valet is a Valet'*. Having trusted to the effect which the true man would produce, in spite of all drawbacks,—and certain that the true man was *lovable* as well as admirable, I have made no direct appeal to the reader's sympathy, nor tried to make out a case in favour of extraordinary virtue.

But the tribute of affectionate applause is claimed now we have arrived at a passage in his life so *characteristic* of the delicacy, generosity, and nobility of his nature, that it is scarcely possible for any one not to love him, after reading it. Of generosity, in the more ordinary sense, there are abundant examples in his history. Riemer has instanced several †, but these are acts of kindness, thoughtfulness, and courtesy, such as one expects to find in a prosperous poet. That he was kind, gave freely, sympathized freely, acted disinterestedly, and that his kindness showed itself in trifles quite as much as in important actions (a most significant trait ‡), is known to all persons moderately acquainted with German literature. But the disposition exhibited in the story I am about to tell is such as few persons would have imagined to be lying beneath the stately prudence, and calm self-mastery of the man so often styled 'heartless'.

This is the story : A man (his name still remains a secret) of a strange, morbid, suspicious disposition, had fallen into destitution, partly from unfortunate circumstances, partly from his own fault. He applied to Goethe for assistance, as so many others did ; and he painted his condition with all the eloquence of despair.

'According to the idea I form of you from your letters', writes Goethe, 'I fancy I am not deceived, and this to me is very painful, in believing that I cannot give help or hope to one who needs so much. But I am not the man to say, "Arise, and go further".

---

* 'Nicht aber darum weil dieser kein Held ist, sondern weil jener der Kammerdiener ist'.—*Philosophie der Geschichte*, p. 40. Goethe repeated this as an epigram; and Carlyle has wrought it into the minds of hundreds ; but Hegel is the originator.

† *Mittheilungen*, vol. I, 102–5.

‡ There is lamentable confusion in our estimate of character on this point of generosity. We often mistake a spasm of sensibility for the strength of lovingness—making an *occasional* act of kindness the sign of a kind nature. Benj. Constant says of himself : '*Je puis faire de bonnes et fortes actions ; je ne puis avoir de bons procédés*'. There are hundreds like him. On the other hand, there are hundreds who willingly perform many little acts of kindness and courtesy, but who never rise to the dignity of generosity ; these are *poor* natures, ignorant of the grander throbbings.

Accept the little that I can give, as a plank thrown towards you for momentary succour. If you remain longer where you are, I will gladly see that in future you receive some slight assistance. In acknowledging the receipt of this money, pray inform me how far you can make it go. If you are in want of a dress, greatcoat, boots, or warm stockings, tell me so; I have some that I can spare.

'Accept this drop of balsam from the compendious medicine chest of the Samaritan, in the same spirit as it is offered'.

This was on the 2nd of November, 1778. On the 11th he writes again, and from the letter we see that he had resolved to do *more* than throw out a momentary plank to the shipwrecked man —in fact he had undertaken to support him.

'In this parcel you will receive a greatcoat, boots, stockings, and some money. My plan for you this winter is this :

'In Jena living is cheap. I will arrange for board and lodging, etc., on the strictest economy, and will say it is for some one who, with a small pension, desires to live in retirement. When that is secured I will write to you ; you can then go there, establish yourself in your quarters, and I will send you cloth and lining, with the necessary money, for a coat, which you can get made, and I will inform the rector that you were recommended to me, and that you wish to live in retirement at the University.

'You must then invent some plausible story, have your name entered on the books of the University, and no soul will ever inquire more about you, neither Burgomaster nor Amtmann. *I have not sent you one of my coats, because it might be recognized in Jena.* Write to me and let me know what you think of this plan, and at all events in what character you propose to present yourself'.

The passage in italics indicates great thoughtfulness. Indeed the whole of this correspondence shows the most tender consideration for the feelings of his protégé. In the postscript he says : 'And now step boldly forth again upon the path of life ! We live but once. . . . Yes, I know perfectly what it is to take the fate of another upon one's own shoulders, but you shall not perish !' On the 23rd he writes :

'I received to-day your two letters of the 17th and 18th, and have so far anticipated their contents as to have caused inquiry to be made in Jena for the fullest details, as for one who wished to live there under the quiet protection of the University. Till the answer arrives keep you quiet at Gera, and the day after to-morrow I will send you a parcel and say more.

'Believe me you are not a burden on me ; on the contrary, it teaches me economy ; *I fritter away much of my income which I might spare for those in want.*   And do you think that your tears and blessings go for nothing? *He who has, must give, not bless; and if the Great and the Rich have divided between them the goods of this world, Fate has counterbalanced these by giving to the wretched the powers of blessing, powers to which the fortunate know not how to aspire*'.

Noble words ! In the mouth of a pharisaical philanthropist *declaiming* instead of *giving*, there would be something revolting in such language ; but when we know that the hand which wrote these words was 'open as a day to melting charity', when we know that (in spite of all other claims) he gave up for some years the sixth part of his very moderate income to rescue this stranger from want, when we know by the irrefragable arguments of deeds, that this language was no hollow phrase, but the deep and solemn utterance of a thoroughly human heart, then, I say, those words awaken reverberations within our hearts, calling up feelings of loving reverence for him who uttered them.

How wise and kind is this also : ' Perhaps there will soon turn up occasions for you to be useful to me where you are, for it is not the Project-maker and Promiser, but he who in trifles affords real service, that is welcome to one who would so willingly do something good and enduring.

' Hate not the poor philanthropists with their precautions and conditions, for one need pray diligently to retain, amid such bitter experience, the good will, courage, and levity of youth, which are the main ingredients of benevolence.   And it is more than a benefit which God bestows when He calls us, who can so seldom do anything to lighten the burden of one truly wretched'.

The next letter, dated December 11th, explains itself :

'Your letter of the 7th I received early this morning.   And first, to calm your mind : you shall be forced to nothing ; the hundred dollars you shall have, live where you may ; but now listen to me.

' I know that to a man his ideas are realities ; and although the image you have of Jena is false, still I know that nothing is less easily reasoned away than such hypochondriacal anxieties.   I think Jena the best place for your residence, and for many reasons.

The University has long lost its ancient wildness and aristocratic prejudices : the students are not worse than in other places, and among them there are some charming people. In Jena, they are so accustomed to the flux and reflux of men that no individual is remarked. And there are too many living in excessively straitened means for poverty to be either a stigma or a noticeable peculiarity. Moreover, it is a city where you can more easily procure all necessities. In the country during the winter, ill, and without medical advice, would not that be miserable ?

'Further, the people to whom I referred you are good domestic people, who, on my account, would treat you well. Whatever might occur to you, I should be in a condition, one way or another, to assist you. I could aid you in establishing yourself ; need only for the present guarantee your board and lodging, and pay for it later on. I could give you a little on New Year's Day, and procure what was necessary on credit. You would be nearer to me. Every market day I could send you something—wine, victuals, utensils, that would cost me little, and would make your existence more tolerable ; and I could thus make you more a part of my household expenses. The objection to Gera is, that communication with it is so difficult ; things do not arrive at proper times, and cost money which benefits no one. You would probably remain six months in Jena before any one remarked your presence. This is the reason why I preferred Jena to every other place, and you will do the same if you could but see things with untroubled vision. How, if you were to make a trial ? However, I know a fly can distract a man with sensitive nerves, and that, in such cases, reasoning is powerless.

'Consider it : it will make all things easier. I promise you, you will be comfortable in Jena. But if you cannot overcome your objections, then remain in Gera. At New Year you shall have twenty-five dollars, and the same regularly every quarter. I cannot arrange it otherwise. I must look to my own household demands ; that which I have given you already, because I was quite unprepared for it, has made a hole, which I must stop up as I can. If you were in Jena, I could give you some little commissions to execute for me, and perhaps some occupation ; I could also make your personal acquaintance, and so on. But act just as your feelings dictate ; if my reasons do not convince you, remain in your present solitude. Commence the writing of your **life, as you talk of doing, and send it me piecemeal, and be** persuaded that I am only anxious for your quiet and comfort, and choose Jena simply because I could there do more for you'.

The hypochondriacal fancies of the poor man were invincible ; and instead of going to Jena he went to Ilmenau, where Goethe secured him a home, and sent him books and money. Having thus seen to his material comforts, he besought him to occupy his mind by writing out the experience of his life, and what he had observed on his travels. In the following letter he refers to his other protégé, Peter Imbaumgarten.

'I am very glad the contract is settled. Your maintenance thus demands a hundred dollars yearly, and I will guarantee the twenty-five dollars quarterly, and contrive also that by the end of this month you shall receive a regular allowance for pocket money. I will also send what I can *in natura*, such as paper, pens, sealing-wax, etc. Meanwhile here are some books.

'Thanks for your news ; continue them. The wish to do good is a bold, proud wish ; we must be thankful when we can secure even a little bit. I have now a proposition to make. When you are in your new quarters I wish you would pay some attention to a boy, whose education I have undertaken, and who learns the huntsman's craft in Ilmenau. He has begun French ; could you not assist him in it? He draws nicely ; could you not keep him to it? I would fix the hours when he should come to you. You would lighten my anxiety about him if you could by friendly intercourse ascertain the condition of his mind, and inform me of it ; and if you could keep an eye upon his progress. But of course this depends on your feeling disposed to undertake such a task. Judging from myself—*intercourse with children always makes me feel young and happy*. On hearing your answer, I will write more particulars. *You will do me a real service, and I shall be able to add monthly the trifle which I have set aside for the boy's education.* I trust I shall be able to lighten your sad condition, so that you may recover your cheerfulness'.

Let me call attention to the delicacy with which he here intimates that he does not mean to occupy Kraft's* time without remunerating it. If that passage be thoroughly considered, it will speak as much for the exquisite kindness of Goethe's nature as any greater act of liberality. Few persons would have considered themselves unentitled to *ask* such a service from one whose

* Herr Kraft was the *assumed* name of this still anonymous protégé.

existence they had secured. To pay for it would scarcely have entered their thoughts. But Goethe felt that to demand a service, which might be irksome, would, in a certain way, be selling benevolence ; if he employed Kraft's time, it was right that he should pay what he would have paid another master. On the other hand, he instinctively shrunk from the indelicacy of making a decided *bargain*. It was necessary to intimate that the lessons would be paid for ; but with that intimation he also conveyed the idea that in undertaking such a task Kraft would be conferring an *obligation* upon him ; so that Kraft might show his gratitude, might benefit his benefactor, and nevertheless be benefited. After reading such a sentence, I could, to use Wieland's expression, 'have eaten Goethe for love !'

Kraft accepted the charge ; and Goethe having sent him some linen for shirts, some cloth for a coat, and begged him to write without the least misgiving, now sends this letter :

'Many thanks for your care of Peter ; the boy greatly interests me, for he is a legacy of the unfortunate *Lindau*. Do him all the good you can quietly. How you may advance him ! I care not whether he reads, draws, or learns French, so that he does occupy his time, and I hear your opinion of him. For the present, let him consider his first object is to acquire the huntsman's craft, and try to learn from him how he likes it, and how he gets on with it. For, believe me, man must have a trade which will support him. The artist is never paid ; it is the artisan. Chodowiecki, the artist whom we admire, would eat but scanty mouthfuls ; but Chodowiecki, the artisan, who with his woodcuts illumines the most miserable daubs, he is paid'.

In a subsequent letter he says, 'Many thanks. By your attention to these things, and your care of Peter, you have performed true service for me, and richly repaid all that I may have been able to do for you. Be under no anxiety about the future, there will certainly occur opportunities wherein you can be useful to me; meanwhile continue as heretofore'. This was written on the *very day* of his return to Wiemar from the Swiss journey ! If this tells us of his attention to his protégé, the next letter tells us of his anticipating even the casualty of death, for he had put Kraft on the list of those whom he left as legacies of benevolence to his friends. It should be remarked that Goethe seems to have preserved profound secrecy with respect to the good he was then doing ; not even in his confidential letters to Frau von Stein is there one hint of Kraft's existence. In short, *nothing* is wanting to complete the circle of genuine benevolence.

The year 1781 began with an increase of Kraft's pension ; or rather, instead of paying a hundred dollars for his board and lodging, and allowing him pocket-money, he made the sum two hundred dollars. 'I can spare as much as that ; and you need not be anxious about every trifle, but can lay out your money as you please. Adieu ; and let me soon hear that your sorrows have left you'. This advance seems to have elicited a demand for *more* money, which produced the following characteristic answer :

'You have done well to disclose the condition of your mind to me ; I can make all allowances, little as I may be able to completely calm you. My own affairs will not permit me to promise you a farthing more than the two hundred dollars, unless I were to get into debt, which in my place would be very unseemly. This sum you shall receive regularly. Try to make it do.

'I certainly do not suppose that you will change your place of residence without my knowledge and consent. Every man has his duty ; make a duty of your love to me, and you will find it light.

'It would be very disagreeable to me if you were to *borrow* from any one. It is precisely this miserable unrest now troubling you which has been the misfortune of your whole life, and you have never been more contented with a thousand dollars than you now are with two hundred ; because you always still desired something which you had not, and have never accustomed your soul to accept the limits of necessity. I do not reproach you with it ; I know, unhappily too well, how it pertains to you, and feel how painful must be the contrast between your present and your past. But enough ! One word for a thousand : at the end of every quarter you shall receive fifty dollars ; for the present an advance shall be made. Limit your wants ; the *Must* is hard, and yet solely by this *Must* can we show how it is with us in our inner man. To live according to caprice requires no peculiar powers*'.

The following explains itself :

'If you once more read over my last letter you will see plainly that you have misinterpreted it. You are neither *fallen in my esteem*, nor have I a *bad opinion* of you, neither have I suffered my *good opinion* to be led astray, nor has your mode of thinking

---

* I will give the original of this fine saying, as I have rendered it but clumsily : 'Das *Muss* ist hart, aber beim *Muss* kann der Mensch allein zeigen wie's inwendig mit ihm steht. Willkürlich leben kann jeder'.

become *damaged* in my eyes : all these are exaggerated expressions, such as a rational man should not permit himself. Because I also speak out my thoughts with *freedom*, because I wish certain traits in your conduct and views somewhat different, does that mean that I look on you as a *bad man*, and that I wish to discontinue our relations ?

'It is these hypochondriacal, weak, and exaggerated notions, such as your last letter contains, which I blame and regret. Is it proper that you should say to me : *I am to prescribe the tone in which all your future letters must be written?* Does one command an honourable, rational man such things as that? Is it ingenuous in you on such an occasion to *underline* the words that you eat *my bread?* Is it becoming in a moral being, when one gently blames him, or names something in him as a malady, to fly out as if one had pulled the house about his ears? Do not misconstrue me, therefore, if I wish to see you contented and satisfied with the little I can do for you. So, if you will, things shall remain just as they were ; at all events I shall not change my behaviour towards you'.

The unhappy man seems to have been brought to a sense of his injustice by this, for although there is but one more letter, bearing the date 1783, that is, two years subsequent to the one just given, the connexion lasted for seven years. When Goethe undertook to write the life of Duke Bernhard he employed Kraft to make extracts for him from the Archives ; which extracts, Luden, when he came to look over them with a biographical purpose, found utterly worthless*. The last words we find of Goethe's addressed to Kraft are, 'You have already been of service to me, and other opportunities will offer. I have no grace to dispense, and my favour is not so fickle. Farewell, and enjoy your little in peace'. It was terminated only by the death of the poor creature in 1785. Goethe buried him at his own expense, but even to the Jena officials he did not disclose Kraft's real name†.

To my apprehension these letters reveal a nature so exquisite in far-thoughted tenderness, so true and human in its sympathies with suffering, and so ready to alleviate suffering by sacrifices rarely made to friends, much less to strangers, that, after reading them, the epithets of 'cold' and 'heartless', often applied to

---

* See LUDEN'S *Rückblicke in Mein Leben.*
† I learn this from a letter to the Judge at Jena, which was exhibited at the *Goethe Austellung* in Berlin, 1861.

Goethe, sound like blasphemies against the noblest feelings of humanity. Observe, this Kraft was no romantic object appealing to the sensibility ; he had no thrilling story to stimulate sympathy ; there was no subscription list opened for him ; there were no coteries weeping over his misfortunes. Unknown, unfriended, ill at ease with himself and with the world, he revealed his wretchedness in secret to the great poet, and in secret that poet pressed his hand, dried his eyes, and ministered to his wants. And he did this not as *one* act, not as one passing impulse, but as the sustained sympathy of seven years.

Pitiful and pathetic is the thought that such a man can, for so many years, both in his own country and in ours, have been reproached, nay even vituperated as cold and heartless ! A certain reserve and stiffness of manner, a certain soberness of old age, a want of political enthusiasm, and some sentences wrenched from their true meaning, are the evidences whereon men build the strange hypothesis that he was an Olympian Jove sitting *above* Humanity, *seeing* life but not *feeling* it, his heart dead to all noble impulses, his career a calculated egotism. How it was that one so heartless became the greatest poet of modern times—how it was that he whose works contained the widest compass of human life, should himself be a bloodless, pulseless diplomatist—no one thought of explaining, till Menzel arose, and with unparalleled effrontery maintained that Goethe had no genius, but only talent, and that the miracle of his works lies in their style—a certain adroitness in representation. Menzel is a man so completely rejected by England—the translation of his work met with such hopeless want of encouragement, that I am perhaps wrong to waste a line upon it ; but the bold style in which his trenchant accusations are made, and the assumption of a certain manliness as the momentum to his sarcasms, have given his attacks on Goethe a circulation independent of his book. To me he appears radically incompetent to appreciate a poet. I should as soon think of asking the first stalwart Kentish farmer for his opinion on the Parthenon. The farmer would doubtless utter some energetic sentences expressing his sense of its triviality ; but the coarse energy of his language would not supply the place of knowledge, feeling, and taste ; nor does the coarse energy of Menzel's style supply those deficiences of nature and education which incapacitate him for the perception of Art.

The paradox still remains, then, in spite of Menzel : a great

poet destitute of the feelings which poetry incarnates—a man
destitute of soul giving expression to all the emotions he has not—
a man who wrote *Werther*, *Egmont*, *Faust*, *Hermann und
Dorothea*, and *Meister*, yet knew not the joys and sorrows of his
kind ; will any one defend that paradox ?* Not only that paradox,
but this still more inexplicable one, that all who knew Goethe,
whether they were his peers or his servants, loved him only as
lovable natures can be loved. Children, women, clerks, professors,
poets, princes—all loved him. Even Herder, bitter against every
one, spoke of him with a reverence which astonished Schiller, who
writes : ' He is by many besides Herder named with a species of
devotion, and *still more loved as a man* than admired as an author.
Herder says he had a clear, universal mind, the truest and deepest
feeling, and the greatest purity of heart †'. Men might learn so
much from his works, had not the notion of his coldness and
indifference disturbed their judgment. ' In no line', says Carlyle,
'does he speak with asperity of any man, scarcely of anything.
He knows the good and loves it ; he knows the bad and hateful
and rejects it ; but in neither case with violence. His love is calm
and active ; his rejection implied rather than pronounced'.

And Schiller, when he came to appreciate by daily intercourse
the qualities of his great friend, thus wrote of him : ' It is not the
greatness of his intellect which binds me to him. If he were not
as a man more admirable than any I have ever known, I should
only marvel at his genius from the distance. But I can truly say
that in the six years I have lived with him, I have never for one
moment been deceived in his character. He has a high truth and
integrity, and is thoroughly in earnest for the Right and the Good ;
hence all hypocrites and phrasemakers are uncomfortable in his
presence'. And the man of whom Schiller could think thus is
believed by many to have been a selfish egotist, ' wanting in the
higher moral feelings' !

But so it is in life : a rumour, originating perhaps in thoughtless
ignorance, and circulated by malice, gains credence in the face of
probability, and then no amount of evidence suffices to dissipate
it. There is an atmosphere round certain names, a halo of glory

---

* I remember once, as we were walking along Piccadilly, talking about the infamous
Büchlein von Goethe, Carlyle stopped suddenly, and with his peculiar look and emphasis, said, ' Yes, it is the wild cry of amazement on the part of all spooneys that the
Titan was not a spooney too ! Here is a godlike intellect, and yet you see he is not an
idiot ! Not in the least a spooney ! '

† *Briefw. mit Körner*, I, p. 136.

or a halo of infamy, and men perceive this halo without seeking to
ascertain its origin.   Every public man is in some respects
mythical ; and the fables are believed in spite of all the contra-
dictions of evidence.   It is useless to hope that men will pause to
inquire into the truth of what they hear said of another, before
accepting and repeating it ; but with respect to Goethe, who has
now been more than a quarter of a century in his grave, one may
hope that evidence so strong as these pages furnish may be held
more worthy of credence than anything which gossip or ignorance,
misconception or partisanship has put forth without proof.

BOOK THE FIFTH

1779 to 1793

CHAPTER I

NEW BIRTH

THE changes slowly determining the evolution of character, when from the lawlessness of Youth it passes into the clear stability of Manhood, resemble the evolution of harmony in the tuning of an orchestra, when from stormy discords wandering in pursuit of concord, all the instruments gradually subside into the true key : round a small centre the hurrying sounds revolve, one by one falling into that centre, and increasing its circle, at first slowly, and afterwards with ever-accelerated velocity, till victorious concord emerges from the tumult. Or they may be likened to the gathering splendour of the dawn, as at first slowly, and afterwards with silent velocity, it drives the sullen darkness to the rear, and with a tidal sweep of light takes tranquil possession of the sky. Images such as these represent the dawn of a new epoch in Goethe's life ; an epoch when the wanderings of an excitable nature are gradually falling more and more within the circle of law ; when aims, before vague, now become clear ; when in the recesses of his mind much that was fluent becomes crystallized by the earnestness which gives a definite purpose to his life. All men of genius go through this process of crystallization. Their youths are disturbed by the turbulence of errors and of passions ; if they outlive these errors they convert them into advantages. Just as the sides of great mountain ridges are rent by fissures filled with molten rock, which fissures, when the lava cools, act like vast supporting ribs strengthening the mountain mass, so, in men of genius, passions first rend, and afterwards buttress life. The diamond, it is said, can only be polished by its own dust ; is not this symbolical of the truth that only by its own fallings-off can genius properly be taught ? And is not our very walk, as Goethe says, a series of falls ?

He was now (1779) entering his thirtieth year. Life slowly emerged from the visionary mists through which hitherto it had been seen; the solemn earnestness of manhood took the place of the vanishing thoughtlessness of youth, and gave a more commanding unity to his existence. He had 'resolved to deal with Life no longer by halves, but to work it out in its totality, beauty, and goodness—*vom Halben zu entwöhnen, und im Ganzen, Guten, Schönen resolut zu leben*'. It is usually said that the residence in Italy was the cause of this change; but the development of his genius was the real cause. The slightest acquaintance with the period we are now considering suffices to prove that long before he went to Italy the change had taken place. An entry in his Diary at this date is very significant. 'Put my things in order, looked through my papers, and burnt all the old chips. Other times, other cares! Calm retrospect of Life, and the extravagances, impulses, and eager desires of youth; how they seek satisfaction in all directions! How I have found delight, especially in mysteries, in dark imaginative connexions; how I only half seized hold of Science, and then let it slip; how a sort of modest self-complacency runs through all I wrote; how short-sighted I was in divine and human things; how many days wasted in sentiments and shadowy passions; how little good I have drawn from them! And now the half of life is over, I find myself advanced no step on my way, but stand here as one who, escaped from the waves, begins to dry himself in the sun. The period in which I have mingled with the world since October 1775 I dare not yet trust myself to look at. God help me further, and give me light, that I may not so much stand in my own way, but see to do from morning till evening the work which lies before me, and obtain a clear conception of the order of things; that I be not as those are who spend the day in complaining of headache, and the night in drinking the wine which gives the headache!'

There is something quite solemn in those words. The same thought is expressed in a letter to Lavater: 'The desire to raise the pyramid of my existence, the basis of which is already laid, as high as practicable in the air, absorbs every other desire, and scarcely ever quits me. I dare not longer delay; I am already advanced in life, and perhaps Death will break in at the middle of my work, and leave the Babylonic tower incomplete. At least men shall say it was boldly schemed, and if I live, my powers shall, with God's aid, reach the completion'. And in a recently published letter to the Duke, he says : ' I let people say what they will, and then I retire into my old fortress of Poetry and work at my *Iphigenia*. By this I am made sensible that I have been treating this heavenly gift somewhat too cavalierly, and there is still time and need for me to become more economical if ever I am to bring forth anything*'.

No better index of the change can be named than his *Iphigenia auf Tauris*, written at this period. The reader will learn with some surprise that this wonderful poem was originally written in prose. It was the fashion of the day. *Götz*, *Egmont*, *Tasso*, and *Iphigenia*, no less than Schiller's *Robbers*, *Fiesco*, *Kabale und Liebe*, were written in prose ; and when *Iphigenia* assumed a poetic form, the Weimar friends were disappointed—they *preferred* the prose.

This was part of the mania for returning to Nature. Verse was pronounced unnatural ; although, in truth, verse is not more unnatural than song. Song is to speech what poetry is to prose ; it expresses a different mental condition. Impassioned prose *approaches* poetry in the rhythmic impulse of its movements ; as impassioned speech in its varied cadences also approaches the intonations of music. Under great emotional excitement, the Arabs give their language a recognizable metre, and almost talk poetry. But prose never *is* poetry, or is so only for a moment ; nor is speech song. Schiller learned to see this, and we find him writing to Goethe, 'I have never before been so palpably convinced as in my present occupation how closely in poetry Substance and Form are connected. Since I began to transform my prosaic language into a poetic rhythmical one, I find myself *under a totally different jurisdiction;* even many motives which in the prosaic execution seemed to me to be perfectly in place, I can no longer use : they were merely *good for the common domestic understanding, whose organ prose seems to be;* but verse absolutely demands reference to the imagination, and thus I was obliged to become poetical in many of my motives'.

That Goethe should have fallen into the sophism which asserted prose to be more natural than verse is surprising. His mind was full of song. To the last he retained the faculty of singing melodiously, when his prose had degenerated into comparative feebleness. And this prose *Iphigenia* is saturated with verses ; which is also the case with *Egmont*. He *meant* to write prose,

---

* *Briefwechsel zwischen Karl August und Goethe*, I, II.

but his thoughts instinctively expressed themselves in verse. The critical reader will do well to compare the prose with the poetic version*. He will not only see how frequent the verses are, but how few were the alterations necessary to be made to transform the prose drama into a poem. They are just the sort of touches which elevate poetry above prose. Thus, to give an example, in prose he says: *unnütz seyn, ist todt seyn* (to be useless is to be dead), which thus grows into a verse—

Ein unnütz Leben ist ein früher Tod†.

Again in the speech of Orestes (Act II, sc. I), there is a fine and terrible allusion to Clytemnestra, 'Better die here before the altar than in an obscure nook where the nets of murderous near *relatives* are placed'. In the prose this allusion is not clear— Orestes simply says, the 'nets of assassins‡'.

The alterations do not touch the substance of this drama ; we must therefore consider it a product of the period now under review ; and as such we may examine it at once.

CHAPTER II

'IPHIGENIA'

IT was very characteristic in Schlegel to call *Iphigenia* 'an echo of Greek song'; he delighted in such rhetorical prettinesses ; but that German scholars should have so often repeated the phrase, and should have so often without misgiving declared *Iphigenia* to be the finest modern specimen of Greek tragedy, is truly surprising, until we reflect on the mass of flagrant traditional errors afloat respecting the Greek drama. For a long while the Three Unities were held to be inseparable from that drama ; in spite of the fact that in several plays Unity of Time is obviously disregarded, and in two or three the Unity of Place is equally so. Again there was the notion that Comedy and Tragedy were not suffered to mingle in the same play ; in spite of the palpable fact of Æschylus and Euripides having mingled them. It was also

---

* See vol. xxxiv of the edition of 1840.
† A life not useful is an early death.
‡ Neither Taylor nor Miss Swanwick appears to have seized the allusion. One translates it, 'by the *knives of avenging kindred*'; the other, 'where *near hands* have spread *assassination's wily net*'.

believed that Destiny formed the tragic-pivot; in spite of the fact, that in the *majority* of these plays Destiny has *no* place, beyond what the religious conceptions of the poets must of necessity have given to it, just as Christianity must of necessity underlie the tragic conceptions of Christian poets.

The very phrase with which critics characterize *Iphigenia* is sufficient to condemn them. They tell us it has 'all the repose of Greek tragedy'. Consider it for a moment : *Repose* in a tragedy ! that is to say, calmness in the terrific upheaving of volcanic passions. Tragedy, we are told by Aristotle, acts through Terror and Pity, awakening in our bosoms sympathy with suffering ; and to suppose *this* effect can be accomplished by the 'meditative repose which breathes from every verse' is tantamount to supposing a battle-song will most vigorously stir the blood of combatants if it borrow the accents of a lullaby.

Insensibly our notions of Greek art are formed from sculpture ; and hence, perhaps, this notion of repose. But acquaintance with the drama ought to have prevented such an error, and taught men not to confound calmnesss of *evolution* with calmness of *life*. The unagitated simplicity of Greek scenic representation lay in the nature of the scenic necessities ; but we do not call the volcano cold, because the snow rests on its top. Had the Greek drama been exhibited on stages like those of modern Europe, and performed by actors without cothurnus and mask, its deep agitations of passion would have welled up to the surface, communicating responsive agitations to the form. But there were reasons why this could not be. In the Grecian drama, everything was on a scale of vastness commensurate with the needs of an audience of many thousands ; and consequently everything was disposed in masses rather than in details ; it thus necessarily assumed something of the sculpturesque form, threw itself into magnificent groupings, and, with a view to its effect, adapted a peculiar eurhythmic construction. It thus assumed slowness of movement, because it could not be rapid without distortion. If the critic doubts this, let him mount on stilts and, bawling through a speaking-trumpet, try what he can make of Shakespeare ; he will then have an approximate idea of the restraints laid upon the Grecian actor, who, clothed so as to aggrandize his person, and speaking through a resonant mask, which had a *fixed* expression, could not *act*, in our modern sense of the word, but could only declaim ; he had no means of representing the *fluctuations* of passion, and the poet therefore was forced to make him represent passion in broad, fixed masses. Hence the movement of the Greek drama was necessarily large, slow, and simple.

But if we pierce beneath scenic necessities and attend solely to the dramatic life which pulses through the Grecian tragedies, what sort of calmness meets us there? Calmness is a relative word. Polyphemus hurling rocks as schoolboys throw cherry-stones, would doubtless smile at our riots, as we smile at buzzing flies; and Moloch howling through the unfathomable wilderness in passionate repentance of his fall, would envy us the wildest of our despair, and call it calmness. But measured by human standards I know not whose sorrow 'can bear such emphasis' as to pronounce those pulses calm which throb in the *Œdipus*, the *Agamemnon*, or the *Ajax*. The Labdacidan Tale is one of the sombrest threads woven by the Parcæ.

The subjects selected by the Greek dramatists are almost uniformly such as to call into play the darkest passions: madness, adultery, and murder in *Agamemnon;* revenge, murder, and matricide in the *Choëphoræ;* incest in *Œdipus;* jealousy and infanticide in *Medea;* incestuous adultery in *Hippolytus;* madness in *Ajax;* and so on throughout the series. The currents of these passions are for ever kept in agitation, and the alternations of pity and terror close only with the closing of the scene. In other words, in spite of the slowness of its scenic presentation this drama is distinguished by the very absence of the repose which is pronounced its characteristic.

Here we meet with the first profound difference separating Goethe from the Greek dramatist. The repose which was forced upon the Greek, which formed one of his restraints, as the hardness of the marble restrains the sculptor, Goethe has adopted under conditions which did *not* force him; while the repose, which the Greek kept only at the surface, Goethe has allowed to settle down to the core. In what was accidental, temporal, he has imitated Greek Art; in the one essential characteristic he has not imitated it. Racine, so unjustly treated by Schlegel, *has* given us the passionate life of the Greek drama, in spite of his *Madame* Hermione and *Monsieur* Oreste; in imitating the slow scenic movement he has also imitated the dramatic agitation of the under-current.

Goethe's *Iphigenia*, then, we must cease to regard according to the Grecian standard. It is a German play. It substitutes profound moral struggles for the passionate struggles of the old legend. It is not Greek in ideas nor in sentiment. It is German, and transports Germany of the eighteenth century into Scythia during the mythic age, quite as absolutely as Racine places the Court of Versailles in the Camp of Aulis; and with the same ample justification*. The points in which Goethe's work resembles the Greek, are, first, the slowness of its scenic movement and simplicity of its action, which produce a corresponding calmness in the dialogue ; and secondly, a saturation of mythic lore. All the rest is German. And this Schiller, as a dramatist, clearly saw. ' I am astonished', he says, 'to find this piece no longer makes the same favourable impression on me that it did formerly ; though I still recognize it as a work full of soul. *It is, however, so astonishingly modern and un-Greek that I cannot understand how it was ever thought to resemble a Greek play. It is purely moral, but the sensuous power, the life, the agitation, and everything which specifically belongs to a dramatic work is wanting.* Goethe has himself spoken slightingly of it, but I took that as a mere caprice or coquetry ; now I understand him'.

Schiller adds, however, that apart from the dramatic form, *Iphigenia* is a marvellous production, which must for ever remain the delight and wonderment of mankind. This is striking the right chord. A drama it is not ; it is a marvellous dramatic poem. The grand and solemn movement of its evolution responds to the large and simple ideas which it unfolds. It has the calmness of majesty. In the limpid clearness of its language, the involved mental processes of the characters are as transparent as the operations of bees within a crystal hive ; while a constant strain of high and lofty music makes the reader feel as if in a holy temple. And above all witcheries of detail there is the one capital witchery, belonging to Greek statues more than to any other works of human cunning—the perfect unity of impression produced by the whole, so that nothing in it seems *made*, but all to *grow;* nothing is superfluous, but all is in organic dependence ; nothing is there for detached effect, but the whole is effect. The poem fills the mind ; beautiful as the separate passages are,

---

* This error of local colouring, which critics more erudite than acute have ridiculed in Racine, is not only an error commanded by the very conditions of Art, but is the very error committed by the Greeks themselves. In this play of *Iphigenia*, Euripides has committed anachronisms as gross as any chargeable to Racine ; and justly : he wrote for the audience of his day, he did not write for antiquity.

admirers seldom think of passages, they think of the wondrous whole.

I cannot in language less than hyperbolical express my admiration for this work considered in itself; as a drama, I think an instructive parallel might be drawn between it and the *Iphigenia* of Euripides. The enormous superiority of Goethe in intellectual stature, even aided by the immeasurable advantage he has of writing in a language which is in some sort our own, would not cover his inferiority as a dramatist.

In Euripides we have this groundwork: Iphigenia, about to be sacrificed at Aulis, was snatched away in a cloud by Diana, and a hind substituted in her place; she is now priestess of Diana in Tauris, where she presides over the bloody sacrifice of every stranger thrown on the inhospitable shores. Orestes and Pylades, in obedience to the oracle, come to Tauris intent on bearing away the Image of Diana: that accomplished, Orestes is to be released from the Furies who pursue him. The two are seized, and brought to Iphigenia for sacrifice. A recognition takes place; and she aids them in their original design of carrying away the goddess. They are pursued by the Scythians, but Minerva appears, to cut the knot and calm the rage of Thoas.

This story Goethe has modernized. The characters are essentially different, the moral elements are different, and the effect is different. His Iphigenia, every way superior to the Greek priestess, has the high, noble, tender, delicate soul of a Christian maiden. Forced to fulfil the duties of a priestess, she subdues by her mild influence the fierce prejudice of Thoas, and makes him discontinue the barbarous practice of human sacrifices. She, who herself had been anointed as a sacrifice, could she preside over the sacrifice of another? This sympathy is modern. No Greek would have suffered her own personal feelings thus to rise up in rebellion against a religious rite. The key-note is struck here, and this tone sounds through the whole piece.

Iphigenia is melancholy, and pines for her native shores, in spite of the honour which attends, and the good she effects by her influence on Thoas. The fate of her family perturbs her. Thoas has conceived a passion for her.

> Thou sharedst **my** sorrow when a hostile sword
> Tore from my side my last, my dearest son;
> *Long as fierce vengeance occupied my heart,*
> *I did not feel my dwelling's dreary void;*

> But now, returning home, my rage appeased,
> My foes defeated and my son avenged,
> I find there's nothing left to comfort me*.

And he expresses a hope to 'bear her to his dwelling as a bride', which she gently evades ; he then taxes her with the mystery in which she has shrouded herself. She answers—

> If I concealed, O king, my name and race,
> 'Twas fear which prompted me, and not mistrust ;
> For didst thou know who stands before thee now,
> And what accursed head thy arm protects,
> A shuddering horror would possess thy heart ;
> And, far from wishing me to share thy throne,
> Wouldst banish me perchance.

Thoas replies with generosity, that nothing shall make him cease his protection.

> In my hands
> The goddess placed thee ; thou hast been to me
> As sacred as to her, and her behest
> Shall for the future also be my law.
> If thou canst hope in safety to return
> Back to thy kindred, I renounce my claims.

This promise becomes an important agent in the *dénouement*, and is skilfully contrived. Iphigenia, urged by him to speak out, utters this tremendous line :

> Know : I issue from the race of Tantalus !†

Thoas is staggered ; but after she has narrated the story of her race, he repeats his offer of marriage, which she will not accept. Irritated by her refusal, he exclaims :

> Be priestess still
> Of the great goddess who selected thee ;
> And may she pardon me that I from her

---

* In all extracts from this work I avail myself of the translation by Miss SWANWICK (*Selections from Goethe and Schiller*), which is many degrees superior to that of the late WILLIAM TAYLOR (*Survey of German Poetry*, vol. III). Feeling, as I profoundly feel, the insuperable difficulties of translating Goethe into English, it would ill become me to criticize Miss Swanwick's version ; but it would also be very unjust not to add, that all versions miss the exquisite beauty of the original, and resemble it no more than a rough woodcut resembles a Titian.

† *Vernimm : ich bin aus Tantalus Geschlecht.*
Miss Swanwick, from metrical necessity, has weakened this into :
> Attend : I issue from the Titan's race.

It was indispensable to preserve the name of Tantalus, so pregnant with terrible suggestion.

Unjustly, and with secret self-reproach,
Her ancient sacrifice so long withheld.
From olden times no stranger near'd our shore
But fell a victim at her sacred shrine ;
But thou with kind affection didst enthral me
That I forgot my duty.   Thou didst rock
My senses in a dream : I did not hear
My people's murmurs : now they cry aloud,
Ascribing my poor son's untimely death
To this my guilt.   No longer for thy sake
Will I oppose the wishes of the crowd
Who urgently demand the sacrifice.

.   .   .   .   .

Two strangers, whom in caverns of the shore
We found concealed, and whose arrival here
Bodes to my realm no good, are in my power :
With them thy goddess may once more resume
Her ancient, pious, long-suspended rites.

Thus ends the first act.

In the conception of Thoas a great dramatic collision is rendered impossible : so high and generous a nature cannot resist an appeal to his generosity ; and thus the spectator foresees there will be no struggle.   In Euripides, on the contrary, the fierce Scythian looms from the dark background, terrible as fate ; and he is artfully withheld from appearing on the scene until the very last.   *How* he is to be appeased no spectator foresees.   To be sure he is appeased by a *Deus ex machina*, and not by a dramatic unravelling of the entangled threads ; but this inferiority is, dramatically speaking, more than compensated by the effect of the collision, and the agitation kept up to the last.   Thoas, in Goethe, is a *moral*, not a *dramatic* figure*.

The carelessness to all dramatic effect which weakens this play is seen in the very avoidance of a path Euripides had opened, viz. the certainty in the mind of the audience that Orestes and Pylades are the two captives to be slaughtered.   In Euripides, Orestes and his companion appear on the scene before they are made prisoners ; in Goethe, not till after their capture has been announced.   The

* The notion of making Thoas in love is not new. LAGRANGE-CHANCEL, in his *Oreste et Pylade* (a real treat to any one with a perception of the ludicrous), has thrown as much 'galanterie' into this play as one may find in an opera. Thoas loves Iphigénie, who loves Pylade ; but while the tyrant sighs in vain, the truculent Scythian is sighed for by Thomyris, *princesse du sang royal des Scythes*. As a specimen of *couleur locale*, I may mention that Thoas in this play has a *capitaine des gardes* and two *ministres d'état*, with an *ambassadeur Sarmante* resident at his Court.

effect of the announcement in Euripides is powerful, in Goethe it is null*.

In the second act Orestes and Pylades appear. The scene between them is very undramatic, but beautiful as a poetic exposition of their mental conditions. Orestes feels—

> It is the path of death that now we tread,
> At every step my soul grows more serene.

But Pylades clings to life, and to his purpose. 'Am I not', he says—

> As ever full of courage and of joy?
> And love and courage are the spirit's wings
> Wafting to noble actions.

Orestes.   Noble actions?
> Time was when fancy painted such before us!
> When oft, the game pursuing, on we roam'd
> O'er hill and valley : hoping that ere long,
> With club and weapon arm'd, we so might chase
> The track of robber or of monster huge.
> And then at twilight, by the glassy sea,
> We peaceful sat reclined against each other ;
> The waves came dancing to our very feet,
> And all before us lay the wide, wide world.
> Then on a sudden one would seize his sword,
> And future deeds shone round us like the stars
> Which gemm'd in countless throngs the vault of night.

Pylades. Endless, my friend, the projects which the soul
> Burns to accomplish. We would every deed
> Perform at once as grandly as it shows
> After long ages, when from land to land
> The poet's swelling song hath rolled it on.
> It sounds so lovely what our fathers did,
> When in the silent evening shade reclined,
> We drink it in with music's melting tones.
> And what we do, is as it was to them
> Toilsome and incomplete.

---

* Compare EURIP. v. 264, *sq.* There is one touch in the peasant's narrative which is very significant of that period when gods walked the earth so familiarly with man that every stranger might be taken for a god :

> ἐνταῦθα δισσοὺς εἶδε τις νεανίας
> βουφορβὸς ἡμῶν κᾳπεχώρησεν πάλιν
> ἄκροισι δακτύλοισι πορθμεύων ἴχνος,
> ἔλεξε δ' οὐχ ὁρᾶτε· δαίμονές τινες
> θάσσουσίν οἵδε.

'There one of our cowboys espied the two youths, and stepping backwards on the points of his toes, retraced his steps, saying, "Do you not see them? they are gods seated there"'.

Pylades fails to inspire him, however, with the resolution which he feels, and with belief in the probability of their escape from the shameful death, which Orestes accepts so calmly. Pylades has heard from the guards the character of Iphigenia, and congratulates himself on the fact that it is a woman who holds their fates in her hands, for even the best of men

> With horror may familiarize his mind ;
> Through custom so transform his character,
> That he at length shall make himself a law
> Of what his very soul at first abhorred.

On some not very intelligible pretext he makes Orestes withdraw, that he may have an interview with Iphigenia ; and as she approaches, unbinds his chains, and speaks, he adroitly bursts forth into these words :

> Delicious music ! dearly welcome tones
> Of our own language in a foreign land !
> With joy my captive eye once more beholds
> The azure mountains of my native coast *.

He then tells her a story something like the real one, but disguising names : the *purpose* of which I do not detect. She inquires after her family, and hears the story of her mother's guilt. Noting her agitation, he asks if she be connected with that family by friendship. She sternly replies :

> Say on : and tell me how the deed was done.

He tells her. All she says is a few brief words, which are terribly significant : when he concludes, she veils herself, and withdraws, saying :

> Enough.   Thou soon wilt see me once again ;

and the act ends in this very *evasive* manner. The third act opens with the visit of Iphigenia to Orestes, in which she requests him to finish the story that Pylades had already half told ; and he does so at some length. Disdaining the guile which had prompted Pylades to conceal their names, he boldly says :

> I am Orestes !

---

* M. PATIN has, I think, mistaken the import of this speech : comparing it with the simple exclamation of Philocletes, he says, 'Philoclète, n'en savait pas tant, il n'était pas si habile à se rendre compte de ses secrets mouvements : tout ce qu'il pouvait était de s'écrier, "O douce parole"'. *Etudes sur les Tragiques Grecs*, III, p. 323.   But Pylades is not expressing *his* sentiments.   His ear is not unfamiliar with the accents of his own language—he has just before heard them from Orestes ; but by picturing Greece to *her*, he adroitly excites her sympathy for *himself*, a Greek.

Here is a proper ἀναγνώρισις,—and naturally, no less than dramatically, it demands a cry from the heart of Iphigenia, who
should at once fling herself into her brother's arms, and confess their relationship. Instead of this, she suffers him to continue talking, and to withdraw; she only reveals herself in
the next scene ! This is more like the dramatic treatment we
find in juvenile writers, than what is expected from a great poet.
Orestes has a return of his madness. He recovers from it, to
feel himself purified by his sister's purity; and Pylades now
suggests that they shall bear away the image, and depart
together.

It is evident that the tragic situation in this story is the slaughter
of a brother by a sister ignorant of a relationship perfectly known
to the audience. So far from having developed the tragedy of
such a situation, Goethe has scarcely touched upon it, and never
once awakened our fears : from first to last we are in no suspense,
our emotions are untouched, our curiosity alone is excited to
watch the process by which the terrible fate will be escaped. In
Euripides, on the contrary, everything conspires to increase the
terror of the situation. Iphigenia, formerly so mild that she wept
with her victims, now rages like a lioness bereaved of her cubs.
She has dreamed that Orestes is dead, and in her desolate condition resolves to wreak her woe on others. Her brother and his
friend are brought before her. She questions them as to their
names. Orestes refuses to tell her. In a rapid interchange of
questions and answers she learns the story of her family; and
then offers to save *one* of their lives, on condition that the
pardoned carry for her a letter to Argos. Here a contest of
generosity ensues, as to who shall accept his life. Pylades is at
length prevailed upon. The discovery is thus managed ; Pylades,
bôund by his oath to deliver the letter, suggests this difficulty,
viz. that should the boat be upset, or should the letter be lost, how
then can he fulfil his promise ? Hereupon, to anticipate such an
accident, Iphigenia tells him the contents of the letter ; and in
telling him reveals her name. This produces the natural cry
from Orestes, who avows himself, and clasps her in his arms.
The dramatic movement of this scene is admirable. From this
point the interest slackens in Euripides, in Goethe it deepens. In
the Greek play it is the culmination of passionate interest ; for
although the stratagem by which Iphigenia contrives to bear
away the sacred image would flatter the propensities of the

cunning Athenian audience*, it must have been, even to them, a delight altogether of a lower kind, addressing lower faculties, than those addressed by the tragic processional grandeur of the earlier portions ; whereas in the German play, the hitherto feeble passionate interest now rises in an ascending scale of high *moral* interest, so that the tragedy evolved addresses the conscience rather than the emotions, being less the conflict of passions than the high conflict with duty.

In the fourth act Iphigenia has to save more than her brother's life ; she has to save him from the Furies ; this is only to be done by deceit, inasmuch as force is impossible under the circumstances.   To a Greek mind nothing could be more satisfactory. The Greek *preferred* deceit to force ; but the Christianized conscience revolts from deceit as cowardly and deeply immoral. Accordingly Iphigenia shudders at the falsehood which is forced upon her, and only requires to be reminded by the king's messenger of the constant kindness and considerateness with which Thoas has treated her, to make her pause.   When, therefore, Pylades arrives, urging her to flight, she communicates to him her scruples.

> *Pylades.*   Him thou dost fly who would have slain thy brother.
> *Iphig.*   To me at least he hath been ever kind.
> *Pylades.*   What fate commands is not ingratitude.
> *Iphig.*   Alas ! it still remains ingratitude,—
>   Necessity alone can justify it.
> *Pylades.*   Thee before gods and men it justifies.
> *Iphig.*   *But my own heart is still unsatisfied.*
> *Pylades.*   Scruples too rigid are a cloak for pride.
> *Iphig.*   *I cannot argue, I can only feel.*

How modern all this is !   Pylades with more worldly views says :

> Life teaches us
> To be less strict with others than ourselves ;
> Thou'lt learn the lesson too.   So wonderful
> Is human nature, and its varied ties
> Are so involved and complicate, that none
> May hope to keep his inmost spirit pure,
> And walk without perplexity thro' life.

---

* Comp. EURIPIDES, v. 1157, *sq.*   Iphigenia pretends that as the image of the goddess has been stained by the impure hands of the two captives, it must be purified, and for this purpose she intends to cleanse it in the sea, but that must be done in solitude.   She then bids Thoas command that every citizen shall remain within doors, carefully avoiding a sight of that which may pollute them—μυσαρὰ γὰρ τὰ τοιάδ' ἐστι :— nay more, with an ingenuity which is almost farcical, she bids Thoas himself remain within the Temple, throwing a veil over his eyes as the captives issue forth, and he is not to consider it at all singular if she is a long while absent.   In this way she contrives to escape with the image, having made fools of Thoas and his guards.

Here, then, lies the tragedy.   Will this soul belie its own high
instincts, even for the sake of saving her brother?   The alternative
is horrible ; and after portraying the temptation in all its force,
and human frailty in all its tenderness, the poet shows us human
grandeur in this fine burst from the unhappy priestess :

> Attend, O king !
> A secret plot is laid ; 'tis vain to ask
> Touching the captives ; they are gone, and seek
> Their comrades, who await them on the shore.
> The eldest—he whom madness lately seized,
> And who is now recovered—is Orestes,
> My brother ! and the other, Pylades,
> His early friend and faithful confidant.
> From Delphi, Phœbus sent them to this shore,
> With a divine command to steal away
> The image of Diana, and to him
> Bear back the sister, promising for this
> Redemption to the blood-stained matricide.
> I have delivered now into thy hands
> The remnants of the house of Tantalus :
> Destroy us—if thou darest !

For anything like this we seek in vain throughout the Greek
Iphigenia; and the mere grandeur of the conception would
produce an overpowering effect on the stage, if delivered with
adequate depth and dignity.

Had Thoas been represented as a fierce Scythian, or even had
he not been hitherto allowed to convince us of his generosity, the
'collision' would have been stronger ; as it is, we have little faith
in his ferocity.   He has nearly relented when Orestes rushes in
with drawn sword to hasten Iphigenia away, because their design
has been discovered.   A scene ensues in which Thoas is resolved
not to suffer the Image of Diana to be borne away ; and as to
carry it away is the object of Orestes, it must be decided by force
of arms.   But now a light suddenly breaks in upon Orestes, who
reads the oracle in another way.   Apollo said—

> 'Back to Greece the sister bring,
> Who in the sanctuary on Tauris' shore
> Unwillingly abides ; so ends the curse'.
> To Phœbus' sister we applied the words,
> And he referred to *thee.*

It was Iphigenia who was to purify him, and to bear *her* away is to
fulfil Apollo's orders.   This interpretation loosens the knot.   Iphi-

genia recalls to Thoas his promise that she should depart if ever she could return in safety to her kindred, and he reluctantly says, 'Then go!' to which she answers—

> Not so, my king ; I cannot part
> Without thy blessing, or in anger from thee.
> Banish us not ! the sacred right of guests
> Still let us claim : so not eternally
> Shall we be severed.   Honour'd and belov'd,
> As my own father was, art thou by me :
> Farewell !   Oh ! do not turn away, but give
> One kindly word of parting in return.
> So shall the wind more gently swell our sails,
> And from our eyes with softened anguish flow
> The tears of separation.   Fare thee well !
> And graciously extend to me thy hand
> In pledge of ancient friendship.
> *Thoas (extending his hand).*   Fare thee well.

This is a very touching, noble close, and is in exquisite harmony with the whole.

The remarks on this masterpiece have already occupied so much space that I could not, were I disposed, pause to examine the various collateral points of criticism which have been raised in Germany.   I will merely allude to the characteristic difference between Ancient and Modern Art exhibited in the treatment of the Furies, which in Euripides are terrible Apparitions, real beings personated by actors ; in Goethe they are Phantasms moving across the stage of an unhappy soul, but visible only to the inward eye ; in like manner the Greek *dénouement* is the work of the actual interference of the Goddess in person, whereas the German *dénouement* is a loosening of the knot by a deeper insight into the meaning of the oracle.

CHAPTER III

PROGRESS

IN the beginning of 1779 we find Goethe very active in his new official duties.   He has accepted the direction of the War Department, which suddenly assumes new importance, owing to the preparations for a war.   He is constantly riding about the country, and doing his utmost to alleviate the condition of the people. 'Misery', he says, 'becomes as prosaic and familiar to me as my own hearth, but nevertheless I do not let go my idea, and will wrestle with the unknown Angel, even should I halt upon my thigh. No man knows what I do, and with how many foes I fight to bring forth a little '.

Among his undertakings may be noted an organization of Firemen, then greatly wanted. Fires were not only numerous, but were rendered terrible by the want of any systematic service to subdue them. Goethe, who in Frankfurt had rushed into the bewildered crowd, and astonished spectators by his rapid peremptory disposition of their efforts into a system—who in Apolda and Ettersburg lent aid and command, till his eyebrows were singed and his feet were burned—naturally took it much to heart that no regular service was supplied; and he persuaded the Duke to institute one.

On this (his thirtieth) birthday the Duke, recognizing his official services, raised him to the place of *Geheimrath*. 'It is strange and dreamlike', writes the Frankfurt burgher in his new-made honour, 'that I in my thirtieth year enter the highest place which a German citizen can reach. *On ne va jamais plus loin que quand on ne sait où l'on va*, said a great climber of this world'. If he thought it strange, Weimar thought it scandalous. 'The hatred of people here', writes Wieland, 'against our Goethe, who has done no one any harm, has grown to such a pitch since he has been made Geheimrath, that it borders on fury'. But the Duke, if he heard these howls, paid no attention to them. He was more than ever with his friend. They started on the 12th of September on a little journey into Switzerland, in the strictest incognito, and with the lightest of travelling trunks. They touched at Frankfurt, and stayed in the old house in the *Hirschgraben*, where Rath Goethe had the pride of receiving not only his son as Geheimrath, but the Prince, his friend and master. Goethe's mother was, as may be imagined, in high spirits—motherly pride and housewifely pride being equally stimulated by the presence of such guests.

From Frankfurt they went to Strasburg. There the recollection of Frederika irresistibly drew him to Sesenheim. In his letter to the Frau von Stein he says : 'On the 25th I rode towards Sesenheim, and there found the family as I had left it eight years ago. I was welcomed in the most friendly manner. The second daughter loved me in those days better than I deserved, and more than others to whom I have given so much passion and faith. I was forced to leave her at a moment when it nearly cost her her life; she passed lightly over that episode to tell me what traces still remained of the old illness, and behaved with such exquisite delicacy and generosity from the moment that I stood before her unexpected on the threshold, that I felt quite relieved. I must do her the justice to say that she made not the slightest attempt to rekindle in my bosom the cinders of love. She led me into the arbour, and there we sat down. It was a lovely moonlight, and I inquired after every one and everything. Neighbours had spoken of me not a week ago. I found old songs which I had composed, and a carriage I had painted. We recalled many a pastime of those happy days, and I found myself as vividly conscious of all, as if I had been away only six months. The old people were frank and hearty, and thought me looking younger. I stayed the night there, and departed at dawn, leaving behind me friendly faces; so that I can now think once more of this corner of the world with comfort, and know that they are at peace with me'.

There is something very touching in this interview, and in his narrative of it forwarded to the woman he *now* loves, and who does not repay him with a love like that which he believes he has inspired in Frederika. He finds this charming girl still unmarried, and probably is not a little flattered at the thought that she still cherishes his image to the exclusion of every other. She tells him of Lenz having fallen in love with her, and is silent respecting her own share in that little episode; a silence which all can understand and few will judge harshly; the more so as her feelings towards Lenz were at that time doubtless far from tender. Besides, apart from the romance of meeting with an old lover, there was the pride and charm of thinking what a world-renowned name her lover had achieved. It was no slight thing even to have been jilted by such a man; and she must have felt that he had not behaved to her otherwise than was to have been expected under the circumstances.

On the 26th Goethe rejoined his party, and 'in the afternoon I called on Lili, and found the lovely *Grasaffen** with a baby of seven weeks old, her mother standing by. There also I was received with admiration and pleasure. I made many inquiries, and to my great delight found the good creature happily married. Her husband, from what I could learn, seems a worthy, sensible fellow,

---

* *Grasaffen*, i.e. 'green monkey', is Frankfurt slang for 'budding miss', and alludes to the old days when he knew Lili.

rich, well placed in the world ; in short, she has everything she needs.   He was absent.   I stayed dinner.   After dinner went with the Duke to see the Cathedral, and in the evening saw Paesiello's beautiful opera, *L'Infante di Zamora*.   Supped with Lili, and went away in the moonlight.   The sweet emotions which accompanied me I cannot describe '.

We may read in these two descriptions the difference of the two women, and the difference of his feeling for them.   From Strasburg he went to Emmendingen, and there visited his sister's grave. Accompanied by such thoughts as these three visits must have called up, he entered Switzerland.   His *Briefe aus der Schweiz*, mainly composed from the letters to the Frau von Stein, will inform the curious reader of the effect these scenes produced on him ; we cannot pause here in the narrative to quote from them. Enough if we mention that in Zurich he spent happy hours with Lavater, in communication of ideas and feelings ; and that on his way home he composed the little opera of *Jery und Bätely*, full of Swiss inspiration.   In Stuttgart the Duke took it into his head to visit the Court, and as no presentable costume was ready, tailors had to be set in activity to furnish the tourists with the necessary clothes.   They assisted at the New Year festivities of the Military Academy, and here for the first time Schiller, then twenty years of age, with the *Robbers* in his head, saw the author of *Götz* and *Werther*.

It is probable that among all the figures thronging in the hall and galleries on that imposing occasion, none excited in the young ambitious student so thrilling an effect as that of the great poet, then in all the splendour of manhood, in all the lustre of an immense renown.   Why has no artist chosen this for an historical picture ?   The pale, sickly young Schiller, in the stiff military costume of that day, with pigtail and papillotes, with a sword by his side, and a three-cornered hat under his arm, stepping forward to kiss the coat of his sovereign Duke, in grateful acknowledgment of the three prizes awarded to him for Medicine, Surgery, and Clinical science ; conscious that Goethe was looking on, and could know nothing of the genius which had gained, indeed, trivial medical prizes, but had failed to gain a prize for German composition.   This pale youth and this splendid man were in a few years to become noble rivals, and immortal friends ; to strive with generous emulation, and the most genuine delight in each other's prowess ; presenting such an exemplar of literary friend-

ship as the world has seldom seen. At this moment, although
Schiller's eyes were intensely curious about Goethe, he was to
the older poet nothing beyond a rather promising medical
student.

Karl August on their return to Frankfurt again took up his abode
in the Goethe family, paying liberal attention to Frau Aja's good
old Rhine wine, and privately sending her a sum of money to
compensate for the unusual expenses of his visit. By the 13th
January he was in Weimar once more, having spent nearly nine
thousand dollars on the journey, including purchases of works
of art.

Both were considerably altered to their advantage. In his
Diary Goethe writes : ' I feel daily that I gain more and more the
confidence of people ; and God grant that I may deserve it, not in
the easy way, but in the way I wish. What I endure for myself
and others no one sees. The best is the deep stillness in which I
live *vis-à-vis* to the world, and thus win what fire and sword
cannot rob me of '. He was crystallizing slowly ; slowly gaining
the complete command over himself. ' I will be lord over myself.
No one who cannot master himself is worthy to rule, and only he
can rule '. But with such a temperament this mastery was not
easy ; wine and women's tears, he felt, were among his weaknesses :

> Ich könnte viel glücklicher seyn,
> Gäb's nur keinen Wein
> Und keine Weiberthränen.

He could not entirely free himself from either. He was a Rhinelander, accustomed from boyhood upwards to the stimulus of wine ;
he was a poet, never free from the fascinations of women. But
just as he was never known to lose his head with wine, so also did
he never lose himself entirely to a woman : the stimulus never
grew into intoxication.

One sees that his passion for the Frau von Stein continues ; but
it is cooling. It was necessary for him to love some one, but he
was loving here in vain, and he begins to settle into a calmer
affection. He is also at this time thrown more and more with
Corona Schröter ; and his participation in the private theatricals
is not only an agreeable relaxation from the heavy pressure of
official duties, but is giving him materials for *Wilhelm Meister*,
now in progress. ' Theatricals ', he says, ' remain among the few
things in which I still have the pleasure of a child and an artist '.

Herder, who had hitherto held somewhat aloof, now draws closer and closer to him, probably on account of the change which is coming over his way of life. And this intimacy with Herder awakens in him the desire to see Lessing; the projected journey to Wolfenbüttel is arrested, however, by the sad news which now arrives that the great gladiator is at peace : Lessing is dead.

Not without significance is the fact that, coincident with this change in Goethe's life, comes the passionate study of science, a study often before taken up in desultory impatience, but now commencing with that seriousness which is to project it as an active tendency through the remainder of his life. In an unpublished *Essay on Granite*, written about this period, he says : 'No one acquainted with the charm which the secrets of Nature have for man, will wonder that I have quitted the circle of observations in which I have hitherto been confined, and have thrown myself with passionate delight into this new circle. I stand in no fear of the reproach that it must be a spirit of contradiction which has drawn me from the contemplation and portraiture of the human heart to that of Nature. For it will be allowed that all things are intimately connected, and that the inquiring mind is unwilling to be excluded from anything attainable. And I who have known and suffered from the perpetual agitation of feelings and opinions in myself and in others, delight in the sublime repose which is produced by contact with the great and eloquent silence of Nature'. He was trying to find a secure basis for his aims ; it was natural he should seek a secure basis for his mind ; and with such a mind that basis could only be found in the study of Nature. If it is true, as men of science sometimes declare with a sneer, that Goethe was a poet in science (which does not in the least disprove the fact that he was great in science, and made great discoveries), it is equally true that he was a scientific poet. In a future chapter we shall have to consider what his position in science truly is ; for the present we merely indicate the course of his studies. · Buffon's wonderful book, *Les Epoques de la Nature*— rendered antiquated now by the progress of geology, but still attractive in its style and noble thoughts—produced a profound impression on him. In Buffon, as in Spinoza, and later on, in Geoffroy St. Hilaire, he found a mode of looking at Nature which thoroughly coincided with his own, gathering many details into a poetic synthesis. Saussure, whom he had seen at Geneva, led him to study mineralogy ; and as his official duties gave him many occasions to mingle with the miners, this study acquired a practical interest, which soon grew into a passion—much to the disgust of Herder, who, with the impatience of one who thought books the chief objects of interest, was constantly mocking him for 'bothering himself about stones and cabbages'. To these studies must be added anatomy, and in particular osteology, which in early years had also attracted him, when he attained knowledge enough to draw the heads of animals for Lavater's *Physiognomy*. He now goes to Jena to study under Loder, professor of anatomy*. For these studies his talent, or want of talent, as a draughtsman, had further to be cultivated. To improve himself he lectures to the young men every week on the skeleton. And thus, amid serious duties and many distractions in the shape of court festivities, balls, masquerades, and theatricals, he found time for the prosecution of many and various studies. He was like Napoleon, a giant-worker, and never so happy as when at work.

Tasso was conceived, and commenced (in prose) at this time, and *Wilhelm Meister* grew under his hands, besides smaller works. But nothing was published. He lived for himself, and the small circle of friends. The public was never thought of. Indeed the public was then jubilant at beerhouses, and scandalized in salons, at the appearance of the *Robbers;* and a certain Küttner, in publishing his *Characters of German Poets and Prose Writers* (1781), could complacently declare that the shouts of praise which intoxicated admirers had once raised for Goethe were now no longer heard. Meanwhile *Egmont* was in progress, and assuming a far different tone from that in which it was originated.

It is unnecessary to follow closely all the details, which letters abundantly furnish, of his life at this period. They will not help us to a nearer understanding of the man, and they would occupy much space. What we observe in them all is, a slow advance to a more serious and decisive plan of existence. On the 27th of May his father dies. On the 1st of June he comes to live in the town of Weimar, as more consonant with his position and avocations. The Duchess Amalia has promised to give him a part of the necessary furniture. He quits his *Gartenhaus* with regret, but makes it still his retreat for happy hours. Shortly afterwards the Duchess Amalia demonstrates to him at great length the necessity of his being ennobled ; the Duke, according to Düntzer, not having dared to break the subject to him. In fact, since he had been for

* Comp. *Brief. zwischen Karl August und Goethe*, I, 25, 26.

six years at court without a patent of nobility, he may perhaps have felt the 'necessity' as somewhat insulting. Nevertheless, I cannot but think that the Frankfurt citizen soon became reconciled to the *von* before his name ; the more so as he was never remarkable for a contempt of worldly rank. Immediately afterwards the President of the Kammer, von Kalb, was suddenly dismissed from his post, and Goethe was the substitute, at first merely occupying the post *ad interim ;* but not relinquishing his place in the Privy Council.

More important to us is the relation in which he stands to Karl August, and the Frau von Stein. Whoever reads with proper attention the letters published in the Stein correspondence will become aware of a notable change in their relation about this time (1781-2). The tone, which had grown calmer, now rises again into passionate fervour, and every note reveals the happy lover. From the absence of her letters, and other evidence, it is impossible to assign the cause of this change with any certainty. It may have been that Corona Schröter made her jealous. It may have been that she feared to lose him. One is inclined to suspect her of some questionable motive, because it is clear that her conduct to him was not straightforward in the beginning, and, as we shall see, became ungenerous towards the close. Whatever the motive, the fact is indubitable. In his letters may be plainly seen the extraordinary fascination she exercised over him, the deep and constant devotion he gave her, the thorough identification of her with all his thoughts and aims. A sentence or two must suffice here. ' O thou best beloved ! I have had all my life an ideal wish of how I would be loved, and have sought in vain its realization in vanishing dreams ; and now, when the world daily becomes clearer to me, I find this realization in thee, and in a way which can never be lost'. Again : 'Dearest, what do I not owe thee ! If thou didst not also love me so entirely, if thou only hadst me as a friend among others, I should still be bound to dedicate my whole existence to thee. For could I ever have renounced my errors without thy aid ? When could I have looked so clearly at the world, and found myself so happy in it, before this time when I have nothing more to seek in it ?' And this : 'As a sweet melody raises us to heaven, so is to me thy being and thy love. I move among friends and acquaintances everywhere as if seeking thee ; I find thee not, and return into my solitude'.

While he was thus happy, thus settling down into clearness, the young Duke, not yet having worked through the turbulence of youth, was often in discord with him. In the published correspondence may be read confirmation of what I have elsewhere learned, namely, that although during their first years of intimacy the poet stood on no etiquette in private with his sovereign, and although to the last Karl August continued the brotherly *thou*, and the most affectionate familiarity of address, yet Goethe soon began to perceive that another tone was called for on his part. His letters become singularly formal as he grows older; at times almost unpleasantly so. The Duke writes to him as to a friend, and he replies as to a sovereign.

Not that his affection diminished ; but as he grew more serious, he grew more attentive to decorum. For the Duchess he seems to have had a tender admiration, something of which may be read in *Tasso.* Her noble, dignified, though somewhat inexpressive nature, the greatness of her heart, and delicacy of her mind, would all the more have touched him, because he knew and could sympathize with what was not perfectly happy in her life. He was often the pained witness of little domestic disagreements, and had to remonstrate with the Duke on his occasional roughness.

From the letters to the Frau von Stein we gather that Goethe was gradually becoming impatient with Karl August, whose excellent qualities he cherishes while deploring his extravagances. ' Enthusiastic as he is for what is good and right, he has, notwithstanding, less pleasure in it than in what is improper; it is wonderful how reasonable he can be, what insight he has, how much he knows ; and yet when he sets about anything good, he must needs begin with something foolish. Unhappily, one sees it lies deep in his nature, and that the frog is made for the water even when he has lived some time on land'. In the following we see that the ' servile courtier' not only remonstrates with the Duke, but refuses to accompany him on his journey, having on a previous journey been irritated by his manners. ' Here is an epistle. If you think right, send it to the Duke, speak to him and do not spare him. I only want quiet for myself, and for him to know with whom he has to do. *You can tell him also that I have declared to you I will never travel with him again.* Do this in your own prudent gentle way'. Accordingly he lets the Duke go away alone : but they seem to have come to some understanding subsequently, and the threat was not fulfilled. Two months after, this sentence informs us of the reconciliation : ' I have had a long and serious conversation with the Duke. In this world, my best one, the dramatic writer has a rich harvest ; and the wise say, Judge no man until you have stood in his place'. Later on we find him complaining of the Duke going wrong in his endeavours to do right. 'God knows if he will ever learn that fireworks at midday produce no effect. I don't like always playing the pedagogue and bugbear, and from the others he asks no advice, nor does he ever tell them of his plans'. Here is another glimpse : 'The Duchess is as amiable as possible, the Duke is a good creature, and one could heartily love him if he did not trouble the intercourse of life by his manners, and did not make his friends indifferent as to what befals him by his breakneck recklessness. It is a curious feeling, that of daily contemplating the possibility of our nearest friends breaking their necks, arms, or legs, and yet have grown quite callous to the idea !' Again : 'The Duke goes to Dresden. He has begged me to go with him, or at least to follow him, but I shall stay here. . . . The preparations for the Dresden journey are quite against my taste. The Duke arranges them in his way, *i.e.*, not always the best, and disgusts one after the other. I am quite calm, for it is not alterable, and I only rejoice that there is no kingdom for which such cards could be played often'.

These are little discordant tones which must have arisen as Goethe grew more serious. The real regard he had for the Duke is not injured by these occasional outbreaks. 'The Duke', he writes, 'is guilty of many follies which I willingly forgive, remembering my own'. He knows that he can at any moment put his horses to the carriage and drive away from Weimar, and this consciousness of freedom makes him contented ; although he now makes up his mind that he is destined by nature to be an author and nothing else. 'I have a purer delight than ever, when I have written something which well expresses what I meant. . . .' 'I am truly born to be a private man, and do not understand how fate has contrived to throw me into a ministry and into a princely family'. As he grows clearer on the true mission of his life, he also grows happier. One can imagine the strange feelings with which he would now take up *Werther*, and for the first time since ten years read this product of his youth. He made some alterations in it, especially in the relation of Albert to Lotte ; and introduced the episode of the peasant who commits suicide from jealousy. Schöll, in his notes to the *Stein Correspondence**, has called attention to a point

* Vol. III, p. 268.

worthy of notice, viz., that Herder, who helped Goethe in the revision of this work, had pointed out to him the very same fault in
its composition which Napoleon two-and-twenty years later laid his
finger on ; the fault, namely, of making Werther's suicide partly
the consequence of frustrated ambition and partly of unrequited
love—a fault which, in spite of Herder and Napoleon, in spite also
of Goethe's acquiescence, I venture to think no fault at all, as will
be seen when the interview with Napoleon is narrated.

CHAPTER IV

PREPARATIONS FOR ITALY

WITH the year 1783 we see him more and more seriously
occupied. He has ceased to be 'the Grand Master of all
the Apes', and is deep in old books and archives. The birth of a
crown prince came to fill Weimar with joy, and give the Duke a
sudden seriousness. The baptism, which took place the 5th of
February, was a great event in Weimar. Herder preached 'like
a God', said Wieland, whose cantata was sung on the occasion.
Processions by torchlight, festivities of all kinds, poems from
every poet, *except* Goethe, testified the people's joy. There is
something very generous in this silence. It could not be attributed
to want of affection. But he who had been ever ready with ballet,
opera, or poem, to honour the birthday of the two Duchesses,
must have felt that now, when all the other Weimar writers were
pouring in their offerings, he ought not to throw the weight of his
position in the scale against them. Had his poem been the worst
of the offerings, it would have been prized the highest because it
was his.

The Duke, proud in his paternity, writes to Merck : 'You have
reason to rejoice with me ; for if there ˈbe any good dispositions
in me they have hitherto wanted a fixed point, but now there is a
firm hook upon which I can hang my pictures. With the help of
Goethe and good luck I will so paint that if possible the next
generation shall say, he too was a painter ! ' And from this time
forward there seems to have been a decisive change in him ;
though he does complain of the 'taciturnity of his *Herr Kammerpräsident*' (Goethe), who is only to be drawn out by the present of
an engraving. In truth, this *Kammerpräsident* is very much

oppressed with work, and lives in great seclusion, happy in love, active in study. The official duties which formerly he undertook so gaily are obviously becoming burdens to him, the more so now his mission rises into greater distinctness. The old desire for Italy begins to torment him. 'The happiest thing is, that I can now say I am on the right path, and from this time forward nothing will be lost.

In his poem *Ilmenau*, written in this year, Goethe vividly depicts the character of the Duke, and the certainty of his metamorphosis. Having seen how he speaks of the Duke in his letters to the Frau von Stein, it will gratify the reader to observe that these criticisms were no 'behind the back' carpings, but were explicitly expressed even in poetry. 'The poem of *Ilmenau*', Goethe said to Eckermann, 'contains in the form of an episode an epoch which in 1783, when I wrote it, had happened some years before; so that I could describe myself historically and hold a conversation with myself of former years. There occurs in it a night scene after one of the breakneck chases in the mountain. We had built ourselves at the foot of a rock some little huts, and covered them with fir branches, that we might pass the night on dry ground. Before the huts we burned several fires and cooked our game. Knebel, whose pipe was never cold, sat next to the fire, and enlivened the company with his jokes, while the wine passed freely. Seckendorf had stretched himself against a tree and was humming all sorts of poetics. On one side lay the Duke in deep slumber. I myself sat before him in the glimmering light of the coals, absorbed in various grave thoughts, suffering for the mischief which my writings had produced'. The sketch of the Duke is somewhat thus to be translated : ' Who can tell the caterpillar creeping on the branch, of what its future food will be ? Who can help the grub upon the earth to burst its shell ? The time comes when it presses out and hurries winged into the bosom of the rose. Thus will the years bring *him* also the right direction of his strength. As yet, beside the deep desire for the True, he has a passion for Error. Temerity lures him too far, no rock is too steep, no path too narrow, peril lies at his side threatening. Then the wild, unruly impulse hurries him to and fro, and from restless activity he restlessly tries repose. Gloomily wild in happy days, free without being happy, he sleeps, fatigued in body and soul, upon a rocky couch'.

While we are at Ilmenau let us not forget the exquisite little

poems written there this September, with a pencil, on the wall of
that hut on the Gickelhahn, which is still shown to visitors :

> Ueber allen Gipfeln
> Ist Ruh,
> In allen Wipfeln
> Spürest du
> Kaum einen Hauch ;
> Die Vögelein schweigen in Walde ;
> Warte nur, balde
> Ruhest du auch.

He had many unpleasant hours as Controller of the Finances,
striving in vain to make the Duke keep within a prescribed definite
sum for expenses ; a thing always found next to impossible with
Princes (not often possible with private men), and by no means
accordant with our Duke's temperament. 'Goethe contrives to
make the most sensible representations', Wieland writes to Merck,
'and is indeed *l'honnête homme à la cour ;* but suffers terribly in
body and soul from the burdens which for our good he has taken
on himself. It sometimes pains me to the heart to see how good
a face he puts on while sorrow like an inward worm is silently
gnawing him. He takes care of his health as well as he can, and
indeed he has need of it'. Reports of this seem to have reached
the ear of his mother, and thus he endeavours to reassure her :
'You have never known me strong in stomach and head ; and that
one must be serious with serious matters is in the nature of
things, especially when one is thoughtful and desires the good and
true. . . . I am, after my manner, tolerably well, am able to do all
my work, to enjoy the intercourse of good friends, and still find
time enough for all my favourite pursuits. I could not wish myself
in a better place, now that I know the world and know how it looks
behind the mountains. And you, on your side, content yourself
with my existence, and should I quit the world before you, I have
not lived to your shame ; I leave behind me a good name and
good friends, and thus you will have the consolation of knowing
that I *am not entirely dead.* Meanwhile live in peace ; fate may
yet give us a pleasant old age, which we will also live through
gratefully'.

It is impossible not to read, beneath these assurances, a tone of
sadness such as corresponds with Wieland's intimation. Indeed,
the Duke, anxious about his health, had urged him in the September of this year to make a little journey in the Harz. He went,

accompanied by Fritz von Stein, the eldest son of his beloved, a boy of ten years of age, whom he loved and treated as a son. ' Infinite was the love and care he showed me', said Stein, when recording those happy days. He had him for months living under the same roof, taught him, played with him, formed him. His instinctive delight in children was sharpened by his love for this child's mother. A pretty episode in the many-coloured Weimar life is this, of the care-worn minister and occupied student snatching some of the joys of paternity from circumstances which had denied him wife and children.

The Harz journey restored his health and spirits : especially agreeable to him was his intercourse with Sömmering, the great anatomist, and other men of science. He returned to Weimar to continue *Wilhelm Meister*, which was now in its fourth book ; to continue his official duties ; to see more and more of Herder, then writing his *Ideen ;* and to sun himself in the smiles of his beloved.

The year 1784 begins with an alteration in the theatrical world. The Amateur Theatre, which has hitherto given them so much occupation and delight, is now closed. A regular troupe is engaged. For the birthday of the Duchess, Goethe prepares the *Planet Dance*, a masked procession ; and prepares an oration for the Reopening of the Ilmenau Mines, which must greatly have pleased him as the beginning of the fulfilment of an old wish. From his first arrival he had occupied himself with these mines, and the possibility of their being once more set working. After many difficulties, on the 24th of February this wish was realized. It is related of him, that on the occasion of this opening speech, made in presence of all the influential persons of the environs, he appeared to have well in his head all that he had written, for he spoke with remarkable fluency. All at once the thread was lost ; he seemed to have forgotten what he had to say. ' This', says the narrator, ' would have thrown any one else into great embarrassment ; but it was not so with him. On the contrary, he looked for at least ten minutes steadily and quietly round the circle of his numerous audience ; they were so impressed by his personal appearance, that during the very long and almost ridiculous pause every one remained perfectly quiet. At last he appeared to have again become master of his subject ; he went on with his speech, and without hesitation continued it to the end as serenely as if nothing had happened '.

His osteological studies brought him this year the discovery of an intermaxillary bone in man, as well as in animals*. In a future chapter† this discovery will be placed in its historical and anatomical light; what we have at present to do with it, is to recognize its biographical significance. Until this discovery was made, the position of man had always been separated from that of even the highest animals, by the fact (assumed) that he had *no* intermaxillary bone. Goethe, who everywhere sought unity in Nature, believed that such a difference did not exist; his researches proved him to be right. Herder was at that time engaged in proving that no structural difference could be found between men and animals; and Goethe, in sending Knebel his discovery, says that it will support this view. 'Indeed, man is most intimately allied to animals. The co-ordination of the Whole makes every creature to be that which it is, and man is as much man through the form of his upper jaw, as through the form and nature of the last joint of his little toe. And thus is every creature but *a note of the great harmony*, which must be studied in the Whole, or else it is nothing but a dead letter. From this point of view I have written the little essay, and that is properly speaking the interest which lies hidden in it'.

The discovery is significant therefore as an indication of his tendency to regard Nature in her unity. It was the prelude to his discoveries of the metamorphosis of plants, and of the vertebral theory of the skull: all three resting on the same mode of conceiving Nature. His botanical studies received fresh impulse at this period. Linnæus was a constant companion on his journeys, and we see him with eagerness availing himself of all that the observations and collections of botanists could offer him in aid of his own. 'My geological speculations', he writes to the Frau von Stein, 'make progress. I see much more than the others who accompany me because I have discovered certain fundamental laws of formation, which I keep secret, and can from them better observe and judge the phenomena before me. . . .' 'Every one exclaims about my solitude, which is a riddle, because no one knows with what glorious unseen beings I hold communion'. It is interesting to observe his delight at seeing a zebra—which was a novelty in Germany—and his inexhaustible pleasure in the

---

* He thus announces it to Herder, 27th March, 1784: 'I hasten to tell you of the fortune that has befallen me. I have found neither gold nor silver, but that which gives me inexpressible joy, the *os intermaxillare* in Man! I compared the skulls of men and beasts, in company with Loder, came on the trace of it, and see there it is!'— *Aus Herder's Nachlass*, I, 75.

† See further on the chapter on 'The Poet as a Man of Science'.

elephant's skull, which he has procured for study. Men confined
to their libraries, whose thoughts scarcely venture beyond the
circle of literature, have spoken with sarcasm, and with pity, of
this waste of time. But—dead bones for dead bones—there is as
much poetry in the study of an elephant's skull as in the study of
those skeletons of the past—history and classics. All depends
upon the mind of the student ; to one man a few old bones
will awaken thoughts of the great organic processes of nature,
thoughts as far-reaching and sublime as those which the fragments
of the past awaken in the historical mind. Impressed with this
conviction, the great Bossuet left the brilliant court of Louis XIV,
to shut himself up in the anatomical theatre of Duverney, that he
might master the secrets of organization before writing his
treatise *De la Connaissance de Dieu**. But there are minds, and
these form the majority, to whom dry bones are dry bones, and
nothing more. ' How legible the book of Nature becomes to me ',
Goethe writes, ' I cannot express to thee ; my long lessons in
spelling have helped me, and now my quiet joy is inexpressible.
Much as I find that is new, I find nothing unexpected ; everything fits in, because I have no system, and desire nothing but the
pure truth '. To help him in his spelling he begins algebra ; but
the nature of his mind was too unmathematical for him to pursue
that study long.

Science and love were the two pillars of his existence in these
days. ' I feel that thou art always with me ', he writes ; ' thy
presence never leaves me. In thee I have a standard of all
women, yea of all men ; in thy love I have a standard of fate.
Not that it darkens the world to me, on the contrary, it makes the
world clear ; I see plainly how men are, think, wish, strive after,
and enjoy ; and I give every one his due, and rejoice silently in
the thought that I possess so indestructible a treasure '.

The Duke increased his salary by 200 thalers, and this, with the
1,800 thalers received from the paternal property, made his
income now 3,200 thalers. He had need of money, both for his
purposes and his numerous charities. We have seen, in the case
of Kraft, how large was his generosity ; and in one of his letters
to his beloved, he exclaims, ' God grant that I may daily become
more economical, that I may be able to do more for others '. The
reader knows this is not a mere phrase thrown in the air. All his

---

* This work contains a little treatise on anatomy, which testifies the patience of the
theologian's study.

letters speak of the suffering he endured from the sight of so much want in the people. 'The world is narrow', he writes, 'and not every spot of earth bears every tree ; mankind suffers, and *one is ashamed to see oneself so favoured above so many thousands.* We hear constantly how poor the land is, and daily it becomes poorer ; but we partly think this is not true, and partly hurry it away from our minds when once we see the truth with open eyes, see the irremediableness, and see how matters are always bungled and botched !' That he did his utmost to ameliorate the condition of the people in general, and to ameliorate particular sorrows as far as lay in his power, is strikingly evident in the concurrent testimony of all who knew anything of his doings. If he did not write dithyrambs of Freedom, and was not profoundly enthusiastic for Fatherland, let us attribute it to any cause but want of heart.

The stillness and earnestness of his life seem to have somewhat toned down the society of Weimar. He went very rarely to Court ; and he not being there to animate it with his inventions, the Duchess Amalia complained that they were all asleep ; the Duke also found society insipid : 'the men have lived through their youth, and the women mostly married'. The Duke altered with the rest. The influence of his dear friend was daily turning him into more resolute paths ; it had even led him to the study of science, as we learn from his letters. And Herder also, now occupied with his great work, shared these ideas, and enriched himself with Goethe's friendship. Jacobi came to Weimar, and saw his old friend again, quitting him with real sorrow. He was occupied at this time with the dispute about Lessing's Spinozism, and tried to bring Goethe into it, who very characteristically told him, 'Before I write a syllable μετα τα φυσικα, I must first have clearly settled my φυσικα'. All controversy was repugnant to Goethe's nature : he said, 'If Raphael were to paint it and Shakespeare dramatize it, I could scarcely find any pleasure in it'. Jacobi certainly was not the writer to conquer such repugnance. Goethe objected to his tone almost as much as to his opinions. 'When self-esteem expresses itself in contempt of another, be he the meanest, it must be repellent. A flippant, frivolous man may ridicule others, may controvert them, scorn them ; but he who has any respect for himself seems to have renounced the right of thinking meanly of others. And what are we all that we can dare to raise ourselves to any height ?' He looks upon Jacobi's metaphysical *tic* as a compensation for all the goods the gods have given him. 'House, riches, children, sister and friends, and a long etc., etc., etc. On the other hand, God has punished you with metaphysics like a thorn in your flesh ; me He has blessed with science, that I may be happy in the contemplation of His works '. How characteristic is this : ' When you say we can only *believe* in God, I answer that I lay great stress on *seeing* (*schauen*), and when Spinoza, speaking of *scientia intuitiva*, says : *Hoc cognoscendi genus procedit ab adequata idea essentiæ formalis quorundam Dei attributorum ad adequatam cognitionem essentiæ rerum*, these few words give me courage to dedicate my whole life to the observation of things which I can reach, and of whose *essentiæ formalis* I can hope to form an adequate idea, without in the least troubling myself how far I can go'. He was at variance, and justly, with those who called Spinoza an atheist.   He called him the most theistical of theists, and the most Christian of Christians—*theissimum et christianissimum.*

While feeling the separation of opinion between himself and Jacobi, he still felt the sympathy of old friendship.   It was otherwise with Lavater.   Their intimacy had been great; no amount of difference had overshadowed it, until the priestly element of Lavater, formerly in abeyance, grew into offensive prominence.   He clouded his intellect with superstitions, and aspired to be a prophet.   He had believed in Cagliostro and his miracles, exclaiming, ' Who would be so great as he, had he but a true sense of the Evangelists?'   He called upon that mystifier, in Strasburg, but was at once sent about his business.   'When a great man', writes Goethe of Lavater, in 1782, 'has a dark corner in him, it is terribly dark'. And the dark corner in Lavater begins to make him uneasy.   ' I see the highest power of reason united in Lavater with the most odious superstition, and that by a knot of the finest and most inextricable kind'.   To the same effect he says in one of the Xenien :—

Wie verfährt die Natur um Hohes und Niedres im Menschen
Zu verbinden ? sie stellt Eitelkeit zwischen hinein.

It was a perception of what he thought the hypocritical nature of Lavater which thoroughly disgusted him, and put an end to their friendship ; mere difference of opinion never separated him from a friend.

His scientific studies became enlarged by the addition of a microscope, with which he followed the investigations of Gleichen, and gained some insight into the marvels of the world of Infusoria. His drawings of the animalcules seen by him were sent to the Frau von Stein ; and to Jacobi he wrote : ' Botany and the microscope are now the chief enemies I have to contend against. But I live in perfect solitude apart from all the world, as dumb as a fish '. Amid these multiform studies,—mineralogy, osteology, botany, and constant ' dipping ' into Spinoza, his poetic studies might seem to have fallen into the background, did we not know that *Wilhelm Meister* has reached the fifth book, the opera of *Scherz, List, und Rache* is written, the great religious-scientific poem *Die Geheimnisse* is planned, *Elpenor* has two acts completed, and many of the minor poems are written. Among these poems, be it noted, are the two songs in *Wilhelm Meister*, *Kennst du das Land*, and *Nur wer die Sehnsucht kennt*, which speak feelingly of his longing for Italy. The preparations for that journey are made in silence. He is studying Italian, and undertakes the revision of his works for a new edition, in which Wieland and Herder are to help him.

Seeing him thus happy in love, in friendship, in work, with young Fritz living with him, to give him, as it were, a home, and every year bringing fresh clearness in his purposes, one may be tempted to ask what was the strong impulse which could make him break away from such a circle, and send him lonely over the Alps? Nothing but the impulse of genius. Italy had been the dream of his youth. It was the land where self-culture was to gain rich material and firm basis. That he was born to be a Poet, he now deliberately acknowledged ; and nothing but solitude in the Land of Song seemed wanting to him. Thither he yearned to go ; thither he would go.

He accompanied the Duke, Herder, and the Frau von Stein to Carlsbad in July 1786, taking with him the works to be revised for Göschen's new edition. The very sight of these works must have strengthened his resolution. And when Herder and the Frau von Stein returned to Weimar, leaving him alone with the Duke, the final preparations were made. He had studiously concealed this project from everyone except the Duke, whose permission was necessary ; but even from him the project was partially concealed. ' Forgive me ', he wrote to the Duke, ' if at parting I spoke vaguely about my journey and its duration. I do not yet know myself what is to become of me. You are happy in a chosen path. Your affairs are in good order, and you will excuse me if I now look after my own ; nay, you have often urged me to do so. I am at this moment certainly able to be spared ; things are so arranged as to go on smoothly in my absence. In this state of things all I

ask is an indefinite furlough'. He says that he feels it necessary
for his intellectual health that he should 'lose himself in a world
where he is unknown'; and begs that no one may be informed of
his intended absence. 'God bless you, is my hearty wish, and
keep me your affection. Believe me that if I desire to make my
existence more complete, it is that I may enjoy it better with you
and yours'.

This was on the 2nd September, 1786. On the third he quitted
Carlsbad incognito. His next letter to the Duke begins thus:
'One more friendly word out of the distance, without date or place.
Soon will I open my mouth and say how I get on. How it will
rejoice me once more to see your handwriting'. And it ends
thus: 'Of course you let people believe that you know where I
am'. In the next letter he says, 'I must still keep the secret of
my whereabouts a little longer'.

CHAPTER V

ITALY

THE long yearning of his life was at last fulfilled: he was in
Italy. Alone, and shrouded by an assumed name from all
the interruptions with which the curiosity of admirers would have
perplexed the author of *Werther*, but which never troubled the
supposed merchant Herr Möller, he passed amid orange trees and
vineyards, cities, statues, pictures, and buildings, feeling himself
'at home in the wide world, no longer an exile'. The passionate
yearnings of Mignon had grown with his growth and strengthened
with his strength, through the early associations of childhood, and
all the ambitions of manhood, till at last they make him sick at
heart. For some time previous to his journey he had been unable
to look at engravings of Italian scenery, unable even to open a
Latin book, because of the overpowering suggestions of the
language; so that Herder could say of him that the only Latin
author ever seen in his hand was Spinoza. The feeling grew and
grew, a mental home-sickness which nothing but Italian skies
could cure. We have only to read Mignon's song, *Kennst du das
Land*, which was written before this journey, to perceive how
trance-like were his conceptions of Italy, and how restless was his
desire to journey there.

And now this deep unrest was stilled. Italian voices were loud around him, Italian skies were above him, Italian Art was before him. He felt this journey was a new birth. His whole being was filled with warmth and light. Life stretched itself before him calm, radiant, and strong. He saw the greatness of his aims, and felt within him powers adequate to those aims.

He has written an account of his journey ; but although no man could have produced a greater work, had he deliberately set himself to do so, and although some passages of this work are among the most delightful of the many pages written about Italy, yet the *Italiänische Reise* is, on the whole, a very disappointing book. Nor could it well have been otherwise, under the circumstances. It was not written soon after his return, when all was fresh in his memory, and when its style had still its warmth and vigour ; but in the decline of his great powers he collected the hasty letters sent from Italy to the Frau von Stein, Herder, and others, and from them he extracted such passages as seemed suitable, weaving them together with no great care, or enthusiasm. Had he simply printed the letters themselves, they would doubtless have given us a far more vivid and interesting picture ; in the actual form of the work we are wearied by various trifles and incidents of the day circumstantially narrated, which in letters would not improperly find a place, but which here want the pleasant, careless, chatty form given by correspondence. The *Italiänische Reise* wants the charm of a collection of letters, and the solid excellence of a deliberate work. It is mainly interesting as indicating the effect of Italy on his mind ; an effect apparently too deep for utterance. He was too completely possessed by the new life which streamed through him, to bestow much time in analysing and recording his impressions.

Curious it is to notice his open-eyed interest in all the geological and meteorological phenomena which present themselves ; an interest which has excited the sneers of some who think a poet has nothing better to do than to rhapsodize. They tolerate his enthusiasm for Palladio, because architecture is one of the Arts ; and forgive the enthusiasm which seized him in Vicenza, and made him study Palladio's works as if he were about to train himself for an architect ; but they are distressed to find him in Padua, once more occupied with 'cabbages', and tormented with the vague conception of a Typical Plant, which will not leave him. Let me confess, however, that some cause for disappointment exists. The poet's yearning is fulfilled; and yet how little literary enthusiasm escapes him! Italy is the land of History, Literature, Painting, and Music; its highways are sacred with associations of the Past; its byways are centres of biographic and artistic interest. Yet Goethe, in raptures with the climate, and the beauties of Nature, is almost silent about Literature, has no sense of Music, and no feeling for History. He passes through Verona without a thought of Romeo and Juliet; through Ferrara without a word of Ariosto, and scarcely a word of Tasso. In this land of the Past, it is the Present only which allures him. He turns aside in disgust from the pictures of crucifixions, martyrdoms, emaciated monks, and all the hospital pathos which makes galleries hideous; only in Raphael's healthier beauty, and more human conceptions, can he take delight. He has no historic sense enabling him to qualify his hatred of superstition by recognition of the painful religious struggles which, in their evolutions, assumed these superstitious forms. He considers the pictures as things of the present, and because their motives are hideous he is disgusted; but a man of more historic feeling would, while marking his dislike of such conceptions, have known how to place them in their serial position in the historic development of mankind.

It is not for Literature, it is not for History, it is not for poetical enthusiasm, we must open the *Italiänische Reise*. There is no eloquence in the book; no, not even when, at Venice, he first stands in presence of the sea. Think of the feelings which the first sight of the sea must call up in the mind of a poet, and then marvel at his reserve. But if the *Italiänische Reise* does not flash out in eloquence, it is everywhere warm with the intense happiness of the writer. In Venice, for example, his enjoyment seems to have been great, as every hour the place ceased to be a *name* and became a *picture*. The canals, lagoons, narrow streets, splendid architecture, and animated crowds, were inexhaustible delights. From Venice he passed rapidly through Ferrara, Bologna, Florence, Arezzo, Perugia, Foligno, and Spoleto, reaching Rome on the 28th October.

In Rome, where he stayed four months, enjoyment and education went hand in hand. 'All the dreams of my youth I now see living before me. Everywhere I go I find an old familiar face; everything is just what I thought it, and yet everything is new. It is the same with ideas. I have gained no new idea, but the old ones have become so definite, living, and connected one with another that they may pass as new'. The riches of Rome are at first bewildering; a long residence is necessary for each object to make its due impression. Goethe lived there among some German artists: Angelica Kaufmann, for whom he had great regard, Tischbein, Moritz, and others. They respected his incognito as well as they could, although the fact of his being in Rome could not long be entirely concealed. He gained, however, the main object of his incognito, and avoided being lionized. He had not come to Italy to have his vanity tickled by the approbation of society; he came for self-culture, and resolutely pursued his purpose.

Living amid such glories of the past, treading each day the ground of the Eternal City, every breath from the seven hills must have carried to him some thought of history. 'Even Roman antiquities', he writes, 'begin to interest me. History, inscriptions, coins, which hitherto I never cared to hear about, now press upon me. Here one reads history in quite another spirit than elsewhere; not only Roman history, but world history'. Yet I do not find that he read much history, even here. Art was enough to occupy him; and for Painting he had a passion which renders his want of talent still more noticeable. He visited Churches and Galleries with steady earnestness; studied Winckelmann, and discussed critical points with the German artists. Unhappily he also wasted precious time in fruitless efforts to attain facility in drawing. These occupations, however, did not prevent his completing the versification of *Iphigenia*, which he read to the German circle, but found only Angelica who appreciated it; the others having expected something *genialisch*, something in the style of *Götz with the Iron Hand*. Nor was he much more fortunate with the Weimar circle, who, as we have already seen, preferred the prose version.

Art thus with many-sided influence allures him, but does not completely fill up his many-sided activity. Philosophic speculations give new and wondrous meanings to Nature; and the ever-pressing desire to discover the secret of vegetable forms sends him meditative through the gardens about Rome. He feels he is on the track of a law which, if discovered, will reduce to unity the manifold variety of forms. Men who have never felt the passion of discovery may rail at him for thus, in Rome, forgetting, among plants, the quarrels of the Senate and the eloquence of Cicero;

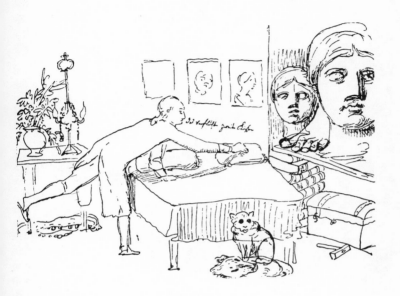

Goethe's studio in Rome

but all who have been haunted by a great idea will sympathize with him, and understand how insignificant is the existence of a thousand Ciceros in comparison with a law of Nature.

Among the few acquaintances he made, let us note that of Monti the poet, at the performance of whose tragedy, *Aristodemo*, he assisted. Through this acquaintance he was reluctantly induced to allow himself to be enrolled a member of the Arcadia*, under the title of *Megalio*, '*per causa della grandezza*, or rather *grandiosità delle mie opere*, as they express it'.

And what said Weimar to this prolonged absence of its poet? Instead of rejoicing in his intense enjoyment, instead of sympathizing with his aims, Weimar grumbled and gossiped, and was loud in disapprobation of his neglect of duties at home, while wandering among ruins and statues. Schiller, who had meanwhile come to Weimar, sends to Körner the echo of these grumblings, 'Poor Weimar! Goethe's return is uncertain, and many here look upon his eternal separation from all business as decided. While he is painting in Italy, the Vogts and Schmidts must work for him like beasts of burden. He spends in Italy for doing nothing a salary of 1800 dollars, and they, for half that sum, must do double work'. One reads such sentences from a Schiller with pain ; and there are several other passages in the correspondence which betray a jealousy of his great rival, explicable, perhaps, by the uneasy, unhappy condition in which he then struggled, but which gives his admirers pain. This jealousy we shall hereafter see openly and even fiercely avowed.

While Weimar grumbled, Weimar's Duke in truer sympathy wrote affectionately to him, releasing him from all official duties, and extending the leave of absence as long as it might be desired. Without Goethe, Weimar must indeed have been quite another place to Karl August ; but no selfishness made him desire to shorten his friend's stay in Italy. Accordingly, on the 22nd of February, Goethe quitted Rome for Naples, where he spent five weeks of hearty enjoyment. Throwing aside his incognito, he mixed freely with society, and still more freely with the people, whose happy careless *far niente* delighted him. He there made the acquaintance of Sir William Hamilton, and saw the lovely Lady Hamilton, the syren whose beauty led the noble Nelson astray. Goethe was captivated by her grace, as she moved through the mazes of the

---

* This is erroneously placed by him during his second residence in Rome. His letter to Fritz von Stein, however, gives the true date.

shawl dance she made famous. He was also captivated in quite another manner by the writings of Vico, which had been introduced to him by his acquaintance Filangierie, who spoke of the great thinker with southern enthusiasm.

'If in Rome one must *study*', he writes, 'here in Naples one can only *live*'. And he lived a manifold life : on the seashore, among the fishermen, among the people, among the nobles, under Vesuvius, on the moonlit waters, on the causeway of Pompeii, in Pausilippo,—everywhere drinking in fresh delight, everywhere feeding his fancy and experience with new pictures. Thrice did he ascend Vesuvius ; and as we shall see him during the campaign in France pursuing his scientific observations undisturbed by the cannon, so here also we observe him deterred by no perils from making the most of his opportunity. Nor is this the only noticeable trait. Vesuvius could make him forget in curiosity his personal safety, but it did not excite one sentence of poetry. His description is as quiet as if Vesuvius were Hampstead Heath.

The enthusiasm breaks out, however, here and there. At Pæstum he was in raptures with the glorious antique temples, the remains of which still speak so eloquently of what Grecian art must have been.

Pompeii, Herculaneum, and Capua interested him less than might have been anticipated. 'The Book of Nature', he says, 'is after all the only one which has in every page important meanings'. It was a book which fastened him as fairy tales fasten children.

> Here about the beach he wandered, nourishing a youth sublime
> With the fairy tales of science and the long result of Time.

Wandering thus lonely, his thoughts hurried by the music of the waves, the long-baffling, long-soliciting mystery of vegetable forms grew into clearness before him, and the typical plant was no more a vanishing conception, but a principle clearly grasped.

On the 2nd of April he reached Palermo. He stayed a fortnight among its orange trees and oleanders, given up to the exquisite sensations which, lotus-like, lulled him into forgetfulness of everything save the present. Homer here first became a living poet to him. He bought a copy of the *Odyssey*, read it with unutterable delight, and translated as he went, for the benefit of his friend Kniep. Inspired by it, he sketched the plan of *Nausikaa*, a drama in which the *Odyssey* was to be concentrated. Like so many other plans, this was never completed. The garden of Alcinous had to yield

Goethe in Italy

to the *Metamorphoses of Plants*, which tyrannously usurped his thoughts.

Palermo was the native city of Count Cagliostro, the audacious adventurer who, three years before, had made so conspicuous a figure in the affair of the Diamond Necklace. Goethe's curiosity to see the parents of this reprobate led him to visit them, under the guise of an Englishman bringing them news of their son. He has narrated the adventure at some length; but as nothing of biographical interest lies therein, I pass on with this brief indication, adding that his sympathy, always active, was excited in favour of the poor people, and he twice sent them pecuniary assistance, confessing the deceit he had practised.

He returned to Naples on the 14th of May, not without a narrow escape from shipwreck. He had taken with him the two first acts of *Tasso* (then in prose), to remodel them in verse. He found on reading them over, that they were soft and vague in expression, but otherwise needing no material alteration. After a fortnight at Naples, he once more arrived in Rome. This was on the 6th of June 1787, and he remained till the 22nd of April 1788: ten months of labour, which only an activity so unusual as his own could have made so fruitful. Much of his time was wasted in the dabbling of an amateur, striving to make himself what Nature had refused to make him. Yet it is perhaps perilous to say that with such a mind any effort was fruitless. If he did not become a painter by his studies, the studies were doubtless useful to him in other ways. Art and antiquities he studied in company with artistic friends. Rome is itself an education; and he was eager to learn. Practice of the art sharpened his perceptions. He learned perspective, drew from the model, was passionate in endeavours to succeed with landscape, and even began to model a little in clay. Angelica Kaufmann told him, that in Art he *saw* better than anyone else; and the others believed perhaps that with study he would be able to do more than see. But all his study and all his practice were vain; he never attained even the excellence of an amateur. To think of a Goethe thus obstinately cultivating a branch of art for which he had no talent makes us look with kinder appreciation on the spectacle, so frequently presented, of really able men obstinately devoting themselves to produce poetry which no cultivated mind can read; men whose culture and insight are insufficient to make them perceive in themselves the difference between aspiration and inspiration.

If some time was wasted upon efforts to become a painter, the rest was well employed. Not to mention his scientific investigations, there was abundance of work executed. *Egmont* was rewritten. The rough draft of the two first acts had been written at Frankfurt, in the year 1775 ; and a rough cast of the whole was made at Weimar, in 1782. He now took it up again, because the outbreak of troubles in the Netherlands once more brought the patriots into collision with the House of Orange. The task of rewriting was laborious, but very agreeable, and he looked with pride on the completed drama, hoping it would gratify his friends. These hopes were somewhat dashed by Herder, who—never much given to praise—would not accept Clärchen, a character which the poet thought, and truly thought, he had felicitously drawn. Besides *Egmont*, he prepared for the new edition of his works new versions of *Claudine von Villa Bella* and *Erwin und Elmire*, two comic operas. Some scenes of *Faust* were written ; also these poems : *Amor als Landschaftsmaler; Amor als Gast; Künstler's Erdenwallen; and Künstler's Apotheose*. He thus completed the last four volumes of his collected works which Göschen had undertaken to publish, and which we have seen him take to Carlsbad and to Italy, as his literary task.

The effect of his residence in Italy, especially in Rome, was manifold and deep. Foreign travel, even to unintelligent, uninquiring minds, is always of great influence, not merely by the presentation of new objects, but also, and mainly, by the withdrawal of the mind from all the intricate connexions of habit and familiarity which mask the real relations of life. This withdrawal is important, because it gives a new standing-point from which we can judge ourselves and others, and it shows how much that we have been wont to regard as essential is, in reality, little more than routine. Goethe certainly acquired clearer views with respect to himself and his career : severed from all those links of habit and routine which had bound him in Weimar, he learned in Italy to take another and a wider survey of his position. He returned home, to all appearance, a changed man. The crystallizing process which commenced in Weimar was completed in Rome. As a decisive example, we note that he there finally relinquishes his attempt to become a painter. He feels that he is born only for poetry, and during the next ten years resolves to devote himself to literature.

One result of his study of art was to reconcile his theories and his tendencies. We have noted on several occasions the objective

Angelika Kauffmann

tendency of his mind, and we now find him recognizing that
tendency as dominant in ancient art. ' Let me ', he writes to
Herder, ' express my meaning in a few words. The ancients
represented *existences*, we usually represent the *effect;* they portrayed the terrible, we terribly ; they the agreeable, we agreeably,
and so forth. Hence our exaggeration, mannerism, false graces,
and all excesses. For when we strive after effect, we never think
we can be effective enough '. This admirable sentence is as inaccurate in an historical, as it is accurate in an æsthetical sense ;
unless by the ancients we understand only Homer and some
pieces of sculpture. As a criticism of Æschylus, Euripides,
Pindar, Theocritus, Horace, Ovid, or Catullus, it is quite wide
of the truth ; indeed, it is merely the traditional fiction current
about ancient art, which vanishes on a steady gaze ; but inaccurate though it be, it serves to illustrate Goethe's theories. If
he found *that* in Italy, it was because that best assimilated with
his own tendencies, which were eminently concrete. ' People talk
of the study of the ancients ', he says somewhere, ' but what does
it mean, except that we should look at the real world, and strive
to express it, for that is what they did '. And to Eckermann he
said : ' All eras in a state of decline are subjective ; on the other
hand, all progressive eras have an objective tendency. Our
present time is retrogade, for it is subjective '. Here, in Rome, he
listens to his critical friends with a quiet smile, ' when in metaphysical discussions they held me not competent. I, being an
artist, regard this as of little moment. Indeed, I prefer that the
principle from which and through which I work should be hidden
from me '. How few Germans could say this ; how few could say
with him, ' *Ich habe nie über das Denken gedacht;* I have never
thought about Thought ' !

Leaving all such generalities, and descending once more to
biographic detail, we meet Goethe again in the toils of an unhappy
passion. How he left the Frau von Stein we have seen. Her
image accompanied him everywhere. To her he wrote constantly.
But he has before confessed that he loved her less when absent from
her, and the length of his absence now seems to have cooled his
ardour. He had been a twelvemonth away from her, when the
charms of a young Milanese, with whom he was thrown together
in Castel Gandolfo, made him forget the coldness, almost
approaching rudeness, with which hitherto he had guarded
himself from female fascination. With the rashness of a boy he

falls in love, and then learns that his mistress is already betrothed. I am unable to tell this story with any distinctness, for he was nearly eighty years old when he wrote the pretty but vague account of it in the *Italiänische Reise*, and there are no other sources come to hand. Enough that he loved, learned she was betrothed, and withdrew from her society to live down his grief. During her illness, which followed upon an unexplained quarrel with her betrothed, he was silently assiduous in attentions; but although they met after her recovery, and she was then free, I do not find him taking any steps towards replacing the husband she had lost. As may be supposed, the tone of his letters to the Frau von Stein became visibly altered: they became less confidential and communicative; a change which did not escape her.

With Herder his correspondence continues affectionate. Pleasant it is to see the enthusiasm with which he receives Herder's *Ideen*, and reads it in Rome with the warmest admiration; so different from the way in which Herder receives what *he* sends from Rome!

On the 22nd April, 1788, he turned homewards, quitting Rome with unspeakable regret, yet feeling himself equipped anew for the struggle of life. 'The chief objects of my journey', he writes to the Duke, 'were these: to free myself from the physical and moral uneasiness which rendered me almost useless, and to still the feverish thirst I felt for true art. The first of these is tolerably, the second quite achieved'. Taking *Tasso* with him to finish on his journey, he returned through Florence, Milan, Chiavenna, Lake Constance, Stuttgard, and Nürnberg, reaching Weimar on the 18th June, at ten o'clock in the evening*.

CHAPTER VI

'EGMONT' AND 'TASSO'

THERE are men whose conduct we cannot approve, but whom we love more than many whose conduct is thoroughly admirable. When severe censors point out the sins of our favourites,

---

* It will be seen from this route that he never was in Genoa; consequently the passage in Schiller's correspondence with Körner (vol. IV, p. 59), wherein a certain G. is mentioned as having an unhappy attachment to an artist's model, cannot allude to Goethe. Indeed the context, and Körner's reply, would make this plain to any critical sagacity; but many writers on Goethe are so ready to collect scandals without scrutiny, that this warning is not superfluous. Vehse, for instance, in his work on the Court of Weimar, has not the slightest misgiving about the G. meaning Goethe; it never occurs to him to inquire whether Goethe ever was in Genoa, or whether the dates of these letters do not point unmistakably in another direction.

reason may acquiesce, but the heart rebels. We make no protest, but in secret we keep our love unshaken. It is with poems as with men. The greatest favourites are not the least amenable to criticism ; the favourites with Criticism are not the darlings of the public. In saying this we do not stultify Criticism any more than Morality is stultified in our love of agreeable rebels. In both cases admitted faults are cast into the background by some energetic excellence.

Egmont is such a work. It is far, very far, from a masterpiece, but it is an universal favourite. As a tragedy, criticism makes sad work with it ; but when all is said, the reader thinks of Egmont and Clärchen, and flings criticisms to the dogs. These are the figures which remain in the memory : bright, genial, glorious creations, comparable to any to be found in the long galleries of Art.

As a Drama—*i.e.*, a work constructed with a view to representation—it wants the two fundamental requisites, viz., a collision of elemental passions, from whence the tragic interests should spring ; and the construction of its materials into the dramatic form. The first fault lies in the conception ; the second in the execution. The one is the error of the dramatic poet ; the other of the dramatist. Had Shakespeare treated this subject, he would have thrown a life and character into the mobs, and a passionate movement into the great scenes, which would have made the whole live before our eyes. But I do not think he would have surpassed Egmont and Clärchen.

The slow, languid movement of this piece, which makes the representation somewhat tedious, does not lie in the length of the speeches and scenes, so much as in the undramatic construction. Julian Schmidt has acutely remarked : 'A dramatic intention hovered before him, but he executed it in a lyrical musical style. Thus in the interview between Egmont and Orange, the two declaim against each other, instead of working on each other'. It is in certain passages dramatic, but the whole is undramatic. It approximates to the novel in dialogue.

Schiller, in his celebrated review of this work, praises the art with which the local colouring of History is preserved ; but most people would willingly exchange this historical colouring for some touches of dramatic movement. The merit, such as it is, belongs to erudition, not to poetry ; for the local colour is not, as in *Götz*, and in Scott's romances, vivid enough to place the epoch before our eyes. Schiller, on the other hand, objects to the departure from history, in making Egmont unmarried, and to the departure from heroic dignity in making him in love. Goethe of course knew that

Egmont had a wife and several children. He rejected such historical details : and although I am disposed to agree with Schiller, that by chance he deprived himself of some powerful dramatic situations, I still think he did right in making the change.

In the first place it has given us the exquisite character of Clärchen, the gem of the piece. In the next place it is dubious whether he would have treated the powerful situations with the adequate dramatic intensity. He knew and confessed that his genius was not tragic. ' I was not born for a tragic poet ', he wrote to Zelter ; ' my nature is too conciliating ; hence no really tragic situation interests me, for it is in its essence irreconcilable '.

The character of Egmont is that of a healthy, noble, heroic man ; and it is his humanity which the poet wishes to place before us. We are made spectators of a happy nature, not of great actions ; the hero, for he is one, presents himself to us in his calm strength, perfect faculties, joyous, healthy freedom of spirit, loving generous disposition ; not in the hours of strenuous conflict, not in the spasms of his strength, not in the altitude of momentary exultation, but in the quiet strength of permanent power. This presentation of the character robs the story of its dramatic collision. The tendency of Goethe's mind, which made him look upon men rather as a Naturalist than as a Dramatist, led him to prefer delineating a character to delineating a *passion;* and his biographical tendency made him delineate Egmont as more like what Wolfgang Goethe would have been under the same circumstances. This same tendency to draw from his own experience, also led him to create Clärchen. Rosenkranz, indeed, seeking to show the profound historical conception of this work, says, that the love for Clärchen was necessary ' as an indication of Egmont's sympathy with the people ' ; but the reason seems to me to have been less critical, and more biographical.

It is a sombre and a tragic episode in history which is treated in this piece. The revolution of the Netherlands was one imperiously commanded by the times ; it was the revolt of citizens against exasperating oppression ; of conscience against religious tyranny ; of the nation against a foreigner. The Duke of Alva, who thought it better the Emperor should lose the Netherlands than rule over a nation of heretics, but who was by no means willing that the Netherlands should be lost, came to replace the Duchess of Parma in the regency ; came to suppress with the sword and scaffold the rebellion of the heretics. The strong contrast of Spaniard and Hollander, of Catholic and Protestant, of despotism and liberty which this subject furnished, are all *indicated* by Goethe ; but he has not used them as powerful dramatic elements.   The characters talk, talk well, talk lengthily ; they do not act.   In the course of their conversations we are made aware of the state of things ; we do not dramatically assist at them.

Egmont opens with a scene between soldiers and citizens, shooting at a mark.   A long conversation lets us into the secret of the unquiet state of the country, and the various opinions afloat. Compare it with analogous scenes in Shakespeare, and the difference between dramatic and non-dramatic treatment will be manifest.   Here the men are puppets ; we see the author's *intention* in all they say ; in Shakespeare the men betray themselves, each with some peculiar trick of character.

The next scene is still more feeble.   The Duchess of Parma and Machiavelli are in conversation.   She asks his counsel ; he advises tolerance, which she feels to be impossible : except in the casual indication of two characters, the whole of this scene is unnecessary : and indeed Schiller, in his adaptation of this play to the stage, lopped away the character of the Duchess altogether, as an excrescence.

The free, careless, unsuspicious nature of Egmont is well contrasted with that of the suspicious Orange ; his character is painted by numerous vivid touches, and we are in one scene made aware of the danger he is in.   But the scene ends as it began, in talk.   The next scene introduces Clärchen and her unhappy lover Brackenburg.   Very pretty is this conception of his patient love, and her compassion for the love she cannot share :—

Mother. Do you send him away so soon ?

Clärchen. I long to know what is going on ; and besides—do not be angry with me, mother—his presence pains me.   I never know how I ought to behave towards him.   I have done him a wrong, and it goes to my very heart to see how deeply he feels it.   Well—it can't be helped now.

Mother. He is such a true-hearted fellow !

Clärchen. I cannot help it, I must treat him kindly.   *Often without a thought I return the gentle, loving pressure of his hand.*   I reproach myself that I am deceiving him, that I am nourishing a vain hope in his heart.   I am in a sad plight.   God knows I do not willingly deceive him. *I do not wish him to hope, yet I cannot let him despair !*

Is not that taken from the life, and is it not exquisitely touched ?

Clärchen. I loved him once, and in my soul I love him still.   I could have married him ; yet I believe I never was really and passionately in love with him.

Mother. You would have been happy with him.

Clärchen. I should have been provided for, and led a quiet life.

Mother. And it has all been trifled away by your folly.

Clärchen. I am in a strange position.   When I think how it has come about, I know it indeed, and yet I know it not.   *But I have only to look on Egmont, and all becomes clear to me;* yes, then even stranger things would seem quite natural.   Oh, what a man he is!   The provinces worship him.   And in his arms am I not the happiest being alive ?

Mother. And the future ?

Clärchen. I ask but this—does he love me ?   *Does* he love me—as if there could be a doubt !

There are reminiscences of Frederika in this simple, loving Clärchen, and in the picture of her devotion to the man so much above her.   This scene, however, though very charming, is completely without onward movement.   It is talk, not action ; and the return of Brackenburg at the close, with his despairing monologue, is not sufficient for the termination of an act.

In act second we see the citizens again ; they are becoming more unruly as events advance.   Vanzen comes to stir their rebellious feelings ; a quarrel ensues, which is quieted by the appearance of Egmont, who, on hearing their complaints, advises them to be prudent.   'Do what you can to keep the peace ; you stand in bad repute already.   Provoke not the King still further.   The power is in his hands.   An honest citizen who maintains himself industriously has everywhere as much freedom as he needs'.   He quits them, promising to do his utmost for them, advising them to stand against the new doctrines, and not to attempt to secure privileges by sedition.   The people's hero is no demagogue.   He opposes the turbulence of the mob, as he opposes the tyranny of the crown.   In the next scene we have him with his secretary ; and here are further manifested the kindness and the *insouciance* of his nature.   'It is my good fortune that I am joyous, live fast, and take everything easily.   I would not barter it for a tomb-like security.   My blood rebels against this Spanish mode of life, nor are my actions to be regulated by the cautious measures of the Court.   Do I live only to think of life ?   Shall I forgo the enjoyment of the present moment that I may secure the next, which, when it arrives, must be consumed in idle fears and anxieties ?'   This is not the language of a politician, but of a happy man. 'Take life too seriously, and what is it worth? If the morning wake us to no new joys, if the evening bring us not the hope of new pleasures, is it worth while to dress and undress? Does the sun shine on me to-day that I may reflect on yesterday? That I may endeavour to foresee and to control what can neither be foreseen nor controlled—the destiny of to-morrow?' The present is enough for him. 'The sunsteeds of Time, as if goaded by invisible spirits, bear onward the light car of Destiny. Nothing remains for us but, with calm self-possession, firmly to grasp the reins, and guide the car now right, now left, here from the precipice, there from the rock. Who knows Whither he is hasting? Who reflects from Whence he came?'

Very poetic, and tragic too, is this contrast of character with circumstance. We know the peril which threatens him. We feel that this serenity is in itself the certain cause of his destruction; and it affects us like the joyousness of Romeo, who, the moment before he hears the terrible news of Juliet's death, feels 'his bosom's lord sit lightly on its throne'. In the scene which follows between Egmont and Orange, there is a fine argumentative exposition of their separate views of the state of affairs; Orange warns him to fly while there is yet safety; but he sees that flight will hasten civil war, and he remains.

Act the third once more brings the Duchess and Machiavelli before us, and once more they talk about the troubles of the time. The scene changes to Clärchen's house, and we are spectators of that exquisite interview which Scott has borrowed in *Kenilworth*, where Leicester appears to Amy Robsart in all his princely splendour. Beautiful as this scene is, it is not enough to constitute one act of a drama, especially the *third* act; for nothing is done in it, nothing is indicated even in the development of the story which had not been indicated before; the action stands still that we may see childish delight, womanly love, and manly tenderness.

The poetic reader, captivated by this scene, will be impatient at the criticism which espies a fault in it, and will declare such a picture infinitely superior to any dramatic effect. 'What pedantry', he will exclaim, 'to talk of technical demands in presence of a scene like this!' and with a lofty wave of the hand dismiss the critic into contempt. Nevertheless, the critic is forced by his office to consider what are the technical demands. If the poet has attempted a drama, he must be tried by dramatic standards. However much we may delight in the picture Goethe has presented in this third act, we cannot but feel that Shakespeare, while giving the picture, would have made it subservient to the progress and development of the piece; for Shakespeare was not only a poet, he was also a dramatic poet.

Act the fourth again shows us citizens talking about the times, which grew more and more ominous. In the next scene Alva, the terrible Alva, appears, having laid all his plans. Orange has fled, but Egmont comes. A long discussion, very argumentative but utterly undramatic, between Alva and Egmont, is concluded by the arrest of the latter.

Act the fifth shows us Clärchen in the streets trying to rouse Brackenburg and the citizens to revolt and to the rescue of Egmont. There is great animation in this scene, wherein love raises the simple girl into the heroine. The citizens are alarmed, and dread to hear Egmont named:

Clärchen. Stay! stay! Shrink not away at the sound of his name, to meet whom ye were wont to press forward so joyously! When rumour announced his approach, when the cry arose, 'Egmont comes! he comes from Ghent!' then happy were they who dwelt in the streets through which he was to pass. And when the neighing of his steed was heard, did not every one throw aside his work, while a ray of hope and joy, like a sunbeam from his countenance, stole over the toil-worn faces which peered from every window. Then as ye stood in doorways ye would lift up your children and pointing to him exclaim, 'See! that is Egmont! he who towers above the rest!' 'Tis from him ye must look for better times than those your poor fathers have known!'

Clärchen, unable to rouse the citizens, is led home by Brackenburg. The scene changes to Egmont's prison, where he soliloquizes on his fate; the scene again changes, and shows us Clärchen waiting with sickly impatience for Brackenburg to come and bring her the news. He comes; tells her Egmont is to die; she takes poison, and Brackenburg, in despair, resolves also to die. The final scene is very weak and very long. Egmont has an interview with Alva's son, whom he tries to persuade into aiding him to escape; failing in this, he goes to sleep on a couch, and Clärchen appears in a vision as the figure of Liberty. She extends to him a laurel crown. He wakes—to find the prison filled with soldiers who lead him to execution.

There are great inequalities in this work, and some disparities of style. It was written at three different periods of his life; and although, when once completed, a work may benefit by careful revision extending over many years, it will inevitably suffer from fragmentary composition; the delay which favours revision is fatal to composition. A work of Art should be completed before the paint has had time to dry; otherwise the changes brought by time in the development of the artist's mind will make themselves felt in the heterogeneous structure of the work. *Egmont* was conceived in the period when Goethe was under the influence of Shakespeare; it was mainly executed in the period when he had taken a classical direction. It wants the stormy life of *Götz* and the calm beauty of *Iphigenia*. Schiller thought the close was too much in the opera style; and Gervinus thinks that preoccupation with the opera, which Goethe at this period was led into by his friendly efforts to assist Kayser, has given the whole work an operatic turn. I confess I do not detect this; but I see a decided deficiency in dramatic construction, which is also to be seen in all his later works; and that he really did not know what the drama properly required, to *be* a drama as well as a poem, we shall see clearly illustrated in a future chapter. Nevertheless, I end as I began with saying that find what faults you will with *Egmont*, it still remains one of those general favourites against which criticism is powerless.

Still less satisfactory from the dramatic point of view is *Tasso;* of which we may say what Johnson says of *Comus*, 'it is a series of faultless lines, but no drama'. Indeed, for the full enjoyment of this exquisite poem, it is necessary that the reader should approach it as he approaches *Comus*, or *Manfred*, or *Philip von Artevelde*, with no expectations of finding in it the qualities of *Othello*, or *Wallenstein*. It has a charm which few can resist; but it wants all the requisites of stage representation. There is scarcely any action; and what little there is only serves as a vehicle of struggle which goes on in Tasso's mind, instead of the struggle and collision of two minds. Even the dramatic elements of love and madness are not dramatically treated. We feel their presence in Tasso's mind; we never see their flaming energy fusing the heterogeneous materials of circumstance into fiery unity; we are thus spectators of a disease, not of an acted story. Hence the beauty of this work lies in its poetry, and cannot be reproduced in a translation.

The moment chosen by Goethe is when Tasso having just completed his 'Jerusalem Delivered', gives unmistakable signs of the unhappy passion and unhappy malady which have made his biography one of the saddest in the sad list of 'mighty poets in their misery dead'. German critics have affirmed that the piece is saturated with historical facts and local colour. But it is clear that great liberties have been taken both with history and local colour. Indeed, there was too obvious a superficial resemblance between the position of Tasso at the Court of Ferrara and Goethe at the Court of Weimar not to make these liberties necessary. Had Goethe painted the actual relation between Tasso and Alphonso, the public might have read between the lines reflections on Karl August. Moreover, it is difficult to deny the truth of Madame de Stael's remark, that 'les couleurs du Midi ne sont pas assez prononcées'. The tone of the work is German throughout, and would considerably have surprised an Italian of the Court of Ferrara.

Tasso was finally completed shortly after the rupture with the Frau von Stein, presently to be related ; but I have noticed it here, as the most convenient place. It is in truth to be regarded as one of the products of his early Weimar years, having been merely versified in Italy, and after his return home.

CHAPTER VII

RETURN HOME

GOETHE came back from Italy greatly enriched, but by no means satisfied. The very wealth he had accumulated embarrassed him, by the new problems it presented, and the new horizons it revealed :

> For all experience is an arch wherethrough
> Gleams that untravelled world, whose margin fades
> For ever and for ever as we move.

He had in Rome become aware that a whole life of study would scarcely suffice to still the craving hunger for knowledge ; and he left Italy with deep regret. The return home was thus, in itself, a grief; the arrival was still more painful. Every one will understand this, who has lived for many months away from the circle of old habits and old acquaintances, feeling in the new world a larger existence more consonant with his nature and his aims ; and has then returned once more to the old circle, to find it unchanged,— pursuing its old paths, moved by the old impulses, guided by the old lights,—so that he feels himself a *stranger*. To return to a great capital, after such an absence, is to feel ill at ease ; but to return from Italy to Weimar !　If we, on entering London, after a residence abroad, find the same interests occupying our friends which occupied them when we left, the same family gossip, the same books talked about, the same placards loud upon the walls of the unchanging streets, the world seeming to have stood still while we have lived through so much : what must Goethe have felt coming from Italy, with his soul filled with new experience and new ideas, on observing the quiet unchanged Weimar?　No one seemed to understand him ; no one sympathized in his enthusiasm, or in his regrets.　They found him changed.　He found them moving in the same dull round, like blind horses in a mill.

First, let us note that he came back resolved to dedicate his life to Art and Science, and no more to waste efforts in the laborious duties of office.　From Rome he had thus written to Karl August : ‘ How grateful am I to you for having given me this priceless leisure !　My mind having from youth upwards had this bent, I should never have been at ease until I had reached this end.　My relation to affairs sprang out of my personal relation to you ; now let a new relation, after so many years, spring from the former.　I can truly say, that in the solitude of these eighteen months I have found my own self again.　But as what?　As an Artist !　What else I may be, you will be able to judge and use.　You have shown throughout your life that princely knowledge of what men are, and what they are useful for ; and this knowledge has gone on increasing, as your letters clearly prove to me : to that knowledge I gladly submit myself.　Ask my aid in that Symphony which you mean to play, and I will at all times gladly and honestly give you my advice.　Let me fulfil the whole measure of my existence at your side, then will my powers, like a new-opened and purified spring, easily be directed hither and thither.　Already I see what this journey has done for me, how it has clarified and brightened my existence.　As you have hitherto borne with me, so care for me in future ; you do me more good than I can do myself, more than I can claim.　I have seen a large and beautiful bit of the world, and the result is, that I wish only to live with you and yours. Yes, I shall become more to you than I have been before, if you let me do what I only can do, and leave the rest to others.　Your sentiments for me, as expressed in your letters, are so beautiful, so honourable to me, that they make me blush,—that I can only say : Lord, here am I, do with thy servant as seemeth good unto thee ’.

The wise Duke answered this appeal nobly. He released his friend from the Presidency of the Chamber, and from the direction of the War Department, but kept a distinct place for him in the Council, 'whenever his other affairs allowed him to attend'. The poet remained the adviser of his Prince, but was relieved from the more onerous duties of office. The direction of the Mines, and of all Scientific and Artistic Institutions, he retained ; among them that of the Theatre.

It was generally found that he had grown colder in his manners since his Italian journey. Indeed, the process of crystallization had rapidly advanced ; and beyond this effect of development, which would have taken place had he never left Weimar, there was the further addition of his feeling himself at a different standing-point from those around him. The less they understood him, the more he drew within himself. Those who understood him, Moritz, Meyer, the Duke and Herder, found no cause of complaint.

During the first few weeks he was of course constantly at Court. Thus the *Hof-Courier Buch* tells us that the day after his arrival he dined at Court. This was the 19th of June. Again on the 20th, 22nd, 25th, 27th, 28th, 29th, 30th. In July, on the 1st, 2nd, 4th, 5th, 6th, 7th, 8th, 11th, 12th, 14th, 15th, 16th, 17th, 18th, 19th, 20th, and 21st, and so on almost uninterruptedly till September. His official release made the bond of friendship stronger. Besides, every one was naturally anxious to hear about his travels, and he was delighted to talk of them.

But if Weimar complained of the change, to which it soon grew accustomed, there was one who had deeper cause of complaint, and whose nature was not strong enough to bear it—the Frau von Stein. Absence had cooled the ardour of his passion. In Rome, to the negative influence of absence, was added the positive influence of a new love. He returned to Weimar, still grateful to her for the happiness she had given him, still feeling for her the affection which no conduct of hers could destroy, and which warmed his heart towards her to the last ; but he returned also with little of the passion she had for ten years inspired ; he returned with a full conviction that he had outlived it. Nor did her presence serve to rekindle the smouldering embers. Charlotte von Stein was now five-and-forty. It is easy to imagine how much he must have been struck with the change in her. Had he never left her side, this change would have approached with gradual steps, stealthily escaping observation ; but the many months' absence removed a veil from his eyes. She was five-and-forty to him, as to others. In this perilous position she adopted the very worst course. She found him changed, and told him so, in a way which made him feel more sharply the change in her. She thought him cold, and her resource was—reproaches. The resource was more feminine than felicitous. Instead of sympathizing with him in his sorrow at leaving Italy, she felt the regret as an offence ; and perhaps it was; but a truer, nobler nature would surely have known how to merge its own pain in sympathy with the pain of one beloved. He regretted Italy ; she was not a compensation to him ; she saw this, and her self-love suffered. The coquette who had so long held him captive, now saw the captive freed from her chains. It was a trying moment. But even in the worst aspect of the position, there was that which a worthy nature would have regarded as no small consolation : she might still be his dearest friend ; and the friendship of such a man was worth more than the love of another. But this was not to be.

Before the final rupture, he went with her to Rudolstadt, and there for the first time spoke with Schiller, who thus writes to Körner, 12th September, 1788: 'At last I can tell you about Goethe, and satisfy your curiosity. The first sight of him was by no means what I had been led to expect. He is of middle stature, holds himself stiffly and walks stiffly ; his countenance is not open, but his eye very full of expression, lively, and one hangs with delight on his glances. With much seriousness his mien has nevertheless much goodness and benevolence. He is brown complexioned, and seemed to me older in appearance than his years. His voice is very agreeable, his narrations are flowing, animated, and full of spirit ; one listens with pleasure ; and when he is in good humour, as was the case this time, he talks willingly and with great interest. We soon made acquaintance, and without the slightest effort ; the circle, indeed, was too large, and every one too jealous of him, for me to speak much with him alone, or on any but general topics. . . . . On the whole, I must say that my great idea of him is not lessened by this personal acquaintance ; but I doubt whether we shall ever become intimate. Much that to me is now of great interest, he has already lived through ; he is, less in years than in experience and self-culture, so far beyond me that we can never meet on the way ; and his whole being is originally different from mine, his world is not my world, our conceptions are radically different. Time will show '.

Could he have looked into Goethe's soul he would have seen there was a wider gulf between them than he imagined. In scarcely any other instance was so great a friendship ever formed between men who at first seemed more opposed to each other. At this moment Goethe was peculiarly ill-disposed towards any friendship with Schiller, for he saw in him the powerful writer who had corrupted and misled the nation. He has told us how pained he was on his return from Italy to find Germany jubilant over Heinse's *Ardinghello*, and Schiller's *Robbers*, and *Fiesco*. He had pushed far from him, and for ever, the whole *Sturm und Drang* creed ; he had outgrown that tendency, and learned to hate his own works which sprang from it ; in Italy he had taken a new direction, hoping to make the nation follow him in this higher region, as it had followed him before. But while he advanced, the nation stood still ; he 'passed it like a ship at sea'. Instead of following him, the public followed his most extravagant imitators. He hoped to enchant men with the calm ideal beauty of an *Iphigenia*, and the sunny heroism of an *Egmont*; and found every one enraptured with *Ardinghello* and *Karl Moor*. His publisher had to complain that the new edition of his works, on which so much time and pains had been bestowed, went off very slowly, while the highly spiced works of his rivals were bought by thousands.

> Schüler macht sich der Schwärmer genug, und rühret die Menge
> Wenn der vernünftige Mann einzelne Liebende zählt.
> Wunderthätige Bilder sind meist nur schlechte Gemälde,
> Werke des Geists und der Kunst sind für den Pöbel nicht da*.

In this frame of mind it is natural that he should keep aloof from Schiller, and withstand the various efforts made to bring about an intimacy. ' To be much with Goethe ', Schiller writes in the February following, ' would make me unhappy ; with his nearest friends he has no moments of overflowingness : I believe, indeed, he is an egoist, in an unusual degree. He has the talent of conquering men, and of binding them by small as well as great attentions : but he always knows how to hold himself free. He makes his existence benevolently felt, but only like a god, without giving himself : this seems to me a consequent and well-planned conduct, which is calculated to ensure the highest enjoyment of

---

* Dreamers make scholars enough, they flatter the weakness of thousands,
  While the intelligent man counts his disciples by tens.
  Poor indeed are the pictures famous for miracle-working :
  Art in its loftiest forms ne'er can be prized by the mob.

self-love. . . . Thereby is he hateful to me, although I love his genius from my heart, and think greatly of him. . . . It is quite a peculiar mixture of love and hatred he has awakened in me, a feeling akin to that which Brutus and Cassius must have had for Cæsar. I could kill his spirit, and then love him again from my heart'. These sentences read very strangely now we know how Schiller came to love and reverence the man whom he here so profoundly misunderstands, and whom he judges thus from the surface. But they are interesting sentences in many respects; in none more so than in showing that if he, on nearer acquaintance, came to love the noble nature of his great rival, it is a proof that he had seen how superficial had been his first judgment. Let the reader who has been led to think harshly of Goethe, from one cause or another, take this into consideration, and ask himself whether he too, on better knowledge, might not alter his opinion.

'With Goethe', so runs another letter, 'I will not compare myself, when he puts forth his whole strength. He has far more genius than I have, and greater wealth of knowledge, a more accurate sensuous perception (*eine sichere Sinnlichkeit*), and to all these he adds an artistic taste, cultivated and sharpened by knowledge of all works of Art'. But with this acknowledgment of superiority there was coupled an unpleasant feeling of *envy* at Goethe's happier lot, a feeling which his own unhappy position renders very explicable. 'I will let you see into my heart', he writes to Körner. '*Once for all, this man, this Goethe, stands in my way*, and recalls to me so often that fate has dealt hardly with me. How lightly is *his* genius borne by his fate; and how must *I* even to this moment struggle!'

Fate had indeed treated them very differently. Throughout Schiller's correspondence we are pained by the sight of sordid cares, and anxious struggles for existence. He is in bad health, in difficult circumstances. We see him forced to make literature a trade; and it is a bad one. We see him anxious to do hack-work, and translations, for a few dollars, quite cheered by the prospect of getting such work; nay, glad to farm it out to other writers, who will do it for less than he receives. We see him animated with high aspirations, and depressed by cares. He too is struggling through the rebellious epoch of youth, but has not yet attained the clearness of manhood; and no external aids come to help him through the struggle. Goethe, on the contrary, never knew such cares. All his life he had been shielded from the depressing influence of poverty; and now he has leisure, affluence, renown, social position—little from *without* to make him unhappy. When Schiller therefore thought of all this, he must have felt that Fate had been a niggard stepmother to him, as she had been a lavish mother to his rival.

Yet Goethe had his sorrows, too, though not of the same kind. He bore within him the flame of genius, a flame which consumes while it irradiates. His struggles were with himself, and not with circumstances. He felt himself a stranger in the land. Few understood his language ; none understood his aims. He withdrew into himself.

There is one point which must be noticed in this position of the two poets, namely, that however great Schiller may be now esteemed, and was esteemed by Goethe after awhile, he was not at this moment regarded with anything beyond the feeling usually felt for a rising young author. His early works had indeed a wide popularity ; but so had the works of Klinger, Maler Müller, Lenz, Kotzebue, and others, who never conquered the great critics ; and Schiller was so unrecognized at this time that, on coming to Weimar, he complains, with surprise as much as with offended self-love, that Herder seemed to know nothing of him beyond his name, not having apparently read one of his works. And Goethe, in the official paper which he drew up recommending Schiller to the Jena professorship, speaks of him as 'a Herr Friedrich Schiller, author of an historical work on the Netherlands'. So that not only was Schiller's tendency antipathetic to all Goethe then prized, he was not even in that position which commands the respect of antagonists ; and Goethe considered Art too profoundly important in the development of mankind, for differences of tendency to be overlooked as unimportant.

CHAPTER VIII

CHRISTIANE VULPIUS

ONE day early in July, 1788, Goethe, walking in the much-loved park, was accosted by a fresh, young, bright-looking girl, who, with many reverences, handed him a petition. He looked into the bright eyes of the petitioner, and then, in a conciliated mood, looked at the petition, which entreated the great poet to exert his

influence to procure a post for a young author, then living at Jena
by the translation of French and Italian stories. This young
author was Vulpius, whose *Rinaldo Rinaldini* has doubtless made
some of my readers shudder in their youth. His robber romances
were at one time very popular ; but his name is now only rescued
from oblivion, because he was the brother of that Christiane who
handed the petition to Goethe, and who thus took the first step on
the path which led to their marriage. Christiane is on many
accounts an interesting figure to those who are interested in the
biography of Goethe ; and the love she excited, no less than the
devotedness with which for eight-and-twenty years she served him,
deserve a more tender memory than has befallen her.

Her father was one of those wretched beings whose drunkenness
slowly but surely brings a whole family to want. He would sometimes sell the coat off his back for drink. When his children grew
up, they contrived to get away from him, and to support themselves : the son by literature, the daughters by making artificial
flowers*, woollen work, etc. It is usually said that Christiane was
utterly uneducated, and the epigrammatic pen glibly records that
'Goethe married his servant'. She never was his servant. Nor
was she uneducated. Her social position indeed was very humble,
as the foregoing indications suggest : but that she was not uneducated is plainly seen in the facts, of which there can be no
doubt, namely, that for her were written the *Roman Elegies*, and
the *Metamorphoses of Plants ;* and that in her company Goethe
pursued his optical and botanical researches. How much she
understood of these researches we cannot know : but it is certain
that, unless she had shown a lively comprehension, he would never
have persisted in talking of them to her. Their time, he says, was
not spent only in caresses, but also in rational talk :

> Wird doch nicht immer geküsst, es wird vernünftig gesprochen.

This is decisive. Throughout his varied correspondence we always
see him presenting different subjects to different minds, treating of
topics in which his correspondents are interested, not dragging forward topics which merely interest *him ;* and among the wide range
of subjects he had mastered, there were many upon which he
might have conversed with Christiane, in preference to science, had
she shown any want of comprehension of scientific phenomena.
There is one of the *Elegies*, the eighth, which in six lines gives

---

* This detail will give the reader a clue to the poem *Der neue Pausias*.

us a distinct idea of the sort of cleverness and the sort of beauty which she possessed ; a cleverness not of the kind recognized by schoolmasters, because it does not display itself in aptitude for book-learning ; a beauty not of the kind recognized by conventional taste, because it wants the conventional regularity of feature.

> Wenn du mir sagst, du habest als Kind, Geliebte, den Menschen
> Nicht gefallen, und dich habe die Mutter verschmäht,
> Bis du grösser geworden und still dich entwickelt ; ich glaub' es :
> Gerne denk' ich mir dich als ein besonderes Kind.
> Fehlet Bildung und Farbe doch auch der Blüthe des Weinstocks,
> Wenn die Beere, gereift, Menschen und Götter entzückt*.

Surely the poet's word is to be taken in such a case?

While, however, rectifying a general error, let me not fall into the opposite extreme. Christiane had her charm ; but she was not a highly gifted woman. She was not a Frau von Stein, capable of being the companion and the sharer of his highest aspirations. Quick motherwit, a lively spirit, a loving heart, and great aptitude for domestic duties, she undoubtedly possessed : she was gay, enjoying, fond of pleasures even to excess, and—as may be read in the poems which she inspired—was less the mistress of his Mind than of his Affections. Her golden-brown locks, laughing eyes, ruddy cheeks, kiss-provoking lips, small and gracefully rounded figure, gave her 'the appearance of a young Dionysos'†. Her *naïveté*, gaiety and enjoying temperament, completely fascinated Goethe, who recognized in her one of those free, healthy specimens of Nature which education had not distorted with artifice. She was like a child of the sensuous Italy he had just quitted with so much regret ; and there are few poems in any language which approach the passionate gratitude of those in which he recalls the happiness she gave him.

Why did he not marry her at once? His dread of marriage has already been shown ; and to this abstract dread there must be added the great disparity of station : a disparity so great that not only did it make the liaison scandalous, it made Christiane herself reject the offer of marriage. Stahr reports that persons now living have heard her declare that it was her own fault her marriage was so long delayed ; and certain it is that when—Christmas 1789—

---

* 'When you tell me, dearest, that as a child you were not admired, and even your mother scorned you, till you grew up and silently developed yourself, I can quite believe it. I can readily imagine you as a peculiar child. If the blossoms of the vine are wanting in colour and form, the grapes once ripe are the delight of gods and men'.

† So says Madame Schopenhauer, *not* a prejudiced witness.

Christiane Vulpius. Drawing by Goethe

she bore him a child (August von Goethe, to whom the Duke stood godfather), he took her with her mother and sister to live in his house, and always regarded the connexion as a marriage. But however he may have regarded it, Public Opinion has not forgiven this defiance of social laws. The world blamed him loudly ; even his admirers cannot think of the connexion without pain. 'The Nation', says Schäfer, 'has never forgiven its greatest poet for this rupture with Law and Custom ; nothing has stood so much in the way of a right appreciation of his moral character, nothing has created more false judgments on the tendency of his writings than his half-marriage'.

But let us be just. While no one can refrain from deploring that Goethe, so eminently needing a pure domestic life, should not have found a wife whom he could avow, one who would in all senses have been a wife to him, the mistress of his house, the companion of his life ; on the other hand, no one who knows the whole circumstances can refrain from confessing that there was also a bright side to this dark episode. Having indicated the dark side, and especially its social effect, we have to consider what happiness it brought him at a time when he was most lonely, most unhappy. It gave him the joys of paternity, for which his heart yearned. It gave him a faithful and devoted affection. It gave him one to look after his domestic existence, and it gave him a peace in that existence which hitherto he had sought in vain.

> Oftmals hab' ich geirrt, und habe mich wieder gefunden,
> Aber glücklicher nie ; nun ist diess Mädchen mein Glück !
> Ist auch dieses ein Irrthum, so schont mich, ihr klügeren Götter,
> Und benehmt mir ihn erst drüben am kalten Gestad*.

There is a letter still extant (unpublished) written ten years after their first acquaintance, in which, like a passionate lover, he regrets not having taken something of hers on his journey—even her slipper—that he might feel less lonely !† To have excited such love, Christiane must have been a very different woman from that which it is the fashion in Germany to describe her as being. In conclusion, let it be added that his mother not only expressed herself perfectly satisfied with his choice, received

---

* 'Often have I erred, and always found the path again, but never found myself happier : now in this maiden lies my happiness ! If this, too, is an error, O spare me the knowledge, ye gods, and let me only discover it beyond the grave '.

† My accomplished German translator here adds some passages from Goethe's correspondence with Herder, which indicate the fervour of the passion Christiane excited and sustained.

Christiane as a daughter, and wrote affectionately to her, but refused to listen to the officious meddlers who tried to convince her of the scandal which the connexion occasioned.

The *Roman Elegies* are doubly interesting : first, as expressions of his feelings ; secondly, as perhaps the most perfect poems of the kind in all literature. In them we see how the journey to Italy had saturated his mind with the spirit of ancient Art. Yet while reproducing the past with matchless felicity, he is, at the same time, thoroughly *original*. Nowhere in Greek or Roman literature do I remember this union of great thoughts, giving grandeur to the verse, with individual passion, giving it intensity. They are not simply elegies—outpourings of individual feelings— they are *Roman* elegies, and mirror a world. In modern poems all classical recollections and allusions are for the most part frigid and laboured, springing from study ; not the spontaneous forms of poetic expression. In these *Roman Elegies* the classic world lives again ; indeed at times one can almost say he is more antique than the ancients*. The thirteenth elegy, *Amor der Schalk*, for example, is in Anacreon's manner, but far above anything we have of Anacreon. Antique also is the direct un- misgiving sensuousness of the poet, and his unperplexed earnest- ness of passion, an earnestness which does not absorb the other activities of his nature, but allies itself with them. Thus in the fifth elegy there is a picture of the most vivid sensuousness, aiding, not thwarting, the poetical activity. What a poem, what a world of emotion and thought these lines suggest :

> Ueberfällt sie der Schlaf, lieg' ich und denke mir viel.
> Oftmals hab' ich auch schon in ihren Armen gedichtet,
> Und des Hexameters Mass leise mit fingernder Hand
> Ihr auf dem Rücken gezählt. Sie athmet in lieblichem Schlummer,
> Und es durchglühet ihr Hauch mir bis ins Tiefste die Brust.

This picture of the poet murmuring verses while his beloved sleeps softly by his side, warmed by her breath, yet with fingering hand marking the rhythm of verse, is typical of the whole story of Goethe's love. Passion fed, it never stifled the flame of his genius. He enjoyed ; but in the brief pauses of enjoyment the presence of high aims was felt.

The blending of individual passion with classic forms, making

---

* Schlegel happily says of them, 'they enrich Roman poetry with German poems'. *Charakteristiken und Kritiken*, II, p. 199.

Christiane sleeping.   Drawing by Goethe

the past live again in the feeling of the present, may be illustrated
by the following example :

> Lass dich, Geliebte, nicht reu'n, dass du mir so schnell dich ergeben !
> Glaub' es, ich denke nicht frech, denke nicht niedrig von dir.
> Vielfach wirken die Pfeile des Amor : einige ritzen
> Und vom schleichenden Gift kranket auf Jahre das Herz.
> Aber mächtig befiedert, mit frisch geschliffener Schärfe,
> Dringen die andern ins Mark, zünden behende das Blut.'
> *In der heroischen Zeit, da Götter und Göttinnen liebten,*
> *Folgte Begierde dem Blick, folgte Genuss der Begier.*
> Glaubst du, es habe sich lange die Göttin der Liebe besonnen,
> Als in Idäischen Hain einst ihr Anchises gefiel ?
> *Hätte Luna gesäumt, den schönen Schläfer zu küssen.*
> *O, so hätt' ihn geschwind, neidend, Aurora geweckt*.*

Many of the finest passages are as antique in their directness of
expression as in other qualities. He said justly to Eckermann,
that Metre is a peculiar veil which clothes the nakedness of
expression, and makes that admissible which in prose would be
offensive, and which even in another lighter kind of Metre would
be offensive.   In the *Don Juan* stanza he says the material of the
Roman Elegies would be indelicate.   On the question how far a
poet is justified in disregarding the conventional proprieties of his
age in the portrayal of feeling, let Schiller be heard : 'The
laws of propriety are foreign to innocent nature ; only the experience of corruption has given origin to them.   But as soon as
that corruption has taken place, and natural innocence has
vanished from manners, the laws of propriety are sacred, and
moral feeling will not offend them.   They have the same validity
in an artificial world as the laws of nature have in a world of
innocence.   But the very thing which constitutes the poet is that
he banishes from himself everything which reminds him of an
artificial world, that he may restore Nature in her primitive

---

* In Sir Theodore Martin's volume of privately printed poems and translations, the
passage in the text is thus rendered :—
> Blush not, my love, at the thought, thou yieldest so soon to my passion ;
> Trust me, I think it no shame—think it no vileness in thee !
> Shafts from the quiver of Amor have manifold consequence.   Some scratch,
> And the heart sickens for years with the insidious bane :
> Others draw home to the head, full plumed, and cruelly pointed,
> Pierce to the marrow, and straight kindle the blood into flame.
> In the heroical age, when goddess and god were the lovers,
> Scarce did they look but they long'd, longing they rush'd to enjoy.
> Think'st thou Love's goddess hung back, when deep in the forest of Ida,
> She, with a thrill of delight, first her Anchises beheld ?
> Coyly had Luna delayed to fondle the beautiful sleeper,
> Soon had Aurora in spite waken'd the boy from his dream.

simplicity. And if he has done this, he is thereby absolved from all laws by which a perverted heart seeks security against itself. He is pure, he is innocent, and whatever is permitted to innocent nature is permitted also to him. If thou who readest and hearest him art no longer innocent, and if thou canst not even momentarily become so by his purifying presence, it is thy *misfortune* and not his ; thou forsakest him, he did not sing for thee '.

Had Goethe written nothing but the *Roman Elegies*, he would hold a first place among German poets. These elegies are, moreover, scarcely less interesting in their biographical significance. They speak plainly of the effect of Italy upon his mind. They speak eloquently of his love for Christiane. There are other tributes to her charms, and to the happiness she gave him ; but were there no other tributes, these would suffice to show the injustice of the opinion which the malicious tongues of Weimar have thrown into currency respecting her ; opinions, indeed, which received some countenance from her subsequent life, when she had lost youth and beauty, and when the faults of her nature had acquired painful prominence. It is Goethe's misfortune with posterity that he is mostly present to our minds as the calm old man, seldom as the glorious youth. The majority of busts, portraits, and biographic details, are of the late period of his career. In like manner, it is the misfortune of his wife that testimonies about her come mostly from those who only saw her when the grace and charm of youth had given place to a coarse and corpulent age. But the biographer's task is to ascertain by diligent inquiry what is the truth at the various epochs of a career, not limiting himself to one epoch ; and as I have taken great pains to represent the young Goethe, so also have I tried to rescue the young Christiane from the falsifications of gossip, and the misrepresentations derived from judging her youth by her old age.

It has already been intimated that Weimar was loud in disapprobation of this new liaison ; although it had uttered no word against the liaison with the Frau von Stein. The great offence seems to have been his choosing one beneath him in rank. A chorus of indignation rose. It produced the final rupture between him and the Frau von Stein. Here is a letter wherein he answers her reproaches : ' If you could but listen to me, I would gladly tell you, that although your reproaches pain me at the moment, they leave no trace of anger in my heart against you. Moreover, I can set them right. If you have much to bear from me, it is but just that

I should also bear with you.   It is much better that we should come
to a friendly understanding, than strive constantly to come to unanimity, and when that striving fails, separate again.   It is impossible to clear myself with you, because, on every reckoning, I must
remain your debtor.   But if we consider how much we have all to
bear from each other, we shall still, dearest, forgive one another.
Farewell, and love—me.   On the first opportunity you shall hear
more about the pretty secrets '.

   The pretty secrets here alluded to are probably about Christiane.
The letter produced a reply, which called from him the following :
' Thanks for thy letter, although it has troubled me in more ways
than one.   I delayed answering it, because it is difficult in such
cases to be sincere, and not give pain. . . .   What I left behind in
Italy I will not now repeat ; you have already repulsed my confidence on that subject in a manner sufficiently unfriendly.   When I
first returned, you were, unhappily, in a peculiar mood, and I
honestly confess the way in which you received me was excessively
painful.   I saw Herder and the Duchess depart for Italy ; they
urgently offered me a place in their carriage, but I stayed behind
for the sake of that friend for whom I had returned ; and this, too,
was at a moment when I was incessantly and sarcastically told that
I might as well have remained in Italy,—that I had no sympathy,
and so on.   And all this before there was a hint of the liaison
which now seems to offend you so much.   And what is this liaison?
Who is beggared by it ?   Who makes any claims on the feelings I
give the poor creature ?   Who, on the hours I pass in her society ?
Ask Fritz, ask the Herders, ask any one who knows me intimately,
whether I am less sympathetic, less active, or less friendly than
before ?   Whether I do not rather now, for the first time, rightly
belong to them and to society ?   And it must be by a miracle
indeed if I should have forgotten the best, the deepest relation of
all, that, namely, to thee.   How vividly I have felt my disposition
to be the same, whenever it has happened that we have talked on
some interesting subject !   But I freely confess that the manner in
which you have treated me hitherto is not to be endured.   When
I was inclined to talk, you shut my lips ; when I was communicative about Italy, you complained of my indifference ; when I was
active for my friends, you reproached me with coldness and neglect
of you.   You criticized every look, blamed every movement, and
constantly made me feel ill at ease.   How then can openness and
confidence continue, while you repulse me with predetermined ill

humour? I would add more, did I not fear that in your present mood it might irritate you more than it would tend to reconcile us. Unhappily you have long despised my advice with reference to coffee, and have adopted a regimen eminently injurious to your health. As if it were not already difficult enough to conquer certain moral impressions, you strengthen your hypochondria by physical aids, the evil influence of which you have long acknowledged, and out of love to me had for some time relinquished, to the obvious improvement of your health. May the present journey do you good! I do not quite relinquish the hope that you will again learn to know me. Farewell. Fritz is happy, and visits me constantly'.

Over this letter she wrote *O!!!* It was a terrible letter to receive, and she doubtless was indignant at what she conceived to be its injustice. She had been 'misunderstood'. People always *are* misunderstood in such cases. They are blameless, but their conduct is misrepresented. They are conscious of having felt precisely the reverse of what is attributed to them; and they wonder that they are not known better.

Shifting our position, and reading the letter less from the Frau von Stein's point of view, than from the point of view of by-standers, we read in it the amplest justification of the writer. We see how intensely unamiable must have been her manner of receiving him. Her subsequent conduct but too well confirms this impression. She showed herself worse than unamiable. The final passage of the letter alluding to her hypochondria being aggravated by coffee and bad diet, reads like an impertinence; but those who know how serious he was in his objections to the use of coffee, and how clearly he perceived the influence of physical well-being on moral health, will not be surprised at it. At any rate, whatever accents of harshness may be heard in this letter, there is no mistaking the pain in it; and a week after, he writes the following:

'It is not easy for me to write a letter with more pain than the one I last wrote to thee, which was probably as unpleasant for thee to read as for me to write. Meanwhile at least the lips have been opened, and I hope that never may we henceforth keep them closed against each other. I have had no greater happiness than my confidence in thee, which formerly was unlimited, and since I have been unable to use it, I have become another man, and must in future still more become so. I do not complain of my present condition, I have managed to make myself at home in it, and hope

to keep so, although the climate once more affects me, and will
sooner or later make me unfit for much that is good.   But when I
think of the damp summer and severe winter, and of the combination of outward circumstances which makes existence here difficult,
I know not which way to turn*.   I say this as much in relation to
thee as to myself, and assure thee that it pains me infinitely to give
thee pain under such circumstances.   I will say nothing in my own
excuse.   But I would beg thee to help me so that the relation
which thou objectest to may not become still more objectionable,
but remain as it is.   Give me once more thy confidence ; see the
case from a natural point of view; let me speak to thee quietly and
reasonably about it, and I dare to hope that everything between
us will once more be pure and friendly.   Thou hast seen my
mother and made her happy ; let my return make me happy
also'.

He offered friendship in vain ; he had wounded the self-love of a
vain woman ; there is a relentless venom in ignoble minds, when
the self-love is wounded, which poisons friendship and destroys all
gratitude.   It was not enough for the Frau von Stein that he had
loved her so many years with a rare devotion ; it was not enough
that he had been more to her child than its own father was ; it was
not enough that now the inevitable change had come, he still felt
tenderness and affection for her, grateful for what she *had* been to
him ; the one fact, that he had ceased to love her, expunged the
whole past.   A nature with any nobleness never forgets that once
it loved, and once was happy in that love ; the generous heart is
grateful in its memories.   The heart of the Frau von Stein had no
memory but for its wounds.   She spoke with petty malice of the
' low person ' who had usurped her place ; rejected Goethe's
friendship ; affected to pity him ; and circulated gossip about his
beloved.   They were forced to meet ; but they met no longer as
before.   To the last he thought and spoke of her tenderly ; and I
know on unexceptionable authority that when there was anything
appetizing brought to table, which he thought would please her,
he often said, ' Send some of this to the Frau von Stein '.

There is a letter of hers extant which shows what was the
state of her feelings after a lapse of twelve years.   It may find a
place here as a conclusive document with which to wind up the
strange episode of their history.   It is addressed to her son.

---

* This is a paraphrastic abbreviation of the passage, which if given as in the original
would need long collateral explanations.

Three passages are italicized by way of emphasis, to call attention to the spirit animating the writer.

'*Weimar, January* 12*th*, 1801.

'I did not know that our *former friend Goethe* was still so dear to me that a severe illness, from which he has been suffering for nine days, would so deeply affect me. It is a convulsive cough accompanied with erysipelas ; he can lie in no bed, and is obliged always to be kept in a standing posture, otherwise he would be choked. His neck, as well as his face, is swollen and full of internal blisters, his left eye stands out like a great nut, and discharges blood and matter; he is often delirious. Inflammation of the brain was feared, so he was bled, and had mustard foot-baths, which made his feet swell, and seemed to do him some good ; but last night the convulsive cough returned, I fear from his having been shaved yesterday ; my letter will tell you either of his being better or of his death—I shall not send it before. The Schillers and I have already shed many tears over him in the last few days ; I deeply regret now that *when he wished to visit me on New Year's Day, I, alas! because I lay ill with headache, excused myself,* and now I shall perhaps never see him again.

'14*th*. Goethe is better, but the twenty-first day must be got over ; between this and then something else might happen to him, because the inflammation has injured something in his head and his diaphragm. Yesterday he ate with great appetite some soup which I had sent him ; his eye, too, is better, but he is very melancholy, and they say he wept for three hours ; especially he weeps when he sees August, who has in the meantime taken refuge with me : I am sorry for the poor boy, he was dreadfully distressed, but he is already accustomed to drink away his troubles ; he lately, in *a club belonging to his mother's class*, drank seventeen glasses of champagne, and I had the greatest difficulty in keeping him from wine when he was with me.

'15*th*. Goethe sent to me to-day, thanked me for my sympathy, and hoped he should soon be better ; the doctors consider him out of danger, but his recovery will take a long time yet'.

Who could believe that this was written by one passionately loved for ten years, and written of one who was thought to be dying ? Even here her hatred to Christiane cannot restrain itself.

CHAPTER IX

THE POET AS A MAN OF SCIENCE

TO the immense variety of his studies in Art and Science must now be added a fragmentary acquaintance with the philosophy of Kant. He had neither the patience nor the delight in metaphysical abstractions requisite to enable him to master the Critique of Pure Reason ; but he read here and there in it, as he read in Spinoza ; and was especially interested in the æsthetical portions of the *Kritik der Urtheilskraft.* This was a means of bringing him nearer to Schiller, who still felt the difference between them to be profound ; as we see in what he wrote to Körner : 'His philosophy draws too much of its material from the world of the senses, where I only draw from the soul. His mode of presentation is altogether too sensuous for me. But his spirit works and seeks in every direction, striving to create a whole, and that makes him in my eyes a great man'.

Remarkable indeed is the variety of his strivings. After completing *Tasso,* we find him writing on the Roman Carnival, and on Imitation of Nature, and studying with strange ardour the mysteries of botany and optics. In poetry it is only necessary to name the *Roman Elegies,* to show what productivity in that direction he was capable of ; although, in truth, his poetical activity was then in subordination to his activity in science. He was, socially, in an unpleasant condition ; and, as he subsequently confessed, would never have been able to hold out, had it not been for his studies in Art and Nature. In all times these were his refuge and consolation.

On Art, the world listened to him attentively. On Science, the world would not listen ; but turned away in silence, sometimes in derision. In both he was only an amateur. He had no executive ability in Painting or Sculpture to give authority to his opinions, yet his word was listened to with respect, often with enthusiasm *. But while artists and the public admitted that a man of genius might speak with some authority, although an amateur, men of science were not willing that a man of genius should speak on *their* topics, until he had passed college examinations and re-

* RAUCH, the sculptor, told me that among the influences of his life, he reckons the enthusiasm which Goethe's remarks on Art excited in him. Many others would doubtless say the same.

ceived his diploma. The veriest blockhead who had received a diploma considered himself entitled to sneer at the poet who 'dabbled in comparative anatomy'. Nevertheless that poet made discoveries and enunciated laws, the importance of which the professional sneerer could not even appreciate, so far did they transcend his knowledge.

Professional men have a right to be suspicious of the amateur, for they know how arduous a training is required by Science. But while it is just that they should be *suspicious*, it is absurd for them to shut their eyes. When the amateur brings forward crudities, which he announces to be discoveries, their scorn may be legitimate enough ; but when he happens to bring forward a discovery, and they treat it as crudity, their scorn becomes self-stultification. If their professional training gives them superiority, that superiority should give them greater readiness of apprehension. The truth is, however, that ordinary professional training gives them nothing of the sort. The mass of men, simply because they are a mass of men, receive with difficulty every new idea, unless it lies in the track of their own knowledge ; and this opposition, which every new idea must vanquish, becomes tenfold greater when the idea is promulgated from a source not in itself authoritative.

But whence comes this authority ? From the respect paid to genius and labour. The man of genius who is known to have devoted much time to the consideration of any subject is justly supposed to be more competent to speak on that subject than one who has paid little attention to it. No amount of genius, no amount of study, can secure a man from his native fallibility ; but, after adequate study, there is a presumption in his favour, and it is this presumption which constitutes his authority. In the case of a poet who claims to be heard on the question of science, we naturally assume that he has not given the requisite labour ; and on such topics genius without labour carries no authority. But if his researches show that the labour *has* been given, we must then cease to regard him as a poet, and admit him to the citizenship of science. No one disputes the immense glory of a Haller, or a Redi, on the ground of their being poets. They were poets and scientific workers ; and so was Goethe. This would perhaps have been more readily acknowledged if he had walked in the well-beaten tracks of scientific thought ; but he opened new tracks, ard those who might, perhaps, have accepted him as a colleague, were called upon to accept him as a guide. Human nature could not stand this. The presumption against a poet was added to the presumption against novelty ; singly each of these would have been an obstacle to a ready acceptance ; united they were insuperable.

When Goethe wrote his exquisite little treatise on the *Metamorphoses of Plants**, he had to contend against the twofold obstacle of resistance to novelty and his own reputation. Had an obscure professor published this work, its novelty would have sufficed to render it unacceptable ; but the obscurest name in Germany would have had a *prestige* greater than the name of the great poet. All novelty is *prima facie* suspicious ; none but the young welcome it ; for is not every new discovery a kind of slur on the sagacity of those who overlooked it ? And can novelty in science, promulgated by a poet, be worth the trouble of refutation ? The professional authorities decided that it could not. The publisher of Goethe's works, having consulted a botanist, declined to undertake the printing of the *Metamorphoses of Plants.* The work was only printed at last because an enterprising bookseller hoped thereby to gain the publication of the other works. When it appeared, the public saw in it a pretty piece of fancy, nothing more. Botanists shrugged their shoulders, and regretted the author had not reserved his imagination for his poems. No one believed in the theory, not even his attached friends. He had to wait many years before seeing it generally accepted, and it was then only accepted because great botanists had made it acceptable. A considerable authority on this matter has told us how long the theory was neglected, and how ' depuis dix ans (written in 1838) il n'a peut-être pas été publié un seul livre d'organographie, ou de botanique descriptive, qui ne porte l'empreinte des idées de cet écrivain illustre ' †. It was the fact of the theory being announced by the author of *Werther* which mainly retarded its acceptance ; but the fact also that the theory was leagues in advance of the state of science in that day must not be overlooked. For it is curious that the leading idea had been briefly yet explicitly announced as early as 1759, by Caspar Friedrich Wolff, in his now deservedly celebrated *Theoria Generationis*, and again, in 1764, in his *Theorie von der Generation*‡. I shall have to recur

---

* He has also a poem on this subject, but it is scarcely more poetical.

† AUGUSTE ST. HILAIRE : *Comptes Rendus des Séances de l'Acad.*, VII, 437. See also his work, *Morphologie Végétale*, vol. I, p. 15.

‡ I have only been able to procure this latter work, which is a more popular and excursive exposition of the principles maintained in the Inaugural Dissertation of 1759.

to Wolff; at present it need only be noted that even *his* professional authority and remarkable power could not secure the slightest attention from botanists for the morphological theory—a proof that the age was not ripe for its acceptance.

A few of the eminent botanists began, after the lapse of some years, to recognize the discovery. Thus Kieser declared it to be 'certainly the vastest conception which vegetable physiology had for a long time known'. Voigt expressed his irritation at the blindness of the botanists in refusing to accept it. Nees von Esenbeck, one of the greatest names in the science, wrote in 1818, 'Theophrastus is the creator of modern botany. Goethe is its tender father, to whom it will raise looks full of love and gratitude, as soon as it grows out of its infancy, and acquires the sentiment which it owes to him who has raised it to so high a position'. And Sprengel, in his *History of Botany*, frequently mentions the theory. In one place he says, 'The *Metamorphoses* had a meaning so profound, joined to such great simplicity, and was so fertile in consequences, that we must not be surprised if it stood in need of multiplied commentaries, and if many botanists failed to see its importance'.

It is now, and has been for some years, the custom to insert a chapter on Metamorphosis in every work which pretends to a high scientific character.

'For a half century', says Goethe in the *History of the Botanical Studies*, 'I have been known as a poet in my own country and abroad. No one thinks of refusing me that talent. But it is not generally known, it has not been taken into consideration, that I have also occupied myself seriously through many years with the physical and physiological phenomena of Nature, observing them with the perseverance which passion alone can give. Thus when my essay on the development of plants, published nearly forty years before, fixed the attention of botanists in Switzerland and France, there seemed no expression for the astonishment at the fact of a poet thus going out of his route to make a discovery so important. It is to combat this false notion that I have written the history of my studies, to show that a great part of my life has been devoted to Natural History, for which I had a passion. It is by no sudden and unexpected inspiration of genius, but through long prosecuted studies, I arrived at my results. I might doubtless have accepted the honour which men wished to pay my sagacity, and in secret rejoiced in it. But as it is equally pernicious in science to keep exclusively to facts, or exclusively to abstract theories, I have deemed it my duty to write, for serious men, the detailed history of my studies'.

He was not *much* hurt at the reception of his work. He knew how unwilling men are to accord praise to any one who aims at success in different spheres, and found it perfectly natural they should be so unwilling ; adding, however, that 'an energetic nature feels itself brought into the world for *its own development, and not for the approbation of the public*'.

We shall have occasion to consider his theory of Metamorphosis hereafter ; at present let us follow the biographical path, and note his confession that some of the happiest moments of his life were those devoted to his botanical studies. 'They have acquired an inestimable value in my eyes', he says, 'because to them I owe the most beautiful of all the relations which my lucky star shone on. To them I owe the friendship of Schiller'.

Side by side with botanical and anatomical studies must be placed his optical studies. A more illustrative contrast can scarcely be found than is afforded by the history of his efforts in these two directions. They throw light upon scientific Method, and they throw light on his scientific qualities and defects. If we have hitherto followed him with sympathy and admiration, we must now be prepared to follow him with that feeling of pain which rises at the sight of a great intellect struggling in a false direction. His botanical and anatomical studies were of that high character which makes one angry at their cold reception ; his optical studies were of a kind to puzzle and to irritate the professional public.

He has written the history of these studies also. From youth upwards he had been prone to theorize on painting, led thereto, as he profoundly remarks, by the very absence of a talent for painting. It was not necessary for him to theorize on poetry ; he had within him the creative power. It *was* necessary for him to theorize on painting, because he wanted 'by reason and insight to fill up the deficiences of nature'. In Italy these theories found abundant stimulus. With his painter friends he discussed colour and colouring, trying by various paradoxes to strike out a truth. The friends were all deplorably vague in their notions of colour. The critical treatises were equally vague. Nowhere could he find firm ground. He began to think of the matter from the opposite side—instead of trying to solve the artists' problem, he strove to solve the scientific problem. He asked himself, What is colour? Men of science referred him to Newton ; but Newton gave him little help. Professor Büttner lent him some prisms and optical instruments, to try the prescribed experiments. He kept the prisms a long while, but made no use of them. Büttner wrote to him for his instruments ;

Goethe neither sent him back, nor set to work with them. He delayed from day to day, occupied with other things. At last Büttner became uneasy, and sent for the prisms, saying they should be lent again at a future period, but that at any rate he must have them returned. Forced thus to part with them, yet unwilling to send them back without making one effort, he told the messenger to wait, and taking up a prism, looked through it at the white wall of his room, expecting to see the whole wall coloured in various tints, according to the Newtonian statement. To his astonishment, he saw nothing of the kind. He saw that the wall remained as white as before, and that only there, where an opaque interfered, could a more or less decisive colour be observed ; that the window frames were most coloured, while the light grey heaven without showed no trace of colour. 'It needed very little meditation to discover that to produce colour a *limit* was necessary, and instinctively I exclaimed, "Newton's theory is false!"' There could be no thought of sending back the prisms at such a juncture ; so he wrote to Büttner begging for a longer loan, and set to work in real earnest.

This was an unhappy commencement. He began with a false conception of Newton's theory, and thought he was overthrowing Newton, when, in fact, he was combating his own error. The Newtonian theory does *not* say that a white surface seen through a prism appears coloured, but that it appears white, its edges only coloured. The fancied discovery of Newton's error stung him like a gadfly. He multiplied experiments, turned the subject incessantly over in his mind, and instead of going the simple way to work, and learning the a, b, c, of the science, tried the very longest of all short cuts, namely, experiment on insufficient knowledge. He made a white disc on a black ground, and this, seen through the prism, gave him the spectrum, as in the Newtonian theory ; but he found that a black disc on a white ground also produced the same effect. 'If Light', said I to myself, 'resolves itself into various colours in the first case, then must Darkness also resolve itself into various colours in this second case'. And thus he came to the conclusion that Colour is not contained in Light, but is the product of an intermingling of Light and Darkness.

'Having no experience in such matters, and not knowing the direction I ought to take, I addressed myself to a Physicist of repute, begging him to verify the results I had arrived at. I had already told him my doubts of the Newtonian hypothesis, and hoped to see him at once share my conviction. But how great was my surprise when he assured me that the phenomenon I spoke of was already known, and perfectly explained by the Newtonian theory. In vain I protested and combated his arguments, he held stolidly to the *credo*, and told me to repeat my experiments in a *camera obscura*'.

Instead of quieting him, this rebuff only turned him away from all Physicists, that is, from all men who have special knowledge on the subject, and made him pursue in silence his own path. Friends were amused and interested by his experiments ; their ignorance made them ready adepts. The Duchess Luise showed especial interest ; and to her he afterwards dedicated his *Farben-lehre*. The Duke also shared the enthusiasm. The Duke of Gotha placed at his disposal a magnificent laboratory. Prince August sent him splendid prisms from England. Princes and poetasters believed he was going to dethrone Newton ; men of science only laughed at his pretension, and would not pay his theory the honour of a refutation. One fact he records as very noticeable, namely, that he could count Anatomists, Chemists, Littérateurs, and Philosophers, such as Loder, Sömmering, Göttling, Wolff, Forster, Schelling (and, subsequently, Hegel), among his adherents ; but not one Physicist—*hingegen keinen Physiker !* Nor does he, in recording this fact, see that it is destructive of his pretensions.

What claim had Anatomists, Littérateurs, and philosophers to be heard in such a controversy ? Who would listen to a mathematician appealing to the testimony of zoologists against the whole body of mathematicians past and present ? There is this much, however, to be said for Goethe : he had already experi-enced neglect from professional authorities when he discovered the intermaxillary bone, and when, in the *Metamorphoses of Plants*, he laid before them a real discovery, the truth of which he profoundly felt. He was prepared therefore for a similar disregard of his claims when he not only produced a new theory, but attacked the highest scientific authority. He considered that Newtonians looked on him as a natural enemy. He thought them steadfastly bent on maintaining established prejudice. He thought they were a guild united against all innovation by common interest and common ignorance. Their opposition never made him pause ; their arguments never made him swerve.

He thought them profoundly in error when they imagined optics to be a part of mathematics; and as he did not understand mathematics, he could not appreciate their arguments.

His *Beiträge zur Optik*, which appeared in 1791, was a sort of feeler thrown out to the great public. The public was utterly unsympathizing. The ignorant had no interest in such matters, and certainly would not address themselves to a poet for instruction; the physicists saw that he was wrong. 'Everywhere', he says, 'I found incredulity as to my competence in such a matter; everywhere a sort of repulsion at my efforts; and the more learned and well-informed the men were, the more decided was their opposition'.

For years and years he continued his researches with a patience worthy of admiration. Opposition moved him not: it rather helped to increase his obstinacy. It extorted from him expressions of irritability and polemical bad taste, which astound us in one elsewhere so calm and tolerant. Perhaps, as Kingsley once suggested to me, he had a vague feeling that his conclusions were not sound, and felt the jealousy incident to imperfect conviction. Where his conviction was perfect, he was calm. The neglect of his *Metamorphoses*—the denial of his discovery of the intermaxillary bone —the indifference with which his essays on Comparative Anatomy were treated—all this he bore with philosophic serenity. But on the *Farbenlehre* he was always sensitive, and in old age ludicrously so. Eckermann records a curious conversation, wherein he brings forward a fact he has observed, which contradicts the theory of colours; and Goethe not only grows angry, but refuses to admit the fact. In this matter of Colour he showed himself morally weak, as well as intellectually weak. 'As for what I have done as a poet', said the old man once, 'I take no pride in it whatever. Excellent poets have lived at the same time with myself; more excellent poets have lived before me, and will come after me. But that in my century I am the only person who knows the truth in the difficult science of colours—of that, I say, I am not a little proud'.

The reader will doubtless be curious to know something of this Theory of Colours; and although it must necessarily appear greatly to its disadvantage in the brief abstract for which alone I can find space, an abstract without the numerous illustrations and experiments which give the theory a plausible aspect, yet the kernel of the matter will appear.

The Newtonian theory is that white light is composed of the

seven prismatic colours, *i.e.*, rays having different degrees of re-frangibility. Goethe says it is not composed at all, but is the simplest and most homogeneous thing we know*. It is absurd to call it composed of *colours*, for every light which has taken a colour is darker than colourless light. Brightness cannot therefore be a compound of darkness. There are but two pure colours, *blue* and *yellow*, both of which have a tendency to become *red*, through *violet* and *orange* ; there are also two mixtures, *green* and *purple*. Every other colour is a degree of one of these, or is impure. Colours originate in the modification of Light by outward circumstances. They are not developed *out* of Light, but *by* it. For the phenomenon of Colour, there is demanded Light and Darkness. Nearest the Light appears a colour we name *yellow;* nearest the Darkness, a colour we name *blue*. Mix these two and you have *green*.

Starting from the fundamental error of the simplicity of Light, Goethe undertakes to explain all the phenomena of Colour, by means of what he calls the *Opaques*—the media. He maintains that on the one hand there is Light, and on the other Darkness ; if a semi-transparent medium be brought between the two, from these contrasts and this medium Colours are developed, contrasted in like manner, but soon through a reciprocal relation tending to a point of reunion.

The highest degree of Light seen through a medium very slightly thickened appears *yellow*. If the density of the medium be increased, or if its volume become greater, the light will gradually assume a *yellow-red*, which deepens at last to a *ruby*.

The highest degree of Darkness seen through a semi-transparent medium, which is itself illuminated by a light striking on it, gives a *blue* colour ; which becomes paler as the density of the medium is increased ; but on the contrary becomes darker and deeper as the medium becomes more transparent. In the least degree of dimness short of absolute transparency, the deep *blue* becomes the most beautiful *violet*.

There are many interesting facts adduced in illustration. Thus, smoke appears yellow or red before a light ground, blue before a dark ground ; the blue colour, at the under part of a candle-flame, is also a case of blue seen opposite a dark ground. Light trans-

---

* ' Let us thank the gods ', exclaims Schelling, ' that they have emancipated us from the Newtonian spectrum (*spectrum* truly !) of composed light. We owe this to the genius to whom our debt is already so large'. *Zeitschrift für specul. Philos.*, II, p. 60. To the same effect Hegel in his *Encyclopädie der philos. Wissenschaften.*

mitted through the air is yellow, orange, or red, according to the density of the air ; Darkness transmitted through the air is blue, as is the case of the sky, or distant mountains.

He tells a curious ancdote in illustration of this blueness of darkness. A painter had an old portrait of a theologian to clean ; the wet sponge passing over the black velvet dress, suddenly changed it to a *light blue plush.* Puzzled at this truly remarkable phenomenon, and not understanding how light blue could be the ground of deep black, he was in great grief at the thought of having thus ruined the picture. The next morning, to his joy, he found the black velvet had resumed its pristine splendour. To satisfy his curiosity, he could not refrain from wetting a corner once more, and again he saw the *blue* appear. Goethe was informed of the phenomenon, which was once more produced, in his presence. ' I explained it', he says, ' by my doctrine of the semi-opaque medium. The original painter, in order to give additional depth to his black, may have passed some particular varnish over it ; on being washed, this varnish imbibed some moisture, and hence became semi-opaque, in consequence of which the *black* beneath immediately appeared *blue*'. The explanation is very ingenious ; nor does the *Edinburgh* reviewer's answer seem to meet the question, when he says*: ' As there is no gum or resin, or varnish of any kind that possesses the property of yielding blue or any other colour by being wetted, we have no doubt the varnish had been worn off, or else the picture never had been varnished'. It is not a question of wetted varnish yielding blue, but of wetted varnish furnishing the medium through which black appears blue. His own explanation, however, is probably correct. He assumes that there was no varnish, and that the particles of bodies which produce blackness, on the usual theory, are smaller than those which produce blue or any other colour ; and if we increase the size of the particles which produce blackness by the smallest quantity, they yield the *blue* colour described by Goethe. The action of the water swelled them a little, and thus gave them the size which fitted them to reflect *blue* rays.

The theory loses much of its seductive plausibility when thus reduced to its simplest expression. Let us, however, do the same for the Newtonian theory, and then estimate their comparative value. Newton assumes that white Light is a compound ; and he proves this assumption by decomposing a beam of light into its elements. These elements are rays, having different degrees of refrangibility,

---

* *Edin. Rev.*, Oct. 1840, p. 117.

separable from each other by different media. Each ray produces its individual colour. Not only will the beam of white Light in passing through a prism be separated into its constituent rays, or colours, but these rays may be again collected by a large lens, and, in being thus brought together, again reappear as white Light. There are few theories in science which present a more satisfactory union of logic and experiment.

It cannot be denied that Goethe's theory is also extremely plausible ; and he has supported it with so many accurate experiments and admirable observations, that to this day it has not only found ardent advocates, even among men of science, though these are few, but has very sorely perplexed many Newtonians, who, relying on the mathematical accuracy of their own theory, have contemptuously dismissed Goethe's speculation instead of victoriously refuting it. His obstinacy was excusable, since believing himself to be in the right he challenged refutation, and no one picked up his gauntlet. They declined in contempt ; he interpreted it as bigotry. He tried to get the French Academy to make a report on his work. This honour was withheld : Cuvier disdainfully declaring that such a work was not one to occupy an Academy ; Delambre answering all solicitations with this phrase : 'Des observations, des expériences, et surtout ne commençons pas par attaquer Newton'. As if the *Farbenlehre* were not founded on observations and experiments ! As if the glory of Newton were to stand inviolate before all things ! Goethe might well resent such treatment. If he was wrong in his theory, if his experiments were incomplete, why were these errors not pointed out? To contradict Newton might offer a presumption against the theory ; but Newtonians were called upon not to explain the contradiction between Goethe and Newton, which was vociferously announced, but the contradiction between Goethe and Truth, which they contemptuously asserted.

As this is a branch of science in which I can pretend to no competence, and as I have met with no decisive refutation of Goethe which can be quoted here, I should consider it sufficient to say that the fact of the vast majority of physicists in Europe refusing to pay any attention to the *Farbenlehre*, although not in itself more than a presumption against that theory, is nevertheless a presumption so very strong as only to be set aside by stringently coercive evidence. Looking at the *Farbenlehre* from the impartial, if imperfect, point of view of an outsider, I should say that not only has Goethe manifestly misunderstood Newton, but has presented a theory which is based on a radical mistake. The mistake is that of treating Darkness as a positive quality, rather than as a simple negation of Light. By means of this Darkness, as a *co-operating agent* with Light, colours are said to arise. Stripped of all the ambiguities of language, the theory affirms that Light is itself perfectly colourless until mingled with various degrees of Nothing—or, in other words, until it suffers various diminutions ; and with each diminution the colours become of a deeper hue. This may seem too preposterous for belief; yet what is Darkness but the negation of Light ? It is true that Goethe has in one place named Darkness, in the abstract, a pure negation ; but it is not less true that in the construction of his theory, Darkness plays the part of a positive ; and necessarily so ; for if we once conceive it as a simple negative, the theory falls to the ground. Light being assumed as colourless, no diminution of the colourless can give colours. Unless Darkness be positive,—co-operative,—we are left to seek the elements of colour *in* Light ; and this is precisely where the Newtonian theory finds it.

It was an old idea that the different confines of shadow variously modify light, producing various colours. This Newton has elaborately refuted (*Optics*, part II, book i), proving by simple experiments that all colours show themselves indifferently in the confines of shadow ; and that when rays which differ in refrangibility are separated from one another, and any one is considered apart, 'the colour of the light which it composes cannot be changed by any refraction or reflection whatever, as it ought to be were colours nothing else than modifications of light caused by refractions, reflexions, and shadows'.

It should be emphatically stated that the highest physical authorities have borne testimony to the accuracy of Goethe's facts ; and as these facts are exceedingly numerous, and often highly important, the value of his optical studies must be estimated as considerable. He was a man of genius, and he laboured with the passionate patience of genius. But in awarding our admiration to the man, we may withhold assent from his theory. That which has exasperated men of science, and caused them to speak slightingly of his labours, is the bitterly polemical tone of contempt with which he announced a discovery which they could not recognize as true. He was aggressive and weak. He vociferated that Newton was in error ; and a casual glance at his supposed detection of the error discovered a fundamental misconception. If we stand aloof from these heats of personal conflict, and regard the subject with a calmer eye, we shall see that the question simply reduces itself to this : which of the two theories offers the fullest and clearest explanation of the facts ?

Light and Colours are, like Sound and Tones, to be viewed as as objective phenomena, related to certain external conditions ; or as subjective phenomena, related to certain sensations. Before asking What is Light or Sound ? we must consider whether we seek the objective fact, or the subjective sensation. Every one admits that, apart from a sensitive organism, the objective phenomena of Light and Sound exist, although *not* as the Light and Sound known in our sensations. But as we can only know them through our sensations, it seems eminently philosophical to begin our study with these. And this Goethe has done. He first unfolds the law of physiological colours, *i.e.*, the modifications of the retina ; and his immense services in this direction have been cordially recognized by Physiologists. Since, however, we can never learn thus what are the eternal *conditions* of the phenomena, we have to seek in objective facts such an explanation as will best guide us. The assumption of rays having different degrees of refrangibility may one day turn out to be erroneous ; but it is an assumption which colligates the facts better than any other hitherto propounded, and therefore it is accepted. By regarding both Sound and Light as produced from waves of an elastic medium, acoustic and optic phenomena are reducible to *calculation.* It is true they thus incur Goethe's reproach of ceasing to be concrete objects to the mind, and becoming mathematical symbols ; but this is the very ambition of scientific research : a point to which I shall presently return. Let us compare the objective and subjective facts.

If an elastic rod be made to vibrate, the ear perceives nothing until the vibrations reach eight in a second, at which point the lowest tone becomes audible ; if the rapidity of the vibrations be now constantly accelerated, tones higher and higher in the scale become audible, till the vibrations reach 24,000 in a second, at which point the ear again fails to detect any sound. In like manner, it is calculated that when vibrations reach 483 billions in a second, Light, or rather the red ray, begins to manifest itself to the retina ; with increasing rapidity of vibration, the colours pass into orange, yellow, green, blue, and violet, till 727 billions are reached, at which point no *light* is perceptible. Here chemical action begins; and the rays are called chemical rays: as at the other end of the spectrum they are called heat rays. These are objective *conditions* which have been rigorously ascertained: and most important results have been arrived at through them.

The subjective facts according to Goethe lead to the belief that Tones are the product of Sound and Silence, as Colours are of Light and Darkness. Sound is made various (in tones) by various intermixtures with Silence. Descending from the highest audible note there is a gradual retardation of the vibrations, caused by the gradual encroachments of Silence, until at length Silence predominates and no Sound is heard. Suppose this hypothesis granted, we shall still have to ask what are the *conditions* of this Silence? If these are retardations of vibration, we may dispense with the hypothetical Silence. By similar reasoning we dispense with the hypothetical Darkness.

The assumption of different rays of unequal refrangibility is not only supported by the prismatic decomposition and recomposition of light, but also finds confirmation in the law of Refraction discovered by Snellius. And the consequence drawn from it, namely, that the relation of the sine of incidence, though constant for each colour, *varies* in the different colours of the spectrum, brings the whole question within the domain of mathematical calculation. The phenomena cease to be *qualitative* only, and become *quantitative:* they are measurable, and are measured. On Goethe's theory, granting its truth, the phenomena are not measurable; and whoever glances into a modern work on Optics will see that the precision and extent to which calculation has been carried are in themselves sufficient grounds for assigning the preference to the theory which admits such calculation. For as Copernicus profoundly says, 'It is by no means necessary that hypotheses should be true, nor even seem true; it is enough if they *reconcile calculation with observations**'.

Goethe's want of acquaintance with Mathematics and with the Methods of Physical Science prevented his understanding the defect in his own theory, and the manifest superiority of the theory which he attacked. He opposed every mathematical treatment of the subject as mischievous; and Hegel, who has shown himself still more opposed to the Methods of Science, applauds him on this very point.

* COPERNICUS: *De Revolutionibus Orbium Cælestium*, 1566.

'I raised the whole school of Mathematicians against me', says Goethe, 'and people were greatly amazed that one who had no insight into Mathematics could venture to contradict Newton. *For that Physics could exist independently of Mathematics no one seemed to have the slightest suspicion*'. Nor has that suspicion gained yet any ground with men in the least conversant with Physics, however necessary it may sometimes have been to protest against too exclusive an employment of Mathematics. But the misconception which lies at the bottom of Goethe's polemics was a very natural one to a poet never trained in mathematical or experimental science, and unaware of the peculiar position occupied by Mathematics as the great instrument of research. In his essay, *Ueber Mathematik und deren Misbrauch** , he compares the philosopher employing such an instrument to a man who should invent a machine for drawing a cork, an operation which two arms and hands very easily effect.

To make his error intelligible, let us suppose a man of great intellectual acuteness and energy suddenly to light upon the idea that our chemical theories were vitiated by a false basis—that the atomic theory was not only an hypothesis, but an hypothesis which misrepresented the order of Nature ; there being, in truth, none of the quantitative relations as are presupposed in that theory. Imagine the reformer setting to work, multiplying experiments, inventing explanations, disregarding all that the accumulated experience of ages had stored up on this very matter, and above all despising, as useless or worse, the very instrument which rescues Chemistry from rough guess-work, and elevates it into the possibility of a science—the instrument known as the Balance. It is probable that our reformer would make many curious observations, some of them quite new. It is probable that he would in many directions stimulate research. But it is certain that he would be hopelessly wrong in his theories, for he would necessarily be imperfect in his data. Without the delicate control of the Balance, chemical experiment can never become *quantitative;* and without quantitative knowledge there can be no chemical science strictly so called, but only *qualitative, i.e.* approximative knowledge. No amount of observation will render observation precise unless it can be measured. No force of intellect will supply the place of an instrument. You may watch falling bodies for an eternity, but without Mathematics mere watching

* *Werke*, XL p 468.

will yield no law of gravitation. You may mix acids and alkalis together with prodigality, but no amount of experiment will yield the secret of their composition, if you have flung away the Balance.

Goethe flung away the Balance. Hegel boldly says this is Goethe's merit—*das Prisma heruntergebracht zu haben.* He praises the 'pure sense of Nature', which in the poet rebelled against Newton's 'barbarism of Reflection'. To the same effect Schelling, who does not hesitate to choose it as the very ground for proclaiming Goethe's superiority over the Newtonians, that 'instead of the artificially confused and disfiguring experiments of the Newtonians, he places the purest, simplest verdicts of Nature herself before us'; he adds, 'it is not surprising that the blind and slavish followers of Newton should oppose researches which prove that precisely the very section of Physics, in which up to this time they have imagined the most positive, nay almost geometric evidence, to be on their side, is based on a fundamental error'*.

This point of Method, if properly examined, will help to elucidate the whole question of Goethe's aptitude for dealing with physical science. The native direction of his mind is visible in his optical studies as decisively as in his poetry; that direction was towards the *concrete* phenomenon, not towards abstractions. He desired to explain the phenomena of colour, and in Mathematics these phenomena disappear; that is to say, the very *thing* to be studied is hurried out of sight and masked by abstractions. This was utterly repugnant to his mode of conceiving Nature. The marvellous phenomena of polarized light in the hands of Mathematicians excited his boundless scorn. 'One knows not', he says, 'whether a body or a mere ruin lies buried under those formulas†'. The name of Biot threw him into a rage; and he was continually laughing at the Newtonians about their Prisms and Spectra, as if Newtonians were pedants who preferred their dusty rooms to the free breath of heaven. He always spoke of observations made in his garden, or with a simple prism in the sunlight, as if the natural and simple Method were much more certain than the artificial Method of Science. In this he betrayed his misapprehension of Method. He thought that Nature revealed herself to the patient observer:

> Und was sie deinem Geist nicht offenbaren mag,
> Das zwingst du ihr nicht ab mit Hebeln und mit Schrauben.

* SCHELLING: *Zeitschrift für spekulative Philos.*, II, p. 60.
† *Werke*, XL, 473.

'And what she does not reveal to the Mind will not be extorted from her by Levers and Screws'. Hence his failure ; hence also his success ; for we must not forget that if as a contribution to Optics his *Farbenlehre* be questionable, as a contribution to the knowledge of colour demanded by Artists it is very valuable. Painters have repeatedly acknowledged the advantage they have derived from it ; and I remember hearing Riedel, at Rome, express the most unbounded enthusiasm for it ; averring that, as a colourist, he had learned more from the *Farbenlehre*, than from all the other teachers and books he had ever known. To artists and physiologists—*i.e.* to those who are mainly concerned with the phenomena of colour as perceptions, and who demand qualitative rather than quantitative knowledge—his labours have a high value ; and even physicists must admit, that however erroneous the theory and imperfect the method he has adopted, still the immense accumulation and systematization of facts, and the ingenuity with which he explains them, deserve serious respect. As Bacon felicitously says, a tortoise on the right path will beat a racer on the wrong path ; and if it be true that Goethe was on the wrong path, it is not less true that he shows the thews and sinews of a racer.

It is with other feelings that we contemplate him labouring in the organic sciences. There the native tendencies of his mind and the acquired tendencies of education better fitted him for success. Biology has peculiar fascinations for the poetical mind, and has seduced several poets to become physiologists. Mathematics are not required. Concrete observations furnish the materials for a keen and comprehensive comparison.

Let it be distinctly understood, and that not on the testimony of the admiring biographer, but on some of the highest scientific testimonies in Europe*, that in the organic sciences Goethe holds an eminent place—eminent not because of his rank as a poet, but in spite of it. Let it be understood that in these sciences he is not to be treated as a poet, a facile amateur, but as a *thinker* who, having mastered sufficent knowledge to render his path secure,

---

* In the first edition of this work several passages were quoted in support of the assertion in the text ; but one effect of this chapter has been to render such evidence superfluous, Goethe's position in science becoming daily more widely recognized. The following references are therefore all that need now be given : AUGUSTE ST. HILAIRE : *Morphologie Végétale*, I, p. 15. OSCAR SCHMIDT : *Goethe's Verhältniss zu den organischen Wissenschaften*, p. 10. JOHANNES MUELLER : *Ueber phantastische Gesichtserscheinungen*, p. 104. CUVIER : *Histoire des Sciences Naturelles*, IV, p. 316. ISIDORE, GEOFFROY ST. HILAIRE : *Essais de Zoologie générale*, p. 139. OWEN : *Archetype and Homologies of the Skeleton*, p. 3. HELMHOLTZ : *Allgemeine Monatsschrift*, May 1853. VIRCHOW : *Goethe als Naturforscher*.

gave an impulse to the minds of contemporaries and successors, which is not even yet arrested.

Goethe was a thinker in science, a manipulator of scientific ideas. He was not one of those laborious and meritorious workers who with microscope and scalpel painfully collect the materials from which Science emerges.   He worked, too, in his way, and everywhere sought in the order of nature for verification of the ideas which he had conceived *à priori*.   Do not, however, mistake him for a metaphysician.   He was a positive thinker on the *à priori* Method ; a Method vicious only when the seeker rests contented with his own assumptions, or seeks only a *partial* hasty confrontation with facts—what Bacon calls *notiones temerè à rebus abstractas;* a Method eminently philosophic when it merely *goes before* the facts, anticipating what will be the tardy conclusions of experience.   The *à priori* Method is a bright and brilliant instrument.   It will cut the fingers when clumsily handled.   It will cut deep into the truth if rightly used ; as it was by Kepler and Goethe, who looked upon nature from the heights, but having seen or fancied they saw something in the plains, at once descended to verify the truth of their observation.

We will glance at his achievements in this field.   The intermaxillary bone* was long a bone of contention among anatomists. Vesalius—one of the grandest and boldest of the early pioneers who wrote against Galen, as the philosophers wrote against Aristotle—declared, and with justice, that Galen's anatomy was not founded on the dissection of the *human* body, but on that of animals.   A proof, said he, is that 'Galen indicates a separate bone connected with the maxillary by sutures ; a bone which, as every anatomist can satisfy himself, exists only in animals'.   The Galenists were in arms.   They could bring no fact in evidence, but *that* was of very little consequence ; if facts were deficient, was not hypothesis always ready ?   Sylvius, for example, boldly said that man *had formerly* an intermaxillary bone.   If he has it no longer, he *ought* to have it.   It is luxury, it is sensuality which has gradually deprived man of this bone†.   What has not luxury been made to answer for !   The dispute was carried down through centuries, no one attempting to demonstrate anatomically the

---

* It is the centre bone of the upper jaw—that which contains the incisor teeth.

† This same Sylvius it was who replied to Vesalius that Galen was not wrong when he described man as having seven bones in his sternum (there are only three) : ' for ', said he, ' in ancient times the robust chests of heroes might very well have had more bones than our degenerate day can boast'.   It is impossible to decide upon what might have been ; but the mummies are ancient enough, and they have no more bones than we.

existence of the bone. Camper actually raised this presumed absence of the bone into the one distinguishing mark separating man from the ape ; which is doubly unfortunate, for in the first place the bone is not absent in man, and secondly in as far as it can be considered absent in man it is equally absent in the chimpanzee, the highest of the apes *. Thus was anatomy a treacherous ally in this question, although Camper knew not how treacherous.

This slight historical sketch will serve to show that the discovery, if unimportant, was at least far from easy ; indeed, so little did it lie in the track of general knowledge, that it was at first received with contemptuous disbelief, even by men so eminent as Blumenbach†, and it was forty years gaining general acceptance, although Loder, Spix, and Sömmering at once recognized it. Camper, to whom Goethe sent the manuscript, found that it was *très élégant, admirablement bien écrit, c'est à dire d'une main admirable*, but thought a better Latin style desirable. Goethe began to despise the pedantry of professional men who would deny the testimony of their five senses in favour of an old doctrine ; and he admirably says, ' the phrases men are accustomed to repeat incessantly end by becoming convictions, *and ossify the organs of intelligence* ‡'.

The most remarkable point in this discovery is less the discovery than the Method which led to it. The intermaxillary bone in animals contains the incisor teeth. Man has incisor teeth ; and Goethe, fully impressed with the conviction that there was Unity in Nature, boldly said, if man has the teeth in common with animals, he must have the bone in common with animals. Anatomists, lost in details, and wanting that fundamental conception which now underlies all philosophical anatomy, saw no abstract necessity for such identity of composition ; the more so, because *evidence* seemed wholly against it. But Goethe was not

---

* Blumenbach had already noted that in some young apes and baboons no trace was discoverable of the bone.

† See his *Comparative Anatomy*, translated by Lawrence ; and the translator's note, p. 60.

‡ Since the first edition of this work was published, I have come upon a piquant illustration of the not very honourable tendency in men to plume themselves on the knowledge of a discovery which they had formerly rejected. VICQ D'AZYR : *Discours sur l'Anatomie (Œuvres*, IV, 159), mentioning his discovery of the intermaxillary, adds, ' J'ai appris de M. Camper, dans son dernier voyage à Paris, *que cet os lui est connu depuis très long temps*'. Now this same Camper, on receiving the anonymous dissertation in which Goethe propounded the discovery, said, ' Je dois ré-examiner tout cela ' ; but on learning that Goethe was the author, he wrote to Merck that he had ' convinced himself that the bone did not exist ' (see VIRCHOW : *Goethe als Naturforscher*, p. 79) ; yet no sooner does a great anatomist tell him that the bone exists, than he complacently declares ' I have known it a long while '.

only guided by the true philosophic conception, he was also instinctively led to the true Method of demonstration, namely, Comparison of the various modifications which this bone underwent in the animal series. This Method has now become *the* Method ; and we require to throw ourselves into the historical position to appreciate its novelty, at the time he employed it. He found on comparison that the bone varied with the nutrition of the animal, and the size of its teeth. He found, moreover, that in some animals the bone was not separated from the jaw ; and that in children the sutures were traceable. He admitted that seen from the front no trace of the sutures was visible, but on the interior there were unmistakable traces. Examinations of the fœtal skull has since set the point beyond dispute. I have seen one where the bone was distinctly separated ; and I possess a skull, the ossification of which is far advanced at the parietal sutures, yet internally faint traces of the intermaxillary are visible*.

Goethe made his discovery in 1784, and communicated it to several anatomists. Loder mentions it in his *Compendium* in 1787.

Respecting Goethe's claim to the honour of this discovery, I have recently discovered a fact which is of great or small significance according to the views we hold respecting such claims ; namely, whether the clear enunciation of an idea, though never carried out in detail, suffices to give priority ; or whether, in the words of Owen †, ' He becomes the true discoverer who establishes the truth : and the sign of the proof is the general acceptance. Whoever, therefore, resumes the investigation of a neglected or repudiated doctrine, elicits its true demonstration, and discovers and explains the nature of the errors which have led to its tacit or declared rejection, may calmly and confidently await the acknowledgments of his rights in its discovery '. If we hold the former view, we must assign the discovery of the intermaxillary in man to Vicq d'Azyr ; if we hold the latter, to Goethe. In the *Traité d'Anatomie et de Physiologie*, which the brilliant anatomist published in 1786, we not only find him insisting on the then novel idea of an uniform plan in the structure of organic beings, according to which nature ' semble opérer toujours d'après un

---

* These might be considered abnormal cases. But M. J. Weber has devised a method of treating the skull with dilute nitric acid, which makes the separation of the bones perfect. *Froriep's Notizen*, 1828, bd. 19, 282. VIRCHOW : *l.c.*, p 80.
† OWEN : *Homologies of the Skeleton*, p. 76. Comp. also MALPIGHI : *Opera Posthuma*, 1697, p. 5.

modèle primitif et général dont elle ne s'écarte qu'à regret et dont on rencontre partout des traces*'; but we find this explicit illustration given among others : 'Peut on s'y refuser enfin (*i.e.* to admit the traces of a general plan) en comparant les os maxillaires antérieurs que j'appelle *incisifs* dans les quadrupèdes, avec cette pièce osseuse qui soutient les dents incisives supérieurs dans l'homme, où elle est séparée de l'os maxillaire par une petite fêlure très remarquable dans les fœtus, à peine visible dans les adultes, et dont personne n'avoit connu l'usage'. In a subsequent passage of the second *Discours* he says : 'Toutes ces dents sont soutenues dans la mâchoire antérieure par un os que j'ai décrit sous le nom d'incisif ou labial, que quelques-uns appellent inter-maxillaire, que l'on à découvert depuis peu dans les morses, et *dont j'ai reconnu les traces dans les os maxillaires supérieurs du fœtus humain*'†.

The reader will remark that this is not simply the announcement of the fact, but is adduced in illustration of the very same doctrine which Goethe invoked. The *Traité d'Anatomie*, as we have seen, was published in 1786 ; that is to say, two years after Goethe had made his discovery ; and Sömmering, in writing to Merck ‡, says : 'I have expressed my opinion on Vicq d'Azyr's work in the *Götting. Gelehrt. Anzeig.* It is the best we have. But as far as the work has yet gone Goethe is not mentioned in it'. From which it may be inferred that Sömmering supposed Vicq d'Azyr to have been acquainted with Goethe's contemporary labours ; but against such a supposition we must remember that if Germany took note of what was passing in France, discoveries made in Germany travelled with great slowness across the Rhine ; and in illustration of this slowness we may note that Geoffroy St. Hilaire, who was several years afterwards nobly working out conceptions of Philosphical Anatomy in a spirit so identical with that of Goethe, was utterly unconscious of the existence of a predecessor, and noticing the monograph of G. Fischer, said, '*Goethes* aurait le premier décou-vert l'interpariétal dans quelques rongeurs, et se serait contenté d'en faire mention par une note manuscrite sur un exemplaire d'un traité d'anatomie comparée §'.

But the conclusive point is this : although the *Traité d'Anatomie*

---

* VICQ D'AZYR, *Œuvres*, IV, p. 26. The work is there called *Discours sur l'Anatomie*.
† *Ibid.*, p. 159. ‡ *Briefe an Merck*, p. 493.
§ *Philosophie Anatomique*, II, p. 55. Geoffroy was afterwards very proud to have the suffrage of *Goethes;* and Geoffroy's son has spoken most honourably of the coinci-dence between the speculations of his father and the poet.

did not appear till 1786, the discovery of the intermaxillary was published by Vicq d'Azyr in the Académie des Sciences for 1779*, five years before Goethe announced his discovery to Herder. The question of priority is therefore settled. The Frenchman had no need of any acquaintance with what the German poet had worked out ; and Merck's astonishment at finding Goethe's 'so-called discovery accepted by Vicq d'Azyr' was wholly misplaced ; but can we be equally sure that Goethe was altogether ignorant of his predecessor? I think he was. The sudden enthusiasm, the laborious investigation, the jubilate of triumph, are evidences that if ever his predecessor's discovery had come under his notice (which is highly improbable) it was completely forgotten ; and we may judge how completely Vicq d'Azyr's announcement had been without echo in the scientific world, from the fact that the three most illustrious men of the day, Camper, Blumenbach, and Sömmering, knew nothing of it, and denied the existence of the bone Goethe claimed to have discovered. Thus, in assigning priority to Vicq d'Azyr, we by no means diminish Goethe's merit. He it was who thoroughly worked out the discovery ; he it was who gave it a fixed and definite place in science ; he it is who is always named as the discoverer.

The only importance of this discovery is the philosophic Method which it illustrates ; the firm belief it implies that all organisms are constructed on an uniform plan, and that Comparative Anatomy is only valid because such a plan is traceable. In our day it seems an easy conception. We are so accustomed to consider all the variations in organic structures as modifications of a type, that we can hardly realize to ourselves any other conception. That it was by no means an obvious idea, nor one easy to apply, may be seen in two brilliant applications—the metamorphosis of plants, and the vertebral theory of the skull.

Place a flower in the hands of the cleverest man of your acquaintance, providing always he has not read modern works of science, and assure him that leaf, calyx, corolla, bud, pistil, and stamen, differing as they do in colour and in form, are nevertheless all modified leaves ; assure him that flower and fruit are but modifications of one typical form, which is the leaf ; and if he has any confidence in your knowledge he may accept the statement, but assuredly it will seem to him a most incomprehensible paradox.

* In the first edition I stated that 'from a note to BLUMENBACH'S *Comparative Anatomy* (p. 19), it seems as if Vicq d'Azyr had made this observation as early as 1780'. The date in the text is given by Vicq d'Azyr himself. *Œuvres*, IV, 159.

Place him before a human skeleton, and, calling his attention to its manifold forms, assure him that every bone is either a vertebra, or the appendage to a vertebra, and that the skull is a congeries of vertebræ under various modifications, he will, as before, accept your statement, perhaps ; but he will, as before, think it one of the refinements of transcendental speculation to be arrived at only by philosophers. Yet both of these astounding propositions are first principles in Morphology ; and in the History of Science both of these propositions are to be traced to Goethe. Botanists and anatomists have, of course, greatly modified the views he promulgated, and have substituted views nearer and nearer the truth, without yet being quite at one. But he gave the impulse to their efforts.

While botanists and anatomists were occupied in analysis, striving to distinguish separate parts, and give them distinct names, his poetical and philosophic mind urged him to seek the supreme synthesis, and reduce all diversities to a higher unity. In his poem addressed to Christiane he says :

> Thou, my love, art perplexed with the endless seeming confusion
> Of the luxuriant wealth which in the garden is spread ;
> Name upon name thou hearest, and in thy dissatisfied hearing,
> With a barbarian noise one drives another along.
> All the forms resemble, yet none is the same as another ;
> Thus the whole of the throng points at a deep-hidden law *.

To prove this identity was no easy task. He imagined an ideal typical plant (*Urpflanze*), of which all actual plants were the manifold realizations ; and this I cannot but agree with Schleiden in considering a conception at once misleading and infelicitous. He was happier in the conception of all the various organs of the plant as modifications of one fundamental type ; this type he names the *Leaf.* Not that we are to understand the metamorphosis of plants to be analogous to the metamorphosis of animals ; (an error into which I fell in my first edition, as Ferdinand Cohn properly points out), nor indeed is it such a metamorphosis at all. The pistil and petal are not first developed into leaves, and from these leaves changed into petal and pistil ; as a caterpillar develops into a grub, and the grub into a butterfly. This would be metamorphosis. Instead of this we must conceive the whole plant as a succession of repetitions of the original type variously modified ; in some of these repetitions the modification has been

---

* Whewell's translation : *Hist. Inductive Sciences,* III, 360.

slight, in others considerable. The two typical forms are stem and leaf. From the seed there is an ascending and a descending axis, formed of a succession of stems : the ascending axis is called the aerial stem ; the descending axis is the root. From both of these stems lateral stems or branches are given off; and from these again others. The Leaf is the second type : it forms all the other organs by various modifications. Widely as a pistil differs from a petal, and both from an ordinary leaf, they are disclosed as identical by the history of their development.

It is impossible to be even superficially acquainted with biological speculations, and not to recognize the immense importance of the recognition of a Type. As Helmholtz truly observes, 'the labours of botanists and zoologists did little more than collect materials, until they learned to dispose them in such a series that the laws of dependence and a generalized type could be elicited. Here the great mind of our poet found a field suited to it ; and the time was favourable. Enough material had been collected in botany and comparative anatomy for a clear survey to be taken ; and although his contemporaries all wandered without a compass, or contented themselves with a dry registration of facts, he was able to introduce into science two leading ideas of infinite fruitfulness '.

And here the question presents itself : Is Goethe rightfully entitled to the honour universally awarded to him of having founded the Morphology of Plants? We must again evoke the distinction previously stated. No one denies that the doctrine was so entirely novel that botanists at first rejected it with contempt, and only consented to accept it when some eminent botanists had shown it to be true. No one denies that Goethe worked it out ; if any predecessor had conceived the idea, no one had carried the idea into its manifold applications. But he has himself named Linnæus and Wolff as his precursors ; and it is of some interest to ascertain in what degree these precursors have claim to the honour of the discovery.

It has been remarked by the eminent botanist Ferdinand Cohn*, that the great Linnæus mingled with his observation much fantastic error, which the poet Goethe was the first to eliminate. But Dr. Hooker, while admitting the metaphysical and speculative matter which Linnæus has mixed up with his statements, is

---

* *Goethe und die Metamorphosen der Pflanzen*, in the *Deutsches Museum* of PRUTZ, IV, Jan. 1862.

disposed to value them highly. 'The fundamental passage is in the *Systema Naturæ*, in the introduction to which work the following passage occurs :—" Prolepsis (Anticipation) exhibits the mystery of the metamorphosis of plants, by which the herb, which is the *larva* or imperfect condition, is changed into the declared fructification : for the plant is capable of producing either a leafy herb or a fructification. . . . When a tree produces a flower, nature anticipates the produce of five years where these come out all at once ; forming of the bud leaves of the next year, *bracts;* of those of the following year, the *calyx;* of the following, the *corolla;* of the next, the *stamina;* of the subsequent, the *pistils*, filled with the granulated marrow of the seed, the terminus of the life of a vegetable ". . . . In the *Prolepsis* the speculative matter, which Linnæus himself carefully distinguishes as such, must be separated from the rest, and this may, I think, be done in most of the sections. He starts with explaining clearly and well the origin and position of buds, and their constant presence, whether developed or not, in the axils of the leaf : adding abundance of acute observations and experiments to prove his statements. The leaf he declares to be the first effort of the plant in spring : he proceeds to show, successively, that bracts, calyx, corolla, stamen, and pistils are each of them metamorphosed leaves *'. Dr Hooker adds, 'There is nothing in all this that detracts from the merits of Goethe's re-discovery'; and there can be little doubt that, had not Goethe, or another, proved the doctrine, botanists would to this day have continued to pass over the passage in Linnæus as one of his 'fanciful flights'.

The *aperçu* was in Linnæus ; a spark awaiting the presence of some inflammable imagination ; and when we remember how fond Goethe was of Linnæus, we can hardly suppose that this *aperçu* had not more than once flashed across his mind as a gleam of the truth. With regard to Caspar Friedrich Wolff the evidence is far from satisfactory. It is certain that Wolff in his immortal work on 'Generation' had clearly grasped the morphological principles, and had left Goethe very little to add to them. But it is very uncertain whether Goethe had ever read Wolff. Some years after the publication of his work he mentions with pride the fact of Wolff having been his 'admirable precursor', and says that his attention to the work had been drawn by a namesake of the great embryologist. It was with no little surprise therefore that I

* WHEWELL: *Hist. of Ind. Sciences*, 3rd ed., III, 553.

read in Düntzer*, the unhesitating assertion that in 1785 Herder had made Goethe a present of Wolff's *Theoria Generationis* which contained a rough outline of several of Goethe's favourite ideas. If this statement were correct, Goethe would be under serious suspicion ; but it is not correct. On referring to the passage in Herder's letter to Knebel, which Düntzer pretends is the authority for this statement, I find, in the first place, that Herder does not specify the *Theoria Generationis*, nor indeed can we be sure he refers to C. F. Wolff at all, he merely says, 'Wolf', which is a common name among German authors ; in the second place he does not say that he has *given* the book to Goethe, but that he *intends* doing so when he can get a copy ; meanwhile Knebel is not to mention the book to Goethe. And out of such a sentence as this, Düntzer has constructed a 'fact', which while it gives his pedantry the small delight of correcting in a foot-note Goethe's assertion that F. A. Wolff directed his attention to the *Theoria Generationis*, lays Goethe open to the charges of having borrowed his morphology from Wolff, of having concealed the fact, and of having pretended never to have seen his predecessor's work until his attention was directed to it some years afterwards. Against such charges the following arguments may be urged. First, there is Goethe's own explicit statement—and his veracity is not lightly to be questioned. Secondly, if the work referred to by Herder was the *Theoria Generationis* (which is probable, but not certain), and if it was given as intended (also probable but not certain), we have no evidence that Goethe read it. Thirdly, and conclusively, the date of the very letter in which Herder mentions his intention is ten years *later* (1795) than Düntzer would have us suppose ; and it is thus five years *after* the publication of Goethe's views (1790)†.

The *Metamorphosen* was published in 1790. In 1817 Goethe says that he had requested his scientific friends to make notes of any passages they might meet in earlier writers relative to the topic he had treated, because he was convinced that there was nothing absolutely new. His friend F. A. Wolff directed him to Caspar Friedrich. In expressing his admiration for his great predecessor he is proud to acknowledge how much he had learned from him during five-and-twenty years. Now five-and-twenty

---

* *Goethe und Karl August*, 1861, p. 212.
† See KNEBEL : *Nachlass*, II, 268, which is the authority cited by Düntzer, whose inaccuracy is unpardonable in one so uniformly dull, and so merciless in ferreting out the small inaccuracies of others.

years from 1817 brings us back to 1792—that is to say, two years after the publication of the *Metamorphosen*, and three years before the letter written by Herder*. So that if we assume the work in question to have been the *Theoria Generationis*, Goethe was perfectly correct in mentioning A. F. Wolff, and not Herder, as the friend to whom he was first indebted for a knowledge of its existence.

The tone in which Goethe speaks of Caspar Friedrich Wolff is assuredly not that of a man who had any obligations to conceal ; but of a man who, recognizing a precursor with pleasure, speaks of the two theories as two independent modes of conceiving the phenomena, the theory of his precursor being pre-eminently physiological, while his own was pre-eminently morphological.

With regard both to Linnæus and Wolff it may be said that they anticipated the morphology of plants, but that to Goethe belongs the credit of establishing it. We do not take from the credit of Columbus by showing that five centuries before he discovered the New World, Scandinavian voyagers had repeatedly touched on those shores ; nor do we diminish the value of Goethe's contribution to Science by showing that before him Wolff had perceived the identity of the various organs of the plant. It was not the purpose of the Scandinavians to discover the New World. They did not make their discovery a possession for mankind. Neither was it Wolff's purpose to create a new theory in Botany. He discovered a process of nature while he was seeking the laws of Epigenesis, and he only used his discovery as one of several illustrations. Columbus set out with the distinct purpose of discovery, and made his discovery a possession for all time. So also Goethe set out with the distinct purpose, and Botanists justly declare that to his work they owe the idea of plant metamorphosis.

Goethe's work is very beautiful, and may be read without any previous botanical knowledge. It traces the metamorphoses of the grain into the leaf, and thence into the flower. The morphological part is perfect, except that, as Cohn remarks, he has given an exclusive predominance to the leaf, and overlooked the not less important stem. It is to be regretted that he hampers himself with the following physiological hypothesis : every segment pro-

---

* It should be added that Knebel's editors place a (?) after the date 1795. But we have no reason to suppose they could err by *ten* years in assigning this letter its place ; Düntzer professes no doubt as to the accuracy of the date ; and internal evidence, taken with what is said above, renders it highly probable that 1795 is very little removed from the correct date.

ceeding immediately from that which goes before it, receiving its nourishment through all the segments which have gone before, must, he says, be more perfect, and must send to its leaves and buds a more elaborated sap. The result is that the coarser fluids are rejected, the finer attracted, and the plant grows more and more perfect till it reaches its point of culmination.

This hypothesis of a more elaborated sap, reaching the ultimate segments, is in direct contradiction to the hypothesis of Wolff, which also declares the flower to be modified leaves; but how modified?* they are modified because they are imperfect. Their development has been arrested. They are smaller, have less sap, the sap has lost its chlorophyl, and the colour of the flower is an evidence of *imperfection*. I cannot stop to consider Wolff's ingenious arguments by which he endeavours to show that flowering and fructification are arrests of development. It is enough to indicate the contrast between his and Goethe's views. Both are agreed that inasmuch as a differentiation does take place, it must have some cause; but the cause is by Wolff said to be deficiency of sap, by Goethe elaborated sap.

Goethe agrees with Wolff as regards the passage of the leaf into the flower being dependent on the acceleration or retardation of the sap. It had been noticed by Linnæus that a too abundant supply of food retards the flowering, and accelerates the growth of leaves; whereas a moderate supply, nay, even an approach to starvation, accelerates the flowering and diminishes the number of leaves. Wolff attributes this simply to the fact that so long as there is abundant nutriment there will be abundant growth, and no arrest in the shape of imperfect leaves (*i.e.,* flowers); and when nutriment is scanty, the arrest soon takes place. But unfortunately for this opinion, and indeed for the opinion that flowers are imperfect leaves resulting from a want of nutriment, there is a class of plant which blossom *before* they put forth leaves. Goethe's explanation, hypothetical though it be, is better. He says that as long as there are any of the grosser fluids to be rejected, the organs of the plant are forced to employ themselves in this labour, which labour renders flowering impossible; but no sooner do we limit the nourishment than, by diminishing this process of elaboration, we accelerate the flowering.

We are here touching on the great law of antagonism between Growth and Development which is intimately connected with the

* *Theorie von der Generation,* § 80, *sq.*

law of Reproduction—a subject too vast to be even indicated in this rapid survey. The student will note, however, that although Goethe perils his position by the introduction of an hypothetical elaboration of fluids, without assigning a cause for that elaboration, he nevertheless sees,what many fail to see, that Reproduction is only another form of Growth—a process of differentiation. 'The vital forces of the plant', he says, 'manifest themselves in two ways: on the one hand *vegetation*, issuing in the stem and leaves ; on the other *reproduction*, issuing in flowers and fruits. If we examine vegetation closely, we shall see that the plant continuing itself from articulation to articulation, from leaf to leaf, and putting forth buds, accomplishes a *reproduction* which differs from that ordinary so-named in being *successive*—it manifests itself in a series of isolated developments instead of manifesting itself *simultaneously*. That force which produces buds has the greatest analogy with that which determines simultaneously the higher act of propagation. We can force the plant to produce buds incessantly, or we can accelerate the epoch of flowering ; the first by abundant nourishment, the second by nourishment less abundant. In defining *budding* as "successive propagation", and *flowering* and *fructification* as " simultaneous propagation", we designate the mode in which each manifests itself. Thus, then, whether the plant buds, flowers, or fructifies, it is always by means of *the same organs*, the form and destination of which are changed. The same organ which expands into a leaf upon the stem and presents such varied forms, contracts to make the calyx, expands again to make the petal, to contract once more into the sexual organs, and expand for the last time into fruit'.

Whatever may be the final decision upon the Metamorphoses of Plants, there must ever remain the great and unique glory of a poet having created a new branch of science, and by means as legitimately scientific as those of any other creation. Morphology now counts among its students illustrious names, and crowds of workers. And this science we owe to the author of *Faust*. Nor is this all. He has priority in some of the most luminous and comprehensive ideas which are now guiding philosophic speculation on the science of life. In the historical sketch which Carus prefixes to his *Transcendental Anatomy*, after setting forth the various tentatives men had made to discover by means of *descriptive* anatomy, and occasional comparisons, the true relations of the various parts of the body, he says*: 'If we go

* *Anatomie Comparée*, vol. III, p. 3. French trans.

back as far as possible into the history of the labours undertaken with a view to arrive at the philosophic conception of the skeleton, we find that the first idea of a metamorphosis of the osseous forms,—*i.e.*, that all forms are but modifications more or less traceable of one and the same Type—belongs to Goethe'. After a quotation of Goethe's words, Carus adds: 'It is difficult to express in clearer terms the idea of the Unity which rules over the plurality of the skeleton-forms. Its first great application was the vertebral theory of the skull'.

Let me repeat, as a matter of justice, and not to allow the high praise bestowed on Goethe's efforts to mislead the reader's expectation, that the merit is that of a *thinker in science*, not the merit of an industrious discoverer and collector of details. His great effort was to create a Method, to establish principles upon which the science could be founded. In an admirable little essay on 'Experiment as the mediator between the Object and the Subject', written in 1793, we see how clear were his ideas on Method. 'Man', he says, 'regards at first all external objects with reference to himself; and rightly so, for his whole fate depends on them, on the pleasure or pain which they cause him, on their utility or danger to him'. This is the initial stage of all speculation. Its Method is the determination of the external order according to *analogies drawn from within*. The culmination of this Method is seen in the fundamental axiom of Des Cartes and Spinoza: *all clear ideas are true*. So long as this Method is followed, Metaphysics reigns triumphant, and Science is impossible. It is displaced by the Objective Method. Goethe remarks how much more difficult is the task of discerning objects according to this Method, *i.e.*, not as related to *us*, but as related to one another. Our touchstone of pleasure or pain is given up. With godlike indifference we become *spectators*, and seek that which *is*, not that which touches *us*. Thus the real botanist considers less the beauty, or the use of flowers, than their laws of growth, and their relation to each other. And as the sun shines on them, developing them all impartially, so must the philosopher look on them with calm, contemplative eye, taking the terms of his comparison from the circle he contemplates, not from any figments of his own mind. Goethe sets aside all inquiry into final causes,—by Bacon justly styled 'barren virgins',—and seeks to know what *is*.

It is worthy of remark that the study of Development is quite a modern study. Formerly men were content with the full-statured animal,—the perfected art,—the completed society. The phases of development and the laws of growth were disregarded, or touched on in a vague, uncertain manner. A change has come over the spirit of inquiry. 'The history of Development', says von Baer, 'is the true torchbearer in every inquiry into organic bodies'. In Geology, in Physiology, in History, and in Art, we are all now bent in tracing the phases of development. To understand the *grown* we try to follow the *growth*.

As a thinker in science Goethe was truly remarkable, and as a worker not contemptible. To prove how far he was in advance of his age we have only to cite a single passage which, in its aphoristic pregnant style, contains the clear announcement of biological laws, which have since been named among the glories of Geoffroy St. Hilaire, Von Baer, Milne-Edwards, Cuvier, and Lamarck.

'Every living being is not a unity but a plurality. Even when it appears as an individual, it is the reunion of beings living and existing in themselves, identical in origin, but which may appear identical or similar, different or dissimilar.

'The *more imperfect* a being is, the more do its individual parts *resemble each other*, and the more do these parts *resemble the whole*. The *more perfect* the being is, the more *dissimilar are its parts*. In the former case the parts are more or less a repetition of the whole; in the latter case they are totally unlike the whole.

'The more the parts resemble each other, the less subordination is there of one to the other. *Subordination of parts indicates high grade of organization*'*.

To illustrate by familiar examples. Take a polyp and cut it into several pieces; each piece will live and manifest all those phenomena of nutrition and sensibility which the whole polyp manifested. Turn it inside out like a glove, the internal part becomes its skin, the external part becomes its stomach. The reason is, that in the simple structure of the polyp, the parts resemble each other and resemble the whole. There is no individual organ, or apparatus of organs, performing one function, such as nutrition, and nothing else. Every function is performed by every part; just as in savage societies, every man is his own tailor, his own armourer, his own cook, and his own policeman. But take an animal higher in the scale, and there you find the structure composed of dissimilar parts, and each part having

* *Zur Morphologie*, 1807 (written in 1795), *Werke*, XXXVI, p. 7.

a different office. That animal cannot be hewn in pieces and each piece continue to live as before. That animal cannot have its skin suddenly turned into a stomach. That animal, in the social body, cannot make his own clothes or his own musket ; the division of labour which has accompanied his higher condition has robbed him of his universal dexterity.

The law invoked by Goethe, is now to be met with in every philosophic work on zoology. One form of it is known in England as Von Baer's law, viz., that Development proceeds from the Like to the Unlike, from the General to the Particular, from the Homogeneous to the Heterogeneous. I have too profound an admiration for Von Baer to wish in any way to diminish his splendid claims, but I cannot help remarking that when writers attribute to him the merit of having discovered this law, they are in direct contradiction with Von Baer himself, who not only makes no such claim, but in giving the formula adds, 'this law of development has indeed never been overlooked'*. His merit is the splendid application and demonstration of the law, not the first perception of it.

It is generally known that the law of 'division of labour in the animal organism' is claimed by Milne-Edwards, the great French zoologist, as a discovery of his own. Yet we see how clearly it is expressed in Goethe's formula. And with even more clearness do we see expressed Cuvier's principle of classification, viz., the *subordination of parts*. I do not wish to press this point further, nor do I wish that these great men should be robbed of any merit in order to glorify Goethe with their trophies. The student of history knows how discoveries are, properly speaking, made by the Age, and not by men. He knows that all discoveries have had their anticipations ; and that the world justly credits the man who makes the discovery *available*, not the man who simply perceived that it was possible. I am not here writing the history of science, but the biography of Goethe ; and the purpose of these citations is to show that he placed himself at the highest point of view possible to his age, and that as a thinker he thought the thoughts which the greatest men have subsequently made popular.

Observe, moreover, that Goethe's anticipation is not of that slight and fallacious order which, like so many other anticipations,

---

* ' Dieses Gesetz der Ausbildung ist wohl nie verkannt worden '. *Zur Entwickelungsgeschichte.* Erster Theil, p. 153. Among others, WOLFF has clearly stated it. *Theorie von der Generation,* § 28, p. 163. See also MECKEL, *Traité d'Anatomie Comparée.* French trans., 1, 297. BUFFON also says : ' Un corps organisé dont toutes les parties seraient semblables à lui-même est la plus simple car ee n'est que la répétition de la même forme '. *Hist. Nat.,* 1749, 11, 47.

rests upon a vague or incidental phrase. He did not simply attain an *aperçu* of the truth. He mastered the law, and his mastery of that law sprang from his mastery of the whole series of conceptions in which it finds its place. Thus in his *Introduction to Comparative Anatomy*, written in 1795, he pointed out the essentially sterile nature of the comparisons then made, not only in respect of comparing animals with men and with each other, not only in the abuse of final causes, but also in taking man as the standard, instead of commencing with the simplest organisms and rising gradually upwards. One year after this, Geoffroy St. Hilaire, ignorant of what was passing in the study at Weimar, and in the Museum at Jena, published his *Dissertation sur les Makis*, wherein he began his renovation of the science. He, too, like Goethe, was bent on the creation of a Type according to which all organized structures could be explained. This conception of a Type (*allgemeines Bild*), according to which the whole animal kingdom may be said to be constructed, was a truly scientific conception, and has borne noble fruit. It must not, however, be confounded with a Platonic Idea. It was no metaphysical entity, it was simply a scientific artifice. Goethe expressly says that we are not for an instant to believe in the *existence* of this Type as an objective reality, although it is the generalized expression of that which really exists. This caution has not been sufficiently present to the minds of several speculators ; and the idea of a Type has engendered not a few extravagances. Nevertheless, the net result of these speculations has been good.

One of the most interesting applications of the idea of a Type is the theory of the vertebral structure of the skull. Every cultivated reader knows that transcendental anatomists now conceive the skull as composed of three, or more, vertebræ variously modified ; but very few readers have a distinct conception of what parts of the skull are separable into vertebræ, or what is the amount of resemblance now traceable underneath the modifications ; and this is the less to be wondered at, seeing that even now there is no great unanimity among independent investigators. The principles of Morphology are not always sufficiently attended to. Just as in considering the Metamorphoses of Plants we had to dismiss the idea of the pistil or stamen having been modified from a leaf, so must we dismiss the idea of a skull having been modified from a vertebral column. In both cases we may express the morphological identity—the unity of composition—by considering

every organ in the plant as a modification of the typical leaf, and
every bone in the skeleton as a modification of the typical vertebra
(or part of a vertebra) ; but it is as inaccurate and misleading to
call the skull a vertebral column as it would be to call the brain a
spinal cord.   Between the brain and cord there is a fundamental
identity : both are masses of ganglionic substance, having (as I
have elsewhere shown*) identical properties and similar, though
not the same, functions.   But over and above these fundamental
resemblances there are manifest and important differences.   To
disregard these differences, and fix attention solely on the resemblances, is eminently unphilosophical ; and we can only be justified
in saying that the structure of the skull is on the same *general
plan* as the structure of the rest of the spinal axis, precisely as we
say that the structure of the fish exhibits the same general plan as
the structure of the quadruped.   In other words, every special
vertebra is the *individual* form of a *general* type.   The skull is not,
as Oken maintains, a modified spinal column†.   To maintain this
is to say that the spinal vertebra is the typical form from which
the cranial vertebræ are developed ; whereas, in truth, both are
but variations of one typical form ; and the idea of Kielmeyer
that the spinal column is a skull, is quite as accurate as the idea
of Oken that the skull is a spinal column.   Indeed, Kielmeyer's
idea is the more admissible of the two ; for if we seek our evidence
in embryology, or in that 'permanent embryology' the Animal
Series, we find the cranial vertebræ are *first* in order of time : in
fishes the skull alone presents true osseous development of all the
segments of the typical bone ; and if we go still lower in the series,
we find—in the Cephalopoda—a rudimentary brain, not unlike the
lower forms of the brain in fishes, enclosed in a rudimentary skull,
but without a spinal cord or a spinal column.   We are justified,
therefore, in saying that the skull cannot be a modification of the
spinal column.

Oken and Spix regard the head as a 'repetition' of the trunk ;
the brain is a repetition of the spinal cord ; the mouth repeats the
intestine and abdomen ; the nose repeats the lungs and thorax ;
the jaws the limbs.   Unfortunately for this ingenious scheme,
there are vertebrate animals with heads but without limbs ; and
it would therefore be nearer the mark to call the limbs modified

* *Reports of British Association for the Advancement of Science*, 1859, and
Physiology of Common Life, vol. II.
† 'As the brain is a more voluminously developed spinal cord, so is the brain-case a
more voluminous spinal column '.   OKEN ; cited by OWEN, *Homologies*, p. 74.

jaws, than to call jaws modified limbs.   In presence of such perplexities, we cannot wonder if some men have objected to the vertebral theory, that it amounts to nothing more than saying a vertebra is a bone.

The typical vertebra is thus defined by Owen : ' One of those segments of the endoskeleton which constitutes the axis of the body and the protecting canals of the nervous and vascular trunks'*. A perfect vertebra should therefore contain at least two arches, one to form the protecting walls of a nervous centre, the other to form the protecting walls of the great bloodvessels.   Now if we make a section of the skull, we find that this bony box 'consists of a strong central mass whence spring an upper arch and a lower arch.   The upper arch is formed by the walls of the cavity containing the brain, and stands in the same relation to it as does the neural arch of a vertebra to the spinal cord with which that brain is continuous.   The lower arch encloses the other viscera of the head, in the same way as the ribs embrace those of the thorax. And not only is the general analogy between the two manifest, but a young skull may readily be separated into a number of segments, in each of which it requires but little imagination to trace a sort of family likeness to such an expanded vertebra as the atlas'†.

The luminous guide of anatomical research, by Geoffroy St. Hilaire named 'le principe des connexions', will thus easily lead us to recognize the neural arches of the brain-case as homologues of the neural arches of the spinal axis, and we may ask with Huxley, 'What can be more natural than to take another step to conceive the skull as a portion of the vertebral column still more altered than the sacrum or coccyx, whose vertebræ are modified in correspondence with the expansion of the anterior end of the nervous centre and the needs of the cephalic end of the body?' This was the question which flashed upon the poet's mind, and which indeed is so intimately allied to the morphological doctrines he had already found realized in plants, that far from estimating it as a discovery which reflects singular honour on his sagacity, I am disposed to think more lightly of it than of many a neglected sentence in his little studied essays.   I say this, not because the idea seems obvious now it has been stated, and every one can make the egg stand on end after Columbus, but because in Goethe's attempt to carry his idea into anatomical detail, it

* OWEN : *Homologies*, p. 81.
† HUXLEY : *Croonian Lecture*, 1858.

is universally confessed that he was not successful. This is a point to which we shall presently return. Meanwhile I may add that, on re-examination of this complex subject, I am of opinion that neither Goethe nor Oken has been free from a certain indistinctness of conception, or has sufficiently kept before him all the elements of the problem. A fundamental mistake, already touched upon, is in the supposed relation of the skull to the spinal axis. Anatomists would scarcely venture to affirm that the brain bears the same relation to the cervical enlargement of the spinal cord, as that enlargement bears to the lumbar enlargement of the cord ; yet they affirm, explicitly and implicitly, that the brain-case bears the same relation to the cervical vertebræ as those vertebræ bear to the lumbar. Whereas anatomy very plainly teaches that over and above certain fundamental resemblances between the brain and spinal cord, resemblances not much greater than between the sympathetic ganglia and the brain, there are also manifest and important differences, very early exhibited in the course of embryological development, and bringing with them corresponding differences in the protecting bones. And in this point of view the researches of embryologists, as expounded in Huxley's remarkable Croonian Lecture, seem decisive. I will cite here the conclusion to which Huxley is led : 'The fallacy involved in the vertebral theory of the skull', he says, ' is like that which before Von Baer infested our notions of the relations between fishes and mammals. The mammal was imagined to be a modified fish, whereas, in truth, both fish and mammal start from a common point, and each follows its own road thence. So I conceive what the facts teach us is this : the spinal column and the skull start from the same primitive condition—a common central plate with its laminæ dorsales and ventrales—whence they immediately begin to diverge. The spinal column, in all cases, becomes segmented into its somatomes ; and in the great majority of cases distinct centra and intercentra are developed, enclosing the notocord more or less completely. The cranium never becomes segmented into somatomes ; distinct centra and intercentra, like those of the spinal column, are never developed in it. Much of the basis cranii lies beyond the notocord. In the process of ossification there is a certain analogy between the spinal column and the cranium, but the analogy becomes weaker as we proceed towards the anterior end of the skull '.

Although Huxley insists, perhaps, too much upon the *differences*, in his impatience at the too great emphasis which has been laid on the *resemblances*, his criticism seems to me conclusive against the vertebral theory as generally understood. It is certainly extending the principles of transcendental anatomy to a hazardous limit when the brain is regarded as a 'repetition' of any segments of the spinal cord. The differences between the two are more than differences of volume and shape. In the one the grey matter is inside ; in the other it is outside. From the one sensory and motor nerves, symmetrically in pairs, are given off to supply the skin and muscles ; in the other the sensory and motor nerves are not only distributed in a very different manner—the optic, olfactory, and acoustic having no corresponding motor nerves— but they are limited to ganglia at the base and in the medulla oblongata : the two most voluminous and important parts of the brain (the cerebrum and cerebellum) having *no* nerves whatever. In the presence of such wide diversities as these, not to mention others, it is surely an abuse of language when Oken calls the brain a more voluminously developed spinal cord, and deduces thence that the brain-case is only a repetition of the spinal column.

Having thus endeavoured to convey some idea of the famous vertebral theory of the skull, I have now to consider a somewhat angrily debated question, affecting Goethe's character more than his intellectual pretensions, namely, the charge of mendacious vanity brought against him by Oken, and, I am sorry to say, very inconsiderately countenanced by Professor Owen*, in respect to priority in the discovery.

Fifteen years after Goethe had passed away from this world, and when therefore there was no power of reply, Oken in the *Isis* (1847, *Heft* VII) made his charge. His statement completely staggered me, suggesting very painful feelings as to Goethe's conduct. Indeed, the similarity in the stories of both suggests suspicion. Goethe, during one of his rambles in the Jewish cemetery near Venice, noticed the skull of a ram, which had been cut longitudinally, and on examining it, the idea occurred to him that the face was composed of three vertebræ : 'the transition from the anterior sphenoid to the ethmoid was evident at once'. Now, compare Oken's story. He narrates how in 1802 in a work on the Senses, he had represented these organs as repetitions of lower organs, although he had not then grasped the idea, which lay so close at hand, respecting the skull as a repetition of the spinal column. In

* Art. OKEN in *Encyclopædia Britannica*, 8th edit.

1803 he identified the jaws of insects as limbs of the head ; and in 1806, while rambling in the Harz mountains, he picked up the skull of a deer : on examining it, he exclaimed, 'That is a vertebral column !' Virchow admits that the coincidence in the stories is singular, but adds that the discovery is just as probable in the one case as in the other ; all that is proved by the coincidence being that both minds were on the verge of the discovery. Goethe by long physiognomical and osteological studies was prepared for the idea ; and was naturally led from the Metamorphoses of Plants to those of Insects ; and if Oken reversed this order, passing from insects to mammals, he was, nevertheless, many years later than Goethe, as dates unequivocally prove. It is important to bear in mind that the vertebral theory is only another application of those morphological doctrines which Goethe had developed and applied to plants ; and although it is quite *possible* that he might have held these views without making the special application to the skull, yet we know as a fact that he at once saw how the morphological laws must necessarily apply to animals, since he expressly states this in announcing his discovery to Herder*. Nay, he shortly after- wards wrote, ' In Natural History I shall bring you what you little expect.   I believe myself to be very near the law of organization '. Still it may be objected, this is no proof ; it only shows that Goethe applied his doctrines to the animal organization, not that he made a special application to the skull.   Even this doubt, however, has been finally settled by the recently published correspondence, which gives us a letter from Goethe to Herder's wife, dated 4th May, 1790, from Venice. ' Through a singular and lucky accident I have been enabled to take a step forwards in my explanation of the animal development (*Thierbildung*).   My servant, in jest, took up the fragment of an animal's skull from the Jewish cemetery, pre- tending to offer it me as a Jew's skull '.   Now when we remember that Goethe in after years affirmed that it was in 1790, and in the Jewish cemetery of Venice, that the idea of the vertebral structure of the skull flashed upon him, the evidence of this letter is conclusive.

Oken declares he made his discovery in 1806, and that in 1807 he wrote his Academic Programme.   He was then a *Privat-Docent* in Göttingen, ' at a time, therefore, when Goethe certainly knew nothing of my existence '.   He sent his dissertation to Jena, where he had just been appointed professor.   Of that university Goethe

* *Italiänische Reise*, ii, p. 5.

was curator. Oken considers this fact decisive : namely, that Goethe would assuredly have remonstrated against Oken's claim to the discovery had he not recognized its justice. The fact, however, is by no means decisive : we shall see presently that Goethe had his own reasons for silence. ' I naturally sent Goethe a copy of my programme. This discovery pleased him so much that he invited me, at Easter, 1808, to spend a week with him at Weimar, which I did. As long as the discovery was ridiculed by men of science Goethe was silent, but no sooner did it attain renown through the works of Meckel, Spix, and others, than there grew up a murmur among Goethe's servile admirers that this idea originated with him. About this time Bojanus went to Weimar, and hearing of Goethe's discovery, half believed it, and sent the rumour to me, which I thoughtlessly printed in the *Isis* (1818, p. 509) ; whereupon I announced that I made my discovery in the autumn of 1806'. This is equivocal. He did *not* throw any doubt on Goethe's claim to priority, he only asserted his own originality. ' Now that Bojanus had brought the subject forward', he adds, ' Goethe's vanity was piqued, and he came afterwards, thirteen years subsequent to my discovery, and said he had held the opinion for thirty years'.

Why was Goethe silent when Oken first announced his discovery? and why did not Oken make the charge of plagiarism during Goethe's lifetime? The first question may be answered from Goethe's own works. In a note entitled *Das Schädelgerüst aus sechs Wirbelknochen auferbaut*, after alluding to his recognition first of three and subsequently of six vertebræ in the skull, which he spoke of among his friends, who set to work to demonstrate it if possible, he says : ' In the year 1807 this theory appeared tumultuously and imperfectly before the public, and naturally awakened great disputes and some applause. How seriously it was damaged by the incomplete and fantastic method of exposition History must relate'. This criticism of the exposition will be understood by every one who has read Oken, and who knows Goethe's antipathy to metaphysics.* With all his prepossession in favour of a Type, he could not patiently have accepted an exposition which ' tumultuously' announced that ' The whole man is but a vertebra'. Accordingly he took no notice of the tumultuous metaphysician ; and in his *Tag und Jahres Hefte* he mentions that while he was working out his theory with two friends, Riemer

---

* So also Cuvier's antipathy to this exposition made him blind to the truth which it contained.

and Voigt, they brought him, with some surprise, the news that this idea had just been laid before the public in an academic programme, 'a fact', he adds, '*which they, being still alive, can testify*'. Why did he not claim priority? 'I told my friends to keep quiet, for the idea was not properly worked out in the programme ; and that it was not elaborated from original observations would be plain to all scientific men. I was frequently besought to speak plainly on the subject ; but I was firm in my silence'.

When I first discussed this question, and knew nothing of the decisive evidence which lay unpublished in the letter to Herder's wife, I said that this statement carried complete conviction to my mind. It was published many years before Oken made his charge, and it accused him in the most explicit terms of having prematurely disclosed an idea Goethe was then elaborating with the assistance of his friends. Nor was this all. It appealed to two honourable and respected men, then living, as witnesses of the truth. Oken said nothing when the question could have been peremptorily settled by calling upon Voigt and Riemer. He waited till death rendered an appeal impossible. He says, indeed, that he made no answer to the first passage I have cited, because he was not *named* in it, and he 'did not wish to involve himself in a host of disagreeables'. But this is no answer to the *second* passage. There he is named as plainly as if the name of Oken were printed in full ; and not only is he named, but Goethe's friends speak of Oken's coming forward with Goethe's idea as a matter which 'surprised' them. Those to whom this reasoning was not conclusive are now referred to the confirmation it receives from the letter to Herder's wife.

Having vindicated Goethe's character, and shown that *biographically* we are fully justified in assigning to him the honour of having first conceived this theory, it now remains to be added that *historically* the priority of Oken's claim must be admitted. In writing the poet's biography, it is of some importance to show that he was not indebted to Oken for the discovery. In writing the history of science, it would be to Oken that priority would be assigned, simply because, according to the judicious principles of historical appreciation, priority of publication carries off the prize. No man's claim to priority is acknowledged unless he can bring forward the evidence of publication ; otherwise every discovery might be claimed by those who have no right to it. Moreover, Oken has another claim : to him undeniably belongs the merit of having introduced the idea into the scientific world, accompanied with sufficient amount of detail to make it acceptable to scientific minds, and to set them to work in verifying the idea. On these grounds I think it indisputable that the vertebral theory must be attributed to Oken, and not to Goethe; although it is not less indisputable that Goethe did anticipate the discovery by sixteen years, and would have earned the right to claim it of History, had he made his discovery public, instead of privately discussing it with his friends. Virchow thinks otherwise; he assigns priority to Goethe; but he would, I am sure, admit the generally received principle that priority of publication is the test upon which alone History can rely.

To conclude this somewhat lengthy chapter on the scientific studies, it must be stated that, for the sake of bringing together his various efforts into a manageable whole, I have not attended strictly to chronology. Nor have I specified the various separate essays he has written. They are all to be found collected in his works. My main object has been to show what were the directions of his mind; what were his achievements and failures in Science; what place Science filled in his life, and how false the supposition is that he was a mere dabbler. What Buffon says of Pliny may truly be said of Goethe, that he had *cette facilité de penser en grand qui multiplie la science;* and it is only as a thinker in this great department that I claim a high place for him.

CHAPTER X

THE CAMPAIGN IN FRANCE

WE now return to the narrative, some points of which have been anticipated in the preceding chapter. In 1790 Goethe undertook the government of all the Institutions for Science and Art, and busied himself with the arrangement of the Museums and Botanical Gardens at Jena. In March of the same year he went once more to Italy to meet the Duchess Amalia and Herder in Venice. There he tried in Science to find refuge from troubled thoughts. Italy on a second visit seemed, however, quite another place to him. He began to suspect there had been considerable illusion in the charm of his first visit. The *Venetian Epigrams*, if compared with the *Roman Elegies*, will indicate the difference of

his mood. The yearning regret, the fulness of delight, the newness of wonder which give their accents to the *Elegies*, are replaced by sarcasms and the bitterness of disappointment. It is
true that many of these epigrams were written subsequently, as
their contents prove, but the mass of them are products of the
Venetian visit. Something of this dissatisfaction must be attributed to his position. He was ill at ease with the world. The
troubles of the time, and the troubles of his own domestic affairs,
aggravated the dangers which then threatened his aims of self-
culture, and increased his difficulty in finding that path in Science
and Art whereon the culture of the world might be pursued.

In June he returned to Weimar. In July the Duke sent for him at
the Prussian Camp in Silesia, 'where, instead of stones and flowers,
he would see the field sown with troops'. He went unwillingly,
but compensated himself by active researches into 'stones and
flowers', leaving to the Duke and others such interest as was to be
found in soldiers. He lived like a hermit in the camp, and began to
write an essay on the development of animals, and a comic opera.

In August they returned. The Duchess Amalia and Herder,
impatient at 'such waste of time over old bones', plagued him
into relinquishing osteology, and urged him to complete *Wilhelm
Meister*. He did not, however, proceed far with it. The creative
impulse was past ; and to disprove Newton was a more imperious
desire. In 1791, which was a year of quiet study and domestic
happiness for him, the Court Theatre was established. He
undertook the direction with delight. In a future chapter we
shall follow his efforts to create a national stage, and by bringing
them before the eye in one continuous series, save the tedious
repetition of isolated details. In July the Duchess Amalia
founded her Friday Evenings. Her palace, between the hours
of five and eight, saw the Duke, the Duchess Luise, Goethe and
his circle, with a few favoured friends from the Court, assembled to
hear some one of the members read a composition of his own.
No sort of etiquette was maintained. Each member, on entering,
sat down where he pleased. Only for the Reader was a distinct
place allotted. One night Goethe read them the genealogy of
Cagliostro, which he had brought from Italy ; another night he
gave them a lecture on Colours ; Herder lectured on Immortality ;
Bertuch on Chinese Colours and English Gardens ; Böttiger on
the Vases of the Ancients ; Hufeland on his favourite theme of
Longevity ; and Bode read fragments of his translation of

Montaigne. When the reading was over, they all approached a large table in the middle of the room, on which lay some engravings or some novelty of interest, and friendly discussion began. The absence of etiquette made these reunions delightful.

The mention of Cagliostro in the preceding paragraph recalls Goethe's comedy, *Der Gross Kophta*, in which he dramatized the story of the Diamond Necklace. It had originally been arranged as an opera ; Reichardt was to have composed the music ; and if the reader happens to have waded through this dull comedy, he will regret that it was not made an opera, or anything else except what 'it is. One is really distressed to find such productions among the writings of so great a genius, and exasperated to find critics lavish in their praise of a work which their supersubtle ingenuity cannot rescue from universal neglect. I will not occupy space with an analysis of it.

And now he was to be torn from his quiet studies to follow the fortunes of an unquiet camp. The King of Prussia and the Duke of Brunswick at the head of a large army invaded France, to restore Louis XVI to his throne and save legitimacy from the sacrilegious hands of Sansculottism. France, it is said, groaned under the tyranny of factions, and yearned for deliverance. The emigrants made it clear as day that the allies would be welcomed by the whole nation ; and the German rulers willingly lent their arms to the support of legitimacy. Karl August, passionately fond of the army, received the command of a Prussian regiment. And Goethe, passionately fond of Karl August, followed him into the field. But he followed the Duke—he had no sympathy with the cause. Indeed, he had no strong feeling either way. Legitimacy was no passion with him ; still less was Republicanism. Without interest in passing politics, profoundly convinced that all salvation could only come through inward culture, and dreading disturbances mainly because they rendered culture impossible, he was emphatically the ' Child of Peace', and could at no period of his life be brought to sympathize with great struggles. He disliked the Revolution as he disliked the Reformation, because they both thwarted the peaceful progress of development :

> Franzthum drängt in diesen verworrenen Tagen wie ehmals
> Lutherthum es gethan, ruhige Bildung zurück.

That philosophers and patriots should thunder against such a doctrine, refute its arguments, and proclaim its dangers, is reasonable enough ; but how strangely unreasonable in philosophers and patriots to thunder against Goethe, because he, holding this doctrine, wrote and acted in its spirit ! We do not need this example to teach us how men transfer their hatred of opinions to the holders of the hated opinions, otherwise we might wonder at the insensate howl which has been raised against the greatest glory of the German name, because he did not share the opinions of the howlers ; opinions, too, which they for the most part would not have held, had they not been instructed by the events which have since given approbation to what *then* seemed madness.

It was not in Goethe's nature to be much moved by events, to be deeply interested in the passing troubles of external life. A meditative mind like his naturally sought in the eternal principles of Nature the stimulus and the food, which other minds sought in passing phenomena of the day. A poet and a philosopher is bound to be interested in the great questions of poetry and philosophy ; but to rail at him for not also taking part in politics, is as irrational as to rail at the prime minister because he cares not two pins for Greek Art, and has no views on the transmutation of species. It is said, and very foolishly said, that Goethe turned from politics to art and science, because politics disturbed him, and because he was too *selfish* to interest himself in the affairs of others. But this accusation is on a par with those ungenerous accusations which declare heterodoxy to be the shield of profligacy : as if doubts proceeded only from dissolute habits. How unselfish Goethe was, those best know who know him best ; it would be well if we could say so much of many who devote themselves to patriotic schemes. Patriotism may be quite as selfish as Science or Art, even when it is a devout conviction ; nor is it likely to be less selfish when, as so often happens, patriotism is only an uneasy pauperism.

That Goethe sincerely desired the good of mankind, and that he laboured for it in his way with a perseverance few have equalled, is surely enough to absolve him from the charge of selfishness, because his labours did not take the special direction of politics ? What his opinions were is one thing, another thing his conduct. Jean Paul says, 'he was more far-sighted than the rest of the world, for in the beginning of the French Revolution he despised the patriots as much as he did at the end'. I do not detect any feeling so deep as contempt, either late or early ; but it is certain that while Klopstock and others were madly enthusiastic at the

opening of this terrible drama, they were as madly fanatical against
it before its close; whereas Goethe seems to have held pretty
much the same opinion throughout. It has been finely said:
'Toute période historique a deux faces: l'une assez pauvre, assez
ridicule, ou assez malheureuse, qui est tournée vers le calendrier
du temps; l'autre grande, efficace, et sérieuse, qui regarde celui
de l'éternité'. Of no epoch is this more strikingly true than of
the French Revolution. In it Goethe only saw the temporal
aspect; his want of historical philosophy prevented him from
seeing the eternal aspect.

There were three principles promulgated by the Republicans,
which to him were profound absurdities. The first was the doctrine of equality; not simply of equality in the eye of the law (that
he accepted), but of absolute equality. His study of Nature, no
less than his study of men, led him, as it could not but lead him,
to the conviction that each Individual is perfect in itself, and
in so far equals the highest; but that no one Individual is exactly
like another.

> Gleich sei keiner dem Andern; doch gleich sei Jeder dem Höchsten.
> Wie das zu machen? es sei Jeder vollendet in sich.

The second revolutionary principle was the doctrine of government by the people. He believed in no such governmental
power. Even when you kill the King, he says, you do not know
how to rule in his place.

> Sie gönnten Cäsar'n das Reich nicht,
> Und wussten's nicht zu regieren.

He pointed to the fate of France 'as a lesson both to governors
and the governed, but more even for the latter than the former.
The rulers were destroyed, but who was there to protect the Many
against the Many? The Mob became the Tyrant'.

> Frankreichs traurig Geschick, die Grossen mögen's bedenken;
> Aber bedenken fürwahr sollen es Kleine noch mehr.
> Grosse gingen zu Grunde: doch wer beschützte die Menge
> Gegen die Menge? Da war Menge der Menge Tyrann.

What wonder then if he felt repulsion to all the 'Apostles of
Freedom', when on close scrutiny he found they all sought
nothing but licence?

> Alle Freiheits-Apostel, sie waren mir immer zuwider
> Willkür suchte doch nur Jeder am Ende für sich.

The third revolutionary principle was, that political freedom is necessary to man. In the early days of authorship he had already spoken his conviction that such freedom was by no means necessary. In *Egmont* it reappears ; and through life we find him insisting on the fact that no man *can* be free ; the only freedom necessary is that which enables each to go about his business in security, to rear house and children, to move unconstrained in his small circle. It does not seem to occur to him that even this freedom is impossible without political freedom. It does not occur to him that police-regulations affect the individual, and governmental regulations affect the nation*.

But while he was thus fundamentally opposed to the principles of the Revolution, and the government of the Many, it is equally clear that he had no sympathy with the Royalists ; that he absolved neither their policy nor their acts. The madness of the Terrorists was to him no excuse for the duplicity of the Royalists. 'No, you are not right. No, you must not deceive the Mob, because the Mob is wild and foolish. Wild and foolish are all Mobs which have been duped. Be only *upright* with them, and you will gradually train them to be men'.

> Sage, thun wir nicht recht ?   Wir müssen den Pöbel betrügen.
> Sieh' nur, wie ungeschickt, sieh' nur, wie wild er sich zeigt !—
> Ungeschickt und wild sind alle rohen Betrognen ;
> Seid nur *redlich*, und so führt ihn zum Menschlichen an.

Nor was all the wild oratory so irrational in his eyes as the Royalists proclaimed it. 'These street orators seem to me also mad ; but a madman will speak wisdom in freedom, when in slavery wisdom is dumb'.

> Mir auch scheinen sie toll ; doch redet ein Toller
> Weise Sprüche, wenn, ach !   Weisheit im Sclaven verstummt.

To Eckermann he said : 'A revolution is always the fault of the government, never of the people'.

I might extend these remarks by showing how such political principles naturally grew up in the course of his education, and how he, in the forty-third year of his age, was not likely to become an apostle of Freedom, or to become deeply interested in political

---

* This was Dr. Johnson's opinion : 'Sir, I would not give a guinea to live under one form of government rather than another. It is of no moment to the happiness of an individual. Sir, the danger of the abuse of power is nothing to a private man. What Frenchman is prevented from passing his life as he pleases?' BOSWELL, chap. xxvi. No one thinks this opinion a proof of Johnson's heartless egoism.

disturbances, especially at this period when he had completely emerged from the rebellious strivings of his youth, and had settled the aims of manhood.   But enough has been said to show what his position truly was ; and the reader who will not accept it with that impartiality which it claims, will certainly not accept it more readily, because he is told its origin and growth.   The American who despises the Negro because he is black, will not despise him less on learning that the blackness is nothing but a peculiar modification of the pigment in the skin.

Goethe has himself written a diary of the 'Campaign in France'*, and if I had any belief in the reader's following the advice, I would advise him to read that work, and save some pages of this volume. In well-grounded suspicion that he will do nothing of the kind, I select a few details of interest, and string them on a thread of narrative.

The Allies entered France, believing the campaign would be a mere promenade.   Longwy they were assured would soon surrender, and the people receive them with open arms.   Longwy did surrender ; but the people, so far from showing any disposition to welcome them, everywhere manifested the most determined resistance.   The following passage will let us pretty clearly into the secret of Goethe's views.   ' Thus did the Prussians, Austrians, and a portion of the French, come to carry on their warlike operations on the French soil.   By whose power and authority did they this ? They might have done it in their own name.   War had been partly declared against them—their league was no secret ; but another pretext was invented.   They took the field in the name of Louis XVI : they exacted nothing, but they borrowed compulsorily.   *Bons* had been printed, which the commander signed ; but whoever had them in his possession filled them up at his pleasure, according to circumstances, and Louis XVI was to pay. Perhaps, after the manifesto, nothing had so much exasperated the people against the monarchy as did this treatment.   I was myself present at a scene which I remember as a most tragic one. Several shepherds, who had succeeded in uniting their flocks, in order to conceal them for safety in the forests or other retired places, being seized by some active patrols and brought to the army, were at first well received and kindly treated.   They were asked who were the different proprietors : the flocks were separated

---

* It has been translated by Mr. Robert Farie.   The extracts which follow are from this translation.

and counted. Anxiety and fear, but still with some hope, fluctuated in the countenances of the worthy people. But when this mode of proceeding ended in the division of the flocks among the regiments and companies, whilst, on the other hand, the pieces of paper drawn on Louis XVI were handed over quite civilly to their proprietors, and their woolly favourites were slaughtered at their feet by the impatient and hungry soldiers, I confess that my eyes and my soul have seldom witnessed a more cruel spectacle, and more profound manly suffering in all its gradations. The Greek tragedies alone have anything so purely, deeply pathetic'.

Throughout these pages he is seen interesting himself in men, in science, in nature,—but not at all in the cause of the war. Soldiers fishing attract him to their side, and he is in ecstasies with the optical phenomena observed in the water. The bombardment of Verdun begins, and he enters a battery which is hard at work, but is driven out by the intolerable roar of the cannon ; on his way out he meets the Prince Reuss. ' We walked up and down behind some vineyard walls, protected by them from the cannon balls. After talking about sundry political matters by which we only got entangled in a labyrinth of hopes and cares, the Prince asked me what I was occupied with at present, and was much surprised when, instead of speaking of tragedies and novels, excited by the phenomenon of to-day, I began to speak with great animation of the doctrine of colours'. He has been reproached for this 'indifference', and by men who extol Archimedes for having prosecuted his studies during the siege of Syracuse. It was as natural for Goethe to have his mind occupied with a curious phenomenon amid the roar of cannon, as it was for the soldiers to sing libertine songs when marching to death. The camp too afforded him, with its opportunities for patience, some good opportunities for observing mankind. He notices the injurious influence of war upon the mind: ' You are daring and destructive one day, and humane and creative the next ; you accustom yourself to phrases adapted to excite and keep alive hope in the midst of most desperate circumstances ; by this means a kind of hypocrisy is produced of an unusual character, and is distinguished from the priestly and courtly kind'.

After detailing some of the miseries of the campaigning life, he says : ' Happy is he whose bosom is filled with a higher passion. The colour phenomenon observed at the spring never for a moment left me. I thought it over and over again, that I might be able to make experiments on it. I dictated to Vogel a loose sketch

of my theory, and drew the figures afterwards.   These papers I
still possess with all the marks of the rainy weather, as witnesses
of the faithful study in the dubious path I had entered'.   Very
characteristic of his thirst for knowledge is this daring exposure of
himself: 'I had heard much of the cannon fever, and I wanted to
know what kind of thing it was.   Ennui and a spirit which every
kind of danger excited to daring, nay even to rashness, induced
me to ride up quite coolly to the outwork of La Lune.   This was
again occupied by our people ; but it presented the wildest aspect.
The roofs were shot to pieces, the cornshocks scattered about, the
bodies of men mortally wounded stretched upon them here and
there, and occasionally a spent cannon-ball fell and rattled among
the ruins of the tile-roofs.   Quite alone, and left to myself, I rode
away on the heights to the left, and could plainly survey the favourable position of the French : they were standing in the form of a
semicircle, in the greatest quiet and security ; Kellermann, on the
left wing, being the easiest to reach. . . . I had now arrived quite
in the region where the balls were playing across me : the sound
of them is curious enough, as if it were composed of the humming
of tops, the gurgling of water, and the whistling of birds.   They
were less dangerous by reason of the wetness of the ground ;
wherever one fall it stuck fast.   And thus my foolish experimental
ride was secured against the danger at least of the balls rebound-
ing.   In these circumstances, I was soon able to remark that something unusual was taking place within me : I paid close attention
to it, and still the sensation can be described only by similitude.
It appeared as if you were in some extremely hot place, and at the
same time quite penetrated by the heat of it, so that you feel yourself, as it were, quite one with the element in which you are.   The
eyes lose nothing of their strength or clearness ; but it is as if the
world had a kind of brown-red tint, which makes the situation, as
well as the surrounding objects, more impressive.   I was unable
to perceive any agitation of the blood, but everything seemed
rather to be swallowed up in the glow of which I speak.   From this,
then, it is clear in what sense this condition can be called a fever.
It is remarkable, however, that the horrible uneasy feeling arising
from it is produced in us solely through the ears.   For the cannon
thunder, the howling, whistling crashing of the balls through the
air, is the real cause of these sensations.   After I had ridden back,
and was in perfect security, I remarked with surprise that the glow
was completely extinguished, and not the slightest feverish agitation

was left behind.   On the whole, this condition is one of the least
desirable, as indeed among my dear and noble comrades, I found
scarcely one who expressed a really passionate desire to try it.   Thus
the day had passed away ; the French stood immovable, Kellermann having taken also a more advantageous position.   Our people
were withdrawn out of the fire, and it was exactly as if nothing
had taken place.   The greatest consternation was diffused among
the army.   That very morning they had thought of nothing short
of spitting the whole of the French and devouring them ; nay, I
myself had been tempted to take part in this dangerous expedition
from the unbounded confidence I felt in such an army and in the
Duke of Brunswick ; but now every one went about alone, nobody
looked at his neighbour, or if it did happen, it was to curse or
to swear.   Just as night was coming on, we had accidentally formed
ourselves into a circle, in the middle of which the usual fire even
could not be kindled : most of them were silent, some spoke, and
in fact the power of reflection and judgment was awanting to all.
At last I was called upon to say what I thought of it ; for I had been
in the habit of enlivening and amusing the troop with short sayings.
This time I said : From this place and from this day forth commences a new era in the world's history, and you can all say that
you were present at its birth '.

The night brought rain and wind.   They had lain on the
ground behind a hill which protected them from the cutting wind,
when it was proposed that they should bury themselves in the
earth, covered by their cloaks.   Holes were dug, and even Karl
August himself did not refuse this 'premature burial'.   Goethe
wrapped himself in a blanket and slept better than Ulysses.   In
vain a colonel remonstrated, and pointed out to them that the
French had a battery on the opposite hill with which they could
bury the sleepers in real earnest.   Sleep and warmth for the
present were worth more than security against possible danger.

The defeat at Valmy, slight as it was, discouraged the Prussians,
and exhilarated the French.   The Prussians, startled at the cry of
vive la nation ! with which the republicans charged them, and
finding themselves on a foreign territory without magazines, stores,
or any preparations for a great conflict, perceived the mistake they
had made, and began to retreat.   It was doubtless a great relief
to Goethe to hear that he had not much longer to endure the
hardships of campaigning.   He had no interest in the cause, and
he had not gained, by closer contact with the leaders, a higher

opinion of their characters. 'Although I had already found among the diplomatic corps some genuine and valuable friends, I could not refrain, so often as I saw them in the midst of these great movements, from making some odd comparisons which forced themselves irresistibly upon my mind : they appeared to me as so many playhouse directors, who choose the pieces, distribute the parts, and move about unseen ; while the actors, doing their best, and well prompted, have to commit the result of their exertions to fortune and the humour of the public'.

He fell in with a collection of pamphlets, and among them were the instructions of the Notables. 'The moderation of the people's demands at this time, the modesty with which they were put forward, formed a striking contrast to the violence, insolence, and desperation of the present state of things. I read these papers with genuine emotion, and took copies of some of them'.

His return was slow. Meanwhile, the arms of the French seemed everywhere victorious. Verdun and Longwy were once more occupied by the republicans. On the Rhine, Treves and Mainz had capitulated to Custine. Goethe says :

'In the midst of this misery and confusion, a missing letter of my mother's found me, and reminded me, in a strange manner, of many peaceful passages of my youth, and circumstances connected with my family and native town. My uncle, the Alderman Textor, had died, whose near relationship had excluded me, during his lifetime, from the honourable and useful post of a Frankfurt councillor ; and now, in accordance with an established and laudable custom, they thought immediately of me, I being pretty far advanced among the Frankfurt graduates. My mother had been commissioned to ask me whether I would accept the office of councillor if I were chosen one of those to be balloted for, and the golden ball should fall to me. Such a question could not, perhaps, have arrived at a more singular time than the present ; I was taken by surprise, and thrown back upon myself ; a thousand images started up before me, and prevented me from forming any connected conclusion. But as a sick person or prisoner forgets for the moment his pains and troubles whilst listening to some tale which is related to him, so was I also carried back to other spheres and other times. I found myself in my grandfather's garden, where the espaliers, richly laden with nectarines, were wont to tempt the grandson's longing appetite ; and only the threat of banishment from this paradise, only the hope of receiv-

ing from the good old grandfather's own hand the red-cheeked
fruit when ripe, could restrain this longing within reasonable
bounds till the proper time at length arrived. Then I saw the
venerable old man busied with his roses, and carefully protecting
his hands from the thorns with the antiquarian gloves, delivered
up as tribute by tax-freed cities; like the noble Laertes,—all but
in his longings and his sorrows. Afterwards I saw him in his
mayor's robes, with gold chain, sitting on the throne-seat under
the Emperor's portrait; then, last of all, alas! in his dotage, for
several years in his sick chair; and, finally, in his grave! On my
last journey to Frankfurt, I had found my uncle in possession
of the house, court, and garden; as a worthy son of such a
father, he attained, like him, the highest offices in the government
of this free town. Here, in this intimate family circle, in this
unchanged old well-known place, these boyhood recollections
were vividly called forth, and brought with new emphasis before
me. They were united also with other youthful feelings which
I must not conceal. What citizen of a free city will deny that he
has been ambitious of, sooner or later, rising to the dignity of
councillor, alderman, or burgomaster; and has industriously and
carefully striven, to the best of his ability, to attain to them, or
perhaps other less important offices? For the pleasing thought of
one day filling some post in the government is awakened early in
the breast of every republican, and is liveliest and proudest in the
soul of a boy. I could not, however, abandon myself long to these
pleasing dreams of my childhood. But, too soon aroused, I sur-
veyed the ominous locality which surrounded me, the melancholy
circumstances which hemmed me in, and, at the same time, the
cloudy obscured prospect in the direction of my native town. I
saw Mentz in the hands of the French; Frankfurt threatened,
if not already taken; the way to it obstructed; and within those
walls, streets, squares, dwellings, the friends of my youth, and my
relations, already overtaken perhaps by the same misfortunes from
which I had seen Longwy and Verdun so cruelly suffer: who
would have dared to rush headlong into the midst of such a state
of things? But even in the happiest days of that venerable
corporation, it would have been impossible for me to agree to this
proposal; the reasons for which are easily explained. For twelve
years I had enjoyed singular good fortune,—the confidence as well
as the indulgence of the Duke of Weimar. This highly gifted
and cultivated prince was pleased to approve of my inadequate

services, and gave me facilities for developing myself, which would have been possible under no other conditions in my native country. My gratitude was boundless, as well as my attachment to his august consort and mother, to his young family, and to a country to which I had not been altogether unserviceable. And had I not to think also of newly acquired, highly cultivated friends, and of so many other domestic enjoyments and advantages which had sprung from my favourable and settled position?'

A pleasant surprise was in store for him on his return to Weimar, in the shape of the house in the *Frauenplan*, which the Duke had ordered to be rebuilt during his absence. This house, considered a palace in those days, was a very munificent gift. It was not so far advanced in the reconstruction but that he could fashion it according to his taste; he arranged the splendid stair-case, which was too large for the proportions of the house, but was a pleasant reminiscence of Italy.

The passer-by sees, through the windows, the busts of the Olympian gods, which stand there as symbols of calmness and completeness. On entering the hall, the eye rests upon two noble casts, in niches; or rests on the plan of Rome which decorates the wall, and on Meyer's *Aurora*, which colours the ceiling. The group of Ildefonso stands near the door; and on the threshold, welcome speaks in the word ' SALVE '. On the first floor we enter the Juno room, so called from the colossal bust of Juno which consecrates it; on the walls are the *Loggie* of Raphael. To the left of this stands the Reception room; in it is the harpsichord which furnished many a musical evening : Hummel and the young Mendelssohn played on it, Catalani and Sontag sang to it. Over the doors were Meyer's mythological cartoons; on the walls a copy of Aldobrandi's Wedding, with sketches of the great masters, and etchings. A large cabinet contained the engravings and gems ; a side closet the bronze statuettes, lamps and vases. On the other side, connected with the Juno room and opposite the Reception room, were three small rooms. The first contained sketches of Italian masters, and a picture by Angelica Kaufmann. The second and third contained various specimens of earthenware, and an apparatus to illustrate the *Farbenlehre*. A prolongation of the Juno room backwards was the Bust room, with the busts of Schiller, Herder, Jacobi, Vos, Sterne, Byron, etc. To this succeeded, a few steps lower, and opening on the trellised staircase leading to the garden, a small room in which he was fond of dining with a small party. The garden was tastefully laid out. The summer-houses contained his natural history collections.

But the sanctuary of the house is the study, library, and bedroom. In the rooms just described the visitor sees the tokens of Goethe's position as minister and lover of Art. Compared with the Weimar standard of that day, these rooms were of palatial magnificence ; but compared even with the Weimer standard, the rooms into which we now enter are of a more than bourgeois simplicity. Passing through an ante-chamber, where in cupboards stand his mineralogical collections, we enter the study, a low-roofed narrow room, somewhat dark, for it is lighted only through two tiny windows, and furnished with a simplicity quite touching to behold*. In the centre stands a plain oval table of unpolished oak. No arm-chair is to be seen, no sofa, nothing which speaks of ease. A plain hard chair has beside it the basket in which he used to place his handkerchief. Against the wall, on the right, is a long pear-tree table, with book-shelves, on which stand lexicons and manuals. Here hangs a pin-cushion, venerable in dust, with the visiting cards, and other trifles, which death has made sacred. Here also a medallion of Napoleon, with this circumscription : ' Scilicet immenso superest ex nomine multum '. On the side wall, again, a book-case with some works of poets. On the wall to the left is a long desk of soft wood, at which he was wont to write. On it lie the original manuscripts of *Götz* and the *Elegies*, and a bust of Napoleon, in milk-white glass, which in the light shimmers with blue and flame colour ; hence prized as an illustration of the *Farbenlehre*. A sheet of paper with notes of contemporary history is fastened near the door, and behind this door schematic tables of music and geology. The same door leads into a bedroom, if bedroom it can be called, which no maid-of-all-work in England would accept without a murmur : it is a closet with a window. A simple bed, an arm-chair by its side, and a tiny washing-table with a small white basin on it, and a sponge, is all the furniture. To enter this room with any feeling for the greatness and goodness of him who slept here, and who here slept his last sleep, brings tears into our eyes, and makes the breathing deep.

From the other side of the study we enter the library ; which should rather be called a lumber-room of books. Rough deal shelves hold the books, with paper labels on which are written ' philosophy ', ' history ', ' poetry ', etc., to indicate the classification.

* I describe it as it now stands, just as it was on the day of his death.

Goethe's home in Weimar

The yellow room

Small dining room

The staircase

Juno room

The big collection room

Urbino room

Goethe's workroom

It was very interesting to look over this collection, and the English reader will imagine the feelings with which I took down a volume of Taylor's *Historic Survey of German Poetry*, sent by Carlyle, and found, in the piece of paper used as a book-mark, a bit of Carlyle's own handwriting.

Such was Goethe's house, during the many years of his occupation. At the time of which we now write it was of course somewhat different. The pleasure of reconstructing it, and the happiness of being once more at home with Christiane and his boy, able to pursue his studies in peace, were agreeable contrasts with his life in the camp. Meyer had returned from Italy, and came to live with him. Meyer's historical knowledge and true friendship made him very valuable. Optical studies alternated with discussions upon Art.

In this year, 1793, much was studied, but little produced. The comedy of the *Bürgergeneral* was written, that of the *Aufgeregten* was commenced, and the *Unterhaltungen der Ausgewanderten* planned. More important was the version of *Reinecke Fuchs*. All these are products of the French Revolution. The *Bürgergeneral* is really an amusing little piece, setting forth the absurdity of loud-mouthed patriotism; but it has greatly incensed all those who are angry with Goethe for not having espoused the cause of the Revolution. It is admitted that there was much in the Revolution which was hollow, foolish, and wicked; but the Revolution was too serious a thing to be treated only with ridicule. I quite agree with this opinion. But considering his sentiments and position, it seems to me quite natural that he who neither sympathized with the Revolution, nor absolved the Royalists; who could therefore neither write dithyrambs of freedom nor cries of indignation; who did not fully appreciate the historical import- ance of the event, and only saw its temporal and *personal* aspect, should have taken to Comedy, and to Comedy alone. He did not write invectives; he did not write satires. He saw the comic aspect, and he smiled. As events deepened the shadows of the picture, he, too, became more serious. The *Aufgeregten*, which was never completed, would have given a complete expression to his political views. *Reinecke Fuchs* was commenced as a relief; it was turned to as an 'unholy World-bible', wherein the human race exhibited its unadorned and unfeigned animal nature with mavellous humour, in contrast to the bloody exhibition which the Reign of Terror then offered as a spectacle to the world.

He was now, May 1794, once more to join the army which was besieging Mainz. The narrative, which is also to be found in Mr. Farie's translation, presents him in no new aspect, and may therefore be passed over with this allusion. The city capitulated on the 24th of July, and on the 28th of August—his forty-fifth birthday—he re-entered Weimar, to finish *Reinecke Fuchs* and to pursue his scientific researches. 'I go home', he wrote to Jacobi, 'where I can draw a circle round me, in which nothing can enter, save Love and Friendship, Science and Art. I will not complain of the past, for I have learnt much that was valuable'. Experience is the only schoolmaster ; although, as Jean Paul says, 'the school-fees are somewhat heavy'. Goethe was always willing to pay the fees, if he could but get the instruction.

BOOK THE SIXTH

1794 to 1805

CHAPTER I

GOETHE AND SCHILLER

THERE are few nobler spectacles than the friendship of two great men ; and the History of Literature presents nothing comparable to the friendship of Goethe and Schiller. The friendship of Montaigne and Etienne de la Boëtie was, perhaps, more passionate and entire ; but it was the union of two kindred natures, which from the first moment discovered their affinity, not the union of two rivals incessantly contrasted by partizans, and originally disposed to hold aloof from each other. Rivals Goethe and Schiller were, and are ; natures in many respects directly antagonistic ; chiefs of opposing camps, and brought into brotherly union only by what was highest in their natures and their aims.

To look on these great rivals was to see at once their profound dissimilarity. Goethe's beautiful head had the calm victorious grandeur of the Greek ideal ; Schiller's the earnest beauty of a Christian looking towards the Future. The massive brow, and large-pupilled eyes,—like those given by Raphael to the infant Christ, in the matchless Madonna di San Sisto,—the strong and well-proportioned feature, lined indeed by thought and suffering, yet showing that thought and suffering have troubled, but not vanquished, the strong man,—a certain healthy vigour in the brown skin, and an indescribable something which shines out from the face, make Goethe a striking contrast to Schiller, with his eager eyes, narrow brow,—tense and intense,—his irregular features lined by thought and suffering, and weakened by sickness. The one *looks*, the other *looks out*. Both are majestic ; but one has the majesty of repose, the other of conflict. Goethe's frame is massive, imposing ; he seems much taller than he is. Schiller's frame is disproportioned, he seems less than he is. Goethe holds himself

stiffly erect; the long-necked Schiller 'walks like a camel'*.
Goethe's chest is like the torso of the Theseus; Schiller's is bent,
and has lost a lung.

A similar difference is traceable in details, 'An air that was
beneficial to Schiller acted on me like poison', Goethe said to
Eckermann. 'I called on him one day, and as I did not find him
at home, I seated myself at his writing-table to note down various
matters. I had not been seated long, before I felt a strange indisposition steal over me, which gradually increased, until at last I
nearly fainted. At first I did not know to what cause I should
ascribe this wretched and to me unusual state, until I discovered
that a dreadful odour issued from a drawer near me. When I
opened it, I found to my astonishment that it was full of rotten
apples. I immediately went to the window and inhaled the fresh
air, by which I was instantly restored. Meanwhile his wife came
in, and told me that the drawer was always filled with rotten
apples, because the scent was beneficial to Schiller, and he could
not live or work without it'.

As another and not unimportant detail, characterizing the healthy
and unhealthy practice of literature, it may be added that Goethe
wrote in the freshness of morning, entirely free from stimulus;
Schiller worked in the feverish hours of night, stimulating his
languid brain with coffee and champagne.

In comparing one to a Greek ideal, the other to a Christian
ideal, it has already been implied that one was the representative
of Realism, the other of Idealism. Goethe has himself indicated
the capital distinction between them: Schiller was animated with
the idea of Freedom; Goethe, on the contrary, was animated with
the idea of Nature. This distinction runs through their works:
Schiller always pining for something greater than Nature, wishing
to make men Demigods; Goethe always striving to let Nature
have free development, and produce the highest forms of Humanity.
The Fall of Man was to Schiller the happiest of all events, because
thereby men fell away from pure *instinct* into conscious *freedom;*
with this sense of freedom came the possibility of Morality. To
Goethe this seemed paying a price for Morality which was higher
than Morality was worth; he preferred the ideal of a condition

---

* This picturesque phrase was uttered by Tieck, the sculptor, to Rauch, from whom
I heard it. Let me add that Schiller's brow is called in the text, 'narrow', in defiance
of Dannecker's bust, with which I compared Schiller's skull, and found that the sculptor,
as usual, had grossly departed from truth in his desire to idealize. Artists always believe
they know better than Nature.

wherein Morality was unnecessary. Much as he might prize a good police, he prized still more a society in which a police would never be needed.

But while the contrast between these two is the contrast of real and ideal, of *objective* and *subjective* tendencies, apparent when we consider the men in their totality, this is only true of them relatively to each other. To speak of Goethe as a Realist, pure and simple, is erroneous ; and to speak of Schiller as an Idealist, pure and simple, is not less so. Gervinus strikingly remarks that, compared with Nicolai or Lichtenberg, Goethe appears as an Idealist ; compared with Kant and his followers, Schiller appears as a Realist. If Schiller, in comparison with Goethe, must be called a self-conscious poet, in comparison with the Romanticists, he is *naïve* and instinctive. Indeed, all such classifications are necessarily imperfect, and must only be used as artifices of language, by which certain general and predominant characteristics may be briefly indicated. Goethe and Schiller were certainly different natures ; but had they been so fundamentally opposed, as it is the fashion to consider them, they could never have become so intimately united. They were opposite and allied, with somewhat of the same differences and resemblances as are traceable in the Greek and Roman Mars. In the Greek Mythology the God of War had not the prominent place he attained in Rome ; and the Greek sculptors, when they represented him, represented him as the victor returning, after conflict, to repose : holding in his hand the olive branch, while at his feet sate Eros. The Roman sculptors, or those who worked for Rome, represented Mars as the God of War in all his terrors, in the very act of leading on to victory. But, different as these two conceptions were, they were both conceptions of the God of War ; Goethe may be likened to the one, and Schiller to the other : both were kindred spirits united by a common purpose.

Having touched upon the points of contrast, it will now be needful to say a word on those points of resemblance which served as the basis of their union. It will be unnecessary to instance the obvious points which two such poets must have had in common ; the mention of some less obvious will suffice for our present purpose. They were both profoundly convinced that Art was no luxury of leisure, no mere amusement to charm the idle, or relax the careworn ; but a mighty influence, serious in its aims although pleasurable in its means ; a sister of Religion, by whose aid the great world-scheme was wrought into reality. This was with them no mere sonorous phrase. They were thoroughly in earnest. They believed that Culture would raise Humanity to its full powers ; and they, as artists, knew no Culture equal to that of Art. It was probably a perception of this belief that made Karl Grün say, 'Goethe was the most ideal Idealist the earth has ever borne ; an *æsthetic* Idealist'. And hence the origin of the wide-spread error that Goethe 'only looked at life as an artist', *i. e.*, cared only for human nature inasmuch as it afforded him materials for Art ; a point which will be more fully examined hereafter. (*Book* VII, *ch.* 4.) The phases of their development had been very similar, and had brought them to a similar standing-point. They both began rebelliously ; they both emerged from titanic lawlessness in emerging from youth to manhood. In Italy the sight of ancient masterpieces completed Goethe's metamorphosis. Schiller had to work through his in the gloomy north, and under the constant pressure of anxieties. He, too, pined for Italy, and thought the climate of Greece would make him a poet. But his intense and historical mind found neither stimulus nor enjoyment in plastic Art. Noble men and noble deeds were the food which nourished his great soul. 'His poetic purification came from moral ideals ; whereas in Goethe the moral ideal came from the artistic'*. Plutarch was his Bible. The ancient masterpieces of poetry came to him in this period of his development, to lead him gently by the hand onwards to the very point where Goethe stood. He read the Greek tragedians in wretched French translations, and with such aid laboriously translated the *Iphigenia* of Euripides. Homer, in Voss's faithful version, became to him what Homer long was to Goethe. And how thoroughly he threw himself into the ancient world may be seen in his poem, *The Gods of Greece*. Like Goethe, he had found his religious opinions gradually separating him more and more from the orthodox Christians ; and, like Goethe, he had woven for himself a system out of Spinoza, Kant, and the Grecian sages.

At the time, then, that these two men seemed most opposed to each other, and *were* opposed in feeling, they were gradually drawing closer and closer in the very lines of their development, and a firm basis was prepared for solid and enduring union. Goethe was five-and-forty, Schiller five-and-thirty. Goethe had much to give, which Schiller gratefully accepted ; and if he could not in return

* *Gervinus*, v, p. 152.

Friedrich von Schiller

influence the developed mind of his great friend, or add to the vast stores of its knowledge and experience, he could give him that which was even more valuable, *sympathy* and *impulse*. He excited Goethe to work. He withdrew him from the engrossing pursuit of science, and restored him once more to poetry. He urged him to finish what was already commenced, and not to leave his works all fragments. They worked together with the same purpose and with the same earnestness, and their union is the most glorious episode in the lives of both, and remains as an eternal exemplar of a noble friendship.

Of all the tributes to Schiller's greatness which an enthusiastic people has pronounced, there is perhaps nothing which carries a greater weight of tenderness and authority than Goethe's noble praise. It is a very curious fact in the history of Shakespeare, that he is not known to have written a single line in praise of any contemporary poet. The fashion of those days was for each poet to write verses in eulogy of his friends ; and the eulogies written by Shakespeare's friends are such as to satisfy even the idolatry of admirers in our day ; but there exists no eulogy, no single verse, from him whose eulogy was more worth having than that of all the rest put together*. Had literary gossip, pregnant with literary malice, produced the absurd impression that Shakespeare was cold, selfish, and self-idolatrous, this curious fact would have been made a damning proof. I have so often in these pages used Shakespeare as a contrast to Goethe, that it would be wrong not to contrast him also on this point. Of all the failings usually attributed to literary men, Goethe had the least of what could be called jealousy ; of all the qualities which sit gracefully on great-ness, he had the most of magnanimity. The stream of time will carry down to after ages the memory of several whose names will live only in his praise ; and the future students of Literary History will have no fact to note of Goethe similar to that noted of Shakespeare : they will see how enthusiastic was his admiration of his rivals, Schiller, Voss, and Herder, and how quick he was to perceive the genius of Scott, Byron, Béranger and Manzoni.

But I must quit this attempt to characterize the two rivals, and proceed to narrate their active co-operation in the common work.

---

* There is, indeed, a couplet in the *Passionate Pilgrim* which names Spenser with high praise; but it is doubtful whether the *Passionate Pilgrim* is anything but the attempt of a bookseller to palm off on the public a work which Shakespeare never wrote; and it is certain that Shakespeare is *not* the author of the sonnet in which Spenser is mentioned, that sonnet having been previously published by a Richard Barnfield

While the great world was agitated to its depths by the rapid march of the Revolution, the little world of Weimar pursued the even tenor of its way, very much as if nothing concerning the destinies of mankind were then in action. Because Goethe is the greatest figure in Germany, the eyes of all Germans are turned towards him, anxious to see how he bore himself in those days. They see him—not moving with the current of ideas, not actively sympathizing with events ; and they find no better explanation of what they see than the brief formula that 'he was an Egoist'. If they look, however, at his companions and rivals, they will find a similar indifference. Wieland, the avowed enemy of all despotism, was frightened by the Reign of Terror into demanding a dictatorship. Nor—strange as it may appear—was Schiller, the poet of Freedom, the creator of Posa, more favourable to the French than Goethe himself. The Republic had honoured him in a singular way. It had forwarded him the diploma of citizenship ; a dignity, conferred at the same time on Washington, Franklin, Tom Paine, Pestalozzi, Campe, and Anacharsis Clootz ! The diploma signed by Danton and Roland, dated 6th September, 1792, is now preserved in the Library at Weimar, where visitors will notice the characteristic accuracy of the French in the spelling of Schiller's name—*à Monsieur Gille, publiciste allemand.* This honour Schiller owed to his *Robbers*, or as his admirers called it, *Robert, chef de Brigands.* From the very first he had looked with no favourable eye on the Revolution, and the trial of Louis XVI produced so deep an impression on him, that he commenced an address to the National Convention, which was however outrun by rapid events. Like Wieland, he saw no hope but in a dictatorship.

Such being the position of the leading minds, we are not to wonder if we find them pursuing their avocations just as if nothing were going on in France or elsewhere. Weimar could play no part in European politics. The men of Weimar had their part to play in Literature, through which they saw a possible regeneration. Believing in the potent efficacy of culture, they devoted themselves with patriotism to that. A glance at the condition of German Literature will show how patriotism had noble work to do in such a cause.

The Leipsic Fair was a rival to our Minerva Press : Chivalry romances, Robber-stories and Spectre-romances, old German superstitions, Augustus Lafontaine's sentimental family-pictures, and Plays of the *Sturm und Drang* style, swarmed into the sacred

places of Art, like another invasion of the Goths.   On the stage
Kotzebue was king.   The *Stranger* was filling every theatre, and
moving the sensibilities of a too readily moved pit.   Klopstock was
becoming more and more oracular, less and less poetical.   Jean
Paul indeed gave signs of power and originality ; but except
Goethe and Schiller, Voss, who had written his *Luise* and translated *Homer*, alone seemed likely to form the chief of a school
of which the nation might be proud.

   It was in this state of things that Schiller conceived the plan of
a periodical—*Die Horen*,—memorable in many ways to all students
of German Literature.   Goethe, Herder, Kant, Fichte, the Humboldts, Klopstock, Jacobi, Engel, Meyer, Garve, Matthisson, and
others, were to form a phalanx whose irresistible might should
speedily give them possession of the land.   'The more the narrow
interests of the present', says Schiller, in the announcement of
this work, 'keep the minds of men on the stretch, and subjugate
while they narrow, the more imperious is the need to free them
through the higher universal interest in that which is purely *human*
and removed beyond the influences of time, and thus once more to
re-unite the divided political world under the banner of Truth and
Beauty'.

   Such was the undertaking which formed the first link in the
friendship of Goethe and Schiller.   How they stood towards each
other has been seen in the seventh chapter of the preceding Book.
One day, in May 1794, they met, coming from a lecture given by
Batsch at the Natural History Society in Jena ; in talking over the
matter, Goethe, with pleased surprise, heard Schiller criticize the
fragmentary Method which teachers of Science uniformly adopted.
When they arrived at Schiller's house, Goethe went in with him,
expounding the Theory of Metamorphoses with great warmth.
Taking up a pen, he made a rapid sketch of the typical plant.
Schiller listened with great attention, seizing each point clearly and
rapidly, but shaking his head at last, and saying : 'This is not an
observation, it is an Idea'.   Goethe adds : 'My surprise was painful, for these words clearly indicated the point which separated us.
The opinions he had expressed in his essay on *Anmuth und Würde*
recurred to me, and my old repulsion was nearly revived.   But I
mastered myself, and answered that I was delighted to find I had
Ideas without knowing it, and to be able to contemplate them with
my own eyes'.   There can be no question of Schiller having been
in the right, though perhaps both he and Goethe assigned an ex-

clusively subjective meaning to the phrase. The typical plant Goethe knew very well, was not to be found in nature; but he thought it was *revealed* in plants*. Because he arrived at the belief in a type through direct observation and comparison, and not through *à priori* deduction, he maintained that this type was a perception (*Anschauung*) not an Idea. Probably Schiller was more impressed with the metaphysical nature of the conception than with the physical evidence on which it had been formed. The chasm between them was indeed both broad and deep: and Goethe truly says: ' It was in a conflict between the Object and the Subject, the greatest and most interminable of all conflicts, that began our friendship, which was eternal'. A beginning had been made. Schiller's wife, for whom Goethe had a strong regard, managed to bring them together; and the proposed journal, *Die Horen*, brought their activities and sympathies into friendly union. Rapid was the growth of this friendship, and on both sides beneficial. Schiller paid a fortnight's visit at Weimar; Goethe was frequently in Jena. They found that they agreed not only on subjects, but also on the mode of looking at them. ' It will cost me a long time to unravel all the ideas you have awakened in me', writes Schiller, ' but I hope none will be lost'.

Regretting that he could not give the novel *Wilhelm Meister* for the *Horen*, having already promised it to a publisher, Goethe nevertheless sends Schiller the manuscript from the third book onwards, and gratefully profits by the friendly criticism with which he reads it. He gave him, however, the two *Epistles*, the *Unterhaltungen deutscher Ausgewanderten*, the *Roman Elegies*, and the essay on *Literary Sansculottism*.

The mention of *Wilhelm Meister* leads us to retrace our steps a few months, when the active interest he took in the direction of the Weimar Theatre revived his interest in this novel, over which he had dawdled so many years. He finished it; but he finished it in quite a different spirit from that in which it was commenced, and I do not at all feel that Schiller's criticisms really were of advantage to it. But of this anon.

Towards the end of July he went to Dessau, and from thence to Dresden, where he strove with Meyer to forget the troubles of the time in contemplation of the treasures of Art. 'All Germany',

---

* Goethe, speaking of his labours in another department, says, ' I endeavoured to find the Primitive Animal (Urthier), in other words, the Conception, the Idea of an Animal'. *Werke*, XXXVI, p. 14.

he writes to Fritz von Stein, 'is divided into anxious, croaking, or indifferent men. For myself I find nothing better than to play the part of Diogenes, and roll my tub'. He returned, and daily grew more and more intimate with Schiller. They began the friendly interchange of letters, which have since been published in six volumes, known to every student. In Goethe's letters to other friends at this time, 1795, is noticed an inward contentment, which he rightly attributes to this new influence. 'It was a new spring to me', he says, 'in which all seeds shot up, and gaily blossomed in my nature'. Contact with Schiller's earnest mind and eager ambition gave him the stimulus he so long had wanted. The ordinary spurs to an author's activity—the need of money or the need of fame—pricked him not. He had no need of money; of fame he had enough; and there was no nation to be appealed to. But Schiller's restless striving, and the emulation it excited, acted like magic upon him; and the years of their friendship were for both the most productive. In an unpublished letter from Frau von Stein to Charlotte von Lengefeld, dated 1795, there is this noticeable sentence: 'I also feel that Goethe is drawing nearer to Schiller, for he has appeared to be now a little more aware of my existence. He seems to me like one who has been shipwrecked for some years on one of the South Sea Islands, and is now beginning to think of returning home'. By the shipwreck is of course meant Christiane Vulpius; and by home, the salon of the Frau von Stein. It is possible, however, to reverse these positions.

On the 1st of November another son is born to Goethe. He bids Schiller to bring his contribution in the shape of a daughter, that the poetic family may be united and increased by a marriage. But this child only lives a few days. On the 20th, Schiller writes: 'We have deeply grieved for your loss. You can console yourself with the thought that it has come so early, and thus more affects your *hopes* than your love'. Goethe replies: 'One knows not whether in such cases it is better to let sorrow take its natural course, or to repress it by the various aids which culture offers us. If one decides upon the latter method, *as I always do*, one is only strengthened for a moment; and I have observed that Nature always asserts her right through some other crisis'.

No other crisis seems to have come in this case. He was active in all directions. Göttling, in Jena, had just come forward with the discovery that phosphorus burns in nitrogen; and this drew

Goethe's thoughts to Chemistry, which for a time was his recreation. Anatomy never lost its attraction : and through the snow
on bitter mornings he was seen trudging to Loder's lectures, with
a diligence young students might have envied. The Humboldts,
especially Alexander, with whom he was in active correspondence,
kept alive his scientific ardour ; and it is to their energetic advice
that we owe the essays on Comparative Anatomy. He was constantly talking to them on these subjects, eloquently expounding
his ideas, which would probably never have been put to paper
had they not urged him to it. True it is that he did not finish
the essays ; and only in 1820 did he print what he had written*.
These conversations with the Humboldts embraced a wide field.
'It is not perhaps presumptuous to suppose', he says, 'that many
ideas have thence, through *tradition*, become the common property
of science, and have blossomed successfully, although the gar-
dener who scattered the seeds is never named'.

Poetical plans were numerous ; some of them were carried into
execution. A tragedy on the subject of 'Prometheus Unbound'
was begun, but never continued. The *Hymn to Apollo* was
translated. *Alexis und Dora*, the *Vier Jahres Zeiten*, and several
of the smaller poems, were written and given to Schiller for the
Horen or the *Musen Almanach ;* not to mention translations from
Madame de Stael, and the *Autobiography of Benvenuto Cellini*.
But the product of this time which made the greatest sensation
was the *Xenien*.

It has already been indicated that the state of German Literature was anything but brilliant, and that public taste was very low.
The *Horen* was started to raise that degraded taste by an illustrious
union of 'All the Talents'. It came—was seen—and made *no*
conquest. Mediocrity in arms assailed it in numerous journals.
Stupidity, against which, as Schiller says, 'the gods themselves
are powerless', was not in the least moved. The *Horen* was a
double failure, for it failed to pay its expenses, and it failed to
excite any great admiration in the few who purchased it. Articles
by the poorest writers were attributed to the greatest. Even
Frederick Schlegel attributed a story by Caroline von Wolzogen
to Goethe. The public was puzzled—and somewhat *bored*. 'All
the Talents' have never yet succeeded in producing a successful

---

* This detail is important, as indeed every question of date must be in science.
When the Essays were published, the principal ideas had already been brought before
the world ; when the Essays were written, the ideas were extraordinary novelties.

Wilhelm von Humboldt

periodical, and there are some good reasons for supposing that they never will. The *Horen* met with the fate of *The Liberal*, in which Byron, Shelley, Leigh Hunt, Moore, Hazlitt and Peacock were engaged. But the two great poets who had taken the greatest interest in it were not to be ignored with impunity. They resolved on a literary vengeance, and their vengeance was the *Xenien*.

A small library might be collected of the works called forth by these epigrams ; but for the English reader the topic necessarily has but slender interest. He is not likely to exclaim with Boas : ' On the 31st of October, 1517, was commenced the Reformation of the Church in Germany ; in October, 1796, commenced the Reformation of Literature. As Luther published his Theses in Wittenberg, so Goethe and Schiller published their *Xenien*. No one before had the courage so to confront sacred Dulness, so to lash all Hypocrisy'. One sees that some such castigation was needed, by the loud howling which was set up from all quarters ; but that any important purification of Literature was thereby effected is not so clear.

The idea was Goethe's. It occurred to him while reading the *Xenia* of Martial ; and having thrown off a dozen epigrams, he sent them to Schiller for the *Musen Almanach*. Schiller was delighted, but said there must be a hundred of them, chiefly directed against the journals which had attacked the *Horen;* the hundred was soon thought too small a number, and it was resolved to have a thousand. They were written in the most thorough spirit of collaboration, the idea being sometimes given by one, and the form by another ; one writing the first verse, and leaving the second to the other. There is no accurate separation of their epigrams, giving each to each, although critics have made an approximative selection ; and Maltzahn has recently aided this by collation of the original manuscripts.

The sensation was tremendous. All the bad writers in the kingdom, and they were an army, felt themselves personally aggrieved. The pietists and sentimentalists were ridiculed ; the pedants and pedagogues were lashed. So many persons and so many opinions were scarified, that no wonder if the public ear was startled at the shrieks of pain. Counterblasts were soon heard, and the *Xenien-Sturm* will remain as a curious episode of the war of the ' many foolish heads against the two wise ones'. ' It is amusing', writes Goethe to Schiller, ' to see what has really irritated these fellows, what they believe will irritate us, how empty and low is their conception of others, how they aim their arrows merely at the outworks, and how little they dream of the inaccessible citadel inhabited by men who are in earnest'.   The sensation produced by the *Dunciad* and by the *English Bards and Scotch Reviewers* was mild compared with the sensation produced by the *Xenien;* although the wit and sarcasm of the *Xenien* is as milk and water compared with the vitriol of the *Dunciad* and the *English Bards*.

Read by no stronger light than that which the appreciation of wit *as* wit throws on these epigrams, and not by the strong light of personal indignity, or personal malice, the *Xenien* will appear very weak productions, and the sensation they excited must appear somewhat absurd.   But a similar disappointment meets the modern reader of the *Anti-Jacobin*. We know that its pages were the terror of enemies, the malicious joy of friends. We know that it was long held as a repertory of English wit, and the 'Days of the *Anti-Jacobin*' are mentioned by Englishmen as the days of the *Xenien* are by Germans.   Yet now that the *personal* spice is removed, we read both of them with a feeling of wonder at their enormous influence.   In the *Xenien* there are a few epigrams which still titillate the palate, for they have the salt of wit in their lines.   There are many also which have no pretension to wit, but are admirable expressions of critical canons and philosophic ideas.   If good taste could not be created by attacks on bad taste, there was at any rate some hope that such a castigation would make certain places sore ; and in this sense the *Xenien* did good service.

The publication of *Wilhelm Meister* falls within this period, and we may now proceed to examine it as a work of art.

CHAPTER II

' WILHELM MEISTER '

A FRENCHMAN, an Englishman, and a German, were commissioned, it is said, to give the world the benefit of their views on that interesting animal the Camel.   Away went the Frenchman to the *Jardin des Plantes*, spent an hour there in rapid investigation, returned, and wrote a *feuilleton*, in which there was no phrase the Academy could blame, but also no phrase which

Alexander von Humboldt

added to the general knowledge. He was perfectly satisfied, however, and said, *Le voilà, le chameau !* The Englishman packed up his tea-caddy and a magazine of comforts ; pitched his tent in the East ; remained there two years studying the Camel in its habits ; and returned with a thick volume of facts, arranged without order, expounded without philosophy, but serving as valuable materials for all who came after him. The German, despising the frivolity of the Frenchman, and the unphilosophic matter-of-factness of the Englishman, retired to his study, there *to construct the Idea of a Camel from out of the depths of his Moral Consciousness.* And he is still at it.

With this myth the reader is introduced into the very heart of that species of criticism which, flourishing in Germany, is also admired in some English circles, under the guise of Philosophical criticism, and which has been exercised upon *Wilhelm Meister* almost as mercilessly as upon *Faust.*

My readers, it is hoped, will not generalize this remark so as to include within it all German critics and men of culture ; such an extension of the remark would be almost as unfair in Germany as in England. There are many excellent critics in Germany, and excellent judges who are not critics ; it would be too bad if our laughter at pedants and pretenders were to extend to these. But no one acquainted with Germany or German literature can fail to recognize the widespread and pernicious influence of a mistaken application of Philosophy to Art : an application which becomes a tyranny on the part of real thinkers, and a hideous absurdity on the part of those who merely echo the jargon of the schools. It is this criticism which has stifled art in Germany, and ruined many a young artist who showed promise. It is a fundamental mistake to translate Art into the formulas of Philosophy, and then christen the translation the Philosophy of Art. The critic is never easy until he has shifted his ground. He is not content with the work as it presents itself. He endeavours to get *behind* it, beneath it, into the depths of the soul which produced it. He is not satisfied with what the artist has *given*, he wants to know what he *meant*. He guesses at the meaning ; the more remote the meaning lies on the wandering tracks of thought, the better pleased is he with the discovery ; and he sturdily rejects every simple explanation in favour of this exegetical Idea. Thus the phantom of Philosophy hovers mistily before Art, concealing Art from our eyes. It is true the Idea said to underlie the work

was never conceived by anyone before, least of all by the Artist ;
but *that* is the glory of the critic : he is proud of having plunged
into the depths.   Of all horrors to the German of this school there
is no horror like that of the surface—it is more terrible to him than
cold water.

Wilhelm Meister has been the occasion of so many ideas constructed out of the depths of moral consciousness, it has been
made to *mean* such wondrous (and contradictory) things, that its
author must have been astonished at his unsuspecting depth.
There is some obvious symbolism in the latter part, which I have
little doubt was introduced to flatter the German tendency ; as
I have no sort of doubt that its introduction has spoiled a masterpiece.   The obvious want of unity in the work has given free play
to the interpreting imagination of critics.   Hillebrand boldly says
that the ' Idea of *Wilhelm Meister* is precisely this—that it has no
Idea ',—which does not greatly further our comprehension.

Instead of trying to discover the Idea, let us stand fast by
historical criticism, and see what light may be derived from a consideration of the origin and progress of the work, which, from
first to last, occupied him during twenty years.   The first six
books—beyond all comparison the best and most important—
were written before the journey to Italy : they were written during
the active theatrical period when Goethe was manager, poet, and
actor.   The contents of these books point very clearly to his
intention of representing in them the whole nature, aims, and art
of the comedian ; and in a letter to Merck he expressly states that
it is his intention to portray the actor's life.   Whether at the
same time he meant the actor's life to be symbolical, cannot be
positively determined.   That may, or may not, have been a
secondary intention.   The primary intention is very clear.   Nor
had he, at this time, yielded to the seduction of attempting the
symbolical in Art.   He sang as the bird sings ; his delight was in
healthy objective fact ; he had not yet donned the robes of an
Egyptian priest, or learned to speak in hieroglyphs.   He was
seriously interested in acting, and the actor's art.   He thought
the life of a player a good framework for certain pictures, and he
chose it. Afterwards, the idea of making these pictures symbolical
certainly did occur to him, and he concluded the romance upon
this after-thought.

Gervinus emphatically records his disbelief of the opinion that
Goethe originally intended to make Wilhelm *unfit* for success

as an actor ; and I think a careful perusal of the novel, even in its present state, will convince the reader that Gervinus is right. Instead of Wilhelm's career being represented as the development of a false tendency—the obstinate cultivation of an imperfect talent, such as was displayed in Goethe's own case with respect to plastic Art—one sees, in spite of some subsequent additions thrown in to modify the work according to an after-thought, that Wilhelm has a true inborn tendency, a talent which ripens through practice. With the performance of *Hamlet* the apogee is reached ; and here ends the first plan. Having written so far, Goethe went to Italy. We have seen the changes which came over his views. After a lapse of ten years he resumes the novel ; and having in that period lived through the experience of a false tendency— having seen the vanity of cultivating an imperfect talent—he *alters* the plan of his novel, makes it symbolical of the erroneous striving of youth towards culture ; invents the cumbrous machinery of a Mysterious Family, whose watchful love has guided all his steps, and who have encouraged him in error that they might lead him through error unto truth. This is what in his old age he declared —in the *Tag und Jahres Hefte*, and in his letters to Schiller—to have been the plan upon which it was composed. ' It sprang ', he says, ' from a dim feeling of the great truth that Man often seeks that which Nature has rendered impossible to him. All dilettantism and false tendency is of this kind. Yet it is possible that every false step should lead to an inestimable good, and some intimation of this is given in Meister '. To Eckermann he said : ' The work is one of the most incalculable productions ; I *myself can scarcely be said to have the key to it.* People seek a central point, and that is difficult to find ; nor is it even right. I should think a *rich manifold life brought close to our eyes would be enough in itself without any express tendency*, which, after all, is only for the intellect '. This is piercing to the very kernel. The origin of the symbolical matter, however, lies in the demands of the German intellect for such food. ' But ', he continues, ' if anything of the kind is insisted upon, it will, perhaps, be found in the words which Frederic at the end addresses to the hero, when he says, " Thou seem'st to me like Saul, the son of Kish, who went out to seek his father's asses, and found a kingdom ". Keep only to this ; for, in fact, the whole work seems to say nothing more than that man, despite all his follies and errors, being led by a higher hand, reaches some happy goal at last '.

Schiller, who knew only the *second* plan, objected, and with justice, to the disproportionate space allotted to the players. ' It looks occasionally ', he wrote, ' as if you were writing *for* players, whereas your purpose is only to write *of* them. The care you bestow on certain little details of this subject and individual excellencies of the art, which although important to the player and manager, are not so to the public, give to your representation the false appearance of a particular design ; and even one who does not infer such a design, might accuse you of being too much under the influence of a private preference for these subjects '. If we accept the later plan, we must point out the inartistic composition, which allows five books of Introduction, one of disconnected Episode, and only two of Development. This is against all proportion. Yet Frederick Schlegel expressly says that the two last books are properly speaking the whole work ; the others are but preparations*.

The purpose, or rather purposes, of *Wilhelm Meister* seem first, the rehabilitation of Dramatic Art ; and secondly, the theory of Education. The last two books are full of Education. Very wise and profound thoughts are expressed, and these thoughts redeem the triviality of the machinery. But otherwise these books are lamentably inferior to the first six books in style, in character, in interest. On the whole, *Wilhelm Meister* is, indeed, ' an incalculable work '. Several readings have intensified my admiration (which at first was tepid), and intensified also my sense of its defects. The beauties are ever new, ever wonderful ; the faults press themselves upon notice more sharply than they did at first.

The story opens with great dramatic vivacity. Mariana and old Barbara stand before us, sketched with Shakespearean sharpness of outline and truth of detail. The whole episode is admirable, if we accept the lengthy narrative in which Wilhelm details his early passion for the Marionnettes, which has probably made some readers as drowsy as it made Mariana. There is something painfully trivial in his long narrative ; apart from its artistic error as a digression. The contrast between Wilhelm and the prosaic Werner is felicitously touched. But the happiest traits are those which show Wilhelm's want of decision and

* *Charakteristiken und Kritiken*, p. 168. Schlegel's review is well worth reading as an example of ingenious criticism, and praise artfully presented under the guise of analysis.

incapacity of finishing the work he has begun ; traits which indicate his peculiar temperament. Indeed throughout the novel Wilhelm is not the hero, but a creature of the incidents. He is a mere nose-of-wax. And this is artfully designed. Egmont and Goetz are heroes : living in stormy times, they remain altogether uninfluenced by the times. The poet represents noble characters, and he represents them in their strong, clear individuality, superior to circumstance. With Wilhelm, he shows how some characters change, obedient to every external influence. The metamorphoses of Wilhelm would have been impossible with a character such as Egmont. This seems so obvious, that one is surprised to find critics objecting to the vacillating character of Wilhelm, as if it were a fault in art. It would be as reasonable to object to the vacillations of Hamlet. Wilhelm is not only led with ease from one thing to another, but is always oscillating in his views of himself. Even his emotions are not persistent. He passes from love of the passionate Mariana to an inclination for the coquettish Philina ; from Philina to the Countess, whom he immediately forgets for the Amazon ; he is about to marry Theresa, but relinquishes her as soon as he is accepted, and offers himself to Natalie.

There is in this novel evidence of sufficient humour to have made a decidedly humorous writer, had that faculty not been kept in abeyance by other faculties. Wilhelm's unconscious pedantry, and his predominant desire to see the drama illustrated in ordinary life, and to arrange life into a theatre* ; the Count and his eccentricities ; the adventures of the players in the castle where they arrive, and find all the urgent necessaries wanting ; the costume in which Wilhelm decks himself; the whole character of Philina and that of Frederic—are instances of this humorous power.

To tell the story of this novel would be too great an injustice to it ; the reader has, therefore, it must be presupposed, already some acquaintance with it ; in default thereof, let him at once make its acquaintance†. The narrative being presupposed as known, my task is easy. I have only to refer to the marvellous art with which the characters unfold themselves. We see them, and see through them. They are never described, they exhibit

---

* See especially Book I, cap. 15, for his idea of the private life of players, as if they carried *off* the stage something of their parts *on* the stage.
† It has been translated by Carlyle.

themselves. Philina, for example, one of the most bewitching and original creations in fiction, whom we know as well as if she had flirted with us, and jilted us, is never once described. Even her person is made present to us through the impression it makes on others, not by any direct information. We are not told that she was a strange mixture of carelessness, generosity, caprice, wilfulness, affectionateness, and gaiety; a lively girl, of French disposition, with the smallest possible regard for decorum, but with a true decorum of her own; snapping her fingers at the world, disliking conventions, tediousness and pedantry; without any ideal aspirations, yet also without any affectations; coquetting with all the men, disliked by all the women, turning every one round her finger, yet ready to oblige and befriend even those who had injured her: we are not told this; but as such she lives before us. She is so genuine, and so charming a sinner, that we forgive all her trespasses. On the whole, she is the most original and most difficult creation in the book. Mignon, the great poetical creation, was perhaps less difficult to draw, when once conceived. All the other characters serve as contrasts to Philina. She moves among them and throws them into relief, as they do her. The sentimental sickly Aurelia, and the sentimental Madame Melina, have an earnestness Philina does not comprehend; but they have the faults of their qualities, and she has neither. She has no more sense of earnestness than a bird. With bird-like gaiety and bird-like enjoyment of existence she chirrups through sunshine and rain. One never thinks of demanding morality from her. Morality? she knows it not, nay, has not even a bowing acquaintance with it. Nor can she be called immoral. Contrasting her with Mignon, we see her in contrast with Innocence, Earnestness, Devotion, and vague yearnings for a distant home; for Philina was never innocent, she is as quick and clever as a kitten; she cannot be serious: if she does not laugh she must yawn or cry; devoted she cannot be, although affectionate; and for a distant home, how can that trouble one who knows how to nestle everywhere? It is possible to say very hard words of Philina; but, like many a naughty child, she disarms severity by her grace.

Of Mignon, and her songs, I need say nothing. Painters have tried to give an image of that strange creation which lures the imagination and the heart of every reader; but she defies the power of the pencil. The old Harper is a wild weird figure, bearing a mystery about with him, which his story at the close finely clears up. He not only adds to the variety of the figures in the novel, but by his unforgetable songs gives a depth of passion and suffering to the work which would otherwise move too exclusively in familiar regions. These two poetic figures, rising from the prosaic background, suggest an outlying world of beauty; they have the effect of a rainbow in the London streets. Serlo, Laertes, the selfish Melina, and his sentimental wife, are less developed characters, yet drawn with a masterly skill.

But when we quit their company—that is, when we quit the parts which were written before the journey to Italy, and before the plan was altered—we arrive at characters such as Lothario, the Abbé, the Doctor, Teresa, and Natalie, and feel that a totally new style is present. We have quitted the fresh air of Nature, and entered the philosopher's study; life is displaced by abstractions. Not only does the interest of the story seriously fall off, but the handling of the characters is entirely changed. The characters are described; they do not live. The incidents are crowded, have little vraisemblance and less interest. The diction has become weak—sometimes positively bad. As the men and women are without passion, so is the style without colour. Schiller, writing of the first Book, says: 'The bold poetic passages, which flash up from the calm current of the whole, have an excellent effect; they elevate and fill the soul'. But the style of the last two Books, with the exception of the exquisite Harper's story, is such that in England the novel is almost universally pronounced tedious, in spite of the wonderful truth and variety of character, and the beauty of so many parts. In these later Books the narrative is slow, and carries incidents trivial and improbable. The Mysterious Family in the Tower is an absurd mystification; without the redeeming interest which Mrs. Radcliffe would have thrown into it. With respect to the style, it is enough to open at random, and you are tolerably certain to alight upon a passage which it is difficult to conceive how an artist could have allowed it to pass. The iteration of certain set forms of phrase, and the abstractness of the diction, are very noticeable. Here is a sentence! 'Sie können aber hieraus die unglaubliche Toleranz jener Männer sehen. dass sie eben auch mich auf meinem *Wege* gerade *deswegen*, weil es mein *Weg* ist, keines*wegs* stören'.

One great peculiarity in this work is that which probably made

Novalis call it 'artistic Atheism'*. Such a phrase is easily uttered, sounds well, is open to many interpretations, and is therefore sure to find echoes. I take it to mean that in *Wilhelm Meister* there is a complete absence of all *moral verdict* on the part of the author. Characters tread the stage, events pass before our eyes, things are done and thoughts are expressed ; but no word comes from the author respecting the moral bearing of these things. Life forgets in activity all moral verdict. The good is beneficent, but no one praises it ; the bad works evil, but no one anathematizes it. It is a world in which we see no trace of the preacher, not a glimpse even of his surplice. To many readers this absence is like the absence of salt at dinner. They feel towards such simple objective delineation something of the repugnance felt in Evangelical circles to Miss Edgeworth's Tales. It puts them out. Robert Hall confessed that reading Miss Edgeworth hindered him for a week in his clerical functions ; he was completely disturbed by her pictures of a world of happy active people *without* any visible interference of religion—a sensible, and on the whole, healthy world, yet without warnings, without exhortations, without any apparent terrors concerning the state of souls.

Much has been said about the immorality of *Wilhelm Meister*, which need not be repeated here. Schiller hits the mark in his reply to what Jacobi said on this point : 'The criticism of Jacobi has not at all surprised me ; for it is as inevitable that an individual like him should be offended by the unsparing truth of your pictures, as it is that a mind like yours should give him cause to be so. Jacobi is one of those who seek only their own ideas in the representation of poets, and prize more what *should be* than *what is;* the contest therefore begins in first principles. So soon as a man lets me see that there is anything in poetical representations that interests him more than internal necessity and truth, I give him up. If he could show you that the immorality of your pictures does not proceed from the nature of the subject but from the manner in which you treat it, then indeed would you be accountable, not because you had sinned against moral laws, but against critical laws'.

Wilhelm Meister is not a moral story, that is to say not a story written with the express purpose of illustrating some obvious

---

* 'Das Buch handelt bloss von gewöhnlichen Dingen, die Natur und der Mysticismus sind ganz vergessen. Es ist eine poetisirte bürgerliche und häusliche Geschichte; das Wunderbare darin wird ausdrücklich als Poesie und Schwärmerei behandelt. Künstlerischer Atheismus ist der Geist des Buchs'. *Schriften,* II, p. 367.

maxim. The consequence is that it is frequently pronounced immoral; which I conceive to be an absurd judgment; for if it have no express moral purpose, guiding and animating all the scenes, neither has it an immoral purpose. It may not be written for the edification of virtue; assuredly it is not written for the propagation of vice. If its author is nowhere a preacher, he cannot by his sternest critics be called a pander. All that can be said is that the Artist has been content to paint scenes of life, *without comment;* and that some of these scenes belong to an extensive class of subjects, familiar indeed to the experience of all but children, yet by general consent not much talked of in society. If any reader can be morally injured by reading such scenes in this novel rather than in the newspaper, his moral constitution is so alarmingly delicate, and so susceptible of injury, that he is truly pitiable. Let us hope the world is peopled with robuster natures; a robuster nature need not be alarmed.

But while asserting *Wilhelm Meister* to be in no respect a Moral Tale, I am bound to declare that deep and healthy moral meaning lies in it, pulses through it, speaking in many tones to him who hath ears to hear it. As Wordsworth says of Tam O'Shanter, 'I pity him who cannot perceive that in all this, though there was no moral purpose, there is a moral effect'. What each reader will see in it, will depend on his insight and experience. Sometimes this meaning results from the whole course of the narrative; such for example as the influence of life upon Wilhelm in moulding and modifying his character, raising it from mere impulse to the subordination of reason, from dreaming self-indulgence to practical duty, from self-culture to sympathy; but the way this lesson is taught is the artist's not the preacher's way, and therefore may be missed by those who wait for the moral to be pointed before they are awake to its significance.

The 'Confessions of a Beautiful Soul', which occupy the Sixth Book, have, in some circles, embalmed what was pronounced the corruption of the other books. Stolberg burned all the rest of the work, and kept these chapters as a treasure. Curious indeed is the picture presented of a quiet mystic, who is at the same time an original and strongly marked character; and the effect of religious convictions on life is subtly delineated in the gradual encroachment and final predominance of mysticism on the mind of one who seemed every way so well fitted for the world. Nevertheless, while duly appreciating the picture, I regret that it was not published separately, for it interrupts the story in a most inartistic manner, and has really nothing to do with the rest of the work.

The criticism on *Hamlet*, which Wilhelm makes, still remains the best criticism we have on that wonderful play. Very artfully is *Hamlet* made as it were a part of the novel ; and Rosenkrantz praises its introduction not only because it illustrates the affinity between Hamlet and Wilhelm, both of whom are reflective, vacillating characters, but because Hamlet is further allied to Wilhelm in making the Play a touchstone, whereby to detect the truth, and determine his own actions.

Were space at disposal, the whole of Schiller's criticism on this work might fitly be given here from his enthusiastic letters ; but I must content myself with one extract, which is quite delightful to read : 'I account it the most fortunate incident in my existence, that I have lived to see the completion of this work ; that it has taken place while my faculties are still capable of improvement ; that I can yet draw from this pure spring ; and the beautiful relation there is between us makes it a kind of religion with me to feel towards what is yours as if it were my own, and so to purify and elevate my nature that my mind may be a clear mirror, and that I may thus deserve, in a higher sense, the name of your friend. How strongly have I felt on this occasion that the Excellent is a power ; that by selfish natures it can be felt only as a power ; and that only where there is disinterested love can it be enjoyed. I cannot describe to you how deeply the truth, the beautiful vitality, the simple fulness of this work has affected me. The excitement into which it has thrown my mind will subside when I shall have perfectly mastered it, and that will be an important crisis in my being. This excitement is the effect of the beautiful, and only the beautiful, and proceeds from the fact that my intellect is not yet entirely in accordance with my feelings. I understand now perfectly what you mean when you say that it is strictly the beautiful, the true, that can move you even to tears. Tranquil and deep, clear, and yet, like nature, unintelligible, is this work ; and all, even the most trivial collateral incident, shows the clearness, the equanimity of the mind whence it flowed'.

CHAPTER III

THE ROMANTIC SCHOOL

'AFTER the mad challenge of the *Xenien*', writes Goethe to Schiller, 'we must busy ourselves only with great and worthy works of Art, and shame our opponents by the manifestation of our poetical natures in forms of the Good and Noble'. This trumpet-sound found Schiller alert. The two earnest men went earnestly to work, and produced their matchless ballads, and their great poems, *Hermann und Dorothea* and *Wallenstein*. The influence of these men on each other was very peculiar. It made Goethe, in contradiction to his native tendency, speculative and theoretical. It made Schiller, in contradiction to his native tendency, realistic. Had it not urged Goethe to rapid production, we might have called the influence wholly noxious; but seeing what was produced, we pause ere we condemn. 'You have created a new youth for me', writes Goethe, 'and once more restored me to Poetry, which I had almost entirely given up'. They were both much troubled with Philosophy at this epoch. Kant and Spinoza occupied Schiller; Kant and scientific theories occupied Goethe. They were both, moreover, becoming more and more imbued with the spirit of ancient Art, and were bent on restoring its principles. They were men of genius, and therefore these two false tendencies—the tendency to Reflection, and the tendency to Imitation—were less hurtful to *their* works than to the national culture. Their genius saved them, in spite of their errors; but their errors misled the nation. It is remarked by Gervinus, that ' Philosophy was restored in the year 1781, and profoundly affected all Germany. Let any one draw up a statistical table of our literary productions, and he will be amazed at the decadence of Poetry during the last fifty years in which Philosophy has been supreme'. Philosophy has distorted Poetry, and been the curse of Criticism. It has vitiated German Literature; and it produced, in combination with the tendency to Imitation, that brilliant error known as the Romantic School.

A few words on this much-talked-of school may not be unacceptable. Like its offspring, *L'École Romantique* in France, it had a critical purpose which was good, and a retrograde purpose which was bad. Both were insurgent against narrow critical canons ; both proclaimed the superiority of Mediæval Art ; both sought, in Catholicism and in national Legends, meanings profounder than those current in the literature of the day. The desire to get deeper than Life itself led to a disdain of reality and the present. Hence the selection of the Middle Ages and the East as regions for the ideal : they were not present, and they were not classical ; the classical had already been tried, and against it the young Romantic School was everywhere in arms. In other respects the German and French schools greatly differed. The Schlegels, Tieck, Novalis, and Werner, had no enemy to combat in the shape of a severe National Taste, such as opposed the tentatives of Victor Hugo, Dumas, and Alfred de Vigny. On the contrary, they were supported by a large body of the nation, for their theories only carried further certain tendencies which had become general. Thus in as far as these theories were critical, they were little more than jubilations over the victorious campaigns won by Lessing, Herder, Goethe, and Schiller. The Schlegels stood upon the battlefield, now silent, and sang a hymn of victory over the bodies of the slain. Frederick Schlegel, by many degrees the most considerable critic of this school, began his career with an Anthology from Lessing's works : *Lessing's Geist : eine Blumenlese seiner Ansichten ;* he ended it with admiration for Philip the Second and the cruel Alva, and with the proclamation that Calderon was a greater poet than Shakespeare. Frederick Schlegel thus represents the whole Romantic School from its origin to its close.

Fichte, Schelling, Schleiermacher, and Solger are the philosophers of this school ; from the two former came the most famous, now almost forgotten, principle of ' Irony ', which Hegel * not only disposed of as a principle, but showed that the critics themselves made no use of it. No one, not even Tieck, attempted to exhibit the ' irony ' of Shakespeare, the god of their idolatry. Among the services rendered by Tieck and A. W. Schlegel, the translation of Shakespeare must never be forgotten, for although that translation is by no means so accurate as is generally believed, being often singularly weak, and sometimes grossly mistaken in its interpretation of the meaning, it is nevertheless a translation which, on the whole, has, perhaps, no rival in literature, and has served to make Shakespeare as familiar to the Germans as to us.

In their crusade against the French, in their naturalization

* *Æsthetik,* 1, p. 84–90.

of Shakespeare, and their furtherance of Herder's efforts towards the restoration of a Ballad Literature and the taste for Gothic Architecture, these Romanticists were with the stream.   They also flattered the national tendencies when they proclaimed 'Mythology and Poetry, symbolical Legend and Art to be one and indivisible'*, whereby it became clear that a new religion, or at any rate a new Mythology, was needed, for 'the deepest want and deficiency of all modern Art lies in the fact that the artists have no Mythology' †.

While Fichte, Schelling, and Schleiermacher were tormented with the desire to create a new philosophy and a new religion, it soon became evident that a Mythology was not to be created by programme ; and as a Mythology was indispensable, the Romanticists betook themselves to Catholicism, with its saintly Legends and saintly Heroes ; some of them, as Tieck and A. W. Schlegel, out of nothing more than poetic enthusiasm and dilettantism ; others, as F. Schlegel and Werner, with thorough conviction, accepting Catholicism and all its consequences.

Solger had called Irony the daughter of Mysticism ; and how highly these Romanticists prized Mysticism is known to all readers of Novalis. To be mystical was to be poetical as well as profound ; and critics glorified mediæval monstrosities because of the deep spiritualism which stood in contrast with the pagan materialism of Goethe and Schiller. Once commenced, this movement carried what was true in it rapidly onwards to the confines of nonsense. Art became the handmaid of Religion.   The canon was laid down that only in the service of Religion had Art ever flourished,—only in that service *could* it flourish : a truth from which strange conclusions were drawn.   Art became a propaganda.   Fra Angelico and Calderon suddenly became idols.   Werner was proclaimed a Colossus by Wackenroder, who wrote his *Herzensergiessungen eines Kunstliebenden Klosterbruders*, with Tieck's aid, to prove, said Goethe, that because some monks were artists all artists should turn monks.   Then it was that men looked to Faith for miracles in Art. Devout study of the Bible was thought to be the readiest means of rivalling Fra Angelico and Van Eyck ; inspiration was sought in a hair-shirt. Catholicism had a Mythology, and painters went over in crowds to the Roman Church.   Cornelius and Overbeck lent real genius to the attempt to revive the dead forms of early Christian Art, as Goethe and Schiller did

* F. SCHLEGEL : *Gespräche über Poesie*, p. 263.   † *Ibid.*, p. 274.

to revive the dead forms of Grecian Art. Overbeck, who painted
in a cloister, was so thoroughly penetrated by the ascetic spirit,
that he refused to draw from the living model, lest it should make
his works too *naturalistic;* for to be true to Nature was tantamount to being false to the higher tendencies of Spiritualism.
Some had too much of the artistic instinct to carry their principles
into these exaggerations ; but others less gifted, and more bigoted,
carried the principles into every excess. A band of these reformers
established themselves in Rome, and astonished the Catholics
quite as much as the Protestants. Cesar Masini, in his work *Dei
Puristi in Pittura,* thus describes them : 'Several young men came
to Rome from Northern Germany in 1809. They abjured Protestantism, adopted the costume of the Middle Ages, and began
to preach the doctrine that painting had died out with Giotto, and
to revive it, a recurrence to the old style was necessary. Under
such a mask of piety they concealed their nullity. Servile admirers
of the rudest periods in Art, they declared the pigmies were giants,
and wanted to bring us back to the dry hard style and barbarous
imperfection of a Buffalmacco, Calandrino, Paolo Uccello, when
we had a Raphael, a Titian, and a Correggio'. In spite of their
exaggerated admiration of the Trecentisti, in spite of a doctrine
which was fundamentally vicious, the Romanticists made a decided
revolution, not only in Literature but in Painting, and above all in
our general estimate of painters. If we now learn to look at the
exquisite works of Fra Angelico, Ghirlandajo, and Massacio with
intense pleasure, and can even so far divest ourselves of the
small prejudices of criticism, as to be deeply interested in Giotto,
Gozzoli, or Guido da Arezzo, feeling in them the divine artistic
faculty which had not yet mastered artistic expression, it is to
the preaching of the Romanticists that we owe this source of
noble enjoyment. In poetry the Romanticists were failures, but
in painting they achieved marked success. Whatever may be
thought of the German School, it must be confessed that before
Overbeck, Cornelius, Schadow, Hess, Lessing, Hübner, Sohn, and
Kaulbach, the Germans had no painters at all ; and they have in
these men painters of very remarkable power.

To return to Goethe. He was led by Schiller into endless theoretical discussions. They philosophized on the limits of epic
and dramatic poetry ; read and discussed Aristotle's Poetics ;
discussions which resulted in Goethe's essay, *Ueber epische und
dramatische Poesie;* and, as we gather from their correspondence,

scarcely ventured to take a step until they had seen how Theory justified it. Goethe read with enthusiasm Wolf's *Prolegomena* to Homer, and at once espoused its principles*. The train of thought thus excited, led him from the origin of epic songs to the origin of the Hebrew songs, and Eichhorn's *Introduction to the Old Testament* led him to attempt a new explanation of the wanderings of the people of Israel, which he subsequently inserted in the notes to the *Westöstliche Divan*.

Nor was he only busy with epical theories; he also gave himself to the production of epics. *Hermann und Dorothea*, the most perfect of his poems, was written at this time. *Achilleis* was planned and partly executed; *Die Jagd* was also planned, but left unwritten, and subsequently became the prose tale known as *die Novelle*. This year of 1797 is moreover memorable as the year of ballads, in which he and Schiller, in friendly rivalry, gave Germany lyrical masterpieces. His share may be estimated, when we learn that in this year were written the *Bride of Corinth*, the *Zauberlehrling*, *der Gott und die Bajadere*, and the *Schatzgräber*. In an unpublished letter to Körner, he writes, 'You will have learned from Schiller that we are now making attempts in the ballad line. His are, as you know already, very felicitous. I wish that mine may be in some sort worthy to stand beside them; he is, in every sense, more competent to this species of poetry than I am'.

In the same year *Faust* was once more taken up. The *Dedication*, the *Prologue in Heaven* and the Intermezzo of *Oberon and Titania's Marriage* were written. But while he was in this mood, Hirt came to Weimar, and in the lively reminiscences of Italy, and the eager discussions of Art which his arrival awakened, all the northern phantoms were exorcised by southern magic. He gave up *Faust*, and wrote an essay on the *Laokoon*. He began once more to pine for Italy. This is characteristic of his insatiable hunger for knowledge; he never seemed to have mastered *material* enough. Whereas Schiller, so much poorer in material, and so much more inclined to production, thought this Italian journey would only embarrass him with fresh objects; and urged Meyer to dissuade him from it. He did not go; and I think Schiller's opinion was correct: at the point now reached

* Later on in life he returned to the old conviction of the unity of Homer. It is to be regretted that in England Wolf's masterly work is seldom read, the critics contenting themselves with second-hand statements of his views, which fail to do them justice.

he had nothing to do but to give a form to the material he had accumulated.

In the July of this year he, for the third time, made a journey into Switzerland. In Frankfurt he introduced Christiane and her boy to his mother, who received them very heartily, and made the few days' stay there very agreeable. It is unnecessary for us to follow him on his journey, which is biographically interesting only in respect to the plan of an epic on *William Tell* which he conceived, and for which he studied the localities. The plan was never executed. He handed it over to Schiller for his drama on that subject, giving him at the same time the idea of the character of Tell, and the studies of localities which Schiller managed to employ with a mastery quite astonishing to his friend. The same brotherly co-operation is seen in the composition of *Wallenstein.* It is not true, as was currently supposed in Germany, that Goethe wrote any portions of that work. He has told us himself he only wrote two unimportant lines. But his counsel aided Schiller through every scene ; and the bringing it on the stage was to him like a triumph of his own.

In the spring of 1798 Schelling's Philosophy of Nature, and his own plans for a History of the Theory of Colours, lured him from poetry ; but Schiller again brought him back to it. *Faust* was resumed, and the last tragic scenes of the First Part were written. In the summer he was much at Jena with Schiller, consequently with poetry. Achilles and Tell, the ancient and the modern world, as Schäfer remarks, struggled for priority, but neither obtained it, because he was still perplexed in his epic theories. The studies of the *Iliad* had 'hunted him through the circle of enthusiasm, hope, insight, and despair'. No sooner did he leave Jena than, as he confessed, he was drawn by another polarity. Accordingly, we see him busy with an art-journal, the *Propyläen.* He was also busy with the alteration of the Theatre, the boards of which, on the 12th of October, 1798, were made for ever memorable by the production of *Wallenstein's Camp* and *Prologue.* On the 30th January, 1799, the birthday of the Duchess Louise, the *Piccolomini* was produced ; and, on the 20th of April, *Wallenstein's Tod.*

It was in this year that a young advocate, in Edinburgh, put forth a translation of *Götz von Berlichingen,* and preluded to a fame as great as Goethe's own ; and it was in the December of this year that Karl August's generosity enabled Schiller to quit Jena, and come to Weimar for the rest of his life, there in uninterrupted intercourse with Goethe to pursue the plans so dear to both, especially in the formation of a national stage.   I will take advantage of this change to insert a chapter on *Hermann und Dorothea*, which was published in 1796-7 ; and I will afterwards group together the scattered details of the theatrical management, so as to place them before the reader in a continuous narrative.

CHAPTER IV

'HERMANN UND DOROTHEA'

THE pleasure every one finds in making acquaintance with the original stories from which Shakespeare created his marvellous plays, is the pleasure of detecting how genius can improve upon the merest hint, and how with its own vital forces it converts lifeless material into immortal life.   This pleasure also carries the conviction that there is no lack of subjects for an artist, if he have but the eye to see them.   It shows us that great poets are not accustomed to cast about for subjects worthy of treatment ; on the contrary, the merest hint is enough to form the nucleus of a splendid work : a random phrase will kindle a magnificent conception.

Very like the material offered by Bandello to Shakespeare is the material offered to Goethe by the old narrative* from which he created one of the most faultless of modern poems.   Herein we learn how a rich and important citizen of Altmühl has in vain tried to persuade his son to marry.   The Saltzburg emigrants pass through the town, and among them the son finds 'a maiden who pleases him right well' ; he inquires after her family and bringing up, and as all he hears is satisfactory, away he hies to his father, declaring that unless this Saltzburg maiden be given him, he will remain unmarried all his life.   The father, aided by the pastor, tries to persuade him from such a resolution.   But their efforts being vain, the pastor advises the father to give his consent, which is done.   Away goes the son to the maiden, and asks her if she is willing to enter his father's domestic service.   She accepts, and is presented to the father.   But he, ignorant of his son's *ruse*, and believing he sees before him the betrothed, asked her whether she is fond of his son.

---

* *Das Liebthätige Gera gegen die Salzburgischen Emigranten. Das ist: kurze und wahrhaftige Erzählung wie dieselben in der Gräflich Reuss Plauischen Residenz Stadt angekommen, aufgenommen, und versorget, auch was an und von vielen derselben Gutes gesehen und gehöret worden.* Leipzig : 1732.

The maiden thinks they are laughing at her, but on learning that they are serious in wishing her to belong to the family, declares herself quite ready, and draws from her bosom a purse containing 200 ducats, which she hands to her bridegroom as her dowry.

This is the story out of which grew *Hermann und Dorothea*. An ordinary story, in which the poet alone could see a poem ; *what* he has seen, every reader of German literature well knows ; and those to whom the poem is unknown must be content with the following analysis.

The epoch is changed to that of the French Revolution. The emigrants are driven from home by political events. The scene is on the right side of the Rhine. The streets of a quiet little village are noisy with unaccustomed movement ; every one is crowding to see the sad procession of emigrants passing through, in the heat and dust of a summer afternoon. Mine host of the Golden Lion, sitting at his doorway, marvels at such curiosity, but applauds the active benevolence of his wife, who has sent their son with linen, food and drink, to bestow upon the sufferers, 'for to give is the duty of those who have'.

And now are seen returning some of the curious. See how dusty their shoes ! and how their faces are burning ! They come back wiping the perspiration from their glowing faces ; the old couple rejoice at having sat quiet at home, contending themselves with what will be told them of the sight. Sure enough, here comes the pastor, and with him the apothecary ; seating themselves on the wooden bench, they shake the dust off their shoes, and fan their hot faces with their handkerchiefs. They narrate what they have seen ; and mine host, sighing, hopes his son will overtake the emigrants, and give them what has been sent. But the heat suggests to him that they should retire into the cool back parlour, and, out of the way of the flies, refresh themselves with a bottle of Rhine wine. There, over the wine, mine host expresses his wish to see his son married. This is the whole of the first canto ; and yet, slight as the material is, the wonderful objective treatment gives it substance. The fresh air of the country breathes from the verse.

In the second canto Hermann appears before his father and friends. The pastor's quick eye detects that he is returned an altered man. Hermann narrates how he accomplished his mission. Overtaking the emigrants, he fell in with a cart drawn by oxen, wherein lay a poor woman beside the infant to which she had just

given birth. Leading the oxen was a maiden, who came towards
him with the calm confidence of a generous soul, and begged his
aid for the poor woman whom she had just assisted in her travail.
Touched with pity, and feeling at once that this maiden was the
best person to distribute justly the aid he had brought, Hermann
gave it all into her hands. They parted, she gratefully pursuing
her sad journey, he thoughtfully returning home. Love has leaped
into his heart, and, by the light of his smile, the pastor sees he is
an altered man.

On hearing his tale, the apothecary hugs himself with the consolation of not having wife and children to make him anxious in
these anxious times ; 'the single man escapes the easiest'. But
Hermann reproves him, asking, 'Is it well that a man should feel
himself alone in joy and sorrow, not understanding how to share
these joys and sorrows ? I never was so willing to marry as to-day ;
for many a good maiden needs the protection of a husband, and many
a man needs the bright consolation of a wife, in the shadow of misfortune'. Hereupon the father, smiling, exclaims, 'I hear you with
pleasure ; such a sensible word you have seldom uttered'. And
his mother also applauds him, referring to her marriage as an
example. Memory travels back complacently to the day of her
betrothal. It was in the midst of misfortune—a fire had destroyed
all their property—but in that hour of misfortune their union was
decided. The father here breaks in, and says the story is true, but
evidently wishes to warn his son from any imitation of his own
venture. With admirable art and humour his fatherly anxiety is
depicted. He married a girl who had nothing when he himself had
nothing ; but now, when he is old and well to do in the world, this
idea of beginning life upon no solid foundation of fortune is
alarming to him. He paints the difficulties of keeping house, the
advantages of fortune, and concludes with a decisive intimation to
Hermann that he expects a rich daughter-in-law to be brought into
the house. He indicates the daughters of a rich neighbour, and
wishes Hermann to select one. But Hermann has not only a new
love in his heart, he has an old repugnance to these rich neighbours, who mocked his simplicity, and ridiculed him because he
was not as familiar with the personages of an opera as they were.
This enrages his father, who upbraids him for being a mere peasant without culture, and who angrily declares he will have no
peasant-girl brought into the house as his daughter-in-law, but a
girl who can play the piano, and who can draw around her the

finest people of the town.   Hermann, in silence, quits the room ; and thus closes the second canto.

The third canto carries on the story.   Mine host continues his angry eloquence.   It is his opinion that the son should always rise higher in the social scale than the father : for what would become of the house, or the nation, without this constant progress ?   'You are always unjust to your son', replies the mother, 'and thus frustrate your own wishes.   We must not hope to form children after our own notions.   As God has given them us, so must we have them and love them, bring them up as best we can, and let them have their own disposition.   For some have this and others that gift. One is happy in one way, another in another.   I won't have my Hermann abused.   He is an excellent creature.   But with daily snubbing and blame you crush his spirit'.   And away she goes to seek her son.   'A wonderful race the women', says the host, smiling, as his wife departs, 'just like children.   They all want to live after their own fashion, and yet be praised and caressed !' The old apothecary, carrying out the host's arguments respecting the continual improvement of one's station, happily displays his character by a speech of quiet humour, describing his own anxiety to improve the appearance of his house, and how he has always been hindered by the fear of the expense.   The contrast of characters in this poem is of the finest and sharpest : mother and father, pastor and apothecary, all stand before us in distinctive, yet unobtrusive, individuality, such as only the perfection of art achieves.

In the fourth canto, the mother seeks her son.   The description of this search is a striking specimen of Goethe's descriptive poetry, being a series of pictures without a metaphor, without an image, without any of the picturesque aids which most poets employ ; and yet it is vivid and picturesque in the highest degree. I wish I dared quote it.   But the reader of German can seek it in the original ; and translation is more than ever unjust to a poet, where style is in question.

In the stable she seeks him, expecting to find him with his favourite stallion ; then she goes into the garden (not omitting to set up the tree-props and brush the caterpillars from the cabbages, like a careful housewife as she is !), then through the vineyard until she finds him seated under the pear-tree, in tears.   A charming scene takes place between them.   Hermann declares his intention of setting off in defence of fatherland ; he is eloquent on the duties of citizens to give their blood for their country. But the mother knows very well it is no political enthusiasm thus suddenly moving him to quit his home ; she has divined his love for Dorothea, the maiden whom he met among the emigrants ; she questions him, and receives his confidence. Yes, it is because he loves Dorothea, and because his father has forbidden him to think of any but a rich bride, that he is about to depart. His father has always been unjust to him. Here interposes the mother ; persuades Hermann to make the first advances to his father, certain that the paternal anger is mere hasty words, and that the dearest wish of Hermann's heart will not be disregarded. She brings him back with these hopes.

In the fifth canto the friends are still sipping from green glasses the cool Rhine wine, and arguing the old question. To them enter mother and son. She reminds her husband how often they have looked forward to the day when Hermann should make choice of a bride. That day has arrived. He has chosen the emigrant maiden. Mine host hears this in ominous stillness. The Pastor rises, and heartily backs Hermann in his prayer. He looks upon this choice as an inspiration from above, and knows Hermann well enough to trust him in such a choice. The father is still silent. The Apothecary, cautious ever, suggests a middle course. He does not trust implicitly in these inspirations from above. He proposes to inquire into the character of the maiden, and as he is not easily to be deceived, he undertakes to bring back a true report. I need scarcely point out the superiority of this treatment of the old story, wherein the lover first inquires into the character of the maiden, and then makes up his mind to have her. Hermann needs no inquiry—but neither does he shirk it. He urges the Apothecary to set off, and take the Pastor with him, two such experienced men being certain to detect the truth. For himself he is sure of the result. Mine host, finding wife and friends against him, consents, on a worthy report being brought by Pastor and Apothecary, to call Dorothea his daughter. The two commissioners seat themselves in the cart, and Hermann, mounting the box, drives them swiftly to the village. Arriving there, they get out. Hermann describes Dorothea, that they may recognize her ; and awaits their return. Very graphic is the picture of this village, where the wanderers are crowded in barns and gardens, the streets blocked up with carts, men noisily attending to the lowing cows and horses, women busily washing and drying on every hedge, while the children dabble in the stream. Through this crowd the two friends wander, and witness a quarrel, which is silenced by an old magistrate, who afterwards gives them satisfactory details about Dorothea. This episode is full of happy touches and thoughtful poetry. The friends return joyful to Hermann, and tell him he may take Dorothea home. But while they have been inquiring about her, he, here on the threshold of his fate, has been torturing himself with doubts as to whether Dorothea will accept him. She may love another; what is more probable? She may refuse to come with them into a strange house. He begs them to drive home without him. He will alone ask Dorothea, and return on foot with her if she consent. The Pastor takes the reins, but the cautious Apothecary, willing enough to entrust the Pastor with the care of his soul, has misgivings about his power of saving his body. The Pastor reassures him, and they disappear in a cloud of dust, leaving Hermann to gaze after them motionless, fixed in thought.

The next two cantos are exquisitely poetical. As Hermann stands by the spring, he sees Dorothea coming with a water jug in each hand. He approaches her, and she smiles a friendly smile at his approach. He asks why she comes so far from the village to fetch water. She answers that her trouble is well repaid if only because it enables her to see and thank him for the kindness he has shown to the sufferers; but also adds that the improvident men have allowed oxen and horses to walk into the streams, and so disturb all the water of the village. They then pass to the well, and sit upon the wall which protects it. She stoops, and dips a jug in the water; he takes the other jug and dips it also, and they see the image of themselves mirrored in the wavering blue of the reflected heavens, and they nod and greet each other in the friendly mirror. 'Let me drink', says the joyous youth. And she holds the jug for him. Then they rest, leaning upon the jugs in sweet confidence.*

She then asks him what has brought him here. He looks into

---

* I cannot resist quoting the original of this charming picture :
  Also sprach sie, und war die breiten Stufen hinunter
  Mit dem Begleiter gelangt ; und auf das Mäuerchen setzten
  Beide sich nieder des Quells. Sie beugte sich über, zu schöpfen ;
  Und er fasste den anderen Krug, und beugte sich über.
  Und sie sahen gespiegelt ihr Bild in der Bläue des Himmels
  Schwanken, und nickten sich zu, und grüssten sich freundlich im Spiegel.
  Lass mich trinken, sagte darauf der heitere Jüngling ;
  Und sie reicht' ihm den Krug. Dann ruhten sie Beide vertraulich
  Auf die Gefässe gelehnt.

her eyes, and feels happy, but dares not trust himself with the avowal. He endeavours to make her understand it in an indirect recital of the need there is at home for a young and active woman to look after the house and his parents. She thinks he means to ask her to come as servant in his house, and, being alone in the world, gladly consents. When he perceives her mistake he is afraid to undeceive her, and thinks it better to take her home and gain her affection there. 'But let us go', she exclaims, 'girls are always blamed who stay long at the fountain in gossip'. They stand. up, and once more look back into the well to see their images meeting in its water, and 'sweet desires possess them'.

He accompanies her to the village, and witnesses, in the affection all bear to Dorothea, the best sign that his heart has judged aright. She takes leave of them all, and sets forth with Hermann, followed by the blessings and handkerchief-wavings of the emigrants. In silence they walk towards the setting sun, which tinges the storm-clouds threatening in the distance. On the way she asks him to describe the characters of those she is going to serve. He sketches father and mother. 'And how am I to treat you, you the only son of my future master?' she asks. By this time they had reached the pear-tree, and the moon is shining overhead. He takes her hand, answering, 'Ask your heart, and follow all it tells you'. But he can go no further in his declaration, fearing to draw upon himself a refusal. In silence they sit awhile and look upon the moon. She sees a window—it is Hermann's, who hopes it will soon be hers. They rise to continue their course, her foot slips, she falls into his arms ; breast against breast, cheek against cheek, they remain a moment, he not daring to press her to him, merely supporting her. In a few minutes more they enter the house.

The charm of these cantos, as indeed of the whole poem, cannot of course be divined from the analysis I am making ; the perfume of a violet is not to be found in the description of the violet. But with all drawbacks, the analysis enables a reader of imagination to form a better conception of the poem than he would form from an æsthetical discussion such as philosophical criticism indulges in. With this caveat let our analysis proceed. The mother is uneasy at this long absence of Hermann ; comes in and out, noting the appearances of the storm, and is rather sharp in her blame of the two friends for leaving him without securing the maiden. The Apothecary narrates how he was taught patience in youth; and, the door opening, presents the young couple to their glad eyes. Hermann introduces her, but tells the Pastor aside that as yet there has been no talk of marriage; she only supposes her place to be that of servant. The host, wishing to be gallant, goes at once to the point, treats her as his daughter, and compliments her on her taste in having chosen his son. She blushes, is pained, and replies with some reproach that for such a greeting she was unprepared. With tears in her eyes she paints her forlorn condition, and the secret escapes her, that, touched by Hermann's generosity and noble bearing, she really has begun to feel the love for him they twit her with; but having made that confession, of course she can no longer stay; and she is departing with grief in her heart when the mistake is cleared up; she is accepted, dowerless, by them all, and Hermann, in pressing her to his heart, feels prepared for the noble struggle of life.

Such is the story of *Hermann und Dorothea*, which is written in Homeric hexameters, with Homeric simplicity. In the ordinary course of things, I should be called upon to give some verdict on the much-vexed question as to whether, properly speaking, this poem is an Epic or an Idyll, or, by way of compromise, an Idyllic Epic. The critics are copious in distinctions and classifications. They tell us in what consists the Epos proper, which they distinguish from the Romantic Epos, and from the Bourgeois Epos; and then these heavy batteries are brought to bear on *Hermann und Dorothea*. Well! if these discussions gratify the mind, and further any of the purposes of Literature, let those, whose bent lies that way, occupy themselves therewith. To me it seems idle to trouble oneself whether *Hermann und Dorothea* is or is not an Epic, or what kind of Epic it should be called. It is a poem. One cannot say more for it. If it be unlike all other poems, there is no harm in that; if it resemble some other poems, the resemblance does not enhance its charm. Let us accept it for what it is, a poem full of life, character, and beauty; simple in its materials, astonishingly simple in its handling; written in obvious imitation of Homer, and yet preserving throughout the most modern colour and sentiment. Of all Idylls, it is the most truly idyllic. Of all poems describing country life and country people, it is the most truthful; and on comparing it with Theocritus or Virgil, with Guarini or Tasso, with Florian or Delille, with Gesner or Thomson, the critic will note with interest its absence of poetic ornamenta-

tion, its freedom from all 'idealization'. Its peasants are not
such as have been fashioned in Dresden China, or have solicited
the palette of Lancret and Watteau ; but are as true as poetry
can represent them. The characters are wonderfully drawn, with
a few decisive, unobtrusive touches. Shakespeare himself is not
more dramatic in the presentation of character. The Host, his
wife, the Pastor, the old cautious Apothecary, stand before us in
all their humours. Hermann, the stalwart peasant, frank, simple,
and shy, and Dorothea the healthy, affectionate, robust, simple
peasant girl, are ideal characters in the best sense, viz., in the
purity of nature. Those 'ideal peasants' with Grecian features
and irreproachable linen, so loved of bad painters and poor poets,
were not at all the figures Goethe cared to draw ; he had faith in
nature, which would not allow him to idealize.

Very noteworthy is it that he, like Walter Scott, could find a
real pleasure in talking with the common people, such as astonished
his daughter-in-law (from whom, among others, I learned the
fact), who could not comprehend what pleasure this great intellect
found in conversation with an old woman baking her bread, or an
old carpenter planing a fir-plank. He would talk with his coach-
man, pointing out to him the peculiarities of the scenery, and
delighting in his remarks. Stately and silent as he often was
to travelling bores, and to literary men, with no ideas beyond the
circle of books, he was loquacious and interested whenever one of
the people came in his way ; and the secret of this was his abiding
interest in every individuality. A carpenter, who was a carpenter,
interested him ; but the carpenter in Sunday clothes, aping the
bourgeois, would have found him as silent and stately as every
other pretender found him. What Scott gathered from his intercourse with the people, every one knows who has noticed the rich
soil of humour on which Scott's antiquarian fancies are planted ;
what Goethe gathered from the same source may be read in most
of his works, especially in *Hermann und Dorothea, Faust,* and
Wilhelm Meister.

The same objective truth is noticeable in his delineation of the
scenes. They are not rhetorically or metaphorically described,
they are presented directly to us. Instead of saying what they
are like, he says what they *are.* Hence it is that while this poem
is essentially *popular* (and on its first appearance produced a deep
impression on the people, was reprinted on the coarsest paper, at
the lowest prices, such as only occurs with the people's literature),

it is also one of the greatest favourites with highly cultured readers. Between these two classes there is a third class, cultivated indeed, but not sufficiently cultivated, which finds the simplicity of this poem undistinguishable from baldness. Such readers desire imagery, and cannot see the art which dispenses with it ; they want more stirring incidents, and characters stalking upon stilts.

As I do not enter upon the discussion of whether the poem is or is not an Epic, I may leave undisturbed all the derivative questions respecting the absence of *similes, episodes,* and *supernatural machinery*—which the critics assure us are indispensable to the Epic—as also the other subsidiary matters of action, time, and space. By so doing the bulk of this chapter is materially diminished, and the reader not materially impoverished. Two points only require notice, and those shall be briefly touched.

First of the subject-matter. Taken from the sad experience of the hour, moving amid scenes made desolate by the French Revolution, it was natural that something of political significance should be sought in this story. Schiller would undoubtedly have made it the vehicle of splendid eloquence on Freedom, such as would have made the pulses beat. But that was nowise Goethe's tendency. He told Meyer that he had endeavoured 'in an epic crucible to free from its dross the pure human existence of a small German town, and at the same time mirror in a small glass the great movements and changes of the world's stage'*. While leaving to others the political problem, he confined himself as usual to the purely human and individual interest. Instead of declamations on Freedom, he tried to teach men to be free ; and by Freedom he meant the complete healthy development of their own natures, not a change of political institutions. In one of the *Xenien* he says :

> Zur Nation euch zu bilden, ihr hoffet es, Deutsche, vergebens.
> Bildet, ihr könnt es, dafür freier zu Menschen euch aus †.

And in this sense *Hermann und Dorothea* may be accepted as a Hymn to the Family, a solemn vindication of the eternal claims which, as a first necessity, should occupy men.

With regard to the second point, that namely of style, Schiller's cordial praise, in a letter to Meyer, may here find place. 'Nor have we in the meantime been inactive, as you know, and least of

---

* *Briefe an und von Goethe.*
† 'Germans, you hope in vain to develop yourselves into a nation ; strive, therefore, to develop yourselves all the more freely into men'.

all our friend, who in the last few years has really surpassed himself. His epic poem you have read; you will admit that it is the pinnacle of his and all our modern art. I have seen it grow up, and have wondered almost as much at the manner of its growth as at the completed work. Whilst the rest of us are obliged painfully to collect and to prune, in order slowly to bring forth anything passable, he has only gently to shake the tree, in order to have fall to him the most beautiful fruit, ripe and heavy. It is incredible with what ease he now reaps for himself the fruits of a well-bestowed life and a persistent culture; how significant and sure all his steps now are; how the clearness as to himself and as to objects, preserves him from every idle effort and beating about. But you have him now yourself, and can satisfy your-self of all this with your own eyes. But you will agree with me in this, that on the summit where he now stands, he ought to think more of bringing the beautiful form he has given himself to outward exhibition, than to go out in search of new material; in short, that he now ought to live entirely for poetic execution'.

The Homeric form is admirably adapted to this kind of narrative; and Voss had already made it popular by his *Luise*. Respecting the style of this poem, I will further beg the reader to compare it with that of the last books of *Wilhelm Meister*, composed about the same period, and he will then see Goethe's immense superiority on quitting prose for poetry. None of the faults of his prose are traceable here. The language is as clear as crystal, and as simple; the details are all, without exception, significant; not a line could be lopped away without injury. One feels that the invigorating breezes of Ilmenau have roused the poet out of the flaccid moods of prose, and given him all his quiet strength.

Before finally dismissing the poem, it may amuse the reader to have a specimen of that ingenious criticism which delights in interpreting the most obvious facts into profound meanings. Hegel, in his *Æsthetik*, and after him Rosenkrantz, in his excellent book, *Goethe und seine Werke*, call attention to the fact that Goethe is far truer in his *German* colouring than Voss, whose *Luise* gave the impulse to this poem. Not having read the *Luise*, I am unable to judge of this superiority; but the example cited by these critics is assuredly amusing. Voss, they tell us, makes his people drink copiously of coffee; but, however widespread the custom of coffee drinking, we must remember that coffee, and the sugar which sweetens it, are not *German*, they come from Arabia and the West Indies ; the very cups in which the coffee is drunk are of Chinese origin, not German.   We are miles away from Germany.   How different in Goethe !   His host of the Golden Lion refreshes guests with a glass of wine ; and what wine? Rhine wine ; the German wine, *par excellence;* the wine growing on the hill behind his own house !   And this Rhine wine, is it not drunk out of green glasses, the genuine German glasses?   And upon what do these glasses stand?   Upon a tin tray : that is also genuine German !

It would be the merest prosaism to suggest that in *Luise* the pastor drinks coffee, because coffee is habitually drunk in the parsonage ; while in *Hermann und Dorothea* the characters drink wine, because they are in the *Golden Lion*, and Rhine wine, because they are in the Rhine country ; yet to such prosaisms is the British critic reduced in answering the subtleties of German æsthetics.

CHAPTER V

THE THEATRICAL MANAGER

IT will be briefer, and help to convey a more accurate notion of Goethe's efforts in the direction of the Theatre, if, instead of scattering through this biography a number of isolated details, recording small events in chronological order, I endeavour to present some general view of his managerial efforts.

We have already seen how, on his arrival at Weimar, the Court was given to theatrical entertainments, and how eagerly he entered into them.   The theatre was in ruin from the fire of the previous year.   Theatres were improvised in the Ettersburg woods, and Tiefurt valley, whereon the gay courtiers 'strutted their brief hour' by torchlight, to the accompaniment of horns.   Actors were improvised from the Court circle.   Plays were improvised, and sometimes written with elaborate care.   The public was the public of private theatricals.   All this has been narrated in Book IV. What we have here to do with it is to call attention to the contrast thus presented by the Weimar stage with other German stages, and, above all, with the essential conditions of a stage which is to be anything more than the amusement of a dilettante circle.   The

drama is essentially a national outgrowth.   In Weimar, instead of
growing out of a popular tendency, and appealing to the people,
it grew out of the idleness of a Court, and appealed to dilettantism.
The actors, instead of being recruited from runaway clerks,
ambitious apprentices, romantic barbers, and scapegrace students,
were princes, noblemen, poets, musicians.   Instead of playing to a
Public,—that heterogeneous, but in dramatic matters indispensable,
jury, whose verdicts are in the main always right—they played to
courtiers, whose judgment, even when unfettered, would not have
had much value ; and it never was unfettered.   The consequence
may be foreseen.   As a Court amusement, the theatre was a
pleasant and not profitless recreation ; as an influence, it was
pernicious.   The starting-point was false.   Not so can dramatic
art flourish ; not so are Molières and Shakespeares allowed to
manifest their strength.   The national co-operation is indispensable.   Academies may compile Dictionaries, they cannot create
Literature ; and Courts may patronize Theatres, they cannot
create a Drama.   The reason lies deep in the nature of things.
Germany has never had a Drama, because she has never had
a Stage which could be, or would be, national.   Lessing knew
what was needed, but he had not the power to create it.
Schiller early mistook the path, and all his noble strivings were
frustrated.

Goethe and Schiller, profoundly in earnest, and profoundly convinced of the great influences to be exercised by the stage, endeavoured to create a German Drama which should stand high above
the miserable productions then vitiating public taste.   They
aspired to create an Ideal Drama, in which the loftiest forms
of Art should be presented.   But they made a false step at the
outset.   Disgusted with the rude productions of the day, and
distrusting the instincts of the public, they appealed to the cultivated few.   Culture was set above Passion and Humour, Literature above Emotion.   The stage was to be literary ; which is
saying, in other words, that it was not to be popular.   Nor did
experience enlighten them.   During the whole period of their
reform, the principal performances were of the old style.   At first
a wandering troupe, with a wandering repertory, performed opera,
drama, and farce, as best it could, with more real success than
High Art could boast.   Even when Schiller had ennobled the
stage with his masterpieces, the ever pressing necessity of *amusing*
the public forced the manager to give the vulgar appetite its

vulgar food *. The dramatic problem is : How to unite the demands of an audience insisting on amusement with the demands of Art looking beyond amusement? There are many writers who can amuse, but who reach no higher aim ; and there are writers who have lofty aims, but cannot amuse. In the drama the first class is nearer the mark than the second ; but the true dramatist is he who can unite the two. Shakespeare and Molière— to take the greatest examples—are as amusing as they are profound ; and they live only because they continue to amuse. *Othello, Hamlet, Macbeth, Tartuffe, L'école des Femmes*, and the *Malade Imaginaire*, may be enjoyed by the pit, and by the most cultivated critic. Goethe and Schiller fell into the error which in England, a few years ago, was preached as a gospel by a band of clever writers, who gloried in the title of 'Unacted Dramatists' ; the error of supposing a magnificent dome could be erected without a basis on our common earth ; the error of supposing that a Drama could be more successful as Literature than as the reflection of national life.

It was in 1790 that the Weimar Theatre was rebuilt and reopened. Goethe undertook the direction with powers more absolute than any other director ever had ; for he was independent even of success. The Court paid all expenses ; the stage was left free for him to make experiments upon. He made them, and they all failed. He superintended rehearsals with great care. Shakespeare's *King John* and *Henry IV*, his own *Gross-Kophta, Bürgergeneral, Clavigo, Die Geschwister*, were produced, but without any great effect ; for the actors were mediocre and ill paid, and there was no audience to stimulate actors by enthusiasm and criticism. The audience was chilled by the presence of the Court, and could rarely be emboldened into rapture, which is the life, the pulse, the stimulus of acting. The pit was cowed by the Court, and the Court was cowed by Goethe. His contempt of public opinion was undisguised. 'The direction', he wrote to his second in command, 'acts according to its own views, and not in the least according to the demands of the public. Once for all, understand that the public must be controlled—*will determinirt seyn*'. To Schiller, who was quite of this opinion, he said : 'No one can serve two masters, and of all masters the last that I would select is the public which sits in a German theatre'. It is all very well for a poet or a philosopher to scorn the fleeting fashions of the day, and to rely on the verdict

* Goethe confesses so much. See *Eckermann*, vol. I, p. 305; Oxenford's translation.

of posterity ; but the Drama appeals to the public of the day, and while the manager keeps his eye on posterity, the theatre is empty.

Wer machte denn der Mitwelt Spass?

'Who is to amuse the present?' asks the sensible Merry Andrew, in the Theatre-Prologue to *Faust*. A dramatist appealing to posterity is like an orator hoping to convince the descendants of his audience instead of persuading the listening crowd.

The Weimar audiences might be treated despotically, but they could not be forced into enthusiasm for that which wearied them. They submitted in silence. The riotous gallery and dogged pit of France and England only tolerate the absurdities which delight *them;* they admit no arbiter but their own amusement. An infusion of this rebellious element would have aided Goethe and Schiller in their efforts, by warning them from many a mistake. The Jena students might have supplied this element, had they been more constant visitors, and less controlled. The student is by nature and profession a rebel ; and the Jena student had this tendency cultivated into a system. To be a roaring swashbuckler, with profound contempt for all *Philistines,* and a vast capacity for beer, was not, indeed, enough to constitute a pure judge of art ; but to be young, full of life and impulse, and above all to be independent, were primary qualities in a dramatic audience ; and the students brought such qualities into the pit. 'Without them', says the worthy Klebe in his description of Weimar, 'the house would often be empty. They generally come in the afternoon, and ride or drive back after the play'. If they enlivened the theatre, they scandalized the town. Imagination pictures them arriving covered with dust, in garbs of varied and eccentric device, ambitious of appearing as different from 'humdrum' citizens as might be : adorned with tower-shaped caps, with motley ornaments of tassel, lace, etc., from under which escape flowing locks quite innocent of comb, which mingle with beard and moustache. Their short jackets are lined with stuffs of different colour. Their legs are cased in riding trousers, the inner sides of which are of leather. In their hands is the famous long whip, which they crack as they pour from the Webicht over the bridge into the town, startling its provincial dulness with an uproar by them called 'singing'—a musical entertainment which they vary by insulting the not imposing soldiers, whom they christen 'tree-frogs', on account of the green and yellow uniform. They push to the utmost the licence and pride of the 'Renomist', namely, to be ill-mannered.

When these students poured into the theatre, they carried there something like enthusiasm ; but they were controlled by one who had a very mediocre admiration of their wild ways—the Geheimrath Goethe, who was not only *Geheimrath* and Manager, but their idol *. Of him Edward Devrient, in his excellent history of the German stage †, says : 'He sat in the centre of the pit ; his powerful glance governed and directed the circle around him, and bridled the dissatisfied or neutral. On one occasion, when the Jena students, whose arbitrary judgment was very unseasonable to him, expressed their opinion too tumultuously, he rose, commanded silence, and threatened to have the disturbers turned out by the hussars on guard. A similar scene took place in 1802 on the representation of Fr. Schlegel's *Alarcos*, which appeared to the public too daring an attempt, and the approbation given by the loyal party provoked a loud laugh of opposition. Goethe rose and called out with a voice of thunder : " Let no one laugh ! " At last he went so far as for some time to forbid any audible expression on the part of the public, whether of approval or disapproval. He would suffer no kind of disturbance in what he held to be suitable. Over criticism he kept a tight rein ; hearing that Bötticher was writing an essay on his direction of the theatre, he declared that if it appeared he would resign his post ; and Bötticher left the article unprinted.'

Holding this despotic position towards the public, it may be imagined that he was imperious enough with the actors. Both he and Schiller were of opinion that nothing short of the 'brief imperative' was of any use with actors—*denn durch Vernunft und Gefälligkeit ist nichts auszurichten*, said Schiller. Goethe as director would hear of no opposition, would listen to none of the egotistical claims which usually torment managers ; he insisted on each doing what was allotted to him. Resistance was at once followed by punishment ; he sent the men to the guard house, and had sentinels placed before the doors of the women, confining them to their rooms. With the leading actors he employed other means : once when Becker refused to play a small part in *Wallenstein's Lager*, Goethe informed him that if he did not undertake

* See HEINRICH SCHMIDT : *Erinnerungen eines Weimarischen Veteranen*, p. 46, describing the enthusiasm with which he and DE WETTE and their friends read Goethe's poems, and wrote poems in his praise.
† *Geschichte der deutschen Schauspiel-Kunst.*

Friedrich von Müller

the part, he, Goethe, would play it himself—a threat which at once vanquished Becker, who knew it would be fulfilled.

Nevertheless with all this despotism he was still the great, high-minded, lovable Goethe, and was reverenced by the actors who were under him. Chancellor von Müller says that 'Nowhere did he more freely exercise the spell of his imposing presence ; rigorous and earnest in his demands, unalterable in his determinations, prompt and delighted to acknowledge every successful attempt, attentive to the smallest as to the greatest, and calling forth in every one his most hidden powers—in a narrow circle, and often with slender means, he accomplished what appeared incredible ; his encouraging glance was a rich reward ; his kind word an invaluable gift. Every one felt himself greater and more powerful in the place which he had assigned to him, and the stamp of his approbation seemed to be a sort of consecration for life. No one who has not seen and heard with what pious fidelity the veterans of that time of Goethe's and Schiller's cheerful spirited co-operation treasured every recollection of these their heroes, with what transport they dwelt on every detail of their proceedings, and how the mere mention of their names called forth the flash of youthful pleasure from their eyes, can have an idea of the affectionate attachment and enthusiastic veneration those great men inspired'.

It appears from Edward Devrient's account that the actors were miserably paid. Even Caroline Jagemann—the Duke's mistress —who was prima donna, as well as leading actress, received only six hundred thalers a year, with a retiring pension of three hundred ; and six hundred thalers is about one hundred pounds sterling. Moreover, the actors were not allowed a *congé*, as at other theatres ; so that no money could be made by them beyond their salaries *. Except to confessed mediocrity, Weimar could scarcely have offered a temptation ; nevertheless, the magic names of Goethe and Schiller did attract a few good actors.

The shifts to which the management was forced to have recourse, with so small and insufficient a troupe, may be gathered from this anecdote. The opera of *Die Zauberflöte* was performed, but the Queen of Night was so far advanced in pregnancy that it was impossible to let her appear in that condition. Another singer was not to be had. In this dilemma Goethe actually made her

---

* On the various salaries paid to actors at Weimar, see PASQUÉ : *Goethe's Theater-leitung in Weimar*, I.

sing the music behind the scenes, while an actress on the stage pantomimically represented the character.

When the connexion between Schiller and Goethe grew closer, the theatre began to assume a really earnest aspect. With his natural tendency to interest himself in whatever deeply interested his friends, Goethe caught some of Schiller's dramatic enthusiasm, and began to treat the stage as a means of artistic education for the nation. *Don Carlos* was performed ; somewhat later *Egmont* was adapted to the stage by Schiller (in a melodramatic style which revealed his love of material effects), and the greatest undertaking of all was achieved, namely, the performance of *Wallenstein.* The effect was prodigious, and the Weimar stage seemed really to have achieved something like the establishment of a new and grandiose style of dramatic representation. It was, however, but a flash. The strivings of the two poets were misdirected, as the event soon proved. No drama could so be founded. The dramatic age had passed, and could not be restored —not at least in such forms.

' The Weimar School', says Devrient *, who is here speaking *ex professo*, and is worth attending to, 'although it demanded of the artist "to produce something resembling nature†", nevertheless set up a new standard of nobleness and beauty, by which every phenomenon in the region of art was to be tested. The tendency hitherto dominant had by no means neglected the beautiful, but it had sought only a *beautiful reality*,—now, with subtle distinction, *beautiful truth* was demanded from it. Hitherto *living nature* had served as the standard, now an *enlightened taste* was to be the rule. The actors were to disaccustom themselves to the native German manner, and find a freer, a more universal conception ; they were to raise themselves out of the narrow limits of the special, of the individual, to the contemplation of the general, of the Ideal.

' These were astoundingly new and hard demands on the actor. Hitherto a plain understanding, with vivid and sensitive feelings, had tolerably well sufficed to make this natural talent tell ; for the problems lay within the actor's circle of vision. Now, appeal was principally made to his taste ; he was required to have a refined instinct, and ennobled sentiments, which, to a certain degree, presupposed scientific and antiquarian culture ; for instead of *nature*,

---

* *Geschichte der deutschen Schauspiel-Kunst*, p. 255.
† *Goethe's Vorrede zu den Propyläen.*

as hitherto, the antique was now the model of speech and feature. The actual culture of the histrionic class was not in the remotest degree adequate to these demands ; what then was to be done ? The Weimar School must content itself with *training :* it must seek to supply by external drilling what ought properly to have proceeded from a higher intellectual life, from an intrinsically ennobled nature. Nothing else remained to it. The spirit of our literature was pressing forward with unexampled power to that summit on which it could from thenceforth measure itself with that of all other nations ; it carried along with it theatrical art, such as it was. If the attempt had been made to advance the culture of actors as far as was necessary in order to bring it even with the victorious march of our literature, the moment would have been lost in which the stage could render immeasurable service to the national culture.

'Goethe and Schiller had essentially this mission : to elevate poetry ; to carry the intellectual life of the nation into higher ideal regions ; literature was their *immediate* object, the stage only a secondary one ; nay, it was with them only a means to an end. To work with entire devotion to dramatic art, solely for it and through it, as Molière and Shakespeare did, never occurred to them ; nor would they imitate Lessing, who attached himself closely to art, to what it achieved, and could achieve. They placed themselves and their poems on the standpoint of the independent *literary* drama. The old schism between the *genres* again presented itself: the scholarly in opposition to the popular drama ; and poetic art again won the supremacy over dramatic. *Don Carlos* and *Wallenstein* were not conceived for the actual stage, and could only be adapted to it with great labour and sacrifice ; in writing *Faust, Tasso,* and the *Natürliche Tochter,* Goethe did not contemplate their representation, which must be considered purely as a theatrical experiment. It was a natural consequence that, since the two great poets adapted their works to the theatre just as it was, and were by no means excessively fastidious in their mode of doing it, they, with the same sort of violence, pushed forward the art of representation, and here also had to content themselves with what could be achieved by merely external discipline. Dramatic art had not reached that point of culture which could prepare it perfectly to comprehend and master their poems, and reproduce them independently. . . . Now if this new school was to make its authority in taste acknowledged, that authority must necessarily be exercised with a certain despotism. With despotism towards the actors and the public, since both were deeply imbued with naturalism. Like the unfortunate Neuber, like Schroeder in his eightieth year, Schiller and Goethe placed themselves in decided opposition to the taste of the majority. They maintained a thoroughly aristocratic position with respect to the public, and defended the ideal principle with all the power of their pre-eminent genius ; nay, they did not scorn to attack the prevalent taste with the sharpest weapons of satire. Their correspondence exhibits their contempt for the masses, and for the champions of the popular taste, in all that rudeness which seems inseparable from the enthusiasm of great souls for a more exalted humanity. Nowhere did they sue for the approbation of the multitude ; nowhere did they accommodate themselves to the ruling taste, or even flatter it.

'The despotic energy with which Goethe carried out the ideal principle, in spite of all difficulties, necessarily made itself felt in his direction of the theatre. He had to urge forward dramatic art, and to wring from the public a formal respect for the experiments of his school ; a double task, which obliged him to surpass even Schroeder in the peremptoriness of his commands'.

Not only were there difficulties of rhythm, but also of pronunciation to be overcome. The German language, harsh as it is at the best, becomes hideous in the careless licences of pronunciation which various cities and classes adopt—as people who are too ugly to hope for any admiration, come at last entirely to neglect their appearance. The Suabians, Austrians, and especially the Weimarians, plagued Goethe terribly with their peculiarities of speech. 'One would scarcely believe that b, p, d, and t, are generally considered to be *four* different letters', said the poet to Eckermann, 'for they only speak of a hard and a soft b, and of a hard and a soft d, and thus seem tacitly to intimate that p and t do not exist*. With such people *Pein* (pain) is like *Bein* (leg), *Pass* (pass) like *Bass* (bass), and *Teckel* (a terrier) like *Deckel* (cover)'. Thus an actor in an impassioned moment bidding his mistress cease her reproaches, exclaimed *O ente* (Oh, duck !) meaning *O ende* (Oh, cease !)

The success of *Wallenstein*, which was a theatrical no less than an artistic success, seemed to have decided the battle in favour of

---

* LUDECUS in his book, *Aus Goethe's Leben: Wahrheit und keine Dichtung*, tells a story of GRAF, Schiller's favourite actor, who on seeing the great TALMA exclaimed, '*Dalma ist ein Gott!*'

the Ideal school ; seemed, but did not.   Art was henceforth to be everything.   So far did Goethe carry out his principle of placing Art foremost *, that he would not suffer the actors to 'forget the audience'; his maxim was, that in a scene between two actors, the presence of the spectator should constantly be felt.   Consequently the actors were not allowed to stand in profile, or to turn their backs upon the audience, or to speak at the back of the stage, under any pretext.   They were to *recite*, not to *be* the characters represented.   Heinrich Schmidt narrates how Goethe in giving him lessons in acting, entered into the minutest details.   In the celebrated monologue of Hamlet, 'To be or not to be', he allowed Schmidt to place his right hand upon his chin, while the left hand supported the right elbow ; but would not permit this left hand to be closed like a fist, insisting that the two middle fingers should be held together, the thumb and the other two fingers kept apart †.   In acting, he reversed his old artistic maxim, and insisted on Beauty first, Truth afterwards : *erst schön dann wahr* ‡.

It will surprise no one that this tendency, this pre-occupation with the Ideal, should result in the rehabilitation of the most perfect form of drama which that tendency has produced—I mean the French Tragedy, so pitilessly ridiculed by Lessing.   Nay, Goethe himself translated Voltaire's *Mahomet*, which was played in 1800, and afterwards *Tancred*.   The *Adelphi* of Terence, translated by Einsiedel ; the *Ion* of Schlegel ; the *Phédre* of Racine, translated by Schiller ; and finally Schiller's own *Braut von Messina*, sufficiently show the wide departure from anything like a modern drama into which the Weimar school had wandered.   Nay, even Shakespeare had to suffer the indignity of being elevated by this classical mania.   Schiller translated his *Macbeth* —how he travestied it may be seen by the curious reader ; enough to mention here that he changes the Witches into Fates ; and we learn from Heinrich Voss that these terrible sisters were represented by young girls beautifully dressed !   We need not, therefore, be surprised on hearing that Terence's comedy was actually represented by actors in Roman Masks,—thus entirely getting rid of Expression, which forms the basis of modern acting.

* See his *Rules for Actors* in *Werke*, XXXV, pp. 435-459.
† *Erinnerungen*, p. 110.
‡ Remnants of the old Weimar school still talk of these days, and of the drilling which it was necessary to give the actors.   From one, to whom Goethe was very kind, I heard full confirmation of what is said in the text.

So deplorable a mistake needs only to be mentioned to be appreciated. One step alone remained for dilettantism ; and that step was to give the actors the cothurnus, and make them spout Latin and Greek.

During these antique restorations, experiments were made with Shakespeare, Calderon, Gozzi—with everything but the life of the people—and Weimar was proclaimed a great school of Art, in which the *literary* public religiously believed. But the other public? Goethe himself shall answer. 'Here in Weimar they have done me the honour to perform my *Iphigenia* and my *Tasso*', he said to Eckermann in his old age. 'But how often? Scarcely once in three or four years. The public finds them tedious. Very probably. . . . I really had the notion once that it was possible to found a German Drama ; but there was no emotion or excitement —all remained as it was before'.

To found a German Drama by means of poetic works, and antique restorations, was the delusion of one who was essentially *not* a dramatist. I have more than once denied to Goethe the peculiar genius which makes the dramatist ; and my denial is not only supported by the evidence of his own works, it is, I think, conclusively established by his critical reflections on Shakespeare, and his theatrical treatment of Shakespeare's works. Profoundly as he appreciated the poet, he seems to me wholly to have misunderstood the dramatist. He actually asserts that Hamlet's Ghost, and the witches in *Macbeth*, are examples of Shakespeare's 'representing what would better be imagined' ; that in the reading, these figures are acceptable, but in the acting they disturb, nay repel, our emotion. So radical a misconception need not be dwelt on. The reader, who does not at once perceive it, may rest assured that he is wholly unacquainted with the secrets of dramatic art. As an example of Goethe's entire misunderstanding of Shakespeare's art, I will cite the version he made of *Romeo and Juliet*, of which he was not a little proud. The subject is of sufficient literary interest —considering the two names implicated—to warrant a digression.

It was in 1811 that he undertook to recast *Romeo and Juliet* for the stage ; and as this version has recently been recovered, and printed by Boas*, we can imagine it at leisure. There is scarcely any Shakespearean play which a great poet and dramatist might so reasonably undertake to recast as *Romeo and Juliet;* for while it is instinct with life, character, and dramatic movement, it is in some

* *Nachträge zu Goethe's Werken.*

respects among the worst of Shakespeare's fine plays.   Juvenility
of style is apparent in almost every scene.   The frequence of rhyme,
the forced rhetoric and conceits, the lame expression, and the deficiency in that passionate and profound poetry which illuminates
the great plays, prove it to be an early work.   In most of the great
situations we find long tirades of rhetorical *concetti* in place of the
nervous language, strongly coloured by passion, which Shakespeare
afterwards knew so well how to employ.   Thus when Juliet is in
agony of suspense as to whether Romeo is dead, she says :

> This torture should be roared in dismal hell.
> Hath Romeo slain himself? Say thou but *I*,
> And that bare vowel, *I*, shall poison more
> Than the death-darting *eye* of cockatrice :
> I am not I, if there be such an *I*.

There are critics who will defend this (what will they not defend in
Shakespeare?) and find plausible arguments to show that it is true
passion ; but I do not advise any modern poet to write thus, if he
would win the admiration of these critics.

It will not be supposed, however, that I am dead to the beauty of
this work, which, because of its pre-eminent qualities, is an universal favourite.   It is the work of Shakespeare *young*, but indis-
putably Shakespeare.   He has not only presented the story with
wonderful vividness and variety, but he has crowded it with *characters*, and animated those characters with true dramatic motives.
Think of Old Capulet, Tybalt, the Nurse, Peter, Gregory and
Sampson, and the Apothecary,—all episodical figures, yet each
having his well-marked individuality.   By touches brief yet free
and masterly the figures stand out from the canvas.

One would imagine that a dramatist who undertook to remedy
the defects of this work, would throw all his labour into those parts
where the work is weakest, and thus free the rich harvest of
dramatic thought from all the chaff and stubble ; one would certainly
never expect him to remove any of those vivid touches which give
life to the characters, or any of those dramatic presentations of the
subject which animate the scene.   Yet this, and this only, has
Goethe done*.

Shakespeare opens with one of his life-like expositions, pregnant

* In a letter to Frau von Wolzogen, he speaks of his recently completed version
thus : 'The maxim which I followed was to concentrate all that was most interesting,
and bring it into harmony ; for Shakespeare, following the bent of his genius, his time,
and his public, was forced to bring together much that was not harmonious, to flatter
the reigning taste'. *Literarischer Nachlass der Frau von Wolzogen*, vol. I, p. 437.

with purpose, and arresting attention at the outset. The Capulet servants are swaggering in the streets of Verona, and no sooner do they meet the servants of the Montagues than at once they come to blows. Tybalt and Benvolio quickly join the fray : old Capulet and old Montague are not long behind. The whole feud of the two houses—that which forms the *nodus* of the piece—lives before us. The entrance of the Prince, threatening death to the man who next disturbs the peace of Verona, introduces another tragic motive. The whole exposition is a masterly specimen of dramatic art. But Goethe had so little sense of what was dramatic, that he strikes out this exposition, and opens his version like a comic opera, with a chorus of servants who are arranging lamps and garlands before Capulet's house :

> Zündet die Lampen an
> Windet auch Kränze dran
> Hell sey das Haus !
> etc. etc.

Maskers pass into the house. Romeo and Benvolio enter and *talk*. They *tell* us of that family feud, which Shakespeare made us *see*. Rosalind is alluded to by Romeo, but all the fantastic hyperbole of desire which Shakespeare's Romeo expresses (in direct contrast with the expression of his *passion* for Juliet) is struck out. The two enter Capulet's house, where Benvolio promises to show him a lovelier face than Rosalind's. Before they enter, however, Mercutio arrives ; and at this point the student of Shakespeare will uplift his eyebrows when he sees how Goethe has contrived to destroy this poetic creation. Not only is the celebrated Mab speech omitted, but Mercutio declares he will keep out of the ball-room, lest he should be discovered—by his handsome figure! The whole of this must be translated, or my readers may withhold their credence.

Romeo.   Come with us.
          Get you a mantle, get a stranger's mask.
     Mercutio.   In vain I don the mask, it helps me not.
          I'm known by every child, and must be known.
I am a distinguished man ; there is a character in my figure and voice, in my walk, in my every movement.
     Benvolio.   Truly ! thy paunch has a charming look.
     Mercutio.   It is easy for you to talk—toothpicks, beanstalks as you are ! You hang rag after rag upon you : who will unpack you ? But I with the heaviest mantle, with the most outrageous nose, I have only to appear,

and some one directly whispers behind, 'There goes Mercutio! By my faith, it is Mercutio!' That indeed would be immensely vexatious were it no glory. And since I am Mercutio, let me be Mercutio, and always Mercutio! Now, good-bye to you. Do your business as well as you can, I seek my adventures on my pillow. An airy dream shall delight me, while you run after your dreams, and can no more catch them than I can.

> I shall be brisk when o'er you weeps the dawn,
> While you for weariness, or love, will yawn.   *Exit.*

Into *this* has Mercutio been metamorphosed! The ball scene follows. The Nurse, indeed, is introduced, but all her individuality is destroyed; every one of the characteristic touches is washed out by an unsparing sponge. In his essay on Shakespeare he gives us the clue to these omissions; for he says 'that the Nurse and Mercutio almost entirely destroy the tragic meaning of the story, and are to be regarded as farcical additions, which the modern stage repudiates'*. The alterations in this scene are not important, and are chiefly the presence of the Prince, who comes to the ball with Mercutio, his object being to mix in the society of Capulet and Montague, and so bring about amity between the houses. The old feud is again *talked* of : as if talking could take the place of doing! The rest of the piece follows the original pretty closely; there are only two alterations which call for notice; one an improvement, and one an extraordinary and inexplicable blunder.

To begin with the blunder: The reader knows with what sharpness Shakespeare has contrasted the calm, respectable Paris, who woos Juliet through her parents, and the fervid Romeo, who goes direct to Juliet herself; one seeks the father's consent, without troubling himself about the maid; the other seeks the maid's consent, and braves the enmity of the father. What will the reader think of Goethe's dramatic ideas, on hearing that this contrast is entirely effaced : Paris makes love to Juliet; has long adored her in silence, before he ventured to ask her parents' consent!

The second alteration is a dramatic improvement; although it will certainly make the Shakespeare bigots cry out. It is the closing of the piece with Juliet's death, the Friar in a short soliloquy pointing the moral. Nothing can be more undramatic or more tiresome than the long recapitulation of facts perfectly familiar to the audience, with which Shakespeare ends the piece.

This *Romeo and Juliet* was not only produced at Weimar,

* *Werke*, XXXV, 379.

but it kept the stage in Berlin until within the last few years!
The Berlin critics on its original production were by no means
favourably inclined to it—the dénouement, we learn from Zelter,
especially displeased them. Did they resent being robbed of
their *ennui*?

Enough has been said to characterize the attempt of Goethe
and Schiller to create a German Drama ; which attempt, although
its failure was inevitable, cannot be regarded without sympathy,
were it only for the noble aim animating it. That aim was
misdirected ; but it was the error of lofty minds, who saw *above*
the exigencies of the age. They could not bring themselves to
believe that the Drama, which they held to be so grand a form of
Art, had ceased to be the lay-pulpit, and had become a mere
amusement.

With Schiller's death Goethe's active interest in the theatre
ceased. The Obermarschall Graf von Edeling was adjoined to
him, as acting superintendent, but without absolute power, which
still remained in Goethe's hands. This was towards the end of
1813. And in 1817 his son, August von Goethe, was added to the
direction. Thus was the theatre burdened with a Geheimrath,
absolute but inactive, an Obermarschall, and a Court page. Nor
were matters better behind the scenes. An intrigue had long
been forming, under the direction of Caroline Jagemann, to force
Goethe's resignation. Between the Duke's mistress and the
Duke's friend there had never been a very pleasant feeling. She
was naturally jealous of Goethe's power. As an actress under his
direction, she must have had endless little causes of complaint.
Had the poet been less firmly fixed in the Duke's affections and
interests, this rivalry could not have endured so long. At last a
crisis came.

There was at that period, 1817, a comedian named Karsten,
whose poodle performed the leading part in the well-known
melodrame of *The Dog of Montargis* with such perfection that he
carried the public everywhere with him, in Paris as in Germany.
It may be imagined with what sorrowing scorn Goethe heard of
this. The dramatic art to give place to a poodle! He, who
detested dogs, to hear of a dog performing on all the stages of
Germany with greater success than the best of actors! The
occasion was not one to be lost. The Duke, whose fondness for
dogs was as marked as Goethe's aversion to them, was craftily
assailed, from various sides, to invite Karsten and his poodle to

Weimar. When Goethe heard of this, he haughtily answered, 'In our Theatre regulations stands : *no dogs admitted on the stage*'—and paid no more attention to it. As the Duke had already written to invite Karsten and his dog, Goethe's opposition was set down to systematic arbitrariness, and people artfully 'wondered' how a prince's wishes could be opposed for such trifles. The dog came. After the first rehearsal, Goethe declared that he would have nothing more to do with a theatre on which a dog was allowed to perform ; and at once started for Jena. Princes ill brook opposition ; and the Duke, after all, was a Duke. In an unworthy moment, he wrote the following, which was posted in the theatre, and forwarded to Goethe :

'From the expressed opinions which have reached me, I have come to the conviction that the Herr Geheimrath von Goethe wishes to be released from his functions as Intendent, which I hereby accord. KARL AUGUST'.

A more offensive dismissal could scarcely have been suggested by malice. In the Duke it was only a spurt of the imperious temper and coarseness which roughened his fine qualities. On Goethe the blow fell heavily. 'Karl August never understood me', he exclaimed, with a deep sigh. Such an insult to the greatest man of his age, coming from his old friend and brother in arms, who had been more friend than monarch to him during two-and-forty years, and who had declared that one grave should hold their bodies—and all about a dog, behind which was a miserable greenroom cabal ! The thought of leaving Weimar for ever, and of accepting the magnificent offers made him from Vienna, pressed urgently on his mind.

But, to his credit be it said, the Duke quickly became sensible of his unworthy outbreak of temper, and wrote to Goethe in a tone of conciliation : 'Dear Friend', he wrote, 'From several expressions thou hast let fall, I gather that thou wouldst be pleased to be released from the vexations of theatrical management, but that thou wouldst willingly aid it by thy counsel and countenance, when, as will doubtless often be the case, thou art specially appealed to by the manager. I gladly fall in with thy desire, thanking thee for the great good thou hast effected in this troublesome business, begging thee to retain thy interest in its artistic prosperity, and hoping that the release will better thy health. I enclose an official letter notifying this change, and with best wishes for your health, etc.'. The cloud passed over; but no entreaty could make Goethe resume the direction of the theatre, and he withdrew his son also from his post in the direction. He could pardon the hasty act and unconsidered word of his friend ; but he was prouder than the Duke, and held firmly to his resolution of having nothing to do with a theatre which had once prostituted itself to the exhibition of a clever poodle.

What a sarcasm, and in the sarcasm what a moral, lies in this story ! Art, which Weimar will not have, gives place to a poodle !

CHAPTER VI

SCHILLER'S LAST YEARS

THE current of narrative in the preceding chapter has flowed onwards into years and events from which we must now return. Instead of the year 1817, we must recall the year 1800. Schiller has just come to settle at Weimar, there to end his days in noble work with his great friend. It may interest the reader to have a glimpse of Goethe's daily routine ; the more so, as such a glimpse is not to be had from any published works.

He rose at seven, sometimes earlier, after a sound and prolonged sleep ; for, like Thorwaldsen, he had a 'talent for sleeping', only surpassed by his talent for continuous work. Till eleven he worked without interruption. A cup of chocolate was then brought, and he resumed work till one. At two he dined. This meal was the important meal of the day. His appetite was immense. Even on the days when he complained of not being hungry, he ate much more than most men. Puddings, sweets, and cakes were always welcome. He sat a long while over his wine, chatting gaily to some friend or other (for he never dined alone), or to one of the actors, whom he often had with him, after dinner, to read over their parts, and to take his instructions. He was fond of wine, and drank daily his two or three bottles.

Lest this statement should convey a false impression, I hasten to recall to the reader's recollection the habits of our fathers in espect of drinking. It was no unusual thing to be a 'three-bottle man' in those days in England, when the three bottles were of port or Burgundy ; and Goethe, a Rhinelander, accus-

Schiller's home in Weimar

tomed from boyhood to wine, drank a wine which his English
contemporaries would have called water. The amount he drank
never did more than exhilarate him ; never made him unfit for
work, or for society*.

Over his wine he sat some hours : no such thing as dessert was
seen upon his table in those days : not even the customary coffee
after dinner. His mode of living was extremely simple ; and even
when persons of very modest circumstances burned wax, two poor
tallow candles were all that could be seen in his rooms. In the
evening he went often to the theatre, and there his customary glass
of punch was brought at six o'clock. When he was not at the
theatre, he received friends at home. Between eight and nine
a frugal supper was laid, but he never ate anything except a little
salad or preserves. By ten o'clock he was usually in bed.

Many visitors came to him. From the letters of Christiane to
Meyer we gather that he must have exercised hospitality on a large
scale, since about every month 50 lbs. of butter are ordered from
Bremen, and the cases of wine have frequently to be renewed. It
was the pleasure and the penalty of his fame, that all persons who
came near Weimar made an effort to see him. Sometimes these
visitors were persons of great interest ; oftener they were fatiguing
bores, or men with pretensions more offensive than dullness. To
those who pleased him he was inexpressibly charming ; to the
others he was stately, even to stiffness. While, therefore, we hear
some speak of him with an enthusiasm such as genius alone can
excite, we hear others giving vent to the feelings of disappointment, and even of offence, created by his manners. The stately
minister exasperated those who went to see the impassioned poet.
As these visitors were frequently authors, it was natural they
should avenge their wounded self-love in criticisms and epigrams.
To cite but one example among many : Bürger, whom Goethe had
assisted in a pecuniary way, came to Weimar, and announced himself in this preposterous style : 'You are Goethe—I am Bürger',
evidently believing he was thereby maintaining his own greatness,
and offering a brotherly alliance. Goethe received him with the

---

* ' For the last thousand years, the life of the Rhinelander is as it were steeped in
wine ; he has become like the good old wine-casks, tinted with the vinous green.   Wine
is the creed of the Rhinelander in everything.   As in England, in the days of Cromwell,
the Royalists were known by the meat pasties, the Papists by their raisin soup, the
Atheists by their roast beef; so is the man of the Rhinegau known by his wine-flask.
A jolly companion drinks his seven bottles every day, and with it grows as old as
Methuselah, is seldom drunk, and has at most the Bardolph mark of a red nose'.
LIEBIG : *Letters on Chemistry*.   Appendix.

most diplomatic politeness, and the most diplomatic formality ;
instead of plunging into discussions of poetry, he would be brought
to talk of nothing but the condition of the Göttingen University,
and the number of its students. Bürger went away furious,
avenged this reception in an epigram, and related to all-comers
the experience he had had of the proud, cold, diplomatic Geheimrath. Others had the like experience to recount ; and a public,
ever greedy of scandal, ever willing to believe a great man is
a small man, echoed these voices in swelling chorus. Something
of offence lay in the very nature of Goethe's bearing, which was
stiff, even to haughtiness. His appearance was so imposing, that
Heine humorously relates how, on the occasion of his first interview
with him, an elaborately prepared speech was entirely driven from
his memory by the Jupiter-like presence, and he could only stam-
mer forth 'a remark on the excellence of the plums which grew on
the road from Jena to Weimar'. An imposing presence is irritating to mean natures ; and Goethe might have gained universal
applause, if, like Jean Paul, he had worn no cravat, and had let his
hair hang loose upon his shoulders.

The mention of Jean Paul leads me to quote *his* impression of
Goethe.

' I went timidly to meet him. Every one had described him as cold to
everything upon earth. Frau von Kalb said he no longer admires anything, not even himself. Every word is ice. Nothing but curiosities
warm the fibres of his heart ; so I asked Knebel if he could petrify me,
or encrust me in some mineral spring that I might present myself as a
statue or a fossil '.

How one hears the accents of village gossip in these sentences !
To Weimarian ignorance Goethe's enthusiasm for statues and
natural products seemed monstrous.

' His house ', Jean Paul continues, ' or rather his palace, pleased me ;
it is the only one in Weimar in the Italian style ; with such a staircase !
A Pantheon full of pictures and statues. Fresh anxiety oppressed me.
At last the god entered, cold, monosyllabic. "The French are drawing
towards Paris", said Knebel. "Hm !" said the god. His face is
massive and animated ; his eye a ball of light ! At last, as conversation
turned on art, he warmed, and was himself. His conversation was not
so rich and flowing as Herder's, but penetrating, acute, and calm.
Finally, he read, or rather performed, an unpublished poem, in which the
flames of his heart burst through the external crust of ice ; so that he
greeted my enthusiasm with a pressure of the hand. He did it again as I

took leave, and urged me to call.   By heaven ! we shall love each other !
He considers his poetic career closed.   There is nothing comparable to
his reading.   It is like deep-toned thunder, blended with whispering
rain-drops '.

Now let us hear what Jean Paul says of Schiller.   ' I went yesterday to see the stony Schiller, from whom all strangers spring
back as from a precipice. His form is wasted, yet severely powerful, and very angular. He is full of acumen, but without love.
His conversation is as excellent as his writings '. He never repeated this visit to Schiller, who doubtless quite subscribed to
what Goethe wrote.   ' I am glad you have seen Richter.   His
love of truth, and his wish for self-improvement, have prepossessed
me in his favour ; but the social man is a sort of theoretical man,
and I doubt if he will approach us in a practical way '.

If to pretenders and to *strangers* Goethe was cold and repellent,
he was warm and attractive enough to all with whom he could
sympathize.   Brotherly to Schiller and Herder, he was fatherly in
his loving discernment and protection to such men as Hegel, then
an unknown teacher, and Voss, the son of the translator of Homer*.
He excited passionate attachments in all who lived in his intimacy ;
and passionate hatred in many whom he would not admit to intimacy.

The opening of this century found Schiller active, and anxious
to stimulate the activity of his friend.   But theories hampered the
genius of Goethe ; and various occupations disturbed it.   He was
not like Schiller, a reflective, critical poet, but a spontaneous, instinctive poet.   The consequence was, that Reflection not only
retarded, but misled him into Symbolism—the dark corner of that
otherwise sunny palace of Art which he has reared.   He took up
Faust, and wrote the classic intermezzo of *Helena*.   He was very
busy with the theatre, and with science ; and at the close of the
year fell into a dangerous illness, which created much anxiety in
the Duke and the Weimar circle, and of which the Frau von Stein
wrote in that letter quoted on p. 328. He recovered in a few weeks,
and busied himself with the translation of *Theophrastus on
Colours*, with *Faust*, and the *Natürliche Tochter*.

While the two chiefs of Literature were, in noble emulation and
brotherly love, working together, each anxious for the success of
the other, the nation divided itself into two parties, disputing

* Note Voss's enthusiastic gratitude in his *Mittheilungen über Goethe und Schiller.*

which was the greater poet of the two ; as in Rome the artists dispute about Raphael and Michael Angelo. 'It is difficult to appreciate one such genius', says Goethe of the two painters, 'still more difficult to appreciate both. Hence people lighten the task by partizanship'. The partizanship in the present case was fierce, and has continued. Instead of following Goethe's advice, and rejoicing that it had two such poets to boast of, the public has gone on crying up one at the expense of the other. Schiller himself with charming modesty confessed his inferiority ; and in one of his letters to Körner he says : 'Compared with Goethe I am but a poetical bungler—*gegen Goethe bin und bleib' ich ein poetischer Lump*'. But the majority have placed him higher than his rival, at least higher in their hearts. Gervinus has remarked a curious contradiction in the fate of their works. Schiller, who wrote for men, is the favourite of women and youths ; Goethe, who remained in perpetual youth, is only relished by men. The secret of this is, that Schiller had those passions and enthusiasms which Goethe wanted. Goethe told Eckermann that his works never could be popular ; and, except the minor poems and *Faust*, there are none of his productions which equal the popularity of Schiller's.

To make an instrument of vengeance out of this partizanship, seemed an excellent idea to Kotzebue, who, after being crowned at Berlin, and saluted all over Germany with tributes of tears, now came to his native city of Weimar. He was invited to Court, but he was not admitted into the select Goethe-Schiller circle ; which irritated his vanity the more, because a joke of Goethe's had been repeated to him. In Japan, besides the temporal court of the emperor, there is the spiritual court of the Dalai-Lama, which exercises a superior though secret influence. Goethe, alluding to this, said : 'It is of no use to Kotzebue that he has been received at the temporal court of Japan, if he cannot get admitted to the spiritual court'. Kotzebue thought he could destroy that court, and set up one of his own, of which Schiller should be the Dalai-Lama.

There was at this time a select little circle, composed of Goethe, Schiller, Meyer, and several distinguished women, the Countess von Einsiedel, Fräulein von Imhoff, Frau von Wolzogen, and others. The great preponderance of women in this circle gave a romantic tinge to the laws they imposed on themselves. On Kotzebue's arrival, one of Amalia's maids of honour used her utmost to obtain his admission ; but Schiller and Goethe, resolved on his exclusion, got a bye-law enacted, that 'no member should have the power of introducing another person, native or stranger, without the previously expressed unanimous consent of the other members'. A certain coolness had sprung up between some of the members of the circle, and Goethe, pestered by the iteration of the request that Kotzebue should be admitted, at last said, 'Laws once recognized should be upheld ; if not, it would be better to break up the society altogether ; which, perhaps, would be the more advisable, as constancy is always difficult, if not tedious, to ladies'. The ladies were naturally enough irritated. Kotzebue was ready to inflame them. Schiller had just gone to Leipsic ; and Kotzebue, taking advantage of this absence, organized a fête to celebrate the coronation of Frederick Schiller in the Stadthouse of Weimar. Scenes from *Don Carlos*, the *Maid of Orleans*, and *Maria Stuart*, were to come first. Goethe's favourite, the Countess von Einsiedel (now his foe), was to represent the Joan of Arc ; the Fräulein von Imhoff the Queen of Scots ; Sophie Moreau was to recite the Song of the Bell. Kotzebue was to appear as Father Thibaut in the *Maid of Orleans* and as the Bell Founder, in which latter character he was to strike the mould of the bell (made of pasteboard), and breaking it in pieces, disclose the bust of Schiller, which was to be crowned by the ladies. The preparations for this fête were eagerly carried forward. Weimar was in a state of excitement. The cabal looked prosperous. The Princess Caroline had consented to be present. Schiller was most pressingly invited, but said, in Goethe's house, a few days before, 'I shall send word I am ill'. To this Goethe made no reply. He heard of all the arrangements in perfect silence.

'It was thought', says Falk, to whom we owe this story, 'that a coolness between the two great men would spring out of this cabal ; especially if the simple, unsuspecting Schiller should fall into the toils laid for him. But they who suspected this, knew not the men. Fortunately, however, the whole scheme fell to pieces. The directors of the Library refused to lend Schiller's bust ; the Burgomaster refused to lend the Stadthouse. Rarely has so melancholy, so disastrous a day risen on the gay world of Weimar. To see the fairest, most brilliant hopes thus crushed at a blow when so near their fulfilment, what was it but to be wrecked in sight of port ? Let the reader but imagine the now utterly useless expenditure of crape, gauze, ribbons, lace, beads, flowers which the fair creatures had made ; not to mention the pasteboard for the bell, the canvas colours, brushes for the scenes, the wax candles for lighting, etc. Let him think of the still greater outlay of time and trouble requisite for the learning so many and such varied parts ; let him figure to himself a majestic Maid of Orleans, a captivating Queen of Scots, a lovely Agnes, so suddenly compelled to descend from the pinnacle of glory, and in evil moment to lay aside the crown and sceptre, helm dress and ornament, and he will admit there never was fate more cruel '.

Shortly after this—on the 13th June, 1802—Goethe's son was confirmed. Herder officiated on the occasion ; and this brought him once more into that friendly relation with Goethe, which of late had been cooled by his jealousy of Schiller. Herder had been jealous of the growing friendship of Goethe and Merck ; he was still more embittered by the growing friendship of Goethe and Schiller. He was bitter against Schiller's idol, Kant, and all Kant's admirers, declaring the new philosophy destructive of Christian morals. He was growing old, and the bitterness of his youth was intensified by age and sickness. Schiller was in every way antagonistic to him ; and the representation of *Wallenstein* 'made him ill'. Goethe, whose marvellous tolerance he had so sorely tried, and who never ceased to admire his fine qualities, said, 'one could not go to him without rejoicing in his mildness, one could not quit him without having been hurt by his bitterness'. For some time Goethe was never mentioned in the Herder family, except in an almost inimical tone ; and yet Herder's wife wrote to Knebel : 'Let us thank God that Goethe still lives. Weimar would be intolerable without him'. They lived together in Jena for a few days, and parted never to see each other again. In December, 1803, Herder was no more.

While discussing Physical Science with Ritter, Comparative Anatomy with Loder, Optics with Himly, and making observations on the Moon, the plan of a great poem, *De Natura Rerum*, rose in Goethe's mind, and like so many other plans, remained a plan. Intercourse with the great philologist Wolff led him a willing student into Antiquity ; and from Voss he tried to master the whole principles of Metre with the zeal of a philologist. There is something very piquant in the idea of the greatest poet of his nation, the most musical master of verse in all possible forms, trying to acquire a theoretic knowledge of that which on instinct he did to perfection.   It is characteristic of his new tendency to theorize on poetry.

Whoever reads the *Natürliche Tochter*, which was completed at this period, will probably attribute to this theorizing tendency the absence of all life and vigour which makes it 'marble smooth and marble cold'.   But although it appears marble cold to us, it was the marble urn in which the poet had buried real feelings; and Abeken relates that the actress who originally performed the Heroine, told him how, on one occasion, when she was rehearsing the part in Goethe's room, he was so overcome with emotion, that with tears in his eyes he bade her pause*.   This may seem more strange than the fact that Schiller admired the work, and wrote to Humboldt : 'The high symbolism with which it is handled, so that all the crude material is neutralized, and everything becomes portion of an ideal Whole, is truly wonderful.   It is entirely Art, and thereby reaches the innermost Nature, through the power of truth'.   And Fichte—who, Varnhagen tells me, was with him in the box at the Theatre when the play was performed at Berlin, and was greatly moved by it—declared it to be Goethe's master-piece.   Rosenkranz is amazed at the almost universal condem-nation of the work.   'What pathos, what warmth, what tragic pain !' he exclaims.   Others would echo the exclamation—in irony.   It seems to me that the very praise of Schiller and Fichte is a justification of the general verdict.   A drama which is *so* praised, *i.e.*, for its high symbolism, is a drama philosophers and critics may glorify, but which Art abjures.   A drama, or any other poem, may carry with it material which admits of symbolical interpretation ; but the poet who makes symbolism the substance and the purpose of his work has mistaken his vocation.   The whole Greek Drama has been *interpreted* into symbols by some modern scholars ; but if the Greek Dramatists had written with any such purpose as that detected by these interpreters, they would never have survived to give interpreters the trouble. The *Iliad* has quite recently been once more interpreted into an allegory ; Dante's *Divine Comedy* has been interpreted into an allegory ; Shakespeare's plays have, by Ulrici, been interpreted into moral platitudes ; the *Wahlverwandtschaften* has been interpreted into a 'world history'.   Indeed symbolism being in its very nature *arbitrary*—the indication of a meaning not directly expressed, but arbitrarily thrust *under* the expression—there is no

* ABEKEN : *Goethe in den Jahren 1771-75*, p. 21.

limit to the power of *interpretation*. It is, however, quite certain that the poets had not the meanings which their commentators find ; and equally certain that if poets wrote for commentators they would never produce masterpieces.

In December 1803 Weimar had a visitor whose rank is high among its illustrious guests : Madame de Stael. Napoleon would not suffer her to remain in France ; she was brought by Benjamin Constant to the German Athens, that she might see and know something of the men her work *De l'Allemagne* was to reveal to her countrymen. It is easy to ridicule Madame de Stael ; to call her, as Heine does, 'a whirlwind in petticoats', and a 'Sultana of mind'. But Germans should be grateful to her for that book, which still remains one of the best books written about Germany ; and the lover of letters will not forget that her genius has, in various departments of literature, rendered for ever illustrious the power of the womanly intellect. Goethe and Schiller, whom she stormed with cannonades of talk, spoke of her intellect with great admiration. Of all living creatures he had seen, Schiller said, she was 'the most talkative, the most combative, the most gesticulative' ; but she was 'also the most cultivated, and the most gifted'. The contrast between her French culture and his German culture, and the difficulty he had in expressing himself in French, did not prevent his being much interested. In the sketch of her he sent to Goethe it is well said, 'She insists on explaining everything ; understanding everything ; measuring everything. She admits of no Darkness ; nothing Incommensurable ; and where her torch throws no light, there nothing can exist. Hence her horror for the Ideal Philosophy which she thinks leads to mysticism and superstition. For what we call poetry she has no sense ; she can only appreciate what is passionate, rhetorical, universal. She does not prize what is false, but does not always perceive what is true'.

The Duchess Amalia was enchanted with her, and the Duke wrote to Goethe, who was at Jena, begging him to come over, and be seen by her ; which Goethe very positively declined. He said, if she wished very much to see him, and would come to Jena, she should be very heartily welcomed ; a comfortable lodging and a bourgeoise table would be offered her, and every day they could have some hours together when his business was over ; but he could not undertake to go to Court, and into society ; he did not feel himself strong enough. In the beginning of 1804, however, he came to Weimar, and there he made her acquaintance ; that is to say, he received her in his own house, at first *tête-à-tête*, and afterwards in small circles of friends.

Except when she managed to animate him by her paradoxes or wit, he was cold and formal to her, even more so than to other remarkable people ; and he has told us the reason. Rousseau had been drawn into a correspondence with two women, who addressed themselves to him as admirers ; he had shown himself in this correspondence by no means to his advantage, now (1803) that the letters appeared in print*. Goethe had heard or read of this correspondence ; and Madame de Stael had frankly told him she intended to print his conversation. This was enough to make him ill at ease in her society ; and although she said he was ' un homme d'un esprit prodigieux en conversation . . . quand on le sait faire parler il est admirable', she never saw the real, but a factitious Goethe. By dint of provocation—and champagne—she managed to make him talk brilliantly ; she never got him to talk to her seriously. On the 29th of February she left Weimar, to the great relief both of Goethe and Schiller.†

Nothing calls for notice during the rest of this year, except the translation of an unpublished work by Diderot, *Rameau's Nephew*, and the commencement of the admirable work on *Winckelmann and his Age*. The beginning of 1805 found him troubled with a presentiment that either he or Schiller would die in this year. Both were dangerously ill. Christiane writing to her friend Nicolaus Meyer, says, that for the last three months the Geheimrath has scarcely had a day's health, and at times it seemed as if he must die. It was a touching scene when Schiller, a little recovered from his last attack, entered the sick room of his friend. They walked up to each other, and, without speaking a word, expressed their joy at meeting in a long and manly kiss. Both hoped with the return of spring for return of health and power. Schiller meanwhile was translating the *Phèdre* of Racine ; Goethe was translating the *Rameau's Nephew*, and writing the history of the *Farbenlehre*.

The spring was coming, but on its blossoms Schiller's eyes were

---

* The correspondence alluded to can be no other than that of Rousseau with Madame de la Tour-Franqueville and her friend, whose name is still unknown ; it is one of the most interesting among the many interesting correspondences of women with celebrated men. A charming notice of it may be found in ST. BEUVE's *Causeries du Lundi*, vol. II.

† In the *Tag und Jahres Hefte*, 1804 (*Werke*, XXVII. p. 143), the reader will find Goethe's account of Mad. de Stael and her relation to him.

not to rest. On the 30th of April the friends parted for the last time. Schiller was going to the theatre. Goethe, too unwell to accompany him, said good-bye at the door of Schiller's house. During Schiller's illness, Goethe was much depressed. Voss found him once pacing up and down his garden, crying by himself. He mastered his emotion as Voss told him of Schiller's state, and only said, ' Fate is pitiless, and man but little'.

It really seemed as if the two friends were to be united in the grave as they had been in life. Goethe grew worse. From Schiller life was fast ebbing. On the 8th of May he was given over. 'His sleep that night was disturbed ; his mind again wandered ; with the morning he had lost all consciousness. He spoke incoherently and chiefly in Latin. His last drink was champagne. ·Towards three in the afternoon came on the last exhaustion ; the breath began to fail. Towards four he would have called for naphtha, but the last syllable died upon his lips ; finding himself speechless, he motioned that he wished to write something ; but his hand could only trace three letters, in which was yet recognizable the distinct character of his writing. His wife knelt by his side ; he pressed her hand. His sister-in-law stood with the physician at the foot of the bed, applying warm cushions to the cold feet. Suddenly a sort of electric shock came over his countenance ; the head fell back ; the deepest calm settled on his face. His features were as those of one in a soft sleep.

'The news of Schiller's death soon spread through Weimar. The theatre was closed ; men gathered into groups. Each felt as if he had lost his dearest friend. To Goethe, enfeebled himself by long illness, and again stricken by some relapse, no one had the courage to mention the death of his beloved rival. When the tidings came to Henry Meyer, who was with him, Meyer left the house abruptly lest his grief might escape him. No one else had courage to break the intelligence. Goethe perceived that the members of his household seemed embarrassed and anxious to avoid him. He divined something of the fact, and said at last, " I see—Schiller must be very ill". That night they overheard him—the serene man who seemed almost above human affection, who disdained to reveal to others whatever grief he felt when his son died—they overheard Goethe weep ! In the morning he said to a friend, " Is it not true that Schiller was very ill yesterday ?" The friend (it was a woman) sobbed. " He is dead ", said Goethe faintly. "You have said it", was the answer. "He is dead", repeated Goethe, and covered his face with his hands'*.

'The half of my existence is gone from me', he wrote to Zelter. His first thoughts were to continue the *Demetrius* in the spirit in which Schiller had planned it, so that Schiller's mind might still be with him, still working at his side. But the effort was vain. He could do nothing. 'My diary,' he says, 'is a blank at this period; the white pages intimate the blank in my existence. In those days I took no interest in anything'.

CHAPTER VII

'FAUST'

ALTHOUGH the First Part of *Faust* was not published until 1806, it was already completed before Schiller's death, and may therefore be fitly noticed in this place. For more than thirty years had the work been growing in its author's mind, and although its precise chronology is not ascertainable, yet an approximation is possible which will not be without service to the student.

The Faust-fable was familiar to Goethe as a child. In Strasburg, during 1770-71, he conceived the idea of fusing his personal experience into the mould of the old legend; but he wrote nothing of the work until 1774-5, when the ballad of the King of Thule, the first monologue, and the first scene with Wagner, were written; and during his love affair with Lili, he sketched Gretchen's catastrophe, the scene in the street, the scene in Gretchen's bedroom, the scenes between Faust and Mephisto during the walk, and in the street, and the garden scene. In his Swiss journey, he sketched the first interview with Mephisto and the compact; also the scene before the city gates, the plan of Helena (subsequently much modified), the scene between the student and Mephisto, and Auerbach's cellar. When in Italy, he read over the old manuscript, and wrote the scenes of the witches' kitchen and the cathedral; also the monologue in the forest. In 1797 *the whole was remodelled.* Then were added the two Prologues, the Walpurgis night, and the dedication. In 1801 he completed it, as it now stands, retouching it perhaps in 1806,

* BULWER'S *Life of Schiller.*

when it was published. Let us now with some carefulness examine this child of so much care.

The cock in Esop scratched a pearl into the light of day, and declared that to him it was less valuable than a grain of millet seed. The pearl is only a pearl to him who knows its value. And so it is with fine subjects: they are only fine in the hands of great artists. Where the requisite power exists, a happy subject is a fortune; without that power, it only serves to place the artist's incompetence in broader light. Mediocre poets have tried their prentice hands at Faust; poets of undeniable genius have tried to master it; Goethe alone has seen in it the subject to which his genius was fully adequate; and has produced from it the greatest poem of modern times:

> An Orphic tale indeed,—
> A tale divine, of high and passionate thoughts,
> To their own music chaunted.

Although genius can find material in the trifles which ordinary minds pass heedlessly by, it is only a very few subjects which permit the full display of genius. The peculiarities of a man's organization and education invest certain subjects with a charm and a significance. Such was *Der Freischütz* for Weber; the maternity of the Madonna for Raphael; *Faust* for Goethe. Thus it is that a fine subject becomes the marble out of which a lasting monument is carved.

Quite beyond my purpose, and my limits, would be any account of the various materials, historical and æsthetical, which German literature has gathered into one vast section on Faust, and the Faust legend. There is not a single detail which has not exercised the industry and ingenuity of commentators; so that the curious need complain of no lack of informants. English readers will find in the translations by Hayward and Blackie a reasonable amount of such information pleasantly given; German readers will only have the embarrassment of a choice. Far more important than all learned apparatus, is the attempt to place ourselves at the right point of view for studying and enjoying this wondrous poem, the popularity of which is almost unexampled. It appeals to all minds with the irresistible fascination of an eternal problem, and with the charm of endless variety. It has every element: wit, pathos, wisdom, farce, mystery, melody, reverence, doubt, magic, and irony; not a chord of the lyre is unstrung, not a fibre of the heart untouched. Students earnestly wrestling with doubt, striving to solve the solemn riddles of life, feel their pulses strangely agitated by this poem ; and not students alone, but as Heine, with allowable exaggeration, says, every billiard-marker in Germany puzzles himself over it. In *Faust* we see, as in a mirror, the eternal problem of our intellectual existence ; and, beside it, varied lineaments of our social existence. It is at once a problem and a picture. Therein lies its fascination. The problem embraces questions of vital importance ; the picture represents opinions, sentiments, classes, moving on the stage of life. The great problem is stated in all its nudity ; the picture is painted in all its variety.

This twofold nature of the work explains its popularity ; and, what is more to our purpose, gives the clue to its secret of composition ; a clue which all the critics I am acquainted with have overlooked ; and although I cannot but feel that considerable suspicion must attach itself to any opinion claiming novelty on so old a subject, I hope the contents of this chapter will furnish sufficient evidence to justify its acceptance. The conviction first arose in my mind as the result of an inquiry into the causes of the popularity of *Hamlet*. The two works are so allied, and so associated together in every mind, that the criticism of the one will be certain to throw light on the other.

Hamlet, in spite of a prejudice current in certain circles that if now produced for the first time it would fail, is the most popular play in our language. It *amuses* thousands annually, and it stimulates the minds of millions. Performed in barns and minor theatres oftener than in Theatres Royal, it is always and everywhere attractive. The lowest and most ignorant audiences delight in it. The source of the delight is twofold : First, its reach of thought on topics the most profound ; for the dullest soul can *feel* a grandeur which it cannot *understand*, and will listen with hushed awe to the outpourings of a great meditative mind obstinately questioning fate ; Secondly, its wondrous dramatic variety. Only consider for a moment the striking effects it has in the Ghost ; the tyrant murderer ; the terrible adulterous queen ; the melancholy hero, doomed to so awful a fate ; the poor Ophelia, broken-hearted and dying in madness ; the play within a play, entrapping the conscience of the King ; the ghastly mirth of gravediggers ; the funeral of Ophelia interrupted by a quarrel over her grave betwixt her brother and her lover ; and finally, the hurried bloody dénouement. Such are the figures woven in the tapestry by passion and poetry. Add thereto the absorbing fascination of profound thoughts. It may indeed be called the tragedy of thought, for there is as much reflection as action in it ; but the reflection itself is made dramatic, and hurries the breathless audience along, with an interest which knows no pause. Strange it is to notice in this work the indissoluble union of refinement with horrors, of reflection with tumult, of high and delicate poetry with broad, palpable, theatrical effects. The machinery is a machinery of horrors, physical and mental : ghostly apparitions— hideous revelations of incestuous adultery and murder—madness —Polonius killed like a rat while listening behind the arras— gravediggers casting skulls upon the stage and desecrating the churchyard with their mirth—these and other horrors form the machinery by which moves the highest, the grandest, and the most philosophic of tragedies.

It is not difficult to see how a work so various should become so popular. *Faust*, which rivals it in popularity, rivals it also in prodigality. Almost every typical aspect of life is touched upon ; almost every subject of interest finds an expression in almost every variety of rhythm. It gains a large audience because it appeals to a large audience :

> Die Mass könnt ihr nur durch Masse zwingen,
> Ein jeder sucht sich endlich selbst was aus.
> Wer Vieles bringt wird manchem Etwas bringen,
> Und jeder geht zufrieden aus dem Haus*.

Critics usually devote their whole attention to an exposition of the Idea of Faust ; and it seems to me that in this laborious search after a remote explanation they have overlooked the more obvious and natural explanation furnished by the work itself. The reader who has followed me thus far will be aware that I have little sympathy with that Philosophy of Art which consists in translating Art into Philosophy, and that I trouble myself, and him, very little with 'considerations on the Idea'. Experience tells me that the Artists themselves had quite other objects in view than that of developing an Idea ; and experience further says that the Artist's public is by no means primarily anxious about the Idea, but leaves that entirely to the critics,—who can-

---

* The mass can be compelled by mass alone,
 Each one at length seeks out what is his own.
 Bring much, and every one is sure to find
 From out your nosegay something to his mind.
                                    BLACKIE.

not agree among themselves. In studying a work of Art, we should proceed as in studying a work of nature : after delighting in the effect, we should try to ascertain what are the *means* by which the effect is produced, and not at all what is the Idea lying behind the means. If in dissecting an animal we get clear conceptions of the mechanism by which certain functions are performed, we do not derive any increase of real knowledge from being told that the functions are the final causes of the mechanism, while, on the other hand, if an *à priori* conception of purpose is made to do the work of actual inspection of the mechanism, we find ourselves in a swamp of conjectural metaphysics where no dry land is to be found.

The Theatre Prologue. This opening of the work shows a strolling company of Players about to exhibit themselves in the market-place, to please the motley crowd with some rude image of the Comedy and Tragedy of Life. The personages are three : The Manager, the Poet, and the Merry Andrew : three types representing the question of Dramatic Art in reference to poets and the public. The Manager opposes his hard practical sense to the vague yearnings and unworldly aspirings of the Poet ; he thinks of receipts, the poet thinks of fame. But here, as ever, hard practical sense is not the best judge ; the arbitration of a third is needed, and we have it in the Merry Andrew, who corrects both disputants by looking to the real issue, namely, the *amusement of the public.* When the poet flies off in declamations about Posterity, this wise and merry arbiter slily asks : Who then is to amuse the present? A question we feel repeatedly tempted to ask those lofty writers who, despising a success they have striven in vain to achieve, throw themselves with greater confidence on the Future ; as if the Future in *its* turn would not also be a Present, having its despisers and its Jeremiahs.

The Theatre Prologue, brief though it is, indicates the whole question of poets, managers, and public. It is the wisest word yet uttered on the topic, and seems as fresh and applicable as if written yesterday. No consideration of importance is omitted, and there are no superfluities. Every line is thrown off with the utmost ease, and with the perfect clearness of perfect strength. One might say without exaggeration that the mastery of genius is as distinctly traceable in these easy felicitous touches, as in any other part of the work ; for it is perhaps in the treatment of such trifles that power is most decisively seen : inferior writers always

overdo or underdo such things ; they are inflated or flat. All
bodies at a certain degree of heat become luminous, and in the
exaltation of passion even an inferior mind will have inspirations
of felicitous thought ; but, reduced to normal temperatures, that
which before was luminous becomes opaque, and the inferior
mind, being neither exalted by passion nor moved towards new
issues by the pressure of crowding thoughts, exhibits its normal
strength. And that is why the paradox is true, of real mastery
being most clearly discernible in trifles. When the wind is furiously
sweeping the surface, we cannot distinguish the shallowest from
the deepest stream ; it is only when the winds are at rest that we
can see to the bottom of the shallow stream, and perceive the
deep stream to be beyond our fathom.

We may still call upon the wisdom of this Prologue.   The
Manager wants to know how best to attract the public :

> Sie sitzen schon, mit hohen Augenbraunen
> Gelassen da, und möchten gern erstaunen.
> Ich weiss wie man den Geist des Volks versöhnt ;
> Doch so verlegen bin ich nie gewesen ;
> Zwar sind sie an das Beste nicht gewöhnt
> *Allein sie haben schrecklich viel gelesen**.

The Poet, who never drifts towards Utilitarianism, replies in rhapsodies about his Art ; whereupon the Merry Andrew bids him
prove himself a master of his Art, by *amusing* the public.

> Let Fancy with her many-sounding chorus,
> Reason, Sense, Feeling, Passion, move before us ;
> But mark you well ! a spice of Folly too.

The Manager insists upon 'incidents' above all things :

> They come to see, you must engage their eyes.

And he adds, with true managerial instinct,

> You give a piece—give it at once in pieces !
> In vain into an artful whole you glue it,—
> The public, in the long run, will undo it.

---

* With eyebrows arch'd already they sit there,
And gape for something new to make them stare.
I know how to conciliate the mob,
But ne'er yet felt it such a ticklish job :
'Tis true what they have read is not the best,
But that they much have read must be confessed.
                              BLACKIE'S *Translation.*

I shall generally follow this translation ; but the passage just cited is not of the
usual excellence. The last couplet of the original is one of those couplets which, in
their ease, familiarity, and felicity, are the despair of translators.

So the dispute runs on, till the Manager settles it by resolving to give a grand and motley spectacle, 'From heaven to earth, and thence thro' earth to hell'. This sentence gives us the clue to the composition of the work; a clue which has usually been taken only as a guide through the mental labyrinth, through the phases of the psychological problem, instead of through that, and *also* through the scenes of life represented.

The *Prologue in Heaven* succeeds. In many quarters this Prologue has been strangely misunderstood. It has been called a parody of the Book of Job, and censured as a parody. It has been stigmatized as irrelevant and irreverent, out of keeping with the rest, and gratuitously blasphemous. Some translators have omitted it 'as unfit for publication'. Coleridge debated with himself, 'whether it became his moral character to render into English, and so far certainly to lend his countenance to, language much of which he thought vulgar, licentious, and blasphemous'*. And I will confess that my first impression was strongly against it; an impression which was only removed by considering the legendary nature of the poem, and the legendary style adopted. It is only organic analysis which can truly seize the meaning of organic elements; so long as we judge an organism *ab extra*, according to the Idea, or according to *our* Ideas, and not according to *its* nature, we shall never rightly understand structure and function; and this is as true of poems as of animals. Madame de Stael admirably says of the whole work, ' il serait véritablement trop naïf de supposer qu'un tel homme ne sache pas toutes les fautes de goût qu'on peut reprocher à sa pièce; mais il est curieux de connaître les motifs qui l'ont déterminé à les y laisser, ou plutôt à les y mettre'. And in trying to understand what were the motives which induced Goethe to introduce this prologue, and to treat it in this style, we must dismiss at once the supposition that he meant to be blasphemous, and the supposition that he could not have been as grave and decorous as Klopstock, had he deemed it fitting. Let us look a little closer.

The wager between Mephistopheles and the Deity was part and parcel of the Legend. In adopting the Legend Goethe could not well omit this part, and his treatment of it is in the true mediæval style, as all who are familiar with mediæval legends, and especially those who are familiar with the Miracle-plays of Europe, will recognize at once. In these Miracle-plays we are startled by the

* *Table Talk*, vol. II, p. 118.

coarsest buffoonery, and what to modern ears sounds like blasphemy, side by side with the most serious lessons ; things the most sacred are dragged through the dirt of popular wit ; persons the most sacred are made the subject of jests and stories which would send a shudder through the pious reader of our times. As a specimen of the lengths to which this jesting spirit went, in the works of priests, performed by priests, and used for religious instruction, the following bit of buffoonery may be cited. In one of the plays God the Father is seen sleeping on his throne during the Crucifixion. An Angel appears to him ; and this dialogue takes place :

' *Angel.* Eternal Father, you are doing what is not right, and will cover yourself with shame. Your much beloved son is just dead, and you sleep like a drunkard.

' *God the Father.* Is he then dead ?

' *Angel.* Ay, that he is.

' *God the Father.* Devil take me if I knew anything about it '*.

Nothing is more certain than that such things were not intended as blasphemous ; they were the naïve representations which un-cultured minds naïvely accepted.   In treating a mediæval legend, Goethe therefore gave it something of the mediæval colouring—a faint tint, just enough to effect his purpose, when the real colour would have been an offence. In adopting the idea of the Prologue he followed the old puppet-play of *Faust*, of which there are many versions †. An inferior artist would assuredly have made this Prologue as grand and metaphysical as possible. Goethe intentionally made it naïve. We cannot suppose him unable to treat it otherwise had he so willed ; but he did not will it so. He was led to write this scene by his study of the older literature, and the source of its inspiration is traceable in this naïveté‡. Consider the whole tenor of the work, and see how great a want of keeping there would have been in a prologue which represented Mephistopheles and the Deity according to modern conceptions of severe propriety, when the rest of the work was treated accord-ing to legendary belief ; scenes like that with the poodle, the

---

* Quoted in Scherr: *Geschichte der Deutschen Cultur*, p. 171. In the early forms of the drama I remember nothing so irreverent as this passage, but many of extreme coarseness and ignoble buffoonery. Nor is this strange perversion of the religious ceremony unexampled. In Greece, where the Drama was a religious festival, the same comic licence flourished unrestricted ; the very stage trodden by the Eumenides and solemnized by the presence of the gods, was, in the after-piece, the scene of gross buffoonery, in which the gods were buffoons.

† See Magnin : *Histoire des Marionettes*, p. 325.

‡ It was probably this feeling of its naïveté which made him say that it ought to be translated into the French of Marot.

Walpurgis Night, and the Witches' Kitchen, would have been in open contradiction with a prologue in the modern spirit. It seems to me that the Prologue is just what it should be : poetical, with a touch of mediæval colouring. It strikes the key note ; it opens the world of wonder and legendary belief, wherein you are to see transacted the great and mystic drama of life ; it is the threshold at which you are bidden to lay aside your garments soiled with the dust of the work-day world ; fairy garments are given in exchange, and you enter a new region, where a drama is acted, dream-like in form, in spirit terribly real.

Then, again, the language put into the mouth of Mephistopheles, —which is so irreverent as to make the unreflecting reader regard the whole Prologue as blasphemous,—is it not strictly in keeping ? Here we see the 'spirit that denies' so utterly and essentially irreverent, that even in the presence of the Creator he feels no awe ; the grander emotions are not excitable within his soul ; and, like all his species, he will not believe that others feel such emotions : 'Pardon me', he says, 'I cannot utter fine phrases'. To such spirits, all grandeur of phrase is grandiloquence. Mephisto is not a hypocrite : he cannot pay even *that* homage to virtue. He is a sceptic, pure and simple. In the presence of the Lord he demeans himself much as we may imagine a 'fast' young man behaving when introduced into the presence of a Goethe, without brains enough to be aware of his own insignificance. He offers to lay a wager just as the fast youth would offer to 'back' any opinion of his own ; and the brief soliloquy in which he expresses his feelings on the result of the interview has a levity and a tinge of sarcasm intensely devilish.

There are, it will be observed, two Prologues : one on the Stage, the other in Heaven. The reason of this I take to lie in the two-fold nature of the poem, in the two leading subjects to be worked out. The world and the world's ways are to be depicted ; the individual soul and its struggles are to be portrayed. For the former we have the theatre prologue, because 'All the world's a stage, and all the men and women merely players'. For the latter we have the prologue in heaven, because heaven is the centre and the goal of all struggles, doubts, and reverence ; and because Faust is struggling heavenward :

> Nicht irdisch ist des Thoren Trank noch Speise,
> Ihn treibt die Gährung in die Ferne.

'This fool's meat and drink are not earthly', says Mephisto. 'The ferment of his spirit impels him towards the for ever distant'.

There is also another organic necessity for these two prologues : in the first we see the Manager and his Poet moving the puppets of the scene ; in the second, we see the Lord and Mephistopheles moving the puppets of the drama within a drama. It is from strolling players that the cause of the whole representation proceeds : it is from heaven that the drama of the temptation issues. These two prologues were both written in the same year, and long after the conception of the Faust-legend had taken shape in Goethe's mind. They were afterthoughts, and it becomes us to inquire what purpose they were intended to subserve. I believe that in his first conception he only intended the *individual* element of the work to be developed ; and that the world-picture was an afterthought, the product of reflection. In this subsequent conception the *Second Part* was more or less forecast ; and the two prologues are introductory to the whole poem in this new conception.

But to proceed with our analysis. The first scene is that of *Faust in his study.* The drama here begins. Faust sits amid his books and instruments, vain appliances of vain inquiry. Pale, and worn with midnight toil, he feels his efforts have been vain, feels that science is impotent, feels that no answer to his questions can be extorted by mortal wisdom, and gives himself to magic.

> That I, with bitter-sweating brow,
> No more may teach what I do not know ;
> That I with piercing ken may see
> The world's in-dwelling energy,
> The hidden seeds of life explore,
> And deal in words and forms no more.

The moon, which shines in upon him, recalls him to a sense of the Life without, which he has neglected in his study of parchments and old bones : *Und fragst du noch warum dein Herz*, he exclaims in the well-known lines, and opens the magic book to summon a spirit to his aid :

(*He seizes the book, and pronounces with a mysterious air the sign of the Spirit. A red flame darts forth, and the Spirit appears in the flame.*)

　　Spirit. Who calls me ?

　　Faust (*turning away.*) Vision of affright !

　　Spirit. Thou hast with mighty spells invoked me,
　And to obey thy call provoked me,
　And now—

Faust.   Hence from my sight !
  Spirit. Thy panting prayer besought my form to view,
To hear my voice, and know my semblance too ;
Now bending from my lofty sphere to please thee,
Here am I !—ha ! what shuddering terrors seize thee,
And overpower thee quite ! where now is gone
The soul's proud call ? the breast that scorn'd to own
Earth's thrall, a world in itself created,
And bore and cherish'd ? with its fellow sated
That swell'd with throbbing joy to leave its sphere
And vie with spirits, their exalted peer.
Where art thou, Faust ? whose invocation rung
Upon mine ear, whose powers all round me clung ?
Art *thou* that Faust ? whom melts my breath away,
Trembling ev'n to the life-depths of thy frame,
Now shrunk into a piteous worm of clay !
  Faust. Shall I then yield to thee, thou thing of flame ?
I am thy peer, am Faust, am still the same !
  Spirit. Where life's floods flow,
          And its tempests rave,
          Up and down I wave,
          Flit I to and fro :
          Birth and the grave,
          Life's secret glow,
          A changing motion,
          A boundless ocean,
          Whose waters heave
          Eternally ;
          Thus on the noisy loom of Time I weave
          The living mantle of the Deity.
  Faust. Thou who round the wide world wendest,
Thou busy sprite, how near I feel to thee !
  Spirit. Thou'rt like the spirit whom thou comprehendest,
Not me !   (*vanishes.*)
  Faust (*astounded*). Not thee !
Whom, then ?
I, image of the Godhead,
Not like thee !   (*knocking is heard.*)
Oh, death !—'tis Wagner's knock—he comes to break
The charm that bound me while the Spirit spake !
Thus my supremest bliss ends in delusion
Marr'd by a sneaking pedant-slave's intrusion !

How fine is this transition, the breaking in of prose reality upon
the visions of the poet,—the entrance of Wagner, who, hearing
voices, fancied Faust was declaiming from a Greek drama, and

comes to profit by the declamation. Wagner is a type of the Philister, and pedant ; he sacrifices himself to Books as Faust does to
Knowledge. He adores the letter. The dust of folios is his element ; parchment is the source of his inspiration.

Left once more to himself, Faust continues his sad soliloquy
of despair. The thoughts, and the music in which they are
uttered, must be sought in the original, no translation can be
adequate. He resolves to die ; and seizing the phial which
contains the poison, says :

> I look on thee, and soothed is my heart's pain ;
> I grasp thee, straight is lulled my racking brain,
> And wave by wave my soul's flood ebbs away.
> I see the ocean wide before me rise,
> And at my feet her sparkling mirror lies ;
> To brighter shores invites a brighter day.

He raises the cup to his lips, when suddenly a sound of bells is
heard, accompanied by the distant singing of the choir. It is
Easter. And with these solemn sounds are borne the memories of
his early youth, awaking the feelings of early devotion. Life
retains him upon earth ; Memory vanquishes despair.

This opening scene was *suggested* by the old puppet-play in
which Faust appears, surrounded with compasses, spheres, and
cabalistic instruments, wavering between theology, the divine
science, philosophy, the human science, the magic, the infernal
science. But Goethe has enriched the suggestion from his own
wealth of thought and experience.

The Scene before the Gate. We quit the gloomy study, and the
solitary struggles of the individual, to breathe the fresh air, and
contemplate everyday life, and everyday joyousness. It is Sunday ;
students and maidservants, soldiers and shopkeepers, are thronging out of the city gates on their way to various suburban
beerhouses which line the high road. Clouds of dust and smoke
accompany the throng ; joyous laughter, incipient flirtations,
merry song, and eager debates, give us glimpses of the common
world. This truly German picture is wonderfully painted, and its
place in the poem is significant, showing how life is accepted by
the common mind, in contrast with the previous scene which
showed life pressing on the student, demanding from him an
interpretation of its solemn significance. Faust has wasted his
days in questioning ; the people spend theirs in frivolous

pursuits, or sensual enjoyment; the great riddle of the world
never troubles them, for to them the world is a familiarity and no
mystery. They are more anxious about good tobacco and frothy
beer, about whether this one will dance with that one, and about
the new official dignitaries, than about all that the heavens above
or earth beneath can have of mystery. Upon this scene Faust,
the struggler, and Wagner, the pedant, come to gaze. It affects
Faust deeply, and makes him feel how much wiser these simple
people are than he is—for they enjoy.

> Hier ist des Volkes wahrer Himmel
> Zufrieden jauchzet gross und klein :
> *Hier bin ich Mensch, hier darf ich's seyn.*

Yes, here he feels himself a man, one of the common brotherhood, for here he yearns after the enjoyments which he sees them
pursuing. But Wagner, true pedant, feels nothing of the kind ;
he is only there because he wishes to be with Faust. He is one
of those who, in the presence of Niagara, would vex you with
questions about arrow-headed inscriptions, and in the tumult of a
village festival would discuss the origin of the Pelasgi.

The people crowd round Faust, paying him the reverence always
paid by the illiterate to the 'scholar'. Wagner sees it with envy ;
Faust feels it to be a mockery. Reverence to him, who feels profoundly his own insignificance ! He seats himself upon a stone,
and gazing on the setting sun, pours forth melancholy reflections
on the worthlessness of life, and the inanity of his struggles. The
old peasant has recalled to him the scenes of his youth, when while
the fever raged he was always tending the sick, and saved so many
lives, 'helping, helped by the Father of Good'. Seated on that
stone, the visions of his youth come back upon his mind :

> Here sat I oft, plunged in deep thought, alone,
> And wore me out with fasting and with prayer.
> Rich then in hope, in faith then strong,
> With tears and sobs my hands I wrung,
> And weened the end of that dire pest,
> From the will of Heaven to rest.

His means were unholy.

> Here was the medicine, and the patient died,
> But no one questioned—who survived ?
> And thus have we, with drugs more curst than hell,
> Within these vales, these mountains here,

Raged than the very pest more fell !
I have myself to thousands poisons given ;
They pin'd away, and I must live to hear
Men for the reckless murd'rers thanking heaven !

Wagner does not understand such scruples. He is not troubled, like Faust, with a consciousness of a double nature. The Poodle appears, to interrupt their dialogue, and Wagner, with characteristic stupidity, sees nothing but a *Poodle* in the apparition :

Ich sah ihn lange schon, nicht wichtig schien er mir.

The spiritual insight of Faust is more discerning. They quit the scene, the Poodle following.

Faust's Study. The student and the poodle enter. The thoughts of Faust are solemn ; this makes the poodle restless ; this restlessness becomes greater and greater as Faust begins to translate the Bible—an act which is enough to agitate the best-disposed devil. A bit of incantation follows, and Mephistopheles appears. I must not linger over the details of the scene, tempting as they are, but come to the compact between Faust and Mephistopheles. The state of mind which induces this compact has been artfully prepared. Faust has been led to despair of attaining the high ambition of his life ; he has seen the folly of his struggles ; seen that Knowledge is a will-o'-the-wisp to which he has sacrificed Happiness. He now pines for Happiness, though he disbelieves in it as he disbelieves in Knowledge. In utter scepticism he consents to sell his soul *if* ever he shall realize Happiness. What profound sadness is implied in the compact, that if ever he shall say to the passing moment, ' Stay, thou art fair', he is willing to perish eternally !

This scene of the compact has also its origin in the old Puppet play, and very curious is it to trace how the old hints are developed by Goethe. In the Augsburg version there is one condition among those stipulated by Mephistopheles to the effect that Faust shall never again ascend the theological chair. 'But what will the public say ?' asks Faust. ' Leave that to me', Mephisto replies ; ' I will take your place ; and believe me I shall add to the reputation you have gained in biblical learning '*. Had Goethe known this version, he would probably not have omitted such a sarcastic touch.

I must pass over the inimitable scene which follows between

* *Das Closter*, vol. v, p. 326.

Mephisto and the young Student newly arrived at the University, with boundless desire for knowledge. Every line is a sarcasm, or a touch of wisdom. The *position* of this scene in its relation to the whole deserves, however, a remark. What is the scene, but a withering satire on every branch of knowledge? and where does it occur, but precisely at that juncture when Knowledge has by the hero been renounced, when Books are closed for ever, and Life is to be enjoyed? Thus the words of Mephisto, that Theory is a greybeard, and Life a fresh tree, green and golden—

> Grau, theurer Freund, ist alle Theorie,
> Und grün des Lebens goldner Baum—

prepare us for the utter abjuration of Theory, and the eager pursuit of Enjoyment. This leads to

Auerbach's Cellar, and its scene of Aristophanic buffoonery. The cellar reeks with the fumes of bad wine and stale tobacco ; its blackened arches ring with the sound of boisterous mirth and noisy songs. The sots display themselves in all their sottishness. And *this* is one form of human enjoyment ! A thing still unhappily to be seen in every city of Europe. Faust looks on with a sort of bewildering disgust, which soon wearies him ; and then away ! away ! to the other scene as foul, as hideous—to—

The Witches' Kitchen. Here Faust passes from bestiality to bestiality, from material grossness to spiritual grossness, from the impurity of sots to the impurity of witches. In this den of sorcery he drinks of the witch's potion, which will make him, as Mephisto says, see a Helen in the first woman he meets. Rejuvenescence is accompanied by desires hitherto unknown to him ; he is young, and young passions hurry him into the 'roaring flood of time'.

Meeting with Margaret. The simple girl, returning from church, is accosted by Faust, and answers him somewhat curtly ; here commences the love-episode which gives to the poem a magic none can resist. Shakespeare himself has drawn no such portrait as that of Margaret : no such peculiar union of passion, simplicity homeliness, and witchery. The poverty and inferior social position of Margaret are never lost sight of ; she never becomes an abstraction ; it is Love alone which exalts her above her lowly station and it is only *in* passion that she is so exalted. Very artful and very amusing is the contrast between this simple girl and her friend Martha, who makes love to Mephisto with direct worldly shrewdness. The effect of this contrast in the celebrated garden scene is very fine ; and what a scene that is ! I have no language in which to express its intense and overpowering effect : the picture is one which remains indelible in the memory ; certain lines linger in the mind, and stir it like the memory of deep, pathetic music. For instance, Margaret's asking him to think of her, even if it be for a moment,—she will have time enough to think of *him* :

> Denkt ihr an mich ein Augenblickchen nur,
> *Ich werde Zeit genug an euch zu denken haben :*

What a picture of woman's lonely life, in which the thoughts, not called out by the busy needs of the hour, centre in one object ! And then that exquisite episode of her plucking the flower ' He loves me—loves me not ' ; followed by this charming reflection when Faust has departed :

> Du lieber Gott ! was so ein Mann
> Nicht alles alles denken kann !
> Beschämt nur steh' ich vor ihm da,
> Und sag' zu allen Sachen ja.
> Bin doch ein arm unwissend Kind
> Begreife nicht was er an mir find't *.

Wood and Cavern. I do not understand the relation of this scene to the whole. Faust is alone among the solitudes of Nature, pouring out his rapture and his despair :

> *Faust.* Alas ! that man enjoys no perfect bliss,
> I feel it now. Thou gavest me with this joy,
> Which brings me near and nearer to the gods,
> A fellow, whom I cannot do without ;
> Though, cold and heartless, he debases me
> Before myself, and, with a single breath
> Blows all the bounties of thy love to nought.
> He fans within my breast a raging fire
> For that fair image, busy to do ill.
> Thus reel I from desire on to enjoyment,
> And in enjoyment languish for desire.

Mephisto enters, and the two wrangle. The scene is full of fine things, but its position in the work is not clear to me. It is

---

* The naïveté of expression is not to be translated. Blackie has given the sense :
> Dear God ! what such a man as this
> Can think on any thing you may !
> I stand ashamed, and answer yes
> To every word that he may say.
> I wonder what a man so learned as he
> Can find in a poor simple girl like me.

followed by that scene in Margaret's room which exhibits her at the spinning-wheel, singing *Meine Ruh' ist hin*—'my peace is gone, my heart is sad'; and is succeeded by the second Garden scene, in which she questions Faust about his religion. I must give the famous confession of Faith, though more literally than Blackie renders it :

> Misunderstand me not, thou lovely one.
> Who dare name Him?
> And who confess :
> 'I believe in Him'?
> Who can feel
> And force himself
> To say : 'I believe not in Him'?
> The All-encompasser,
> The All-sustainer
> Encompasses, sustains he not
> Thee, Me, Himself?
> Does not the Heaven arch itself above?
> Lies not the earth firm here below?
> And rise not the eternal stars
> Looking downwards friendly?
> Gaze not our eyes into each other,
> And is not all thronging
> To thy head and heart,
> Weaving in eternal mystery
> Invisibly visibly about thee?
> Fill up thy heart therewith, in all its greatness,
> And when thou'rt wholly blest in this emotion,
> Then call it what thou wilt,
> Call it Joy! Heart! Love! God!
> I have no name for it,
> Feeling is all-in-all.
> Name is sound and smoke,
> Clouding the glow of Heaven.

Margaret feels this confession to be the same in substance as that the Priest tells her, only in somewhat different language :

> Nur mit ein bischen andern Worten.

There is something inexpressibly touching in her solicitude about her lover's faith ; it serves to bring out one element of her character, as her instinctive aversion to Mephisto brings out another element : she sees on his forehead that he feels no sympathy, that 'He never yet hath loved a human soul'. In his presence she almost feels that her own love vanishes; certain it is that in his presence she cannot pray.

The guileless innocence which prattles thus, prepares us for the naïve readiness with which she expresses her willingness to admit her lover to her apartment, and consents to give her mother the sleeping draught. This scene is, with terrible significance, followed by that brief scene at the Well, where Margaret hears her friend Bessy triumph, feminine-wise, over the fall of one of their companions. Women, in all other things so compassionate, are merciless to each other precisely in those situations where feminine sympathy would be most grateful, where feminine tenderness should be most suggestive. Bessy says not a word against the seducer; her wrath falls entirely on the victim, who has been 'rightly served'. Margaret—taught compassion by experience— cannot *now* triumph as formerly she would have triumphed. But now she too is become what she chid, she too is a sinner, and cannot chide! The closing words of this soliloquy have never been translated; there is a something in the simplicity and intensity of the expression which defies translation.

> Doch—alles was dazu mich trieb,
> *Gott! war so gut! ach war so lieb!* *

The next scene shows her praying to the Virgin, the Mother of Sorrows; and this is succeeded by the return of her brother Valentine, suffering greatly from his sister's shame; he interrupts the serenade of Faust, attacks him, and is stabbed by Mephisto, falls, and expires uttering vehement reproaches against Margaret. From this bloodshed and horror we are led to the Cathedral. Margaret prays amid the crowd—the evil spirit at her side. A solemn, almost stifling sense of awe rises through the mind at this picture of the harassed sinner seeking refuge, and finding fresh despair. Around her kneel in silence those who hear with comfort the words to her so terrible:

> Dies iræ, dies illa,
> Solvet sæclum in favilla!

and when the choir bursts forth—

> Judex ergo cum sedebit
> Quidquid latet apparebit,
> Nil inultum remanebit—

---

* The meaning is, 'Yet if I sinned, the sin came to me in shape so good, so lovely, that I loved it'.

she is overpowered by remorse, for the Evil Spirit interprets these words in their most appalling sense.

The Walpurgis Nacht. The introduction of this scene in this place would be a great error if *Faust* were simply a drama. The mind resents being snatched away from the contemplation of human passion and plunged into the vagaries of dreamland. After shuddering with Margaret, we are in no mood for the Blocksberg. But *Faust* is not a drama ; its purpose is not mainly that of unfolding before our eyes the various evolutions of an episode of life ; its object is not to rivet attention through a story. It is a grand legendary spectacle, in which all phases of life are represented. The scene on the Blocksberg is part of the old Legend, and is to be found in many versions of the puppet-play*. Note how Goethe introduces the scene immediately after that in the Cathedral—thus representing the wizard-element in contrast with the religious element ; just as previously he contrasted the Witches' Kitchen and its orgies with the orgies of Auerbach's cellar.

We must not linger on the Blocksberg, but return to earth, and the tragic drama there hastening to its dénouement. Seduction has led to infanticide ; infanticide has led to the condemnation of Margaret. Faust learns it all ; learns that a triple murder lies to his account—Valentine, Margaret, and her child. In his despair he reproaches Mephisto for having concealed this from him, and wasted his time in insipid fooleries. Mephisto coldly says that Margaret is not the first who has so died. Upon which Faust breaks forth : 'Not the first ! Misery ! Misery ! by no human soul to be conceived ! that more than one creature of God should ever have been plunged into the depth of this woe ! that the first, in the writhing agony of her death, should not have atoned for the guilt of all the rest before the eyes of the eternally Merciful ! '

One peculiarity is noticeable in this scene : it is the only bit of prose in the whole work ;—what could have determined him to write it in prose ? At first I thought it might be the nature of the scene ; but the intensity of language seems to demand verse, and surely the scene in Auerbach's cellar is more prosaic in its nature than this ? The question then remains, and on it the critic may exert his ingenuity.

---

* In the Strasburg version, Mephisto promises Hanswurst a steed on which he may gallop through the air ; but, instead of a winged horse, there comes an old goat with a light under his tail.

What painting in the six brief lines which make up the succeeding scene! Faust and Mephisto are riding over a wild and dreary plain; the sound of carpenters at work on the gibbet informs them of the preparations for the execution of Margaret.

And now the final scene opens. Faust enters the dungeon where Margaret lies huddled on a bed of straw, singing wild snatches of ancient ballads, her reason gone, her end approaching. The terrible pathos of this interview draws tears into our eyes after twenty readings. As the passion rises to a climax, the grim, passionless face of Mephistopheles appears—thus completing the circle of irony which runs throughout the poem. Every one feels this scene to be untranslatable. The witchery of such lines as

> Sag' niemand dass du schon bei Gretchen warst,

Mr. Hayward has already pointed out as beyond translation; 'indeed it is only by a lucky chance that a succession of simple, heartfelt expressions or idiomatic felicities are ever capable of exact representation in another language'*.

The survey just taken, disclosing a succession of varied scenes representative of Life, will not only help to explain the popularity of *Faust*, but may help also to explain the secret of its composition. The rapidity and variety of the scenes give the work an air of formlessness, until we have seized the principle of organic unity binding these scenes into a whole. The reader who first approaches it is generally disappointed: the want of visible connexion makes it appear more like a Nightmare than a work of Art. Even accomplished critics have been thus misled. Thus Coleridge, who battled so ingeniously for Shakespeare's Art, was utterly at a loss to recognize any unity in *Faust*. 'There is no whole in the poem', he said, 'the scenes are mere magic-lantern pictures, and a large part of the work is to me very flat'†. Coleridge, combating French critics, proclaimed (in language slightly altered from Schlegel) that the unity of a work of Art is 'organic, not mechanic'; and he was held to have done signal service by pointing out the unity of Shakespeare's conception underlying variety of detail; but when he came to Goethe, whom he disliked, and of whom he always spoke unworthily, he could see nothing but magic-lantern scenes in variety of detail. If *Hamlet* is not a magic-lantern, *Faust* is not. The successive scenes of a magic-lantern have no connexion with a

---

* *Translation of Faust:* Preface, p. xxxi, 3rd Edition.
† *Table Talk*, vol. II, p. 114.

general plan; have no dependence one upon the other. In the analysis just submitted to the reader, both the general plan and the interdependence of the scenes have, it is hoped, been made manifest. A closer familiarity with the work removes the first feeling of disappointment. We learn to understand it, and our admiration grows with our enlightenment. The picture is painted with so cunning a hand, and yet with so careless an air, that Strength is veiled by Grace, and nowhere seems straining itself in Effort.

I believe few persons have read *Faust* without disappointment. There are works which, on a first acquaintance, ravish us with delight: the ideas are new; the form is new; the execution striking. In the glow of enthusiasm we pronounce the new work a masterpiece. We study it, learn it by heart, and somewhat weary our acquaintances by the emphasis of enthusiasm. In a few years, or it may be months, the work has become unreadable, and we marvel at our old admiration. The ideas are no longer novel; they appear truisms or perhaps falsisms. The execution is no longer admirable, for we have discovered its trick. In familiarizing our minds with the work, our admiration has been slowly strangled by the contempt which familiarity is said to breed, but which familiarity only breeds in contemptible minds, or for things contemptible. The work then was no masterpiece? Not in the least*. A masterpiece excites no sudden enthusiasm; it must be studied much and long, before it is fully comprehended; we must grow up to it, for it will not descend to us. Its influence is less sudden, more lasting. Its emphasis grows with familiarity. We never become disenchanted; we grow more and more awestruck at its infinite wealth. We discover no trick, for there is none to discover. Homer, Shakespeare, Raphael, Beethoven, Mozart, never storm the judgment; but, once fairly in possession, they retain it with increasing influence. I remember looking at the Elgin marbles with an indifference which I was ashamed to avow; and since then I have stood before them with a rapture almost rising into tears. On the other hand, works which now cannot detain me a minute before them, excited sudden enthusiasm such as in retrospection seems like the boyish taste for unripe apples. With *Faust* my first feeling was disappointment. Not understanding the real nature of the work, I thought Goethe had missed his aim, because he did not fulfil my conception. It

* ' A deduction must be made from the opinion which even the wise express of a new book or occurrence. Their opinion gives me tidings of their mood, and some vague guess at the new fact, but is nowise to be trusted as the lasting relation between that intellect and that thing '.—*Emerson.*

is the arrogance of criticism to demand that the artist, who never thought of us, should work in the direction of our thoughts. As I grew older, and began to read *Faust* in the original (helped by the dictionary), its glory gradually dawned upon my mind. It is now one of those works which exercise a fascination to be compared only to the minute and inexhaustible love we feel for those long dear to us, every expression having a peculiar and, by association, quite mystic influence.

A masterpiece like *Faust*, because it is a masterpiece, will be almost certain to create disappointment, in proportion to the expectations formed of it.   Sir Joshua Reynolds, on his first visit to the Vatican, could not conceal his mortification at not relishing the works of Raphael, and was only relieved from it on discovering that others had experienced the same feeling. 'The truth is', he adds, 'that if these works had been really what I expected, they would have contained beauties superficial and alluring, but by no means such as would have entitled them to their great reputation'. We need not be surprised therefore to hear even distinguished men express unfavourable opinions of *Faust*.   Charles Lamb, for instance, thought it a vulgar melodrame in comparison with Marlowe's *Faustus;* an opinion he never could have formed had he read *Faust* in the original. He read it in a translation, and no work suffers more from translation. However unwilling a reader may be that his competence to pronounce a judgment should be called in question, it must be said in all seriousness and with the most complete absence of exaggeration and prejudice, that in translation he really has not the work before him.

Several times in these pages I have felt called upon to protest against the adequacy of all translation of poetry.   In its happiest efforts, translation is but approximation ; and its efforts are not often happy. A translation may be good *as* translation, but it cannot be an adequate reproduction of the original.   It may be a good poem ; it may be a good imitation of another poem ; it may be better than the original ; but it cannot be an adequate reproduction ; it cannot be the same thing in another language, producing the same effect on the mind.   And the cause lies deep in the nature of poetry. 'Melody', as Beethoven said to Bettina, 'gives a *sensuous existence to poetry;* for does not the meaning of a poem become embodied in melody?' The meanings of a poem and the meanings of the individual words may be reproduced; but in a poem meaning and form are as indissoluble as soul and body ;

and the form cannot be reproduced. The effect of poetry is a compound of music and suggestion ; this music and this suggestion are intermingled in words, to alter which is to alter the effect. For words in poetry are not, as in prose, simple representatives of objects and ideas : they are parts of an organic whole—they are tones in the harmony ; substitute *other* parts, and the result is a monstrosity, as if an arm were substituted for a wing ; substitute *other* tones or semitones, and you produce a discord. Words have their music and their shades of meaning too delicate for accurate reproduction in any other form ; the suggestiveness of one word cannot be conveyed by another. Now all translation is of necessity a substitution of one word for another ; the substitute may express the meaning, but it cannot accurately reproduce the music, nor those precise shades of suggestiveness on which the delicacy and beauty of the original depend. Words are not only symbols of objects, but centres of associations ; and their suggestiveness depends partly on their sound. Thus there is not the slightest difference in the meaning expressed when I say

> The dews of night began to fall,

or

> The nightly dews commenced to fall.

Meaning and metre are the same ; but one is poetry, the other prose. Wordsworth paints a landscape in this line :

> The river wanders at its own sweet will.

Let us translate it into other words :

> The river runneth free from all restraint.

We preserve the meaning, but where is the landscape? Or we may turn it thus :

> The river flows, now here, now there, at will.

which is a very close translation, much closer than any usually found in a foreign language, where indeed it would in all probability assume some such form as this :

> The river self-impelled pursues its course.

In these examples we have what is seldom found in translations, accuracy of meaning expressed in similar metre ; yet the music and the poetry are gone ; because the music and the poetry are organically dependent on certain peculiar arrangements of sound and suggestion.   Walter Scott speaks of the verse of a ballad by Mickle which haunted his boyhood ; it is this :

> The dews of summer night did fall ;
>   The moon, sweet regent of the sky,
> Silvered the walls of Cumnor Hall,
>   And many an oak that grew thereby.

This verse we will rearrange as a translator would rearrange it :

> The nightly dews commenced to fall ;
>   The moon, whose empire is the sky,
> Shone on the sides of Cumnor Hall,
>   And all the oaks that stood thereby.

Here is a verse which certainly would never have haunted any one ; and yet upon what apparently slight variations the difference of effect depends !   The meaning, metre, rhymes, and most of the words, are the same ; yet the difference in the result is infinite.   Let us translate it a little more freely :

> Sweetly did fall the dews of night ;
>   The moon, of heaven the lovely queen,
> On Cumnor Hall shone silver bright,
>   And glanced the oaks' broad boughs between.

I appeal to the reader's experience whether this is not a translation which in another language would pass for excellent ; and nevertheless it is not more like the original than a wax rose is like a garden rose.   To conclude these illustrations, I will give one which may serve to bring into relief the havoc made by translators who adopt a *different* metre from that of the original*.   Wordsworth begins his famous Ode :

> There was a time when meadow, grove, and stream,
> The earth, and every common sight,
>   To me did seem
>   Apparelled in celestial light,
> The glory and the freshness of a dream.
> It is not now as it hath been of yore ;
>   Turn wheresoe'er I may,
>   By night or day,
> The things which I have seen I now can see no more.

---

* 'Goethe's poems', said Beethoven, 'exercise a great sway over me, not only by their meaning, but by their rhythm also.   It is a language which urges me on to composition'.

The translator, fully possessed with the sense of the passage, makes no mistakes, but adopting another metre, we will suppose, paraphrases it thus :

> A time there was when wood, and stream, and field,
> The earth, and every common sight, did yield
> To me a pure and heavenly delight,
> Such as is seen in dream and vision bright.
> That time is past ; no longer can I see
> The things which charmed my youthful reverie.

These are specimens of translating from English into English* and show what effects are produced by a change of music and a change of suggestion. It is clear that in a foreign language the music must incessantly be changed, and as no complex words are precisely equivalent in two languages, the suggestions must also be different. Idioms are of course untranslatable. Felicities of expression are the idioms of the poet ; but as on the one hand these felicities are essential to the poem, and on the other hand untranslatable, the vanity of translation becomes apparent. I do not say that a translator cannot produce a fine poem in imitation of an original poem ; but I utterly disbelieve in the possibility of his giving us a work which can be to us what the original is to those who read it. If, therefore, we reflect what a poem *Faust* is, and that it contains almost every variety of style and metre, it will be tolerably evident that no one unacquainted with the original can form an *adequate* idea of it from translation ; and if this is true, it will explain why Charles Lamb should prefer Marlowe's *Faustus*, and why many other readers should speak slightingly of the *Faust*.

As useful memoranda for comparison, I will here analyse Marlowe's *Faustus* and Calderon's *El Magico Prodigioso*.

Doctor Faustus has many magnificent passages, such as Marlowe of the 'mighty line' could not fail to write ; but on the whole it is wearisome, vulgar, and ill-conceived. The lowest buffoonery, destitute of wit, fills a large portion of the scenes ; and the serious parts want dramatic evolution. There is no character well drawn. The melancholy figure of Mephistophilis has a certain grandeur, but he is not the Tempter, according to the common conception, creeping to his purpose with the cunning of the serpent ; nor is he the cold, ironical 'spirit that denies' ; he is more like the Satan of

---

* Aristotle has a very similar argument and mode of illustration in the *De Poetica*.

Byron, with a touch of piety and much repentance. The language
he addresses to Faustus is such as would rather frighten than seduce him.

The reader who opens *Faustus* under the impression that he is
about to see a philosophical subject treated philosophically, will
have mistaken both the character of Marlowe's genius and of Marlowe's epoch. *Faustus* is no more philosophical in intention than
the *Jew of Malta*, or *Tamburlaine the Great*. It is simply the
theatrical treatment of a popular legend,—a legend admirably
characteristic of the spirit of those ages in which men, believing in
the agency of the devil, would willingly have bartered their future
existence for the satisfaction of present desires. Here undoubtedly
is a philosophical problem, which even in the present day is constantly presenting itself to the speculative mind. Yes, even in the
present day, since human nature does not change,—forms only
change, the spirit remains ; nothing perishes,—it only manifests
itself differently. Men, it is true, no longer believe in the devil's
agency ; at least, they no longer believe in the power of calling up
the devil and transacting business with him ; otherwise there would
be hundreds of such stories as that of *Faust*. But the spirit which
created that story and rendered it credible to all Europe remains
unchanged. The sacrifice of the future to the present is the spirit
of that legend. The blindness to consequences caused by the imperiousness of desire ; the recklessness with which inevitable and
terrible results are braved in perfect consciousness of their being
inevitable, provided that a temporary pleasure can be obtained, is
the spirit which dictated Faust's barter of his soul, which daily dictates the barter of men's souls. We do not make compacts, but
we throw away our lives ; we have no Tempter face to face with us
offering illimitable power in exchange for our futurity : but we have
our own Desires, imperious, insidious, and for them we barter our
existence,—for one moment's pleasure risking years of anguish.

The story of Faustus suggests many modes of philosophical
treatment, but Marlowe has not availed himself of any : he has
taken the popular view of the legend, and given his hero the vul-
garest motives. This is not meant as a criticism, but as a statement. I am not sure that Marlowe was wrong in so treating his
subject ; I am only sure that he treated it so. Faustus is disappointed with logic, because it teaches him nothing but debate,
—with physic, because he cannot with it bring dead men back to
life,—with law, because it concerns only the 'external trash',—and

with divinity, because it teaches that the reward of sin is death, and that we are all sinners. Seeing advantage in none of these studies he takes to necromancy, and there finds content ; and how ?

> *Faust.* How am I glutted with conceit of this !
> Shall I make spirits fetch me what I please?
> Resolve me of all ambiguities ?
> Perform what desperate enterprise I will?
> I'll have them fly to India for gold,
> Ransack the ocean for orient pearl,
> And search all corners of the new-found world
> For pleasant fruits and princely delicates.
> I'll have them read me strange philosophy ;
> And tell the secrets of all foreign kings :
> I'll have them wall all Germany with brass,
> And make swift Rhine circle fair Wittenburg :
> I'll have them fill the public schools with skill,
> Wherewith the students shall be bravely clad :
> I'll levy soldiers with the coin they bring,
> And chase the prince of Parma from our land,
> And reign sole king of all the provinces :
> Yea, stranger engines for the brunt of war,
> Than was the fiery keel at Antwerp bridge,
> I'll make my servile spirits to invent.

There may in this seem something trivial to modern apprehensions, yet Marlowe's audience sympathized with it, having the feelings of an age when witches were burned, when men were commonly supposed to hold communication with infernal spirits, when the price of damnation was present enjoyment.

The compact signed, Faustus makes use of his power by scampering over the world, performing practical jokes and vulgar incantations,—knocking down the Pope, making horns sprout on the heads of noblemen, cheating a jockey by selling him a horse of straw, and other equally vulgar tricks, which were just the things the audience would have done had they possessed the power. Tired of his buffooneries he calls up the vision of Helen ; his rapture at the sight is a fine specimen of how Marlowe can write on a fitting occasion.

His last hour now arrives : he is smitten with remorse, like many of his modern imitators, when it is too late ; sated with his power, he now shudders at the price. After some tragical raving, and powerful depicted despair, he is carried off by devils. The close is in keeping with the commencement : Faustus is damned because he made the compact. Each part of the bargain is fulfilled ; it is a tale of sorcery, and Faustus meets the fate of a sorcerer.

The vulgar conception of this play is partly the fault of Marlowe, and partly of his age. It might have been treated quite in conformity with the general belief ; it might have been a tale of sorcery, and yet magnificently impressive. What would not Shakespeare have made of it ? Nevertheless, we must in justice to Marlowe look also to the state of opinion in his time ; and we shall then admit that another and higher mode of treatment would perhaps have been less acceptable to the audience. Had it been metaphysical, they would not have understood it ; had the motives of Faustus been more elevated, the audience would not have believed in them. To have saved him at last, would have been to violate the legend, and to outrage their moral sense. For, why should the black arts be unpunished? why should not the sorcerer be damned? The legend was understood in its literal sense, in perfect accordance with the credulity of the audience. The symbolical significance of the legend is entirely a modern creation.

Let us now turn to Calderon's *El Magico Prodigioso*, often said to have furnished Goethe with the leading idea of his *Faust*, which, however, does *not* resemble *El Magico* in plot, incidents, situations, characters, or ideas. The *Faustus* of Marlowe has a certain superficial resemblance to the *Faust*, because the same legend is adopted in both ; but in *El Magico* the legend is altogether different ; the treatment different. Calderon's latest editor, Don Eugenio de Ochoa, is quite puzzled to conceive how the notion of resemblance got into circulation, and gravely declares that it is *enteramente infundada.*

The scene lies in the neighbourhood of Antioch, where, with 'glorious festival and song', a temple is being consecrated to Jupiter. Cyprian, a young student, perplexing himself with the dogmas of his religion (polytheism), has retired from the turmoil of the town to enjoy himself in quiet study. Pliny's definition of God is unsatisfactory, and Cyprian is determined on finding a better. A rustling amongst the leaves disturbs him, caused by the demon, who appears in the dress of a cavalier. They commence an argument, Cyprian pointing out the error of polytheism, the demon maintaining its truth. We see that Cyprian has been converted to monotheism—a step towards his conversion to Christianity ; and this conversion operated by the mere force of truth, this change of opinion resulting from an examination of polytheism, was doubtless flattering to Calderon's audience,—a flattery carried to its acmé in the feeble defence of the demon, who on his entrance declares, aside, that Cyprian shall never find the truth. Calderon would not let the devil have the best of the argument even for a moment. Instead of the 'spirit that denies', he presents us with a malignant fiend, as impotent as he is malignant, —a fiend who acknowledges himself worsted in the argument, and who resolves to conquer by lust the student whom he cannot delude by sophisms. He has power given him to wage enmity against Justina's soul ; he will make Justina captivate Cyprian, and with one blow effect two vengeances. We need not point out the dissimilarity between such a fiend, and the fiend Mephistopheles.

Cyprian is left alone to study, but is again interrupted by the quarrel of Lelio and Floro, two of his friends, who, both enamoured of Justina, have resolved to decide their rivalry by the sword. Cyprian parts them, and consents to become arbiter. He then undertakes to visit Justina, in order to ascertain to whom she gives the preference. In this visit he falls in love with her himself. There is an underplot, in which Moscon, Clarin, and Libia, according to the usual style of Spanish comedies, parody the actions and sentiments of their masters ; I omit it, as well as the other scenes which do not bear on the subject-matter of the drama.

Justina, a recent convert to Christianity, is the type of Christian innocence. She rejects Cyprian's love, as she had rejected that of her former admirers. This coldness exasperates him :

> So beautiful she was—and I,
> Between my love and jealousy,
> And so convulsed with hope and fear,
> Unworthy as it may appear,—
> So bitter is the life I live
> That, hear me, Hell ! I now would give
> To thy most detested spirit
> My soul, for ever, to inherit,
> To suffer punishment and pine,
> So this woman may be mine,
> Hear'st thou, Hell ? Dost thou reject it ?
> My soul is offered.
> 　　*Demon (unseen).* I accept it.
> 　　　　　(*Tempest, with thunder and lightning.*)

In another writer we might pause to remark on the 'want of keeping' in making a polytheist address such a prayer to hell ; but

Calderon is too full of such things to cause surprise at any individual instance. The storm rages,—a ship goes down at sea ; the demon enters as a shipwrecked passenger, and says aside :

> It was essential to my purposes
> To wake a tumult on the sapphire ocean,
> That in this unknown form I might at length
> Wipe out the blot of the discomfiture
> Sustained upon the mountain, and assail
> With a new war the soul of Cyprian,
> Forging the instruments of his destruction
> Even from his love and from his wisdom.

Cyprian addresses words of comfort to him on his misfortune ; the demon says it is in vain to hope for comfort, since all is lost that gave life value. He then tells his story ; describing, by means of a very transparent equivocation, the history of his rebellion in heaven and his chastisement. In the course of his narrative he insinuates his power of magic, hoping to awaken in Cyprian's breast a love of the art. Cyprian offers him the hospitality due to a stranger, and they quit the scene.

In their next scene the demon asks Cyprian the reason of his constant melancholy. This is an opportunity for the display of fustian, never let slip by a Spanish dramatist. Cyprian describes his mistress and his passion for her with the volubility of a lover, and the taste of an Ossian. He very circumstantially informs the demon that the ' partes que componen a esta divina muger '—the charms which adorn this paragon—are the charms of Aurora, of fleecy clouds and pearly dews, of balmy gales and early roses, of meandering rivulets and glittering stars, of warbling birds and crystal rocks, of laurels and of sunbeams ; and so forth through the space of more than fifty lines, in a style to captivate magazine poets, and to make other readers yawn. Having described her, he declares that he is so entranced with this creature as to have entirely forsaken philosophy ; he is willing to give away his soul for her. The demon accepts the offer, splits open a rock and shows Justina reclining asleep. Cyprian rushes towards her, but the rock closes again, and the demon demands that the compact shall be signed before the maiden is delivered. Cyprian draws blood from his arm, and with his dagger writes the agreement on some linen. The demon then consents to instruct him in magic, by which, at the expiration of one year, he will be able to possess Justina.

This temptation-scene is very trivial,—feeble in conception and bungling in execution. Remark the gross want of artistic keeping in it : Cyprian had before addressed a vow to hell that he would give his soul for Justina ; the demon answered, 'I accept it !' Thunder and lightning followed,—effective enough as a melodramatic *coup de théâtre*, utterly useless to the play ; for although the demon appears, it is not to make a compact with Cyprian, it is not even to tempt him ; it is simply to become acquainted with him, gain his confidence, and *afterwards* tempt him. The time elapses, and the demon then tempts Cyprian as we have seen. How poor, feeble, and staggering these outlines ! What makes the feebleness of this scene stand out still more clearly is the gross and senseless parody of Clarin, the *gracioso*. Like his master, he too is in love ; like his master he offers to sell his soul to the demon, and strikes his nose, that with the blood he may write the compact on his handkerchief.

It is in this temptation-scene, however, that the single point of resemblance occurs between the plays of Calderon and Goethe. It is extremely slight, as every one will observe; but slight as it is, some critics have made it the basis of their notion of plagiarism. The compact is the point which the legend of St. Cyprian and the legend of Faust have in common. In all other respects the legends differ and the poems differ. It is curious however to compare the motives of the three heroes, Faustus, Cyprian, and Faust ; to compare what each demands in return for his soul ; and in this comparison Calderon 'shows least bravely' ; his hero is the most pitiful of the three.

To return to our analysis : The year's probation has expired, and Cyprian is impatient for his reward. He has learned the arts of necromancy, in which he is almost as proficient as his master ; boasts of being able to call the dead from out their graves, and of possessing many other equally wonderful powers. Yet with this science he does nothing, attempts nothing. Of what use then was the year's probation ? of what use this necromantic proficiency ? Had the question been put to Calderon he would probably have smiled, and answered, 'to prolong the play and give it variety',—a sensible answer from a rapid playwright, but one which ill accords with the modern notion of his being a profound artist. Perhaps it is too much to expect that a man who wrote between one and two hundred plays should have produced one that could be regarded as a work of art ; nor should we have judged him by any higher

standard than that of a rapid and effective playwright, had not the
Germans been so hyperbolical in criticism, which the English,
who seldom read the poet, take for granted must be just.

The demon calls upon the spirits of hell to instil into Justina's
mind impure thoughts, so that she may incline to Cyprian.   But
this could have been done at first, and so have spared Cyprian his
year's probation and his necromantic studies,—studies which are
never brought to bear upon Justina herself, though undertaken
expressly for her conquest.   Justina enters in a state of violent
agitation : a portion of the scene will serve as a specimen.   I
borrow from the translation of this scene which appeared in the
Monthly Chronicle, vi, p. 346.

The demon enters and Justina asks him :

> Say if thou a phantom art,
> Formed by terror and dismay?
>   *Dæm.* No ; but one call'd by the thought
> That now rules, with tyrant sway,
> O'er thy faltering heart,—a man
> Whom compassion hither brought,
> That he might point out the way
> Whither fled thy Cyprian.
>   *Just.* And so shalt thou fail.   This storm
> Which afflicts my frenzied soul
> May imagination form
> To its wish, but ne'er shall warm
> Reason to its mad control.
>   *Dæm.* If thou hast the thought permitted,
> Half the sin is almost done !
> Wilt thou, since 'tis all committed,
> Linger ere the joy be won?
>   *Just.* In our power abides not thought,
> (Thought, alas ! how vain to fly) ;
> But the deed is, and 'tis one
> That we sin in mind have sought
> And another to have done :
> I'll not move my foot to try.
>   *Dæm.* If a mortal power assail
> Justina with all its might,
> Say will not the victory fail
> When thy wish will not avail,
> But inclines thee in despite?
>   *Just.* By opposing to thee now
> My free will and liberty,
>   *Dæm.* To my power they soon shall bow.

> *Just.* If it could such power avow,
> Would our free will then be free?
>   *Dæm.* Come, 'tis bliss that thou wilt prove.
>   *Just.* Dearly would I gain it so.
>   *Dæm.* It is peace, and calm, and love. (*Draws, but cannot*
>   *Just.* It is misery, death, despair !   *move her.*)
>   *Dæm.* Heavenly joy !
>   *Just.*   'Tis bitter woe !
>   *Dæm.* Lost and shamed, forsaken one !
> Who in thy defence shall dare?
>   *Just.* My defence is God alone.
>   *Dæm.* Virgin, virgin, thou hast won !   (*Loosens his hold.*)

How delighted must the audience have been at this victory
over the demon, by the mere announcement of a faith in God !
Unable to give Cyprian the real Justina, the demon determines on
deceiving him with a phantom. A figure enveloped in a cloak
appears, and bids Cyprian follow. In the next scene Cyprian
enters with the fancied Justina in his arms. In his transport he
takes off the cloak, and instead of Justina discovers a Skeleton,
who replies to his exclamation of horror :—

> Así, Cipriano, son
> Todas las glorias del mundo !

'Such are the glories of this world'. In this terrific situation we
recognize the inquisitor and the playwright, but the artist we do
not recognize. As a piece of stage effect this skeleton is powerfully conceived ; as a religious warning it is equally powerful ; as
art it is detestable. It is a fine situation, though he has used it
twice elsewhere ; but the consistency of the play is violated by it.
If the demon wished to seduce Cyprian, would he have attempted
to do so by *such* means? No. But Calderon here, as elsewhere,
sacrifices everything to a *coup de théâtre*.

Cyprian, exasperated at the deception, demands an explanation.
The demon confesses that he is unable to force Justina, as she is
under the protection of a superior power. Cyprian asks who that
power is. The demon hesitates, but is at length obliged to own
that it is the God of the Christians. Cyprian seeing that God
protects those who believe in him, refuses to own allegiance to
any other. The demon is furious, and demands Cyprian's soul,
who contends that the demon has not fulfilled his share of the
compact. Words run high : Cyprian draws his sword and stabs

the demon, of course without avail,—another stage effect. The
demon drags him away, but, like Justina, he calls God to his aid,
and the demon rushes off discomfited.

Cyprian becomes a Christian, and Justina assures him of his
salvation in spite of his sins, for—

> . . . no tiene
> Tantas estrellas el cielo,
> Tantas arenes el mar,
> Tantas centelles el fuego,
> Tantos átomes el dia,
> Como él perdona pecados.

Justina and Cyprian are condemned as heretics, and burned at
Antioch, martyrs of the Christian faith.   The demon appears
riding on a serpent in the air, and addresses the audience, telling
them that God has forced him to declare the innocence of Justina,
and the freedom of Cyprian from his rash engagement.   Both
now repose in the realms of the blessed.

These analyses will enable the reader to perceive how Marlowe
and Calderon have treated the old story, each in a spirit conformable with his genius and his age ; the one presenting a legend in its
naïveté, the other a legend as the vehicle for religious instruction.
Goethe taking up the legend in an age when the naïve belief could no
longer be accepted, treated it likewise in a way conformable with his
genius and his age.   The age demanded that it should be no simple
legend, but a symbolical legend ; not a story to be credited as *fact*,
but a story to be credited as *representative* of fact ; for although the
rudest intellect would reject the notion of any such actual compact
with Satan, the rudest and the loftiest would see in that compact a
symbol of their own desires and struggles.

To adapt the legend to his age, Goethe was forced to treat it
symbolically, and his own genius gave the peculiar direction to that
treatment.   We shall see in the Second Part, how his waning vigour
sought inspiration more in symbolism than in poetry, more in reflection than in emotion ; but for the present, confining ourselves to
the First Part, we note in his treatment a marvellous mingling of
the legendary and the symbolical, of the mediæval and the modern.
The depth of wisdom, the exquisite poetry, the clear bright painting, the wit, humour, and pathos, every reader will distinguish ; and
if this chapter were not already too long, I should be glad to linger
over many details, but must now content myself with the briefest
indication of the general aspects of the poem.

And first of the main theme : 'The intended theme of Faust', says Coleridge, 'is the consequences of a misology or hatred and depreciation of knowledge caused by an originally intense thirst for knowledge baffled. But a love of knowledge for itself and for pure ends would never produce such a misology, but only a love of it for base and unworthy purposes'. Having stated this to be the theme, Coleridge thus criticizes the execution : 'There is neither causation nor proportion in Faust ; he is ready-made conjuror from the beginning ; the *incredulus odi* is felt from the first line. The sensuality and thirst after knowledge are unconnected with each other'*. Here we have an example of that criticism before alluded to, which imposes the conceptions of the critic as the true end and aim of the artist. Coleridge had formed the plan of a Faust of his own, and blames Goethe for not treating the topic in the way Coleridge conceived it should be treated. A closer scrutiny would have convinced him that misology is not the intended theme. After the first two scenes knowledge is never mentioned ; misology is exhausted as a topic in the initial stages of the work. And what says Goethe himself? 'The marionette fable of Faust murmured with *many voices* in my soul. I too had wandered into every department of knowledge, and had returned early enough satisfied with the vanity of science. And life, too, I had tried under various aspects, and always came back sorrowing and unsatisfied'. Here, if anywhere, we have the key to *Faust*. It is a reflex of the struggles of his soul. Experience had taught him the vanity of philosophy ; experience had early taught him to detect the corruption underlying civilization, the dark undercurrents of crime concealed beneath smooth outward conformity. If then we distinguish for a moment one of the two aspects of the poem—if we set aside the picture, to consider only the problem—we come to the conclusion that the theme of *Faust* is the cry of despair over the nothingness of life. Misology forms a portion, but only a portion of the theme. Baffled in his attempts to penetrate the *mystery* of Life, Faust yields himself to the Tempter, who promises that he shall penetrate the *enjoyment* of Life. He runs the round of pleasure, as he had run the round of science, and fails. The orgies of Auerbach's cellar, the fancies of the Blocksberg, are unable to satisfy his cravings. The passion he feels for Gretchen is vehement, but feverish, transitory ; she has no power to make him say to the passing moment, 'Stay, thou art fair'. He is restless because he

* *Table Talk*, vol. II, p. III.

seeks,—seeks the Absolute, which can never be found. This is the doom of humanity :

Es irrt der Mensch so lang' er strebt.

It has been said reproachfully that in *Faust* the problem is stated but not solved. I do not think this reproach valid, because I do not think a poem was the fit vehicle for a solution. When the Singer becomes a Demonstrator, he abdicates his proper office, to bungle in the performance of another. But very noticeable it is that Goethe, who has so clearly stated the problem, has also, both practically, in his life, and theoretically, in his writings, given us the nearest approach to a solution by showing how the 'heavy and the weary weight' of this great burden may be wisely borne. His doctrine of Renunciation—*dass wir entsagen müssen*—applied by him with fertile results in so many directions, both in life and theory, will be found to approach a solution, or at any rate to leave the in- soluble mystery without its perplexing and tormenting influence. Activity and sincerity carry us far, if we begin by Renunciation, if we at the outset content ourselves with the Knowable and Attainable, and give up the wild impatience of desire for the Unknowable and Unattainable. The mystery of existence is an awful problem, but it *is* a mystery and placed beyond the boundaries of human faculty. Recognize it as such, and renounce ! Knowledge can only be relative, never absolute. But this relative knowledge is infinite, and to us infinitely important : in that wide sphere let each work according to ability. Happiness, ideal and absolute, is equally unattainable : renounce it ! The sphere of active Duty is wide, sufficing, ennobling to all who strenuously work in it. In the very sweat of labour there is stimulus which gives energy to life ; and a consciousness that our labour tends in some way to the lasting benefit of others, makes the rolling years endurable.

CHAPTER VIII

THE LYRICAL POEMS

THE *Faust* and the Lyrics suffice to give Goethe pre-eminence among the poets of modern times, Shakespeare excepted ; and had they stood alone as representatives of his genius, no one would ever have disputed his rank. But he has given the world many other works : in other words, he has thrown open many avenues through which the citadel of his fame may be attacked. His fame is lessened by his wealth ; the fact of his doing so much, has lessened the belief in his power ; for as the strength of a beam is measured by its weakest part, so, but unjustly, are poets tested by their weakest works, whenever enthusiasm does not drown criticism. Thus does mere wealth endanger reputation ; for when many targets are ranged side by side, the clumsiest archer will succeed in striking one; and that writer has the best chance with the critics who presents the smallest surface.   Greek Literature is so grand to us mainly because it is the fragment of fragments ; the master-pieces have survived, and no failures are left to bear counter-witness. Our own contemporary Literature seems so poor to us, not because there are no good books, but because there are so many bad, that even the good are hidden behind the mass of mediocrity which obtrudes itself upon the eye.   Goethe has written forty volumes on widely different subjects.   He has written with a perfection no German ever achieved before, and he has also written with a feebleness which it would be gratifying to think no German would ever emulate again.   But the weak pages are prose.   In verse he is always a *singer;* even the poorest poems have something of that grace which captives us in his finest.   The gift of Song, which is the especial gift of the poet, and which no other talents can replace, makes his trifles pleasant, and his best lyrics matchless.

The lyrics are the best known of his works, and have by their witchery gained the admiration even of antagonists.   One hears very strange opinions about him and his works ; but one never hears anything except praise of the minor poems.   They are instinct with life and beauty, against which no prejudice can stand. They give musical form to feelings the most various, and to feelings that are *true*.   They are gay, coquettish, playful, tender, passionate, mournful, reflective, and picturesque ; now simple as the tune which beats time to nothing in your head, now laden with weighty thought ; at one moment reflecting with ethereal grace the whim and fancy of caprice, at another sobbing forth the sorrows which press a cry from the heart.   'These songs', says Heine, himself a master of song, 'have a playful witchery which is inexpressible.   The harmonious verses wind round your heart like a tender mistress. The Word embraces you while the Thought imprints a kiss'*.

---

* 'Die harmonischen Verse umschlingen dein Herz wie eine zärtliche Geliebte ; das Wort umarmt dich, während der Gedanke dich küsst'.

Part of this witchery is the sincerity of the style. It does not seek surprises in diction, nor play amid metaphors, which, in most poets, are imperfect expressions of the meaning they are thought to adorn. It opens itself like a flower with unpretending grace, and with such variety as lies in the nature of the subject. There is no ornament in it. The beauties which it reveal are organic, they form part and parcel of the very tissue of the poem, and are not added as ornaments. Read, for example, the ballad of the *Fisherman* (translated above). How simple and direct the images, and yet how marvellously pictorial ! Turning to a totally different poem, the *Bride of Corinth*,—what can surpass the directness with which every word indicates the mysterious and terrible situation ? Every line is as a fresh page in the narrative, rapidly and yet gradually unfolded. A young man arrives at Corinth from Athens, to seek the bride whom his and her parents have destined for him. Since that agreement of the parents her family has turned Christian ; and, 'when a new faith is adopted, love and truth are often uprooted like weeds'. Ignorant of the change, he arrives. It is late in the night. The household are asleep ; but a supper is brought to him in his chamber, and he is left alone. The weary youth has no appetite ; he throws himself on his bed without undressing. As he falls into a doze the door opens, and by the light of his lamp he sees a strange guest enter—a maiden veiled, clothed in white, about her brow a black and gold band. On seeing him, she raises a white hand in terror. She is about to fly, but he entreats her to stay—points to the banquet, and bids her sit beside him and taste the joys of the gods, Bacchus, Ceres, and Amor. But she tells him she belongs no more to joy ; the gods have departed from that silent house where One alone in Heaven, and One upon the Cross, are adored ; no sacrifices of Lamb or Ox are made, the sacrifice is that of a human life. This is a language the young pagan understands not. He claims her as his bride. She tells him she has been sent into a cloister. He will hear nothing. Midnight—the spectral hour—sounds ; and she seems at her ease. She drinks the purple wine with her white lips, but refuses the bread he offers. She gives him a golden chain, and takes in return a lock of his hair. She tells him she is cold as ice, but he believes that Love will warm her, even if she be sent from the grave :

> Wechselhauch und Kuss !
> Liebesüberfluss !
> Brennst du nicht und fühlest mich entbrannt ?

Love draws them together ; eagerly she catches the fire from his
lips, and each is conscious of existence only in the other; but
although the vampire bride is warmed by his love, no heart beats
in her breast. It is impossible to describe the weird voluptuousness
of this strange scene ; this union of Life and Death ; this altar of
Hymen erected on the tomb.   It is interrupted by the presence of
the mother, who, hearing voices in the bridegroom's room, and the
kiss of the lovers mingling with the cockcrow, angrily enters to
upbraid her slave, whom she supposes to be with the bridegroom.
She enters angry 'and sees—God ! she sees her own child !' The
vampire rises like a Shadow, and reproaches her mother for having
disturbed her. 'Was it not enough that you sent me to an early
grave?' she asks. But the grave could not contain her : the
psalms of priests—the blessings of priests had no power over her ;
earth itself is unable to stifle Love. She has come ; she has
sucked the blood from her bridegroom's heart ; she has given him
her chain and received the lock of his hair. To-morrow he will
be grey; his youth he must seek once more in the tomb. She bids
her mother prepare the funeral pyre, open her coffin, and burn the
bodies of her bridegroom and herself, that they together may
hasten to the gods.

   In the whole of this wondrous ballad there is not a single image.
Everything is told in the most direct and simple style. Everything
stands before the eye like reality. The same may be said of the
well-known *Gott und die Bajadere*, which is, as it were, the inverse
of the *Bride of Corinth*. The Indian god passing along the banks
of the Ganges is invited by the Bajadere to enter her hut, and
repose himself. She coquettes with him, and lures him with the
wiles of her caste. The god smiles and sees with joy, in the
depths of her degradation, a pure human heart. He gains her love ;
but, to put her to the severest proof, he makes her pass through

Lust und Entsetzen und grimmige Pein.

She awakes in the morning to find him dead by her side. In an
agony of tears she tries in vain to awaken him. The solemn,
awful sounds of the priests chanting the requiem break on her ear.
She follows his corpse to the pyre, but the priests drive her away ;
she was not his wife ; she has no claim to die with him. But
Passion is triumphant ; she springs into the flames, and the god
rises from them with the rescued one in his arms.

   The effect of the changing rhythm of the poem, changing from tender lightness to solemn seriousness, and the art with which the whole series of events is unfolded in successive pictures, are what no other German poet has ever attained. The same art is notice-able in the *Erl King*, known to every reader through Schubert's music, if through no other source. The father riding through the night, holding his son warm to his breast ; the child's terror at the Erl King, whom the father does not see ; and the bits of landscape which are introduced in so masterly a way, as explanations on the father's part of the appearances which frighten the child ; thus mingling the natural and supernatural, as well as imagery with narrative : all these are cut with the distinctness of plastic art. The *Erl King* is usually supposed to have been original ; but Viehoff, in his *Commentary on Goethe's Poems*, thinks that the poem Herder translated from the Danish, *Erlkönigs Tochter*, suggested the idea. The verse is the same. The opening line and the concluding line are nearly the same ; but the story is different, and none of Goethe's art is to be found in the Danish ballad, which tells simply how Herr Oluf rides to his marriage, and is met on the way by the Erl King's daughter, who invites him to dance with her ; he replies that he is unable to stop and dance, for to-morrow is his wedding-day. She offers him golden spurs and a silk shirt, but he still replies, 'To-morrow is my wedding-day'. She then offers him heaps of gold. 'Heaps of gold will I gladly take ; but dance I dare not—will not'. In anger she strikes him on the heart, and bids him ride to his bride. On reaching home, his mother is aghast at seeing him so pallid. He tells her he has been in the Erl King's country. 'And what shall I say to your bride ?' 'Tell her I am in the wood with my horse and hound'. The morning brings the guests, who ask after Herr Oluf. The bride lifts up the scarlet cloak ; 'there lay Herr Oluf, and he was dead'. I have given this outline of the Danish ballad for the reader to compare with the *Erlkönig:* a comparison which will well illustrate the difference between a legend and a perfect poem.

It is not in the ballads alone, of which three have just been men-tioned, that Goethe's superiority is seen. I might go through the two volumes of Lyrics, and write a commentary as long as this Biography, without exhausting so fertile a topic. Indeed his Bio-graphy is itself but a commentary on these poems, which are real expressions of what he has thought and felt :

> Spät erklingt was früh erklang,
> Glück und Unglück wird Gesang.

Even when, as in the ballads, or in poems such as the exquisite Idyl of *Alexis and Dora*, he is not giving utterance to any personal episode, he is scarcely ever *feigning*.   Many of the smaller poems are treasures of wisdom ; many are little else than the carollings of a bird 'singing of summer in full-throated ease'.   But one and all are inaccessible through translation ; therefore I cannot attempt to give the English reader an idea of them ; the German reader has already anticipated me, by studying them in the original.

BOOK THE SEVENTH

1805 to 1832

CHAPTER I

THE BATTLE OF JENA

THE death of Schiller left Goethe very lonely. It was more than the loss of a friend; it was the loss also of an energetic stimulus which had urged him to production; and in the activity of production he lived an intenser life. During the long laborious years which followed—years of accumulation, of study, of fresh experience, and of varied plans—we shall see him produce works of which many might be proud; but the noonday splendour of his life has passed, and the light which we admire is the calm effulgence of the setting sun.

As if to make him fully aware of his loss, Jacobi came to Weimar; and although the first meeting of the old friends was very pleasant, they soon found the chasm which separated them intellectually had become wider and wider, as each developed in his own direction. Goethe found that he understood neither Jacobi's ideas nor his language. Jacobi found himself a stranger in the world of his old friend. This is one of the penalties we pay for progress; we find ourselves severed from the ancient moorings; we find our language is like that of foreigners to those who once were dear to us, and understood us.

Jacobi departed, leaving him more painfully conscious of the loss he had sustained in losing Schiller's ardent sympathy. During the following month, Gall visited Jena, in the first successful eagerness of propagating his system of Phrenology, which was then a startling novelty. All who acknowledge the very large debt which Physiology and Psychology owe to Gall's labours (which acknowledgment by no means implies an acceptance of the premature, and, in many respects, imperfect, system founded on those labours) will be glad to observe that Goethe not only attended Gall's lectures, but in private conversations showed so much sympathy, and such ready appreciation, that Gall visited him in his sick-room and dissected the brain in his presence, communicating all the new views to which he had been led.   Instead of meeting this theory with ridicule, contempt, and the opposition of ancient prejudices— as men of science, no less than men of the world, were and are still wont to meet it—Goethe saw at once the importance of Gall's mode of dissection (since universally adopted), and of his leading views*; although he also saw that science was not sufficiently advanced for a correct verdict to be delivered.   Gall's doctrine pleased him because it determined the true position of Psychology in the study of man.   It pleased him because it connected man with Nature more intimately than was done in the old schools, showing the identity of all mental manifestation in the animal kingdom†.

But these profound and delicate investigations were in the following year interrupted by the roar of cannon.   On the 14th of October, at seven o'clock in the morning, the thunder of distant artillery alarmed the inhabitants of Weimar.   The battle of Jena had begun.   Goethe heard the cannon with terrible distinctness; but as it slackened towards noon, he sat down to dinner as usual. Scarcely had he sat down, when the cannon burst over their heads. Immediately the table was cleared.   Riemer found him walking up and down the garden.   The balls whirled over the house; the bayonets of the Prussians in flight gleamed over the garden wall. The French planted a few guns on the heights above Weimar, from which they could fire on the town.   It was a calm bright day.   In the streets everything appeared dead.   Every one had retreated under cover.   Now and then the boom of a cannon broke silence; the balls, hissing through the air, occasionally struck a house.   The birds were singing sweetly on the esplanade; and the deep repose of nature formed an awful contrast to the violence of war.

In the midst of this awful stillness a few French hussars rode into the city, to ascertain if the people were there.   Presently a whole troop galloped in.   A young officer came to Goethe to assure him that his house would be secure from pillage; it had been selected as the quarters of Marshal Augereau.   The young hussar who brought this message was Lili's son!   He accompanied

---

* Compare *Freundschaftliebe Briefe von Goethe und seine Frau, an N. Meyer*, p. 19.
† Gall's assertion that Goethe was born for political Oratory more than for Poetry has much amused those who know Goethe's dislike of politics; and does not, indeed, seem a very happy hit.

Goethe to the palace. Meanwhile several of the troopers had made themselves at home in Goethe's house. Many houses were in flames. Cellars were broken open. The pillage began.

Goethe returned from the palace, but without the Marshal, who had not yet arrived. They waited for him till deep in the night. The doors were bolted, and the family retired to rest. About midnight two tirailleurs knocked at the door, and insisted on admittance. In vain they were told the house was full, and the Marshal expected. They threatened to break in the windows, if the door were not opened. They were admitted. Wine was set before them, which they drank like troopers, and then they insisted on seeing their host. They were told he was in bed. No matter ; he must get up ; they had a fancy to see him. In such cases, resistance is futile. Riemer went up and told Goethe, who, putting on his dressing-gown, came majestically down stairs, and by his presence considerably awed his drunken guests, who were as polite as French soldiers can be when they please. They talked to him ; made him drink with them, with friendly clink of glasses ; and suffered him to retire once more to his room. In a little while, however, heated with wine, they insisted on a bed. The other troopers were glad of the floor ; but these two would have nothing less than a bed. They stumbled up stairs ; broke into Goethe's room, and there a struggle ensued, which had a very serious aspect. Christiane, who throughout displayed great courage and presence of mind, procured a rescue, and the intruders were finally dragged from the room. They then threw themselves on the bed kept for the Marshal ; and no threats would move them. In the morning the Marshal arrived, and sentinels protected the house. But even under this protection, the disquiet may be imagined when we read that twelve casks of wine were drunk in three days ; that eight-and-twenty beds were made up for officers and soldiers, and that the other costs of this billeting amounted to more than 2,000 dollars.

The sun shining with continuous autumnal splendour in these days looked down on terrible scenes in Weimar. The pillage was prolonged, so that even the palace was almost stripped of the necessaries of life. In this extremity, while houses were in flames close to the palace, the Duchess Luise manifested that dauntless courage which produced a profound impression on Napoleon, as he entered Weimar, surrounded by all the terrors of conquest, and was received at the top of the palace stairs by her,—calm, dignified, unmoved. *Voilà une femme à laquelle même nos deux cent canons n'ont pu faire peur!* he said to Rapp.   She pleaded for her people ; vindicated her husband ; and by her constancy and courage prevailed over the conqueror, who was deeply incensed with the Duke, and repeatedly taunted him with the fact that he spared him solely out of respect for the Duchess.

The rage of Napoleon against the Duke was as unwise as it was intemperate ; but I do not allude to it for the purpose of showing how petty the great conqueror could be ; I allude to it for the purpose of quoting the characteristic outburst which it drew from Goethe. ' Formed by nature to be a calm and impartial spectator of events, even I am exasperated', said Goethe to Falk, 'when I see men required to perform the impossible.   That the Duke assists wounded Prussian officers robbed of their pay ; that he lent the lion-hearted Blücher four thousand dollars after the battle of Lübeck—that is what you call a conspiracy !—that seems to you a fit subject for reproach and accusation !   Let us suppose that to-day misfortune befalls the grand army ; what would a general or a field-marshal be worth in the Emperor's eyes, who would act precisely as our Duke has acted under these circumstances ?   I tell you the Duke *shall* act as he acts !   He *must* act so !   He would do great injustice if he ever acted otherwise !   Yes ; and even were he thus to lose country and subjects, crown and sceptre, like his ancestor, the unfortunate John ; yet must he not deviate one hand's breadth from his noble manner of thinking, and from that which the duty of a man and a prince prescribes in the emergency.   Misfortune ! What is misfortune ?   This is a misfortune—that a prince should be compelled to endure such things from foreigners.   And if it came to the same pass with him as with his ancestor, Duke John ; if his ruin were certain and irretrievable, let not that dismay us : we will take our staff in our hands, and accompany our master in adversity, as old Lucas Kranach did : we will never forsake him. The women and children when they meet us in the villages, will cast down their eyes, and weep, and say to one another, " That is old Goethe, and the former Duke of Weimar, whom the French Emperor drove from his throne, because he was so true to his friends in misfortune ; because he visited his uncle on his death-bed ; because he would not let his old comrades and brothers in arms starve ! " '

'At this', adds Falk, 'the tears rolled in streams down his cheeks. After a pause, having recovered himself a little, he continued : " I will sing for bread !   I will turn strolling ballad singer, and put our misfortunes into verse ! I will wander into every village and into every school wherever the name of Goethe is known ; I will chant the dishonour of Germany, and the children shall learn the song of our shame till they are men ; and thus they shall sing my master upon his throne again, and your's off his ! " '

I shall have to recur to this outburst on a future occasion, and will now hasten to the important event which is generally supposed to have been directly occasioned by the perils of the battle of Jena. I mean his marriage.

CHAPTER II

GOETHE'S WIFE

THE judgments of men are singular. No action in Aristotle's life subjected him to more calumny than his generous marriage with the friendless Phythia ; no action in Goethe's life has excited more scandal than his marriage with Christiane. It was thought disgraceful enough in him to have taken her into his house (a liaison out of the house seeming, in the eyes of the world, a venial error, which becomes serious directly it approaches nearer to the condition of marriage) ; but for the great poet, the Geheimrath, actually to complete such an enormity as to crown his connection with Christiane by a legal sanction, *this* was indeed more than society could tolerate.

I have already expressed my opinion of this unfortunate connexion, a *mésalliance* in every sense ; but I must emphatically declare my belief that the redeeming point in it is precisely that which has created the scandal. Better far had there been no connexion at all ; but if it was to be, the nearer it approached a real marriage, and the farther it was removed from a fugitive indulgence, the more moral and healthy it became. The fact of the *mésalliance* was not to be got over. Had he married her at first, this would always have existed. But many other and darker influences would have been averted. There would have been no such 'skeleton in the closet of his life' as, unfortunately, we know to have existed. Let us for a moment look into that closet.

Since we last caught a glimpse of Christiane Vulpius, some fifteen years have elapsed, in the course of which an unhappy change has taken place. She was then a bright, lively, pleasure-loving girl. Years and self-indulgence have now made havoc with her charms; The evil tendency, which youth and animal spirits kept within excess, has asserted itself with a distinctness which her birth and circumstances may explain, if not excuse, but which can only be contemplated in sadness. Her father, we know, ruined himself by intemperance ; her brother impaired fine talents by similar excess ; and Christiane, who inherited the fatal disposition, was not saved from it by the checks which refined society imposes, for in Weimar she was shut out from society by her relation to Goethe. Elsewhere, as we learn from her letters to Meyer, she was not quite excluded from female society. Professor Wolff and Kapellmeister Reichardt present her to their daughters ; and she dances at public balls. But in Weimar this was impossible. There she lived secluded, shunned ; and had to devote herself wholly to her domestic duties, which for one so lively and so eager for society must have had a depressing influence. Fond of gaiety, and especially of dancing, she was often seen at the students' balls at Jena ; and she accustomed herself to an indulgence in wine, which rapidly destroyed her beauty, and which was sometimes the cause of serious domestic troubles. I would fain have passed over this episode in silence ; but it is too generally known to be ignored ; and it suggests a tragedy in Goethe's life little suspected by those who saw how calmly he bore himself in public. The mere mention of such a fact at once suggests the conflict of feelings hidden from public gaze ; the struggle of indignation with pity, of resolution with weakness. I have discovered but one printed indication of this domestic grief, and that is in a letter from Schiller to Körner, dated 21st October, 1800. ' On the whole he produces very little now, rich as he still is in invention and execution. His spirit is not sufficiently at ease ; his wretched domestic circumstances, which he is too weak to alter, make him so unhappy '.

Too weak to alter ! Yes, there lies the tragedy, and there the explanation. Tender, and always shrinking from inflicting pain, he had not the sternness necessary to put an end to such a condition. He suffered so much because he could not inflict suffering. To the bystander such endurance seems inexplicable ; for the bystander knows not how the insidious first steps are passed over, and how endurance strengthens with repeated trials ; he knows not the hopes of a change which check violent resolutions, nor how affection prompts and cherishes such hopes against all evidence.

The bystander sees certain broad facts, which are inexplicable to him only because he does not see the many subtle links which bind those facts together ; he does not see the mind of the sufferer struggling against a growing evil, and finally resigning itself, and trying to put a calm face on the matter. It is easy for us to say, Why did not Goethe part from her at once ? But parting was not easy. She was the mother of his child ; she had been the mistress of his heart, and still was dear to him. To part from her would not have arrested the fatal tendency ; it would only have accelerated it. He was too weak to alter his position. He was strong enough to bear it. Schiller divined this by his own moral instincts. 'I wish', he writes in a recently discovered letter, 'that I could justify Goethe in respect to his domestic relations as I can confidently in all points respecting literature and social life. But unfortunately, by some false notions of domestic happiness, and an unlucky aversion to marriage, he has entered upon an engagement which weighs upon him in his domestic circle, and makes him unhappy, yet to shake off which, I am sorry to say, he is too weak and soft-hearted. This is the only shortcoming in him ; but even this is closely connected with a very noble part of his character, and he hurts no one but himself'.

And thus the years rolled on. Her many good qualities absolved her few bad qualities. He was sincerely attached to her, and she was devoted to him ; and now, in his fifty-eighth year, when the troubles following the battle of Jena made him 'feel the necessity of drawing all friends closer', who, among those friends, deserved a nearer place than Christiane ? He resolved on marrying her.

It is not known whether this thought of marriage had for some time previous been in contemplation, and was now put in execution when Weimar was too agitated to trouble itself with his doings ; or whether the desire of legitimizing his son in these troublous days suggested the idea. Riemer thinks the motive was gratitude for her courageous and prudent conduct during the troubles ; but I do not think that explanation acceptable, the more so as, according to her own statement, marriage was proposed in the early years of their acquaintance. In the absence of positive testimony, I am disposed to rely on psychological evidence ; and, assuming that the idea of marriage *had* been previously entertained, the delay in execution is explicable when we are made aware of one peculiarity in his nature, namely, a singular hesitation in adopting any decisive course of action—singular, in a man so resolute and imperious when once his decision had been made. This is the weakness of imaginative men. However strong the volition, when once it is set going, there is in men of active intellects, and especially in men of imaginative, apprehensive intellects, a fluctuation of motives keeping the volition in abeyance, which practically amounts to weakness ; and is only distinguished from weakness by the strength of the volition when let loose. Goethe, who was aware of this peculiarity, used to attribute it to his never having been placed in circumstances which required prompt resolutions, and to his not having educated his will ; but I believe the cause lay much deeper, lying in the nature of psychological actions, not in the accidents of education.

But be the cause of the delay this or any other, it is certain that on the 19th of October, *i.e.* five days after the battle of Jena, and *not*, as writers constantly report, 'during the cannonade', he was united to Christiane, in the presence of his son, and of his secretary, Reimer.

The scandal which this act of justice excited was immense, as may readily be guessed by those who know the world. His friends, however, loudly applauded his emergence from a false position. From that time forward, no one who did not treat her with proper respect could hope to be well received by him. She bore her new-made honours unobtrusively, and with a quiet good sense, which managed to secure the hearty goodwill of most of those who knew her.

CHAPTER III

BETTINA AND NAPOLEON

I T is very characteristic that during the terror and the pillage of Weimar, Goethe's greatest anxiety on his own account was lest his scientific manuscripts should be destroyed. Wine, plate, furniture, could be replaced ; but to lose his manuscripts was to lose what was irreparable. Herder's posthumous manuscripts *were* destroyed ; Meyer lost everything, even his sketches ; but Goethe lost nothing, except wine and money*.

The Duke, commanded by Prussia to submit to Napoleon, laid

---

* It is at once ludicrous and sad to mention that even *this* has been the subject of malevolent sneers against him. His antagonists cannot forgive him the good fortune which saved *his* house from pillage, when the houses of others were ransacked. They seem to think it a mysterious result of his selfish calculations !

down his arms and returned to Weimar, there to be received with the enthusiastic love of his people, as some compensation for the indignities he had endured. Peace was restored. Weimar breathed again. Goethe availed himself of the quiet to print his *Farbenlehre* and *Faust*, that they might be rescued from any future peril. He also began to meditate once more an epic on William Tell; but the death of the Duchess Amalia on the 10th April drove the subject from his mind.

On the 23rd of April Bettina came to Weimar. We must pause awhile to consider this strange figure, who fills a larger space in the literary history of the nineteenth century than any other German woman. Everyone knows 'the Child' Bettina Brentano, —daughter of the Maximiliane Brentano with whom Goethe flirted at Frankfurt in the *Werther* days—wife of Achim von Arnim, the fantastic Romanticist—the worshipper of Goethe and Beethoven— for some time the privileged favourite of the King of Prussia—and writer of that wild, but unveracious book, *Goethe's Correspondence with a Child*. She is one of those phantasts to whom everything seems permitted. More elf than woman, yet with flashes of genius which light up in splendour whole chapters of nonsense, she defies criticism, and puts every verdict at fault. If you are grave with her, people shrug their shoulders, and saying 'she is a Brentano', consider all settled. 'At the point where the folly of others ceases the folly of the Brentanos begins', runs the proverb in Germany.

I do not wish to be graver with Bettina than the occasion demands; but while granting fantasy its widest licence, while grateful to her for the many picturesque anecdotes she has pre-served from the conversation of Goethe's mother, I must consider the history of her relation to Goethe seriously, because out of it has arisen a charge against his memory which is very false and injurious. Many unsuspecting readers of her book, whatever they may think of the passionate expressions of her love for Goethe, whatever they may think of her demeanour towards him, on first coming into his presence, feel greatly hurt at his coldness; while others are still more indignant with him for keeping alive this mad passion, feeding it with poems and compliments, and doing this out of a selfish calculation, in order that *he might gather from her letters materials for his poems!* In both these views there is complete misconception of the actual case. True it is that the *Correspondence* furnishes ample evidence for both opinions; and against that evidence there is but one fact to

Bettina Brentano

be opposed, but the fact is decisive : the *Correspondence* is a
romance.

A harsher phrase would be applied were the offender a man, or
not a Brentano, for the romance is put forward as biographical
fact, not as fiction playing around and among fact.   How much
is true, how much exaggeration, and how much pure invention,
I am in no position to explain.   But Riemer, the old and trusted
friend of Goethe, living in the house with him at the time of
Bettina's arrival, has shown the *Correspondence* to be a 'romance
which has only borrowed from reality the time, place, and circumstances'; and from other sources I have learned enough to see
both Goethe's conduct and her own in quite a different light from
that presented in her work.

A young, ardent, elfin creature worships the great poet at a
distance, writes to tell him so, is attentive to his mother, who
gladly hears praises of her son, and is glad to talk of him.   He
is struck with her extraordinary mind, is grateful to her for the
attentions to his mother, and writes as kindly as he can without
compromising himself.   She comes to Weimar.   She falls into
his arms, and, according to her not very credible account, goes to
sleep in his lap on their first interview ; and is ostentatious of her
adoration and her jealousy ever afterwards.   If true, the position
was very embarrassing for Goethe : a man aged fifty-eight worshipped by a girl who, though a woman in years, looked like a
child, and worshipped with the extravagance, partly mad, and
partly wilful, of a Brentano—*what* could he do?   He could take
a base advantage of her passion ; he could sternly repress it ; or
he could smile at it, and pat her head as one pats a whimsical,
amusing child.   These three courses were open to him, and only
these.   He adopted the last, until she forced him to adopt the
second ; forced him by the very impetuosity of her adoration.   At
first the child's coquettish, capricious ways amused him ; her bright-
glancing intellect interested him ; but when her demonstrations
became obtrusive and fatiguing, she had to be 'called to order' so
often, that at last his patience was fairly worn out.   The con-
tinuation of such a relation was obviously impossible.   She gave
herself the licence of a child, and would not be treated as a child.
She fatigued him.

Riemer relates that during this very visit she complained to him
of Goethe's coldness.   This coldness, he rightly says, was simply
patience ; a patience which held out with difficulty against such

assaults. Bettina quitted Weimar, to return in 1811, when by her own conduct she gave him a reasonable pretext for breaking off the connexion ; a pretext, I am assured, he gladly availed himself of. It was this. She went one day with Goethe's wife to the Exhibition of Art, in which Goethe took great interest ; and there her satirical remarks, especially on Meyer, offended Christiane, who spoke sharply to her. High words rose, gross insult followed. Goethe took the side of his insulted wife, and forbade Bettina the house. It was in vain that on a subsequent visit to Weimar she begged Goethe to receive her. He was resolute. He had put an end to a relation which could not be a friendship, and was only an embarrassment*.

Such being the real story, as far as I can disentangle it, we have now to examine the authenticity of the *Correspondence*, in as far as it gives support to the two charges : 1st, of Goethe's alternate coldness and tenderness ; 2nd, of his using her letters as material for his poems. That he was ever tender to her is denied by Riemer, who pertinently asks how we are to believe that the coldness, of which she complained during her visit to Weimar, grew in her absence into the lover-like warmth glowing in the sonnets addressed to her. This is not credible ; but the mystery is explained by Riemer's distinct denial that the sonnets were addressed to her. They were *sent* to her, as to other friends ; but the poems which she says were inspired by her, were in truth written for another. The proof is very simple. These sonnets were written before she came to Weimar, and had already passed through Riemer's hands, like other works, for his supervision. Riemer moreover knew to *whom* these passionate sonnets were addressed, although he did not choose to name her. I have no such cause for concealment, and declare the sonnets to have been addressed to Minna Herzlieb, of whom we shall hear more presently ; as indeed the charade on her name, which closes the series (*Herz-Lieb*), plainly indicates. Not only has Bettina appropriated the sonnets which were composed at Jena while Riemer was with Goethe, and inspired by one living at Jena, but she has also appropriated poems known by Riemer to have been written in 1813–19, she then being the wife of Achim von Arnim, and having since 1811 been resolutely excluded from Goethe's house.

---

* I give this story as it was told me, by an authority quite unexceptionable ; nevertheless, in all such narratives there is generally some inaccuracy, even when relating to contemporary events, and the details above given may not be absolutely precise, although the net result certainly is there expressed.

To shut your door against a woman, and yet write love-verses to
her; to respond so coldly to her demonstrations that she complains of it, and yet pour forth sonnets throbbing with passion, is
a course of conduct certainly not credible on evidence such as the
Correspondence with a Child. Hence we are the less surprised
to find Riemer declaring that some of her letters are 'little more
than meta-and-paraphrases of Goethe's poems, *in which both
rhythm and rhyme are still traceable'.* So that instead of Goethe
turning her letters into poems, Riemer accuses her of turning
Goethe's poems into her letters. An accusation so public and so
explicit—an accusation which ruined the whole authenticity of the
Correspondence—should at once have been answered. The production of the originals with their post marks might have silenced
accusers. But the accusation has been fourteen years before the
world, and no answer attempted.

Although the main facts had already been published, a perfect
uproar followed the first appearance of this chapter in Germany.
Some ardent friend of Bettina's opened fire upon me in a pamphlet *,
which called forth several replies in newspapers and journals †;
and I believe there are few Germans who now hesitate to acknowledge that the whole correspondence has been so tampered with
as to have become, from first to last, a romance. For the sake
of any still unconvinced partizans in England, a few evidences of
the manipulation which the correspondence has undergone may
not be without interest.

In the letter bearing date 1st March, 1807, we read of the King
of Westphalia's Court, when, unless History be a liar, the kingdom of Westphalia was not even in existence. Goethe's mother,
in another letter, speaks of her delight at Napoleon's appearance,
—four months before she is known to have set eyes upon him.
The letters of Goethe, from November to September, all imply
that he was at Weimar; nay, he invites her to Weimar on the
16th July; she arrives there at the end of the month; visits him,
and on the 16th August he writes to her from thence. Düntzer
truly says, that these letters *must* be spurious, since Goethe left
for Karlsbad on the 25th May, and did not return till September.
Not only does Bettina visit Goethe at Weimar at a time when he
is known to have been in Bohemia, but she actually receives letters
from his mother dated the 21st September and 7th October, 1808,

---

* *An G. H. Lewes: Eine Epistel von Heinrich Siegfried.* Berlin, 1858.
† See in particular the article by DUENTZER: *Allgemeine Zeitung,* 20 April, 1858.

although the old lady died on the 13th September. One may over-look Bettina's intimating that she was only thirteen, when the parish register proves her to have been two-and-twenty; but it is impossible to place the slightest reliance on the veracity of a book which exhibits flagrant and careless disregard of facts; and if I have been somewhat merciless in the exposure of this fabrication, it is because it has greatly helped to disseminate very false views respecting a very noble nature.

In conclusion, it is but necessary to add that, Bettina's work thus deprived of its authenticity, all those hypotheses which have been built on it respecting Goethe's conduct, fall to the ground. Indeed, when one comes to think of it, the hypothesis of his using her letters as poetic materials does seem the wildest of all figments; for not only was he prodigal in invention and inexhaustible in material, but he was especially remarkable for always expressing his own feelings, his own experience, not the feelings and experience of others.

We part here from Bettina; another and very different figure enters on the scene : Napoleon at the Congress of Erfurt. It was in September 1808 that the meeting of the Emperors of France and Russia, with all the minor potentates forming the *cortège*, took place at the little town of Erfurt, a few miles from Weimar. It was a wonderful sight. The theatre was opened, with Talma and the Parisian troupe, performing the finest tragedies of France before a parterre of Kings. 'Exactly in front of the pit sat the two Emperors, in arm-chairs, in familiar conversation; a little in their rear, the Kings; and then the reigning Princes and hereditary Princes. Nothing was seen in the whole pit but uniforms, stars, and orders. The lower boxes were filled with staff officers and the most distinguished persons of the imperial bureaux; the upper front with Princesses; and at their sides foreign ladies. A strong guard of grenadiers of the imperial guard was posted at the entrance. On the arrival of either Emperor the drum beat thrice; on that of any King, twice. On one occasion the sentinel, deceived by the outside of the King of Würtemburg's carriage, ordered the triple salute to be given, on which the officer in command cried out, in an angry tone, *Taisez-vous—ce n'est qu'un roi !'*[*]

Napoleon, on this occasion, gave a friendly reception to the Duke of Weimar, and to Goethe and Wieland, with whom he talked

[*] Kanzler von Müller in Mrs. AUSTIN's *Germany from 1760 to 1814*, p. 307.

Friedrich Wilhelm Riemer

about literature and history.   Goethe went to Erfurt on the 29th of
September, and that evening saw *Andromaque* performed.   On the
30th, there was a grand dinner given by the Duke, and in the evening *Britannicus* was performed.   In the *Moniteur* of the 8th of
October he is mentioned among the illustrious guests : ' Il paraît
apprécier parfaitement nos acteurs, et admirer surtout les chefs-
d'œuvre qu'ils représentent '.   On the 2nd of October he was summoned to an audience with the Emperor, and found him at breakfast, Talleyrand and Daru standing by his side ; Berthier and
Savary behind.   Napoleon, after a fixed look, exclaimed : ' *Vous
êtes un homme*'; a phrase which produced a profound impression on
the flattered poet.   ' How old are you?' asked the Emperor.   'Sixty'.
' You are very well preserved '.   After a pause—' You have written
tragedies ? '   Here Daru interposed, and spoke with warmth of
Goethe's works, adding that he had translated Voltaire's *Mahomet*.
' It is not a good piece ', said Napoleon, and commenced a critique
on *Mahomet*, especially on the unworthy portrait given of that conqueror of a world.   He then turned the conversation to *Werther*,
which he had read seven times, and which accompanied him to
Egypt.   'After various remarks, all very just', says Goethe, 'he
pointed out a passage and asked me why I had written so : it was
contrary to nature.   This opinion he developed with great clearness.
I listened calmly, and smilingly replied that I did not know whether
the objection had ever been made before, but that I found it perfectly just.   The passage was unnatural ; but perhaps the poet
might be pardoned for the artifice which enabled him to reach his
end in an easier, simpler way.   The Emperor seemed satisfied and
returned to the drama, and criticized it like a man who has studied
the tragic stage with the attention of a criminal judge, and who
was keenly alive to the fault of the French in departing from Nature.
He disapproved of all pieces in which fate played a part.   " Ces
pièces appartiennent à une époque obscure.   Au reste, que veulent-
ils dire avec leur fatalité ?   La politique est la fatalité " '.
   The interview lasted nearly an hour.   Napoleon inquired after
his children and family ; was very gracious ; and wound up almost
every sentence with *qu'en dit M. Goet ?*   As Goethe left the room,
Napoleon repeated to Berthier and Caru, *Voilà un homme !*
   A few days after, Napoleon was in Weimar, and great festivities
were set on foot to honour him ; among them a *chasse* on the battlefield of Jena ; a grand ball at Court ; and *La Mort de César* at the
theatre, with Talma as Brutus.   During the ball, Napoleon talked

at great length with Goethe and Wieland. Speaking of ancient and modern literature, Napoleon touched on Shakespeare, whom he was too French to comprehend, and said to Goethe : ' Je suis étonné qu'un grand esprit, comme vous, n'aime pas les genres tranchés '. Goethe might have replied that *les grands esprits* have almost universally been the very reverse of *tranchés* in their tastes ; but of course it was not for him to controvert the Emperor. As Johnson said on a similar occasion : ' Sir, it was not for me to bandy words with my sovereign '. After speaking magniloquently of tragedy, Napoleon told him he ought to write a *Death of Cæsar*, but in a grander style than the tragedy of Voltaire. ' Ce travail pourrait devenir la principale tâche de votre vie. ' Dans cette tragédie il faudrait montrer au monde comment César aurait pu faire le bonheur de l'humanité si on lui avait laissé le temps d'exécuter ses vastes plans '. One cannot help thinking of Goethe's early scheme to write *Julius Cæsar*, and how entirely opposed it would have been to the *genre tranché* so admired by Napoleon.

A proposition more acceptable than that of writing tragedies at his age, was that of accompanying Napoleon to Paris. ' Venez à Paris, je l'exige de vous ; là vous trouverez un cercle plus vaste pour votre esprit d'observation ; là vous trouverez des matières immenses pour vos créations poétiques '. He had never seen a great capital like Paris or London, and there was something very tempting in this invitation. F. von Müller says he often spoke with him on the probable expense of the journey, and of the Parisian usages ; but the inconvenience of so long a journey (in those days), and his own advanced age, seem to have checked his desire.

On the 14th of October he and Wieland received the cross of the Legion of Honour—then an honour ; and the two Emperors quitted Erfurt. Goethe preserved complete silence on all that had passed between him and Napoleon. Indeed when he recorded the interviews, many years later, in the annals of his life, he did so in the most skeleton-like manner. To the oft-repeated question, What was the passage in *Werther* indicated by Napoleon as contrary to Nature, he always returned a playful answer, referring the questioner to the book, on which to exercise his own ingenuity in discovery. He would not even tell Eckermann. He was fond, in this later period of his life, of playing hide-and-seek with readers, and enjoyed their efforts to unravel mysteries. The present mystery has been cleared up by the Chancellor von Müller, to whom we owe most of the details respecting this Napoleon interview.

The objection raised by Napoleon was none other than the objection raised by Herder when *Werther* was revised by him in 1782,—viz. that Werther's melancholy which leads him to suicide, instead of proceeding solely from frustrated love, is complicated by his frustrated ambition.   Herder thought this a fault in art, Napoleon thought it contrary to Nature; and strange to say, Goethe agreed with both, and altered his work in obedience to Herder's criticism, though he forgot all about it when Napoleon once more brought the objection forward.   Against Herder, Napoleon, and Goethe himself, it is enough to oppose the simple fact: Werther (*i.e.* Jerusalem) *was* suffering from frustrated ambition, as well as from frustrated love; and what Goethe found him, that he made him.   We have only to turn to Kestner's letter, describing Jerusalem and his unhappy story, to see that Goethe, in *Werther*, followed with the utmost fidelity the narrative which was given him.   This anec- dote affords a piquant commentary on the value of criticism: three men so illustrious as Napoleon, Goethe, and Herder, pointing to a particular treatment of a subject as contrary to Art and contrary to Nature; the treatment being all the while strictly in accordance with Nature.

That he was extremely flattered by the attentions of Napoleon has been the occasion of a loud outcry from those who, having never been subjected to any flattery of this nature, find it very con- temptible.   But the attentions of a Napoleon were enough to soften in their flattery even the sternness of a republican; and Goethe, no republican, was all his life very susceptible to the gratification which a Frankfurt citizen must feel in receiving the attention of crowned heads.   There is infinite insincerity uttered on this subject; and generally the outcry is loudest from men who would themselves be most dazzled by Court favour of any kind.   To hear them talk of Goethe's servility and worship of rank, one might fancy that they stood on a moral elevation, looking down upon him with a superior pity which in some sort compensated their inferiority of intellect. There is one anecdote which they are very fond of quoting, and which I will therefore give, that we may calmly consider what is its real significance.   Beethoven, writing to Bettina in 1812, when he made Goethe's acquaintance in Töplitz, says: 'Kings and princes can to be sure make professors, privy councillors, etc., and confer titles and orders, but they cannot make great men—minds which rise above the common herd—these they must not pretend to make, and therefore must these be held in honour.   When two men, such as Goethe and I, come together, even the high and mighty perceive what is to be considered great in men like us. Yesterday, on our way home, we met the whole imperial Family. We saw them coming from a distance, and Goethe separated from me to stand aside : say what I would, I could not make him advance another step. *I pressed my hat down upon my head, buttoned up my great coat, and walked with folded arms through the thickest of the throng.* Princes and pages formed a line, the Archduke Rudolph took off his hat, and the Empress made the first salutation. Those gentry know me. I saw to my real amusement the procession file past Goethe. He stood aside with his hat off, bending lowly. I rallied him smartly for it ; I gave him no quarter '*.

This anecdote is usually quoted as evidence of Beethoven's independence and Goethe's servility. A very little consideration will make us aware that Beethoven was ostentatiously rude in the assertion of his independence, and that Goethe was simply acting on the dictates of common courtesy, in standing aside and taking off his hat, as all Germans do when Royalty passes them. It is as much a matter of courtesy to stand still, and take off the hat, when a Royal personage passes in carriage or on foot, as it is to take off the hat when an acquaintance passes. Beethoven might choose to ignore all such courtesies ; indeed his somewhat eccentric nature would not move in conventional orbits ; and his disregard of such courtesies might be pardoned as the caprices of an eccentric nature ; but Goethe was a man of the world, a man of courtesies, and a minister ; to have folded his arms, and pressed down his hat upon his head, would have been a rudeness at variance with his nature, his education, his position, and his sense of propriety.

It is possible, nay probable, that the very education Goethe had received may have given to his salutation a more elaborate air than was noticeable in other bystanders. In bowing, he may have bowed very low, with a certain formality of respect ; for I have no wish to deny that he did lay stress on conventional distinctions. Not only was he far from republican sternness, but he placed more value on his star and title of Excellency than his thorough-going partizans are willing to admit. If that be a weakness, let him be credited with it ; but if he were as vain of such puerilities as an English Duke is of the Garter, I do not see any cause for serious reproach in it. So few poets have been Excellencies, so few have worn stars

* Schindler's *Life of Beethoven*, edited by Moscheles, vol. 1, pp. 133-5.

on their breasts, that we have no means of judging whether
Goethe's vanity was greater or less than we have a right to expect.
Meanwhile it does seem to me that sneers at his title, and epigrams
on his stars, come with a very bad grace from a nation which is
laughed at for nothing more frequently than for its inordinate love
of titles.   Nor are Englishmen so remarkable for their indifference
to rank, as to make them the fittest censors of this weakness in a
Goethe.

CHAPTER IV

'ELECTIVE AFFINITIES'

AMONG the Jena friends whom Goethe saw with constant
pleasure was Frommann, the bookseller, in whose family there
was an adopted child, by name Minna Herzlieb, strangely interesting to us as the original of Ottilie in the *Wahlverwandtschaften*.
As a child she had been a great pet of Goethe's ; growing into
womanhood, she exercised a fascination over him which his reason
in vain resisted.   The disparity of years was great : but how
frequently are young girls found bestowing the bloom of their
affections on men old enough to be their fathers ! and how
frequently are men at an advanced age found trembling with the
passion of youth !   In the Sonnets addressed to her, and in the
novel of *Elective Affinities*, may be read the fervour of his passion,
and the strength with which he resisted it.   Speaking of this novel,
he says : 'No one can fail to recognize in it a deep passionate wound
which shrinks from being closed by healing, a heart which dreads
to be cured. . . . In it, as in a burial-urn, I have deposited with
deep emotion many a sad experience.   The 3rd of October 1809
(when the publication was completed) set me free from the work ;
but the feelings it embodies can never quite depart from me '.   If
we knew as much of the circumstances out of which grew the
Elective Affinities as we do of those out of which grew *Werther*,
we should find his experience as clearly embodied in this novel as
it is in *Werther;* but conjecture in such cases being perilous, I will
not venture beyond the facts which have been placed at my disposal ; and may only add therefore that the growing attachment was
seen by all with pain and dismay.   At length it was resolved to send
Minna to school*, and this absolute separation saved them both.

* In the novel, Ottilie also is sent back to school.

It is very curious to read *Die Wahlverwandtschaften* by this light ; to see not only the sources of its inspiration, but the way in which Goethe dramatizes the two halves of his own character. Eduard and Charlotte loved each other in youth. Circumstances separated them ; and each made a *mariage de convenance* from which, after a time, they were released by death. The widower and the widow, now free to choose, naturally determine on fulfilling the dream of their youth. They marry. At the opening of the story we see them placidly happy. Although a few quiet touches make us aware of a certain disparity between their natures, not enough to create unhappiness, but enough to prevent perfect sympathy, the keenest eye would detect no signs which threatened the enduring stability of their happiness. Eduard has a friend, almost a brother, always called 'The Captain', whom he invites to come and live with them. Charlotte strongly opposes this visit at first, having a dim presentiment of evil ; but she yields, the more so as she desires that her adopted daughter, Ottilie, should now be taken from school, and come to live with them.

Thus are the four actors in the drama brought together on the stage ; and no sooner are they brought together, than the natural *elective affinities* of their natures come into play. Charlotte and the Captain are drawn together ; Eduard and Ottilie are drawn together. This is shown to be as inevitable as the chemical combinations which give the novel its title. A real episode in the tragedy of life is before us ; felt to be inevitable ; felt to be terrible ; felt also to present a dilemma to the moral judgment, on which two parties will pronounce two opposite opinions.

Those critics who look at human life, and consequently at Art, from the abstract point of view, who, disregarding fact and necessity, treat human nature as a chess-board on which any moves may be made which the player chooses, the player himself being considered an impersonal agent untroubled by rashness, incapable of overlooking what is palpable to the bystanders,—those critics, I say, will unhesitatingly pronounce the situation an immoral situation, which the poet should not have presented, and which in real life would at once have been put an end to by the idea of Duty.

Others, again, who look at life as it *is*, not as it might be ; who accept its wondrous complexity of impulses, and demand that Art should represent reality—consider this situation as terribly true, and although tragic, by no means immoral ; for the tragedy lies in

Minna Herzlieb

the collision of Passion with Duty—of Impulse with Social Law.
Suppose Charlotte and Eduard unmarried, and these 'affinities'
would have been simple impulses to marriage. But the fact of
marriage stands as a barrier to the impulses : the collision is
inevitable.

The divergence of opinion, here indicated, must necessarily
exist among the two great classes of readers. Accordingly in
Germany and in England the novel is alternately pronounced
immoral and profoundly moral. I do not think it is either the one
or the other. When critics rail at it, and declare it saps the whole
foundation of marriage, and when critics enthusiastically declare it
is profoundly moral because it sets the sacredness of marriage in
so clear a light, I see that both have drawn certain general
conclusions from an individual case ; but I do not see that they
have done more than put *their* interpretations on what the author
had no intention of being interpreted at all. Every work of Art
has its moral, says Hegel ; but the *moral depends on him that
draws it.* Both the conclusion against marriage, and the conclusion
in favour of. marriage, may therefore be drawn from this novel ;
and yet neither conclusion be correct — except as the private
interpretation of the reader. Goethe was an Artist, not an Advocate ; he painted a true picture, and because he painted it truly, he
necessarily presented it in a form which would permit men to draw
from it those opposite conclusions which might be drawn from
the reality itself. Suppose the story actually to have passed before
our eyes, the judgments passed on it, even among those thoroughly
acquainted with all the facts, would have been diametrically
opposite. It is not difficult to write a story carrying the moral
legible in every page ; and if the writer's object be primarily that
of illustrating a plain moral, he need not trouble himself about
truth of character. And for this reason : he employs character as
a *means* to an end, he does not make the delineation of character
his end ; his purpose is didactic, not artistic. Quite otherwise is
the artist's purpose and practice : for him human life is the end and
aim ; for him the primary object is character, which is, as all know,
of a mingled woof, good and evil, virtue and weakness, truth and
falsehood, woven inextricably together.

Those who object to such pictures, and think that truth is no
warrant, may reasonably consider Goethe blameable for having
chosen the subject. But he chose it because he had experienced it.
And once grant him the subject, it is difficult to blame his treatment

of it, as regards the social problem.   He did his utmost to present
this truthfully.

There is, it is true, one scene, which, although true to nature,
profoundly true, is nevertheless felt to be objectionable on moral
and æsthetical grounds.   The artist is not justified in painting every
truth ; and if we, in this nineteenth century often carry our exclusion
of subjects to the point of prudery, that error is a virtue compared
with the demoralizing licence exhibited in French literature.   The
scene I refer to has probably roused more indignation against the
Wahlverwandtschaften than all the rest of the book.

It is a painful story.   Two of the actors represent Passion in its
absorbing, reckless, irresistible fervour, rushing onwards to the
accomplishment of its aims.   The two other actors represent with
equal force, and with touching nobleness, the idea of Duty.   Eduard
and Ottilie love rapidly, vehemently, thoughtlessly.   Not a doubt
troubles them.   Their feeling is so natural, it so completely absorbs
them, that they are like two children entering on a first affection.
But, vividly as they represent Instinct, Charlotte and the Captain
as vividly represent Reason ; their love is equally profound, but it
is the love of two rational beings, who, because they reason, reason
on the circumstances in which they are placed ; recognize society,
its arrangements and its laws ; and sacrifice their own desires to
this social necessity.   They subdue themselves ; upheld by Conscience they face suffering ; Conscience dictates to them a line of
conduct never dreamt of by the passionate Eduard, and but vaguely
apprehended by Ottilie.

Eduard no sooner knows that he is loved than he is impatient
for a divorce, which will enable him to marry Ottilie, and enable
Charlotte to marry the Captain.   Unfortunately Charlotte, who has
hitherto had no children by Eduard, feels that she is about to be a
mother.   This complicates a position which before was comparatively simple.   Childless, she might readily have consented to a
divorce ; she cannot now.   Every argument fails to persuade
Eduard to relinquish the one purpose of his life ; and he only consents to test by absence the durability of his passion.

He joins the army, distinguishes himself in the field, and returns
with desires as imperious as ever.   Meanwhile the Captain has
also absented himself.   Charlotte bears her fate, meekly, nobly.
Ottilie in silence cherishes her love for Eduard, and devotes herself with intense affection to Charlotte's child.   This child, in accordance with a popular superstition (which, by the way, physiology

emphatically discredits), resembles in a striking manner both
Ottilie and the Captain, thus physically typifying the passion felt
by Eduard for Ottilie and the passion felt by Charlotte for the
Captain.

Charlotte, who is strong enough to bear her fate, never relinquishes the hope that Eduard will learn to accept his with like forti-
tude. But he remains immovable. Opposition only intensifies his
desire. At length the child is drowned while under Ottilie's charge.
In the depth of her affliction a light breaks in upon her soul ; and
now, for the first time, Ottilie becomes conscious of being wrong in
her desire to be Eduard's wife. With this consciousness comes a
resolution never to be his. The tragedy deepens. She wastes
away. Eduard, whose passion was his life, lingers awhile in mute
sorrow, and then is laid to rest by her side.

Such, in its leading motives, is the terrible tragic drama which
Goethe has worked out with indefatigable minuteness in *Die Wahlverwandtschaften*. The story moves slowly, as in life, through
various episodes and circumstances ; but if slow, it is always intelligible.

We need only a hint of the origin of this story to read in it how
Goethe has represented himself under the two different masks of
the impulsive Eduard and the reasonable, strong-willed Captain.
These characters are drawn from the life, drawn from himself. Considered only as characters in a novel, they are masterly creations.
Eduard—weak, passionate, and impatient—still preserves our interest even in his weakest moments. How admirable a touch is
that where, in the early uneasiness of his position, he hears of the
Captain's having criticized his flute playing, and 'at once feels himself freed from every obligation of duty' ! It is precisely those
passionate natures which leap at any excuse, no matter how frivolous, that they may give them the semblance of justification.
Charlotte and the Captain stand as representatives of Duty and
Reason, in contrast with Ottilie and Eduard, who represent Impulse
and Imagination ; in the two reasonable personages Goethe has
achieved the rare success of making reason lovable.

Rosenkrantz has noticed how well the various forms of marriage
are represented in this novel. Eduard and Charlotte each tried
mariage de convenance ; they then tried a *marriage of friendship ;*
if the former was unhappy, the latter was not sufficing : it was not
the *marriage of love.* Moreover, in the liaison of the count and
the baroness, we see marriage as it is so often found in the world—

as a mere convention conventionally respected. Hence the count is painted as a frivolous, careless man of fashion, who plays with St. Simonian theories, and thinks marriage ought to be an apprenticeship terminable every five years.

Besides such points, the critic will note admiringly how the characters present themselves in thought, speech, and act, without any description or explanation from the author. The whole representation is so objective, so simple, and the march of the story is so quiet, moving amid such familiar details, that except in the masterpieces of Miss Austen, I know not where to look for a comparison. And if English and French readers sometimes feel a little wearied by the many small details which encumber the march of the story, and irritate the curiosity which is impatient for the dénouement, no such weariness is felt by German readers, who enjoy the details, and the purpose which they are supposed to serve. A dear friend of mine, whose criticism is always worthy of attention, thinks that the long episodes which interrupt the progress of the story during the interval of Eduard's absence and return, are artistic devices for impressing the reader with a sense of the slow movement of life ; and, in truth, it is only in fiction that the dénouement usually lies close to the exposition. I give this opinion, for the reader's consideration ; but it seems to me more ingenious than just. I must confess that the stress Goethe lays on the improvements of the park, the erection of the moss hut, the restoration of the chapel, the making of new roads, etc , is out of all proportion, and somewhat tedious. Julian Schmidt calls attention to the inartistic device of dragging in pages of detached aphorisms and reflections on life under the pretence of their being extracts from Ottilie's journal. The pretence of a connexion—namely, the 'red thread'—which is to run through these extracts, and exhibit the development of her feelings, is entirely lost sight of, and instead of the feelings of an impassioned girl, we have the thoughts of an old man. The original intention was simply to write a *novelle*, a little tale ; and for that there was abundant material. In expanding the *novelle* into a novel, he has spoiled a masterpiece. Indeed, I must frankly say that, either from want of constructive instinct, or from an indolent and haughty indifference towards the public, his novels are quite unworthy of a great artist in point of *composition*. He seems to have regarded them as vehicles for the expression of certain views, rather than as organic wholes.

The style of *Die Wahlverwandtschaften* is greatly admired by Germans ; Rosenkrantz pronounces it classical. We must remember, however, that Germany is not rich in works written with the perfection which France and England demand ; we must remember, moreover, that most German opinions on Goethe are to be received with the same caution as English opinions about Shakespeare ; and bearing these two facts in mind, we shall lend a more willing ear to those native critics who do not regard the style of the *Wahlverwandtschaften* as classical. It is a delicate point for a foreigner to venture on an opinion in such a case ; and if I wrote for Germans, I should simply quote the current verdict ; but writing for Englishmen who read German, there may be less temerity in alluding to the signs of age which the style of this novel betrays. Englishmen comparing this prose with the prose of his earlier works, or with the standard of admirable prose—and so great a writer must only be measured by the highest standards—will find it often weak, cold, mechanical in the construction of its sentences, and somewhat lifeless in the abstractness of its diction. There is also a fatiguing recurrence of certain set forms of phrase. Passages of great beauty there are, touches of poetry no reader will overlook. The last chapter is a poem. Its pathos is so simple that one needs to be in robust mood to read it. The page also where Charlotte and the Captain are on the lake together under the faint light of appearing stars, is a poem the music of which approaches that of verse.

CHAPTER V

POLITICS AND RELIGION

MINNA HERZLIEB, to whom we owe the *Wahlverwandtschaften*, lived to be a happy wife. Goethe long carried the arrow in his heart. In 1810, he once more gave poetic expression to his experience in an erotic poem, setting forth the conflict of Love and Duty. The nature of this poem, however, prevented its publication, and it still exists only as a manuscript. In this year also he commenced his *Autobiography*, the first part of which appeared in 1811. The public, anxious for autobiography, received it with a disappointment which is perfectly intelligible ; charming as the book is in every other respect, it is tantalizing to a reader curious to see the great poet in his youth.

Before writing this *Autobiography* he had to outlive the sorrow for his mother's death. She died on the 13th of September, 1808, in her 78th year. To the last, her love for her son, and his love for her, had been the glory and sustainment of her happy old age. He had wished her to come and live with him at Weimar; but the circle of old Frankfurt friends, and the influence of old habits, kept her in her native city, where she was venerated by all.

A volume would be required to record with anything like fulness the details of the remaining years. There is no deficiency of material: in his letters, and the letters of friends and acquaintances, will be found an ample gleaning; but unhappily the materials are abundant precisely at the point where the interest of the story begins to fade. From sixty to eighty-two is a long period; but it is not a period in which persons and events influence a man; his character, already developed, can receive no new direction. At this period biography is at an end, and necrology begins. For Germans, the details to which I allude have interest; but the English reader would receive with mediocre gratitude a circumstantial narrative of all Goethe did and studied; all the excursions he made; every cold and toothache which afflicted him; every person he conversed with *.

I may mention, however, his acquaintance with Beethoven, on account of the undying interest attached to the two names. They were together for a few days at Töplitz, with the most profound admiration for each other's genius. The biographer of Beethoven adds: ' But though Beethoven has praised Goethe's patience with him (on account of his deafness), still it is a fact, that the great poet, and minister, too soon forgot the great composer; and when, in 1823, he had it in his power to render him an essential service with little trouble to himself, he did not even deign to reply to a very humble epistle from our master'. This is the way accusations are made; this is the kind of evidence on which they are believed. The only *facts* here established are, that Beethoven wrote to Goethe, and that Goethe did not reply. Beethoven's letter requested Goethe to recommend the Grand Duke to subscribe to his Mass. It was doubtless very mortifying not to receive a reply; such things always are mortifying, and offended self-love is apt to suggest bad motives for the offence. But a bystander, knowing how many motives may

---

* The period which is included in this Seventh Book occupies no less than 563 pages of Viehoff's Biography; yet, while I have added a great many details to those collected by Viehoff, I do not think any of interest have been omitted.

Life mask of Goethe

actuate the conduct, and unwilling to suppose a bad motive for which there is no evidence, will at once see that the inferences of Goethe's 'not deigning to reply', and of having 'forgotten the great composer', are by no means warranted by the facts.   We know that Goethe was naturally of an active benevolence ; we know that he was constantly recommending to the Grand Duke some object of charitable assistance ; we know that he profoundly admired Beethoven, and had no cause to be offended with him ; and, knowing this, we must accept any interpretation of the fact of silence in preference to that which the angry Beethoven, and his biographer, have inferred.

To pursue our narrative : The year 1813, which began the War of Independence, was to Goethe a year of troubles.   It began with an affliction—the death of his old friend Wieland ; which shook him more than those who knew him best were prepared for. Herder ; Schiller ; the Duchess Amalia ; his mother ; and now Wieland,—one by one had fallen away, and left him lonely, advancing in years.

Nor was this the only source of unhappiness.   Political troubles came to disturb his plans.   Germany was rising against the tyranny of Napoleon ; rising, as Goethe thought, in vain.   'You will not shake off your chains', he said to Körner, 'the man is too powerful ; you will only press them deeper into your flesh'.   His doubts were shared by many ; but happily the nation shared them not.   While patriots were rousing the wrath of the nation into the resistance of despair, he tried to 'escape from the present, because it is impossible to live in such circumstances and not go mad' ; he took refuge, as he always did, in Art.   He wrote the ballads *Der Todtentanz*, *Der getreue Eckart*, and *die wandelnde Glocke* ; wrote the essay *Shakespeare und kein Ende*, and finished the third volume of his *Autobiography*.   He buried himself in the study of Chinese history.   Nay, on the very day of the battle of Leipsic, he wrote the epilogue to the tragedy of *Essex*, for the favourite actress, Madame Wolf *.

Patriotic writers are unsparing in sarcasms on a man who could thus seek refuge in Poetry from the bewildering troubles of politics, and they find no other explanation than that he was an Egoist.   Other patriotic writers, among them some of ultra-republicanism, such as Karl Grün, have eloquently defended him.   I do

---

* Curiously enough, on that very day of Napoleon's first great defeat, his medallion, which was hung on the wall of Goethe's study, fell from its nail on to the ground.

not think it necessary to add arguments to those already suggested respecting his relations to politics. Those who are impatient with him for being what he was, and not what they are, will listen to no arguments. It is needless to point out how, at sixty-four, he was not likely to become a politician, having up to that age sedulously avoided politics. It is needless to show that he was not in a position which called upon him to *do* anything. The grievance seems to be that he wrote no war songs, issued no manifestos, but strove to keep himself as much as possible out of the hearing of contemporary history. If this was a crime, the motive was not criminal. Judge the act as you will, but do not misjudge the motive. To attribute such an act to cowardice, or fear of compromising himself, is unwarrantable, in the face of all the evidence we have of his character.

When the mighty Napoleon threatened the Grand Duke, we have seen how Goethe was roused. That was an individual injustice, which he could clearly understand, and was prepared to combat. For the Duke he would turn ballad-singer ; for the Nation he had no voice; and why? Because there was no Nation. He saw clearly then, what is now seen clearly, that Germany had no existence as a Nation : it was a geographical fiction ; and such it remains in our day. And he failed to see what is now clearly seen, that the German Peoples were, for the time, united by national enthusiasm, united by a common feeling of hatred against France ; failing to see this, he thought that a collection of disunited Germans was certain to be destroyed in a struggle with Napoleon. He was wrong ; the event has proved his error ; but his error of opinion must not be made an accusation against his sincerity. When Luden the historian, whose testimony is the weightier because it is that of a patriot, had that interview with him, after the battle of Leipsic, which he has recorded with so much feeling*, the impression left was, he says, ' that I was deeply convinced they are in grievous error who blame Goethe for a want of love of country, a want of German feeling, a want of faith in the German people, or of sympathy with its honour and shame, its fortune or misery. His silence about great events was simply a painful resignation to which he was necessarily led by his position and his knowledge of mankind'. Luden came to him to speak of a projected journal, the *Nemesis*, which was to excite the nation's hatred of France. Goethe dissuaded him. 'Do not believe', he said, after a pause, 'that I am indifferent to the great

* *Luden's Rückblicke in mein Leben*, p. 113 seq.

ideas—Freedom, Fatherland, and People. No; these ideas are in us; they form a portion of our being which no one can cast off. Germany is dear to my heart. I have often felt a bitter pain at the thought that the German people, so honourable as individuals, should be so miserable as a whole. A comparison of the German people with other peoples awakens a painful feeling, which I try to escape in any way I can; and in Art and Science I have found such escapes; *for they belong to the world at large, and before them vanish all the limits of nationality.* But this consolation is after all but a poor one, and is no compensation for the proud conviction that one belongs to a great, strong, honoured, and dreaded people'. He spoke also of Germany's future, but he saw that this future was still far distant. 'For us, meanwhile, this alone remains: let every one, according to his talents, according to his tendencies and according to his position, *do his utmost to increase the culture and development of the people,* to strengthen and widen it on all sides, that the people may not lag behind other peoples, but may become competent for every great action when the day of its glories arrives'. Very wise words, however unpalatable to enthusiastic patriotism. Turning from such abstract considerations to the question of the journal, and the probability of 'awakening' the German People to Freedom, 'But *is* the people awakened?' he continued. 'Does it know what it wants and what it wills? Have you forgotten what that honest Philister in Jena said to his neighbour, as in his joy he called out, that the French were departed, and his rooms were ready for the reception of the Russians? The sleep has been too deep for a mere shaking to alter it. And is every agitation an elevation? We are not now considering the cultivated youth, but the many, the millions. And what will be won? Freedom, you say; but perhaps it would be more correct to call it a setting free— *not, however, a setting free from the yoke of foreigners, but from a foreign yoke.* True, I no longer see Frenchmen, no longer see Italians; but *in their place I see Cossacks, Baschkirs, Croats, Magyars and other Hussars'.*

He who thought thus, was not likely to be found among the enthusiasts of that day, had he been at the age of enthusiasm. But, as he said to Eckermann, who alluded to the reproaches against him for not having written war songs, 'How could I take up arms without hatred, and how could I hate without youth? If such an emergency had befallen me when twenty years old, I should certainly not have been the last; but it found me past sixty. Besides we cannot all serve our country in the same way, but each does his best according as God has endowed him. I have toiled hard enough during half a century. I can say, that in those things which Nature has appointed for my daily work, I have permitted myself no relaxation or repose, but have always striven, investigated, and done as much, and as well, as I could. If every one can say the same of himself, it will prove well with all. To write military songs, and sit in a room! That forsooth was my duty! To have written them in the bivouac when the horses at the evening's outposts are heard neighing at night, would have been well enough; that was not my way of life nor my business, but that of Theodore Körner. His war songs suit him perfectly. But to me, who am not of a warlike nature, and who have no warlike sense, war songs would have been a mask which would have fitted my face very badly. I have never affected anything in my poetry. I have never uttered anything which I have not experienced, and which has not urged me to production. I have only composed love songs when I have loved; and how could I write songs of hatred without hating?'

Connected with this political indifference, and mainly the cause of it, was his earnestness in Art; an earnestness which has been made the evidence of this most extraordinary charge against him, namely, that he 'looked on life only as an artist'. The shallow phrase has become stereotyped. Every one has heard it who has heard anything of him. It is uttered with the confidence of conviction, and is meant to convey a volume of implicit reprobation. When a man devotes himself to a special science, gives to it the greater part of his time, his thoughts, and sympathies, we marvel at his energy, and laud his passionate devotion; we do not make his earnestness a crime; we do not say of a Faraday that he 'looks at life only as a Chemist'; of an Owen 'that he looks at life only as a Zoologist'. It is understood that any great pursuit must necessarily draw away the thoughts and activities from other pursuits. Why then is Art to be excluded from the same serious privilege? Why is the artist, who is in earnest, excluded from the toleration spontaneously awarded to the Philosopher? I know but of one reason, and that is the indisposition in men to accept Art as serious. Because it ministers directly to our pleasures, Art is looked on as the child of luxury, the product of idleness; and those who cannot rise to the height of the conception which animated a Goethe and a Schiller, are apt to treat it as mere rhetoric and self-importance in men who speak of Art as the noblest form of

Culture. Indeed, those who regard Painting and Sculpture as means of supplying their dining-rooms and galleries with costly ornaments, Music as furnishing the excuse for a box at the opera, and Poetry as an agreeable pastime, may be justified in thinking lightly of painters, sculptors, musicians, and poets. But I will not suppose the reader to be one of this class ; and may therefore appeal to his truer appreciation for a verdict in favour of the claims made by Art to serious recognition, as one among the many forms of national culture. This granted, it follows that the more earnestly the artist accepts and follows his career, the more honour does he claim from us.

Now Goethe was a man of too profoundly serious a nature not to be in earnest with whatever he undertook ; he led an earnest and laborious life, when he might have led one of pleasure and luxurious idleness. 'To scorn delights and live laborious days', with no other reward than the reward of activity, the delight of development, was one of the necessities of his nature. He worked at Science with the patient labour of one who had to earn his bread ; and he worked in the face of dire discouragement, with no reward in the shape of pence or praise. In Art, which was the main region of his intellectual strivings, he naturally strove after completeness. If the Philosopher is observed drawing materials for his generalizations out of even the frivolities of the passing hour, learning in the theatre, the ball-room, or in the incoherent talk of railway passengers, to detect illustrations of the laws he is silently elaborating, we do not accuse him of looking on life only as a Philosopher, thereby implying that he is deficient in the feelings of his race ; yet something like this is done by those who make a crime of Goethe's constant endeavour to collect from life material for Art.

If when it is said 'he looked on life only as an artist', the meaning is that he, as an artist, necessarily made Art the principal occupation of his life—the phrase is a truism ; and if the meaning is that he isolated himself from the labours and pursuits of his fellow-men, to play with life, and arrange it as an agreeable drama —the phrase is a calumny. It is only through deep sympathy that a man can become a great artist ; those who play with life can only play with art. The great are serious. That Goethe was a great artist all admit. Has the life we have narrated shown him to be deficient in benevolence, in lovingness, in sympathy with others and their pursuits? Has it shown any evidence of a nature so wrapped in self-indulgence, and so coldly calculating, that life *could* become a mere playing to it? If the answer be No, then let us hear no more about Goethe's looking on life only as an artist. The vulgar may blame a devotion which they cannot understand ; do not let us imitate the vulgar. ' Le monde comprend peu un pareil stoïcisme ', says a thoughtful and sympathetic writer, ' et voit souvent une sorte de sécheresse dans l'âpreté de ces grandes âmes,— dures pour elles-mêmes et par conséquent un peu pour les autres, qui ont l'air de se consoler de tout, pourvu que l'univers reste livré à leur contemplation. Mais au fond c'est là le plus haut degré du désintéressement et le plus beau triomphe de l'âme humaine. Ce que la conscience timorée des âmes tendres et vertueuses appelle l'égoisme du génie, n'est d'ordinaire que le détachement des jouissances personnelles et l'oubli de soi pour l'idéal ' *.

While one party has assailed him for his political indifference, another, and still more ungenerous party, has assailed him for what they call his want of religion. The man who can read Goethe's works and not perceive in them a spirit deeply religious, must limit the word religion to the designation of his own doctrines ; and the man who, reading them, discovers that Goethe was not orthodox, is discovering the sun at mid-day. Orthodox he never pretended to be. His religious experiences had begun early, and his doubts began with them. There are those who regard Doubt as criminal in itself; but no human soul that has once struggled, that has once been perplexed with baffling thoughts which it has been too sincere to huddle away and stifle in precipitate conclusions dreading to face the consequences of doubt, will speak thus harshly and unworthily of it.

> There lives more faith in honest doubt,
> Believe me, than in half the creeds :
> He fought his doubts and gathered strength ;
> He would not make his judgment blind ;
> He faced the spectres of the mind,
> And laid them : thus he came at length
> To find a stronger faith his own †.

The course of his opinions, as we have seen, was often altered. At times he approached the strictness of strict sects ; at times he went great lengths in scepticism. The Fräulein von Klettenberg taught him to sympathize with the Moravians ; but Lavater's unconscious hypocrisy, and the moral degradation of the Italian

---

* **Ernest Renan** : *Essais de Morale*, p. 138. † *In Memoriam.*

Johann Heinrich Meyer

priesthood, gradually changed his respect for the Christian Churches into open and sometimes sarcastic contempt of priests and priesthoods.   In various epochs of his long life he expressed himself so variously that a pietist may claim him, or a Voltairian may claim him : both with equal show of justice.   The secret of this contradiction lies in the fact that he had deep religious sentiments, with complete scepticism on most religious doctrines.   Thus, whenever the Encyclopædists attacked Christianity he was ready to defend it * ; but when he was brought in contact with dogmatic Christians, who wanted to force their creed upon him, he resented the attempt, and answered in the spirit of his scepticism.   To the Encyclopædists he would say, ' Whatever frees the intellect, without at the same time giving us command over ourselves, is pernicious ' ; or he would utter one of his profound and pregnant aphorisms, such as

Nur das Gesetz kann uns die Freiheit geben,

i.e., only within the circle of Law can there be true Freedom.   We are not free when we acknowledge no higher power, but when we acknowledge it, and in reverence raise ourselves by proving that a Higher lives in us.

But against dogmatic teachings he opposed the fundamental rule, that all conceptions of the Deity must necessarily be *our* individual conceptions, valid for us, but not to the same extent for others. Each soul has its own religion ; must have it as an individual possession ; let each see that he be true to it, which is far more efficacious than trying to accommodate himself to another's !

Im Innern ist ein Universum auch ;
Daher der Völker löblicher Gebrauch
Dass Jeglicher das Beste was er kennt
Er Gott, ja seinen Gott benennt.

' I *believe* in God ' was, he said, ' a beautiful and praiseworthy phrase ; but to *recognize* God in all his manifestations, *that* is true holiness on earth '.   He declared himself in the deepest sense of the word a Protestant, and as such claimed ' the right of holding his inner being free from all prescribed dogma, the right of developing himself religiously ! '   With reference to the genuineness of Scripture, he maintained with the modern Spiritualists that nothing is genuine but what is truly excellent, which stands in harmony with

* ABEKEN was told by a lady that she once heard Goethe soundly rate a respected friend, because she spoke of sacred persons in the tone of vulgar rationalism.

the purest nature and reason, and which even now ministers to our highest development. He looked upon the Four Gospels as genuine, 'for there is in them a reflection of a greatness which emanated from the person of Jesus, and which was of as divine a kind as was ever seen upon earth. If I am asked whether it is in my nature to pay Him devout reverence, I say—certainly! I bow before Him as the divine manifestation of the highest morality. If I am asked whether it is in my nature to reverence the sun, I again say—certainly! For he is likewise a manifestation of the highest Being. I adore in him the light and the productive power of God; by which we all live, move, and have our being. But if I am asked whether I am inclined to bow before a thumb bone of the apostle Peter or Paul, I say—away with your absurdities! * * * Let mental culture go on advancing, let science go on gaining in depth and breadth, and the human intellect expand as it may, it will never go beyond the elevation and moral culture of Christianity as it shines forth in the Gospels. The mischievous sectarianism of Protestants will one day cease, and with it the hatred between father and son, sister and brother; for as soon as the pure doctrine and love of Christ are comprehended in their true nature, and have become a living principle, we shall feel ourselves great and free as human beings, and not attach special importance to a degree more or less in the outward forms of religion. Besides, we shall all gradually advance from a Christianity of words and faith to a Christianity of feeling and action'. He was eighty-two when those words were uttered to Eckermann. Ten years before, he wrote to his old friend the Countess von Stolberg: 'I have meant honestly all my life both with myself and others, and in all my earthly strivings have ever looked upwards to the Highest. You and yours have done so likewise. Let us continue to work thus while there is daylight for us; for others another sun will shine by which they will work, while for us a brighter Light will shine. And so let us remain untroubled about the future! In our Father's kingdom there are many provinces, and as He has given us here so happy a resting-place, so will He certainly care for us above; perhaps we shall be blessed with what here on earth has been denied us, to know one another merely by seeing one another, and thence more thoroughly to love one another'.

There are two aspects under which religion may be considered: the divine aspect, and the human aspect; in the one it is Theosophy, in the other Ethics. Goethe's Theosophy was that of Spinoza, modified by his own poetical tendencies; it was not a geometrical, but a poetical Pantheism. In it the whole universe was conceived as divine ; not as a lifeless mass, but as the living manifestation of Divine Energy ever flowing forth into activity. St. Paul tells us that God lives in everything, and everything in God. Science tells us that the world is always *becoming*. Creation continues. The world was not made, once and for ever, as a thing completed, and afterwards serenely contemplated. The world is still amaking. The primal energies of Life are as young and potent as of old, issuing forth under new forms through metamorphoses higher and ever higher, as dawn broadens into day.

Goethe's religion was eminently concrete, and devout in its worship of realities. He believed in fact ; he thought reality in itself holier than any fiction could make it. Human nature was to him a holy fact, and man's body a temple of holiness. This is Hellenic, but its kinship with Spinoza's system is also obvious. Spinoza had no sympathy with those philosophers who deride or vilify human nature : in his opinion it was better to try to understand it ; and disregarding the clamours of those who conceived the emotions and actions of human nature to be chaotic and absurd, he analysed its properties as if it had been a mathematical figure. In other words he inquired without passion, reasoned without foregone conclusions, interrogated the facts as they presented themselves, and recorded the simple answers *. And this did Goethe. He strove above all things to understand fact, because fact was divine manifestation. The mystic change of birth and death—the sweet influences of opening life and orderly development—the restless strivings and the placid rests—the ever-moving shuttles of the 'roaring Loom of Time, which weaves for God the garment we see him by '—were to him the 'freshly uttered word of God'.

Goethe's moral system was intimately connected with this Theosophy. His worship was Nature worship, his moral system an idealization of Humanity. The human being was the highest manifestation of the Divine on earth, and the highest manifestation of Humanity was therefore the ideal to which morality tended. We must first learn Renunciation ; we must learn to limit ourselves to the Possible ; in this first restraint lies the germ of self-sacrifice : in giving up claims too high for attainment, we learn to give up

---

* *Ethices*, Pars III, præfatio: 'Nam ad illos revertere volo, qui hominum affectus et actiones detestari vel ridere malunt, quam intelligere. His sine dubio mirum videbitur, quod hominum vitia et ineptias more geometrico tractare aggrediar, et certa ratione demonstrare velim ea quæ rationi repugnare, quæque vana, absurda, et horrenda esse clamitant. Sed mea hæc ratio est '.

claims for the sake of others.   True piety springs from human love.
' If certain phenomena of nature', he says, 'looked at from the
moral standing point, force us to assume the existence of a primitive Evil, so on the other hand many phenomena force us to assume
a primitive Good.   This spring of goodness, when flowing into life,
we name *Piety;* as the ancients did, who regarded it as the basis
of all virtue.   It is the force which counterbalances egoism ; and
if by a miracle it could for a moment suddenly be active in all men,
the earth would at once be free from evil'.

It would be no difficult task to select from his works a series of
moral propositions of the noblest character ; but indeed his works
are saturated with a morality such as speaks to every heart not
prejudiced, and are even more remarkable for the absence of any
mean, grovelling, selfish, and narrow views than for their direct
teaching.   The cry of 'Immorality' which has been sometimes
raised against his works, springs from that uncharitableness which
denounces every thought not taught by the denouncing sect.   If
any one can read Goethe's works and not feel the writer to have
been one strengthened by noble sentiments and warmed by the
purest love for human nature in its most generous forms, I have
nothing to add to the words of the spirit in *Faust,*—

Du gleichst dem Geist den du begreifst,—

' You resemble the Spirit which you understand '*.

Whatever else he has been accused of, he has never been accused
of not having striven incessantly to reach a full development of his
own being, and to aid the culture of his nation.   There is something truly grand in the picture of his later years ; so calm, and
yet so active.   His sympathy, instead of growing cold with age,
seems every year to become more active.   Every discovery in
Science, every new appearance in Literature, every promise in Art
finds him eager as a child to be instructed, and ready with aid or
applause to further it.

Old age indeed is a relative term.   Goethe at seventy was younger

---

* I heard a capital story of Carlyle at a dinner-party in Berlin, silencing the cant
about Goethe's want of religion, by one of his characteristic sarcasms.   For some time
he sat quiet, but not patient, while certain pietists were throwing up their eyes, and
regretting that so great a genius! so godlike a genius! should not have more purely
devoted himself to the service of Christian Truth ! and should have had so little, etc.,
etc.   Carlyle sat grim, ominously silent, his hands impatiently twisting his napkin,
until at last he broke silence, and in his slow, emphatic way said, ' *Meine Herren*, did
you never hear the story of that man who vilified the sun because it would not light his
cigar?'   This bombshell completely silenced the enemy's fire.   Not a word was spoken
in reply.   ' I could have kissed him ! ' exclaimed the enthusiastic artist who narrated the
anecdote to me.

than many men at fifty ; and at eighty-two he wrote a scientific review of the great discussion between Cuvier and Geoffroy St. Hilaire on Philosophic Zoology, a review which few men in their prime could write. But there are Physiologists who deny that seventy is old age. M. Flourens, for example, maintains that from fifty-five to seventy man is at his most virile period ; and M. Reveillé Parisse, in his work *La Vieillesse*, declares that between fifty-five and seventy-five, and sometimes beyond, the mind acquires an extension, a consistence, and a solidity truly remarkable, 'c'est véritablement l'homme ayant atteint toute la hauteur de ses facultés'. And the history of Science and Literature furnishes several striking examples of intellectual activity in old age—the activity being doubtless a cause of this prolongation of power. Sophocles, who is said to have written his masterpiece at eighty, is an example of great poetic capacity thus prolonged. The reflective powers often retain their capacity, and by increase of material seem to *increase* it ; but not so the productive powers. Yet in Goethe we see extraordinary fertility, even in the latest years ; the Second Part of *Faust* was completed in his eighty-first year, and the *West-östliche Divan* was written in his sixty-fifth. Although we cannot by any means consider these works as equal to the works of his earlier days, we must still consider them as marvellous productions to issue under the sunset of a poet.

The *West-östliche Divan* was a refuge from the troubles of the time. Instead of making himself unhappy with the politics of Europe, he made himself happy studying the history and poetry of the East. He even began to study the Oriental languages, and was delighted to be able to copy the Arabic manuscripts in their peculiar characters. Von Hammer, De Sacy, and other Orientalists had given him abundant material ; his poetic activity soon gave that material shape. But while donning the Turban, and throwing the Caftan over his shoulders, he remained a true German. He smoked opium and drank *Foukah ;* but his dreams were German and his songs were German. This forms the peculiarity of the Divan—it is West-Eastern ; the images are Eastern, the feeling is Western. Precisely as in the Roman Elegies he had thrown himself into the classical past, reproducing its forms with unsurpassed ease and witchery, yet never for a moment ceasing to be original, never ceasing to be German ; so also in this Eastern world we recognize the Western poet. He follows the Caravan slowly across the desert ; he hears the melancholy chant of the Bulbul singing on the borders of sparkling fountains ; he listens devoutly to the precepts of Mohammed, and rejoices in the strains of Hafis. The combination is most felicitous. It produced an epoch in German Literature. The Lyrists, according to Gervinus, suddenly following this example, at once relinquished their warlike and contemporary tone to sing the songs of the East. Rückert and Platen, following the trace of the German Hafis, wandered among Roses and Ghazels ; other poets gladly imitated them. Does it not seem as if there were a natural tendency in the German character to turn the back upon active political life, when we see that in the two great crises of history, in the Crusades and in the War of Independence, the poets fled from the stormy contemplation of their time, seeking inspiration in an order of ideas completely opposed to the time? The Minnesingers, amid the clang of knightly achievements, could only sing of Love and Pleasure ; the modern poets, amid the storms of an European struggle, could find no inspiration but in Romanticism, or in Orientalism ! This is the more noticeable because Goethe has been angrily reproached for his flight into the East ; although surely the aged poet might find an excuse when the young poets were applauded ?

The *West-östliche Divan* is divided into twelve Books : the Singer, Hafis, Love, Contemplation, Sadness, Proverbs, Timour, Suleika, Wine-house, Parables, Persians, and Paradise ; very various in contents, and of various excellence. Truly may be applied to Goethe the epigraph he applies to Hafis : 'Let us call the Word the Bride, and the Spirit will be the Bridegroom ; he who has known Hafis has seen this marriage'.

> Sey das Wort die Braut genannt
> Bräutigam der Geist ;
> Diese Hochzeit hat gekannt
> Wer Hafisen preis't.

How much of his own experience he has clothed in these Eastern forms we cannot know ; but in one case, in the *Buch Suleika*, he has placed the name of Hatem where the rhyme plainly tells us to read Goethe :

> Du beschämst, wie Morgenröthe
> Jener Gipfel ernste Wand,
> Und noch einmal fühlet *Hatem*
> Frühlingshauch und Sommerbrand.

The grace with which many of these poems are lightly touched ; the admirable wisdom which smiles so serenely under them ; the calm, hot, noonday stillness, interchanging with the careless gaiety of the Wine-house mirth, cannot be indicated by translation ; nor will I attempt it. For the sake of the German reader, however, here is one brief specimen :

> Trunken müssen wir alle seyn !
> *Jugend ist Trunkenheit ohne Wein ;*
> Trinkt sich das Alter wieder zu Jugend
> So ist es wundervolle Tugend.
> Für Sorgen sorgt das liebe Leben
> Und Sorgenbrecher sind die Reben.

To these poems is added a volume of Historical Notes, which show indeed a conscientious study of the East, but which also show how immeasurably inferior he was in prose to poetry. Age is visible in every page.

In the early chapters of his *Autobiography* he had presented a picture of Frankfurt, which was very gratifying to the people of that city ; and when, in the year 1814, he passed through the city he was received with an ovation which recalls the last visit of Voltaire to Paris. *Tasso* was performed at the theatre with great pomp. No sooner did he make his appearance in the box which had been prepared for him, and which was hung with flowers and laurel-crowns, than Haydn's symphony struck up, and the whole house rose with a burst of enthusiastic cheering. The symphony continued, and the shouts rose tumultuously above it. At length the curtain rolled up, and gradually a solemn stillness settled through the house. A prologue greeted the great poet, and was the signal for more shouting. After *Tasso* came an epilogue, during which the laurel-crowns were taken from the busts of Ariosto and Tasso, and handed to Goethe. And when all was over, the corridors and staircases of the theatre were crowded with admirers, through whom he passed smiling his thanks.

CHAPTER VI

THE ACTIVITY OF AGE

IN the year 1816 he began to publish an Art Journal, *Kunst und Alterthum*, which continued till 1828, a curious monument of the old man's studies and activity. It is curious, moreover, as indicating a change in the direction of his ideas. We have seen what his relation was to the Romantic School, and. how the tendencies of his nature and education led him to oppose to the characteristics of that School the characteristics of Greek Art. The *Propylaen* represents the Greek tendency : *Kunst und Alterthum* represents a certain leaning towards the Romantic. Gothic Art, the old German and Netherland painters, no longer seemed to him objectionable ; but the discovery of the Elgin marbles once more awakened his enthusiasm for that perfection of form which was the ideal of Greek Art* ; and I have heard Rauch, the sculptor, humorously narrate Goethe's whimsical outbreaks when the young sculptor Rietschl seemed in danger of perverting his talent by executing designs in the spirit of the Romantic School.

Strong, however, as the opposition was which he felt to the vagaries of the so-called Christian Art, he had too much of the *Faust* spirit to keep entirely aloof from the Romanticists. In his old age the tendency to substitute Reflection for Inspiration naturally assumed greater force ; and his love of mystification was now wearing a serious aspect, duping himself perhaps as much as it duped others. The German nation had persisted in discovering profound meanings in passages which he had written without any recondite meaning at all ; finding himself a prophet when he meant only to be a poet, he gradually fell into the snare, and tried to be a prophet now he could no longer be so great a poet as before. Every incident was to be typical. Every phrase was of importance. Whether the lion should roar at a particular time (in the *Novelle*), or whether he should be silent, were subjects of long deliberation. The *Wanderjahre* was one great arsenal of symbols, the *Second Part of Faust* another. He delighted in seeing the philosophic critics outdoing each other in far-fetched ingenuity, 'explaining' his *Faust* and *Meister* ; and very astutely he refused to come to their aid. He saw libraries filled with discussions as to what he had intended ; but no one ever seduced him into an explanation which would have silenced these discussions. Instead of doing so, he seemed disposed to furnish the world with more riddles. In a word, he mystified the public ; but he did so in a grave, unconscious way, with a certain belief in his own mystification.

In the year 1816, Saxe Weimar was made a Grand Duchy ; and he received the Falcon Order, together with an increase of salary, which now became three thousand thalers, with extra allowance for

* See his letter to Haydon in the *Life of Haydon*, vol. II, p. 295.

Ottilie von Goethe

his equipage. Two other events made this year memorable. Lotte—Werther's Lotte—now a widow in her sixtieth year, and mother of twelve children, pays him a visit at Weimar. They had not met since her marriage, and what a meeting this must have been for both ! how strange a mingling of feelings recurrent to a pleasantly agitated past, and of feelings perplexed by the surprise at finding each other so much changed !

The second and far more serious event of the year is the death of his wife. Many affected to consider this 'a happy release'. People are fond of arranging the lives of others according to their own conceptions, interpreting afflictions like these without regard to the feelings of the afflicted. The blow was heavy to bear. She who for eight-and-twenty years had loved and aided him, who—whatever her faults—had been to him what no other woman was, could not be taken from him without making him deeply feel the loss. His self-mastery was utterly shaken. He kneeled at her bedside, seizing her cold hands, and exclaiming : 'Thou wilt not forsake me ! No, no ; thou must not forsake me !' He has expressed his feelings in two passages only ; in the exquisite lines he wrote on the day of her death, and in a letter to Zelter. These are the lines :—

> Du versuchst, O Sonne, vergebens
> Durch die düstern Wolken zu scheinen !
> Der ganze Gewinn meines Lebens
> Ist, ihren Verlust zu beweinen *.

And to Zelter the words were these: 'When I tell thee, thou rough and sorely tried son of earth, that my dear little wife has left me, thou wilt know what that means'.

In Science he strove to find forgetfulness ; and the loneliness of his house was next year changed into an unaccustomed liveliness by the marriage of his son with Ottilie von Pogwisch, one of the gayest and most brilliant of the Weimar circle. She was always a great favourite with her father-in-law, and during the remainder of his life not only kept his house for him, and received his numerous guests, but became a privileged favourite, to whom everything was permitted. In the year following he sang a cradle song over his first grandchild.

His ministerial duties were not heavy, but were punctiliously

---

* ' In vain, O Sun, you struggle to shine through the dark clouds ; the whole gain of my life is to bewail her loss '.

performed. Here are two anecdotes which exhibit his imperious and determined character in a strong light. He had long laboured for the improvement of Jena. The library, he told Eckermann, 'was in very bad condition. The situation was damp and close, and by no means fit to contain its treasures in a proper manner; particularly as by purchase of the Büttner library on the part of the Grand Duke, an addition had been made of 13,000 volumes, which lay in heaps upon the floor, because there was no room to place them properly. I was really in some distress on that account. An addition should have been made to the building, but for this the means were wanting; and moreover this addition could easily be avoided, since adjoining the library there was a large room standing empty, and quite calculated to supply our necessities. However, this room was not in possession of the library, but was used by the medical faculty, who sometimes employed it for their conferences. I therefore applied to these gentlemen with the very civil request that they would give up this room for the library. To this they would not agree. They were willing, they said, to give it up if I would have a new room built for their conferences, and that immediately. I replied that I should be very ready to have another place prepared for them, but that I could not promise them a new building immediately. This did not satisfy them, for when next morning I asked them for the key, I was told it could not be found! There now remained no other course but to enter as conqueror. I therefore sent for a bricklayer, and took him into the library before the wall of the adjoining room. "This wall, my friend", said I, "must be very thick, for it separates two different parts of the building: just try how strong it is". The bricklayer went to work, and scarcely had he given five or six hearty blows, when bricks and mortar fell in, and one could see through the opening some venerable perukes with which the room was decorated. "Go on, my friend", said I. "I cannot yet see clearly enough. Do not restrain yourself, but act as if you were in your own house". This friendly encouragement so animated the bricklayer, that the opening was soon large enough to serve perfectly for a door; when my library attendants rushed into the room each with an armful of books, which they threw upon the ground as a sign of possession. Benches, chairs, and desks vanished in a moment; and my assistants were so quick and active, that in a few days all the books were arranged along the walls. The doctors, who soon after entered the room through the usual door, were quite confounded at so un-

Karl Friedrich Zelter

expected a change. They did not know what to say, but retired in silence; but they all harboured a secret grudge against me. When I related this to the Grand Duke, he laughed heartily and quite approved me. Afterwards, when on account of the great dampness of the library I wished to take down and remove the whole of the old city wall, which was quite useless, I found no better success. My entreaties, reasons, and representations found no hearing ; and I was forced at last to go to work as a conqueror. When the city authorities saw my workmen destroying their old wall, they sent a deputation to the Grand Duke, with the humble request that his Highness would be pleased, by a word of command, to check my violent destruction of their venerable wall. But the Grand Duke, who had secretly authorized me, said : " I do not intermeddle with Goethe's affairs. He knows what he has to do, and must act as he thinks right. Go to him and speak to him yourself if you have the courage ! " '

The other anecdote is recorded by Luden. In 1823 the *Landtag* (or Parliament, to use the nearest English equivalent) assembled, and demanded the Finance accounts. Goethe, who was at the head of the Commission for Art and Science, to which a sum of 11,787 thalers was allotted, at first took no notice of the demand made for his accounts ; but was heard to express himself angrily at this Landtag with its pedantic fuss about a paltry sum. At length he was prevailed upon to send in his accounts. What was the surprise of the Landtag to read a few lines to this effect : ' Received, so much ; Expended, so much ; Remains, so much. *Signed* Grossherzogl. Immediatcommission für Wissenschaft und Kunst, *Goethe!* ' At this cavalier procedure some of the members burst out laughing ; others were indignant, and proposed to refuse the grant for the following year : a proposition which was all the more acceptable because the Landtag had a great idea of economy, and but a small idea of the value of science and art. Luden strove to convince them this was an unwise procedure. He urged indeed the necessity of the Landtag being put in possession of all the details of expenditure, not that any doubt could arise respecting the judicious mode in which the expenditure had been made, but because in public affairs it was indispensable men should see as well as believe. Against him it was argued that the mere statement of every groschen received and expended was not sufficient ; it was also necessary that the Landtag should be convinced that the expenditure had been solely for useful and desirable purposes, not permitting any favouritism or luxury to enjoy the benefit of public money.

Although the sittings of the Landtag were strictly private, one cannot be surprised at these debates having oozed out and formed the topic of gossip. Goethe was very indignant. He had been so long accustomed to an imperial sway, before which every one gave way, that the idea of his actions being controlled and questioned by a Landtag was very irritating to him. Nor, although he was obviously in the wrong in this instance, were the Grand Duke and Duchess inclined to side against him. Karl August himself spoke earnestly to the Land Marshall, urging on him the impropriety of so offending Goethe ; the Grand Duchess sent for Luden, who thus reports the interview : ' She spoke to me with that dignified simplicity which made her so imposing, and which was imposing even to Napoleon in his anger. It would be a serious evil, she said, if our friendly relations should be disturbed by any misunderstanding. It would be the more unpleasant to me, because I fear it would much annoy the Grand Duke. The Landtag is unquestionably in the right ; but the Geheimrath Goethe undoubtedly thinks he too is in the right. Above or beyond the written laws there is still another law—*the law for poets and women.* The Landtag is assuredly convinced that the whole of the money granted has been truly employed by Goethe? You admit that? Well, then, the only question that now can arise is whether the money has been properly expended. But here one must remember the position held by the Geheimrath in relation to the world, to this country, to our Court, and to the Grand Duke through a long series of years : this position very naturally has influenced his mode of looking at affairs. I find it perfectly intelligible that he can well believe he has before all others the right of deciding for himself what is the best means of employing the money placed at his disposal. I do not understand these matters, and far be it from me to pretend to set any one right ; my only wish is that friendly relations be preserved, and that the old Geheimrath may be spared every annoyance. How this is to be done I do not see. But the Landtag need be under no uneasiness lest this should become a precedent. *We have but one Goethe, and who knows how long we may preserve him ;* a second will not perhaps be soon found again '.

Is this not very charming ? And can we wonder that Luden was conquered, and that in turn the whole Landtag was brought over

to a sort of sullen acquiescence? While relating such characteristic anecdotes, place must be found for another, which is indeed
less interesting in itself, but which circulates in Germany and
England under a very absurd and very injurious form. The first
time I heard it gravely stated as a fact, of which proof could be
brought, the reader may imagine with what indignation I at once
denied it, and insisted on the proof being produced, although proof
must have been indeed overwhelming which could make me believe
that Goethe had *stolen an ingot of gold*. No proof, however,
came. The accusation slipped from my mind, until it was once
more gravely adduced, and that too in Weimar. The requisite
inquiries having been made, this story emerged as the foundation
of the scandal.

The Emperor of Russia had forwarded to Döbereiner, the great
chemist, a bar of platinum. It was given to Goethe, who was to
examine it, and make any experiment on it he pleased, and then
transmit it to Döbereiner. Goethe, whose passion for minerals is
well known, and who had the 'collector's mania', placed this bar
of platinum among his treasures, and delighted himself with
contemplating it, till at last he could not be brought to part with it.
Döbereiner, impatient, wrote to him, begging to have it sent. But
no answer came. He wrote again, without success. He was,
indeed, placed in a position very similar to that in which we saw
Professor Büttner, who having lent Goethe his prisms and optical
instruments, wrote in vain to have them returned, and was forced
to send his servant with an order to bring them away. Goethe
delayed and delayed, and could not bring himself to part with the
platinum ; and when Döbereiner, out of patience, complained to
the Grand Duke, Karl August laughed and said, 'Leave the old
donkey in peace! you'll never get it from him. I will write to the
Emperor for another'.

To this may be added, that in the early *genialische* period Goethe
carried off a hundred engravings by Albrecht Dürer from Knebel's
collection, to study them at leisure at home, and these engravings
Knebel never saw in his own house again. Now these cases,
although coming under the category of that much abused licence
which men permit themselves, namely, the licence of borrowing
books, umbrellas, and money, are not defensible, nor will I palliate
them. Let the reader pass any sentence he will upon such
infractions of the rule of conscientiousness ; but let us not hear
such things uttered as that Goethe stole a bar of gold or platinum.

With Döbereiner, he followed all the new phenomena which chemistry was then bringing before the astonished world. He also prepared his own writings on morphology for the press ; and studied Greek mythology, English literature, and Gothic art. Byron's *Manfred* he reviewed in the *Kunst und Alterthum*, and enthusiastically welcomed our great poet as the greatest product of modern times. Scott also he read with ever-increasing admiration. Homer, always studied with delight, now reassumed to him that individuality which Wolff had for a time destroyed ; Schubarth's *Ideen über Homer*, having brought him round once more to the belief in the existence of 'the blind old man of Scio's rocky isle '*. Painting, sculpture, architecture, geology, meteorology, anatomy, optics, Oriental literature, English literature, Calderon, and the romantic school in France—these were the subjects which by turns occupied his inexhaustible activity. 'Life ', he says, 'resembles the Sybilline Books ; it becomes dearer the less there remains of it '. To one who could so worthily occupy the last remaining years of a long life, they must indeed have been precious. As he grew older, he worked harder. He went less into society. To Court he very seldom went. ' I wouldn't send the picture ', writes the Duke to him, 'because I hoped it might lure thee out, now Candlemas is over, a day when every bear and badger leaves his lair '. But in lieu of his going to Court, the Court went to him. Once every week the Grand Duchess paid him a visit, sometimes bringing with her a princely visitor, such as the late Emperor of Russia, then Grand Duke, or the King of Wurtemberg. He had always something new and interesting set aside for this visit, which was doubly dear to him, because he had a tender regard for the Grand Duchess, and it pleased him to be able to show her a new engraving, medallion, book, poem, or some scientific novelty. Karl August came often, but not on particular days. He used to walk up into the simple study, and chat there as with a brother. One day Goethe had a Jena student paying him a visit ; the student saw an elderly gentleman walk unannounced into the room, and quietly seat himself on a chair ; the student continued his harangue, and when it was concluded, Goethe quietly said, 'But I must introduce the gentlemen : his Royal Highness the Grand Duke of Saxe Weimar, Herr ——, student from Jena '. Never did the student forget the embarrassment of that moment !

The first edition of *Wilhelm Meister's Wanderjahre* falls in this

* See the little poem *Homer wider Homer.*

period, 1821, and as this edition is the one best known in England through Carlyle's translation, it may now be criticized, the more so, as what was afterwards *thrown into* the book (I will not say worked into it) only made it still more fragmentary and imperfect.

There are pages in the *Wanderjahre* which he alone could have written ; but I cannot bring myself to regard the whole book as anything better than a collection of sketches and studies, often incomplete, and sometimes not worth completing. It is very unequal, some parts being as feeble as others are admirable. The story of *The Man of Fifty* has capital points, and the *New Melusina* is a charming fairy tale ; but much of what is symbolical seems to me only fantastic ; and as a composition the work is feeble, and careless even to impertinence. Not only are the various little stories 'dragged in' with the transparent artifice of juvenile productions ; not only are these stories for the most part tiresome and sometimes trivial, but there is one story (*Nicht zu weit*) which, beginning with considerable animation, is actually left unfinished in the work, just as it lay unfinished in his portfolio. Observe it is not given as a fragment—the conclusion is promised, but never comes. This is an impertinence to the public ; all the more remarkable as coming from a writer who thought so much of Art. He might have published the stories separately, as they were written separately ; and if he could not work out the great scheme of the *Wanderjahre*, he might have left it a fragment, or left it unpublished.

It is easy for admirers of this work to cite very beautiful passages ; and it is by no means difficult to read under its symbolical dullness any profound meanings the interpreter wishes to read there. But for my own part, greatly as I admire Goethe, and profoundly as his works affect me, I do not recognize in the *Wanderjahre* the old magic, nor can my love for the writer persuade me that it is well written, well conceived, or intelligibly executed. I quarrel with no man who finds delight in the book ; but candour compels me to own that I find in it almost every fault a work can have : it is unintelligible, it is tiresome, it is fragmentary, it is dull, and it is often ill-written. When particular passages are cited for their wisdom or their beauty one is apt to fancy that one has been unjust to a strange work ; but a *re*-reading of the work as a whole soon restores the original verdict. Irving said that there was more true religion in the episode of the Three Reverences than in all the theological writings of the day. And Carlyle has on more than one occasion noticed the profound wisdom which shines through many of the pages. How can it be otherwise, when Goethe is the author? But separate passages do not make a book ; and to show how this book was made, a passage from Eckermann will suffice. 'When he began to remodel and finish this novel, which had previously appeared in one volume*, Goethe intended to expand it into two. But as the work progressed the manuscript grew beyond expectation ; and as his secretary wrote widely, Goethe was deceived, and thought he had enough for three volumes, and accordingly the manuscript went in three volumes to the publishers. However, when the printing had reached a certain point, it was found that a miscalculation had been made, and that the two last volumes were too small. The publishers sent for more manuscript, and as the course of the novel could not be altered, and it was impossible to write a new tale in the hurry of the moment, Goethe was really in some perplexity. Under these circumstances he sent for me, told me the state of the case, and mentioned how he thought of helping himself out of the difficulty, laying before me two large bundles of manuscripts. " In these two parcels ", said he, " you will find various papers hitherto unpublished, detached pieces finished and unfinished ; opinions on natural science, art, literature, and life, all mingled together. Suppose you were to make up from these six or eight printed sheets to fill the gaps in my *Wanderjahre*. Strictly speaking, they have nothing to do with it, but the proceeding may be justified by the fact that mention is made of an archive in Makaria's house in which such detached pieces are preserved. Thus we shall not only get over a difficulty, but find a fitting vehicle for sending a number of interesting things into the world". I approved of the plan, set to work at once, and completed the desired arrangement in a short time. Goethe seemed well satisfied. I had put together the whole into two principal parts ; one under the title *From Makaria's Archive*, the other under the title *According to the Views of the Wanderer*. And as Goethe, at this time, had just finished two poems—one on *Schiller's Skull*, and the other *Kein Wesen kann zu Nichts zerfallen*—he was desirous to bring out these also, and we added them at the close of the two divisions. But when the *Wanderjahre* came out, no one knew what to make of it. The progress of the romance was interrupted by a number of enigmatical sayings, the explanation of which

---

* This is the volume Carlyle translated. See *German Romance*, vol. IV. It is superior to the expanded work.

Johann Peter Eckermann

could be expected from men only of special studies, such as artists, litterati, men of science ; this greatly annoyed all other readers, especially those of the fair sex. Then, as for the two poems, people could as little understand them as they could guess how they got into such a place. Goethe laughed at this'.

No other criticism of the *Wanderjahre* is needed after such a story. Had Goethe stood in awe of the public, had he lived in England or France, where 'Reviewers' exercise at least the duty of Police, he would not thus have ventured to play with his own reputation and to mystify the public.

Nor did he escape without punishment even into Germany. He had mystified the public, but the public was not pleased. His friends were not pleased. No one accepted the work with satisfaction. It remained for writers of our day to see in it a social Bible—a Sybilline Book. The first symptoms of dissatisfaction came from his nearest friends ; but their objections were of course mild, and were praise compared with the objections raised by his enemies. A certain Pustkuchen, a clergyman of Lieme, imitated Nicolai's parody of *Werther*, but in a serious spirit, bringing out a *Wanderjahre*, in which Goethe's views of life were held up to the execration of all good Christians. It had become the watchword of one party to say Goethe was no Christian ; as it afterwards became the watchword of another party to say he was no patriot ; and, finally, there came Menzel, who said he was not only no Christian, no Patriot, no Moralist, but also no Genius,—only a man of talent ! Goethe contented himself with an epigram or so on Pustkuchen, and continued his way. To his opponents generally he said, ' If they could judge me, I should not be the man I am '.

> Hätten sie mich beurtheilen können
> So wär' ich nicht was ich bin.

And the barking of the curs, he said, which follows us as we leave the stable, proves nothing more than that we are on horseback :

> Es bellt der Spitz aus unserm Stall
> Und will uns stets begleiten.
> Und seiner lauten Stimme Schall
> Beweist nur dass wir reiten.

While a strong feeling of opposition was growing up in his own nation, a feeling which such works as the *Wanderjahre* were not likely to mitigate, his fame began to extend to Italy, England, and

France. His active interest in the important productions of foreign literature, was reciprocated in the admiration expressed for him by men like Manzoni, Scott, Byron, Carlyle, Stapfer, Ampère, Soret, and others. He had written of Manzoni's *Carmagnola*, defending it against adverse criticism, with a fervour which, according to Manzoni, secured his reputation in Europe. 'It is certain that I owe to Goethe's admiration all the praise I have received. I was very ill treated until he so nobly defended me, and since then I have not only seen public opinion change, but I myself have learned to look at my productions in a new light'. How profound was his admiration for Byron, and how flattered Byron was by it, is well known. The poem he sent to Byron, in answer to the dedication of *Werner*, reached him just as he was setting out on the expedition to Greece.

Nor was his activity confined to reading. Oersted's magnificent discovery of electro-magnetism awakened his keenest interest. He made Döbereiner exhibit the phenomena, and shortly afterwards had Oersted to visit him. D'Alton's anatomical work on the Sloth and Megatherium found him as ready as a young reviewer to proclaim its importance to the world. He wrote also the account of his *Campaign in France;* the *Annals* of his Life; Essays on Art; smaller poems; the epigrams, *Zahme Xenien;* translated modern Greek songs; and sketched a restoration of the lost drama *Phaëton*, by Euripides.

It is evident then that there was abundant life in the old Jupiter, whose frame was still massive and erect; whose brow had scarcely a wrinkle of old age; whose head was still as free from baldness as ever; and whose large brown eyes had still that flashing splendour which distinguished them. Hufeland, the physician, who had made a special study of the human organization with reference to its powers of vitality, says, that never did he meet with a man in whom bodily and mental organization were so perfect as in Goethe. Not only was the prodigious strength of vitality remarkable in him, but equally so the perfect *balance* of functions. 'One can truly say that his distinguishing characteristic was the harmony with which all mental faculties worked together, so that his creative Imagination was always under the control of his Reason; and the same is true of his physical faculties: no function was predominant, all worked together for the continuance of a marvellous balance. But *productivity* was the fundamental character of his bodily and mental organization; and the former showed itself in a rich nutritive power,

Ulrike von Lewetzow

a rapid sanguinification and reproduction.   He made much blood even as an old man '.

Not only life, but the life of life, the power of loving was still preserved to him.   *Quisquis amat, nulla est conditione senex*, says old Pontanus ; and the Marquis de Lassay prettily makes the loss of love-dreams a sign of the last sleep :—'Hélas, quand on commence à ne plus rêver, ou plutôt à rêver moins, on est près de s'endormir pour toujours'.   In the seventy-fourth year of his age, Goethe had still youth enough to love.   At Marienbad he met with a Fräulein von Lewezow.   A passion grew up between them, which, returned on her side with almost equal vehemence, brought back to him once more the exaltation of the *Werther* period.   It was thought he would marry her, and indeed he wished to do so ; but the representations of his friends, and perhaps the fear of ridicule, withheld him. He tore himself away ; and the Marienbad Elegy, which he wrote in the carriage as it whirled him away, remains as a token of the passion and his suffering.

Nor does the Fräulein von Lewezow appear to have been the only one captivated by the 'old man eloquent'.   Madame Szymanowska, according to Zelter, was 'madly in love' with him ; and however figurative such a phrase may be, it indicates, coming from so grave a man as Zelter, a warmth of enthusiasm one does not expect to see excited by a man of seventy-four.

On the 7th of November 1825, Goethe, who had a few weeks before prepared a Jubilee for the fiftieth anniversary of Karl August's reign, was in turn honoured by a Jubilee celebrating the fiftieth anniversary of his arrival at Weimar.   'At dawn of day, when he opened the shutters of his bedroom, the first sound that met his ears was a morning song, sung by voices concealed in his garden. His first glance fell on the various tasteful gifts of neat-handed friends.   At half-past eight all the carriages in the town were in motion ; all persons of consideration in Court and city were in pilgrimage to the poet's house.   A party of musicians, and fourteen female friends, had assembled in his salon, to perform a morning ode written by Professor Riemer, and set to music by Eberwein. At nine, when Goethe was conducted from his study by a friend and his own son, the crowd in every room was so great that they were obliged to lead him unobserved by a side entrance.   Scarcely was that honoured head beheld than the music began, and heightened the emotion which beamed from all eyes.   The nymphs of the Ilm greeted the golden day of their faithful poet, and sang his immortality. The whole throng of auditors was deeply affected. The tones melted away in solemn silence. With modest dignity, the venerable man turned to his friends and expressed his thanks by eloquent pressure of the hands and affectionate words. Baron von Fritsch then stepped forward, and delivered the autograph letter of the Duke, and the golden medal which had been secretly struck in Berlin ; it bore the likeness of Karl August and Luise on one side ; on the other the laurel-crowned head of the poet : the names of Karl August and Luise were engraved on the rim.

' Goethe, who expected some memorial worthy of the giver, held both for some time unopened in silent emotion. The various deputations now advanced. There were deputations from Jena, Weimar, Eisenach, and from the Lodge of Freemasons. The Jena students addressed him through two deputies.

' Shortly after ten, Karl August and Luise came to offer their congratulations. They remained with him an hour alone ; when the hereditary Grand Duke and Grand Duchess, with their two Princesses, arrived. Meanwhile the ministers of state, the chiefs of the courts of justice, the most distinguished persons of the Court, and the deputations had collected together ; the principal ladies of Weimar, among whom were the daughters and grand-daughters of Wieland and Herder, assembled in an upper room. As soon as all the invited had arrived, they were conducted, two by two, into the great room in which were placed the statue of the Grand Duke and Rauch's bust of Goethe, on a handsome pedestal, with a laurel crown beside it. Just as the procession reached the centre of the hall, music was heard from the galleries. The effect of this harmony in the lofty and beautiful hall, decorated with the busts and portraits, was indescribable.

' At two o'clock a banquet was prepared for more than two hundred persons in the hall of the Stadthaus. In the evening *Iphigenia* was performed at the theatre. At the end of the third act, Goethe, warned by his physician, retired ; and now a beautiful conclusion to this extraordinary day awaited him. A serenade was performed in front of his house by the orchestral band of the Grand Ducal Chapel. Hummel had with great feeling and taste combined the triumphal March in Titus, Gluck's overture to *Iphigenia,* and a masterly Adagio of his own, with an echo for horns. The opening expressed the triumphant glories of the day, while the melting tones of the Adagio seemed to invite to the tranquillity which follows the accomplishment of work.

'All the houses in the *Frauenplan*, where Goethe lived, were illuminated. A numerous company repaired to his house, where an elegant entertainment awaited them, and Goethe remained one hour with his guests before retiring for the night. This day was likewise celebrated at Leipsic and Frankfurt. In Frankfurt the consul-general Bethmann marked the day by placing in his museum a statue of Goethe, as large as life, which Rauch had executed for him'*.

Reading this and such anecdotes as the one formerly narrated about the Landtag, how can we wonder if the man, who was treated so like a god, adopted something of the imperiousness and assumption of the part thus thrust upon him?

In the following year Germany showed her gratitude to him by a privilege which in itself is the severest sarcasm on German nationality—the privilege, namely, of a protection of his copyright. He announced a complete edition of his works, and the *Bundestag* undertook to secure him from piracy in German cities! Until that time his works had enriched booksellers; but this tardy privilege secured an inheritance for his children.

In the way of honours, he was greatly flattered by the letter which Walter Scott sent to him, in expression of an old admiration; and on the 28th of August, 1827, Karl August came into his study accompanied by the King of Bavaria, who brought with him the Order of the Grand Cross as a homage. In strict etiquette a subject was not allowed to accept such an Order without his own sovereign granting permission, and Goethe, ever punctilious, turned to the Grand Duke, saying: 'If my gracious sovereign permits'. Upon which the Duke called out: '*Du alter Kerl! mache doch kein dummes Zeug!* Come, old fellow, no nonsense'.

On the 6th January, 1827, the Frau von Stein died, in her eighty-fifth year.

And now the good old Duke was to be taken from him whom he affectionately styled his *Waffenbruder*—his brother in arms. On the 14th of June, 1828, he was no more. Humboldt's letter to Goethe contains so interesting an account of the Duke's last hours, that some sentences may here be cited: 'As if this great brightness, as with the lofty snow-capped Alps, were the forerunner of departing

* These details and many others are given in *Goethe's Goldener Jubeltag*. Weimar: 1826. I have abridged the abridgment given by Mrs. Austin, *Goethe and his Contemporaries*, vol. III.

light, never have I seen the great humane prince more animated, more intelligent, more mild, more sympathizing with the further development of the people than in the last days when we had him here. I frequently said to my friends, anxiously and full of misgivings, that this animation, this mysterious clearness of intellect, combined with so much bodily weakness, was to me a fearful phenomenon. He himself evidently vacillated between hope of recovery and expectation of the great catastrophe. In Potsdam I sat many hours with him. He drank and slept alternately, then drank again then rose to write to his consort, and then slept again. He was cheerful, but much exhausted. In the intervals he overpowered me with the most difficult questions upon physics, astronomy, meteorology, and geology ; upon the atmosphere of the moon ; upon the coloured double stars ; upon the influence of the spots in the sun upon the temperature ; upon the appearance of organized forms in the primitive world ; and upon the internal warmth of the earth. He slept at intervals during his discourse and mine, was often restless, and then said, kindly excusing his apparent inattention, " You see, Humboldt, it is all over with me ! " Suddenly he began to talk desultorily upon religious matters. He regretted the increase of pietism, and the connexion of this species of fanaticism with a tendency towards political absolutism, and the suppression of all free mental action. " Then ", he exclaimed, " there are false-hearted fellows, who think that by means of pietism they can make themselves agreeable to princes, and obtain places and ribbons. They have smuggled themselves in with a poetical predilection for the middle ages ". His anger soon abated, and he said that he had found much consolation in the Christian religion. " It is a humane doctrine ", said he, " but has been distorted from the beginning. The first Christians were the free thinkers among the ultras " '.

Knowing Goethe's love for the Duke, his friends entertained great fears that the shock of this event would be terrible. He was seated at dinner when the news arrived. It was whispered from one to the other. At length it was gently broken to him. They were breathless with suspense. But his face remained quite calm—a calmness which betrayed him. ' Ah ! this is very sad ', he sighed : ' let us change the subject '. He might banish the subject from conversation, he could not banish it from his thoughts. It affected him deeply ; all the more so, because he did not give expression to his grief. '*Nun ist alles vorbei!* Nothing now remains ',

Goethe at 78

he said. When Eckermann came in the evening, he found him utterly prostrate *.

Retiring to the pleasant scenes of Dornburg, the old man strove in work and in contemplation of Nature to call away his thoughts from his painful loss. The next year—1829—he finished the *Wanderjahre* in the form it now assumes, worked at the *Second Part of Faust*, and in conjunction with a young Frenchman, Soret, who was occupied translating the *Metamorphoses of Plants*, revised his scientific papers.

In February 1830, the death of the Grand Duchess once more overshadowed the evening of his life. These clouds gathering so fast are significant warnings of the Night which hurries on for him —'the night in which no man can work'!

Before narrating the last days of this long career, it will be necessary to say something of the *Second Part of Faust*, which was not indeed finally completed until the 20th July, 1831, but which may be noticed here to avoid interruption of the closing scene.

CHAPTER VII

THE 'SECOND PART OF FAUST'

IN the presence of this poem, I feel more embarrassment than with any other of Goethe's works. Difficult as the task has been in each instance to convey an adequate idea of the work before me, and to give expression to the critical opinions I had formed respecting it, that difficulty becomes complicated in the present instance by the consciousness of the opposition existing between a certain class of admirers and myself, a class not of ignorant, prejudiced, but of enlightened and ingenious intellects. These admirers speak of the *Second Part of Faust* as a work of transcendent merit, surpassing all that Goethe has written, a storehouse of profound and mystic philosophy, a miracle of execution. Others again, and these among Goethe's most loving

---

* The calmness with which he received the announcement recalls those grand scenes in Marston's *Malcontent* and Ford's *Broken Heart*, where the subordination of emotion to the continuance of offices of politeness rises into sublimity. Herodotus has touched the same chord in his narrative of the terrific story of Thyestes (*Clio*, 119). Harpagus on discovering that he has feasted on his own children in the banquet set before him by Thyestes remains quite calm. Shakespeare has expressed the true philosophy of the matter in his usual pregnant language:

Give sorrow words: the grief that does not speak
Whispers the o'erfraught heart, and bids it break.

students, declare it to be of mediocre interest, very far inferior to the *First Part*, and both in conception and execution an elaborate mistake. And of these I am one. I have tried to understand the work ; tried to place myself at the right point of view for perfect enjoyment ; but repeated trials, instead of clearing up obscurities and deepening enjoyment, as with the other works, have more and more confirmed my first impressions. Now although it needs but little experience to suggest that the fault may be wholly mine, 'the most legible hand', as Goethe says, 'being illegible in the twilight' ; although I might learn from what I have felt, and from what others have felt about the *First Part*, not to be hasty in pronouncing judgment, nevertheless I must express my real convictions, and not withhold them on the chance that future enlightenment may cause me to alter them. What Channing says of opinions generally, is applicable to critical opinions : we are answerable for their *uprightness*, not for their *rightness*.

Moreover, comparing the impressions produced by *Faust* and by the *Second Part*, although it is true that in both cases a sense of disappointment is created, the kind of objection made to each is entirely different. In *Faust*, a want of familiarity with the work may cause it to appear fragmentary, discordant, irreverent, not sufficiently metaphysical, and so forth ; but a single reading is enough to impress us with a sense of its interest, its pathos, its poetry, its strongly-marked character. In other words, the substance of the work lays hold of us ; it is only the execution upon which criticism exercises itself. If we think it fragmentary, the fragments are at any rate of deep significance. If we think it deficient in taste, we never reproach it with want of power. The reverse is the case with this *Second Part*. Our objections are not raised by the details, but by the body of the poem ; it is not the execution, but the whole conception, both in respect to the story itself, and to the mode of working out that story. What is the consequence? The consequence is that familiarity with *Faust* removes our objections and intensifies our admiration ; but familiarity with the *Second Part* confirms our objections, and discloses their source.

If we remember that all Goethe's works are biographical, are parts of his life, and expressions of the various experiences he underwent, and the various stages of culture he passed through, there will be a peculiar interest in examining this product of his old age ; and at the same time the reader will see the motive which made me reserve for this chapter what has to be said on the *Second Part*, instead of affixing it to the criticism of the *First Part*; for indeed the two poems are two, not two parts of one poem ; the interval between them in conception and treatment is as wide as the interval of years between their composition. Taking up the biographical clue, we have seen in previous chapters the gradual development of a tendency towards mysticism and over-reflectiveness, which, visible as a germ in his earliest years, grew with his growth, and expanded in the later years, till its overgrowth shadowed and perplexed his more vigorous concrete tendencies, and made this clearest and most spontaneous of poets as fond of symbols as a priest of Isis. To those—and they are many—who think the aim and purpose of Art is to create symbols for Philosophy, this development will be prized as true progress. Others who do not thus subordinate the artist to the thinker, must regard the encroachment of Reflection as a sign of decay. It is quite true that modern Art, as representative of the complexity of Modern Life, demands a large admixture of Reflection ; but the predominance of the reflective tendency is a sign of decay. It is true that for an organism of a certain degree of complexity, an internal osseous structure is necessary ; but the increase of ossification is cause and consequent of decay of vital power.

With the two parts of *Faust* we have very much the same critical questions to debate as with the earlier and later books of *Wilhelm Meister;* questions too wide and deep for thorough discussion here, and which I must content myself with indicating. One cardinal consideration must, however, be brought forward, which lies at the very basis of all argument on the subject. It is this: If the artist desire to express certain philosophic conceptions by means of symbols, he must never forget that, Art being Representation, the symbols chosen must possess *in themselves* a charm independent of what they mean. The forms which are his materials, the symbols which are his language, must in themselves have a beauty, and an interest, readily appreciable by those who do not understand the occult meaning. Unless they have this they cease to be Art; they become hieroglyphs. Art is picture-painting, not picture-writing. Beethoven, in his Symphonies, may have expressed grand psychological conceptions, which, for the mind that interprets them, may give an extra charm ; but if the strains in themselves do not possess a magic, if they do not sting the soul with a keen delight, then let the meaning be never so profound, it will

pass unheeded, because the *primary requisite* of music is not that
it shall present grand thoughts, but that it shall agitate the audience
with musical emotions. The poet who has only profound meanings,
and not the witchery which is to carry his expression of those
meanings home to our hearts, has failed. The primary requisite
of poetry is that it shall move us ; not that it shall instruct us.

The *Second Part of Faust*, if the foregoing be correct, is a
failure, because it fails in the primary requisite of a poem.
Whatever else it may be, no one will say it is interesting. The
scenes, incidents, and characters do not *in themselves* carry that
overpowering charm which masters us in the *First Part*. They
borrow their interest from the meanings they are supposed to
symbolize. Only in proportion to your ingenuity in guessing the
riddle is your interest excited by the means. Mephisto, formally
so marvellous a creation, has become a mere mouthpiece ; Faust
has lost all traces of individuality, every pulse of emotion. The
philosophic critics will point out how this change is necessary,
because in the *Second Part* all that was individual has become
universal. But this is only a description, not a justification ; it is
dignifying failure with a philosophic purpose. Goethe has himself declared this to have been his intention : ' I could not help
wondering ', he says, ' that none of those who undertook a con-
tinuation and completion of my fragment should have conceived
the idea, which seemed so obvious, that the *Second Part* must
necessarily be carried into a more elevated sphere, conducting
Faust into higher regions under worthier circumstances '. Right
enough : but in changing the ground there was no necessity for
such a change of treatment; to conduct Faust into a higher
region it was not necessary to displace the struggles of an
individual by representative abstractions ; above all, it was not
necessary to forsake the real domain of Art for that of Philosophy,
and sacrifice beauty to meaning. The defect of this poem does
not lie in its occult meanings, but in the poverty of poetic life,
which those meanings are made to animate. No matter how
occult the meaning, so that the picture be fine. A lion may be
the symbol of wakefulness, of strength, of kindness, of solitari-
ness, and of many other things, according to the arbitrary fancy
of the artist ; and it matters comparatively little whether we
rightly or wrongly interpret the artist's meaning ; but his lion
must be finely executed, must excite our admiration *as* a lion, if
we are to consider it a work of Art.

Respecting the philosophic meaning of the *First Part* critics battle, and will battle perhaps for ever ; but they are tolerably unanimous respecting its beauty. The passion, poetry, sarcasm, fancy, wisdom, and thrilling thoughts as from some higher world ; the pathos and naïveté of Gretchen ; the cruel coldness of Mephisto ; the anguish of the restless student ; these are what all understand, and, understanding, enjoy. We may baffle ourselves with the mystery ; we all are enchanted with the picture. We are moved by it as children are moved while reading the *Pilgrim's Progress*, believing all its allegorical persons and incidents to be real. When the child grows older, and learns to read beneath the allegory a series of grand representative abstractions, a new enjoyment is added ; but even then the enjoyment depends less on the meaning than on the form. In all attempts at allegory which make the meaning prominent, and neglect the form, the effect is cold, lifeless, uninteresting. Allegory which has been said to tell the story of a mind while seeming to tell the story of a life, is only acceptable on the condition of its story being interesting in itself. The *Second Part of Faust* fails in this first requisite ; you must have the key to it. There is no direct appeal to the emotions. There is no intrinsic beauty in the symbols. In saying this I speak of it as a whole ; in detail there are many passages of exquisite beauty, some lines of profound thought, and some happy sarcasm ; but there is no incident, no character, no one scene which lives in the memory like the incidents, characters, and scenes of the *First Part*.

The work opens with Faust on a flowery turf trying to calm his restlessness in sleep. It is twilight, and around him hover celestial spirits. Ariel sings, accompanied by an Æolian harp ; the other spirits join in chorus, and Faust, awakened by the sun-rise, pours forth his feelings in beautiful verse. This may represent the awakening from the dark Night of his soul which has followed on the death of Margaret, and which now vanishes as Time, the consoler, brings round the Day, and as the fresh morning air inspires fresh energies.

> Du regst und rührst ein kräftiges Beschliessen
> Zum höchsten Daseyn immerfort zu streben.

The scene changes to the Emperor's Court. Things are in a bad state. The Lord Chancellor complains that the laws are disregarded ; the Generalissimo complains of the army ; and the

First Lord of the Treasury complains of the empty exchequer. This is a very amusing scene, full of sarcasm and sly wisdom. Mephisto appears in the guise of a Court Fool, and the Emperor asks his advice. Gold, says Mephisto, is abundant in the earth, and can be brought to light by man's nature and spiritual power. No sooner are these words Nature and Spirit pronounced than the Lord Chancellor, with sensitive orthodoxy, prescient of heresy, exclaims :

> Natur und Geist—so spricht man nicht zu Christen.
> Desshalb verbrennt man Atheisten.

' Nature and Spirit—words not fit for Christian ears. It is for such words we burn Atheists'. He adds, that there are but two classes who worthily support the throne—the clergy and aristocracy: they withstand the storm,—and take Church and State in payment of their services. The fun of this scene would be more relished if it were visibly woven into the plot; but one fails to see any connecting link: the more so as Faust is not even present. The next scene is equally obscure. It is a mask got up for the Emperor, and is as wild and variegated as may be. It contains some light happy verses and some satire ; but the reader is bewildered. The next scene is the Emperor's pleasure grounds : a satire on Law's scheme of paper money is introduced. Mephisto has declared man's mind will bring money to light ; and this is proved by man resolving to attach the value of gold to paper. The people, thus suddenly enriched with cheap wealth, run into the wildest extravagances. Fine material for the commentator here ; but the reader is not greatly elated. In the next scene, Faust has drawn Mephistopheles apart, much to the devil's surprise, who asks him if there has not been amusement enough for him in the motley throng ; but Faust has promised the Emperor to show him Helen of Troy, and calls upon Mephisto to fulfil that promise. Mephisto says he has no power over the heathen world ; and Helen is not so easily brought on the stage as paper money is. But there is nevertheless a way : Faust must seek The Mothers who dwell in terrible solitudes :

> Ins Unbetretene
> Nicht zu Betretende.

Faust departs. The scene changes, and again presents the Court. Mephisto there removes the freckles from a fair one's face, cures another of lameness, gives a philtre to the third. The lights begin to burn dimly in the hall, and the spectacle commences. Faust appears on the stage and calls up Paris, who is variously criticized by the company ; then Helen appears, and Mephisto, who sees her for the first time, confesses she is beautiful, but not exactly to his taste. But Faust is in uncontrollable rapture, and expresses what may be interpreted as the feelings of a German Artist brought into the presence of Grecian Art. He is jealous of Paris, and interferes. Then follows an explosion : the spirits disappear, and Faust is borne off senseless by Mephisto. Thus closes the first act.

If we disregard for a moment the symbolical significance of these scenes, and the occasional charm of the writing, there will be little to admire ; and this consideration is all important, because even if the symbolism be accepted by us, as it is by certain critics, if we marvel at the profound thought and searching sarcasm underlying the phantasmagoria, we are still only admiring the Philosopher, and have not the Artist before us ; we are praising the poem for other than poetic qualities. Nor must we be surprised if readers, who do not perceive the meaning intended to be conveyed, or seeing it, do not highly esteem it, are lukewarm in their admiration.

In the second act Faust is discovered lying in bed in his old Study, Mephisto by his side. A servant comes in, from whom we learn that Wagner has taken Faust's place, and acquired almost as great a reputation. He has long been busied in attempts to discover the vital principle, by means of which he will create a man. Our old friend the Student now enters: he whom Mephisto instructed years ago. He is an Idealist, and presents an occasion for some quizzing of Fichte's philosophy. We are then led into Wagner's laboratory. He has just completed his manufacture of an Homunculus, which he keeps in a bottle. There is very admirable writing in this scene ; especially quaint and characteristic is the language of Wagner, who, in the pride of science, declares the old methods of generation to be idle and frivolous :

> Wie sonst das Zeugen Mode war
> Erklären wir für eitel Possen.

It may be all very well for animals, but man with his high gifts must have a purer, higher origin.

The Homunculus, however, turns out to be an imp, and a very irreverent imp, who undertakes to instruct Mephisto and conducts him and Faust into the Classical Walpurgis Night, which occupies

the rest of the act.   This Walpurgis Night, which is a classical
pendant to the Brocken scene in the *First Part*, is a sort of olla
podrida.   It contains the gathered fragments of many years, thrown
together without much care, and with infinite obscurity.   It is an
inexhaustible field for Commentators.   A capital touch is that of
making Mephisto feel quite a stranger among the classical figures,
and very humorous his disapprobation of the Antique Nude !

> Zwar sind auch wir von Herzen unanständig,
> *Doch das Antike find' ich zu lebendig!*

In the Brocken scene of the *First Part* we had the German world
of Witchcraft, and the German ideal of female loveliness and simplicity in Gretchen.   In this *Second Part* we have the Classical
world of Supernaturalism, and the Greek ideal of loveliness in
Helen.   The third act is occupied with *Helena*, which was originally published as a separate poem, and was reviewed at some length
by Carlyle in the *Foreign Review**.   He says of it truly enough
that 'it by no means carries its significance written on its forehead
so that he who runs may read ; but on the contrary, it is enveloped
in a certain mystery, under coy disguises, which to hasty readers
may be not only offensively obscure, but altogether provoking and
impenetrable'.   We should not quarrel with its obscurity, if the
opaque forms themselves had transcendent beauty : an alabaster
vase may give as much delight as a vase of crystal.   Carlyle, indeed, is forced to add that the 'outward meaning seems unsatisfactory enough, were it not that ever and anon we are reminded of
a cunning, manifold meaning which lies hidden under it ; and incited by capricious beckonings to evolve this more completely from
its quaint concealment'.   The question at issue here rests entirely
on the share to be allotted to Meaning in a work of Art.   Carlyle
refers to Bunyan as 'nowise our best theologian ; neither unhappily
is theology our most attractive science ; yet which of our compends
and treatises, nay which of our romances and poems, lives in such
mild sunshine as the good old *Pilgrim's Progress* in the memory
of so many men ?'   But this, if I have not altogether mistaken the
point, is a condemnation ; for who can say that the memories of
men are fondly occupied with the *Second Part of Faust* in general,
or with *Helena* in particular ?

But while I am thus thrown into a position of antagonism both
with respect to the work itself and to its eulogists, I must guard

* Subsequently reprinted in his *Miscellanies*, vol. I.

against the supposition that I do not admire this *Helena*. The style of Art is one which requires for perfect success qualities absent from the whole *Second Part;* but no lover of poetry will fail to recognize the poetry and the charm here to a great degree thrown away. To those who love riddles, to those who love interpretations, the work is inexhaustible ; to those who love beautiful verses, and glimpses of a deeply meditative mind, the work is, and always will be, attractive ; but those who open it expecting a masterpiece will, I think, be perpetually disappointed. Some minds will be delighted with the allegorical Helen embracing Faust, and in the embrace leaving only her veil and vest behind, her body vanishing into thin air—typical of what must ever be the embrace of the defunct Classical with the living Romantic, the resuscitated Past with the actual Present—and in their delight at the recognition of the meaning, will write chapters of commentary. But the kiss of Gretchen is worth a thousand allegories.

The analysis need not be prolonged, the more so as nothing worthy of special notice occurs in the two last acts. Faust, who has viewed many of the aspects of life, is now grown jealous of the encroachments of the sea, and determines to shut it out. He is old, sad, reflective. Four grey old women—Want, Guilt, Misery, and Care—appear to him. On Care asking him if he has ever known her, he answers : 'I have gone through the world, seized every enjoyment by the hair—that which did not satisfy me I let go, that which ran away from me I would not follow. I have only wished and realized my wish, and wished again, and thus have stormed through life : first great and mighty ; but now I take things wisely and soberly. I know enough of this life, and of the world to come we have no clear prospect. A fool is he who directs his blinking eyes *that* way, and imagines creatures like himself above the clouds ! Let him stand firm and look around him here, the world is not dumb to the man of real sense. What need is there for him to sweep eternity ? All he can know lies within his grasp'. These concluding words contain Goethe's own philosophy, and I must quote the original :

> Thor ! wer dorthin die Augen blinzend richtet
> Sich über Wolken seines Gleichen dichtet !
> Er stehe fest und sehe hier sich um ;
> Dem Tüchtigen ist diese Welt nicht stumm.
> Was braucht er in die Ewigkeit zu schweifen !
> Was er erkennt lässt sich ergreifen.

Faust refusing to recognize the omipotence of Care, she breathes on him, and blinds him ; but, blind though he be, he resolves that the work he has planned shall be concluded. 'A marsh', he says, 'extends along the mountain's foot, infecting all that is already won : to draw off the noisome pool would be a crowning success. I lay open a space for many millions to dwell upon, not safely it is true, but in free activity. * * * Yes, heart and soul am I devoted to this wish ; this is the last resolve of wisdom. He only deserves freedom and life who is daily compelled to conquer them for himself; and thus here, hemmed round by danger, bring childhood, manhood, and old age their well-spent years to a close. I would fain see such a busy multitude stand upon free soil with free people. I might then say to the moment, "Stay, thou art fair !" The trace of my earthly days cannot perish in centuries. In the presentiment of such exalted bliss, I now enjoy the most exalted moment'. He has thus said to the passing moment, 'Stay ! thou art fair', and with this he expires.

Venit summa dies et ineluctabile fatum,—

the troubled career is closed. And as far as the problem of *Faust* can receive a solution more general than the one indicated at the close of the criticism on the *First Part*, the solution is I think given in this dying speech ; the toiling soul, after trying in various directions of *individual* effort and *individual* gratification, and finding therein no peace, is finally conducted to the recognition of the vital truth that man lives for man, and that only in as far as he is working for Humanity can his efforts bring permanent happiness.

CHAPTER VIII

THE CLOSING SCENES

THE spring of 1830 found Goethe in his eighty-first year, busy with *Faust*, writing the preface to Carlyle's *Life of Schiller*, and deeply interested in the great philosophical contest which was raging in Paris, between Cuvier and Geoffroy St. Hilaire, on the question of Unity of Composition in the Animal Kingdom. This question, one of the many important and profound questions which are now agitated in Biology, which lies indeed at the bottom of almost all speculations on Development, had for very many years been answered by Goethe in the spirit which he recognized in Geoffroy St. Hilaire ; and it was to him a matter of keen delight to observe the world of science earnestly bent on a solution of the question. The anecdote which M. Soret narrates in the supplemental volume to Eckermann's conversations, is very characteristic.

'Monday, 1st August, 1830. The news of the Revolution of July reached Weimar to-day, and set every one in commotion. I went in the course of the afternoon to Goethe. "Now", exclaimed he, as I entered, "what do you think of this great event? The volcano has come to an eruption ; everything is in flames". "A frightful story", I answered ; "but what could be expected otherwise under such notoriously bad circumstances and with such a ministry, than that the whole would end in the expulsion of the royal family?" "We do not appear to understand each other, my good friend", said Goethe ; "I am not speaking of those people, but of something quite different. I am speaking of the contest so important for science between Cuvier and Geoffroy St. Hilaire, which has come to an open rupture in the Academy". This expression of Goethe's was so unexpected that I did not know what to say, and for some minutes was perfectly at a standstill. "The matter is of the highest importance", he continued ; "and you can form no conception of what I felt at the intelligence of the *séance* of the 19th July. We have now in Geoffroy a powerful and permanent ally. I see how great must be the interest of the French scientific world in this affair ; because notwithstanding the terrible political commotion, the *séance* of the 19th July was very fully attended. However, the best of it is that the synthetic manner of looking at Nature, introduced by Geoffroy into France, cannot be kept back any longer. From the present time Mind will rule over Matter in the scientific investigations of the French. There will be glances of the great maxims of creation—of the mysterious workshop of God ! Besides, what is all intercourse with Nature, if we merely occupy ourselves with individual material parts, and do not feel the breath of the spirit which prescribes to every part its direction, and orders or sanctions every deviation by means of an inherent law ! I have exerted myself in this great question for fifty years. At first I was alone, then I found support, and now at last to my great joy I am surpassed by congenial minds"'

Instead of exclaiming against the coldness of the man who at such a moment could turn from politics to science, let us glance at a somewhat parallel case. Englishmen will be slow in throwing stones at the immortal Harvey; let them hear what Dr. Ent reports. Soon after the most agitating event in English history—— the execution of Charles I.—Dr. Ent called on Harvey, and found him seeking solace in anatomical researches. 'Did I not', said the great philosopher, 'find a balm for my spirit in the memory of my observations of former years, I should feel little desire for life. But so it has been that this life of obscurity, this vacation from public business, which causes tedium and disgust to so many, has proved a sovereign remedy to me'.

Goethe was not a politician, and he was a biologist. His view of the superior importance of such an event as the discussion between Geoffroy and Cuvier, to the more noisy but intrinsically less remarkable event, the Revolution of July, is a view which will be accepted by some philosophers, and rejected by all politicians. Goethe was not content with expressing in conversation his sense of the importance of this discussion ; he also commenced the writing of his celebrated review of it, and finished the first part in September.

In November another great affliction smote him : it was the last he had to bear : the news arrived that his only son, who had a little while before gone to Italy in failing health, had died in Rome on the 28th of October. The sorrowing father strove, as usual, to master all expression of emotion, and to banish it by restless work. But vain was the effort to live down this climbing sorrow. The trial nearly cost him his life. A violent hæmorrhage in the lungs was the result. He was at one time given over ; but he rallied again, and set once more to work, completing the *Autobiography* and continuing *Faust*.

Ottilie von Goethe, the widow of his son, and his great favourite, devoted herself to cheer his solitude. She read Plutarch aloud to him ; and this, with Niebuhr's Roman History, carried him amid the great pageantries of the past, where his antique spirit could wander as among friends. Nor was the present disregarded. He read with the eagerness of youth whatever was produced by remarkable writers, such as Béranger, Victor Hugo, Delavigne, Scott, or Carlyle. He received the homage of Europe ; his rooms were constantly brightened by the presence of illustrious visitors, among whom the English were always welcome.

Rambling over the wild moors, with thoughts oftentimes as wild and dreary as those moors, the young Carlyle, who had been cheered through his struggling sadness, and strengthened for the part he was to play in life, by the beauty and the wisdom which Goethe had revealed to him, suddenly conceived the idea that it would be a pleasant and a fitting thing if some of the few admirers in England forwarded to Weimar a trifling token of their admiration. On reaching home, Mrs. Carlyle at once sketched the design of a seal to be engraved: the serpent of eternity encircling a star, with the words *ohne Hast ohne Rast* (unhasting, unresting), in allusion to the well-known verses.

> Wie das Gestirn,
> Ohne Hast
> Aber ohne Rast,
> Drehe sich jeder
> Um die eigne Last.

'Like a star, unhasting, unresting, be each one fulfilling his God-given hest'. Fifteen English admirers subscribed to have a handsome seal made, on the golden belt of which was engraved: *To the German Master: From friends in England: 28th August*, 1831. This letter accompanied it:

'*To the Poet Goethe, on the* 28*th August,* 1831.

'Sir,—Among the friends whom this so interesting anniversary calls round you, may we English friends, in thought and symbolically, since personally it is impossible, present ourselves to offer you our affectionate congratulations. We hope you will do us the honour to accept this little Birthday Gift, which, as a true testimony of our feelings, may not be without value.

'We said to ourselves: As it is always the highest duty, and pleasure, to show reverence where reverence is due, and our chief, perhaps our only benefactor, is he who by act and word instructs us in wisdom ; so we, undersigned, feeling towards the Poet Goethe as the spiritually taught towards their spiritual teacher, are desirous to express that sentiment openly and in common ; for which end we have determined to solicit his acceptance of a small English gift, proceeding from us all equally, on his approaching birthday ; so that while the venerable man still dwells among us, some memorial of the gratitude we owe him, and we think the whole world owes him, may not be wanting.

'And thus our little tribute, perhaps among the purest that men could offer to man, now stands in visible shape, and begs to be received. May it be welcome, and speak permanently of a most close relation, though wide seas flow between the parties !

'We pray that many years may be added to a life so glorious, that all happiness may be yours, and strength given to accomplish your high task, even as it has hitherto proceeded, like a star, without haste yet without rest.
'We remain, Sir, your friends and servants,
'FIFTEEN ENGLISHMEN'*.

The sentiment expressed in this letter, which every one will see comes from Carlyle, namely, the reverence felt for the spiritual teacher by the spiritually taught, is a manifestation that Goethe's teaching had already borne fruit, and that even in different lands men discerned the quality in which his works are pre-eminent above those of any modern writer—the quality of deep and far-reaching insight.

The English tribute was extremely gratifying, because for England and Englishmen his admiration was very hearty. Among the English who lived at Weimar during those days was a youth whose name is now carried in triumph wherever English Literature is cherished—I allude to William Makepeace Thackeray; and Weimar Albums still display with pride the caricatures which the young satirist sketched at that period. He has kindly enabled me to enrich these pages with a brief account of his reminiscences, gracefully sketched in the following letter :

'*London, 28th April*, 1855.

'DEAR LEWES,—I wish I had more to tell you regarding Weimar and Goethe. Five-and-twenty years ago, at least a score of young English lads used to live at Weimar for study, or sport, or society; all of which were to be had in the friendly little Saxon capital. The Grand Duke and Duchess received us with the kindliest hospitality. The Court was splendid, but yet most pleasant and homely. We were invited in our turns to dinners, balls, and assemblies there. Such young men as had a right, appeared in uniforms, diplomatic and military. Some, I remember, invented gorgeous clothing : the kind old Hof Marschall of those days, M. de Spiegel (who had two of the most lovely daughters eyes ever looked on) being in nowise difficult as to the admission of these young Englanders. Of the winter nights we used to charter sedan chairs, in which we were carried through the snow to those pleasant Court entertainments. I for my part had the good luck to purchase Schiller's sword, which formed a part of my Court costume, and still hangs in my study, and puts me in mind of days of youth the most kindly and delightful.

* The names of these Englishmen, as far as I have been able to ascertain, are Carlyle and his brother Dr. Carlyle, Walter Scott, Lockhart, Wordsworth, Southey, Churchill, Frazer, Professor Wilson, Jerdan, Heraud, Lord Leveson Gower, and Procter (Barry Cornwall).

' We knew the whole society of the little city, and but that the young ladies, one and all, spoke admirable English, we surely might have learned the very best German. The society met constantly. The ladies of the Court had their evenings. The theatre was open twice or thrice in the week, where we assembled, a large family party. Goethe had retired from the direction, but the great traditions remained still. The theatre was admirably conducted ; and besides the excellent Weimar company, famous actors and singers from various parts of Germany performed *Gastrolle** through the winter. In that winter I remember we had Ludwig Devrient in Shylock, Hamlet, Falstaff, and the *Robbers ;* and the beautiful Schröder in *Fidelio.*

' After three-and-twenty years' absence, I passed a couple of summer days in the well-remembered place, and was fortunate enough to find some of the friends of my youth. Madame de Goethe was there, and received me and my daughters with the kindness of old days. We drank tea in the open air at the famous cottage in the Park†, which still belongs to the family, and had been so often inhabited by her illustrious father.

' In 1831, though he had retired from the world, Goethe would nevertheless very kindly receive strangers. His daughter-in-law's tea-table was always spread for us. We passed hours after hours there, and night after night with the pleasantest talk and music. We read over endless novels and poems in French, English, and German. My delight in those days was to make caricatures for children. I was touched to find that they were remembered, and some even kept until the present time ; and very proud to be told, as a lad, that the great Goethe had looked at some of them.

' He remained in his private apartments, where only a very few privileged persons were admitted ; but he liked to know all that was happening, and interested himself about all strangers. Whenever a countenance struck his fancy, there was an artist settled in Weimar who made a portrait of it. Goethe had quite a gallery of heads, in black and white, taken by this painter. His house was all over pictures, drawings, casts, statues, and medals.

' Of course I remember very well the perturbation of spirit with which, as a lad of nineteen, I received the long expected intimation that the Herr Geheimrath would see me on such a morning. This notable audience took place in a little ante-chamber of his private apartments, covered all round with antique casts and bas-reliefs. He was habited in a long grey or drab redingote, with a white neck-cloth and a red ribbon in his buttonhole. He kept his hands behind his back, just as in Rauch's statuette. His complexion was very bright, clear and rosy. His eyes extraordinarily dark‡, piercing and brilliant. I felt quite afraid before them, and recollect comparing them to the eyes of the hero of a certain

---

* What in England are called 'starring engagements'.
† The *Gartenhaus.*
‡ This must have been the effect of the position in which he sat with regard to the light. Goethe's eyes were dark brown, but not very dark.

romance called *Melmoth the Wanderer*, which used to alarm us boys thirty years ago ; eyes of an individual who had made a bargain with a Certain Person, and at an extreme old age retained these eyes in all their awful splendour.   I fancied Goethe must have been still more handsome as an old man than even in the days of his youth.   His voice was very rich and sweet.   He asked me questions about myself, which I answered as best I could.   I recollect I was at first astonished, and then somewhat relieved, when I found he spoke French with not a good accent.

'*Vidi tantum.*   I saw him but three times.   Once walking in the garden of his house in the *Frauenplan;* once going to step into his chariot on a sunshiny day, wearing a cap and a cloak with a red collar. He was caressing at the time a beautiful little golden-haired grand-daughter, over whose sweet fair face the earth has long since closed too.

'Any of us who had books or magazines from England sent them to him, and he examined them eagerly.   *Frazer's Magazine* had lately come out, and I remember he was interested in those admirable outline portraits which appeared for awhile in its pages.   But there was one, a very ghastly caricature of Mr. Rogers, which, as Madame de Goethe told me, he shut up and put away from him angrily.   "They would make me look like that", he said; though in truth I can fancy nothing more serene, majestic, and *healthy* looking than the grand old Goethe.

'Though his sun was setting, the sky round about was calm and bright, and that little Weimar illumed by it.   In every one of those kind salons the talk was still of Art and letters.   The theatre, though possessing no very extraordinary actors, was still conducted with a noble intelligence and order.   The actors read books, and were men of letters and gentlemen, holding a not unkindly relationship with the *Adel.*   At Court the conversa-tion was exceedingly friendly, simple and polished.   The Grand Duchess (the present Grand Duchess Dowager), a lady of very remarkable endowments, would kindly borrow our books from us, lend us her own, and graciously talk to us young men about our literary tastes and pursuits.   In the respect paid by this Court to the Patriarch of letters, there was something ennobling, I think, alike to the subject and sovereign.   With a five-and-twenty years' experience since those happy days of which I write, and an acquaintance with an immense variety of human kind, I think I have never seen a society more simple, charitable, courteous, gentlemanlike, than that of the dear little Saxon city, where the good Schiller and the great Goethe lived and lie buried.

'Very sincerely yours,
'W. M. THACKERAY'.

Thackeray's testimony is not only borne out by all that I learn elsewhere, but is indeed applicable to Weimar in the present day, where the English visitor is received by the reigning Grand Duke and Duchess with exquisite grace of courtesy ; and where he still feels that the traditions of the classic period are *living*.

To return to Goethe : His last secretary, Kräuter, who never speaks of him but with idolatry, describes his activity even at this advanced age as something prodigious. It was moreover systematic. A certain time of the day was devoted to his correspondence ; then came the arrangement of his papers, or the completion of works long commenced. One fine spring morning, Kräuter tells me Goethe said to him : ' Come, we will cease dictation ; it is a pity such fine weather should not be enjoyed, let us go into the park and do a bit of work there '. Kräuter took the necessary books and papers, and followed his master, who, in his long blue overcoat, a blue cap on his head, and his hands in the customary attitude behind his back, marched on, upright and imposing. Those who remember Rauch's statuette will picture to themselves the figure of the old man in his ordinary attitude ; but perhaps they cannot fully picture to themselves the imposing effect of that Jupiter-head which, on this occasion, arrested an old peasant, and so absorbed him, that leaning his hands upon his rake, and resting his chin upon his hands, he gazed on the spectacle in forgetfulness so complete that he did not move out of the way, but stood gazing immovable, while Kräuter had to step aside to pass.

It is usually said indeed that Goethe showed no signs of age ; but this is one of the exaggerations which the laxity of ordinary speech permits itself. His intellect preserved a wonderful clearness and activity, as we know ; and indeed the man who wrote the essay on Cuvier and Geoffroy's discussion, and who completed the *Faust* in his eighty-second year, may fairly claim a place among the Nestors for whom remains

> Some work of noble note,
> Not unbecoming men who strove with gods.

But the biographer is bound to record that in his intellect, as in his body, the old man showed unmistakably that he was old. His hearing became noticeably impaired ; his memory of recent occurrences was extremely treacherous ; yet his eyesight remained strong, and his appetite good. In the later years of his life he presented a striking contrast to the earlier years, in his preference for close rooms. The heated and impure atmosphere of an unventilated room was to him so agreeable that it was difficult to persuade him to have a window open for the purpose of ventilation. Always disliking the cold, and longing for warmth like a child of the south, he sat in rooms so heated that he was constantly taking cold. This did not prevent his enjoyment of the fresh air when he was in the country. The mountain air of Ilmenau, especially, seemed to give him health and enjoyment. It was to Ilmenau he went to escape from the festivities preparing for his last birthday. He ascended the lovely heights of the Gickelhahn, and went into the wood hut where so many happy days had been spent with Karl August. There he saw on the wall those lines he had years before written in pencil,—

> Ueber allen Gipfeln
> Ist Ruh,
> In allen Wipfeln
> Spürest du
> Kaum einen Hauch ;
> Die Vögelein schweigen im Walde.
> Warte nur, balde
> Ruhest du auch.

And wiping the tears from his eyes, tears which rose at the memory of Karl August, Charlotte von Stein, and his own happy youth, he repeated the last line, '*Ja, warte nur, balde ruhest du auch*—Yes, wait but a little, thou too soon wilt be at rest'.

That rest was nearer than any one expected. On the 16th of March following, his grandson, Wolfgang, coming into his room as usual to breakfast with him, found him still in bed. The day before, in passing from his heated room across the garden, he had taken cold. The physician on arriving found him very feverish, with what is known in Weimar as the 'nervous fever', which acts almost like a pestilence. With the aid of remedies, however, he rallied towards evening, and became talkative and jocose. On the 17th he was so much better that he dictated a long letter to W. von Humboldt. All thought of danger ceased. But during the night of the 19th, having gone off into a soft sleep, he awoke about midnight with hands and feet icy cold, and fierce pain and oppression of the chest. He would not have the physician disturbed, however, for he said there was no danger, only pain. But when the physician came in the morning, he found that a fearful change had taken place. His teeth chattered with the cold. The pain in his chest made him groan, and sometimes call out aloud. He could not rest in one place, but tossed about in bed, seeking in vain a more endurable position. His face was ashen grey ; the eyes, deep sunk in the sockets, were dull, and the glance was that of one conscious of the presence of death. After a time these fearful symptoms were

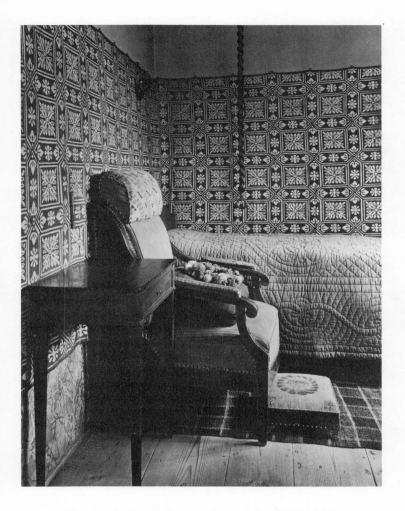

Goethe's bedroom, showing the chair in which he died

allayed, and he was removed from his bed into the easy chair which stood at his bedside. There, towards evening, he was once more restored to perfect calmness, and spoke with clearness and interest of ordinary matters ; especially pleased he was to hear that his appeal for a young artist, a protégé, had been successful ; and with a trembling hand, he signed an official paper which secured a pension to another artist, a young Weimar lady, for whom he had interested himself.

On the following day the approach of death was evident. The painful symptoms were gone. But his senses began to fail him, and he had moments of unconsciousness. He sat quiet in the chair, spoke kindly to those around him, and made his servant bring Salvandy's *Seize Mois, ou la Révolution et les Révolutionnaires*, which he had been reading when he fell ill ; but after turning over the leaves, he laid it down, feeling himself too ill to read. He bade them bring him the list of all the persons who had called to inquire after his health, and remarked that such evidence of sympathy must not be forgotten when he recovered. He sent every one to bed that night, except his copyist. He would not even allow his old servant to sit up with him, but insisted on his lying down to get the rest so much needed.

The following morning—it was the 22nd March, 1832—he tried to walk a little up and down the room, but, after a turn, he found himself too feeble to continue. Reseating himself in the easy chair, he chatted cheerfully with Ottilie on the approaching spring, which would be sure to restore him. He had no idea of his end being so near.

The name of Ottilie was frequently on his lips. She sat beside him, holding his hand in both of hers. It was now observed that his thoughts began to wander incoherently. ' See ', he exclaimed, ' the lovely woman's head—with black curls—in splendid colours— a dark background ! ' Presently he saw a piece of paper on the floor, and asked them how they could leave Schiller's letters so carelessly lying about. Then he slept softly, and on awakening, asked for the sketches he had just seen. These were the sketches seen in a dream. In silent anguish the close now so surely approaching was awaited. His speech was becoming less and less distinct. The last words audible were : *More light !* The final darkness grew apace, and he whose eternal longings had been for more Light, gave a parting cry for it, as he was passing under the shadow of death.

He continued to express himself by signs, drawing letters with his forefinger in the air, while he had strength, and finally, as life ebbed, drawing figures slowly on the shawl which covered his legs. At half-past twelve he composed himself in the corner of the chair. The watcher placed a finger on her lip to intimate that he was asleep. If sleep it was, it was a sleep in which a great life glided from the world.

FINIS

Goethe on his deathbed

INDEX